The Economics of Tax Policy

The Economics of Tax Policy

Edited by Alan J. Auerbach
and
Kent Smetters

OXFORD
UNIVERSITY PRESS

OXFORD
UNIVERSITY PRESS

Oxford University Press is a department of the University of Oxford. It furthers the University's objective of excellence in research, scholarship, and education by publishing worldwide. Oxford is a registered trade mark of Oxford University Press in the UK and certain other countries.

Published in the United States of America by Oxford University Press
198 Madison Avenue, New York, NY 10016, United States of America.

CIP data is on file at the Library of Congress
ISBN 978–0–19–061972–5

CONTENTS

ACKNOWLEDGMENTS

The papers in this volume were prepared for a conference held at the Brookings Institution on December 3–4, 2015, sponsored by the University of California, Berkeley's Burch Center for Tax Policy and Public Finance and the Penn Wharton Public Policy Initiative. We are grateful to the Urban-Brookings Tax Policy Center for providing analysis prepared specially for several papers in the volume, to Chelsey Crim of Brookings for handling local arrangements and to Camille Fernandez for conference organizing and help in shepherding this volume into print.

LIST OF CONTRIBUTORS

Rosanne Altshuler
Department of Economics
Rutgers University
New Brunswick, NJ

Alan Auerbach
Department of Economics
University of California, Berkeley
Berkeley, CA

Daniel Berger
Urban Institute and Tax Policy Center
Washington, DC

Len Burman
Urban Institute and Tax Policy Center
Washington, DC

Dhammika Dharmapala
University of Chicago Law School
Chicago, IL

Susan Dynarski
Gerald R. Ford School of Public Policy
University of Michigan
Ann Arbor, MI

David Figlio
Institute for Policy Research
Northwestern University
Evanston, IL

John N. Friedman
Department of Economics and Watson Institute for International and Public Affairs
Brown University
Providence, RI

Don Fullerton
Department of Finance
University of Illinois at Urbana-Champaign
Urbana, IL

William G. Gale
Brookings Institution and Tax Policy Center
Washington, DC

Kevin Hassett
American Enterprise Institute
Washington, DC

James R. HinesJr.
University of Michigan Law School
Ann Arbor, MI

Hilary Hoynes
Goldman School of Public Policy
University of California at Berkeley
Berkeley, CA

Louis Kaplow
Harvard University Law School
Cambridge, MA

Wojciech Kopczuk
Department of Economics
Columbia University
New York, NY

Brigitte C. Madrian
John F. Kennedy School of Government
Harvard University
Cambridge, MA

James M. Poterba
Department of Economics
Massachusetts Institute of Technology
Cambridge, MA

Jeffrey Rohaly
Urban Institute and Tax Policy Center
Washington, DC

Jesse Rothstein
Institute for Research on Labor and Employment
University of California at Berkeley
Berkeley, CA

Andrew A. Samwick
The Nelson A. Rockefeller Center
Dartmouth College
Hanover, NH

Diane Whitmore Schanzenbach
Institute for Policy Research
Northwestern University
Brookings Institution
Evanston, IL

Judith Scott-Clayton
Teachers College
Columbia University
New York, NY

Joel Slemrod
Department of Economics and the Stephen M. Ross School of Business
University of Michigan
Ann Arbor, MI

Kent Smetters
The Wharton School
The University of Pennsylvania
Philadelphia, PA

Eric Toder
Urban Institute and Tax Policy Center
Washington, DC

Alan D. Viard
American Enterprise Institute
Washington, DC

David Weisbach
University of Chicago Law School
Chicago, IL

Roberton C. WilliamsIII
University of Maryland
Resources for the Future
College Park, MD

1

TAX REFORM IN A CHANGING ECONOMY

Alan Auerbach and Kent Smetters

In 1954, the nation's tax code was reorganized and renamed, becoming the Internal Revenue Code of 1954. Three decades later, the Tax Reform Act of 1986 (TRA86) was so fundamental, US tax law was again renamed by Congress to be the Internal Revenue Code of 1986. TRA86 has been widely credited for simplifying the tax code and reducing special deductions. It lowered the top personal income tax rate from 50% to 28%, while reducing the top corporate rate from 46% to 34%, although it was increased to 39.6% in 2013.

Another thirty years have now passed since the United States undertook a significant reform of its tax system. A lot has changed since 1986. Some of the 1986 reforms have been rolled back. More important, the United States and world economies have changed substantially during the past thirty years:

- **Globalization**: Due to increased trading, by 2014, 48% of revenue earned by the largest 500 publicly traded US firms came from non-US purchasers (Silverblatt 2015). The interconnectedness of economies across countries is one reason why capital markets have also become more integrated. For example, the correlation between the S&P500 (US large-cap stocks) and the EAFE (large-cap stocks in Europe, Australia, and the Fair East) was 50% or lower a few decades ago, but has increased to above 80% (Chen 2008). Cross-country selling also makes it substantially easier for US firms to locate core parts of their business outside of the United States, often to shift earnings to lower tax countries.
- **Tax competition**: Globalization and the concomitant enhanced ability to move production across borders has also produced considerable international tax competition. The weighted average statutory corporate tax rate in non-US OECD countries dropped from about 50% in 1986 to 32% by 2008 (Carroll 2008). The US federal tax rate of 35% now ranks as the highest in the OECD (table 1.1). That figure does not include state tax rates. The US average federal-state statutory corporate rate is closer to 40% (Carroll 2008).
- **Environmental awareness**: Concerns about greenhouse gas emissions have also increased over time. For example, US political contributions for environmental reasons (including contributions made by individuals, political action committees [PACs], and in the form of soft money) have increased sixty-five-fold since 1990

Table 1.1 Top corporate tax rates, by OECD country

OECD Country	*Top Corporate Tax Rate (percent)*
United States	35.00
France	33.33
Belgium	33.00
Australia	30.00
Mexico	30.00
Greece	29.00
New Zealand	28.00
Spain	28.00
Italy	27.50
Norway	27.00
Israel	26.50
Austria	25.00
Netherlands	25.00
Japan	23.90
Denmark	23.50
Chile	22.50
Korea	22.00
Slovak Republic	22.00
Sweden	22.00
Luxembourg	21.00
Portugal	21.00
Estonia	20.00
Finland	20.00
Iceland	20.00
Turkey	20.00
United Kingdom	20.00
Czech Republic	19.00
Hungary	19.00
Poland	19.00
Slovenia	17.00
Canada	15.00
Germany	15.00
Ireland	12.50
Switzerland	8.50

(Center for Responsive Politics 2016). The November 2015 international climate talks in Paris discussed in detail how to prevent the earth's temperature from rising an additional two degrees. Such focus and specificity in objectives was uncommon three decades ago.

- **Growth in tax-preferred retirement accounts**: In 1990, about 19.5 million Americans actively participated in tax-preferred retirement accounts provided by their employers, like 401(k) and 403(b) plans. Total tax-deferred assets in employer-based defined-contribution plans stood at around $385 billion (Employee Benefit Research Institute 2005). By 2012, participation has more than doubled and assets have increased by almost tenfold. Now, 52 million Americans are participating in employer-based tax-deferred accounts, and assets stand at $2.2 trillion. Adding in IRA accounts, annuities, and defined-benefit plans, assets in tax-preferred accounts total $4.4 trillion (Investment Company Institute 2014).
- **Increasing college wage premium**: The value of wages and employer-provided health care has increased for college and post-college graduates relative to people with education that is less than a college degree (figure 1.1). People without a college degree have seen their inflation-adjusted compensation remain flat or even decrease during the past three decades. In contrast, college graduates and post-graduates have experienced compensation increases between one-fifth and one-third. Not surprisingly, more high-school graduates are now seeking a college education. At the same time, US total student debt now exceeds $1.2 trillion, a tripling in value since 2006 (Bricker, Brown, and Pence 2015).
- **The "1%"**: Besides an increasing college wage premium, the top 1% of households take in a larger share of total income than they did thirty years ago. According to the Congressional Budget Office (2014), average inflation-adjusted market income

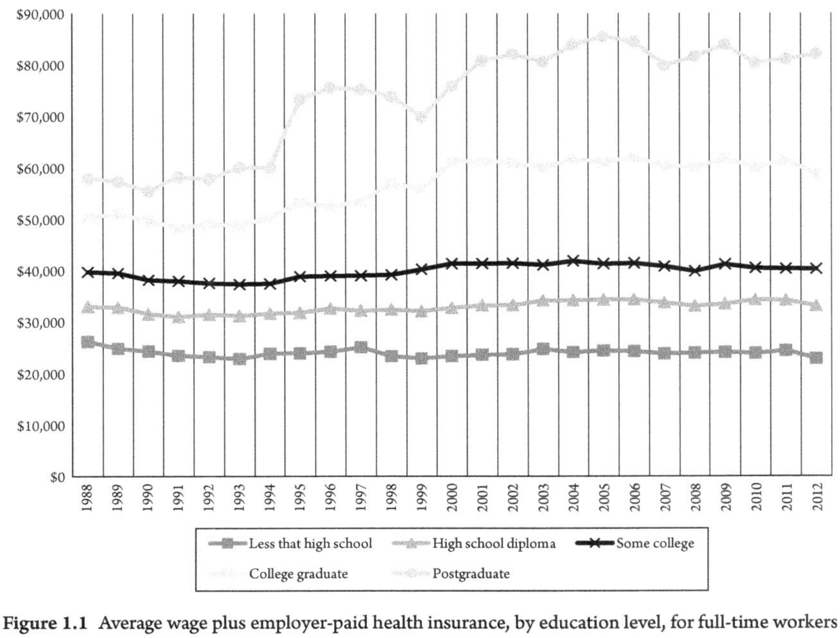

Figure 1.1 Average wage plus employer-paid health insurance, by education level, for full-time workers aged 40 to 55 in 1995 dollars, 1988–2012. *Source*: Penn Wharton Public Policy Initiative calculations based on the Current Population Survey. Health insurance costs provided by data source are imputed.

rose by 174% between 1980 and 2012 for those in the top 1%, while increasing by 16% for those households in the 21st–80th percentiles.

- **Tax expenditures**: "Tax expenditures" are a form of implicit government spending, taking the form of tax revenue that is not collected because of deductions, exemptions, and other exclusions for businesses and individuals. The Joint Committee on Taxation (1986) estimates that the revenue lost from tax expenditures was $450 billion in 1987, a year after the 1986 TRA was passed. Of that amount, about $97 billion represented lower taxes paid by corporations while $353 was due to individuals. By 2014, total tax expenditures increased to $1.4 trillion, almost doubling in value after adjusting for inflation (Joint Committee on Taxation 2015). Some of the expansion was legislative in nature, which expanded tax expenditure opportunities. But a significant rise is due to the greater use of existing tax expenditures such as the exclusion from income of employer-based health care premiums.
- **Growth of small business**: Small business accounts for almost half of US GDP. The number of small businesses grew by 24% between 1986 and 2013 (figure 1.2), reaching about 5,000,000 today. Historically, tax enforcement has been especially challenging with respect to small businesses, which often deal in cash. Across all types of taxpayers, the US Department of Treasury (2009) estimates that it lost about $345 billion in 2001 from unpaid taxes, before enforcement, and $290 billion after enforcement, equal to about 14% of all taxes paid. Its most recent study, using 2006 tax returns, put these values at $450 billion before enforcement and $385 billion after enforcement (Slemrod, this volume).
- **Government debt**: The US federal government debt held by the public now stands at 74% of GDP, well above its fifty-year average historical value of 38% of GDP (Congressional Budget Office 2015). (Gross debt, which includes monies owed to Social Security and other government programs with trust funds, currently exceeds 100% of GDP.) The Congressional Budget Office estimates that, by

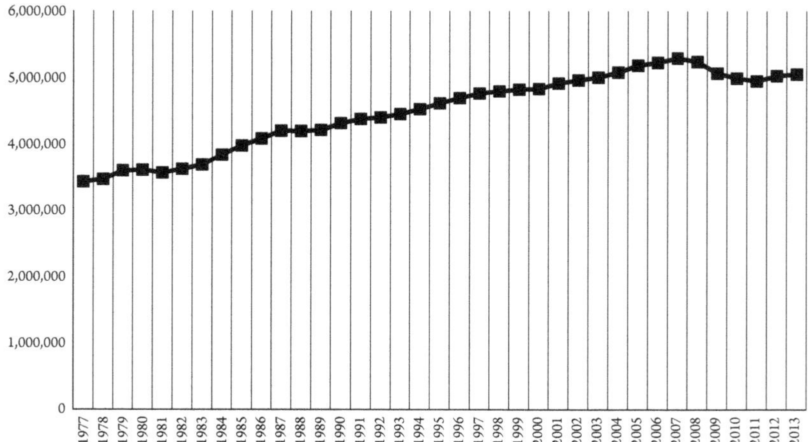

Figure 1.2 Number of small businesses, 1977–2013. *Source:* US Census, Business Dynamic Statistics.

2040, debt held by the public will increase to 107% of GDP under current law, and to 175% of GDP under an "alternative" baseline that includes plausible scenarios about how policy might change.

The current US tax system has not kept up with the immense changes in the US and worldwide economies since the TRA86. The chapters in this volume, sponsored by the Burch Center for Tax Policy and Public Finance at Berkeley and the Penn Wharton Public Policy Initiative, address these deficiencies, providing non-technical reviews of the insights gained from recent economic research, with the intent to inform the policy process and to offer academics an overview of the major areas of tax analysis. Like the authors of each chapter, the discussants, who provide further insights on the respective issues, are leading scholars in the areas of research they evaluate.

1.1 THE EFFECT OF TAXES ON ECONOMIC GROWTH

One of the most spirited debates in the tax literature is whether changes in tax rates have a large impact on economic growth by changing the labor supply, savings and investment decisions of households. To be sure, there is little debate among economists that very high tax rates would reduce growth. The real question is whether the type of tax rate variation that we have seen in the past fifty years or so has had much of an effect. This issue has generated heightened interest as new congressional rules require the Congressional Budget Office to conduct "dynamic scoring" of tax legislation, that is, to include its impact on revenues of induced changes in economic growth.

William Gale and Andrew Samwick (chapter 2, with discussion by Kevin Hassett) review the empirical evidence and find that the net impact on growth has historically been small. One reason is that many past tax cuts have also increased budget deficits, which produce an offsetting drag on capital accumulation. Some past reforms have also simply rewarded previous investment decisions, thereby producing windfalls for investors, rather than encouraging new investment. Gale and Samwick argue that tax rate reductions, therefore, are not all created equally. In particular, tax reforms that improve incentives, reduce distortions, avoid windfalls, and do not increase the deficit are more likely to increase the long-term size of the economy.

1.2 ENVIRONMENTAL TAXATION

Taxing environmental pollution differs from other forms of taxation in one very important way. "Green" taxes can help correct externalities associated with the costs that pollution, congestion, and global warming impose on society, and therefore can actually reduce economic distortions rather than increasing them. Rising atmospheric CO_2 levels have helped renew interest recently in such taxes.

Roberton Williams (chapter 3, with discussion by Don Fullerton) draws on the recent theoretical and empirical research to evaluate the effects of various environmental tax reforms on tax revenue, pollution emissions, economic efficiency, and income distribution. He compares a carbon tax to a range of other possible changes.

These other options include revising or eliminating various energy and environmental tax credits and deductions (many of which might become unnecessary in the presence of a carbon tax), as well as changes to energy taxes such as the federal gasoline tax. Of the competing policy options, he finds that a carbon tax represents the most cost-effective way of reducing greenhouse gas emissions. While such a tax might slow economic growth, the impact could be mitigated if additional tax revenue were used to reduce other tax rates, reduce the budget deficit, or finance growth-enhancing public investments. While a carbon tax would also be mildly regressive, this disadvantage could be overcome if some of the revenue were used in a progressive way.

1.3 TAX ENFORCEMENT

Policy attention to tax evasion and enforcement picked up after the financial crisis of 2008, the Great Recession, and the large deficits that followed. High-income individuals, sole proprietors, and corporations are receiving additional scrutiny, especially in light of growing income inequality. Using 2006 tax returns, the IRS estimates that it lost \$450 billion due to noncompliance before enforcement and \$385 billion after enforcement. These monies, if fully captured, could, for example, finance half of all Social Security benefits paid in 2015. Alternatively, the lost money is twice the amount paid in disability benefits in the same year.

Joel Slemrod (chapter 4, with discussion by David Weisbach) reviews the academic research on tax compliance and the most promising methods for enforcement. During the past decade, academic research in tax evasion and enforcement has greatly expanded, facilitated by increased academic access to administrative tax-return data. Tax authorities have also been more willing to partner with researchers, including conducting randomized field trials. Randomized experiments offer considerable potential to assess the impact of alternative enforcement strategies. Slemrod examines recent findings, reviews innovative enforcement initiatives around the world, and provides some reflections on the most efficient policy directions for the United States to pursue.

1.4 BASE BROADENING BY LIMITING TAX EXPENDITURES

As noted earlier, tax expenditures represent tax revenue that is not collected because of deductions, exemptions, and other exclusions. According to the Joint Committee on Taxation, tax expenditures now account for almost \$1.4 trillion in lost revenue. Martin Feldstein, Daniel Feenberg, and Maya MacGuineas (2011) proposed limiting tax savings from selected provisions to 2% of adjusted gross income (AGI). President Obama proposed to limit tax savings to 28% of the amount of certain deductions and exemptions, and former Ways and Means chairman Dave Camp proposed a 25% limit.

Len Burman, Eric Toder, Daniel Berger, and Jeffrey Rohaly (chapter 5, with discussion by Louis Kaplow) examine how individual income tax expenditures are distributed by income. They compare alternative proposals for limiting tax expenditures and estimate their effects on economic incentives and the distribution of after-tax income.

They find that repealing several of the major individual tax expenditures alone could raise $282 to $366 billion in 2016, depending on the exact design. The 2% AGI limit approach would raise roughly half of that amount. The impact on progressivity also varies by the type of reform. However, because tax expenditures are not very effective at targeting low-income households, various progressive tax expenditure reforms can increase revenue.

1.5 TAX POLICY TOWARD EDUCATION

Along with the rising college premium noted earlier, college enrollments have sharply increased since 1960 (figure 1.3). In 1960, less than 5% of women aged 22 to 24 were enrolled in an accredited college. By 2014, it increased sixfold to 30%. For males, the percentage of enrollment doubled during this period. National efforts to promote college enrollment are increasingly delivered through tax-based assistance, including tax credits and deductions for tuition and fees, tax-advantaged college savings plans, and student loan interest deductions.

Susan Dynarski and Judith Scott-Clayton (chapter 6, with discussion by David Figlio) review the main programs and their history and document their growth over time. Altogether, federal support for postsecondary education costs taxpayers over $180 billion per year. However, Dynarski and Scott-Clayton present evidence that several of the most costly tax-incentive programs, namely tax credits and tuition tax deductions and exclusions ($32 billion), "have precisely zero effect on human capital accumulation." In fact, they conclude that "if their intent is to increase schooling, they are a failure." These programs appear merely to be subsidizing the families of students

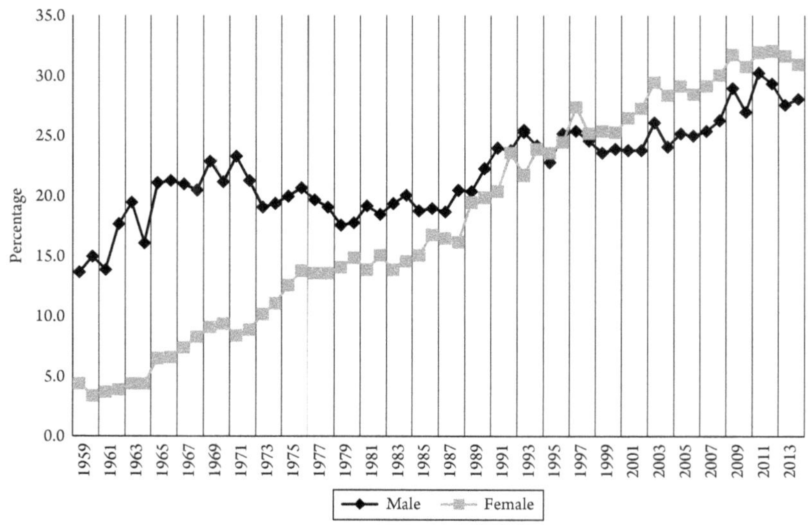

Figure 1.3 Percentage of enrollment of 22–24 year-olds, by sex, 1959–2014. *Source:* US Census Bureau, Current Population Survey.

who otherwise would have attended college. Dynarski and Scott-Clayton argue that traditional Department of Education-based student aid programs are more effective and show how various simplifications could increase the effectiveness of efforts to increase human capital.

1.6 TAX POLICY TOWARD LOW-INCOME FAMILIES

The Earned Income Tax Credit (EITC), introduced in 1975, is one of the few public policies that, historically, has achieved fairly strong bipartisan support. Eligibility for the credit is restricted to low-income households who work. A critical feature of the credit is that it is refundable, meaning that poor families with no tax liability can still receive a transfer. The Child Tax Credit (CTC), introduced in 1997, provides credits to families with children. However, CTC eligibility extends to households with incomes as high as $110,000, and so it targets the poor less than the EITC. The combined tax expenditures on the EITC and CTC exceeded $120 billion in 2013.

Hilary Hoynes and Jesse Rothstein (chapter 7, with discussion by Diane Schanzenbach) explain these programs in detail and review the extensive literature around their effectiveness. They conclude that the EITC has, for the most part, achieved its goals. It has successfully redistributed money and promoted work without inducing unreasonable amounts of compliance and administrative costs. However, the CTC is less effective at redistribution, with most of the benefits going to the non-poor. Hoynes and Rothstein also identify gaps left by both of the programs and suggest potential reforms, including expanding the EITC for workers without children.

1.7 CORPORATE AND BUSINESS TAX REFORM

US corporate tax rates have changed over the years (although not recently). But the basic structure of the US corporate income tax was devised over a century ago, when, unlike today, there was little trading across national borders and little activity among multinational corporations. The United States is now the only major economy that taxes its resident multinational firms on a worldwide basis, where profits repatriated from abroad are subject to US taxes. The United States also has the highest statutory corporate tax rate among OECD countries. Both of these factors lead to considerable economic distortions. For example, US firms are now holding over $2 trillion in profits earned offshore, in large part to avoid paying US taxes. Just eight technology companies alone, including Microsoft, Apple, and Google, are holding over $400 billion offshore.

Dhammika Dharmapala (chapter 8, with discussion by Rosanne Altshuler) provides a framework for navigating these challenging issues. He starts by identifying ten inefficiencies caused by the current US corporate tax system. He then discusses three different potential reforms. The first potential reform involves moving away from worldwide taxes to a territorial regime along with lower corporate tax rates. The second potential reform adopts a formula apportionment system. This system replaces the current separate accounting standard for each affiliate of a multinational corporation with a simple formula where, for example, earnings are apportioned according to sales within each country. The third reform is the destination-based tax, recently introduced by Alan Auerbach (2010) and Auerbach, Michael Devereux, and Helen Simpson (2010). This type of tax system focuses on a firm's cash flow instead of income, while levying taxes based on where the goods are actually consumed (the final destination). This reform is much larger than the previous two approaches. But Dharmapala argues that this reform would eliminate all or most of the inefficiencies of corporate taxation, whereas the first two reforms would only address some of the distortions that he identifies.

1.8 ESTATE AND CAPITAL GAINS TAXATION

In 2001, estates above a personal exemption of $675,000 were taxed at 55%. Today, the tax rate is 40% and the personal exemption for a married couple is close to $11 million. In 2014, there were only 5,158 taxable returns with estates above the personal exemption level, about one-tenth of the number in 2001. There are other tax breaks in the treatment of estates, notably the basis step-up at death where the cost basis of transferred assets is stepped up to the market value at the time of death. This means that neither the decedent nor the recipient of an inheritance owes capital gains taxes on the growth in asset values during the decedent's lifetime.

Wojciech Kopczuk (chapter 9, with discussion by James Poterba) discusses these issues, documenting how changes in estate taxation have reduced tax revenue and arguing that these changes might have contributed to the increasing concentration of wealth over time. He then argues that the basis step-up at death serves little economic purpose, and that the additional revenue received from its elimination could be used to fund a reduced tax rate. He points out how the treatment of spousal transfers at death, however, is a critical factor to consider, especially its revenue implications.

1.9 RETIREMENT TAX INCENTIVES

As noted earlier, participant assets in US tax-deferred retirement accounts have exploded during the past thirty years. Savers contributing to traditional tax-deferred accounts, like 401(k)s, 403(b)s, and IRAs, are able to reduce their reported taxable income by an amount equal to their contributions, up to a yearly maximum. Regular income taxes are then paid only when the money is eventually withdrawn at age 59½ or later. Savers who contribute to newer Roth-style 401(k) and IRA accounts receive no immediate tax reduction but, in exchange, face no tax liability upon eventual withdrawals. Roth accounts are more advantageous, therefore, to individuals who face lower income tax rates today than they expect to at retirement.

John Friedman (chapter 10, with discussion by Brigitte Madrian) reports that these tax breaks are quite costly to federal and state governments, exceeding over $150 billion in FY2014 alone, and projected to increase steeply to over $300 billion within a decade. Such a costly tax break might be efficient, though, if it leads to increases in household saving. However, Friedman argues that the tax incentives mostly reward people who would otherwise have saved. To be sure, previous empirical studies point to a wide range of estimates, but Friedman argues that the best studies suggest little impact on the overall savings rate. He suggests that "nudges," such as the automatic enrollment of participants (which became easier for companies to implement after the Pension Protection Act of 2006), are more effective at increasing contributions.

1.10 FUNDAMENTAL REFORM WITH CONSUMPTION TAXES

Projected future increases in the federal government's debt are primarily driven by the increased spending in the nation's largest entitlement programs, including Medicare, Social Security, and Medicaid. Barring benefit cuts, new revenue will be needed to pay for the added expenses to avoid a significant debt increase. However, for top earners, the average combined federal and state marginal income tax rate is 48%, with values exceeding 50% for residents in California and New York (Prante and John 2013). A parallel concern is that the United States already taxes the returns to capital (corporate and personal) at high levels compared to other countries. Recent discussions, therefore, have looked toward the potential of taxing consumption to raise additional revenue or to even replace some revenue currently obtained from income taxes. Taxing consumption instead of income avoids placing a larger burden on capital income. One major concern, however, is whether consumption taxes can be implemented in a progressive manner.

Alan Viard (chapter 11, with discussion by James Hines) examines three potential progressive forms of consumption taxes: the VAT (as in Europe), the Bradford "X" tax, and a personal expenditure tax. A VAT is levied at the business level. The X tax maintains progressive taxation of individuals and firms, potentially even increasing progressivity, while converting the tax base from income to consumption. With a personal expenditure tax, a household's taxable income is reduced by its level of savings. Viard demonstrates that while all three schemes effectively tax consumption rather than income, they differ in several important respects, including transition effects and the treatment of international transactions.

1.11 CONCLUDING REMARKS

There is general agreement among economists that the United States faces new challenges in its tax system. Since the TRA86, the US tax system has become less competitive internationally, concerns about the environment have grown, tax expenditures have exploded, income inequality has increased, and the nation's growing debt-to-GDP ratio is on an unsustainable path. We hope that this volume provides the basic analysis that policymakers need in order to address these critical issues, without further delay.

REFERENCES

Auerbach, Alan J. 2010. *A Modern Corporate Tax*. Washington, DC: Center for American Progress and the Hamilton Project.

Auerbach, Alan J., Michael P. Devereux, and Helen Simpson. 2010. "Taxing Corporate Income." In *Dimensions of Tax Design: The Mirrlees Review*, edited by James A. Mirrlees, Stuart Adam, Tim Besley, Richard Blundell, Steve Bond, Robert Chote, Malcolm Gammie, Paul Johnson, Gareth Myles, and James Poterba, 837–93. Oxford: Oxford University Press.

Carroll, Robert. 2008. "Fiscal Fact: No. 143." Tax Foundation, August. Washington, DC.

Center for Responsive Politics. 2016. "Environment: Long-Term Contribution Trends." http://www.opensecrets.org/industries/totals.php?cycle=2016&ind=q11

Chen, Peng. 2008. "Reevaluating Asset Allocation in a One-Basket World." Ibbotson Associates, Morningstar, May.

Congressional Budget Office. 2014. "The Distribution of Household Income and Federal Taxes, 2011." CBO Study, November. Washington, DC.

Congressional Budget Office. 2015. "The 2015 Long-Term Budget Outlook." CBO Study, June. Washington, DC.

Employee Benefit Research Institute. 2005. "History of 401(k) Plans: An Update." FACTS from EBRI, February. Washington, DC.

Feldstein, Martin, Daniel Feenberg, and Maya MacGuineas. 2011. "Capping Individual Tax Expenditure Benefits." National Bureau of Economic Research Working Paper No. 16921. Cambridge, MA.

Investment Company Institute. 2014. "Frequently Asked Questions about 401(k) Plans." https://www.ici.org/policy/retirement/plan/401k/faqs_401k

Joint Committee on Taxation. 1986. "Estimates of Federal Tax Expenditures for Fiscal Years 1987–1991." Washington, DC.

Joint Committee on Taxation. 2015. "Estimates of Federal Tax Expenditures for Fiscal Years 2015–2019." Washington, DC.

Prante, Gerald, and Austin John. "Top Marginal Effective Tax Rates by State and by Source of Income, 2012 Tax Law vs. 2013 Tax Law (as enacted in ATRA)" SSRN Working Paper #2176526.

Silverblatt, Howard. 2015. "S&P 500 2014: Global Sales." Research Paper, S&P Dow Jones Indices, McGraw Hill Financial, July.

US Department of the Treasury. 2009. "Update on Reducing the Federal Tax Gap and Improving Voluntary Compliance." July. Washington, DC.

2

EFFECTS OF INCOME TAX CHANGES ON ECONOMIC GROWTH

William G. Gale and Andrew A. Samwick

2.1 INTRODUCTION

Policymakers and researchers have long been interested in how potential changes to the personal income tax system affect the size of the overall economy. In 2014, for example, former Representative Dave Camp (R-MI) proposed a sweeping reform to the income tax system that would reduce rates, greatly pare back subsidies in the tax code, and maintain revenue levels and the distribution of tax burdens across income classes (Committee on Ways and Means 2014).

In this chapter, we focus on how tax changes affect economic growth. We focus on two types of tax changes—reductions in individual income tax rates and "income tax reform." We define the latter as changes that broaden the income tax base and reduce statutory income tax rates, but nonetheless maintain the overall revenue levels and the distribution of tax burdens implied by the current income system. Our focus is on individual income tax reform, leaving consideration of reforms to the corporate income tax (for which, see Toder and Viard 2014) and reforms that focus on consumption taxes for other analyses.

By "economic growth," we mean expansion of the supply side of the economy and of potential Gross Domestic Product (GDP). This expansion could be an increase in the annual growth rate, a one-time increase in the size of the economy that does not affect the future growth rate but puts the economy on a higher growth path, or both. Our focus on the supply side of the economy in the long run is in contrast to the short-term phenomenon, also called "economic growth," by which a boost in aggregate demand, in a slack economy, can raise GDP and help align actual GDP with potential GDP.

The importance of the topics addressed here derive from the income tax's central role in revenue generation, its impact on the distribution of after-tax income, and its effects on a wide variety of economic activities. The importance is only heightened by concerns about the long-term economic growth rate (Gordon 2016; Summers 2014) and concerns about the long-term fiscal status of the federal government (Auerbach and Gale 2016).

We find that, while there is no doubt that tax policy can influence economic choices, it is by no means obvious, on an ex ante basis, that tax rate cuts will ultimately lead to a larger economy in the long run. While rate cuts would raise the after-tax return to working, saving, and investing, they would also raise the after-tax income people receive from their current level of activities, which lessens their need to work, save, and invest. The first effect normally raises economic activity (through so-called substitution effects), while the second effect normally reduces it (through so-called income effects).

The financing of tax cuts significantly affects its impact on long-term growth. Tax cuts financed by immediate cuts in unproductive government spending could raise output, but tax cuts financed by reductions in government investment could reduce output. If they are not financed by spending cuts, tax cuts will lead to an increase in federal borrowing, which in turn, will reduce long-term growth. The historical evidence and simulation analyses suggest that tax cuts that are financed by debt for an extended period of time will have little positive impact on long-term growth and could reduce growth.

Tax reform is more complex, as it involves tax rate cuts as well as base-broadening changes. There is a theoretical presumption that such changes should raise the overall size of the economy in the long term, though the effect and magnitude of the impact are subject to considerable uncertainty. One fact that often escapes unnoticed is that broadening the tax base by reducing or eliminating tax expenditures raises the effective tax rate that people and firms face and hence will operate, in that regard, in a direction opposite to rate cuts and mitigate their effects on economic growth. But base-broadening has the additional benefit of reallocating resources from sectors that are currently tax-preferred to sectors that have the highest economic (pre-tax) return, which should increase the overall size of the economy.

A fair assessment would conclude that well-designed tax policies have the potential to raise economic growth, but there are many stumbling blocks along the way and certainly no guarantee that all tax changes will improve economic performance. Given the various channels through which tax policy affects growth, a tax change will be more growth-inducing to the extent that it involves (i) large positive incentive (substitution) effects that encourage work, saving, and investment; (ii) small or negative income effects, including a careful targeting of tax cuts toward new economic activity, rather than providing windfall gains for previous activities; (iii) reductions in distortions across economic sectors and across different types of income and consumption; and (iv) minimal increases in, or reductions in, the budget deficit.

The remainder of the chapter is organized as follows. Section 2.2 provides a conceptual framework by discussing the channels through which tax changes can affect economic performance, including the many ways in which a positive substitution effect in response to a tax rate cut might be dissipated or even reversed by other factors.

Section 2.3 provides an empirical starting point. We show that growth rates over long periods of time in the United States have not changed in tandem with the massive changes in the structure and revenue yield of the tax system that have occurred. We also report findings from Piketty, Saez, and Stantcheva (2014) that, across advanced countries, even large changes in the top marginal income tax rate over time do not appear to be strongly correlated with rates of growth.

Section 2.4 explores empirical evidence on taxes and growth from studies of major income tax changes in the United States. Consistent with the discussion in section 2.3, the studies find little evidence that tax cuts or tax reform since 1980 have impacted the long-term growth rate significantly.

Section 2.5 examines the new "narrative" approach to identifying tax changes that are exogenous to current economic conditions, stemming from the seminal work of Romer and Romer (2010). The literature, which generally uses vector autoregression (VAR) models, finds that tax cuts that meet the exogeneity criteria raise short-term output and other economic activity. The narrative literature does not speak to the long-term effects, though.

Section 2.6 discusses the results from the literature on simulation models, which has generated two main results. First, debt-financed tax cuts will tend to boost short-term growth (as in standard Keynesian models and in the literature using the narrative approach), but also tend to reduce long-term growth, if they are financed eventually by higher taxes. Second, revenue-neutral income tax reform can provide a modest boost to economic growth.

Section 2.7 concludes.[1]

2.2 FRAMEWORK

Not surprisingly, the overall relationship between tax changes and economic activity over the long term contains many pathways. In this section, we highlight the main channels through which income taxes affect economic growth.[2]

2.2.1 Reductions in Income Tax Rates

Reductions in income tax rates affect the behavior of individuals and businesses through both income and substitution effects. The positive effects of tax rate cuts on the size of the economy arise because lower tax rates raise the after-tax reward to working, saving, and investing. These higher after-tax rewards induce more work effort, saving, and investment through substitution effects. This is typically the "intended" effect of tax cuts on the size of the economy. Another positive effect of pure rate cuts is that they reduce the value of existing tax distortions and induce an efficiency-improving shift in the composition of economic activity (even holding the level of economic activity constant) away from currently tax-favored sectors, such as health and housing.

[1] There are a number of related issues that are both interesting and important, but beyond the scope of the chapter—including, for example, the elasticity of taxable income, the relationship between inequality (especially as it is affected by the tax system) and growth, the effects of corporate income tax reform on growth, and the detailed literatures on the effects of taxes on labor supply, saving, and investment.

[2] Gravelle (2014) provides extensive discussion of the channels through which tax changes affect economic growth, revenues, and other factors.

But pure rate cuts may also provide positive income (or wealth) effects, which reduce the need to work, save, and invest.

An across-the-board cut in income tax rates, for example, incorporates all of these effects. It raises the marginal return to work—increasing labor supply through the substitution effect. It reduces the value of existing tax subsidies and thus would likely alter the composition of economic activity. It also raises a household's after-tax income at every level of labor supply, which in turn, reduces labor supply through the income effect. The net effect on labor supply is ambiguous. Similar effects also apply to the impact of tax rate cuts on saving and other activities.[3]

The initial tax rate will affect the impact of a tax cut of a given size. For example, if the initial tax rate—on wages, say—is 90%, a 10 percentage point reduction in taxes doubles the after-tax wage from 10% to 20% of the pre-tax wage. If the initial tax rate is 20%, however, the same 10 percentage point reduction in taxes only raises the after-tax wage by one-eighth, from 80% to 90% of the pre-tax wage. Although income effects would be the same in the two cases, the substitution effect on labor supply and saving would be larger when tax rates are higher, so that the net gain in labor supply from a tax cut would be larger (or the net loss would be smaller in absolute value) when tax rates are high. In addition, because the economic cost of the tax rises with the square of the tax rate, the efficiency gains from reducing tax rates are larger when tax rates are higher to begin with.

2.2.2 Tax Reform

Tax reform, as defined in section 2.1, involves reductions in income tax rates as well as measures to broaden the tax base; that is, to reduce the use of tax expenditures or other items that narrow the base.[4] By removing the special treatment for various types of income or consumption, base-broadening will tend to raise the average effective marginal tax rates on labor supply, saving, and investment. This has two effects: the average substitution effect will be smaller from a revenue-neutral tax reform than from a tax rate cut, because the lower tax rate raises incentives to work and so on, while the base-broadening reduces such incentives; and the average income effect from a truly revenue-neutral reform should be zero.

Base-broadening has an additional effect that should help expand the size of the economy. Specifically, it would also reduce the allocation of resources to sectors and

[3] Many authors have examined the taxable income elasticity (TIE) (see, e.g., Saez, Slemrod, and Giertz 2012). The TIE combines a taxpayer's labor supply and avoidance responses to tax changes and thus is typically larger than the labor supply elasticity. Thus, a small TIE implies a small effect of taxes on growth (as in Romer and Romer 2014), but a large TIE does not imply a large effect of taxes on growth, as the TIE might arise due to avoidance activities, which do not have a direct effect on economic growth.

[4] Personal exemptions, the standard deduction, and lower marginal tax rates at low incomes are not considered tax expenditures.

industries that currently benefit from generous tax treatment. A flatter-rate, broader-based system would encourage resources to move out of currently tax-preferred sectors and into other areas of the economy with higher pre-tax returns. The reallocation would increase the size of the economy.

2.2.3 Financing

Besides their effects on private agents, tax changes also affect the economy through changes in federal finances. If the tax change is revenue-neutral, there is no issue with financing effects, since the reformed system would raise the same amount of revenue as the existing system.

However, any tax cut must be financed by some combination of future tax increases or current or future spending cuts—with borrowing to bridge the timing of spending and receipts. The associated, necessary policy changes are often not specified in the original tax cut legislation, but they have to be present in some form in order to meet the government's intertemporal budget constraint. Because fiscally unsustainable policies cannot be maintained forever, the financing of a tax cut must be incorporated into analyses of the effect of the tax cut itself.

In the absence of current spending changes, tax cuts are likely to raise the federal budget deficit.[5] The increase in federal borrowing will likely reduce national saving and hence the capital stock owned by Americans and future national income. In most economic environments, the increase in the deficit is also likely to raise interest rates. These changes—lower national saving and the associated increase in interest rates—create a fiscal drag on the economy's ability to grow (Congressional Budget Office 2013; Economic Report of the President 2003; Engen and Hubbard 2004; Gale and Orszag 2004a; Laubach 2009). The financing of tax cuts turns out to be extremely important in the simulation studies of tax rate changes discussed in section 2.6.

Of course, changes in one tax can be financed by changes in other taxes, too. A related literature considers the relationship between economic growth and the mix of taxes used. Arnold et al. (2011) use a panel data set of twenty-one OECD countries over the 1971–2004 period and find that corporate and personal income taxes have the most negative consequences for growth, while consumption taxes and property taxes are less harmful. Acosta-Ormaechea and Yoo (2012) use similar methods and a broader data set of sixty-nine countries over the 1970–2009 period and obtain similar results. As in the case of income tax cuts that are financed by reductions in government spending rather than budget deficits, the growth potential of income tax cuts is higher when the income tax cuts are financed by increases in other taxes that have lesser disincentives for work, saving, and investment.

[5] There are potentially important differences on the size of the economy in the form of spending cuts that could finance tax reductions, but they are beyond the scope of this chapter.

2.2.4 Other Governmental Entities

Federal tax cuts can also generate responses from other governmental entities—including the central bank, state governments, and foreign governments. The Joint Committee on Taxation (2014), for example, examines how different Federal Reserve Board policies would affect the impact of Camp's tax reform proposals on economic growth.

The potential responses of foreign governments are often overlooked. Cuts in US taxes that induce capital inflows from abroad, for example, may encourage other countries to reduce their taxes to retain capital or attract US funds. To the extent that other countries respond, the net effect of income tax cuts on growth will be smaller than otherwise.

2.2.5 Summary

The popular discussion of the link between tax cuts and economic growth often starts with the presumption that tax cuts will boost growth. While substitution effects of tax cuts will boost labor supply and saving, it is not at all clear that this will translate into a stronger supply side of the economy because of several other effects. The first is the income effect, which will at least partially offset the substitution effect. The second is, in the case of tax reform, the higher taxes on the other activities that are now included in the broadened tax base. The third is, in the case of tax cuts not paid for by reduced government spending, the offsetting effects of higher budget deficits and thus interest rates on economic activity.

For individuals on the supply side of the economy, there are two key elasticities—labor supply and saving. Most of the literature finds small effects of taxes on labor supply, but Keane (2011) challenges the presumption that the elasticity of labor supply for males is small. He shows that modeling human capital investment—a positive effect of the current period's labor supply on later periods' wages—allows for labor supply elasticities sufficient to generate large efficiency costs of taxation. He further shows that for women, labor supply elasticities that allow for the dynamic effects of wages on fertility, marriage, education, and work experience are generally quite large. Thus, there remains the potential for some tax cuts to generate behavioral responses on labor supply that lead to higher economic activity.[6]

Bernheim (2002) surveys the literature on the response of savings to generic changes in the after-tax return and concludes that there is little evidence for a large effect. In the case of savings, there must also be a link between the behavioral response of higher savings to the tax cut and economic activity. Chetty et al. (2014) review the uncertain literature on saving incentives and present new evidence that the incentives

[6] See also Keane and Rogerson (2012) and Chetty, Guren, Manoli, and Weber (2011, 2013) on reconciliations of the (small) micro elasticities with (larger) macro labor supply elasticities.

do not raise overall saving. Many studies have considered the causal link between savings and growth. The general conclusion in the literature, well-articulated by Carroll and Weil (1994), is that the observed positive relationship reflects a causal pathway from growth to savings, rather than savings to growth.

2.3 AN EMPIRICAL STARTING POINT

There are at least three concepts to which the term "economic growth" might refer. The narrowest concept is that economic growth is the steady-state rate of growth that emerges from an economic model of supply and demand over time. This concept is too narrow for our purposes, as it ignores all growth that may occur in the (possibly quite lengthy) transition between a steady-state under one tax regime and the steady-state to which the economy converges after some tax policy has been changed. The broadest concept is any change in the level of economic activity over any period of time. This concept implicitly, if not explicitly, underlies analyses of the role of tax changes in stabilization policy, to smooth out economic fluctuations at business cycle frequencies. This concept is too broad, given our focus on the supply side of the economy, as over some short periods of time the level of economic activity may increase because, for example, tax cuts boost demand to align actual and potential GDP rather than increase potential GDP.

A third concept, intermediate between the first two, considers any change in the level of economic activity for periods longer than the business cycle. This could include something that boosts the economy on a one-time, permanent basis, something that alters the steady-state growth rate of the economy, or something that does both. Restricting attention to longer periods is appropriate for several reasons. First, looking at longer periods averages out the impact of tax policy over the business cycle. Second, as discussed in the context of simulation analyses below, tax cuts might have positive effects on economic activity in the short run but negative effects over the long run as higher interest rates from the ensuing deficits crowd out other economic activity. Third, focusing on a longer period helps ensure that the full impact of tax changes can be considered.

Using this concept of economic growth, a first cut at the US historical data and the cross-country data on growth rate differences across countries suggest no strong relationship between economic growth and income tax policy.

2.3.1 Historical Trends

US historical data show huge shifts in taxes with virtually no observable shift in growth rates. From 1870 to 1912, the United States had no income tax, and tax revenues were just 3% of GDP. From 1913 to 1946, the economy experienced an especially volatile period, including two World Wars and the Great Depression, along with the introduction and expansion of the income and payroll taxes and expansion of estate and corporate taxes.

By 1947, the economy had entered a new period with permanently higher taxes and government spending. From 1947 to 2000, the highest marginal income tax rate averaged 66% and federal revenues averaged about 18% of GDP (Gale and Potter 2002). In addition, estate and corporate taxes were imposed at high marginal rates and state-level taxes rose significantly over earlier levels.

The vast differences between taxes before 1913 and after World War II can therefore provide at least a first-order sense of the importance of tax policy on growth. However, the growth rate of real GDP per capita was identical—2.2%–in the 1870–1912 period and between 1947 and 1999 (Gale and Potter 2002).

More formally, Stokey and Rebelo (1995) look at the significant increase in income tax rates during World War II and its effect on the growth rate of per capita real Gross National Product (GNP). Figure 2.1 shows the basic trends they highlight—namely, a massive increase in income tax and overall tax revenues during World War II that has persisted and since proven to be more or less permanent. There is, as shown in figure 2.1, no corresponding break in the growth rate of per capita real GNP before or after World War II (though it is less volatile). A variety of statistical tests confirm formally what figure 2.1 shows; namely, the finding that the increase in tax revenue around World War II had no discernible impact on the long-term per-capita GNP growth rate.[7]

Hungerford (2012) plots the annual real per-capita GDP growth rate against the top marginal income tax rate and the top capital gains tax rate from 1945 to 2010 (see figure 2.2), a period that spanned wide variation in the top rate. The fitted values suggest that higher tax rates are not associated with higher or lower real per-capita GDP growth rates to any significant degree. In multivariate regression analysis, neither the top income tax rate nor the top capital gains tax rate has a statistically significant association with the real GDP growth rate. An obvious caveat to this result is that the share of households facing the top rate is generally quite small. However, historically, the highest several marginal tax rates were moved together, so that changes in the top rate per se proxy for changes in a broader set of higher tax rates that do affect many taxpayers.

To be clear, many factors affect economic growth rates. Nonetheless, if taxes were as crucial to long-term growth as is sometimes claimed, the large historical increases in tax burdens and marginal tax rates that occurred between World War I and the end of World War II, as well as the historic reduction in top marginal income tax rates that has occurred since then, might be expected to affect the aggregate growth rate of the economy.

[7] GNP growth did spike downward immediately after the war, but that was related to a massive demilitarization effort. Overall, the economy grew massively during World War II (for reasons other than taxes, of course) and then maintained its former growth rate in the relatively high-tax post–World War II period.

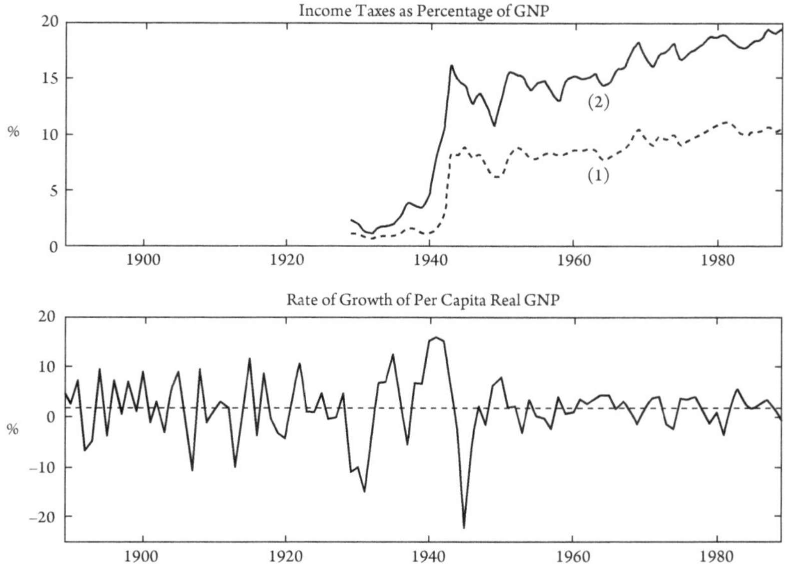

Figure 2.1 Taxes as a share of GNP and growth of real GNP per capita. *Note:* In the top graph, line 1 consists of federal, state, and local individual income taxes. Line 2 adds social security and retirement taxes as well as federal corporate taxes. *Source:* Stokey and Rebelo (1995).

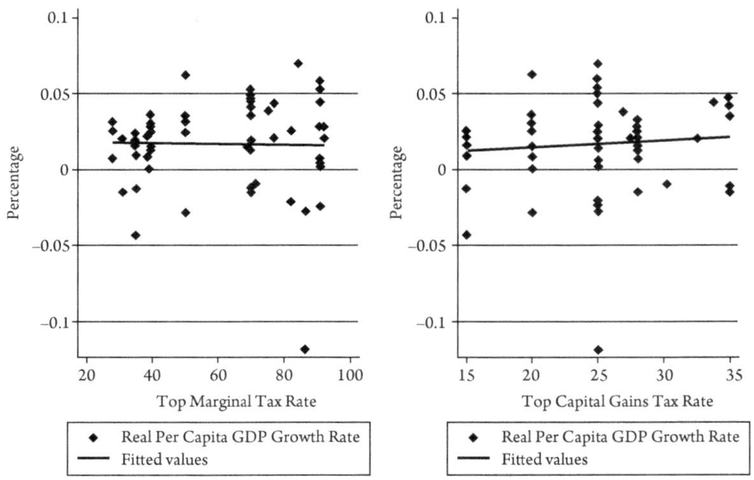

Figure 2.2 Real per capita GDP growth rate and top tax rates, 1945–2010. *Note:* The vertical axis is the real per capita GDP growth rate. *Source:* Hungerford (2012).

2.3.2 Cross-Country Evidence

Cross-country studies generally find very small long-term effects of taxes on growth among developed countries (Slemrod 1995).[8] Countries vary, of course, not just in their level of revenues and spending but also in the composition of taxes and outlays. Nevertheless, a large literature has developed aiming to compare tax effects across countries.

Evidence shows that pooling data from developed and developing countries is inappropriate because the growth processes differ (Garrison and Lee 1992; Grier and Tullock 1989) and that taxes have little or no effect on economic growth in developed countries. Mendoza et al. (1997) and Garrison and Lee (1992) find no tax effects on growth in developed countries. Padovano and Galli (2001) find that a 10 percentage point reduction in marginal tax rates raises the growth rate by 0.11 percentage point in OECD countries. Engen and Skinner (1992) find significant effects of taxes on growth in a sample of 107 countries, but the tax effects are tiny and insignificant when estimated only on developed countries.

Piketty, Saez, and Stantcheva (2014) look at evidence from eighteen OECD countries on tax rates and economic growth for the 1960–2010 time period. Figure 2.3, taken from their study, conveys the idea that there is little correlation between growth in real GDP per capita and the drop in the top marginal rate for the 1960–2010 period. Their regression analysis confirms this result.

Thus, a reasonable summary from the simple correlations of economic growth and income tax policy over long periods is that the presence of strong tax effects on economic growth is hard to reconcile with observations from the US historical record and international comparisons.[9]

2.4 EMPIRICAL ANALYSES OF PARTICULAR TAX REFORMS

Ultimately, the impact of specific tax changes on the size of the economy is an empirical question. Rigorous empirical studies of actual US tax changes are relatively rare, however, for several reasons. First, the United States has only had a few major tax policy changes over the past fifty years. Second, most major tax changes alter many features of the code simultaneously. Third, it is difficult to isolate the impact of tax changes relative to other changes in policy and the economy, an issue addressed directly in section 2.5.

[8] In his comments on Slemrod (1995), Easterly (1995) concludes, "the data mock attempts to discern the growth effects of taxes."

[9] That the weak relationships between economic growth and tax rates in these simple correlations inform the current literature is evident from recent theoretical contributions. Consider Jaimovich and Rebelo (2012), who derive an endogenous growth model in which, over a broad range of tax parameters (including those chosen by the median voter), there is no important relationship between the rate of growth and the tax structure. Only when tax rates get to extremely high levels does the negative effect of taxes on growth appear. The original insight that changes in taxes might have little effect on growth is attributed to Harberger (1964).

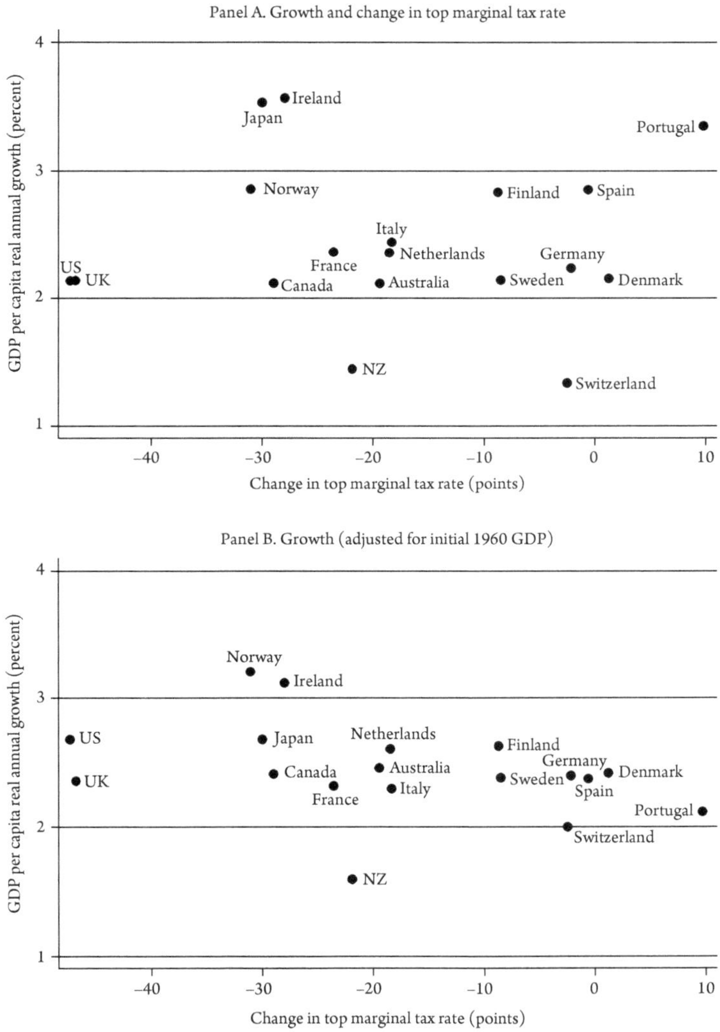

Figure 2.3 Economic growth rates and top marginal tax rates, 1960–2010. *Note*: The figure depicts the average real GDP per capita annual growth rate from 1960–1964 to 2006–2010 plotted against the change in the top marginal tax rate. Panel A considers the raw growth rate while panel B controls for initial real GDP per capita as of 1960. *Source*: Piketty, Saez, and Stantcheva (2014).

In this section, we review studies of specific tax policy changes.[10] It is worth noting that historical reforms do not represent "pure" textbook tax reform efforts, since they all took place in the real world, subject to the compromises that the political process imposes. However, future tax reforms will also be affected by political factors, so the history of reform efforts and their effects is relevant.

[10] See McBride (2012) and Huang and Frentz (2014) for recent surveys that reach different conclusions on the effects of taxes on economic growth.

2.4.1 Effects of Tax Cuts and Tax Increases

Several studies have aimed to disentangle the impact of the major tax cuts that occurred in 1981, 2001, and 2003, as well as the tax increases that occurred in 1990 and 1993. The Economic Recovery Act of 1981 (ERTA) included a 23% across-the-board reduction in personal income tax rates, a deduction for two-earner families, expanded IRAs, numerous reductions in capital income taxes, and indexed the income tax brackets for inflation. Many features of ERTA, particularly some of the subsidies for capital income, were trimmed back in the 1982 and 1984 tax acts.

Feldstein (1986) provides estimates indicating that all of the growth of nominal GNP between 1981 and 1985 can be explained by changes in monetary policy. Of the change in real GNP during that period, he finds that only about 2 percentage points of the 15 percentage point rise cannot be explained by monetary policy. But he also notes that the data do not strongly support either the traditional Keynesian view that the tax cuts significantly raise aggregate demand or traditional supply-side claims that they significantly increase labor supply. He finds, rather, that exchange rate changes and the induced changes in net exports account for the small part of growth not explained by monetary policy.

Feldstein and Elmendorf (1989) find that the 1981 tax cuts had virtually no net impact on economic growth. They find that the strength of the recovery over the 1980s could be ascribed to monetary policy. In particular, they find no evidence that the tax cuts in 1981 stimulated labor supply.

A Center on Budget and Policy Priorities study looks at the relationship between the 1993 tax hikes and the 2001 tax cuts with respect to employment and GDP growth over the periods following the respective reforms (Huang 2012). As figure 2.4 shows,

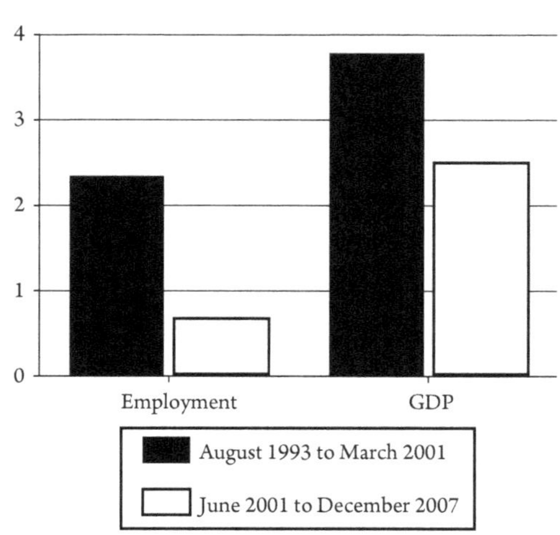

Figure 2.4 Employment and GDP growth following the 1993 tax increases and the 2001 tax cuts. *Note:* The vertical axis is the average annual growth rate during the time period. *Source:* Huang (2012).

job creation and economic growth were significantly stronger in the years following the marginal income tax increases enacted in 1993 (the top marginal tax rate went up from 31% to 39.6%) than they were following the 2001 tax cuts. While correlation does not imply causation, and while the 1993 and 2001 tax changes occurred at different times in the business cycle, making comparisons between the two of them more difficult, the evidence at the very least discredits the argument that higher growth cannot take place during a period of higher tax rates.

The tax cuts in 2001 (The Economic Growth and Tax Relief Reconciliation Act of 2001, or EGTRRA) reduced income tax rates, phased out and temporarily eliminated the estate tax, expanded the child credit, and made other changes. The 2003 tax cut (The Jobs and Growth Tax Relief Reconciliation Act of 2003, or JGTRRA) reduced rates on dividends and capital gains.

A variety of forms of evidence suggest that the impact on growth of these changes was negligible. A cursory look at growth between 2001 and 2007 (before the onset of the Great Recession) suggests that overall growth rate was both mediocre—real per-capita income grew at an annual rate of 1.5% during that period, compared to 2.3% from 1950 to 2001—and was concentrated in housing and finance, two sectors that were not favored by the tax cuts. There is, in short, no first-order evidence in the aggregate data that these tax cuts generated growth.

Careful microeconomic analyses give similar conclusions. Eissa (2008) tabulates the unconditional distribution of hours worked over the 2000–2006 period using the March Current Population Surveys. Her results, displayed in figure 2.5, show that hours worked by prime-age males did not change over this period, while the distributions of hours worked for women—married women and particularly single mothers—shifted lower. This is reflected in the second and third panels of figure 2.5 by the increase in the probability mass at zero hours of work. This lower likelihood of labor force participation is inconsistent with the view that lower tax rates encourage labor supply. The lack of a positive shift in the years following the Bush tax cuts occurred despite the economic recovery from the recession in the early part of the period, suggesting that any impact of tax cuts on average hours worked was minimal.

Gale and Potter (2002) estimate that the 2001 tax cut would have little or no net effect on GDP over the next ten years and could have even reduced it; that is, they find that the negative effect of higher deficits and the decline in national saving would outweigh the positive effect of reduced marginal tax rates. The intuition behind these results is noteworthy. Gale and Potter (2002) do not show that reductions in tax rates have no effect, or negative effects, on economic behavior. Rather, the improved incentives of reduced tax rates—analyzed in isolation—increase economic activity by raising labor supply, human capital, and private saving. Indeed, these factors are estimated to increase the size of the economy in 2011 by almost 1%. But EGTRRA and JGTRRA were sets of tax incentives financed by increased deficits. The key point is that the tax cut reduced public saving (through higher deficits) by more than it increased private saving. As a result, national saving fell, which reduced the capital stock, even after

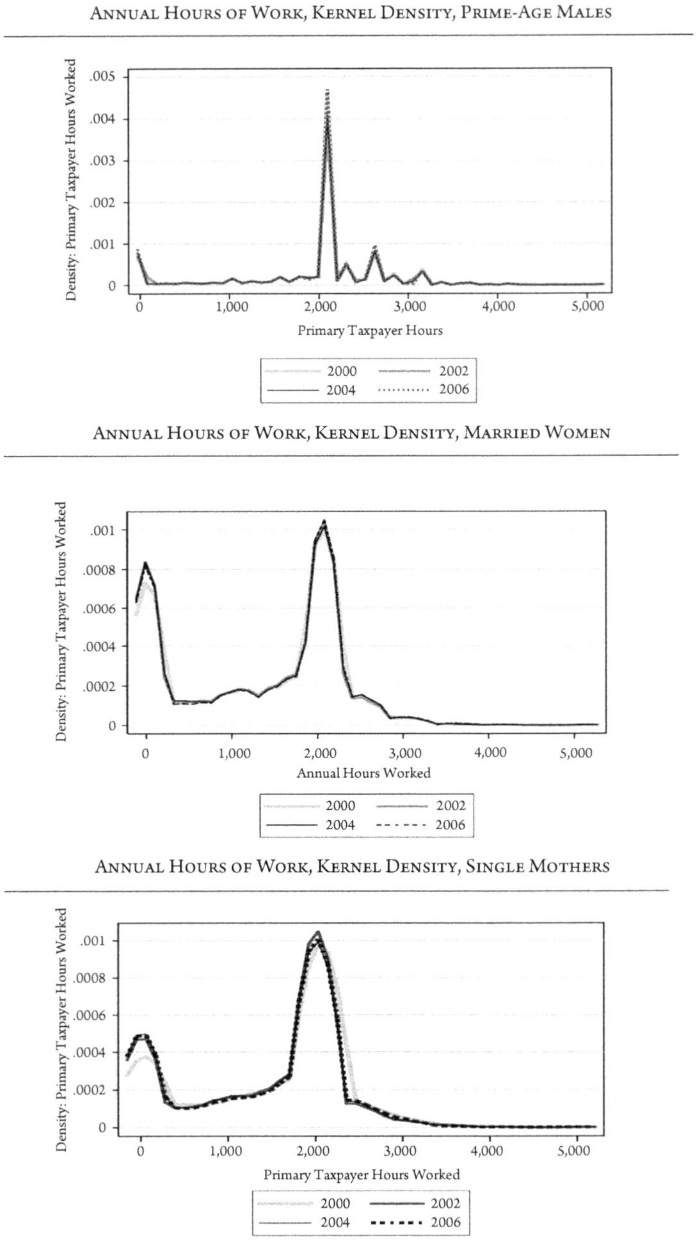

Figure 2.5 Changes in annual hours of work around the tax cuts in 2001 and 2003. *Source:* Eissa (2008), using the March Current Population Surveys, 2001–2007.

adjusting for international capital flows, and lowered GDP and GNP. Thus, the effects on the deficit are central to the findings.[11]

Based on analysis in Gale and Potter (2002) and Gale and Orszag (2005), the 2001 tax cut raised the cost of capital for investments in residential housing, sole proprietorships, and corporate structures because the higher deficits raised interest rates. By contrast, the cost of capital for corporate equipment fell slightly because the tax act also contained provisions for bonus depreciation that more than offset the rise in interest rates.

It might also be thought that the 2003 tax cut would have more beneficial effects on investment, since it focused on dividend and capital gains tax cuts, but Desai and Goolsbee (2004) argue that the effects were likely to be small and Yagan (2015) presents empirical evidence that the 2003 tax cuts had little impact on investment or employment.

2.4.2 Tax Reform

If "tax reform" is defined as base-broadening, rate-reducing changes that are neutral with respect to the pre-existing revenue levels and distributional burdens of taxation, then tax reform is a rare event in modern US history. While virtually every commission that looks at tax reform suggests proposals along these lines—see, for example, the Bowles-Simpson National Commission on Fiscal Responsibility and Reform (2010), the Domenici-Rivlin Debt Reduction Task Force (2010), and President Bush's tax reform commission (President's Advisory Panel 2005)—policymakers rarely follow through. Indeed, only the Tax Reform Act of 1986 (TRA86) would qualify, among all legislative events in the last fifty years. Representative Camp's recent proposal would also qualify, but, of course, it has not been enacted.

Auerbach and Slemrod (1997) address numerous features of TRA86 on economic growth and its components. They suggest that, although there may have been substantial impacts on the timing and composition of economic activity—for example, a reduction in tax-sheltering activity—there was little effect on the overall level of economic activity. They conclude that there were small impacts on saving, labor supply, entrepreneurship, and other productive activities. Although they do not provide an overall estimate for the impact on economic growth, it seems clear from their conclusions about microeconomic impacts and from the lack of aggregate growth in the data that any growth impact of TRA86 was quite small. Evidence from one historical

[11] An earlier study by Engen and Skinner (1996) simulates that a generic 5 percentage point reduction in marginal tax rates would raise annual growth rates by 0.2 to 0.3 percentage points for a decade. But the tax cut that Engen and Skinner examine is financed by immediate reductions in government consumption, not deficits, and the 5 percentage point drop in effective marginal tax rates that they analyze is roughly 3 (10) times the size of the cut in effective economy-wide marginal tax rates on wages (capital income) induced by EGTRRA and JGTRRA. See Gale and Potter (2002) for additional discussion of the Engen and Skinner results and differences between the tax cuts they analyze and the 2001 and 2003 tax changes.

episode is always subject to qualification and one-time circumstances. Nevertheless, the Auerbach-Slemrod analysis is important to consider precisely because TRA86 considerably broadened the tax base and substantially reduced marginal income tax rates, consonant with the very notion of tax reform.

2.5 THE NARRATIVE APPROACH

In a novel study, Romer and Romer (2010) use the narrative record from presidential speeches, executive branch documents, and congressional reports to identify the size, timing, and principal motivation for all major tax policy actions in the post–World War II United States. Focusing on tax changes made to promote long-run growth or to reduce an inherited budget deficit, rather than tax changes made for other reasons (such as to boost the economy in the short run), they find that tax changes have large and persistent effects, with a tax increase of 1% of GDP lowering real GDP by roughly 2% to 3% over the next several years. That is, they show that exogenous tax cuts can boost the economy in the short term. The impacts are rapid enough (with effects taking place over the first few quarters) to suggest an aggregate demand response, but they may also be long-lived enough (with the effects lasting through twenty quarters) to suggest that supply-side responses may be at work as well. As they note:

> Our results are largely silent concerning whether the output effects operate through incentives and supply behavior or through disposable income and demand stimulus. The persistence of the effects is suggestive of supply effects. But other studies have found that monetary policy, which necessarily works through demand, also has highly persistent output effects (for example, Ben S. Bernanke and Ilian Mihov 1998 and Romer and Romer 2004). The speed of the effects is suggestive of demand effects. But rapid supply responses are not out of the question. (2010: 799)

Subsequent work has nested the Romer and Romer framework in the more traditional VAR approach to studying the effect of policy changes (monetary and fiscal) on economic outcomes. Favero and Giavazzi (2012) show that when analyzed in a multivariate VAR, the fiscal multiplier of shocks identified through the narrative method is not different from that obtained through the traditional approach. Using this framework and an average marginal tax rate series constructed by Barro and Redlick (2011), Mertens (2015) estimates that an unanticipated decrease in taxes (associated with an increase of 1 percentage point in the net-of-tax rate) leads to an increase in real GDP of 0.44% in the first year and 0.78% in the third year, after which it slowly declines in magnitude and loses statistical significance.[12]

[12] Barro and Redlick (2011) find that taxes affect short-term growth, but they do not examine long-term issues.

This literature represents an important step forward in that it aims to identify tax policies that are exogenous to current economic circumstances, and the papers show convincingly that such tax policies can have short-term effects on the economy. But the literature is clear that it is not addressing long-term effects. Mertens and Ravn (2012), for example, find that "implemented tax cuts, regarding of their timing, have expansionary effects on output. . . . Tax shocks are important impulses *to the U.S. business cycle*" (emphasis added). Hayo and Uhl (2014) use the same framework to study "the short-term macro-economic effects of legislated tax changes" in Germany. Cloyne (2013) follows a similar approach for the United Kingdom and focuses on business cycle issues.

Zidar (2015) shows that the exogenous tax cuts identified by Romer and Romer (2010) tend to boost subsequent employment growth when the tax cuts are aimed at low-income households but not when they are aimed at high-income households. This pattern seems more consistent with an aggregate demand channel than with a traditional supply-side story.

Mertens and Ravn (2010) find that the economy responds in the same time frame to changes in government spending as it does to taxes in the studies listed above. This pattern also seems consistent with an aggregate demand story. Just as one would not want to draw long-term conclusions about spending and growth from that study, one would not want to draw long-term conclusions about taxes and growth from the studies above.

This is especially true because theory and simulation analyses, presented in section 2.6, suggest that empirical findings of economically significant short-term impacts of tax changes on economic activity are not necessarily inconsistent with long-term impacts that are small, zero, or the opposite sign of the short-term effects. As noted, a reduction in tax rates that increases the government's budget deficit will have negative effects on future economic growth as higher interest rates crowd out economic activity. Whether these future reductions in growth will ultimately outweigh the short-run increases can be considered in a simulation framework, which we discuss in the next section. Thus, the narrative approach, coupled with VAR methodology, represents an important advance in the econometrics of studying the short-term effects of tax policy changes, but the results tell us little with respect to the long-term impacts of tax changes on economic growth.

2.6 SIMULATIONS

Given the various difficulties of empirically estimating the impacts of tax cuts and tax reform using historical data, economists have often turned to simulation analyses to pin down the impacts. The advantage of simulation analysis is the ability to hold other factors constant. The disadvantage is the need to specify a wide variety of features of the economy that may be tangential to tax policy or for which little reliable evidence is available.

2.6.1 Tax Cuts or Increases

Formal analyses confirm the intuition that deficit-financed tax cuts are poorly designed to stimulate long-term growth and that tax cuts financed by spending cuts are more likely to have a positive impact on economic growth.

A simple extrapolation based on earlier published results from the Federal Reserve Board model of the US economy implies that a cut in income tax rates that reduces revenues by 1% of GDP will raise GDP by just 0.1% after ten years if the Fed follows a Taylor (1993) rule for monetary policy (Reifschneider et al. 1999).

Elmendorf and Reifschneider (2002) use a large-scale econometric model developed at the Federal Reserve and find that a reduction in taxes that is somewhat similar to the personal income tax cuts in the 2001 law reduces long-term output and has only a slight positive effect on output in the first ten years.

Auerbach (2002) estimates that a deficit-financed tax cut similar in structure to the 2001 tax cut (which originally was slated to last only until 2010) would reduce the long-term size of the economy if is financed by tax rate increases after it expires. Even if the deficits are eventually offset partially or wholly by reductions in federal outlays (government consumption in the model), the tax cuts would either reduce the size of the per-capita capital stock or slightly raise it by 0.5% in the long term.

The Congressional Budget Office (2001) projected that the 2001 tax legislation may raise or reduce the size of the economy, but the net effect was likely to be less than 0.5% of GDP in either direction in 2011, again depending primarily on how the deficit was financed in the long run. Analysis of the 2003 capital gains tax cuts suggests that the net long-term growth effects are negative—that is, that the negative effects of deficits on capital accumulation outweigh the positive incentive effects of such policies (Joint Committee on Taxation 2003; Macroeconomic Advisers 2003). Similar effects for deficit-financed tax cuts have been found by the Congressional Budget Office (2010).

Diamond and Viard (2008) estimate the effects of a variety of deficit-financed tax cuts, concluding that even when the tax cuts do raise the size of the economy in the long term, they nonetheless often lower the welfare of members of future generations. That combination can occur because deficit-financed tax cuts can shift fiscal burdens to future generations, who then have to pay for the tax cuts via higher distortionary taxes. In addition, a switch in tax bases—say, from income to consumption—will impose different burdens on different generations, since the income and consumption have different timing patterns over the life-cycle.

The most comprehensive aggregate analysis of the long-term effects of deficit-financed tax cuts was undertaken by the Congressional Budget Office (Dennis et al. 2004). This study examines the effects of a generic 10% statutory reduction in all income tax rates, including those applying to dividends, capital gains, and the alternative minimum tax.[13] As Dennis et al. (2004) note in their study, "the reduction in

[13] The authors do not examine the 2001 and 2003 tax cuts per se. Because the Congressional Budget Office study focuses on "pure" rate cuts, rather than the panoply of additional credits and subsidies enacted in EGTRRA, the growth effects reported probably overstate the impact of making the 2001

Table 2.1 Long-term effects of a deficit-financed 10% cut in income tax rates (percentage change in GDP and GNP)

	Financed in the Long-Run by			
	Csuts in Spending		*Increase in Income Tax Rates*	
Model	GDP	GNP	GDP	GNP
OLG-Closed[a]	−0.1	−0.1	−1.5	−1.5
OLG-Open	0.5	−0.4	0.2	−2.1
Ramsey[a]	0.8	0.8	−1.2	−1.2

[a] GNP and GDP are the same in these models. *Source:* Dennis et al. (2004).

marginal tax rates is large compared with the overall budget cost." Thus, the positive growth effects of better incentives are large relative to the negative growth effects on higher deficits. The study uses three different models to examine the long-term effects: a closed- economy overlapping generations (OLG) model; an open economy OLG model; and the Ramsey model. The authors assume that the tax cuts are financed with deficits for ten years; then the budget gaps are closed gradually with either by reductions in government consumption or increases in tax rates. Thus, deficits are allowed to build for the first decade of the tax cut and much of the second decade as well.

The results are reported in table 2.1. In the three scenarios where the tax cuts are financed in the long run by increases in income taxes, the long-term effects are generally negative. In the Ramsey model and the closed economy OLG model, GDP (and GNP) falls significantly. In the open economy OLG model, GDP rises slightly, but GNP falls by even more than in the other models. The chain of events creating this outcome is that the tax cuts reduce national saving and hence increase capital inflows. The inflow, in conjunction with increased labor supply, is sufficient to slightly raise (by 0.2%) the output produced on American soil. The capital inflows, however, must eventually be repaid and doing so reduces national income (GNP) even though domestic production rises.

Ultimately, of course, future living standards of Americans depend on GNP, not GDP (Elmendorf and Mankiw 1999). GNP represents income accruing to Americans, whereas GDP records production that occurs within the country. In the three scenarios where the tax cuts are financed with cuts in government consumption in the long run, the effects are less negative. In the closed-economy OLG model, there is virtually

and 2003 tax cuts permanent because in EGTRRA, many people did not receive marginal rate cuts and some received higher child credits, which should have induced reductions in labor supply via the income effect. In their analysis, every taxpayer receives a reduction in marginal tax rates, so 100% of taxpayers and taxable income is affected, whereas 20% of filers did not receive a tax cut under EGTRRA (Gale and Potter 2002).

no effect on growth. In the open-economy OLG model, GDP rises by 0.5% in the long run, but GNP falls by 0.4%.

A number of studies suggest that the greater the extent to which tax cuts are financed by contemporaneous spending cuts, the greater the likelihood that the policy change raises economic growth. Auerbach (2002) finds that the larger the share of a tax cut is financed by cuts in contemporaneous government purchases, the larger the impact is on national saving. Foertsch (2004) obtains similar results using Congressional Budget Office models. In the Congressional Budget Office (2004) study cited above, the sole exception to the result that tax cuts lower long-term size of the economy occurs when the tax cuts are financed by reductions in government purchases and the policy is run through the Ramsey model, in which case long-term GDP would rise by about 0.8%. However, as the authors note, the Ramsey model implies that the reduction in government saving due to the tax cuts in the first decade is matched one-for-one with increases in private saving (Dennis et al. 2004). Empirical evidence rejects this view (see Gale and Orszag 2004b).[14]

The analysis of tax cuts financed by reductions in government purchases is subject to an important caveat. The models assume that government purchases either represent resources that are destroyed or that government purchases enter utility in a separable fashion from private consumption. For some purposes, like national defense, the latter assumption might be appropriate. In those cases, the cut in spending would reduce households' utility and thus impose welfare costs but would not affect choices at the margin. However, in all of the analyses, it is assumed that there is no investment component of the government purchases—so the analysis would not be representative of the effects of cuts in, for example, education, research and development, or infrastructure investment.

2.6.2 Tax Reform

There is a cottage industry in economics of simulating the impact of broad-based income tax reform on growth. The analysis of tax reform can be broken up conceptually into two distinct parts—how the tax changes affect individual or firm choices regarding the level of work, saving, and investment, and how the changes affect the allocation of such activity across sectors of the economy. There is a long tradition of studies implying that the impact of tax reform on the changing sectoral allocation of resources can be important, starting from Harberger's (1962) classic analysis of the corporate tax and including Fullerton and Henderson (1987), Gravelle and Kotlikoff (1989), and Diamond and Zodrow (2008).[15]

[14] Jones et al. (1993) estimate that the removal of all taxes would raise growth substantially. However, Stokey and Rebelo (1995) show that the result is sensitive to a number of parameter choices and that the most defensible parameter values imply that flatter tax rates have little impact on growth. Lucas (1990) obtains a similar result to Stokey and Rebelo (1995).

[15] The Congressional Budget Office (2005, 2006) published estimates of how effective tax rates vary across types of capital assets. The studies do not report the welfare effects of tax reform but do provide evidence that the tax code favors some sectors of the economy over others.

Lim Rogers (1997) finds that a revenue-neutral shift to a flat-rate income tax with no deductions, exclusions, or credits other than a personal exemption of $10,000 per filer plus $5,000 per dependent would raise the long-term size of the economy by between 1.8% and 3.8%, depending on assumptions about the relevant behavioral elasticities.

Auerbach et al. (1997) find that moving to the same flat-rate income tax (i.e., with the personal exemptions noted above) would reduce the size of the economy by 3% in the long run. However, Altig et al. (2001) use a similar model to evaluate a more extreme policy reform—a revenue-neutral switch to a flat income tax—but with no personal deductions or exemptions. They find that this would raise output immediately by 4.5%, and then by another 1% over the ensuing fifteen years, although it would hurt the poor in current and future generations. The model illustrates two interesting results. First, tax reform can raise the overall size of the economy with a one-time change that puts the economy on a new growth path even if it does not affect the long-term growth rate. In this model, the one-time effect of tax reform on the size of the economy dominates the effect on the overall growth rate.

Second, there is often a trade-off between growth and progressivity in that model. However, more recent work has highlighted the role of uncertainty in tax reform, noting that a progressive income tax system provides insurance against fluctuating income by making the percentage variation of after-tax income less than the percentage variation in pre-tax income (Kneiser and Ziliak 2002; Nishiyama and Smetters 2005). This finding may change the terms of the trade-off between progressivity and growth effects.

The most recent example of simulation of comprehensive tax reform is the Joint Committee on Taxation's (2014) analysis of the Camp plan. The Joint Committee on Taxation offers eight different scenarios depending on how the Federal Reserve responds, the underlying model of the economy used, and assumptions about behavioral elasticities. They find that Camp's plan would raise the size of the economy from 0.1% to 1.6% over the next ten years, with the results depending heavily on the model used and the assumptions made about monetary policy.

2.7 CONCLUSION

Both changes in the level of revenues and changes in the structure of the tax system can influence economic activity, but not all tax changes have equivalent, or even positive, effects on long-term growth.

The argument that income tax cuts raise growth is repeated so often that it is sometimes taken as gospel. However, theory, evidence, and simulation studies tell a different and more complicated story. Tax cuts offer the potential to raise economic growth by improving incentives to work, save, and invest. But they also create income effects that reduce the need to engage in productive economic activity, and they may subsidize old capital, which provides windfall gains to asset holders that undermine incentives for new activity. In addition, tax cuts as a stand-alone policy (that is, not accompanied by spending cuts) will typically raise the federal budget deficit. The increase in the deficit will reduce national saving—and with it, the capital stock owned by Americans and future national income—and raise interest rates, which will negatively affect investment. The net effect of the tax cuts on growth is thus theoretically uncertain and depends on both the structure of the tax cut itself and the timing and structure of its financing.

Several empirical studies have attempted to quantify the various effects in different ways and used different models, yet mostly come to the same conclusion: Long- persisting tax cuts financed by higher deficits are likely to reduce, not increase, national income in the long term. By contrast, cuts in income tax rates that are financed by spending cuts can have positive impacts on growth, according to the simulation models. In modern US history, however, major tax cuts (in 1964, 1981, and 2001/2003) have been accompanied by increases in federal outlays rather than cutbacks.

The effects of income tax reform—revenue- and distributionally neutral base-broadening, rate-reducing changes—build off of the effects of tax cuts but are more complex. The effects of reductions in rates are the same as described in section 2.2.1. Broadening the base in a revenue-neutral manner will eliminate the effect of rate cuts on budget deficits. It will also reduce the impact of the rate cuts on effective marginal tax rates and thus reduce the impact on labor supply, saving, and investment. However, broadening the base will have one other effect as well; by reducing the extent to which the tax code subsidizes alternative sources and uses of income, base-broadening will reallocate resources toward their highest-value economic use and hence will raise the overall size of the economy and result in a more efficient allocation of resources.

These effects can be big in theory and in simulations, especially for extreme policy reforms such as eliminating all personal deductions and exemptions and moving to a flat-rate tax. But there is little empirical analysis of broad-based income tax reform in the United States, in part because there has only been one major tax reform in the last fifty years. Still, there is a sound theoretical presumption—and substantial simulation results—indicating that a base-broadening, rate-reducing tax reform can improve long-term performance. The key, however, is not that it boosts labor supply, saving, or investment—since it raises the same amount of revenue from the same people as before—but rather that it leads to be a better allocation of resources across sectors of the economy by closing off targeted subsidies.

An admittedly less than fully scientific source of evidence is simply asking economists what they think. In a survey of 134 public finance and labor economists, the estimated median effect of the TRA86 on the long-term size of the economy was 1% (Fuchs et al. 1998). Note that TRA86 did not reduce public saving, so the growth effect was entirely due to changes in marginal tax rates and the tax base. The median response also suggested that the 1993 tax increases had no effect on economic growth. The 1993 act raised tax rates on the highest income households but also reduced the deficit and thereby increased national saving.

One strong finding from all of the analysis is that not all tax changes will have the same impact on growth. Reforms that improve incentives, reduce existing subsidies, avoid windfall gains, and avoid deficit financing will have more auspicious effects on the long-term size of the economy, but in some cases may also create trade-offs between equity and efficiency.

These findings illustrate both the potential benefits and the potential perils of income tax reform on long-term economic growth.

ACKNOWLEDGMENTS

Corresponding author: wgale@brookings.edu. We thank Erin Huffer, Bryan Kim, Aaron Krupkin, Bryant Renaud, and Fernando Saltiel for research assistance and Alan Auerbach, Leonard Burman, Jane Gravelle, Douglas Hamilton, Kevin Hassett, Diane Lim, Donald Marron, David Romer, Eric Toder, Kevin Wu, and conference participants at the Tax Policy Center and the Brookings Institution for helpful comments. This research was made possible by a grant from the Peter G. Peterson Foundation. The statements made here and views expressed are solely those of the authors.

REFERENCES

Acosta-Ormaechea, Santiago, and Jiae Yoo. 2012. "Tax Composition and Growth: A Broad Cross-Country Perspective." IMF Working Paper No. 12/257.

Altig, David, Alan J. Auerbach, Laurence J. Kotlikoff, Kent A. Smetters, and Jan Walliser. 2001. "Simulating U.S. Tax Reform." *American Economic Review* 91 (3): 574–95.

Arnold, Jens Matthias, Bert Brys, Christopher Heady, Åsa Johansson, Cyrille Schwellnus, and Laura Vartia. 2011. "Tax Policy for Economic Recovery and Growth." *Economic Journal* 121 (550): F59–F80.

Auerbach, Alan J. 2002. *The Bush Tax Cut and National Saving*. Berkeley: University of California, Berkeley and NBER.

Auerbach, Alan J., and William G. Gale. 2016. "Once More unto the Breach: The Deteriorating Fiscal Outlook." Washington, DC: Brookings Institution.

Auerbach, Alan J., Laurence J. Kotlikoff, Kent A. Smetters, and Jan Walliser. 1997. "Fundamental Tax Reform and Macroeconomic Performance." Washington, DC: Congressional Budget Office.

Auerbach, Alan J., and Joel Slemrod. 1997. "The Economic Effects of the Tax Reform Act of 1986." *Journal of Economic Literature* 35 (2): 589–632.

Barro, Robert J., and Charles J. Redlick. 2011. "Macroeconomic Effects from Government Purchases and Taxes." *Quarterly Journal of Economics* 126 (1): 51–102.

Bernanke, Ben S., and Ilian Mihov. 1998. "Measuring Monetary Policy." *Quarterly Journal of Economics* 108 (3): 869–902.

Bernheim, B. Douglas. 2002. "Taxation and Saving." *Handbook of Public Economics* 3:1173–1249.

Carroll, Christopher D., and David N. Weil. 1994. "Saving and Growth: A Reinterpretation." *Carnegie-Rochester Conference Series on Public Policy* 40:133–92.

Chetty, Raj, John Friedman, Soren Leth-Petersen, Torben Nielsen, and Tore Olsen. 2014. "Active vs. Passive Decisions and Crowd-out in Retirement Savings Accounts: Evidence from Denmark." *Quarterly Journal of Economics* 129 (3): 1141–1219.

Chetty, Raj, Adam Guren, Day Manoli, and Andrea Weber. 2011. "Are Micro and Macro Labor Supply Elasticities Consistent? A Review of Evidence on the Intensive and Extensive Margins." *American Economic Review* 101 (3): 471–75.

Chetty, Raj, Adam Guren, Day Manoli, and Andrea Weber. 2013. "Does Indivisible Labor Explain the Difference between Micro and Macro Elasticities? A Meta-Analysis of Extensive Margin Elasticities." *NBER Macroeconomics Annual* 27 (1): 1–56.

Cloyne, James. 2013. "Discretionary Tax Changes and the Macroeconomy: New Narrative Evidence from the United Kingdom." *American Economic Review* 103 (4): 1507–28.

Committee on Ways and Means. 2014. "Tax Reform Act of 2014: Discussion Draft." Washington, DC: 113th Congress, 2nd Session.

Congressional Budget Office. 2001. "The Budget and Economic Outlook: An Update."

Congressional Budget Office. 2005. "Taxing Capital Income: Effective Rates and Approaches to Reform."

Congressional Budget Office. 2006. "Computing Effective Tax Rates on Capital Income."

Congressional Budget Office. 2010. "The Budget and Economic Outlook: An Update."

Congressional Budget Office. 2013. "The 2013 Long-Term Budget Outlook."

Debt Reduction Task Force. 2010. "Restoring America's Future: Reviving the Economy, Cutting Spending and Debt, and Creating a Simple, Pro-Growth Tax System." Washington, DC: Bipartisan Policy Center.

Dennis, Robert, Douglas Hamilton, Robert Arnold, Ufuk Demiroglu, Tracy Foertsch, Mark Lasky, Shinichi Nishiyama, Larry Ozanne, John Peterson, Frank Russek, John Sturrock, and David Weiner. 2004. "Macroeconomic Analysis of a 10 Percent Cut in Income Tax Rates." Technical Paper Series. Washington, DC: Congressional Budget Office.

Desai, Mihir A., and Austan D. Goolsbee. 2004. "Investment, Overhang, and Tax Policy." *Brookings Papers on Economic Activity* 2:285–355.

Diamond, John W., and Alan D. Viard. 2008. "Welfare and Macroeconomic Effects of Deficit-Financed Tax Cuts: Lessons from CGE Models." In *Tax Policy Lessons from the 2000s*, edited by Alan D. Viard, 145–93. Washington, DC: AEI Press.

Diamond, John W., and George R. Zodrow. 2008. "Consumption Tax Reform: Changes in Business Equity and Housing Prices." In *Fundamental Tax Reform: Issues, Choices and Implications*, edited by John W. Diamond and George R. Zodrow, 227–60. Cambridge, MA: MIT Press.

Easterly, William. 1995. Comment on "What Do Cross-Country Studies Teach about Involvement, Prosperity, and Economic Growth?" *Brookings Papers on Economic Activity* 2:419–24.

Economic Report of the President. 2003. Washington, DC: United States Government Printing Office.

Eissa, Nada. 2008. "Evidence on Labor Supply and Taxes, and Implications for Tax Policy." In *Tax Policy Lessons from the 2000s*, edited by Alan D. Viard, 45–91. Washington, DC: AEI Press.

Elmendorf, Douglas W., and N. Gregory Mankiw. 1999. "Government Debt." In *Handbook of Macroeconomics* 1C, edited by John B. Taylor and Michael Woodford, 1615–69. Amsterdam: Elsevier Science B.V.

Elmendorf, Douglas W., and David Reifschneider. 2002. "Short Run Effects of Fiscal Policy with Forward-Looking Financial Markets." *National Tax Journal* 55 (3): 357–86.

Engen, Eric, and R. Glenn Hubbard. 2004. "Federal Government Debts and Interest Rates." Cambridge, MA: National Bureau of Economic Research Working Paper 10681.

Engen, Eric M., and Jonathan Skinner. 1992. "Fiscal Policy and Economic Growth." Cambridge, MA: National Bureau of Economic Research Working Paper 4223.

Engen, Eric M., and Jonathan Skinner. 1996. "Taxation and Economic Growth." *National Tax Journal* 49 (4): 617–42.

Favero, Carlo, and Francesco Giavazzi. 2012. "Measuring Tax Multipliers: The Narrative Method in Fiscal VARs." *American Economic Journal: Economic Policy* 4 (2): 69–94.

Feldstein, Martin. 1986. "Supply Side Economics: Old Truths and New Claims." *American Economic Review* 76 (2): 26–30.

Feldstein, Martin, and Douglas W. Elmendorf. 1989. "Budget Deficits, Tax Incentives, and Inflation: A Surprising Lesson from the 1983–1984 Recovery." In *Tax Policy and the Economy* (3), edited by Lawrence H. Summers, 1–23. Cambridge, MA: National Bureau of Economic Research.

Foertsch, Tracy. 2004. "Macroeconomic Impacts of Stylized Tax Cuts in an Intertemporal Computable General Equilibrium Model." Washington, DC: Congressional Budget Office.

Fuchs, Victor R., Alan B. Krueger, and James M. Poterba. 1998. "Economists' Views about Parameters, Values, and Policies: Survey Results in Labor and Public Economics." *Journal of Economic Literature* 36 (3): 1387–1425.

Fullerton, Don, and Y. K. Henderson. 1987. "The Impact of Fundamental Tax Reform on the Allocation of Resources." In *The Effects of Taxation on Capital Accumulation*, edited by Martin Feldstein, 401–43. Chicago: University of Chicago Press.

Gale, William G., and Peter R. Orszag. 2004a. "Budget Deficits, National Saving, and Interest Rates." *Brookings Papers on Economic Activity* 2:101–87.

Gale, William G., and Peter R. Orszag. 2004b. "Tax Cuts, Interest Rates, and the User Cost of Capital." Washington, DC: Brookings Institution.

Gale, William G., and Peter R. Orszag. 2005. "Deficits, Interest Rates, and the User Cost of Capital: Reconsidering the Effects of Tax Cuts on Investment." *National Tax Journal* 58 (3): 409–26.

Gale, William G., and Samara Potter. 2002. "An Economic Evaluation of the Economic Growth and Tax Relief Reconciliation Act." *National Tax Journal* 55 (1): 133–86.

Garrison, Charles B., and Feng-Yao Lee. 1992. "Taxation, Aggregate Activity and Economic Growth: Further Cross-Country Evidence on Some Supply-Side Hypotheses." *Economic Inquiry* 30 (1): 172–76.

Gordon, Robert J. 2016. *The Rise and Fall of American Growth: The U.S. Standard of Living since the Civil War*. Princeton, NJ: Princeton University Press.

Gravelle, Jane G. 2014. "Dynamic Scoring for Tax Legislation: A Review of Models." Washington, DC: Congressional Research Service.

Gravelle, Jane G., and Laurence J. Kotlikoff. 1989. "Corporate Taxation and the Efficiency Gains of the 1986 Tax Reform Act." Cambridge, MA: National Bureau of Economic Research.

Grier, Kevin B., and Gordon Tullock. 1989. "An Empirical Analysis of Cross-National Economic Growth, 1951–80." *Journal of Monetary Economics* 24 (2): 259–76.

Harberger, Arnold. 1962. "The Incidence of the Corporation Income Tax." *Journal of Political Economy* 70 (3): 215–40.

Harberger, Arnold. 1964. "Taxation, Resource Allocation, and Welfare." In *The Role of Direct and Indirect Taxes in the Federal Reserve System: A Conference Report of the NBER and the Brookings Institution*, 25–80. Princeton, NJ: Princeton University Press.

Hayo, Bernd, and Matthias Uhl. 2014. "The Macroeconomic Effects of Legislated Tax Changes in Germany." *Oxford Economic Papers* 66 (2): 397–418.

Huang, Chye-Ching. 2012. "Recent Studies Find Raising Taxes on High-Income Households Would Not Harm the Economy: Policy Should Be Included in Balanced Deficit-Reduction Effort." Washington, DC: Center on Budget and Policy Priorities.

Huang, Chye-Ching, and Nathaniel Frentz. 2014. "What *Really* is the Evidence on Taxes and Growth." Washington, DC: Center on Budget and Policy Priorities.

Hungerford, Thomas. 2012. "Taxes and the Economy: An Economic Analysis of the Top Tax Rate Since 1945." Washington, DC: Congressional Research Service.

Jaimovich, Nir, and Sergio Rebelo. 2012. "Non-linear Effects of Taxation on Growth." Cambridge, MA: National Bureau of Economic Research Working Paper 18473.

Joint Committee on Taxation. 2003. "Macroeconomic Analysis of H.R. 2, The Jobs and Growth Reconciliation Tax Act of 2003." Washington, DC: 108th Congress, 1st Session.

Joint Committee on Taxation. 2014. "Macroeconomic Analysis of the Tax Reform Act of 2014." Washington, DC: 113th Congress, 2nd Session.

Jones, Larry E., Rodolfo E. Manuelli, and Peter E. Rossi. 1993. "Optimal Taxation in Models of Endogenous Growth." *Journal of Political Economy* 101 (3): 485–517.

Keane, Michael P. 2011. "Labor Supply and Taxes." *Journal of Economic Literature* 49 (4): 961–1075.

Keane, Michael P., and Richard Rogerson. 2012. "Micro and Macro Labor Supply Elasticities: A Reassessment of Conventional Wisdom." *Journal of Economic Literature* 50 (2): 464–76.

Kneiser, Thomas J., and James P. Ziliak. 2002. "Tax Reform and Automatic Stabilization." *American Economic Review* 92 (36): 590–612.

Laubach, Thomas. 2009. "New Evidence on the Interest Rate Effects of Budget Deficits and Debt." *Journal of the European Economic Association* 7 (4): 858–85.

Lim Rogers, Diane (now Diane Lim). 1997. "Assessing the Effects of Fundamental Tax Reform with the Fullerton-Rogers General Equilibrium Model." Washington, DC: Congressional Budget Office.

Lucas, Robert E. 1990. "Supply-Side Economics: An Analytical Review." *Oxford Economic Papers* 42 (2): 293–316.

Macroeconomic Advisors. 2003. "A Preliminary Analysis of the President's Jobs and Growth Proposals." Washington, DC.

McBride, William. 2012. "What Is the Evidence on Taxes and Growth." Special Report No. 207. Washington, DC: Tax Foundation.

Mendoza, Enrique G., Gian-Maria Milesi-Ferretti, and Patrick Asea. 1997. "On the Ineffectiveness of Tax Policy in Altering Long-Run Growth: Harberger's Superneutrality Conjecture." *Journal of Public Economics* 66 (1): 99–126.

Mertens, Karel. 2015. "Marginal Tax Rates and Income: New Time Series Evidence." Manuscript. Cornell University. September.

Mertens, Karel, and Morten Ravn. 2010. "Measuring the Impact of Fiscal Policy in the Face of Anticipation: A Structural VAR Approach." *Economic Journal* 120 (5): 393–413.

Mertens, Karel, and Morten Ravn. 2012. "Empirical Evidence on the Aggregate Effects of Anticipated and Unanticipated U.S. Tax Policy Shocks." *American Economic Journal: Economic Policy* 4 (2): 145–81.

National Commission on Fiscal Responsibility and Reform. 2010. "The Moment of Truth." Washington, DC: The White House.

Nishiyama, Shinichi, and Kent Smetters. 2005. "Consumption Taxes and Economic Efficiency with Idiosyncratic Wage Shocks." *Journal of Political Economy* 113 (5): 1088–115.

Padovano, Fabio, and Emma Galli. 2001. "Tax Rates and Economic Growth in the OECD Countries (1950–1990)." *Economic Inquiry* 39 (1): 44–57.

Piketty, Thomas, Emmanuel Saez, and Stefanie Stantcheva. 2014. "Optimal Taxation of Top Labor Incomes: A Tale of Three Elasticities." *American Economic Journal: Economic Policy* 6 (1): 230–71.

President's Advisory Panel on Federal Tax Reform. 2005. "Simple, Fair, and Pro-Growth: Proposals to Fix America's Tax System." Washington, DC.

Reifschneider, David, Robert Tetlow, and John Williams. 1999. "Aggregate Disturbances, Monetary Policy, and the Macroeconomy: The FRB/US Perspective." *Federal Reserve Bulletin*, January: 1–19.

Romer, Christina D., and David H. Romer. 2004. "A New Measure of Monetary Shocks: Derivation and Implications." *American Economic Review* 94 (4): 1055–84.

Romer, Christina D., and David H. Romer. 2010. "The Macroeconomic Effects of Tax Changes: Estimates Based on a New Measure of Fiscal Shocks." *American Economic Review* 100 (3): 763–801.

Romer, Christina D. and David H. Romer. 2014. "The Incentive Effects of Marginal Tax Rates: Evidence from the Interwar Era." *American Economic Journal: Economic Policy* 6 (2): 242–81.

Saez, Emmanuel, Joel Slemrod, and Seth H. Giertz. 2012. "The Elasticity of Taxable Income with Respect to Marginal Tax Rates: A Critical Review." *Journal of Economic Literature* 50 (1): 3–50.

Slemrod, Joel. 1995. "What Do Cross-Country Studies Teach about Involvement, Prosperity, and Economic Growth?" *Brookings Papers on Economic Activity* 2:373–415.

Stokey, Nancy L., and Sergio Rebelo. 1995. "Growth Effects of Flat-Rate Taxes." *Journal of Political Economy* 103 (3): 519–50.

Summers, Lawrence H. 2014. "U.S. Economic Prospects: Secular Stagnation, Hysteresis, and the Zero Lower Bound." *Business Economics* 49 (2): 65–73.

Taylor, John. 1993. "Discretion versus Policy Rules in Practice." *Carnegie-Rochester Conference Series on Public Policy* 39:195–214.

Toder, Eric, and Alan D. Viard. 2014. "Major Surgery Needed: A Call for Structural Reform of the U.S. Corporate Income Tax." Washington, DC.

Yagan, Danny. 2015. "Capital Tax Reform and the Real Economy: The Effects of the 2003 Dividend Tax Cut." *American Economic Review* 105 (12): 3531–63.

Zidar, Owen. 2015. "Tax Cuts for Whom? Heterogeneous Effects of Income Tax Changes on Growth and Employment." NBER Working Paper No. 21035. March.

COMMENTARY ON CHAPTER 2

Kevin Hassett

2C.1 INTRODUCTION

Gale and Samwick review simulation, traditional econometric, and more modern "narrative" literatures and discuss the strengths and weaknesses of the evidence in each subfield. In this comment, I reexamine the evidence and at times suggest different conclusions.

2C.2 THE RECENT ECONOMETRIC LITERATURE EXPLORING THE LINK BETWEEN TAXES AND GROWTH

There has been a recent surge in the production of macroeconometric papers finding a strong link between taxes and economic growth using a narrative approach to identify exogenous tax changes. Romer and Romer (2010) find that a tax increase of 1% of GDP lowers output by 3% over ten quarters when one examines only the exogenous tax changes. Others have pursued a similar strategy with data from other countries. The United Kingdom, Cloyne (2013) notes, offers a centralized legislative process with centralized documentation that eases narrative analysis and a sample that includes five times as many post–World War II tax changes as the United States. In an echo of the original estimates of Romer and Romer (2010), Cloyne (2013) estimates that a 1% cut in taxes as a share of GDP increases output by up to 2.5% over three years based on this UK sample. As Cloyne (2013) turns to the United Kingdom, Hayo and Uhl (2014) focus on Germany, examining a sample from 1974 to 2010. They estimate that a tax increase of 1% of GDP cumulatively lowers output by as much as 2.4% over eight quarters. These estimated output effects from US, UK, and German samples only range from 2.4% over eight quarters to 3% over ten quarters.

Other studies distinguish between average tax rates and marginal tax rates, the latter of which tends to be the most relevant for policy discussions. Constructing a time series of average marginal US federal income tax rates from 1912 to 2006, Barro and Redlick (2011) repurpose a variation of the Romer and Romer (2010) identification strategy to construct an instrument for changes in average marginal tax rates (AMTRs). They find that a 1% decrease in the AMTR increases per capita GDP by 0.5% after one year. Deploying a vector autoregression, Mertens (2015) estimates a peak output effect of a 1.5% increase in real GDP from a 1% decrease in the AMTR. The sample does include only changes to personal tax rates and, in the interest of avoiding anticipation effects, excludes tax reforms with an implementation gap between the time of legislation and the time of implementation of one year or more.

Gale and Samwick point out that the long-run effects of tax reform depend on supply-side effects, but that the typical empirical estimate of the output effects of tax reform, which tends to find statistically significant short-run growth effects, does not necessarily imply that this type of effect is present. They also suggest that the immediate short-run responses are more consistent with Keynesian effects than supply-side tax effects. I find the evidence in favor of supply-side effects more compelling than they suggest for a number of reasons.

First, the existing evidence is consistent with the presence of long-run effects on the level of output. That is, the estimates suggest that the growth rate of output following a tax cut increases relative to what it would have been in the absence of the tax shock—and these elevated growth rates are not fully offset by output developments in later time periods. Thus, there is a permanent effect on the level of output, just as the tax models would suggest. Evidence of even a temporary and significant increase in the growth rate of output, then, serves as evidence of a long-run effect on the level of output (assuming that the increase in the growth rate of output is not offset by negative growth effects in later time periods). The baseline specification, for example, in Romer and Romer (2010) is a linear regression that uses the growth rate of real output as its dependent variable. Hayo and Uhl (2014) note that "due to concerns about the non-stationarity of our data, we estimate the model using first differences of macroeconomic variables."

Second, the authors fail to factor in the attempt of Mertens and Ravn (2013) to disentangle supply and demand-based effects. The response of inflation to cuts in the average corporate income tax rate offers insight into whether observed output effects operate through demand or supply-based channels. If cuts to the average personal income tax rate (APITR) or the average corporate income tax rate (ACITR) increase output but also raise inflation, this would suggest that demand-driven channels are at work. If, on the other hand, cuts increase output but also reduce inflation, this would constitute evidence that supply-side channels are at work. Consistent with the dominance of the supply-side channel, Mertens and Ravn (2013) find a reduction in inflation following a 1% cut to the ACITR. Although the estimated cumulative decline after one quarter of 0.35% then increases for the duration of the sample, the point estimate for the effect of the ACITR on inflation still remains negative for the whole of the sample. And this combination of positive growth effects and disinflationary effects only makes sense if the growth rate of supply is exceeding the growth rate of demand as it also works to increase output.

The third reason why these results seem unlikely to be driven by cyclical factors is that the timing of the tax changes appears to be exogenous to the business cycle, as the authors in the narrative-based literature have assumed. If the output effects were generated through demand-side channels, then one might expect that tax cuts tended to occur during times of weak economic growth. However, if the tax cuts are truly exogenous, then they should be distributed through the business cycle evenly.

To test whether this was the case, we turned to data on the arrival of "bad times" in the business cycle and the dates of exogenous tax cuts in the United States, the United Kingdom, and Germany taken from the papers already cited. As our proxy for the arrival of "bad times," we turned to the OECD Composite Leading Indicators (CLI) series for each of the three countries (e.g., OECD 2015). According to the OECD, the CLI series identify business cycle downturns through a deviation-from-trend approach that determines when output measures deviate from their trend (OECD 2016). We then divided the total number of quarters for which the OECD indicator indicated a cyclical downturn by the total number of quarters in the country's exogenous tax shock series. This offers a "placebo" benchmark of how frequent business cycle slowdowns tend to occur in that country during the sample period.

If the occurrence of an "exogenous" tax cut were unrelated to business cycle conditions, after all, we would expect the frequency with which exogenous tax cuts coincided with business cycle downturns to match the frequency with which business cycle downturns occurred in general. To gauge if and how a country's historical experience of exogenous tax cuts compares to this *a priori* benchmark, we then divide the number of quarters in which there was both an exogenous tax cut and a negative reading on the OECD indicator by the total number of exogenous tax cuts that occurred in the sample period. You can think of this as measuring the odds of an exogenous tax cut happening during a period when the OECD indicator turned negative.

Together, these metrics allow us to gauge whether the frequency of an "exogenous" tax cut coinciding with a negative reading on the OECD indicator exceeds the frequency that one would expect to observe if an exogenous cut were equally likely to happen during all states of the cyclical economic conditions. And as one can see in figure 2C.1, the frequency with which exogenous tax cuts during business cycle downturns precisely matches the frequency with which they occur in general in the case of the United States and the United Kingdom, and is not far off in the case of Germany. This lends credence to the notion that what the literature regards as exogenous tax cuts are truly exogenous, rather than endogenous tax cuts masquerading as "exogenous" tax cuts.

Further evidence against the claim that exogenous tax cuts tend to happen during recessions comes from the lack of a correlation between their occurrence in the United States, United Kingdom, and Germany. Given the well-known co-movement of business cycles in each country, if exogenous tax shocks were in fact responses to business cycle movements, then one would expect to observe substantive correlations. Yet, as table 2C.1 shows, the correlations between the exogenous tax shock measures in different countries is remarkably close to zero. Table 2C.1 is based on the author's calculations and data extracted from the individual papers that construct exogenous tax shock series in each of the three countries.[1]

[1] Specifically, the data on exogenous changes are from data posted online in conjunction with Romer and Romer (2010) in the case of the United States; from data posted online in conjunction with Cloyne (2013) in the case of the United Kingdom; and were constructed based on data delineated in table A1 of Uhl (2013), a companion paper of Hayo and Uhl (2014), in the case of Germany. All

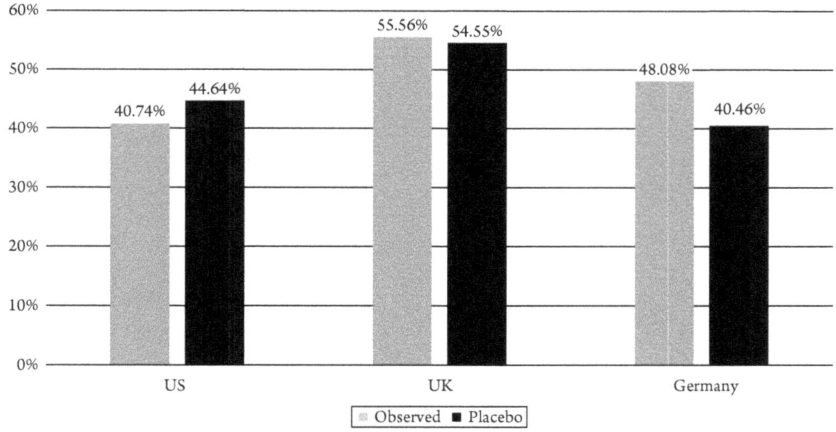

Figure 2C.1 Exogenous tax cuts through the business cycle. The fraction of "exogenous" tax cuts that took place during an OECD-indicated business cycle downturn for each of the United States, United Kingdom, and Germany compared to the "placebo" fraction that one would expect to observe if this relationship were due only to chance.

Table 2C.1 Cross-country correlations of exogenous tax shock incidence

	United States	*United Kingdom*	*Germany*
United States	1.000000	−0.054390	0.014655
United Kingdom	−0.054390	1.000000	0.044819
Germany	0.014655	0.044819	1.000000

2C.3 CAN THEORY EXPLAIN THE LARGE EFFECTS IN THE LITERATURE?

Gale and Samwick suggest that the literature supports the notion that labor elasticities tend to be lower than those who believe output responses to tax cuts would be large would be inclined to believe. While it is true that the literature has in general tended to favor lower elasticities, recent developments suggest that heterogeneity may play an important role, and models that account for it can lead to very large labor supply responses to taxation.

Keane and Rogerson (2012) summarize the key arguments. When human capital is present, the costs borne by an individual who chooses to reduce labor supply are more than just the opportunity cost of the lost wages. Rather, the opportunity cost of time is the sum of the direct cost of the lost wages and the present value of the human capital that would have accrued to the worker, had that worker worked the extra hour.

correlations are for the longest sample permitted by each pair of exogenous tax series. And the data span Q1 1945 through Q4 2007 in the case of the United States; Q1 1948 through Q4 2009 in the case of the United Kingdom; Q1 1964 through Q4 2007 in the case of Germany.

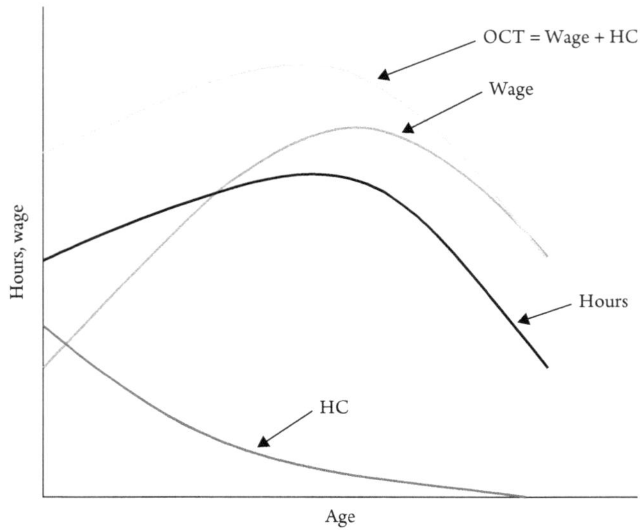

Figure 2C.2 Wages, human capital, and the life-cycle. *Note:* Figure 2C.2 plots, on the horizontal axis, age. On the vertical axis, it plots either hours or wage.

The chart in figure 2C.2, from Keane and Rogerson (2012), illustrates how the role of human capital changes the wage schedule over the course of the life cycle.

Early in life, the opportunity cost of time includes a large human capital component. This means that the opportunity cost of time (the grey line) has a different shape than the wage profile. Hours (the black line) tend to move with the opportunity cost of time but not so clearly with wages. If one estimates the labor response with the wage curve, then, one acquires a downwardly biased estimate of the response. And as the figure would suggest, the literature finds that older workers respond much more than younger workers to changes in tax rates.

It is easy to generate very large effects from taxes once one relies on these larger effects. For example, DeBacker et al. (2015) model the effects of an across-the-board 10% statutory cut to marginal tax rates, they estimate that such a reform would result in a contemporaneous GDP increase of 1.64%.[2] Although the growth rate effects diminish as time goes on, it remains 1.56% even five years after the tax cut and sits at 1.55% in the steady-state. This evidence provides some theoretical support for the large responses found in the narrative literature. Most interesting, it suggests that the effects can be immediate even in a model with no demand-side Keynesian effects. They get large responses up-front because the labor response happens immediately. Thus, there is no reason not to believe the large immediate effects in the narrative approach.

[2] They deploy OG-USA, an overlapping generations model of the US economy, incubated by the Open Source Policy Center and available for wide use through a web application at http://www.ospc.org/taxbrain.

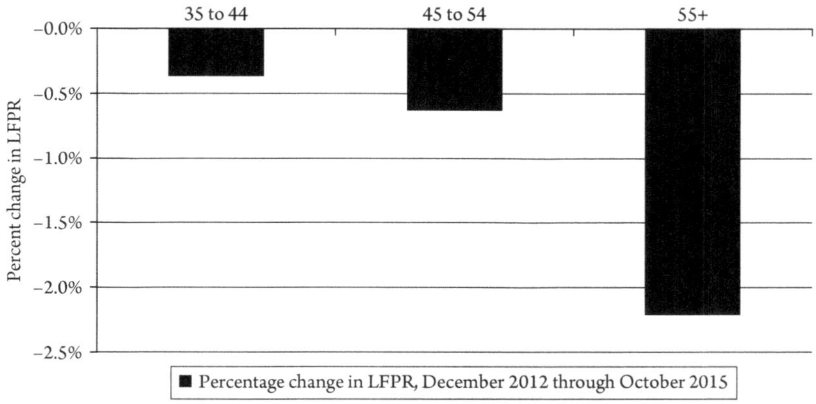

Figure 2C.3 Percentage change in labor force participation rate. Percentage change in the labor force participation rate between December 2012 and October 2015 for each of the three age groups.

2C.4 THE RECENT TAX INCREASES

Let us now consider the experience of the recent marginal tax rate hikes under President Obama.

First, as can be seen in figure 2C.3, labor force participation has changed in the way suggested by the human capital framework developed in Keane and Rogerson (2012). According to that framework, younger individuals are less responsive to changes in marginal tax rates because the present value of human capital accumulation increases as the quantity of an individual's expected future years in the labor force increases. Since current tax rates do not affect the present value of human capital, this would suggest that the labor force participation of younger individuals would drop less than the labor force participation of older individuals in response to the Obama-era marginal tax rate increases. The data, from the Bureau of Labor Statistics (2015), evince precisely this pattern.

So the apparent labor force participation effects are consistent with the Keane and Rogerson (2012) theory. This suggests that the economic effects could have been significant. Figure 2C.4 plots the forecast error of Obama administration growth forecasts on top earners against the effects of the marginal tax rate increase as estimated by Mertens (2015). The Obama administration, which seems to have shared the view of the authors, missed the economic forecast by almost exactly the estimated impact of the tax hikes. Figure 2C.4 is based on the author's calculations using data from the Office of Management and Budget (2013) and Mertens (2015).[3]

As such, it seems that much of the Obama administration's forecast errors for growth in 2013 and 2014 could be explained if they held the same belief that Gale and Samwick are arguing in favor of: that tax rates do not affect growth.

[3] Specifically, the data from Mertens (2015) used are the estimates of the effects of a 1 percentage point increase in the marginal tax rate featured in the middle-left panel of figure 8.

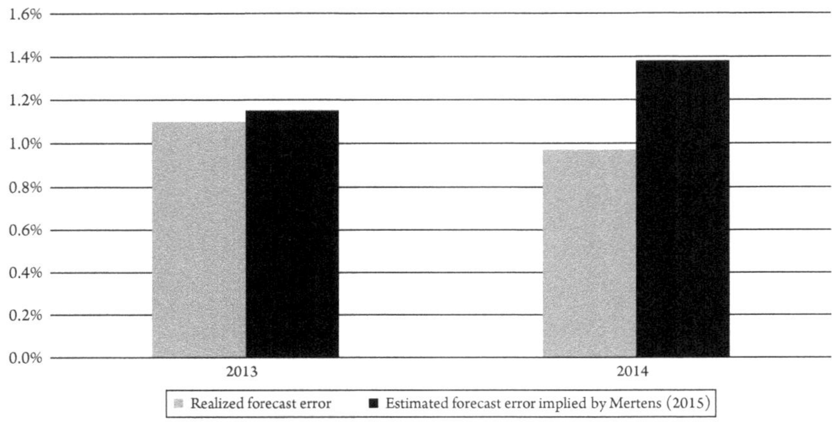

Figure 2C.4 Realized versus expected GDP forecast error. *Note:* Figure 2C.4 plots realized Obama administration growth forecast errors versus the errors that one would expect the Obama administration to make if one estimated the effect of the Obama-era marginal tax rate hikes based on the estimated tax effects in Mertens (2015), but assumed that the Obama administration would not incorporate this negative effect of tax rate increases into their growth forecast.

As a final observation, the authors discuss at great length the importance in simulations of the method of "squaring the circle" when taxes are cut. If future tax hikes are used to restore the revenue, then according to economic theory the effects of the tax change today should be small. If government spending cuts are used, by contrast, then according to economic theory the tax effects should be large. It is worth noting that the empirical literature does not explore this question of ultimate "pay-for," yet still finds large effects. This seems best explained by one of two explanations. Either the markets assume that the shortfall will be paid for with future spending cuts or, alternatively, economic agents who observe massive and persistent deficits that dwarf the magnitude of many tax changes simply assume that the long-run situation is little changed by current policy.

REFERENCES

Barro, R. J., and C. J. Redlick. 2011. "Macroeconomic Effects from Government Purchases and Taxes." *Quarterly Journal of Economics* 126 (1): 51–102.

Bureau of Labor Statistics. 2015. "Labor Force Statistics from the Current Population Survey (LNS11300000)." Data extracted in December 2015.

Cloyne, James. 2013. "Discretionary Tax Changes and the Macroeconomy: New Narrative Evidence from the United Kingdom." *American Economic Review* 103 (4): 1507–28.

DeBacker, Kason, Richard W. Evans, and Kerk L. Phillips. "Macroeconomic Effects of a 10% Cut in Statutory Marginal Income Tax Rates on Ordinary Income." AEI Economic Policy Working Paper Series 2015-15.

Hayo, Bernd, and Matthias Uhl. 2014. "The Macroeconomic Effects of Legislated Tax Changes in Germany." *Oxford Economic Papers* 66 (2): 397–418.

Keane, Michael, and Richard Rogerson. 2012. "Micro and Macro Labor Supply Elasticities: A Reassessment of Conventional Wisdom." *Journal of Economic Literature* 50 (2): 464–76.

Mertens, Karel. 2015. "Marginal Tax Rates and Income: New Time Series Evidence." National Bureau of Economic Research Working Paper 19171.

Mertens, Karel, and Morten O. Ravn. 2013. "The Dynamic Effects of Personal and Corporate Income Tax Changes in the United States." *American Economic Review* 103 (4): 1212–47.

Office of Management and Budget. 2013. "Economic and Budget Analyses: FY 2014." https://www.whitehouse.gov/sites/default/files/omb/budget/fy2014/assets/econ_analyses.pdf

Office of Management and Budget. 2015. "Economic Assumptions FY 1986–FY 2017," in Supplemental Materials: History of Economic Assumptions. Extracted online in December 2015.

Organization for Economic Cooperation and Development. 2015. "OECD Based Recession Indicators for Germany from the Peak through the Trough (DEURECM); OECD Based Recession Indicators for the United Kingdom from the Peak through the Trough (GBRRECM); OECD Based Recession Indicators for the United States from the Peak through the Trough (USARECM)." Data accessed through Federal Reserve Economic Data (FRED) Excel add-on.

Organization for Economic Cooperation and Development. 2016. "OECD Composite Leading Indicators: Reference Turning Points and Component Series." http://www.oecd.org/std/leading-indicators/oecdcompositeleadingindicatorsreferenceturningpointsandcomponent-series.htm

Romer, Christina D., and David H. Romer. 2007. "The Macroeconomic Effects of Tax Changes: Estimates Based on a New Measure of Fiscal Shocks." National Bureau of Economic Research Working Paper 13264.

Romer, Christina D., and David H. Romer. 2009. "A Narrative Analysis of Postwar Tax Changes." http://www.aeaweb.org//articles.php?doi=10.1257/aer.100.3.763

Romer, Christina D., and David H. Romer. 2010. "The Macroeconomic Effects of Tax Changes: Estimates Based on a New Measure of Fiscal Shocks." *American Economic Review* 100 (3): 763–801.

Solt, Frederick. 2014. "The Standardized World Income Inequality Database." Working paper. SWIID Version 5.0, October 2014. Data extracted in May 2015.

Uhl, Matthias. 2013. "A History of Tax Legislations in the Federal Republic of Germany." MAGKS Discussion Papers 11-2013, Marburg.

World Bank World Development Indicators. 2015. "GNI per capita, PPP (constant 2011 international $)." Data extracted in May 2015.

3

ENVIRONMENTAL TAXATION

Roberton C. Williams III

3.1 INTRODUCTION

Long-term projections of the US federal budget show an increasingly large deficit, which would be difficult to address using spending cuts alone. But tax reform proposals tend to be much more concrete about tax cuts than about how those cuts will be paid for (much less how to achieve a net increase in tax revenues). Thus, potential new sources of tax revenue are in demand.

There is also increasing recognition of the need to take action to limit emissions of greenhouse gases (GHGs) and to further reduce emissions of local air pollutants. Using traditional command-and-control environmental regulation to accomplish those goals would be costly.

Environmental taxes have the potential to address both of those issues, providing a source of new tax revenue and a cost-effective way to reduce pollution emissions.

This chapter examines potential environmental tax policy reforms. It focuses primarily on a carbon tax, which is the largest and most important potential new environmental tax. It also more briefly considers a range of other potential reforms. These include revising or eliminating various energy and environmental tax credits and deductions (many of which might become unnecessary in the presence of a carbon tax), as well as changes to energy taxes that have substantial environmental implications (such as the federal gasoline tax). The chapter draws on recent theoretical and empirical research to evaluate the effects of such reforms on tax revenue, pollution emissions, economic efficiency, and income distribution.

The next section of this chapter provides some background on the theory and practice of environmental taxation. Section 3.3 discusses carbon taxes. Section 3.4 considers changes to taxes on motor fuels (gasoline and diesel fuel). Section 3.5 briefly looks at reforms to existing environment- and energy-related tax credits and deductions. The final section summarizes and concludes.

3.2 BACKGROUND

This section provides first an overview of the theory of environmental taxation and then a short discussion of the existing environmental tax provisions in the United States.

3.2.1 Theory of Environmental Taxation

This subsection discusses the theory of environmental taxation and the key implications of that theory for the design and implementation of environmental taxes. It starts by considering environmental taxes as corrective taxes, providing incentives to lower pollution emissions. It then goes on to consider the role of environmental taxes within the larger tax system, considering both the potential for using environmental tax revenue to lower other taxes (or prevent raising them) and how environmental taxes interact with the rest of the tax system. Finally, it compares environmental taxes to alternative policy instruments.

3.2.1.1 Corrective Taxation

The concept of using taxation to correct negative externalities such as pollution is generally credited to Pigou (1920), and such corrective taxes are sometimes referred to as Pigouvian Taxation. The basic idea is simple. A negative externality—a case in which production or consumption of some good harms someone other than the buyer or seller of that good—represents a market failure because the buyer's and seller's decisions fail to take into account that external cost. Consequently, an unregulated free market will generally result in an inefficiently high quantity of any good with an associated negative externality. Imposing a tax on the externality-generating good can correct the externality. If the tax rate is set equal to marginal external damage (the total harm to parties other than the buyer and seller from one additional unit of the good), it brings that external cost into the transaction, ensuring that the buyer pays the full marginal social cost of the good. Thus, the incentive provided by the tax ensures that the market produces the efficient level of the good (in the absence of any other uncorrected market failures).

One complication would be if the marginal external damage from a good varies based on who produces the good or how it is produced. For example, the carbon-dioxide (CO_2) emissions from a megawatt-hour of electricity produced from a power plant that burns natural gas are much lower than the CO_2 emissions if the same quantity of electricity is produced by burning coal (and much lower still if produced by a wind turbine). But that apparent complication is easily incorporated into this simple theory, either by viewing those as different goods (and thus charging different tax rates on electricity produced from different sources), or, more simply, by viewing CO_2 emissions as the good with the negative externality, and imposing a tax per ton of CO_2 emissions. Similarly, if the marginal damage from local air pollutants varies based on where those pollutants are emitted,[1] then emissions in different locations should face different tax rates.

[1] For example, the marginal damage from emissions immediately upwind of a major city tend to be much higher than those in a sparsely populated rural area because the number of people affected is much greater.

In practice, imposing a theoretically ideal tax can be challenging. Estimating marginal damage is difficult, particularly in cases where the harm will occur in the future (as with GHG emissions) or where damage varies widely across space or time (as with local air pollutants). And in many cases, it is difficult for taxing authorities to directly measure emissions, and thus imposing the tax on some proxy for emissions (such as the amount of fuel burned) makes it much easier to enforce. In such cases, any tax will need to depart from the theoretical ideal, but the theory provides some general principles: set tax rates based on the best estimate of marginal damage; and when it is impractical to tax emissions directly, choose a proxy that is as close as practicable to what matters for marginal damage. Taxing based on those principles will most efficiently correct the negative externality from pollution.

Note that I have not yet mentioned the use of revenue from an environmental tax. Many non-economists would define an environmental tax as a tax whose revenue is used to address environmental goals. But to most economists, an environmental tax is a tax on pollution emissions (or on a good proxy for pollution emissions). This latter definition focuses on the corrective role of environmental taxes. In general, the revenue raised by efficient levels of taxes on emissions could be greater or less than the efficient level of spending to address environmental goals, and thus economic theory argues that environmental tax revenue should not necessarily be spent on environmental ends, nor should environmental spending necessarily be financed by environmental taxes.

3.2.1.2 Environmental Taxes as Part of the Broader Tax System

Of course, environmental taxes don't just correct externalities. They also raise revenue, and that can be a major advantage. That revenue can be used to cut (or prevent increasing) other taxes, to reduce the budget deficit, to pay for public goods, to address distributional goals, or for many other purposes. At the same time, interactions between environmental taxes and other pre-existing taxes (primarily income and payroll taxes) can significantly raise the efficiency costs of environmental taxes (or any other excise tax or similar policy). This subsection reviews research on the potential gains from using environmental tax revenue, as well as the potential extra costs implied by interactions with other taxes.

The argument that the revenue-raising role of environmental taxes is a substantial additional reason to implement such taxes first came to prominence in the "double dividend" literature.[2] The idea is simple: if revenue from an environmental tax can be used to finance a cut in the tax rate for a pre-existing distortionary tax (such as the income tax), that cut produces an efficiency gain in addition to the other effects of the environmental tax. The term "double dividend" refers to the claim that environmental taxes raise economic efficiency through two separate channels, both by correcting an externality and by raising revenue that can be used to cut other taxes. That second

[2] See, e.g., Tullock (1967), Pearce (1991), Repetto (1992), and Oates (1995).

"dividend" has since come to be known as the "revenue-recycling effect."[3] And that basic concept also applies to a broader range of uses for the revenue: spending the revenue on public goods or using it to cut the budget deficit could produce similar gains in economic efficiency.[4]

Early papers in the double dividend literature argued that because of that gain from recycling revenue, environmental taxes would still be worthwhile even if the pollutant being taxed turned out to be harmless: that the efficiency gain from revenue-recycling would more than cover the efficiency cost of the tax. That was a particularly attractive argument in the case of a carbon tax, because at the time the early double-dividend papers were written, there was still significant scientific uncertainty about the relationship between anthropogenic carbon emissions and climate change (and it remains a potentially attractive political argument even today, given that many Americans still doubt that relationship). However, subsequent work showed that argument—now referred to as the "strong double-dividend"—does not generally hold.

What those early double-dividend studies missed was the general-equilibrium interactions between environmental taxes and pre-existing distortionary taxes. Environmental taxes lower the real returns to factors of production such as capital and labor, either directly by reducing wages and returns on capital, or indirectly by pushing up the prices of polluting goods. This discourages the supply of those factors, and because pre-existing taxes have already distorted those factor markets (causing the marginal social cost of supplying those factors to be lower than their marginal product), this creates a welfare loss.

Under central-case assumptions, the extra cost from this "tax-interaction effect" is actually slightly larger than the gain from the revenue-recycling effect, and thus not only is there no strong double dividend, but the efficient level of an environmental tax is slightly lower than marginal pollution damage. The intuition for that result is that broader taxes are generally more efficient revenue-raising instruments, and an environmental tax is a narrower tax than an income tax (because the income tax covers all production, whereas the environmental tax covers only polluting production).

More recent work has pushed back to some extent against that conclusion. To pick just one example, Parry and Bento (2000) suggest that inefficient tax preferences within the income tax system (tax deductions, credits, and exemptions that are not justified by market failures) narrow the tax base of the income tax, and that taking this into account means that environmental taxes are more efficient at raising revenue than the income tax—and thus that the optimal environmental tax is more than marginal damage. A major problem with that argument is that it compares the existing (inefficiently designed) income tax to an efficiently designed environmental tax. If a

[3] The terms "revenue-recycling effect" and "tax-interaction effect" are due to Goulder (1995).

[4] If the levels of the budget deficit and of spending on public goods are efficient *ex ante*, then at the margin, using environmental tax revenue to cut the deficit or increase public good provision will have the same efficiency benefit as using it to cut other taxes. To the extent that those levels are not optimal, those alternative uses could produce larger or smaller gains.

real-world environmental tax also includes inefficient deductions or exemptions, then this would weaken or overturn Parry and Bento's argument.

This literature has not come to a single clear and unambiguous conclusion about whether interactions with the broader tax system cause the optimal environmental tax to be slightly higher or lower than marginal damage: it depends on many aspects of the situation at hand. But the literature has generally rejected arguments that such effects cause the optimal tax to be dramatically different from marginal damage.

3.2.1.3 Environmental Taxes versus Other Environmental Policy Instruments

There are many other alternative policies beyond taxes that can be used to reduce pollution emissions, including tradable permits, technology or emissions standards, and subsidies for less-polluting alternatives. In general, the most efficient policies provide an incentive to reduce emissions, while giving the market flexibility about how to accomplish that emissions reduction—flexibility both across different methods of reducing emissions for a given emitter and across different emitters.

Emissions pricing policies—emissions taxes or tradable permits—provide that combination of incentives with flexibility. Other policies generally do not. For example, a technology standard (such as a requirement that all new automobiles have a catalytic converter) requires the use of emissions control technology, but provides little or no incentive to reduce emissions in any other way (such as by improving fuel economy or driving less). Standards also typically aren't flexible across emitters (i.e., there's no option for one emitter to reduce pollution further than the standard requires in return for another emitter being allowed to reduce pollution by less). Similarly, subsidizing a less-polluting alternative (such as subsidies for ethanol) provides an incentive only for switching to that alternative, not for any other way to reduce emissions.

The flexibility provided by emissions pricing policies provides a cost advantage because polluters can choose the lowest-cost combination of methods of reducing emissions. Policies that provide less flexibility will generally be more expensive (for a given level of emissions reductions), because they don't take advantage of all of the possible channels for reducing emissions.

There are some potential efficiency arguments for those less-flexible policies. One such argument is ease of monitoring and enforcement: if it is much easier to check whether a particular technology is in place (e.g., if a car has a catalytic converter installed) than it is to monitor emissions levels, that could outweigh the cost advantage that would come with greater flexibility. A few decades ago, this was a major consideration in many cases. But given advances in monitoring technology, this argument has much less bite than it used to. Another argument is that poorly informed emitters given flexibility may not choose the lowest-cost option, and if regulators are better informed, then a regulation that provides incentives only on the low-cost options could be more efficient than a fully flexible policy. But while this might hold in some cases, the claim that regulators know a business's or consumer's costs better than that business or consumer does should be regarded with some skepticism.

3.2.2 Environmental Taxes in the United States

Metcalf (2009) says that "environmental taxes in the United States are like virtue: much discussed but little practiced." Williams (2009) notes that definitions of what constitutes an environmental tax vary, and measures of the magnitude of environmental taxation will vary correspondingly.[5] But under any reasonable definition, the current level of environmental taxation in the United States is very low, relative either to environmental taxation in other developed countries or to the levels that would efficiently correct major pollution externalities.

By far the largest existing environmental tax in the United States is the motor fuels excise tax: state and federal taxes on motor fuels accounted for approximately $70 billion in 2005, which was roughly 94% of all US environmental tax revenue (Metcalf 2009). The remainder comes from a variety of much smaller taxes. While some of these are intended to provide incentives (e.g., the "gas guzzler" tax on cars with especially low fuel mileage), most are designed simply to raise money to remediate environmental problems (e.g., an excise tax on oil to fund the Oil Spill Liability Trust Fund, or the excise tax on coal which funds the Black Lung Disability Fund). Fullerton (1996) notes that this latter group provides only relatively weak incentives to reduce pollution because the tax bases for these taxes are not tightly connected to pollution emissions.

Metcalf (2009) compared environmental tax revenue in the United States to other OECD countries, using data from the mid-2000s. Environmental tax revenue as a share of GDP was lower for the United States than for all but one other country (Mexico), and was far less than the average (US environmental tax revenue was 0.9% of GDP, compared to 2.23% for the average OECD country). Looking at environmental tax revenue relative to total tax revenue yields a similar picture: the United States was the lowest of all countries in the sample. Using more recent data would, if anything, strengthen that pattern: the United States has not imposed any substantial new federal environmental taxes, and the tax rate for the biggest environmental tax in the United States—the motor fuels excise tax—has remained constant in nominal terms per gallon since 1993, thus falling in real terms.

An alternative comparison would be to the level of environmental taxation that would efficiently correct major environmental externalities. Again, current levels of environmental taxation look very low. First consider motor fuel taxes. Rates for these taxes are well below the efficient level (i.e., marginal external damage). The current

[5] Williams suggests three possible definitions for what constitutes an environmental tax: a tax whose revenue is spent on an environmental goal, as a tax intended to reduce pollution, or as a tax on pollution emissions (or on some quantity closely correlated with pollution emissions. The first two definitions would likely exclude motor fuel taxes, which account for the vast majority of "environmental tax" revenue in the United States and in most other industrialized nations.

have on this measure. Emissions are then generally expressed in terms of CO_2 equivalent quantities (CO_{2e}), typically based on a one-hundred-year time-horizon GWP estimate. Adopting this approach for a tax would imply taxing CO_{2e} emissions, or, equivalently, taxing emissions of each gas based on its GWP.

A more important problem is that monitoring emissions of many of these gases is difficult. CO_2 is relatively straightforward in this regard because the vast majority of anthropogenic CO_2 emissions come from combustion of fossil fuels (e.g., 94% of US CO_2 emissions in 2013 were from combustion[12]), and the CO_2 emitted by combustion is simply proportional to the quantity of carbon in the fuel.[13] Thus, a tax on fossil-fuel combustion, based on the carbon in the fuel, is equivalent to a tax on combustion-related CO_2 emissions. Moreover, much of the non-combustion CO_2 emissions are from large industrial uses such as cement manufacture and use, which are also relatively easy to monitor. Thus, including nearly all CO_2 emissions is relatively easy.

Mansur (2012) provides an excellent discussion of important considerations in choosing the point in the supply chain to apply a corrective tax. Because combustion-related CO_2 emissions depend only on the carbon content of the fuel, these considerations argue for imposing the tax at natural choke points in the fossil-fuel supply chain, where the number of entities subject to the tax would be relatively small, thus minimizing enforcement and compliance costs. For example, there are roughly 150 refineries in the United States, so taxing the carbon content of oil at the refinery level (and applying an equivalent tax to imports of refined petroleum products when they enter the country) would be vastly simpler than taxing consumer purchases of refined petroleum products. Metcalf and Weisbach (2009) suggest that if the tax is applied in this manner, taxing a few thousand fossil-fuel firms could cover roughly 80% of US CO_{2e} emissions.

Adding some other GHGs to the base of a carbon tax could also be easy. Chlorofluorocarbons are already regulated and taxed (because of their role in depleting the ozone layer), so they would be easy to include in a carbon tax, and extending that to cover the closely related hydrochlorofluorocarbons (which are much less damaging to the ozone layer but similar in terms of GHG effects) would also be straightforward.

However, including most other GHGs (which made up roughly 18% of US CO_{2e} emissions in 2013) is substantially more difficult. Advances in remote sensing could help to track methane and nitrous oxide emissions, but it is still likely that including these gases in the base for a carbon tax would need to rely on taxing readily observable proxies for emissions, rather than emissions itself—and to the extent that those aren't perfect proxies, this could entail potentially significant inefficiencies (which would

[12] The emissions figures here and in the next paragraph come from US EPA (2015).

[13] This is because all of the CO_2 produced by combustion is released into the atmosphere. Carbon capture and storage (CCS) technology could change this. CCS would capture CO_2 released by combustion and store it so it is not released into the atmosphere. But CCS will only become cost-effective if technology advances dramatically or if carbon tax rates are much higher than the range of current proposals.

need to be weighed against the inefficiency of leaving those emissions out of the tax base[14]). Including these gases could also be politically difficult because agriculture is responsible for a substantial share of emissions of these gases and is very politically powerful.

3.3.1.2 Initial Tax Rate and Time Path of Rate

As discussed earlier, the basic theory of corrective taxes suggests that the optimal corrective tax rate should equal the marginal damage per unit of emissions. Interactions with the broader tax system may raise or lower this somewhat, but don't dramatically alter that basic conclusion.

The key question, then, is: What is the marginal damage from GHG emissions? This is a complex and difficult question to answer, both because the exact climate effects of a given level of GHGs remain uncertain and because changes to the climate have a wide range of effects, most occurring well into the future, and these are both uncertain and difficult to value accurately. Thus, any estimate will necessarily be highly uncertain.

A recent US inter-agency working group report (US IAWG 2013) estimated the marginal damage from carbon emissions (also referred to as the social cost of carbon, or SCC) to be roughly $43/ton. Because this report could not follow all potential channels for climate change damages, this is likely to be an underestimate, though it is obviously difficult to predict the degree of underestimation. And the report has generally been highly controversial. Nonetheless, this represents the best available estimate, and thus is a good general guideline for the efficient carbon tax rate, suggesting a rate of $43/ton CO_{2e}.

This SCC estimate includes damages to the entire world (which is quite unusual: cost-benefit analysis by the US government typically considers only costs and benefits to the United States). Thus, setting a worldwide tax rate equal to that SCC estimate would be efficient from a global perspective (that is, including costs and benefits to the entire world). Setting the US tax rate is a more complex problem. If one only considers costs and benefits to the United States, and if other countries don't adjust their policies in response to US policy, then the optimal tax would be equal just to the marginal damage to the United States, which is in the vicinity of $4–$5/ton, roughly one-tenth of the SCC estimate. However, if the United States puts any weight on damage to the rest of the world, or if other countries will react to more stringent US climate policy by making their own policies more stringent, then the optimal tax would be higher than marginal damage to the United States, perhaps as high as (or if the latter effect is strong enough, even higher than) marginal damage to the entire world.

[14] For example, leaks from the natural gas extraction and distribution system are responsible for a substantial share of methane emissions. Natural gas has lower CO_2 emissions per unit of energy than other fossil fuels, so a carbon tax would likely cause a shift from other fossil fuels toward natural gas. If methane leaks are significant, and are not taxed, then it's possible that the shift toward natural gas could actually raise CO_{2e} emissions. But taxing leaks is difficult.

Weitzman (2009) argues that risk aversion and uncertainty about climate-change damages together should imply a much more aggressive policy to limit climate change. The argument is that the probability distribution of damage from climate change is "fat-tailed"—put simply, that as we consider very unlikely, highly catastrophic outcomes, the probability of those outcomes falls as we consider more and more severe possible outcomes, but falls relatively slowly compared to most commonly used probability distributions. This means that those catastrophic outcomes—even though they are very unlikely—are still enormously important in determining the expected harms from climate change. And thus, including those potentially catastrophic outcomes implies a much higher SCC estimate (indeed, in its most extreme form, Weitzman's argument implies an infinitely high SCC). More intuitively, Weitzman's argument suggests that we should view climate change policy more as buying insurance against the worst possible outcomes than as trying to reduce damages in the relatively likely moderate-damage cases. Including such effects in a numerical estimate is very difficult, and thus the IAWG did not incorporate them, another reason why it might represent an underestimate.

A closely related question is what the optimal time path for the tax rate is. Should the tax start immediately at the SCC, or should it be gradually phased in? And once it is fully in place, how should it change over time?

Williams (2012) shows that the efficient carbon tax would not be pre-announced or gradually phased in, but would start immediately at the SCC, even when households and firms would face substantial capital adjustment costs in responding to the tax (e.g., the cost of retiring coal-fired electric plants before the end of their useful lives). Shimer (2013) finds an analogous result for labor adjustment costs such as layoffs in fossil-fuel industries.

The intuition for these results is simple: while those adjustments are costly, and affect the optimal quantity path for emissions (with higher adjustment costs implying a slower drop in emissions), the adjustment costs are not market failures, and thus they don't influence the optimal corrective tax, which still equals marginal damage. Williams (2012) notes, however, that these adjustment costs can be important for the distribution of costs, and that while other approaches such as direct transfers would be more efficient, if such alternatives are not possible, a gradual phase-in could be useful for meeting distributional objectives.

In general, the efficient carbon tax will rise over time at the same rate as marginal damage. The IAWG estimates suggest that the SCC rises at roughly 1.5% to 2% per year (in real terms), which would imply a similar rate of increase for the efficient carbon tax rate. Moreover, Daniel et al. (2015) and Lontzek et al. (2015) each add uncertainty about climate change (including the risk of climate tipping points) to integrated assessment models and find that this implies a substantially different time profile for the SCC (and therefore for the optimal carbon tax), one that starts much higher and rises much more slowly than without any uncertainty. Indeed, Daniel et al. (2015) find that this effect is so strong that the SCC actually falls over time.

Sinn (2008) observes that a rapidly rising carbon tax could actually accelerate GHG emissions. Consider the problem that an owner of fossil-fuel reserves faces when a rising carbon tax is imposed. If the tax is high enough, then it might make sense to leave the fuel in the ground forever. But if not, the sooner that fossil fuel is extracted and burned, the less tax will be charged on it—and if the tax is rising faster than the rate of interest, then even the present discounted value of the tax will be rising over time, thus providing an incentive to extract and burn the fuel sooner. This leads to a "green paradox": a carbon tax that starts lower and rises rapidly can cause more emissions in the short run than if there were no tax at all. However, as noted earlier, estimates of the SCC rise substantially more slowly than the rate of interest, so a tax rising with the SCC won't trigger the "green paradox."[15] Thus, the "green paradox" is a real worry only for taxes that rise much faster than the SCC.

While there are some carbon-tax proposals that set the carbon tax based on estimates of the SCC,[16] most proposals include rates that rise more quickly than that. Many call for a tax that rises at 4% or 5% in real terms (e.g., Morris's [2013] proposal for the Hamilton Project suggests a 4% real rise), and it is not uncommon to see proposals that rise far faster than that (recent proposals from the Carbon Tax Center, for example, start at $10/ton and rise by $10/ton each year, an extremely fast rate of increase). There are three main reasons for this.

First, many of these proposals start at rates below the SCC and thus must rise more quickly in order to catch up. It would be more efficient to start at a higher rate and rise more slowly, but if distributional or political considerations prevent that, then starting low and rising quickly may be the next best alternative.

Second, some proposals are aimed at emissions reduction pledges (e.g., an 80% reduction in US emissions by 2050) or at specific temperature-change limits (e.g., a 2° C rise in global temperatures), and these typically entail very modest short-term reductions and very aggressive longer-term reductions in emissions, which are consistent with a very rapidly rising carbon price. These targets are generally arbitrary and rarely based even in part on any analysis of costs and benefits. Thus, the tax paths necessary to follow these emissions trajectories are often far from efficient. Nonetheless, such targets may have substantial political value. And the carbon tax is still a cost-effective approach for following any arbitrary trajectory.

Third—and most common among proposals by economists—proposals are sometimes based on the idea that the tax rate should rise at the real rate of interest. This is the tax path that minimizes present-discounted costs of hitting a given total quantity of emissions over time (and is also the price path—in the absence of uncertainty—that a

[15] If the SCC were rising faster than the rate of interest, then the "green paradox" could be optimal. A rapidly rising SCC would indicate that future carbon emissions are expected to cause much more damage than emissions today, and in such a case, burning the fuel now rather than later would reduce the damage it causes. But estimates suggest that case is more of a theoretical curiosity than a real possibility.

[16] A notable recent example is the American Opportunity Carbon Fee Act, proposed in 2015 by Senators Sheldon Whitehouse and Brian Schatz.

system of bankable and tradable carbon permits would follow). This has some appeal on cost-effectiveness grounds. But looking only at total emissions over a long period (rather than year-by-year emissions) makes sense only if the present-discounted marginal damage from emissions is constant over time. Put differently, this approach minimizes the discounted costs of hitting a target expressed in undiscounted tons, a combination that doesn't generally make sense. Again, there may be political value to hitting this kind of target, but it's not efficient.

3.3.2 Effects on Greenhouse Gas Emissions, Tax Revenue, Growth, and Efficiency

This section looks at estimates for important aggregate effects of a carbon tax: how it affects GHG emissions, the potential tax revenue, and effects on economic growth.

3.3.2.1 Greenhouse Gas Emissions

The primary purpose of a carbon tax is to reduce emissions of GHGs. Thus, a key question for carbon tax models to answer is the extent to which a given carbon tax will actually reduce emissions. Estimates vary somewhat for a given carbon tax across different models. And they obviously vary substantially based on the details of the carbon tax, with the tax rate being the most important and the time path also playing an important role, while other details, such as the use of revenue from the tax play less important roles. The degree of coverage of the tax (the fraction of total GHG emissions that are in the tax base) is also potentially important, though differences here come mostly from whether the tax misses major fossil-fuel uses rather than the extent to which it includes non-CO_2 gases.

Two key points to note when evaluating estimates of emissions reductions are what year or years are under consideration, and what reference point is used for measuring reductions. In general, a given tax rate will generate larger emissions reductions further into the future because some responses to the tax take a significant period of time, and thus the long-run elasticity of emissions with respect to the tax rate is much higher than the short-run elasticity. The point of reference for reductions also matters. National pledges to reduce emissions are typically expressed relative to emissions in some base year (e.g., under the UN Framework Convention on Climate Change the United States pledged to reduce emissions in 2025 to 26%–28% below 2005 levels), and model estimates are sometimes also expressed this way. More commonly, estimates from economic models are reported as reductions below "business-as-usual" (BAU) emissions, meaning the level that would have occurred in a given year in the absence of the policy.[17] The latter measures the effect of the policy, whereas the former shows the actual level of emissions.

[17] A further complication is that BAU sometimes refers to emissions in the absence of the particular policy under consideration, and sometimes to emissions in the absence of any GHG emissions reduction policies.

Hafstead and Kopp (2015) find that a $45/ton carbon tax, starting in 2016 and rising at 2% per year in real terms, would reduce US emissions in 2025 by 41% relative to BAU, which is equivalent to 45% below 2005 levels. In contrast, Carbone et al. (2013) estimate that a $50/ton carbon tax (starting in 2015 and held constant in real terms) would reduce US emissions in 2025 by roughly 23% below BAU. Part of that difference reflects differences in the tax rate under consideration, but more of the difference comes from differences in the models used. Estimating the responsiveness of large sectors of the economy to a carbon tax is very difficult, given that the United States has never imposed such a policy, and thus estimates vary significantly across models.

By way of comparison, the latter study also finds that a $30/ton tax would reduce emissions by roughly 17% below BAU, and a $20/ton tax by roughly 12%. In general, the effect on emissions rises less than linearly with the tax rate (e.g., doubling the tax rate will less than double the emissions reductions). These estimates vary somewhat based on how the revenue from the tax is used, but those differences are relatively small: for example, the estimated emissions reduction from a $30/ton carbon tax is 14.92% if the carbon tax revenue is recycled to finance tax cuts on capital income, versus 16.61% if it is returned to households via lump-sum transfers. That difference arises largely because of differences in overall economic growth caused by the different uses of revenue.

Most models suggest that the vast majority of emissions reductions will come from the electricity sector, at least for moderate carbon tax rates. For example, the same Hafstead and Kopp (2015) study find that 72% of the emissions reductions in 2025 come from the electricity sector. This is because switching away from coal to lower-carbon sources of electricity is one of the least expensive ways to reduce carbon emissions.

An alternative approach when considering the emissions effect of a carbon tax is to look at the question from the other direction: What tax rate is necessary to achieve a particular level of emissions reductions in a given year (or a particular path of emissions over a range of years)? Fawcett et al. (2015) report results from a Stanford Energy Modeling Forum exercise that took this approach, using eight different models under a range of different assumptions about technology changes and other key influences. The exercise looked at what carbon tax rate would be needed to achieve a 17% reduction (relative to 2005) by 2020 and 50% reduction by 2050. On average across the different models and assumptions, this required a tax rate of $41/ton in 2020 and $192/ton in 2050 (both expressed in 2012 dollars). This again shows the non-linearity of the response to the tax: getting a reduction roughly three times as large requires a tax rate more than three times as high. Those estimates also ranged widely across models, with a standard deviation of $35/ton in 2020 and $113/ton in 2050, which again demonstrates the degree of uncertainty about how large the response to any given tax would be.

3.3.2.2 Carbon Tax Revenue

Given an estimate of the emissions effects of a carbon tax, estimating the gross revenue the tax will raise is simple: the tax rate times the emissions subject to the tax. The revenue from a moderate carbon tax is potentially substantial. Carbone et al. (2013) estimates that a $30/ton carbon tax (held constant in real terms) would raise a total of $2.26 trillion in gross revenue over the first ten years. Marron et al. (2015) scale a Congressional Budget Office estimate and find that a $25/ton carbon/ton tax (rising at 2% per year in real terms) would raise $1.6 trillion in gross revenue over ten years.

However, imposing a carbon tax can change the revenues from other taxes and the cost of goods and services that the government buys. Thus, the most relevant question isn't the level of gross revenue, but the net revenue: the amount of revenue left after compensating for those other changes to the government budget. The Joint Committee on Taxation (JCT) and Congressional Budget Office impose a standard offset factor (informally known as a "haircut") to account for effects of indirect taxes (such as a carbon tax) on revenue from other taxes, which reduces the amount of revenue available by 25%.[18] To the extent that the carbon tax affects the overall size of the economy, those effects will also influence net revenue (with greater economic growth implying more net revenue relative to gross revenue from the tax).

Applying that standard offset reduces the gross estimates above to net revenue of $1.7 and $1.2 trillion, respectively, over the next ten years. This still represents a large amount of revenue. By way of comparison, the corporate income tax is estimated to bring in $4.6 trillion in revenue over that period, the total of all excise taxes $1.1 trillion, and the estate and gift tax $246 billion, and the primary budget deficit over that period is projected to be $2 trillion (CBO 2015). Thus, a carbon tax could finance substantial reductions in other taxes or in the budget deficit.

3.3.2.3 Effects of a Carbon Tax on Economic Growth

By itself, a carbon tax is likely to slow economic growth slightly. Fossil fuels are used throughout the economy, and thus taxing carbon acts as an implicit tax on all production. This lowers the return to factors of production such as capital and labor (either directly, through effects on wages and profits, or indirectly, by raising product prices and thus lowering real returns), and thus discourages work, saving, and investment.

[18] The rationale for this standard offset is that for a given total amount of total economic activity, each dollar of indirect tax revenue will reduce total wage and profit income by a dollar, thus reducing revenue by the amount of tax that would have been collected on that dollar. If tax rates average roughly 25%, then this implies a correction factor of roughly 25%. Note that this does not include any effects on the overall size of the economy.

This effect is significant but not dramatic: Carbone et al. (2013) estimates that a $30/ton carbon tax would reduce GDP by roughly 3.5% in 2050.[19] Note that figure expresses a difference in GDP levels, whereas we usually hear about GDP growth rates. A 3.5% difference in GDP levels thirty-five years from now is equivalent to roughly a 0.1% difference in average annual growth rates over that time.

That estimate assumes that the entire revenue from the tax is returned to households in lump-sum transfers. If the revenue is used in some alternative way that provides a boost to growth, such as cutting marginal tax rates, reducing the budget deficit, or funding growth-enhancing public goods, then this would reduce or even reverse the drag on GDP. For example, Carbone et al. (2013) find that if the net revenue from the carbon tax is used to fund cuts in taxes on capital income, that reverses the effect on GDP, leading to a roughly 1.3% higher level of GDP in 2050.

Williams and Wichman (2015) review estimates for the effect of a carbon tax on growth from a range of different models, carbon tax rates, and uses of revenue, and all of them lie between the two estimates cited in the previous two paragraphs. Most cluster around a 0.5% to 0.7% lower level of GDP by 2040, with higher GDP estimates associated with revenue used for capital tax cuts and lower estimates associated with revenue used for lump-sum rebates or with extremely high carbon tax rates.[20]

3.3.3 Distribution of the Cost of a Carbon Tax

While the aggregate effects of a carbon tax are important, they are certainly not all that matters. The distribution of those effects is also important because of both equity and political considerations. This subsection considers how the costs of a carbon tax are distributed across income groups and across states and regions of the United States. Note that this section focuses only on the distribution of the costs of the tax (and distributional effects of potential uses of the carbon tax revenue). It does not consider the distribution of the environmental benefits from a carbon tax (the avoided damage from climate change), which could easily be just as important as the distribution of costs, but is much harder to estimate.

[19] This section focuses on effects on GDP because it is an easily understood measure of economic growth. However, it is worth noting that GDP only measures the value of market goods and services, and leaves out many other goods that are valuable but not sold in the market (e.g., the value of leisure time or of goods produced at home, such as childcare and home-cooked meals). Many studies find that using GDP overstates the cost of a carbon tax relative to more complete measures of economic well-being (such as equivalent variation).

[20] For example, NERA Economic Consulting (2013) estimates a 3.4% lower GDP in 2050 for a case that reduces carbon emissions by 80% in 2050—which in their model requires a carbon price of almost $1,000/ton.

3.3.3.1 Distribution across Income Groups

It is natural to think that a carbon tax will be quite regressive. The most obvious effect of a carbon tax is to raise the prices that consumers pay for direct energy goods: electricity, natural gas, gasoline, heating oil, and so on. And these goods represent a larger share of the budget for poor households than for wealthier households.

Williams et al. (2015) show that the burden imposed by higher direct energy good prices caused by a carbon tax, expressed as a percentage of income, is roughly five times as large for the bottom income quintile (the poorest 20% of households in the United States) as it is for the top income quintile. Those figures are based on current-year income, and it is well-known that such measures tend to overstate how regressive increases in consumer prices are, relative to measures based on income over a longer term (or proxies for longer-term income such as current-year consumption). But even using estimates from Hassett et al. (2009) based on current-year consumption, the burden from direct energy good price increases is 2.5 times as large for the bottom decile as for the top decile.

However, the effects of a carbon tax on consumer prices go well beyond just the effects on direct energy goods. Every good in the economy has some energy use somewhere in its production process, and almost certainly some associated carbon emissions, so one would expect a carbon tax to influence the prices of all goods. Direct energy goods account for only about half of all carbon emissions in the United States. And the effects on the prices of other goods are spread much more evenly through the income distribution. Hassett et al. (2009) find that when using measures based on current-year consumption, the distribution of this indirect burden is slightly progressive, though very close to equal across the income distribution. Thus, taking into account the effects on all prices, not just on prices of direct energy goods, shows that the carbon tax is not as regressive as it might first appear.[21]

Moreover, a carbon tax doesn't just affect prices of consumer goods; it can also affect sources of income such as wages and returns to capital. Most studies of the distributional effects of carbon taxes (or carbon pricing in general) miss those effects because they assume that the entire carbon tax is passed forward into produce prices. In fact, some portion of it will be passed backward, affecting the prices of factors of production used to produce carbon-intensive goods.

The few studies that include effects on sources of income find that these effects make the carbon tax more progressive. Carbon-intensive goods tend also to be capital-intensive in production, so a carbon tax causes a drop in capital demand relative to demand for labor. Moreover, even to the extent that the tax is passed forward into

[21] Grainger and Kolstad (2010) and Mathur and Morris (2014) find generally similar results to Hassett et al. (2009). In addition, Grainger and Kolstad (2010) find that adjusting for household size makes the carbon tax somewhat more regressive, and both papers look at policy options to reduce the regressivity of the tax.

product prices, this also raises the price of capital goods, acting as an implicit tax on capital.[22] Together, these effects cause the carbon tax to fall disproportionately on capital income relative to labor income, and capital income goes disproportionately to higher income people. Moreover, income from government transfers—which goes disproportionately to poorer households—are typically indexed for inflation, and this helps to compensate poorer households for the consumer price effects of the carbon tax.[23]

Williams et al. (2015) finds that effects on incomes substantially reduce the regressivity of a carbon tax, though the tax remains slightly regressive. Rausch et al. (2011) finds an even stronger result, with these effects sufficient to make the carbon tax slightly progressive.

Finally, the use of the revenue from the carbon tax can dramatically influence the overall distributional implications of the policy. Williams et al. (2015) find, for example, that using carbon tax revenue to cut taxes on capital income makes the top income quintile better off (even ignoring any environmental gains), while making the other four quintiles worse off (with the loss getting larger as a percentage of income as one moves down the income distribution). Conversely, returning the revenue via equal-per-capita lump-sum transfers to households makes the bottom three quintiles better off and the top two worse off (with the gain getting smaller or the loss getting larger as one moves up the income distribution). Returning the revenue via cuts in labor taxes falls in between, with a roughly flat distribution of burden. Marron et al. (2015) find quite similar results using a substantially different model.

These results indicate that the use of the carbon tax revenue is more important than the effect of the carbon tax itself in determining the overall distributional effect of the policy. The carbon tax by itself is mildly regressive. Combining it with a regressive use of revenue (such as a cut in taxes on capital) makes it substantially more regressive. Combining it with a progressive use of revenue (such as lump-sum transfers) makes it substantially progressive.

3.3.3.2 Distribution across States or Regions

The distribution of costs of a carbon tax across states or regions of the United States is generally more even than the distribution across income groups. While there are strong geographic patterns to the use of particular energy goods (e.g., heating oil use is strongly concentrated in the northeast, and electricity use is highest in the south due to air-conditioning demand), consumption of energy goods as a whole is spread relatively evenly across the country. And just as with the distribution across income groups, the effects of a carbon tax on the prices of goods that are not direct energy

[22] Many economists incorrectly view a carbon tax as having similar effects to a broad-based consumption tax such as a VAT because they see it as raising consumer good prices. But the carbon tax implicitly taxes all production—whether used for consumption or investment.

[23] This point was first made by Parry and Williams (2010) and then was studied in more detail by Fullerton et al. (2011).

goods are spread more evenly across the economy. Thus, estimates are that the effect of a carbon tax on consumer prices is relatively flat across different regions of the country.

For example, Hassett et al. (2009) estimate that the burden of a carbon tax varies by only 20% across regions (that is, the region with the lightest burden bears a tax burden that is 20% smaller as a percentage of income than the region with the heaviest burden), a range that is much narrower than the variation across income groups. Moreover, that study finds that which regions bear the heaviest and lightest burdens varies substantially from year to year. Mathur and Morris (2014) find similar results.

Williams et al. (2014) looks not just at the effects on consumer prices but also incorporates effects on sources of income (wages, returns to capital, and government transfers) by linking to a computable-general equilibrium model. Again, the distribution of burdens across states is relatively flat. And, just as with the distribution across income groups, the use of the revenue from the carbon tax is important for the distribution of costs across states. Returning the revenue via lump-sum transfers benefits relatively low-income states, such as the southeast and Appalachia. Using revenue to cut taxes on capital income benefits states with large shares of income from capital, such as Florida and relatively high-income coastal states. Returning the revenue via cuts in taxes on labor income leads to a net cost that is nearly flat across states.

3.4 MOTOR FUEL TAXES

While a carbon tax is the largest and likely most important potential new environmental tax, motor fuel taxes (taxes on gasoline and diesel fuel) are by far the most important existing environmental tax, accounting for more than 90% of environmental tax revenue in the United States (and playing a similarly dominant role in nearly all other industrialized nations). This section focuses on motor fuel taxes, with the first subsection considering research on the efficient rates for these taxes, and the second subsection focusing on their distributional effects.

3.4.1 The Efficient Level of Motor Fuel Taxes

There are many negative externalities associated with motor vehicle use, including environmental externalities such as emissions of GHGs and local air pollutants, as well as other externalities such as traffic congestion and vehicle accidents. The most economically efficient approach would be to correct each of these externalities with a policy specifically targeting that externality, for example, a corrective tax aimed at traffic congestion would charge tolls that vary across roads and times of day, with the toll being highest when traffic congestion is at its worst, and falling to zero when a road is empty. The gasoline tax is a very blunt instrument by comparison. But there are practical difficulties with imposing a full set of policies to address those externalities, and it is much easier to adjust the level of existing motor fuel taxes. And regardless of why, to the extent that those other externalities are not fully corrected, they will influence the efficient level of taxes on motor fuels.

A naïve analysis would simply estimate the average level of each of those externalities on a per-gallon basis and add them up to calculate the efficient level for a corrective tax. For externalities that are directly proportional to the amount of fuel burned (such as carbon emissions), that's the correct approach, but not for other externalities. For example, suppose that a particular driver's contribution to traffic congestion is proportional to how much driving he does. If he responds to a higher gasoline tax only by driving less, then the reduction in the externality is directly proportional to the drop in fuel use. But if the higher tax also causes the driver to buy a more fuel-efficient car, then the reduction in the traffic externality is smaller than the drop in fuel use—and in that case, because the gas tax does less to address the traffic externality, that externality adds less to the efficient level of the tax.

Parry and Small (2005) review the various externalities associated with driving, taking into account interactions with the rest of the tax system (as discussed earlier, in section 3.2.1.2), and calculate the efficient tax on gasoline to be approximately $1.01/gallon (in 2000 dollars).[24] West and Williams (2007) find that higher gasoline prices boost household labor supply (more than one would expect simply based on income effects), and that this further raises the efficient gas tax, to $1.12/gallon.[25] Converting that to 2015 dollars implies an efficient tax rate of $1.55/gallon. That is far above the current combined federal and state tax on gasoline, which averages 48.69 cents/gallon and ranges as high as 73.7 cents/gallon (in Pennsylvania).[26]

Far fewer studies look at the efficient level of taxes on diesel fuel, but the efficient tax on diesel fuel used by passenger cars should be roughly similar to that for gasoline, with some upward adjustment based on the greater GHG and local air pollution emissions per gallon, and the higher average miles per gallon (which magnifies per-mile externalities when converted to a per-gallon basis). Parry (2008) finds that the optimal tax on diesel fuel used by heavy-duty trucks is $1.12/gallon (a figure that appears to be in year 2000 dollars, equivalent to $1.55/gallon in 2015). Again, this is well above the current average combined federal and state diesel tax rate of 54.41 cents/gallon (American Petroleum Institute 2015).

3.4.2 Distributional Implications of Motor Fuel Taxes

One major argument against increasing taxes on gasoline is that such a tax is regressive: lower-income households spend a larger fraction of their budgets on gasoline than do wealthier households. Unlike with other energy goods, this doesn't hold throughout the entire income distribution—the very poorest households are less likely to own cars—but it does hold for most of the income distribution.

[24] In comparison, they find that a naïve calculation, simply adding up the externalities, would suggest a much higher rate of $1.76/gallon.

[25] This figure again is in 2000 dollars and is based on the externality estimates taken from Parry and Small. Of that total, 5 cents comes from carbon-dioxide emissions, 16 cents from emissions of local air pollution, 29 cents from traffic congestion, 24 cents from accidents, and an additional 26 cents because the gasoline tax is a more efficient revenue-raising tax than the income tax.

[26] See American Petroleum Institute (2015).

As noted earlier, in section 3.3.3, studies based on one year's income tend to make taxes on consumer goods look more regressive than studies based on income over a longer time period (or proxies for longer-term income, such as expenditures). Poterba (1991) showed that this effect was important for analysis of the gas tax. West (2004) and West and Williams (2004) pointed out that lower-income households have more elastic gasoline demand than higher-income households, and that this lowers the burden they bear from a price increase, making the gas tax less regressive than if the elasticity were constant across incomes.

Nonetheless, even after taking those effects into account, the gas tax is still somewhat regressive. West and Williams (2004) find that the burden of a gas tax is highest for the second-lowest income quintile and lowest for the top quintile, though it is relatively flat across the bottom four quintiles: they estimate that raising the gas tax to the efficient rate (an increase of roughly $1/gallon) would impose a burden of 2.78% of annual expenditures for the bottom quintile, and 3.01%, 2.88%, 2.49%, and 1.60% for the second through fifth quintiles, respectively.

3.5 ENVIRONMENTAL AND ENERGY TAX CREDITS AND DEDUCTIONS

Many of the current environmental and energy provisions within the US tax code are not environmental or energy taxes, but rather tax credits, exemptions, and deductions. Rather than taxing pollution, energy use, or similar activities that government wants to discourage, these tax expenditures are implicit subsidies. This section briefly reviews two of the larger energy/environmental tax expenditures, discusses their effects, and considers whether they could be removed or replaced with more efficient alternatives.

3.5.1 Tax Credits for Renewable Electricity Generation

The renewable energy production tax credit (PTC) provides a tax credit of 2 cents/kWh of electricity generated from qualifying renewable sources (primarily solar, wind, and biomass). Alternatively, firms can take an investment tax credit (ITC) of 30% of the cost of investing in qualifying generating equipment. These credits substantially lower the cost of generating power from renewable sources, and thus encourage use of renewable energy.

This policy can be viewed as correcting a pollution externality, to the extent that renewable power substitutes for other more polluting sources of electricity (and that those pollution externalities are not already corrected by other policies). One might also argue that the policy addresses externalities in technology development (such as research and development spillovers), though that justification is more tenuous, given that these are not brand-new technologies and that the United States represents a relatively small share of world demand.

Nordhaus et al. (2013) looked at the effects of the PTC and ITC on carbon emissions and found relatively small effects: eliminating these provisions would increase carbon emissions by roughly 360 million metric tons, less than 0.3% of US energy-sector emissions. Moreover, this is a relatively expensive way to reduce carbon emissions: the government gives up more than $250 in tax revenue per ton of CO_2 reductions.[27]

Thus, if the goal of the PTC and ITC is to reduce carbon emissions, these credits are a relatively expensive way to achieve that goal. A carbon tax—even one with a very low rate—would do much more to reduce emissions and at a lower cost.

3.5.2 Depletion Allowances for Oil and Gas Wells

Owners of oil and gas wells can deduct a depletion allowance, which is intended to reflect the decline in the value of oil and gas reserves as those reserves are extracted and sold. That depletion is a cost, and thus should be deductible, just as other business costs are. However, independent companies producing in the United States are allowed to use percentage depletion—deducting a percentage of gross income associated with the sale of the oil and/or gas—which typically allows for deductions that exceed the actual cost of acquiring and developing the resource. Thus, the difference between percentage and cost depletion represents an implicit subsidy to oil and gas production by independent producers. The JCT estimates that the difference reduced tax revenue by $4.1 billion over the 2010–2014 period.

This subsidy is difficult to justify on economic grounds. There is no obvious positive externality associated with domestic oil and gas production. "Energy security" is sometimes used as an argument for domestic production, but it is not clear why this represents an externality, nor is it clear that promoting depletion of reserves enhances energy security (indeed, one could argue that energy security is greater if those reserves are left in the ground so they can be used later in case of an energy crisis). The subsidy today largely benefits natural gas producers, and gas is a relatively clean fuel, which suggests there might be some environmental justification. But Nordhaus (2013) finds that eliminating percentage depletion would actually reduce GHG emissions slightly (a net drop of 37 million metric tons per year).

3.6 CONCLUSIONS

This chapter has reviewed major potential environmental and energy tax changes. It focused primarily on a carbon tax but also considered potential changes to the taxes on motor vehicle fuels (currently by far the largest environmental taxes in the United States) and to two of the largest environmental and energy tax expenditures.

A carbon tax represents a cost-effective way of reducing GHG emissions. Research suggests that an efficient carbon tax would be imposed on the carbon content of fossil fuels at a rate equal to the SCC, which is currently estimated at roughly $45/ton,

27 Note that revenue cost is not the same thing as the economic cost of the policy, and unfortunately the model used could not provide estimates of social cost. Nonetheless, this suggests that the policy is quite costly relative to its modest effects, which is consistent with theoretical results that such subsidies are inefficient relative to emissions pricing policies.

and would rise slowly over time, reflecting the projected rise over time in the SCC of roughly 1.5% to 2% per year.

Such a tax would likely slow economic growth, but that effect is very small, especially if the tax revenue is used in ways that promote economic growth, such as cutting marginal rates of other taxes, reducing the budget deficit, or financing growth-enhancing public goods. The tax would also be mildly regressive, imposing a slightly higher burden on lower-income households than on higher-income households, though much less regressive than it is widely perceived to be. Moreover, this regressivity could be overcome if some of the revenue is used in a progressive way.

Taxes on motor fuels are also well below economically efficient levels, by roughly $1/gallon. These taxes are somewhat regressive.

Finally, the two tax expenditures considered—the production and investment tax credits (PTC and ITC) for renewable energy and percentage depletion for oil and gas—have relatively small environmental effects. The PTC and ITC provide environmental benefits, but at relatively high cost: a carbon tax would do far more to reduce pollution emissions and in a much more cost-effective way. Percentage depletion is slightly damaging to the environment and is generally difficult to justify based on economic efficiency arguments.

ACKNOWLEDGMENTS

This chapter was written for the 2015 Conference on the Economics of Tax Policy, sponsored by the Robert D. Burch Center at UC Berkeley, the Penn Wharton Public Policy Initiative, and the Urban-Brookings Tax Policy Center. I am grateful to Alan Auerbach, Don Fullerton, and participants at the conference for their comments and suggestions.

REFERENCES

American Petroleum Institute. 2015. "State Motor Fuel Taxes, Rates Effective 10/01/2015." http://www.api.org/~/media/Files/Statistics/StateMotorFuel-OnePagers-October-2015.pdf

Carbone, Jared C., Richard D. Morgenstern, Roberton C. Williams III, and Dallas Burtraw. 2013. "Deficit Reduction and Carbon Taxes: Budgetary, Economic, Distributional and Economic Impacts." Resources for the Future Report.

Congressional Budget Office. 2015. "Options for Reducing the Deficit: 2015 to 2024."

Daniel, Kent D., Robert B. Litterman, and Gernot Wagner. 2015. "Applying Asset Pricing Theory to Calibrate the Price of Climate Risk." Unpublished.

Fawcett, Allen A., Leon C. Clarke, and John P. Weyant. 2015. "Carbon Taxes to Achieve Emissions Targets: Insights from EMF 24." In *Implementing a US Carbon Tax: Challenges and Debates*, edited by Ian Parry, Adele Morris, and Roberton C. Williams III, 62–82. London and New York: International Monetary Fund and Routledge.

Forster, P., V. Ramaswamy, P. Artaxo, T. Berntsen, R. Betts, D. W. Fahey, J. Haywood, J. Lean, D. C. Lowe, G. Myhre, J. Nganga, R. Prinn, G. Raga, M. Schulz, and R. Van Dorland. 2007.

"Changes in Atmospheric Constituents and in Radiative Forcing." In *Climate Change 2007: The Physical Science Basis. Contribution of Working Group I to the Fourth Assessment Report of the Intergovernmental Panel on Climate Change*, edited by S. Solomon, D. Qin, M. Manning, Z. Chen, M. Marquis, K. B. Averyt, M. Tignor, and H. L. Miller, 129–234. Cambridge: Cambridge University Press.

Fullerton, Don. 1996. "Why Have Separate Environmental Taxes?" *Tax Policy and the Economy* 10:33–70.

Fullerton, Don, Garth Heutel, and Gilbert E. Metcalf. 2011. "Does the Indexing of Government Transfers Make Carbon Pricing Progressive." *American Journal of Agricultural Economics* 94 (2): 347–53.

Goulder, Lawrence H. 1995. "Environmental Taxation and the 'Double Dividend': A Reader's Guide." *International Tax and Public Finance* 2 (2): 157–83.

Grainger, Corbett A., and Charles D. Kolstad. 2010. "Who Pays a Price on Carbon?." *Environmental and Resource Economics* 46 (3): 359–76.

Hafstead, Marc A. C., and Raymond J. Kopp. 2015. "Analysis of the American Opportunity Carbon Fee Act." Resources for the Future issue brief 2015-01.

Hassett, Kevin A., Aparna Mathur, and Gilbert E. Metcalf. 2009. "The Incidence of a U.S. Carbon Tax: A Lifetime and Regional Analysis." *Energy Journal* 30 (2): 155–78.

Lontzek, Thomas S., Yongyang Cai, Kenneth L. Judd, and Timothy M. Lenton. 2015. "Stochastic Integrated Assessment of Climate Tipping Points Indicates the Need for Strict Climate Policy." *Nature Climate Change* 5:441–4.

Mansur, Erin. 2012. "Upstream versus Downstream Implementation of Climate Policy." In *The Design and Implementation of U.S. Climate Policy*, edited by Don Fullerton and Catherine Wolfram, 179–93. Chicago: University of Chicago Press.

Marron, Donald, Eric Toder, and Lydia Austin. 2015. "Taxing Carbon: What, Why, and How." Urban-Brookings Tax Policy Center. http://taxpolicycenter.org/publications/url.cfm?ID=2000274

Mathur, Aparna, and Adele Morris. 2014. "Distributional Effects of a Carbon Tax in Broader U.S. Fiscal Reform." *Energy Policy* 66:326–34.

Metcalf, Gilbert E. 2009. "Environmental Taxation: What Have We Learned in This Decade?" In *Tax Policy Lessons from the 2000s*, edited by Alan Viard, 7–44. Washington, DC: AEI Press.

Metcalf, Gilbert E., and David Weisbach. 2009. "The Design of a Carbon Tax." *Harvard Environmental Law Review* 33:499–556.

Morris, Adele C. 2013. "The Many Benefits of a Carbon Tax." In *15 Ways to Rethink the Federal Budget*, edited by Michael Greenstone, Max Harris, Karen Li, Adam Looney, and Jeremy Patashnik, 63–69. Washington, DC: Brookings Institution.

NERA Economic Consulting. 2013. "Economic Outcomes of a U.S. Carbon Tax." http://www.nera.com/content/dam/nera/publications/archive2/PUB_Smith_NAM_FinalReport_0213.pdf

Nordhaus, William D., Stephen A. Merrill, and Paul T. Beaton, eds. 2013. *Effects of US Tax Policy on Greenhouse Gas Emissions*. Washington, DC: National Academies Press.

Oates, Wallace. 1995. "Green Taxes: Can We Protect the Environment and Improve the Tax System at the Same Time." *Southern Economic Journal* 61: 914–22.

Parry, Ian. 2008. "How Should Heavy-Duty Trucks Be Taxed?" *Journal of Urban Economics* 63 (2): 651–68.

Parry, Ian W. H., and Antonio M. Bento. 2000. "Tax Deductions, Environmental Policy, and the 'Double Dividend' Hypothesis." *Journal of Environmental Economics and Management* 39:67–96.

Parry, Ian, and Kenneth Small. 2005. "Does Britain or the United States Have the Right Gasoline Tax?" *American Economic Review* 95:1276–89.

Parry, Ian W. H., and Roberton C. Williams III. 2010. "What Are the Costs of Meeting Distributional Objectives for Climate Policy?" *B. E. Journal of Economic Analysis & Policy* 10 (2): Article 9.

Pearce, David. 1991. "The Role of Carbon Taxes in Adjusting to Global Warming." *Economic Journal* 101: 938–48.

Pigou, Arthur C. 1920. *The Economics of Welfare*. London: Macmillan.

Rausch, Sebastian, Gilbert E. Metcalf, and John M. Reilly. 2011. "Distributional Impacts of Carbon Pricing: A General Equilibrium Approach with Micro-Data for Households." *Energy Economics* 33 (S1): S20–S33.

Repetto, Robert, Roger C. Dower, Robin Jenkins, and Jacqueline Geoghegan. 1992. *Green Fees: How a Tax Shift Can Work for the Environment and the Economy*. Washington, DC: World Resources Institute.

Sinn, Hans-Werner. 2008. "Public Policies against Global Warming: A Supply Side Approach." *International Tax and Public Finance* 15 (4): 360–94.

Tullock, Gordon. 1967. "Excess Benefit." *Water Resources Research* 3:643–4.

US EPA. 2015. *Inventory of US Greenhouse Gas Emissions and Sinks, 1990–2013*. United States Environmental Protection Agency Report EPA 430-R-15-004.

US IAWG. 2013. *Technical Support Document: Technical Update of the Social Cost of Carbon for Regulatory Impact Analysis under Executive Order 12866*. Washington, DC: Interagency Working Group on Social Cost of Carbon, United States Government.

Weitzman, Martin. 2009. "On Modeling and Interpreting the Economics of Catastrophic Climate Change." *Review of Economics and Statistics* 91 (1): 1–19.

West, Sarah. 2004. "Distributional Effects of Alternative Vehicle Pollution Control Policies." *Journal of Public Economics* 88 (3–4): 735–57.

West, Sarah, and Roberton C. Williams III. 2004. "Estimates from a Consumer Demand System: Implications for the Incidence of Environmental Taxes." *Journal of Environmental Economics and Management* 47 (3): 535–58.

West, Sarah, and Roberton C. Williams III. 2007. "Optimal Taxation and Cross-Price Effects on Labor Supply: Estimates of the Optimal Gas Tax." *Journal of Public Economics* 91:593–617.

Williams, Roberton C., III. 2009, "A Response to Gilbert E. Metcalf." In *Tax Policy Lessons from the 2000s*, edited by Alan Viard, 35–44. Washington, DC: AEI Press.

Williams, Roberton C., III. 2012. "Setting the Initial Time-Profile of Climate Policy: The Economics of Environmental Policy Phase-Ins." In *The Design and Implementation of U.S. Climate Policy*, edited by Don Fullerton and Catherine Wolfram, 245–54. Chicago: University of Chicago Press.

Williams, Roberton C., III, Hal Gordon, Dallas Burtraw, Jared Carbone, and Richard Morgenstern. 2014. "The Initial Incidence of a Carbon Tax across U.S. States." *National Tax Journal* 67 (4): 807–30.

Williams, Roberton C., III, Hal Gordon, Dallas Burtraw, Jared Carbone, and Richard Morgenstern. 2015. "The Initial Incidence of a Carbon Tax across Income Groups." *National Tax Journal* 68 (1): 195–214.

Williams, Roberton C., III, and Casey J. Wichman. 2015. "Macroeconomic Effects of Carbon Taxes." In *Implementing a US Carbon Tax: Challenges and Debates*, edited by Ian Parry, Adele Morris, and Roberton C. Williams III, 62–82. London and New York: International Monetary Fund and Routledge.

COMMENTARY ON CHAPTER 3

Don Fullerton

The chapter by Rob Williams is a joy to read. It's particularly well written and informative, while integrating and explaining all the important topics of environmental taxation. Great job, Rob! Reading it brings me back to a "history of thought" in this field, or at least a history of my own thinking in environmental taxation, with all of the developments from initial thoughts about each of these issues, revisions of that thinking, wholesale replacement of that thinking, and the beginnings of new beliefs about the efficacy and distributional effects of taxes on pollution or on pollution-related activities.

In this discussion, I'll start with a little more background on why this whole topic and especially climate policy is important, and then I'll frame the historical development of thinking about environmental taxation in five "phases." None of this discussion is inconsistent with Rob's points—it's merely a bit of reinterpretation and new emphasis.

3C.1 BACKGROUND

Here is my 60-second imitation of Al Gore in "An Inconvenient Truth"; plenty of further detail is in various reports from the Intergovernmental Panel on Climate Change (e.g., IPCC 2014). Without significant mitigation action, worldwide CO_2 and other greenhouse gas (GHG) emissions will continue to rise exponentially; CO_2 concentrations in the atmosphere have already increased from 320 parts per million (ppm) and are expected to hit 450 ppm by 2030; the ensuing temperature increase is expected to exceed the 2°C target set by politicians at international conferences; sea levels are expected to rise more than a couple feet by 2100; increased frequency and severity of storms and storm surges on top of that higher sea level will wreak havoc on coastal cities worldwide; increased frequency and severity of droughts will ruin crops worldwide; and most important, the state of Illinois where I now live will have its climate move to that of Austin, Texas—where I lived for thirteen years already and moved out because it's too damn hot!

In November 2014, President Obama agreed with President Xi Jinping of China that the United States would cut CO_2 emissions by at least 26% from 2005 levels by 2025 (Davenport 2014). In return, President Xi agreed that China's emissions would continue to increase but peak "around 2030." That particular wording makes it sound like not much of a deal for the United States, but for two factors. First, US emissions already peaked in 2005, fell with the recession, and were already on course for continued reductions, so it's not much further commitment on the part of the United States. Second, a plot of China's emissions and projections heads straight through the roof, so cutting that projected growth to zero might well be the most important contribution to worldwide reductions. In any case, those two promises were incorporated into the Paris Agreement of December 2015, along with 184 other nations of the world (Revkin 2015).

The purpose of this background, of course, is just to point out the importance of Rob Williams and others studying the economic effects of environmental taxation to solve these problems while minimizing economic costs, disruptions, and adverse distributional effects.

3C.2 THE FIVE PHASES OF "THE ENVIRONMENTAL TAX LEARNING CURVE"

Figure 3C.1 is a simple schematic representation of what I would call the five phases of "The Environmental Tax Learning Curve," where the horizontal axis shows the progression of time studying this field, and the vertical axis shows the total knowledge or understanding of the advantages of environmental taxation.

Phase I (Steep Learning): this history of thought begins with Pigou (1920) who points out that a tax on pollution can fix an externality completely by inducing cost-minimizing abatement choices by private agents—with no need for government officials to try to figure out the cost-minimizing choices and to craft regulations that require the right use of each technology. Since politicians cannot know what technologies minimize cost, economists have found that command and control regulations can be many times as expensive as the cost-minimizing incentive policies like a pollution tax or cap-and-trade (e.g., Newell and Stavins 2003).

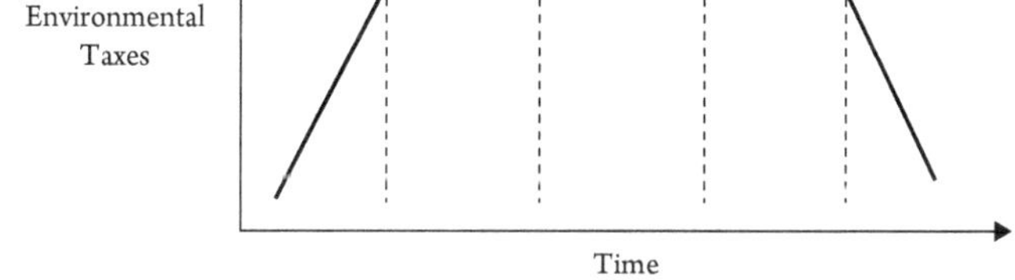

Figure 3C.1 Five phases of the environmental tax learning curve

Another early development was Weitzman's (1974) explanation of when to use a price instrument (like a tax on pollution) or a restriction on quantity (as in a cap-and-trade permit system). With uncertainty about abatement costs, the simple logic is that a tax would fix the price and leave the quantity uncertain, which could be a problem in the case of a threshold quantity—above which are steep damages from illness and deaths. In contrast, the permit system would fix the quantity and leave the price uncertain, which could be a problem if the cost curve is steep and the cost to firms could soar—especially if the damages from pollution are not steep.

These points are important, so we all entered the 1980s thinking that environmental taxation was pretty well understood. The policy prescription seemed straightforward: market economists dislike "Soviet-style" command and control regulation. Despite political difficulties, any pollution problem can be fixed by putting a price on pollution.

Phase II (Still Learning): The early 1990s saw the beginning of a huge literature on the "double dividend" hypothesis that an environmental tax could both improve the environment and raise revenue for use to cut distorting taxes on labor, raise the net-of-tax wage, encourage labor supply, and reduce deadweight loss of the tax system (see Goulder 1995).

A refinement on the choice between a price and quantity instrument is to combine them and get the best of both worlds. A hybrid policy could set the number of permits but also a price ceiling (at which point government simply sells more permits at that price), and even a price floor (at which point government simply buys and retires all available permits at that price).

We also learned that all of these environmental policies tend to have regressive distributional effects, since low-income families spend a relatively high fraction of their income (or total consumption) on electricity, gasoline, and other fossil-fuel-intensive goods. Figure 3C.2 shows that this percentage spent on electricity falls from about 4% to 5% in the lowest annual income group to about 2% in the highest group. These refinements constitute additional learning, but nothing that shattered academic researchers' basic view of environmental taxation.

Phase III (Not Sure What We Are Learning): Some pollutants cannot be measured, however, and so cannot be taxed per unit of pollution as prescribed by Pigou. A prime example is automobile exhaust of local pollutants such as NO_X, SO_2, volatile organic compounds (VOC), and particulate matter. Government cannot require retrofit of monitoring devices on a hundred million existing vehicles; the technology is too expensive even for new cars, and Americans would view it as an invasion of privacy. Moreover, half of auto emissions are not from the tailpipe but simply evaporate off the engine. Thus, as it turns out, "Soviet-style" command and control regulation is unavoidable. Researchers turn to study optimal combinations of regulations on manufacturers to set emissions per mile plus a gasoline tax to reduce miles driven.

The double dividend is also thrown into doubt. As explained by Goulder (1995) and others, the pollution tax itself raises product prices, which can reduce the real net wage as much as the labor tax reduction raises the real net wage. Thus, a double dividend is possible but only if the revenue is used to cut an egregious tax.

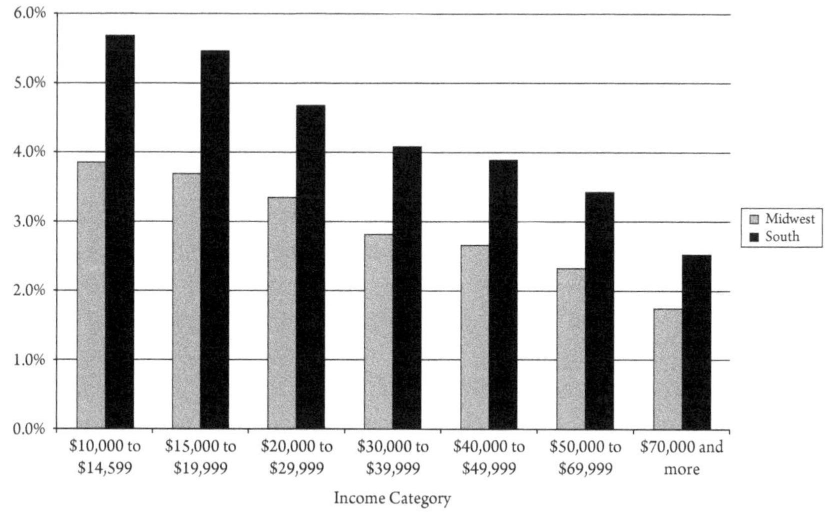

Figure 3C.2 Electricity as a percent of total consumption, by US region and income group. *Source:* US Bureau of Labor Statistics, Consumer Expenditure Survey, http://www.bls.gov/cex/2013/aggregate/quintile.pdf.

Also during this phase, limits are placed on the standard view of distributional effects. Yes, pollution taxes are regressive, when evaluated on the basis of tax paid divided by annual income (figure 3C.2). But other considerations change that story. First of all, the "burden" is not really "tax paid," but a money measure of the change in utility such as an equivalent variation. Second, this burden includes not just effects on the "uses side" of income from higher product prices but also effects on the "sources side" from changes in factor returns—including general equilibrium changes in returns to capital, natural resource rents, and even the high-skilled wage relative to the low-skilled wage. Required abatement technology may increase the demand for high-skilled labor relative to low-skilled labor, for example, further increasing wage disparity. And third, annual income is not the best measure to arrange households from low to high. Best is a measure of permanent income. If consumers engage in consumption smoothing, then annual consumption is better than annual income as a proxy for permanent income.

Phase IV (Unlearning): Effects on the sources side might even be progressive, if labor is better than capital as a substitute for the use of pollution in production. Firms might reduce use of pollution by hiring more labor, which could increase the equilibrium wage. Depending on the pollutant and abatement technology, however, firms may react to pollution policy by increasing demand for abatement capital, which could increase the required rate of return (Fullerton and Heutel 2007).

And even if some of the burden is on capital income, that does not imply the burden is on those with high income. Those with the lowest annual income include many retired individuals who have no labor income at all, while those with medium to high annual income include many other individuals at the top of their earnings trajectory (i.e., doctors, lawyers, bankers, and other professionals with high labor income). Only the very highest annual income group has a lot of capital income. Thus, the ratio of capital income to labor income is U-shaped across income groups, and any change to the rental-wage ratio is neither strictly progressive nor regressive.

Consider a life-cycle model with heterogeneous endowments but where everybody has a hump-shaped wage profile and desires a fairly flat consumption profile (Fullerton and Rogers 1993). Bequests are small, except for the very richest, so almost everybody borrows early in life (e.g., for education). They pay off that borrowing and save during the middle of each career, and then dis-save during retirement. If the wage profile of those with large lifetime endowment is simply a multiple of the profile for those with less lifetime income, then changes in the rental-wage ratio have no differential effects between rich and poor. Therefore, a key consideration is the timing of the peak: any lifetime income group with an earlier wage peak will have to save for longer periods during their life and is more affected by changes in capital income. That effect is not on the rich, in preliminary calculations by Fullerton and Rogers (1993).

Phase V (Steep Unlearning): The environmental tax is not regressive at all, to the extent that social security and other safety net transfers are indexed to the price level. If so, indexing means that low-income transfer recipients are protected against a carbon tax or other policy that raises the cost of electricity and gasoline (Fullerton et al. 2012).

Even more unsettling, the distributional effects of a pollution tax do not even depend much on the pollution tax itself, but on the use of the revenue. Williams et al. (2015), for example, show that use of the revenue to cut capital taxes can increase welfare for the top income group (negative burden of the pollution tax reform), while using the revenue to provide all households an equal per capita lump sum transfer implies gains for the bottom three quintiles.

With regard to prices versus quantities, it turns out that this policy choice probably does not matter at all. Weitzman (1974) focused on a simple but unrealistic permanent choice between one extreme or the other. In fact, either a price policy or a quantity policy can be enacted and subsequently modified: any tax rate that turns out to be too low can be raised. If a set quantity of permits generates a price viewed as too high or too low, then the parliament or legislature will likely change it.

And finally, the whole idea of an environmental tax may be no better or worse than a mandate or regulation (as long as it's not a "technology standard" that requires an expensive type of scrubber or abatement equipment). Consider a "performance standard" that requires a firm not to exceed a certain threshold for emissions per unit of output. Well, that policy requirement can be met by cutting emissions in the numerator, by raising output in the denominator, or by some combination of the two. Thus, it can be shown to be equivalent to the combination of a tax on emissions and a subsidy to output (e.g., Goulder et al. 2016).

In other words, that performance standard version of command and control regulation is equivalent to an emissions tax, with the revenue used to provide a subsidy to output. And everything we thought we knew is gone; now we know nothing; we need new research!

REFERENCES

Davenport, Coral. 2014. "Deal on Carbon Emissions by Obama and Xi Jinping Raises Hopes for Upcoming Paris Climate Talks." *New York Times*, November 12. http://www.nytimes.com/2014/11/13/world/asia/deal-on-carbon-emissions-by-obama-and-xi-jinping-raises-hopes-for-upcoming-paris-climate-talks.html

Fullerton, Don, and Garth Heutel. 2007. "The General Equilibrium Incidence of Environmental Taxes." *Journal of Public Economics* 91 (3–4) (April): 571–91.

Fullerton, Don, Garth Heutel, and Gilbert E. Metcalf. 2012. "Does the Indexing of Government Transfers Make Carbon Pricing Progressive?." *American Journal of Agricultural Economics* 94 (2) (January): 347–53.

Fullerton, Don, and Diane Lim Rogers. 1993. *Who Bears the Lifetime Tax Burden?*. Washington, DC: Brookings Institution.

Goulder, Lawrence H. 1995. "Environmental Taxation and the Double Dividend: A Reader's Guide." *International Tax and Public Finance* 2 (2) (August): 157–83.

Goulder, Lawrence H., Marc A. C. Hafstead, and Roberton C. Williams III. 2016. "General Equilibrium Impacts of a Federal Clean Energy Standard." *American Economic Journal: Economic Policy* 8 (2): 186–218.

IPCC. 2014. "Climate Change 2014: Synthesis Report." Contribution of Working Groups I, II, and III to the Fifth Assessment Report of the Intergovernmental Panel on Climate Change, Core Writing Team, R. K. Pachauri and L. A. Meyer, eds. Geneva, Switzerland: IPCC. https://www.ipcc.ch/report/ar5/syr/

Newell, Richard G., and Robert N. Stavins. 2003. "Cost Heterogeneity and the Potential Savings from Market-Based Policies." *Journal of Regulatory Economics* 23 (1): 43–59.

Pigou, Arthur C. 1920. *The Economics of Welfare*. London: MacMillan.

Revkin, Andrew C. 2015. "Wrangling Appears to Give Way to a Deal in Paris Climate Talks." *New York Times*, December 11. http://dotearth.blogs.nytimes.com/2015/12/11/in-paris-climate-talks-push-is-coming-to-shove-as-the-clock-ticks-down/

Weitzman, Martin L. 1974. "Prices vs. Quantities." *Review of Economic Studies* 41 (4) (October): 477–91.

Williams, Roberton C., III, Hal Gordon, Dallas Burtraw, Jared C. Carbone, and Richard D. Morgenstern. 2015. "The Initial Incidence of a Carbon Tax across Income Groups." *National Tax Journal* 68 (1) (March): 195–214.

4

TAX COMPLIANCE AND ENFORCEMENT
AN OVERVIEW OF NEW RESEARCH AND ITS POLICY IMPLICATIONS

Joel Slemrod

4.1 INTRODUCTION

Policy attention to tax evasion and enforcement picked up after the financial crisis of 2008, the Great Recession, and the large deficits that followed. Particular attention on high-income individuals and corporations has accompanied heightened attention to income and wealth inequality. In the United States, this momentum led to a major initiative aimed at reducing income tax evasion via unreported foreign accounts, albeit in the context of a shrinking Internal Revenue Service (IRS) budget.

Academic research in tax evasion and enforcement has exploded in the new millennium, perhaps inspired by the renewed policy interest and certainly facilitated by increased academic access to administrative tax-return data and increased willingness of tax authorities to partner with researchers on randomized field trials that hold the promise of compelling identification of the impact of alternative enforcement strategies.

In this chapter, I review and discuss the policy implications of a selection of recent economic research on tax compliance and enforcement, mostly but not only regarding income tax issues related to individuals and small businesses.

4.2 THE ECONOMICS OF TAX EVASION

Tax evasion is an important issue because it affects the distribution of the tax burden as well as the resource cost of raising taxes—bread-and-butter concerns of public economics. If the tax gap could somehow be costlessly eliminated and the true liability remitted, the additional money collected could be used to finance worthy government projects, or used to finance an across-the-board cut in tax rates that would benefit most compliant taxpayers. But expanding government programs could be financed in a number of other ways, such as by raising tax rates or by broadening the income tax base, and a tax reduction could be financed by cuts in overall spending. The real question is whether curbing evasion would improve the equity and efficiency implications of the public finances.

Why would an individual or business evade taxes? To an economist, the natural starting point is to consider the private costs and benefits of evasion. And indeed the standard framework for considering whether and how much to evade taxes is a deterrence model. This was first formulated by Allingham and Sandmo (1972), who adapted Becker's (1968) model of criminal behavior to the economics of tax evasion. In this model, a risk-averse taxpayer decides whether and how much to evade taxes in the same way she would approach any risky decision or gamble. People are influenced by possible legal penalties no differently than any other contingent cost: there is nothing per se about the illegality of tax evasion that matters. Nor is there any intrinsic willingness to meet one's tax obligations, sometimes referred to as "tax morale." The model predicts that an increase in either the probability of detection or the penalty if detected will reduce evasion, but does not pin down how big these effects are, so it becomes the task of empirical analysis. The effect of a change in the marginal tax rate is less clear, and depends on the form of the penalty function, as shown by Yitzhaki (1974).

Some social scientists have argued that the deterrence framework misses important elements of the tax evasion decision, and its central assumptions that nothing per se about the illegality of evasion matters, and everyone acts as a free rider, so that there is no issue of intrinsic willingness to pay, or "tax morale." Some have gone further to suggest that, in thinking about tax evasion, it is necessary to abandon the standard expected utility maximization model and incorporate "behavioral" considerations. The models that abandon one or both of these assumptions take different tacks. One approach stresses that some people may fully comply with their legal obligation because of a sense of civic duty regardless of, or in addition to, the possible expected pecuniary gains and argue that the tendency to perform one's duty is susceptible to aspects of the enforcement process. Another approach suggests that, rather than behaving as free riders, some individuals' behavior depends on the process by which the tax and tax enforcement system are formulated and its features, holding constant the incentives the system provides.

Research by the IRS on the tax gap suggests that noncompliance is nontrivial. According to their most recent estimates, based on 2006 returns, the overall gross tax gap is estimated as $450 billion.[1] The IRS expected to eventually collect $65 billion of the $450 billion gross tax gap estimate, which results in a "net tax gap" of $385 billion, so that 14.5% of the estimated tax liability will never be paid. The noncompliance rate varies widely by the source of information reporting to the IRS. When there is little to no third-party-reported information (such as self-employment income), the noncompliance rate is as high as 56%. It is 11% when there is "some" reporting, 8% when there is "substantial" information reporting, and as low as 1% when there is both withholding and substantial reporting (such as wages and salaries).[2]

1 Of note is the fact that the IRS's 2014–2017 strategic plan states a target voluntary compliance rate of 87% by 2017 (IRS 2014).

2 As a comparison, the HM Revenue & Customs (2015) recently calculated the overall tax gap in the United Kingdom as of 2013–2014 to be 6.4% of true liability: 5.0% for the individual income tax, 6.4% for the corporation tax, and 11.1% for the value-added tax. Small- and medium-sized enterprises account for over half of the overall tax gap.

4.3 METHODOLOGY—HOW HAVE WE LEARNED NEW THINGS?

For policy purposes, we are interested in the level and nature of noncompliance, in part to broadly guide where enforcement resources might go. Of more importance is the response of noncompliance to enforcement policy initiatives. To be sure, the empirical analysis of evasion is highly challenging due, fairly obviously, to tax evaders' concealment activities. The threat of punishment and perhaps social shame make taxpayers unwilling to respond accurately even to surveys. Almost all the empirical analyses of evasion, including the most credible ones, don't actually have a reliable measure of evasion, but instead rely on indirect measures of evasion. But scholars have risen to the challenge, and there are several promising developments in measuring tax evasion and, more important, measuring the determinants of tax evasion and how different policies might affect tax evasion. I discuss some of these developments next.

4.3.1 Randomized Field Experiments

Randomized field experiments have been heralded as being in the vanguard of the "credibility revolution" (Angrist and Pischke 2010) in empirical economics because they facilitate identification of the causal impact of, for example, a policy intervention. When implemented appropriately, the researcher need not worry about getting a control group because the control group is built into the randomization: there are two otherwise statistically identical groups, one that gets the policy treatment of interest and the other that doesn't. Although tax rates and bases are unlikely to be randomized in the field, for other tax-system instruments policy randomization is possible and, more important, has become a reality.

4.3.2 Wider Availability of Administrative Data

A very promising recent development is the wider availability for analysis of administrative tax-return data, sometimes linked to other administrative records, often on the whole population of a country. These kinds of data first became available in Nordic countries, but now they're available under varying protocols in Canada, in the United Kingdom, some other European countries, and the United States (here explicitly not generally linked to other administrative data). Compared to having small samples of tax-return data, when a researcher has *all* returns, she has much more (statistical) power to reach reliable conclusions about the effect of taxation and to investigate such issues as the heterogeneity among groups defined by geography or other demographic variables. The fact that tax-return data generally contain what the taxpayer reported, rather than the "truth," is a particular advantage when studying the elasticity of taxable income, which crucially includes evasion and avoidance responses to tax policy instruments, although it can be a hindrance for other purposes, such as measuring the distribution of income when evasion is not distributionally benign.

4.3.3 Kinks, Notches, and Regression Discontinuity Research Designs

The availability of administrative data has facilitated research designs that examine sharp breaks in tax policy parameters. In a regression discontinuity design, there is a cutoff or threshold above or below which a treatment is assigned. By comparing observations lying closely on either side of the threshold and therefore arguably quite similar, one can estimate the average effect of the treatment in that local area of the threshold, even in environments where randomization is not feasible. Note that it is crucial that the assignment of people to treatment is random, and that it is impossible for the people to manipulate their treatment status.

When policy introduces kinks in budget sets, so that the marginal tax rate changes discontinuously around the kink, identification of local behavioral response is credible because in many cases the people on either side of the kink are on average fairly similar. How many people "bunch" at the kink provides, under some assumptions, a measure of how elastic choices are on average with respect to the tax rate. Even more potentially powerful is the analysis of behavior in the presence of policy-induced notches, where the budget set itself is discontinuous, so, for example, reporting one additional dollar of income increases one's tax liability by a few hundred dollars. What makes the study of notches particularly promising is that their presence implies that there is some region of behavior that is always dominated by another region, regardless of one's preferences. The fact that in all cases so far examined there are some people residing in the dominated region sheds light on the constellation of reasons that might interfere with the kind of behavioral responses a standard price-theoretical model would apply: irrationality, cluelessness, adjustment costs, and so on.[3]

4.3.4 Traces of True Income and Evasion with Micro Data

In a traces-of-income approach, one identifies an indicator of the true tax base, say income, and compares that to reported income. The classic research design is due to Pissarides and Weber (1989), who use food consumption as an income indicator. They assume (reasonably) that how much food someone purchases is a function of income, but doesn't depend on what *kind* of income—salary versus self-employment—a person has. Next they look at what the ratio of food purchases to reported income is, separately for employees and self-employed people. Thus, they infer (relative) income from food, and compare this "trace" of true income to (relative) reported income. Under a traces-of-evasion approach, one looks for behavior that can reasonably only be explained by tax evasion, for example, the hoarding of high-value currency.

[3] See Kleven and Waseem (2013).

4.4 WHAT HAVE WE LEARNED?

4.4.1 The Extent and Nature of Evasion

The apparent wide divergence between the compliance rates of employees and the self-employed has attracted a lot of research attention on the latter group. Pissarides and Weber (1989) estimated that self-employed people in the United Kingdom on average underreported their income by about one-third.[4] Feldman and Slemrod (2007) follow a similar approach, but avoid the need to use survey data by instead using as the trace of income charitable donations reported on income tax returns. They find that, other things equal, reported positive self-employment income of $1 is associated with the same level of contributions as $1.54 of wage and salary income, which implies—assuming a negligible wage and salary noncompliance rate and that the self- employed are not inherently more charitable than others—a self-employment noncompliance rate of 35% (0.54/1.54), very similar to the Pissarides-Weber estimate but below the IRS figure of 56%. Note that the key assumption, that the conditional charity-income ratio does not vary by employment status, is stronger than the equivalent assumption about food; for example, Glazer and Konrad (1996) argue that some people give to charities to signal wealth (or integrity), a motive that is arguably more relevant for self-employed people.

Gorodnichenko et al. (2009) employed a similar approach to estimate the effect of Russia's 2001 flat tax reform on the extent of evasion and find that the consumption–income gap fell by about 10% more for a treatment group that had a relatively large decline in marginal tax rates. Assuming that the true relative consumption–income gap did not change over this period, one can interpret this finding as indicating a relative increase in reported income by those whose tax rate declined. Cabral et al. (2014) find a similar pattern of underreporting among the self-employed in the United Kingdom; assuming that salaried workers report truthfully, self-employed workers' true income is on average 28% higher than what they report.

Artavanis et al. (2012) employ a clever research design that takes advantage of household microdata from one of ten large banks in Greece to estimate the extent of underreported income for self-employed Greek workers by type of occupation. They rely on the fact that financial-sector formalization coexists with widespread underreporting of income and note that southern European banks have had to become skilled at inferring true income from reported income in order to remain competitive. Using this insight, and assuming that income is accurately reported for wage and salary earners, they estimate a credit supply equation for wage earners using reported income, hard information (such as credit history, borrower characteristics), and soft

[4] Tax evasion estimates for other countries using this method include Schuetze (2002) for Canada, Johansson (2005) for Finland, Engström and Holmlund (2009) and Engström and Hagen (2015) for Sweden, Martinez-Lopez (2013) for Spain, Paulus (2015) for Estonia, and Hurst et al. (2014) for the United States.

information (such as local economic growth) available to the bank. Supposing this credit supply equation to be valid for wage earners, they infer the "multipliers" that the bank implicitly applies to reported self-employment income. They estimate multipliers in excess of two for doctors, lawyers, engineers and scientists, and accountants and financial service agents, indicating that for these professions reported income is less than half of true income as inferred by the bank.

4.4.2 The Impact of Deterrence

4.4.2.1 Audits

As already mentioned, one of the stimulants to the wave of recent empirical research in tax compliance has been the willingness of some tax authorities to partner with researchers to design and implement randomized controlled trials to learn about aspects of tax enforcement. The most prominent example is threat-of-audit letters, which I discuss next.[5]

In the first application to tax compliance of an RCT design, Slemrod et al. (2001) analyzed the results of a randomized controlled experiment conducted by the State of Minnesota Department of Revenue (MDOR). Randomly selected taxpayers who filed a return for tax year 2013 were sent a letter from the MDOR in January 1995. A treatment group was informed that their 1994 federal and state income tax returns would be "closely examined" for any irregularities. The effect of this statement on the beliefs of the treatment group depends on their prior beliefs about the probability of an audit. If the individual expected that their returns were examined every year, then there would be no change in behavior. Others may have correctly perceived the letter as increasing the probability of an audit. The letter was timed so that individuals generally could only respond by changing their reporting behavior. The authors compared the change in income reported by this treatment group to that of a control group that did not receive any communication from the MDOR. The study found that low- and middle- income taxpayers who received a letter promising a certain audit reported slightly more, but statistically significantly more, income than those who did not receive such a letter, and the difference was larger for those with greater opportunities to evade in the form of income not subject to information reporting. Strikingly, though, high-income taxpayers receiving an audit threat on average reported *lower* income. The authors speculate that sophisticated, high-income taxpayers (and their accountants) understand an audit to be a negotiation, and view reported taxable income as the opening (low) bid in a negotiation that does not necessarily result in the determination and penalization of all noncompliance; this implies that the initial lower tax liability report might not indicate that the eventual tax remittance was lower, as well. This result provides a caveat that the dynamics of tax evasion for very high-income individuals may be different than for others.

[5] Hallsworth (2014) reviews several recent RCTs addressed to tax compliance.

Kleven et al. (2011) conduct a similar audit experiment in Denmark. In the first year of their study, one-half of their sample was randomly chosen to be thoroughly audited (100% audit group) while the rest were not audited or contacted in any way (0% audit group). The following year, randomly chosen individuals from both groups received letters announcing either a 100% probability of audit or a 50% probability of audit. A control group received no letter. The initial unannounced audit found overall evasion equal to 2.2% of net income, but a much higher rate of 14% for self-employment income. The threat-of-audit experiment was conducted only on a sample of employees (i.e., it excluded any self-employed individuals) for administrative reasons. The individuals received the letter shortly after they received their pre-populated returns and had one month to make adjustments to the return. The baseline probability of an adjustment to net income is 13.3%. Among the 0% audit group, those who received a letter were 1.5 percentage points more likely to make an upward adjustment to net income than those who didn't receive a letter. The effect of the threat was similar in the 100% audit group, raising the probability of adjustment of net income by 1.6 percentage points. The experiment also tests the effect of different probabilities of audit. Individuals who were threatened with a 50% probability of audit were about 1.1 percentage points more likely to adjust net income upwards than those who received no letter. Those who received the 100% probability of audit were 0.9 percentage points more likely than the 50% threat of audit to adjust net income upwards. Thus, although a positive audit probability influenced reporting behavior, going from a 50% to 100% probability had little apparent effect.

Many of the tax compliance RCT treatments involve letters about, for example, audit threats sent by the tax authority. Ortega and Scartascini (2015a) investigate the impact of the delivery mechanism. They conduct a field experiment in Colombia that varies the way the National Tax Agency contacts taxpayers with due payments for income, value-added, and wealth taxes (tax delinquencies). Taxpayers were randomly assigned to a control, or to one of three possible delivery mechanisms: letter, email, and personalized visit by a tax inspector. They find sizable differences across delivery methods. Personal visits by a tax inspector are more effective than the impersonal methods; they are, alas, also much more expensive. Ortega and Scartascini (2015b) find that the effect of phone calls falls between those of the impersonal methods and the personal visits.

To combat sales and profit tax evasion by small firms and the self-employed, many developing countries have adopted some form of "reverse withholding," where large firms remit to the tax authority a fixed share of their purchases from small firms and these sellers can apply the withheld amount as a credit against their self-reported income tax liability. While withholding does not affect the firms' true tax liability, there is typically a discontinuity in the audit probability at the withholding rate; firms seeking tax refunds (because self-reported tax liability is lower than the withheld amount) are audited at a higher rate than firms making additional tax remittances. Examining data from Ecuador, Carrillo et al. (2011) find evidence of bunching in reported tax liability just above the 1% withholding threshold, suggesting firms manipulate their self-reported tax liability and possibly real economic choices to minimize tax payments subject to the discontinuity in the audit probability. Third-party data on sales and intermediate input costs filed by large firms as withholding agents indicate bunching is indeed associated with tax evasion: self-reported sales are smaller than third-party reports for at least 10% of firms.

4.4.2.2 Specific Deterrence: The Impact of Audits

To this point I have been discussing the impact on compliance of a change in the perceived probability of detection of noncompliance, usually referred to as general deterrence. Another issue of interest is the effect of audits on the audited, referred to as specific deterrence.[6] A priori taxpayers' behavior following an audit is ambiguous. On the one hand, a taxpayer may assume that the probability of getting audited a second time might be low, sometimes referred to as the "crater effect," which would mean that taxpayers are less likely to comply in the years following an audit. On the other hand, taxpayers may revise upward their prior income tax returns assessment of the probability of an audit; these taxpayers would be more likely to comply in the years following an audit. Moreover, if taxpayers consider the possibility that past returns will be audited upon detection of current-year noncompliance, they will find future noncompliance more attractive because the expected cost of audits of past returns is now much lower.[7]

Two recent studies have examined this issue. DeBacker et al. (2015), using IRS data from the random-audit National Research Program (NRP), found that an audit increases reported wage income of the audited individual over three years after the audit by 0.4% and increases reported Schedule C (self-employment) income by 7.5%. However, this large immediate effect on Schedule C income is short-lived; indeed, five or six years following the audit, the treated group actually reports lower Schedule C income as compared to the control group. The external validity of these results is somewhat problematic. Because taxpayers audited under the NRP are informed that they have been randomly selected for research purposes, these audits may not have the same impact on the perceived probability of a future audit as an operational audit. Moreover, these taxpayers are not representative of those who are typically subject to audit, and their behavior may not be representative of those who are normally targeted for operational audits.

Advani et al. (2015) pursue a similar research strategy using data from the United Kingdom. As DeBacker et al., they find that those who are audited increase their reported tax liability more than the control group in years following the audit. Allowing for the lag between when the return is selected for audit and when the audit is completed, four years after the audit there is a 26% increase in reported liabilities in the treatment group compared to the control group.

[6] It might be useful to define an intermediate concept of deterrence, which includes the impact on those taxpayers who learn of specific enforcement actions directed to others, and possibly thereby modify their behavior. The links may be by word-of-mouth via taxpayers through various networks, including tax preparers. Let me tentatively propose "network deterrence."

[7] Engel and Hines (1999) draw out the implications of this dynamic aspect of decision-making.

4.4.3 Third-Party Information Reporting

The previous section focused on attempts to understand the effect of increasing the perceived probability of detection via a direct communication from the tax authority to the taxpayer. Another set of studies makes explicit why the probability has gone up. Next I review research where the reason is increased information reporting.

Carrillo et al. (2014) examine the effect of a change of the tax authority's use of third-party information on reported firm revenues for the corporate tax in Ecuador. The government has a few sources to verify firms' self-reports of revenue, including other firms' reports of purchases from the firm in question, credit-card sales from credit-card companies, as well as exports and imports information from the Ecuadorian customs authority. For a few years, the revenue service had collected such third-party reports of firm revenues, but had not utilized this information to verify firms' self-reported revenue. In the episode they study, the Ecuadorian tax authority (SRI) informed some firms of the discrepancy between the two reports and offered them the opportunity to file an amended return. The authors compare the reporting behavior of firms before and after notification. They find that 24% of firms underreport revenue in years when the government did not use the third-party-verified information. They also find no bunching of reporting revenue around the third-party reported amount, suggesting that firms did not believe the government was using this information. In the three rounds of the experiment, between 11% and 19% of notified firms filed an amended return. In amended returns, firms correctly report their revenues, but they increased their reported costs almost one-for-one with the increase in revenues (96 cents for each dollar!). The offset of reported expenses is similar to a finding regarding the US 1099-K requiring credit-card companies to report business receipts, discussed next.

In an effort to reduce understatement of revenues, in 2011 the IRS began to require credit-card companies and other third-party payment organizations to report electronic payments received by businesses. Analyzing administrative data on the universe of individual income tax returns that report sole proprietor income, Slemrod et al. (2015) find a large increase in the number of businesses reporting income that is exactly equal to the amount in the 1099-K report, consistent with a simple model of reporting behavior. Although the new reporting requirement increased reported receipts of this relatively small group by up to 24%, this was offset by a 13% increase in reported expenses. They also find that at least 20% of the group in 2011 were induced to file Schedule C by the introduction of Form 1099-K. Thus, information reporting seems to have had the intended effect of increasing compliance on the income that is subject to third-party reports, but the overall effect on evasion was dampened by increased reported expenses, which are not directly observable to the tax authority[8] and may also

[8] Note, though, that in an audit the burden of proof for expenses rests on the taxpayer, while it rests on the IRS for receipts.

have been offset by firms moving to cash receipts that are not covered by this information-reporting regime.

4.4.4 Take-up

Although IRS enforcement efforts (and this chapter) focus mainly on tax evasion, what limits take-up of credits and other tax benefits is also of both policy and intellectual interest. Bhargava and Manoli (2015) address the determinants of incomplete take-up with the Earned Income Tax Credit (EITC) in the United States with a comprehensive randomized field experiment involving 35,050 eligible individuals. They investigate, using alternative mailings, the role of program information (regarding benefits, costs, and rules), informational complexity, and stigma. They find that the take-up rate increases due to the mere receipt of a plain-vanilla mailing, suggesting—consistent with other studies discussed here—that routine contact from the tax authority can have a significant effect on taxpayer behavior, at least in the short run. In addition, both simplification and the visual display of benefits increase take-up. All in all, Bhargava and Manoli suggest that the tested interventions could reduce incomplete EITC take-up by about 25%. Notably, though, a follow-up study by Manoli and Turner (2014) found little to no long-term increases in EITC take-up. Guyton et al. (2015) extend this work to non-filers using an RCT to induce filing among non-filers who are eligible to receive credits, even if they owe tax on net. They find similar results: there is a concurrent effect, but one that does not persist in future years when the mailed reminders stop.

4.4.5 Non-Deterrence Policies to Reduce Noncompliance

Many of the threat-of-audit letter RCTs discussed so far also contained a non-deterrence treatment. Blumenthal et al. (2001) find no evidence that either of two written appeals to taxpayers' consciences had a significant effect on compliance. One letter stressed the beneficial effects of tax-funded projects, while the other conveyed the message that most taxpayers were compliant. Torgler (2004), using a controlled field experiment in Switzerland, also found that moral suasion has hardly any effect on taxpayers' compliance behavior, nor did Fellner et al. (2013). Pomeranz (2015) found that a mailing appealing to tax morale, but promising no increased enforcement, had little effect on VAT remittances. In Castro and Scartascini (2015), messages that emphasized fairness (taxes are used to pay for public services, which the individuals benefits from) or equity (most citizens fulfill their tax obligations) do not have a significant effect. Bhargava and Manoli (2015) also find that the social stigma does not affect take-up of the EITC. In sum, it has been difficult to find evidence that appeals to tax morale, defined broadly, affect taxpayer behavior in the short run when delivered via a one-time mailing. As discussed below, part of the reason could be the wording of these appeal-to-conscience letters; psychological research suggests that using terms with wording such as "cheater," as in "Please don't be a cheater," might affect behavior more than the standard letter-based appeal to conscience wording such as "the entire community suffers." Whether any government would be willing to employ such loaded terms remains to be seen.

Recently a few studies have broken the solid set of field-experimental evidence finding no effect of such appeals. Bott et al. (2014) report the results from a randomized field experiment in Norway conducted with 18,000 taxpayers who the tax authority deemed were likely to have misreported their foreign income and find that including a moral appeal in a letter almost doubled the average foreign income reported compared to a base letter without such an appeal; the moral appeal mainly worked on the intensive margin, by increasing the amount reported of those who report any foreign income. Hallsworth et al. (2014) ran two large natural field experiments using administrative data from more than 200,000 individuals in the United Kingdom and concluded that including social norms and public goods messages in standard tax payment reminder letters can considerably enhance tax compliance; wording that emphasized that the individual was in the minority of non-payers was the most effective in getting individuals to remit their taxes. They also find that mentioning financial penalties and remittance plans significantly increased the likelihood of compliance. Note, though, that Hallsworth et al.'s outcome is the timing of payment of *already reported* liabilities, while most letter-based interventions look at the effect on truthful reporting behavior. It might be that a taxpayer who is simply procrastinating on paying their taxes is more likely to be persuaded by social norms than one who is evading taxes. Second, Hallsworth et al. (like Perez-Truglia and Troiano 2015) specifically study taxpayers who missed payment deadlines. Finally, there are important differences in how the treatment could have been perceived by the recipients. In Hallsworth et al., the letter informs the taxpayer that the UK tax authority (HMRS) is aware of their delinquency. It says, "Nine out of ten people in the U.K. remit their tax on time. You are currently in the very small minority of people who have not paid us yet." In contrast, for example, the letter in the Blumenthal et al. (2001) Minnesota experiment says, "people who file tax returns report correctly and pay voluntarily 93% of income taxes they owe . . . a small number of tax payers who deliberately cheat owe the bulk of unpaid taxes." In this case, the letter does not convey to the taxpayer that the IRS is aware of any wrongdoing by the individual. Thus the difference in results could be due to the difference between informing an individual that the government has evidence of their actual evasion and appealing to their sense of duty without conveying any information on their avoidance behavior.

This set of results has somewhat moved my pre-2013 belief that the evidence overwhelmingly supported that deterrence inhibits noncompliance but that manipulation of norms has no measurable effect. In some settings norm-directed letter interventions seem to matter. It now behooves us to understand better why this can work in some settings, but not others.

One recent paper investigates the impact of shaming on tax compliance. Twenty-three US states currently try to encourage tax delinquents to remit their tax by publishing their names and amount owed online. Perez-Truglia and Troiano (2015) compare the effect of shaming to the effect of financial penalties through an experiment where letters sent to delinquents are worded to emphasize one or the other. They contact all delinquents with names and addresses published online in three states: Kentucky, Kansas, and Wisconsin. In theory, individuals will be more likely to pay off their debt if their perceived shaming adversely impacts their social capital, but shaming might shift their motivation to pay from an intrinsic to an extrinsic one and therefore decrease the likelihood that they remit. The authors find that both shaming and financial penalties increase the likelihood of payment within ten weeks of receiving the letter. The effect of shaming varies by the size of their initial debt, and matters most for those with small amounts of debt (between \$250 and \$2,273), increasing the likelihood of payment by 2.1 percentage points. The effect declines for higher amounts of debt suggesting that there is a limit to the value of preventing social stigma. Because tax authorities warn individuals and give them an opportunity to clear their debts before publishing their names online, one may consider this effect as a lower bound.

4.4.6 Public Disclosure

Public disclosure of tax information is designed to reduce the attractiveness of tax noncompliance as well as aggressive, but arguably legal, tax avoidance. Disclosure may complement deterrence by encouraging people with relevant information about others' true tax liability to come forward, and the fear of that and subsequent tax noncompliance penalties (explicit and shaming) dampens such behavior. Disclosure may also affect tax reporting because taxpayers reduce reported taxable income in order to minimize the attention of the press and of unsavory characters wishing to take advantage of their economic situation. On the other hand, some people might get satisfaction (bragging rights, if you will) from public appreciation of their level of affluence and may be willing to pay for it in the form of a higher tax liability. The empirical evidence on public disclosure in the income tax context is sparse, but growing. Hasegawa et al. (2013) study the effect of the Japanese income tax disclosure system that was abolished in 2004/2005 on tax reports of individuals and businesses. They take advantage of the abolition and the fact that disclosure applied only to taxable incomes above 40,000,000 yen (about \$400,000). They find strong evidence based on bunching of observations right below the disclosure threshold that, on average, individuals and businesses prefer to avoid disclosure; for the latter, this is consistent with the local characterization of so-called "39 companies," whose reported taxable income is kept below the disclosure threshold so as not to provide evidence about their profitability, which might affect the deals they can make with other companies. However, the authors uncover no evidence that disclosure increased reported business taxable income generally.

Bø et al. (2015) explore the effect of public disclosure in Norway, which has a long history of disclosing tax filings, and beginning in 2001 anyone with access to the Internet could obtain individual information on other Norwegians' taxable income and income tax liability. They exploit this change in the degree of exposure to identify the effects of public disclosure on income reporting. Identification of the deterrence effects of public disclosure is facilitated by the fact that, prior to the shift to the

Internet in 2001, in some municipalities something close to the Internet type of public disclosure existed because tax information was distributed widely through paper catalogues that were locally produced and disseminated. Bø et al. observe income changes that are consistent with public disclosure deterring tax evasion: an approximately 3% higher average increase in reported income is found among business owners living in areas where the switch to Internet disclosure represented a relatively large change in access.

4.5 WHAT SHOULD BE DONE?

In what follows I summarize what I conclude about policy from the recent academic literature and observations about policies in place in other countries, plus the unquantifiable value judgments that all policy pronouncements unavoidably involve and the unquantifiable non-pecuniary values, such as privacy and intrusiveness that come into play under some enforcement strategies.

4.5.1 Increase the IRS Budget

I can't prove it's optimal, but I believe the IRS budget should be increased. If the budget was anywhere close to optimal in 2010, it must be too small now. Since then the budget has declined by more than 10%, while the responsibilities of the IRS have expanded, due to the Affordable Care Act, the FATCA, and other new initiatives. To cope with the budget cuts, the IRS has had to reduce their workforce by 12.3% in the last year. This smaller workforce is also less prepared because the training budget is 83% lower than what it was in 2010.[9]

4.5.2 Focus on Deterrence

The recent evidence has strengthened my belief that deterrence remains the most crucial policy instrument in addressing noncompliance, and thus attention must focus on one of its two crucial parameters: the probability that evasion will be detected and punished.[10] By saying this I do not intend to dismiss the importance of the non-deterrence aspects of tax administration. IRS agents should treat taxpayers with respect and civility. The IRS should provide taxpayers with education through its website, phone services, and outreach, and should provide taxpayers with information about what purposes tax revenues are used. I doubt, though, that a tax authority can do much at the margin to enhance such potentially important factors such as the legitimacy of

[9] OECD (2015: 173). Not that this makes it right or wrong, but tax agencies in many countries have also been facing cuts. For example, staffing at the UK tax authority, the HMRC, fell from 91,167 in 2005 to 61,370 in 2014.

[10] The severity of punishment is the other crucial parameter, but little empirical research has been devoted to this topic. Blank (2014) and Paramonova (2015a, b) discuss "collateral tax sanctions" such as revoking from tax evaders drivers' licenses, professional licenses, and passports.

government. The recent literature, with recent exceptions noted earlier, does not find compelling evidence that sending letters emphasizing the duty to be tax-compliant or stressing the civic duty aspects affects tax compliance. What provides the biggest deterrence bang per buck?

4.5.3 Expanded Information Reporting

The United States is probably not ready to, for example, reintroduce[11] public disclosure of income tax information, although the evidence suggests that in other countries, this has at least modest pro-compliance effects. The 1099-K initiative regarding credit-card receipts apparently increased compliance of a small segment of sole proprietors, but its effectiveness was reduced by its lack of coverage of expenses or of cash receipts. The Foreign Account Tax Compliance Act (FATCA) initiative takes information reporting to another level, by requiring/inducing foreign financial institutions to report to the IRS, directly or through their home government, about the foreign accounts of US citizens.

4.5.4 Better Discriminant Function Scores

One of the methods the IRS uses to select returns for examination is computer scoring. The Discriminant Function System (DIF) provides numeric scores for each return that rates the potential for change in tax liability upon audit, based on past IRS experience with similar returns. The Unreported Income DIF (UIDIF) score rates the return for the potential of unreported income. This score is a principal criterion, supplemented by many "compliance filters," used by IRS personnel to select returns for audit and identifying the items on these returns that are most likely to need review. The IRS puts considerable effort into getting the right formula.

Because the DIF and UIDIF are tightly guarded secrets (but see just below), I have no standing to say that the IRS could do better. But I do have a suggestion. The suggestion is that the IRS make available to academics and private firms (on a controlled basis, of course) a large sample of anonymized returns as filed and as "corrected" by auditors, indicate a menu of possible objective functions (e.g., maximize dollars of noncompliance discovered, number of noncompliant returns discovered, number of noncompliant returns with the amount above a certain threshold discovered), and let them submit a new discriminant formula (NDIF). The IRS would then evaluate these NDIFs on a separate large sample of tax returns as filed and as amended by audit. The reward for discovering a better NDIF is to be specified. I suggest that this would, at relatively small cost, lead us to a better DIF.[12] There is substantial precedent for such a venture, the most famous being the Netflix Prize, a $1 million prize offered (and

[11] The United States had public disclosure of income tax returns in its Civil War income tax, and again in 1923 and 1924.

[12] A team of computer scientists claims that artificial intelligence techniques can ascertain whether a corporation has used a particular sophisticated tax shelter. See Browning (2015).

awarded in 2009) by Netflix to the algorithm that provided the most accurate predictions about how much someone is going to enjoy a movie based on their movie preferences. The idea of an open competition for predictive modelling is now institutionalized in the form of kaggle.com, which provides a platform for several such competitions, recently including predicting who survived the Titanic sinking.[13]

4.5.5 Getting the Money

Although public finance textbooks pooh-pooh its importance, the remittance system can be of first-order importance in efficiently enforcing and administering a tax system. Getting the money from what Logue and Slemrod (2009) call the "low-cost remitters" matters. This lesson has been recognized most clearly in the system of employer withholding most countries use for income and payroll taxes: it is cheaper to deal with collecting the tax liability from a small number of organizations with relatively efficient bookkeeping done for non-tax reasons. As mentioned earlier, we now have evidence from diesel taxes that shifting the remittance responsibility can affect the volume of tax evasion.[14] A primary tax difference between classifying, say, Uber drivers as employees or as independent contractors is that only in the former case would Uber be responsible for withholding (i.e., remitting) an approximation of the income tax liability the driving produces. Recently, Airbnb, Inc. has entered into agreements with certain cities that it would remit the hotel tax liability, rather than the property hosts themselves.[15] The policy message is that, for tax compliance reasons, the borders between efficient and inefficient remittance responsibility need to be defended.

Another aspect of getting the money is collection of undisputed taxpayer debts to the tax authority. After all, the deterrence model focuses on the perceived probability that an evading taxpayer will be penalized, which includes ultimately having to pay up. The field experiments recently done suggest that frequent contact, shaming, and face-to-face contact can accelerate payments. The IRS is to be commended for its participation in field experiments to help determine optimal collection strategy. This is an area where more creative efforts might be rewarded; for example, several states publish the names of the biggest debtors and believe it helps with payments.

4.5.6 Informal Economy

A nontrivial fraction of tax evasion in the United States is tied to the informal economy, although that fraction is probably lower than in most other countries. Because other countries have a bigger informal economy problem than the United States (and have different standards about permissible government intrusion), some enforcement strategies have been tried elsewhere already. As of 2012, it is illegal in Norway to purchase

[13] See also the survey on forensic economics by Zitzewitz (2012).

[14] Kopczuk et al. (forthcoming).

[15] Wilking (2015) examines the impact of these agreements on the prices of Airbnb properties.

cleaning services from companies not approved by the labor inspectorate. In many European countries certified cash registers have been used. Since 2010 in Sweden, businesses selling for cash (including debit cards) must have a certified cash register that includes a special black box that only can be accessed by the tax authority; this is in part to counter the use of zappers, software installed on electronic cash registers or other electronic point of sales that allows users to erase recorded transactions.[16] Since 2008 for home renovation and domestic services, consumers can apply for a scheme where they pay the supplier for materials but only half of the labor portion of the fee. The company performing the work then applies to the tax authority for the other half, thus revealing to the tax authority their existence and some of their taxable income and VAT base. Introducing similar policies on a pilot basis would reveal whether they can be effective in limiting noncompliance.

4.5.7 Discouraging Cash and Encouraging Engagement with the Financial Sector

Some types of tax evasion are facilitated by transacting in cash. In response, many governments have introduced a ceiling for cash transactions. Others have required POS terminals in, for example, taxis. Alternatively, one could consider providing incentives to use cards; Argentina offers a 5% VAT discount on debit-card transactions and a 3% discount on credit-card purchases, while South Korea offers a lump-sum refund if card usage exceeds 20% of individual gross income for credit cards and 25% for debit cards.[17] Either a tax on cash or a subsidy to the use of electronic payment could be justified as a Pigouvian policy to address the marginal social cost of difficult-to-monitor-for-tax-purposes transactions. Note that the United States has recently gone in the opposite direction, due to the District Court ruling that allowed stores to charge purchasers a surcharge of up to 4% for using a credit card.[18]

It is, however, wrong to think that electronization of payments always facilitates tax enforcement. A case in point is electronic cash and cryptocurrencies, such as Bitcoin. According to its press clippings, cryptocurrency is about privacy and resistance to oversight, but it also becomes difficult to enforce certain taxation and financial regulations when online transactions cannot be tracked.[19] The 1099-K initiative discussed

[16] These policies are discussed in greater detail in Williams (2014: 101–3). Zappers and appropriate policy responses are discussed by Ainsworth (e.g., 2010).

[17] See Williams (2014: 104).

[18] Note that most credit cards now offer purchasers rewards related to usage. These rewards programs offset to some degree any surcharge for credit-card use, and it is notable that the reward percentage is often higher for purchases at gas stations, where cash discounts abound. In-kind rewards for cash payments extend to Ann Arbor, MI, where my favorite take-out Chinese restaurant offers a free eggroll with a cash payment and, most recently, exempts the cash-paying customer from a 49-cent "convenience charge."

[19] See Marian (2013).

earlier also has this disadvantage, cracking down on underreporting of credit-card sales while leaving cash sales untouched.

4.5.8 Process

The IRS is now fully on board with electronic filing, as a way to process returns at lower cost. About 65% of all returns processed by the IRS in 2014 were filed electronically. It could do more. Two options stand out. The first is the system known alternatively as pre-filled or pre-populated returns, already used to some extent in at least twenty-six countries, and piloted in California. It provides, at no cost to taxpayers upon filing, the information the government already has access to through information returns. It has been attacked as an unwarranted intrusion into the private tax preparation software business; on these arguments, see Holtzblatt (2007) and Bankman (2008). Indirectly it would help compliance if it freed up IRS resources to devote to enforcement, and if it provided taxpayers with a warm glow that ignited their intrinsic motivation to comply (don't hold your breath on that). As discussed earlier, the direct effect of pre-population on compliance is unclear, but saving in collection costs is almost certain.

Another option, discussed by Bankman (2008) and Ventry (2011), would involve a centralized database maintained by the federal government containing most of the information required to file a tax return such as wages information, common deductions, and taxes paid. Taxpayers, professional preparers, and authorities could all access this shared source of information to file taxes. Some filers would still need to input information like charitable deductions. For most taxpayers, however, the "data retrieval system" would considerably simplify the process because they would no longer have to gather the information required from disparate sources.

The IRS could also take advantage of improved information technology by offering a "smart" tax return. Bankman et al. (forthcoming) discuss three ways that a smart return could improve compliance. The first involves changing the wording on existing returns to increase the psychological cost of evasion and increase the perceived expectation of detection by, for example, placing the attestation of honesty to the top of the form. The second builds appeals to morality in the return itself through the use of a short phrase containing a "self-relevant" noun, such as "cheater," as in "please don't be a cheater." Research suggests that this approach might affect behavior more than the standard letter-based appeal to conscience wording such as "the entire community suffers" from evasion or referring to the "compliant majority." The third uses online "conversational agents" to ask adaptive questions that incorporate information known about the taxpayer, including information from answers to previous questions. This would allow the IRS to ask more focused questions, which should reduce evasion and audit costs and it could also benefit taxpayers by reducing filing time and eliminating the risk of subsequent audit. Adaptive questioning that is part of a data-driven system allows for continuous experimentation and real-time modification of algorithms to incorporate the results of that experimentation.

4.6 AN EXCERPT FROM THE STATE OF THE UNION[20] ADDRESS OF 2017

"My tax system proposals do not end with bringing the income tax rate structure in line with our values and eliminating unfair and inefficient loopholes. The fairness of the tax system and its impact on economic growth also depend on how well the laws are enforced. Whatever the top tax rate is, it does not contribute to progressivity if high-income people park their money in foreign financial accounts and don't report the income, and it does not help the economy if investment is diverted from Main Street USA."

"Law-abiding Americans should not have to pay the bills left unopened and unpaid by those who do not play by the rules. That goes for most owners of small businesses, whose contribution to the U.S. economy is so important. The thousands of honest housepainters should not have to struggle to compete with others who shirk their tax obligations and can thereby underprice the honest service providers. Complying with the tax laws is an obligation of all citizens."

"The government has an obligation, as well, to make the tax system as simple and efficient as possible while fairly enforcing the laws. Here are some concrete steps we will take. First, the IRS will be allocated a budget that allows it to do its job well, and continue to do it while respecting taxpayers and providing them with the information they need to comply. Modern data analysis techniques will be employed to identify honest taxpayers and leave them be, while bringing to justice those who are not honest. American taxpayers will also benefit by a modernization of the tax-filing process that will save time and money, and will have the opportunity to go to a highly secure, password-protected website that contains the information the government already has; for most, tax filing will require just a click of a button to prepare as well as file their return."

(Standing ovation from both sides of the aisle.)

ACKNOWLEDGMENTS

Prepared for the conference "The Economics of Tax Policy," held in Washington, DC, on December 3–4, 2015, jointly sponsored by the Robert D. Burch Center at the University of California, Berkeley, the Penn Wharton Public Policy Initiative, and the Urban-Brookings Tax Policy Center. I am grateful to Tejaswi Velayudhan for excellent research assistance. Helpful comments on an earlier draft were received from Claudio Agostini, Alan Auerbach, Wei Cui, Brian Erard, Christian Gillitzer, John Guyton, Anders Jensen, Ben Meiselman, Daniel Reck, Carlos Scartiscini, Christian Traxler, Eleanor Wilking, and David Weisbach. The author has an unpaid contractual relationship with the IRS to make research use of anonymized tax-return data. The views expressed here are not necessarily held by the IRS or the U.S. Department of

[20] In recent decades, newly inaugurated presidents have chosen to deliver speeches to joint sessions of Congress but have not officially considered them State of the Union addresses.

the Treasury. A much longer, more comprehensive version of this paper entitled "Tax Compliance and Enforcement: New Research and Its Policy Implications, is available at http://ssrn.com/abstract=2726077.

REFERENCES

Advani, Arun, William Elming, and Jonathan Shaw. 2015. "How Long-lasting Are the Effects of Audits?" Discussion Paper No. 011-15, Tax Administration Research Centre, University of Exeter.

Ainsworth, Richard. 2010. "Zappers—Retail VAT Fraud." Boston University School of Law Working Paper No. 10-04.

Allingham, Michael, and Agnar Sandmo. 1972. "Income Tax Evasion: A Theoretical Analysis." *Journal of Public Economics* 1 (3–4): 323–38.

Angrist, Joshua, and Jorn-Steffen Pischke. 2010. "The Credibility Revolution in Empirical Economics: How Better Research Design is Taking the Con out of Econometrics." *Journal of Economic Perspectives* 24 (2): 3–30.

Artavanis, Nikolaos, Adair Morse, and Margarita Tsoutsoura. 2012. "Tax Evasion across Industries: Soft Evidence from Greece." Chicago Booth Research Paper No. 12-25, Fama-Miller Center for Finance Working Paper.

Bankman, Joseph. 2008. "Using Technology to Simplify Individual Tax Filing." *National Tax Journal* 61 (4/2): 773–89.

Bankman, Joseph, Clifford Nass, and Joel Slemrod. Forthcoming. "Using the Smart Return to Reduce Tax Evasion." *Tax Law Review*.

Becker, Gary S. 1968. "Crime and Punishment: An Economic Approach." *Journal of Political Economy* 76 (2): 169–217.

Bhargava, Saurabh, and Dayanand Manoli. 2015. "Psychological Frictions and Incomplete Take-up of Social Benefits: Evidence from an IRS Field Experiment." *American Economic Review* 105 (11): 3489–529.

Blank, Joshua D. 2014. "Collateral Compliance." *University of Pennsylvania Law Review* 162:719–800.

Blumenthal, Marsha, Charles Christian, and Joel Slemrod. 2001. "Do Normative Appeals Affect Tax Compliance? Evidence from a Controlled Experiment in Minnesota." *National Tax Journal* 54 (1): 125–38.

Bø, Erlend, Joel Slemrod, and Thor Olav Thoresen. 2015. "Taxes on the Internet: Deterrence Effects of Public Disclosure." *American Economic Journal: Economic Policy* 7 (1): 36–62.

Bott, Kristina, Alexander W. Cappelen, Erik Ø. Sørensen, and Bertil Tungodden. 2014. "You've Got Mail: A Randomized Field Experiment on Tax Evasion." NHH Norwegian School of Economics Working Paper 26/2014.

Browning, Lynne. 2015. "Computer Scientists Wield Artificial Intelligence to Battle Tax Evasion." *New York Times*, October 9.

Cabral, Ana Cinta G., Christos Kotsogiannis, and Gareth Myles. 2014. "Self-Employment Underreporting in Great Britain: Who and How Much?" Tax Administration Research Centre, University of Exeter Discussion Paper No. 010-14.

Carrillo, Paul, Dina Pomeranz, and Monica Singhal. 2014. "Dodging the Taxman: Firm Misreporting and Limits to Tax Enforcement." National Bureau of Economic Research Working Paper No. 20624.

Carrillo, Paul, M. Shahe Emran, and Anita Rivadeneira. 2011. “Do Cheaters Bunch Together? Profit Taxes, Withholding Rates and Tax Evasion.” Working Paper, George Washington University.

Castro, Lucio, and Carlos Scartascini. 2015. “Tax Compliance and Enforcement in the Pampas: Evidence from a Field Experiment.” *Journal of Economic Behavior & Organization* 116:65–82.

DeBacker, Jason, Bradley T. Heim, Anh Tran, and Alexander Yuskavage. 2015. “Once Bitten, Twice Shy? The Lasting Impact of IRS Audits on Individual Tax Reporting.” Working Paper, Indiana University.

Engel, Eduardo M. R. A., and James R. HinesJr. 1999. “Understanding Tax Evasion Dynamics.” National Bureau of Economic Research Working Paper No. w6903.

Engström, Per, and Johannes Hagen. 2015. “Income Underreporting among the Self-Employed: A Permanent Income Approach.” Uppsala University, Department of Economics Working Paper No. 2015: 2.

Engström, Per, and Bertil Holmlund. 2009. “Tax Evasion and Self-Employment in a High-Tax Country: Evidence from Sweden.” *Applied Economics* 41 (19): 2419–30.

Feldman, Naomi, and Joel Slemrod. 2007. “Estimating Tax Noncompliance with Evidence from Unaudited Tax Returns.” *Economic Journal* 117 (518): 327–52.

Fellner, Gerald, Rupert Sausgruber, and Christian Traxler. 2013. “Testing Enforcement Strategies in the Field: Legal Threat, Moral Appeal, and Social Information.” *Journal of the European Economic Association* 11 (3): 634–60.

Glazer, Amihai, and Kai A. Konrad. 1986. “A Signaling Explanation for Charity.” *American Economic Review* 86 (4): 1019–28.

Gorodnichenko, Yuriy, Jorge Martinez-Vazquez, and Klara Sabirianova Peter. 2009. “Myth and Reality of Flat Tax Reform: Micro Estimates of Tax Evasion Response and Welfare Effects in Russia.” *Journal of Political Economy* 117 (3): 504–54.

Guyton, John, Dayanand Manoli, Brenda Schafer, and Michael Sebastiani. 2015. “Reminders and Recidivism: Evidence from Tax Filing and EITC Participation among Low-Income Nonfilers.” Working paper, IRS Office of Research.

Hallsworth, Michael. 2014. “The Use of Field Experiments to Increase Tax Compliance.” *Oxford Review of Public Policy* 30 (4): 658–79.

Hallsworth, Michael, John List, Robert Metcalfe, and Ivo Vlaev. 2014. “The Behavioralist as Tax Collector: Using Natural Field Experiments to Enhance Tax Compliance.” National Bureau of Economic Research Working Paper No. 20007.

Hasegawa, Makoto, Jeffrey L. Hoopes, Ryo Ishida, and Joel Slemrod. 2013. “The Effect of Public Disclosure on Reported Taxable Income: Evidence from Individuals and Corporations in Japan.” *National Tax Journal* 66 (3): 571–608.

HM Revenue & Customs. 2015. “Measuring Tax Gaps 2015 Edition: Tax Gap Estimates for 2013–14.”

Holtzblatt, Janet. 2007. “Implications of Return-free Tax Systems for the Structure of the Individual Income Tax.” *FinanzArchiv/Public Finance Analysis* 63 (3): 327–49.

Hurst, Eric, Geng Li, and Benjamin Pugsley. 2014. “Are Household Surveys Like Tax Forms? Evidence from Income Underreporting of the Self-Employed.” *Review of Economics and Statistics* 96 (1): 19–33.

Internal Revenue Service. 2014. *Strategic Plan FY2014–2017*. Washington, DC: IRS Publication 3744.

Johansson, Edvard. 2005. "An Estimate of Self-Employment Income Underreporting in Finland." *Nordic Journal of Political Economy* 31 (1): 99–109.

Kleven, Henrik J., Martin B. Knudsen, Claus T. Kreiner, Søren Pedersen, and Emmanuel Saez. 2011. "Unwilling or Unable to Cheat? Evidence from a Randomized Tax Audit Experiment in Denmark." *Econometrica* 79 (3): 651–92.

Kleven, Henrik J., and Mazhar Waseem. 2013. "Using Notches to Uncover Optimization Frictions and Structural Elasticities: Theory and Evidence from Pakistan." *Quarterly Journal of Economics* 128 (2): 669–723.

Kopczuk, Wojciech, Justin Marion, Erich Muehlegger, and Joel Slemrod. Forthcoming. "Does Tax-Collection Invariance Hold? Evasion and the Pass-through of State Diesel Taxes." *American Economic Journal: Economic Policy.*

Logue, Kyle D., and Joel Slemrod. 2009. "Of Coase, Calabresi, and Optimal Tax Liability." *Tax Law Review* 63:797–866.

Manoli, Dayanand, and Nicholas Turner. 2014. "Nudges and Learning: Evidence from Notifications for Low-Income Taxpayers." National Bureau of Economic Research Working Paper No. 20718.

Marian, Omri Y. 2013. "Are Cryptocurrencies 'Super' Tax Havens?" *Michigan Law Review First Impressions* 112: 38.

Martinez-Lopez, Diego. 2013. "The Underreporting of Income by Self-employed Workers in Spain." *SERIEs* 4 (4): 353–71.

OECD. 2015. *Tax Administration 2015: Comparative Information on OECD and Other Advanced and Emerging Economics*. Paris: OECD Publishing.

Ortega, Daniel, and Carlos Scartascini. 2015a. "Don't Blame the Messenger: A Field Experiment on Delivery Methods for Increasing Tax Compliance." Working Paper, Inter-American Development Bank.

Ortega, Daniel, and Carlos Scartascini. 2015b. "Who's Calling? The Effect of Phone Calls as a Deterrence Mechanism." Working Paper, Inter-American Development Bank.

Paramonova, Yulia. 2015a. "Tax Debt Collection Enforcement: When Does Suspension of a Driver's License Help?" Working Paper, University of Michigan.

Paramonova, Yulia. 2015b. "Collateral Tax Sanctions: A Way to Correlate Punishment with Ability." Working Paper, University of Michigan.

Paulus, Alari. 2015. "Tax Evasion and Measurement Error: An Econometric Analysis of Survey Data Linked with Tax Records." Institute for Social and Economic Research, University of Essex Working Paper No. 2015–10.

Perez-Truglia, Ricardo, and Ugo Troiano. 2015. "Tax Debt Enforcement: Theory and Evidence from a Field Experiment in the United States." Working Paper, University of Michigan.

Pissarides, Christopher A., and Guglielmo Weber. 1989. "An Expenditure-Based Estimate of Britain's Black Economy." *Journal of Public Economics* 39 (1): 17–32.

Pomeranz, Dina. 2015. "No Taxation without Information: Deterrence and Self-Enforcement in the Value Added Tax." *American Economic Review* 105 (8): 2539–69.

Schuetze, Herb J. 2002. "Profiles of Tax Non-Compliance among the Self-employed in Canada: 1969 to 1992." *Canadian Public Policy/Analyse de Politiques* 28 (2): 219–38.

Slemrod, Joel, Marsha Blumenthal, and Charles Christian. 2001. "Taxpayer Response to an Increased Probability of Audit: Evidence from a Controlled Experiment in Minnesota." *Journal of Public Economics* 79 (3): 429–53.

Slemrod, Joel, Brett Collins, Jeffrey Hoopes, Daniel Reck, and Michael Sebastiani. 2015. "Does Credit-Card Information Reporting Improve Small-Business Tax Compliance?" Working Paper, University of Michigan.

Torgler, Benno. 2004. "Moral Suasion: An Alternative Tax Policy Strategy? Evidence from a Controlled Field Experiment." *Economics of Governance* 5 (3): 235–53.

Ventry, Dennis J. 2011. "Americans Don't Hate Taxes, They Hate Paying Taxes." *University of British Columbia Law Review* 44 (3): 835–89.

Wilking, Eleanor. 2015. "Hotel Tax Incidence: Evidence from Airbnb Remittance Agreements." Working Paper, University of Michigan.

Williams, Colin C. 2014. *Confronting the Shadow Economy: Evaluating Tax Compliance and Behaviour Policies*. Cheltenham, UK: Edward Elgar.

Yitzhaki, Shlomo. 1974. "A Note on 'Income Tax Evasion: A Theoretical Analysis.'" *Journal of Public Economics* 3 (2): 201–2.

Zitzewitz, Eric. 2012. "Forensic Economics." *Journal of Economic Literature* 50 (3): 731–69.

COMMENTARY ON CHAPTER 4

David Weisbach

It is a great pleasure to comment on Joel Slemrod's survey of new research on tax compliance and enforcement. What comes across clearly from his survey is that the field is flourishing. Perhaps what is not so clear is that this flourishing is largely due to his efforts. Much of what we know about compliance and enforcement can be traced to work by Slemrod, his co-authors, and his numerous students.

It is also clear from Slemrod's survey that the credibility revolution has made its way into this area. Modern studies now use a range of techniques to better understand how features of the tax system or policy interventions affect compliance.

What did we learn from these new studies? To a great extent, the studies confirm my priors on issues of compliance and enforcement. First, most evasion is in the self-employed and other informal sectors. We suspected this from a number of sources including information from the Internal Revenue Service. New studies using approaches such as the traces of income approach confirm this. Second, reporting and withholding is effective, which is likely an important reason for the informal/formal compliance differences. And finally, audits and deterrence are important. Enforcement matters. If there are no cops on the highway, people will speed.

The recent work that Slemrod surveys, though, gives us a better sense of some of the nuances. For example, third-party reporting increases the amounts of the reported items that taxpayers state on their returns, but may also induce offsetting behavior. In Carrillo, Pomeranz, and Singhal (2014), firms in Ecuador subject to reporting increased their stated income but almost completely offset the increase by also increasing costs which were not subject to information reporting. The Slemrod et al. (2015) study of credit card reporting in the United States finds a similar although smaller effect.

The effects of enforcement are more subtle than the speeding analogy lets on. In Slemrod, Blumenthal, and Christian (2001), a randomized control trial involving threat of audit letters caused middle and low-income taxpayers to report more income but high-income taxpayers reported lower income. The authors speculate that these taxpayers viewed their initial tax return as a negotiation rather than an attestation and wanted to start the negotiation from a more extreme position.

Slemrod's discussion of the effect of norms on compliance is interesting. I think most people not familiar with the previous literature would have guessed that norms about compliance are important. If you think all of your friends and neighbors are cheating, you may be more likely to cheat because (1) the social sanctions from being caught will be lower and (2) if relative income matters, not cheating puts you at a disadvantage.

Prior studies that attempt to manipulate norms, however, have not found an effect. Slemrod discusses two new studies, Bott et al. (2014) and Hallsworth (2014) which do find effects from attempts to change norms. Bott et al. consider a randomized field experiment in Norway in which a moral appeal in a letter almost doubled the average foreign income reported. Hallsworth et al. considered a randomized field experiment in the United Kingdom that included an appeal to social norms and found an increase in compliance.

Slemrod says that his priors on norms are moved somewhat by these results. Mine are not, at least not by much. The Hallsworth et al. study examined a very special situation involving the payment of an already reported liability, so I think it has little relevance to general reporting or compliance issues. This leaves just Bott et al., which took place in Norway. It is not clear the extent to which a study of the norms of Norwegians will have external validity.

As has been well-discussed in the literature outside of tax compliance, the shift toward better identification in economics, while greatly increasing the credibility of reported results, has not come without costs, and these costs are loom large when studying tax compliance. There are two primary costs. The first is that better identification has led to offsetting concerns about external validity. To identify an effect, studies look for a feature of a tax system, such as a discontinuity or notch, or they manipulate a feature of a tax system such as the risk of audit in a particular circumstance. These features are embedded in a larger tax system and culture, which may be unique. To take some examples from the studies, researchers have considered compliance issues in Ecuador (Carrillo, Pomeranz, and Singhal 2014), Norway (Bo, Slemrod, and Thoresen 2015), Greece (Artavanis, Morse, and Tsoutsoura 2015) Estonia (Paulus et al. 2015), the United Kingdom (Hallsworth 2014), Pakistan (Best et al. 2015; Kleven and Waseem 2013), and Japan (Hasegawa et al. 2013). If one is concerned with the design of a tax system or the enforcement rules in say, the United States, it is not clear the extent to which we can learn from studies of, say, norm manipulation in a country with a completely different culture and tax system. To go back to the Bott et al. (2014) study of norm manipulation in Norway, if we have studies in the United States showing no effect, to what extent should we take the information from Bott et al. to mean we should modify our priors about how US taxpayers will behave? To what extent should we take the differences in results to mean Norwegians are different from Americans? The problems get worse as the development levels, culture, and tax systems get further apart. Evasion may be very sensitive to details. How much can the Norwegians take from a study about Pakistan and how much can the French learn from studies of Ecuador?

A second concern is that an insistence on careful identification means that some effects that may be of central importance cannot be studied. Take norms once again. It may take a very long time to change norms about tax compliance. The changes may only take effect on a large scale as people's perceptions of overall compliance change. There is no way to measure these changes while meeting modern standards for identification even if the effects of norms are real and large. It may be very cost-beneficial for the Internal Revenue Service to focus on norms of compliance even if we cannot determine this within modern standards of identification.

Notwithstanding the extensive work surveyed by Slemrod, there remains much that I would like to know about enforcement and compliance. I would like to know more about the distributional impacts of evasion. How much evasion is the wealthy using Swiss bank accounts (see Zucman 2014) and how much is middle-class small businesses using cash? What is the elasticity of evasion for different income groups? And, how does the marginal cost of reducing evasion vary across income groups? To design optimal systems, we need estimates of parameters of this sort.

I would also want to know how evasion and avoidance relate to one another (and the distributional impact of avoidance). I would guess that they are substitutes. On the margin, if people are optimizing the mix of the two, they may be very good substitutes. The social consequences, however, may be different.

Can we say anything about why some people evade while others comply when they are similarly situated? What characteristics would cause one small cash business to evade when other cash businesses do not? Are there network effects, so, say, dry cleaners in New Jersey evade while accountants in Minnesota comply?

Studies of evasion take tax systems as basically fixed and consider small perturbations, such as random assignment of audit letters or an increase in reporting for a particular type of income. The possibilities for evasion, however, should be central elements in the design of the overall system. For example, as is widely discussed, a retail sales tax has substantially larger evasion opportunities than a VAT even though both are theoretically (i.e., without evasion) the same tax base. The widespread preference for a VAT over a retail sales tax is driven by this concern about avoidance. There are likely to be many other design choices that are similarly driven by evasion or avoidance. The choice between an origin and destination base may be determined by the evasion and avoidance opportunities in an origin base because an origin base requires transfer pricing, which is notoriously subject to manipulation (rarely treated as criminal so falling into the avoidance category). What about the choice between a firm-level business income tax like the Comprehensive Business Income Tax from Department of the Treasury (1992) and an individual-level business income tax like that proposed by Toder and Viard (2014). We have intuitions about these issues. Given the flowering of research into evasion, is there anything modern research techniques can say about these central design issues?

Slemrod in his conclusion includes a hypothetical State of the Union speech in which the president lays out the case for fighting evasion. The argument is straightforward: fighting tax evasion helps the innocent taxpayer who complies with his obligations. People should want the government to fight evasion.

The speech ends with a standing ovation from both sides of the aisle. The case seems compelling to me but the prospect of the standing ovation not so much. But why? If the speech were about some other type of crime that was on the order of magnitude as tax evasion, the standing ovation would be plausible. Everyone hates paying their taxes, but they should like it if others pay theirs. I don't want to have to pay more taxes to support the cheaters. The sheer unlikeliness of Slemrod's hypothetical State of the Union, though, shows that somehow this reasoning is not widespread.

My experience is with the United States, where this odd dynamic seems clear. Do other cultures have the same dynamic where tax evasion is seen as a different sort of crime than other, facially similar, financial crimes? That is, is this dynamic something special to the United States or something special about taxation?

In all, Slemrod provides us with an excellent survey of recent developments in the field. I am looking forward to ten more years of research and Slemrod's next survey.

REFERENCES

Artavanis, Nikolaos, Adair Morse, and Margarita Tsoutsoura. 2015. "Tax Evasion across Industries: Soft Credit Evidence from Greece." National Bureau of Economic Research Working Paper No. 21552.

Best, Michael Carlos, Anne Brockmeyer, Henrik Jacobsen Kleven, Johannes Spinnewijn, and Mazhar Waseem. 2015. "Production versus Revenue Efficiency with Limited Tax Capacity: Theory and Evidence from Pakistan." *Journal of Political Economy* 123:1311–55.

Bo, Erlend E., Joel Slemrod, and Thor O. Thoresen. 2015. "Taxes on the Internet: Deterrence Effects of Public Disclosure." *American Economic Journal: Economic Policy* 7:36–62.

Bott, Kristina, Alexander W. Cappelen, Erik Ø Sørensen, and Bertil Tungodden. 2014. "You've Got Mail: A Randomised Field Experiment on Tax Evasion." NHH Norwegian School of Economics, Discussion Paper 26/2014.

Carrillo, Paul, Dina Pomeranz, and Monica Singhal. 2014. "Dodging the Taxman: Firm Misreporting and Limits to Tax Enforcement." National Bureau of Economic Research Working Paper No. 20624.

Department of the Treasury. 1992. "Report of the Department of the Treasury on Integration of the Individual and Corporate Tax Systems." Department of the Treasury. Washington, DC.

Hallsworth, Michael. 2014. "The Use of Field Experiments to Increase Tax Compliance." *Oxford Review of Economic Policy* 30:658–79.

Hasegawa, Makoto, Jeffrey L. Hoopes, Ryo Ishida, and Joel Slemrod. 2013. "The Effect of Public Disclosure on Reported Taxable Income: Evidence from Individuals and Corporations in Japan. *National Tax Journal* 66:571–608.

Kleven, Henrik J., and Mazhar Waseem. 2013. "Using Notches to Uncover Optimization Frictions and Structural Elasticities: Theory and Evidence from Pakistan." *Quarterly Journal of Economics* 128:669–723.

Paulus, Alari, et al. 2015. "Tax Evasion and Measurement Error: An Econometric Analysis of Survey Data Linked with Tax Records." Institute for Social and Economic Research, University of Essex Working Paper No. 2015.

Slemrod, Joel, Marsha Blumenthal, and Charles Christian. 2001. "Taxpayer Response to an Increased Probability of Audit: Evidence from a Controlled Experiment in Minnesota." *Journal of Public Economics* 79:455–83.

Slemrod, Joel, Brett Collins, Jeffrey Hoopes, Daniel Reck, and Michael Sebastiani. 2015. "Does Credit-Card Information Reporting Improve Small-business Tax Compliance?" National Bureau of Economic Research Working Paper No. 21412.

Toder, Eric J., and Alan D. Viard. 2014. "Major Surgery Needed: A Call for Structural Reform of the U.S. Corporate Income Tax." SSRN Scholarly Paper, Social Science Research Network. Rochester, NY.

Zucman, Gabriel. 2014. "Taxing across Borders: Tracking Personal Wealth and Corporate Profits." *Journal of Economic Perspectives* 28:121–48.

5

ECONOMIC AND DISTRIBUTIONAL EFFECTS OF TAX EXPENDITURE LIMITS

Len Burman, Eric Toder, Daniel Berger, and Jeffrey Rohaly

5.1 INTRODUCTION

Tax expenditures are special tax rules in the form of deductions, exclusions, credits, and favorable rates that benefit selected activities, industries, or groups of taxpayers. Since Stanley Surrey originally popularized the concept in the 1970s, tax policy experts have recognized that special tax benefits represent a form of public spending disguised as tax reductions. Because of this, it is often easier to enact tax breaks to promote policy agendas than to enact equivalent direct spending programs that are more transparent. As a result, many tax expenditures are poorly targeted, distort economic choices of households and businesses, and make the tax law more complicated. Reducing or eliminating many of them to pay for lower rates, deficit reduction, or higher priority spending programs has long been a goal of tax reformers.

Tax expenditure reduction has proven politically difficult, however. The most costly tax expenditures, including the exclusion for employer-sponsored health insurance, itemized deductions for home mortgage interest, charitable contributions, and state and local taxes, and the exemption of interest on municipal bonds benefit many taxpayers and have the support of powerful constituencies. As an alternative, policymakers and commentators have expressed interest in approaches, analogous to direct spending caps, to limit the costs of tax expenditures without targeting single provisions.

This chapter examines the effects of alternative ways of imposing global limitations on groups of tax expenditures that benefit individual taxpayers. We begin by providing some general background on the adverse effects of tax expenditures and past efforts of tax reform proposals to reduce them. We review existing limits on tax expenditures—the alternative minimum tax and the limitation on itemized deductions—and discuss alternative and more comprehensive limitations that would be preferable to existing ones. We then provide estimates of the effects of alternative global limitations on federal revenues and on how much tax rates could be reduced while maintaining revenue neutrality. We estimate the effects of alternative limitations on the distribution of tax burdens, marginal tax rates on capital and labor income, and incentives to engage in tax-subsidized activities. A final section concludes.

5.2 BACKGROUND

The tax expenditure concept dates back to 1967 when Treasury Assistant Secretary Stanley Surrey directed his staff to compile lists of "government spending for favored activities or groups, effected through the tax system rather than through direct grants, loans, or other forms of government assistance" (Surrey and McDaniel 1985).[1]

Some critics object to the notion that letting taxpayers keep more of their own money could be construed as spending. But most economists readily see the duality between tax expenditures and traditional spending programs in the sense that they have nearly identical effects on the budget, resource allocation, relative prices, and the distribution of income. The only difference, typically, is in who administers the program.

The late economist, David Bradford (2003), famously illustrated this point by proposing, with tongue firmly in cheek, a Weapons Supply Tax Credit, which would allow arms manufacturers to sell their ordinance to the Pentagon in exchange for tax credits rather than cash. Instantly, the Defense Department's budget would decline by the amount of transformed spending. Tax revenues would fall by a similar amount (or more, if weapons suppliers demanded a premium on account of the complexities and uncertainties associated with the tax credit mechanism). But government would be doing exactly the same thing. Only the accounting would change.

A more substantive debate relates to the baseline against which tax expenditures are measured. (Donald Marron [2011] has an especially lucid discussion of the baseline and measurement issues.) Surrey thought a very comprehensive income tax should be the baseline, but others have pointed out that, against that yardstick, tax incentives for saving and "bonus depreciation" (partial expensing) provisions are counted as tax expenditures when those provisions would be the norm under a consumption-based tax system. Since the US income tax is really a hybrid combining aspects of income and consumption taxes—and many economists favor a consumption tax on efficiency grounds—it is not clear which baseline is more appropriate. Donald Marron and Eric Toder (2012), however, have estimated that about 70% of tax expenditures would be treated as such against either baseline. At 2016 levels, that would amount to almost $1 trillion of spending.

While the principal function of the tax code is to raise revenue to finance the government, there may be good reasons to run some programs through the IRS. For example, when information on eligibility is already reported on tax returns or easily obtainable by the tax authorities, a tax expenditure might be easier to administer and comply with than a traditional spending program. Running targeted assistance programs like the earned income tax credit through the tax code also has the advantage that individuals do not need to apply in welfare offices, which may be especially burdensome for low-wage workers for whom time away from the job may be impossible during normal working hours. Also, the anonymity of tax filing avoids welfare stigma.

[1] The material in this sections draws heavily from Burman (2013).

However, tax expenditures have numerous drawbacks. Some forms of tax expenditures raise special problems. Itemized deductions are only of value for the minority of tax filers with more deductions than the standard deduction. Even for filers whose deductions just barely exceed the threshold for itemizing, the benefits are miniscule. The value of both deductions and exclusions rises with marginal tax rates—a $100 deduction is worth $10 at a 10% tax rate but $40 at a 40% rate—and thus income. This means that tax expenditures designed to encourage certain behaviors, such as home ownership, charitable giving, or participating in a health insurance or retirement saving plan, provide much bigger incentives to higher- than to lower-income families. Often, lower-income people get little or no benefit from such upside-down subsidies.

Political scientists argue that a key drawback is that tax expenditures are mostly hidden from public view. Chris Howard (1997) aptly named them "The Hidden Welfare State." Suzanne Mettler (2011), referred to "The Submerged State." Mettler contends that the relative invisibility of tax expenditures undermines democracy because their relative obscurity makes it more difficult for citizens to understand how government programs affect them. Lobbyists can sneak expensive ineffective subsidies into the tax code that would never pass muster as direct spending programs (e.g., ethanol tax credits). Moreover, even relatively worthwhile programs (Mettler cites the Affordable Care Act) may be less understood when important provisions are run through the tax code.

Notwithstanding their drawbacks, the use of tax expenditures has increased dramatically over time. Burman and Phaup (2012) report that the number grew from 140 in 1987 to 202 in 2009, a 44% increase in a little over two decades. All told, estimated tax expenditures total about $1.4 trillion in fiscal year 2016.

Burman and Phaup (2012) argue that tax expenditures may have proliferated because voters do not fully perceive their cost. This results in a government that is larger and less efficient than would prevail if citizens had full information. Tax expenditures have a privileged status in the budget process. A new tax credit or deduction is considered a "tax cut," and thus relatively immune from the "tax and spend" critique that would apply to a similar spending program. Tax expenditures are scored as reductions in revenues rather as new spending programs. As a result, both spending and taxes are understated. In a political context where both are considered bad, this clearly creates a bias in favor of tax expenditures over traditional spending.

Nonetheless, proposals for reform abound. Virtually all income tax reform proposals would trim tax expenditures. Several high-profile deficit reduction commissions proposed radical paring of tax expenditures. This would surely make the late Stanley Surrey smile. When he invented the term "tax expenditure," he instructed the Treasury Department to compile a list and tally up their cost. He viewed cuts in tax expenditures as the "pathway to tax reform," and in 1973 made the case in a book of that title (Surrey 1973).

Surrey and latter-day reformers are surely right that cutting tax expenditures could raise revenue while reducing the economic cost of the tax system and making it simpler and fairer. The primary drawback is political: voters like tax expenditures, the biggest of which include the tax exclusion for employer-sponsored health insurance and the mortgage interest deduction. Simply eliminating people's favorite tax breaks is unlikely to win much public support.

As a result, many reform proposals take an indirect approach to limiting them. Martin Feldstein, Daniel Feenberg, and Maya MacGuineas (2011) proposed to limit the tax benefits from selective tax expenditures to 2% of income. Another approach is to limit the value of itemized deductions and selected other deductions and exemptions to 28% of the amount deducted or excluded (US Treasury 2015). A variant is to tax-adjusted gross income (AGI—income before most deductions) at a higher rate than taxable income (after deductions). And some proposals would create a new minimum tax as a percentage of AGI or some other broad measure of income (e.g., the so-called "Buffett Rule"—which would raise the top effective tax rate on capital gains and dividends and cut the value of deductions and exclusions). This chapter explores the policy, revenue, and distributional issues associated with such indirect approaches to limiting tax expenditures.

5.3 LIMITING TAX EXPENDITURES: PRINCIPLES AND TRADE-OFFS

A common theme in many tax reform proposals is to eliminate and reduce many tax expenditures in order to finance a reduction in marginal tax rates on individual and corporate income. Reformers point to the 1986 tax reform as the model for future reform efforts. That reform eliminated or reined in numerous tax subsidies while reducing the top individual rate from 50% to 28% and the top corporate rate from 46% to 34%. Advocates of this type of reform argue that it would promote efficiency, fairness, and simplicity. Efficiency would be advanced because producers, investors, and consumers would make choices based on social costs and benefits instead of engaging in less socially productive activities to reduce their tax liabilities. Fairness would be promoted because people with the same ability to pay, as measured by a broad definition of income or consumption, would face the same tax liability. And the tax law would be simpler because fewer activities would qualify for favorable tax treatment, reducing recordkeeping and reporting obligations.

The 1986 tax reform was, however, far from comprehensive. Most of the savings came from cutting large business tax breaks such as the investment tax credit and accelerated depreciation and preferences for capital income of individuals, such as special rates for capital gains and universal eligibility for contributions to individual retirement accounts. The most popular individual income tax expenditures survived largely unscathed. They include items such as the tax exclusion for employer-sponsored health insurance (with a revenue loss of $342 billion in FY2016, including lost payroll taxes) and the deductions for mortgage interest ($62 billion), charitable contributions ($54 billion), and state and local income and property taxes ($84 billion) (US Treasury 2015). Ronald Reagan stipulated few parameters to the Treasury Department in 1984 when he commissioned the study that ultimately led to the Tax Reform Act of 1986, but one was to preserve tax incentives for homeownership (Birnbaum and Murray 1987). The law Congress enacted did slightly trim the tax break for homeownership, but only for those with mortgages over $1 million.[2] President Bush gave similar instructions to members of his tax reform commission. Former Joint Committee on Taxation Chief of Staff John Buckley (2011) argues forcefully that raising significant revenue from eliminating individual income tax expenditures would be politically difficult, if not impossible.

An alternative approach would apply global limits to a group of tax expenditures, without eliminating any of them. This approach has been in part motivated by the lack of political success in recent years of broader tax reform proposals. We discuss both approaches below.

5.3.1 Global Tax Reform Proposals

In spite of Buckley's caution, there has been no shortage of proposals to combine lower marginal tax rates with broad cuts in tax expenditures. Proposals in this spirit include those advanced by the tax reform panel established by President George W. Bush, the Bipartisan Policy Center (2010), and the National Commission on Fiscal Responsibility and Reform (2010).

In 2005, President George W. Bush convened a blue ribbon panel, which proposed two fundamental tax reform options (President's Advisory Panel on Federal Tax Reform 2005). The first, dubbed the "Simplified Income Tax," was classic tax reform—broader tax base with lower rates. It would have radically simplified the tax code by eliminating many tax expenditures and converting many of the remaining tax deductions to flat credits. The second option, the "Growth and Investment Tax" (GIT) plan, would have limited many of the same expenditures as the simplified income tax plan and would also have allowed firms to expense capital investments, while eliminating interest deductibility. This would have converted the tax system from one mostly based on income to one primarily based on consumption. In a concession to political reality, it would have retained a low rate of tax on dividends, interest, and capital gains of individual taxpayers.[3]

A more radical option is to simplify the tax code so much that many households would no longer have to file income tax returns. The Bipartisan Policy Center (2010) would have imposed a flat 15% tax rate on most taxpayers and limited the value of some tax expenditures to the same 15% rate while eliminating others. Instead of personal exemptions and deductions, which effectively create a zero tax rate bracket, the

[2] The law also limited the use of mortgage debt to finance other, non-housing spending and capped the deduction for home equity lines of credit and second mortgages at $100,000. The IRS has since ruled that the two mortgage limits may be combined, so homeowners may deduct interest on a mortgage up to $1.1 million if they don't deduct other mortgage debt (Ebeling 2010).

[3] GOP presidential candidate Jeb Bush proposed a plan very similar in overall design to the GIT (Burman et al. 2015).

plan would have provided fully refundable credits that increased in value with the number of children.[4] This approach would have allowed employers to withhold at a flat 15% tax rate that would match most employees' tax liability before the refundable credits.

President Obama empaneled the National Commission on Fiscal Responsibility and Reform (2010), commonly called the Bowles-Simpson Commission (after its two heads) with the mandate to reform the tax code and reduce the deficit.[5] (The Bush panel had been instructed to produce a revenue-neutral plan.) Bowles-Simpson would have eliminated even more tax expenditures than the Bipartisan Policy Center Task Force, allowing it to cut tax rates substantially and raise revenue without the need for a supplemental revenue source.[6]

A common thread of these proposals is that none has come close to being enacted. Voters are unenthusiastic about trading their favorite tax breaks for lower tax rates. Any revenue-neutral swap (e.g., President's Advisory Panel 2005) would result in some, and perhaps many, households owing more tax after the reform. Despite all the theoretical clamor for simplicity and fairness, it's not clear that voters are willing to pay much for those salutary attributes.

And if the tax reform is intended to increase revenues, as Bowles-Simpson and the Bipartisan Policy Center set out to do, taxpayers as a group will owe more tax after than before reform. Possibly they can be convinced that this is worthwhile to avoid a debt catastrophe or for the sake of future generations, but the idea of shared sacrifice is likely to run into resistance if many people decide that their share is greater than that of their neighbors (who didn't take as much advantage of tax subsidies).

[4] The plan also included a new value-added tax (dropped in later iterations) and cut top individual and corporate income tax rates to 27%.

[5] President Obama also commissioned a tax reform study under the direction of former Federal Reserve Board chairman Paul Volcker (President's Economic Recovery Advisory Board 2010). The report laid out a laundry list of options the administration might consider as part of a tax reform plan, but did not actually produce such a plan itself. According to the report, "the Board was not asked to recommend a major overarching tax reform, such as the 1986 tax reform, the tax plans proposed by the 2005 Tax Reform Panel, or proposals for introducing a value-added tax in addition to or in lieu of the current income tax system" (p. v).

[6] In Congress, Senators Ron Wyden (D-OR) and Dan Coats (R-IN) produced a more incremental tax reform plan (Wyden and Coats 2011), designed to be revenue-neutral and preserve the most popular tax breaks. It would have eliminated the AMT and cut the corporate tax rate to 24% while capping individual income tax rates at 35%. The cost of these provisions would have been offset by eliminating or scaling back various tax expenditures. The proposal would have raised tax rates on high-income taxpayers' long-term capital gains and dividends to 22.75%. It would have revised the formula the federal government uses to adjust tax parameters for inflation, generally cutting the cost of annual inflation adjustments. The plan would also have reduced businesses' interest deductions. It would have consolidated and simplified individual tax breaks for saving and education. The most radical change is that the plan would have required the IRS to prepare pre-filled tax returns for lower-income filers.

5.3.2 Limiting Tax Expenditures

Rather than repealing or reforming tax expenditures outright, another approach is to apply aggregate limits to a group of them, without singling out separate provisions. Feldstein, Feenberg, and MacGuineas (2011) argue that this type of approach could raise substantial revenue, improve economic efficiency—by reducing distortions caused by "wasteful tax spending"—and significantly simplify the tax system for most taxpayers, all in a progressive way. They also argue that there are significant political economy benefits:

> Singling out one or a small number of tax expenditures to eliminate strikes many taxpayers as unfair. This paper considers a way of reducing the major individual tax expenditures by capping the total amount that the tax expenditures as a whole can reduce the individual's tax burden. More specifically, we examine the effect of limiting the total value of the tax reduction resulting from tax expenditures to two percent of the individual's adjusted gross income. Each individual can benefit from the full range of tax expenditures but can receive tax reduction only up to 2 percent of his AGI. (Feldstein, Feenberg, and MacGuineas 2011: 10)

In other words, the claimed advantage of this approach is that it is indiscriminate. Note, however, that the authors are making a *political* and not an economic argument. It applies to tax expenditures the same logic used by those who advocate (and have sometimes achieved) across-the-board cuts in discretionary spending. Of course, across-the-board cuts in tax expenditures or direct expenditures could only be justified on second-best grounds. Obviously, it would be better to reduce programs (whether conveyed through tax expenditures or direct outlays) that are wasteful, inefficient, or outmoded, while retaining or even expanding programs with net social benefits. The political logic, however, argues that powerful constituencies backing specific programs will always prevail because the gains from eliminating the spending program or tax break (in the form of freed up resources for tax cuts or other programs) are so diffuse that no one would mobilize against them. If, however, in the aggregate either discretionary spending or spending on tax breaks is larger than the economically efficient level, then global limitations could improve efficiency, even if they are not optimal.

5.3.3 Ways of Limiting Tax Expenditures

We identify four generic approaches that limit tax expenditures. Each can be characterized by how they affect (1) the degree to which tax expenditures continue to subsidize favored activities at the margin (the marginal subsidy rate) and (2) the marginal tax rate people pay on additional dollar of earning or investment income (the marginal income tax rate). The four generic approaches are income-based phase-out, alternative tax schedule, overall limits on tax expenditures, and restructured subsidy schedule.

5.3.3.1 Income-Based Phase-Out

Under this approach, tax expenditures are phased out as a taxpayer's income increases. An income-based phase-out of this type has no effect on the marginal subsidy rate for most taxpayers because the phase-out is based solely on income, not the value of deductions.[7] An additional dollar of deductible expenses raises itemized deductions by a dollar while having no effect on the amount of deductions reduced by the phase-out. Instead, the phase-out raises the marginal income tax rate because taxpayers lose deductions (and therefore pay some additional tax in excess of the statutory marginal rate) as their incomes increase.

An example in current law is the limitation on itemized deductions: the total amount of itemized deductions taxpayers may claim declines by 3 cents for every dollar of adjusted gross income in excess of $258,250 for single returns and $309,900 for joint returns (in 2015), up to a maximum of 80% of itemized deductions. For a taxpayer in the 39.6% rate bracket, this effectively raises her marginal income tax rate by 3% to 40.8% because each dollar of additional income raises her taxable income by $1.03. The limitation, however, has no effect on the marginal incentive to give to charity or borrow more to finance a home because each additional dollar of deduction still saves the taxpayer 39.6 cents.

5.3.3.2 Alternative Tax Schedule

Under this approach, taxpayers face a minimum tax amount based on an alternative tax schedule with a lower rate that applies to a broader tax base. Examples of this approach are the individual alternative minimum tax (AMT) in current law and the so-called "Buffett rule," under which taxpayers with income above a specified amount would pay at least 30% of adjusted gross income (instead of taxable income). This approach has mixed effects on both subsidy rates and marginal tax rates on income, as explained in the discussion below of the individual AMT. Thus, its effect on efficiency is ambiguous and could be negative.

The AMT calculation is complex, but it basically amounts to adding certain "preference items," such as state and local taxes and personal exemptions to taxable income, subtracting an AMT exemption that phases out with income, and then applying an alternative rate schedule to calculate tentative AMT (Burman, Gale, and Rohaly 2003). If that amount is higher than regular tax, the difference is an additional tax. The statutory AMT rates are modest—26% and 28%—but the phase out of the AMT exemption raises effective marginal tax rates by 25% to 32.5% and 35%

[7] The phase-out formula limits the reduction in itemized deductions to 80% of the value of certain deductions. A very small number of taxpayers have very high incomes and modest deductions and are thus bound by this limit. In those unusual cases, an additional dollar of itemized deductions only reduces taxable income by 20 cents. However, since the value of itemized deductions—especially charitable donations and state and local taxes—tends to rise with income, very few taxpayers are in this situation.

in the phase-out range. As a result, most AMT taxpayers face higher marginal tax rates than under the regular tax. This reduces the incentive to earn taxable income and actually increases the subsidy rate on tax expenditures allowed under the AMT rules, such as the deduction for charitable contributions for many taxpayers. The subsidy on disallowed tax expenditures, such as the deduction for state and local taxes, is reduced or eliminated. To the extent that those tax expenditures are inefficient, limiting them raises economic efficiency. There is no marginal subsidy on AMT preference items for taxpayers on the AMT. But Gravelle and Marples (2015) point out that some tax subsidies such as state income tax deductions rise in value as income rises. Thus, capping them raises the effective marginal tax rate on income.

The "Buffett rule," which has been included in President Obama's budgets, is very similar. It would set a minimum average tax rate for millionaires of 30% of gross income.[8] This proposal would complicate tax compliance as taxpayers would have to calculate the floor on taxes due and pay that amount if it is higher than the tax calculated under the normal rules. It would also make it hard for taxpayers close to the threshold to predict their marginal effective tax rate or the value of deductions. The marginal tax rate on some kinds of income would rise and others fall precipitously when the cap is reached. The marginal tax rate on capital gains would rise from the lower capital gains tax rate (currently at 23.8% including the surtax on investment income) to 30%, whereas the marginal tax rate on ordinary income (such as wages and salaries) would fall from the top individual income tax rate to 30%. Meanwhile, the marginal value of tax preferences (with the exception of charitable contributions, which are exempt from the Buffett Rule) would fall to zero as long as ordinary income tax is less than the Buffett Rule threshold.

Proposals that set complicated rules to limit tax expenditures depending on circumstances of an individual taxpayer are not in the spirit of base-broadening income tax reform. They may reflect strategic first steps insofar as they reduce the value of tax expenditures, which might diminish the intensity of resistance to base-broadening measures, but they are similar to the complicated limits under current law and often supplement instead of replacing them. The Buffett Rule is really just a somewhat simpler (and more draconian) AMT. And there already is a limitation on itemized deductions, which phase out at higher income levels. These measures have complicated the tax system without necessarily increasing efficiency and fairness.[9]

5.3.3.3 Overall Limits on Tax Expenditures

Compared to the complexity of the Buffett rule, the current law AMT, and the limitation on itemized deductions, a simpler way to limit tax expenditures is simply to place a ceiling on how much any taxpayer may benefit from them. The limit may be a fixed dollar amount or a percentage of income. This approach eliminates the marginal

[8] The president has called the Buffett Rule a principle for tax reform rather than a specific proposal, but Sen. Sheldon Whitehouse (D-RI) made a specific proposal, which the president endorsed.

[9] See Burman, Gale, and Rohaly (2003) for a critique of the AMT.

subsidy for taxpayers claiming tax benefits in excess of the limitation, while retaining the full marginal subsidy for taxpayers with tax expenditures below the limit. Overall limits can raise or reduce marginal income tax rates.

Martin Feldstein, Daniel Feenberg, and Maya MacGuineas (2011) have proposed one type of global limit—a ceiling of 2% of AGI on the tax saving any taxpayer can gain from tax expenditures. The proposal would retain the standard deduction, which simulations suggest would be a more advantageous option for most taxpayers—only 9% would elect to itemize deductions under the proposal. For those who continue to itemize, the calculation of tax liability would be very complex, although presumably manageable with the aid of tax preparation software.

In 2012, presidential candidate, Mitt Romney, floated a variant of the Feldstein et al. proposal. Tax expenditures would be capped at a fixed dollar amount (the exact amount suggested ranged from $17,000 to $50,000). Governor Romney also proposed to eliminate the AMT, which would have made his version much simpler than the Feldstein et al. proposal.[10]

Both of these approaches would eliminate the marginal tax subsidy for the proscribed items for most taxpayers—either because the value of the standard deduction is above the ceiling or because the value of the tax expenditures is above it. Only taxpayers who choose to itemize but have tax expenditures worth less than the ceiling would have a marginal incentive to use more of them. In the Feldstein et al. proposal, this would be a very small group. The Romney variant, however, would have placed many more taxpayers in the unconstrained range. The rationale for limiting subsidies in this particular manner (100% for some, none for others) has not been advanced by designers of these proposals.

If the cap on tax expenditures could be enacted, it would facilitate broader tax reform because the vast majority of taxpayers would receive little or no incentive from the subsidies subject to the limit—either because their current itemizable expenses are so low that they are better off claiming the standard deduction or because they are high enough to exceed the limitation. So it could be a stepping stone to the kind of simplification that Surrey envisioned. However, the political feasibility rests on the assumption that taxpayers and interest groups that benefit from taxpayer behavior that the subsidies promote don't really understand the proposal.[11] Otherwise, one might expect nearly as much opposition to it as to the sweeping cuts in tax expenditures under Bowles-Simpson.

5.3.3.4 Restructured Subsidy Schedule

This approach would reduce the benefit taxpayers could receive from an additional dollar of deduction or exclusions. Examples are President Obama's proposal to limit the tax saving from certain deductions and exclusions to 28% of amount of the deductions

[10] Professor Feldstein advised the Romney campaign, as reported by various media outlets.

[11] For example, limitations on itemized deductions would be vigorously opposed by charitable organizations, home builders, and political representatives from high-tax states.

or exclusions and a more far-reaching proposal by Batchelder, Goldberg, and Orszag (2006) to replace deductions and exclusions with uniform refundable credits. These proposals would reduce marginal subsidy rates for taxpayers in high marginal rate bracket and may slightly increase marginal income tax rates for taxpayers who move into higher brackets because their taxable income increases.

For decades, the Congressional Budget Office has included an option to cap the value of itemized deductions at 15% in its periodic Deficit Reduction volumes. (See Congressional Budget Office 2011, for example.) President Obama has proposed a more modest limit—capping the value of certain tax expenditures at 28%—but he would apply the limit to a much broader list of items, including employer-sponsored health insurance, interest on municipal bonds, and employee contributions to retirement accounts (US Treasury 2016). The proposal certainly would not qualify as a simplification as it would require calculating tax liability with and without the specified deductions and exclusions and limiting the tax savings to 28%. Taxpayers with relatively modest amounts of deductions and exclusions would also have to compare their tax calculated this way with the tax they'd owe if they claimed the standard deduction. While tax software could perform these calculations, many taxpayers would likely be even more confused about the income tax than they are at present.

The intent of the proposal is to limit the disparity in the value of the selected tax expenditures. The maximum value would be 28%, compared with 39.6% under current law. There would still be a marginal subsidy on the proscribed activities, but it would be capped at 28%.

A simpler variant would tax gross income at a higher rate than taxable income for high-income filers. For example, retired Ways and Means Committee chairman, Dave Camp (R-MI) produced a sweeping tax reform draft (Committee on Ways and Means, 2014) that would have set a top ordinary income tax rate of 25%, but included an income surtax on high-income taxpayers. The surtax would have applied to income before most deductions and also would have applied to certain forms of excluded income. In consequence, the Camp plan effectively capped the value of most tax expenditures at 25%.

Batchelder, Goldberg, and Orszag (2006) suggest a different and more far-reaching approach: converting most individual income tax expenditures into refundable tax credits. The authors argue that completely aside from distributional concerns, the change would be desirable on efficiency grounds because the justification for most subsidies would imply an equal subsidy rate regardless of the income of the recipient. Providing subsidies by means of deductions or exclusions introduces substantial variation in subsidy rates because the effective subsidy varies with the marginal income tax bracket, which rises with income. Itemized deductions introduce another source of variation. Those deductions are only valuable to the extent that total itemized deductions exceed the standard deduction. For high-income people with large deductions for state and local taxes, mortgage interest, and charity, the marginal subsidy rate is approximately the income tax rate bracket. However, for middle-income households with modest deductions, the value of the itemized deduction can be reduced or even eliminated. Indeed, 70% of tax filers do not itemize deductions and get no tax benefit from them. Even for those who do itemize, the effective subsidy rate can be substantially reduced because only the amount of itemized deductions in excess of the standard deduction reduces tax liability.[12]

Nonrefundable tax credits are more uniform because their face value does not vary with the income tax rate or itemization status, but those credits are of little or no benefit to households that do not owe income tax. Making those credits refundable would eliminate the variation in value among taxpayers in different tax situations. (When refundable credits exceed tax liability, they are "refunded" to taxpayers.)

Beyond the efficiency argument, refundable credits are more progressive than deductions or nonrefundable credits. Faricy and Ellis (2013) find evidence that such a change could be popular. Self-identified Democrats and liberals care about the progressivity of tax expenditures, whereas Republicans appear to be indifferent to distributional arguments. In addition, the credit rate could be set well below the top income tax rate and still provide as much or more benefit to most taxpayers than a deduction. The Tax Policy Center estimates that more than 80% of tax units (including non-filers) were in the 15% tax bracket or lower in 2015.[13] Since the benefits of most individual income tax expenditures accrue mostly to those with high incomes (because they are in the highest tax brackets and tend to make larger charitable contributions, have larger mortgages, and pay more in taxes), a flat refundable tax credit can redirect the subsidy to lower and middle-income households while actually reducing the cost to the Treasury. In addition, to the extent that the subsidies are aimed at encouraging activities such as homeownership or health insurance coverage, most high-income people need less subsidy to be induced to participate than those with more modest incomes. Thus, a flat refundable tax credit may be able to achieve the objectives of the subsidies at much lower cost.

Refundable tax credits can also be much simpler than current law. Indeed their value could generally be determined without doing any tax calculations, since they do not vary with tax status.[14] However, that can also be a drawback since some people may have to file a tax return solely for the purpose of the claiming the credit.[15] This creates costs for the IRS and for the new tax filers and may also create new avenues for fraud.

[12] For example, suppose the standard deduction for a married couple is $12,000 and that they would have $10,000 of itemized deductions before including charitable contributions. If they make less than $2,000 of charitable contributions, they would get no benefit from itemizing deductions. If they donate $4,000 to charity, the contributions would lower their taxable income by $1,000 (the portion in excess of the $12,000 standard deduction). The effective tax subsidy rate is one-third of the statutory rate. If the household is in a 25% tax bracket, the contributions will save them $250 in federal income tax, or 8.3% of the $3,000 in contributions.

[13] Tax Policy Center table T15-0032.

[14] Note that this is not true for the EITC and the partially refundable child tax credit, since they phase out at higher income levels.

[15] This is generally not true for the EITC and the refundable portion of the child tax credit, since they are only available to families with earnings, and most workers must file to claim refunds of withheld income taxes even if they do not owe any income tax.

5.4 SIMULATIONS OF EFFECTS OF GLOBAL LIMITS ON SELECTED TAX EXPENDITURES

In this section, we simulate the effects of three kinds of global tax expenditure limits on federal receipts, the distribution of the tax burden, marginal tax rates on capital and labor income, and the incentive to donate to charities.

In the illustrative simulations, we include among the selected tax expenditures subject to the limits the following provisions:

- all itemized deductions, but with some variants that exclude from the limits the deductions for charitable contributions and home mortgage interest;
- the exclusion from income of employer-provided health insurance benefits;[16]
- the exemption of interest on state and local bonds; and
- tax benefits for higher education, including tuition credits and the deductibility of student loan interest.

We simulate three ways of limiting these provisions:

- Limiting the tax savings from the provisions to a fixed percentage of modified adjusted gross income (AGI), a design similar to one originally proposed by Feldstein, Feenberg, and MacGuineas (2011). Modified AGI is defined as AGI plus employer-provided health benefits and interest on state and local bonds.
- Imposing a fixed dollar ceiling on the total amount by which the provisions can reduce taxable income. The limit does not apply to tax credits, only to deductions and exclusions.
- Limiting the tax saving per dollar of exemption or deduction similar to one included in Dave Camp's tax reform plan in 2014. Our version would impose a surtax on modified AGI in excess of the current threshold for the 33% rate bracket, combined with a reduction in marginal tax rates.

We also simulate three ways of using the revenue raised by limiting tax expenditures:

- an across the board constant percentage cut in marginal income tax rates;
- an across the board constant percentage point cut in marginal tax rates (i.e., a constant rate cut as a percentage of income);
- a reduction in the top marginal income tax rates only.

[16] This also includes deductible employee contributions to health insurance plans under cafeteria plans.

In all of the options we consider, we eliminate the individual alternative minimum tax (AMT) and the current law limitation on itemized deductions. Thus, the options we consider would substitute improved ways of limiting tax expenditures for the highly flawed existing methods.

We use the Tax Policy Center (TPC) micro-simulation model to simulate these proposals. The appendix briefly describes TPC's methodology and incidence assumptions.

5.4.1 Revenue Effects of Alternative Limits

Replacing the individual alternative minimum tax (AMT) and the current law limitation on itemized deductions with full elimination of selected tax expenditures would increase individual income tax liabilities by $366 billion (table 5.1). (Repealing AMT

Table 5.1 Tax expenditure options, baseline: Current law, impact on tax revenue, 2016 calendar year

Proposal	*2016 Calendar Year*
Option 1: Repeal AMT and limitation on itemized deductions ()	−46.2[a]
Option 2: Option 1 plus repeal certain tax expenditures[b]	366.2
Option 3: Option 2 but allow deduction for charitable contributions	327.7
Option 4: Option 2 but allow deductions for charitable contributions and mortgage interest	281.7
Option 5: Option 1 plus limit tax benefit of certain tax expenditures to 2% of modified AGI[c]	204.7
Option 6: Option 5 but allow full benefit of deduction for charitable contributions	168.7
Option 7: Option 5 but allow full benefit of deductions for charitable contributions and mortgage interest	128.2
Option 8: Option 1 plus limit benefit of certain tax expenditures to 28%[d]	−14.3

[a] Estimates assume a micro-dynamic response using a taxable income elasticity of 0.25; [b] Proposal would repeal all itemized deductions, the exclusion for employer-sponsored health benefits, the exclusion of state and local bond interest, education credits, and the deduction for student loan interest; [c] Proposal would limit the tax benefit of all itemized deductions, the exclusion of employer-sponsored health benefits, the exclusion of interest on state and local bonds, education credits, and the deduction for student loan interest. Modified AGI is AGI plus employer-sponsored health benefits and tax-exempt interest; [d] Proposal would limit the benefit of all itemized deductions, the exclusion of employer-sponsored health benefits, the exclusion of interest on state and local bonds, and the deduction for student loan interest. *Source:* Urban-Brookings Tax Policy Center Microsimulation Model (version 0515-2).

and the limitation on itemized deductions alone would lose $46 billion.) The net revenue gain from eliminating selected tax expenditures would decline to $328 billion if the charitable deduction were retained and to $282 billion if the deductions for charitable contributions and mortgage interest were both retained.

If instead of full elimination, the tax saving from the selected tax expenditures were limited to 2% of modified AGI, tax liabilities would increase by $205 billion. The revenue pickup would drop to $169 billion if the charitable deduction were retained and to $128 billion if the deductions for charitable contributions and mortgage interest were retained.

Finally, replacing the AMT and the limitation on itemized deductions with a proposal to limit the tax benefit per dollar of reduced table income from the selected tax expenditures to 28% would reduce tax liability by about $14 billion.

5.4.2 Distributional Effects of Replacing the AMT and the Limitation on Itemized Deductions with Full Repeal of Selected Tax Expenditures

Eliminating the selected tax expenditures, while repealing the AMT and the limitation on itemized deductions, would raise average tax rates the most for upper-middle income taxpayers,[17] who gain substantial benefits from deductions and exemptions (table 5.2). Tax rates would increase by 3.27% in the 80–90 percentiles and by 3.11% in the 90–95 percentiles, compared with 2.60% for all taxpayers. Net tax increases are less in the top 5% because these taxpayers benefit the most as a share of their income from elimination of the AMT and the limitation on itemized deductions. The overall distributional pattern is similar for proposals that exclude the charitable and mortgage interest deductions, but the relative tax increases among groups differ somewhat. Taxpayers in the top 1% of the distribution benefit the most from retaining the charitable deduction, while taxpayers in the 80–99 percentiles benefit the most from retaining the mortgage interest deduction.

5.4.3 Distributional Effects of Full Repeal and a Percentage of AGI Limit with Alternative Ways of Cutting Marginal Rates

Many reform proposals would limit tax expenditures to help pay for reducing marginal income tax rates. The net effects of these proposals on the distribution of the tax burden depend on how the rates are cut. Simply repealing AMT and the limitation

[17] The term "taxpayer" as used in this chapter includes both tax filers and non-filers who are grouped into tax units. The TPC micro-simulation model supplements tax return data from the public use file (PUF) of individual tax returns produced by the IRS Statistics of Income Division with non-filing tax units created from household data in the Current Population Survey (CPS) of the US Census Unit, based on a statistical match between the PUF and the CPS.

Table 5.2 Replacing the alternative minimum tax and the limitation on itemized deductions (the limitation on itemized deductions) with elimination of selected tax expenditures: Change in average tax rates, calendar year 2016

Income Group	*Repeal AMT and the Limitation on Itemized Deductions (%)*	*Repeal AMT, the Limitation on Itemized Deductions, and Selected Tax Expenditures (%)*	*Repeal AMT, the Limitation on Itemized Deductions, and Selected Tax Expenditures Except Charitable Deduction (%)*	*Repeal AMT, the Limitation on Itemized Deductions, and Selected Tax Expenditures Except Charitable and Mortgage Interest Deductions (%)*
Bottom quintile	0.00	0.55	0.55	0.54
Second quintile	0.00	1.47	1.45	1.40
Third quintile	0.00	2.39	2.31	2.12
Fourth quintile	−0.01	2.75	2.60	2.21
80–90 percentiles	−0.05	3.27	3.09	2.57
90–95 percentiles	−0.19	3.11	2.94	2.40
95–99 percentiles	−0.96	2.74	2.50	1.90
Top 1%	−1.16	2.69	1.81	1.58
All	−0.34	2.60	2.34	1.99

Note: Proposal repeals all itemized deductions (except where otherwise stated), the exclusion for employer-sponsored health benefits, the exclusion of state and local bond interest, education credits, and the deduction for student loan interest. *Source:* Urban-Brookings Tax Policy Center Microsimulation Model (version 0515-2).

on itemized deductions would lose revenue and therefore require offsetting tax rate increases to achieve budget balance. Taxpayers in the top 5% of the distribution receive a disproportionate share of the benefits from repealing AMT and the limitation on itemized deductions, so they would come up net winners if increasing marginal tax rates across the board by 3.68% paid for repeal (table 5.3). If, in contrast, only the top marginal rate were increased, the rate would have to rise to 44.6%. Taxpayers in the 95–99 percentiles (who bear the biggest burdens from the individual AMT) would be the biggest winners (because they are mostly below the top rate bracket), while taxpayers in the top 1% would be the biggest losers.

Repeal of the AMT, the limitation on itemized deductions, and all the selected tax expenditures could pay for an across the board cut in marginal tax rates of 22.4% (lowering the top rate from 39.6 to 30.7%). Taxpayers in the top 10% of the distribution

Table 5.3 Revenue neutral repeal of AMT and the limitation on itemized deductions: Change in average tax rates, calendar year 2016

Income Group	*Increase All Marginal Tax Rates by 3.68% (%)*	*Increase All Marginal Tax Rates by 0.74 Percentage Points (%)*	*Increase Top Two Rates to 39.6% and 46.0% (%)*	*Increase Top Rate to 44.6% (%)*
Lowest quintile	0.02	0.04	0.00	0.00
Second quintile	0.09	0.16	0.00	0.00
Middle quintile	0.20	0.29	0.00	0.00
Fourth quintile	0.29	0.38	−0.01	−0.01
80–90 percentiles	0.33	0.38	−0.05	−0.05
90–95 percentiles	0.28	0.27	−0.18	−0.18
95–99 percentiles	−0.35	−0.45	−0.82	−0.87
Top 1%	−0.41	−0.73	1.43	1.56
All	0.06	0.04	0.11	0.13

Note: Revenue estimates include micro-dynamic responses, but distributional estimates are static. Because proposal on balance raises marginal tax rates and therefore has negative revenue feedback, aggregate tax burdens must rise to keep revenue constant. *Source:* Urban-Brookings Tax Policy Center Microsimulation Model (version 0515-2).

would see their average tax rates decline, while average tax rates would increase for the bottom 90% (table 5.4a). The biggest average tax rate cut would go to taxpayers in the top 1% of the income distribution. If, in contrast, all marginal tax rates were cut by the same number of percentage points, the top rate would fall by only 4.7 percentage points, to 34.9%. Higher income taxpayers would still fare better than lower-income taxpayers, but the differences in tax rate changes among income groups would be much smaller. Finally, if only the top rate were reduced, subject to the constraint that rates could not decline with income, then all marginal rates now at 25% or over would drop to 20.4%. That is, the rate schedule would be 10%, 15%, and 20.4%. Only taxpayers in the top 5% would see tax cuts, with the average tax rate for the top 1% dropping by 7.8%.

The pattern of winners and losers would be similar if the charitable deductions or both charitable and mortgage interest deductions were retained, but the rate reductions would be smaller (tables 5.4b and 5.4c). The highest income groups would fare better than others, especially if tax rates were capped or all rates were cut by the same percentage. Low- and middle-income tax filers would do best when all rates declined by the same number of percentage points, although they still tend to face higher taxes under any of the options.

Table 5.4a Revenue neutral repeal of AMT, the limitation on itemized deductions, and selected tax expenditures: Change in average tax rates, calendar year 2016

Income Group	*Reduce All Marginal Tax Rates by 22.4% (%)*	*Reduce All Marginal Tax Rates by 4.73 Percentage Points (%)*	*Reduce All Marginal Rates 25% and Above to 20.4% (%)*
Lowest quintile	0.37	0.17	0.55
Second quintile	0.70	0.12	1.47
Middle quintile	0.77	−0.02	2.16
Fourth quintile	0.40	−0.31	2.05
80–90 percentiles	0.28	−0.07	1.70
90–95 percentiles	−0.38	−0.33	0.51
95–99 percentiles	−1.58	−0.79	−2.46
Top 1%	−2.61	−0.40	−7.82
All	−0.37	−0.25	−0.47

Note: Proposal repeals all itemized deductions, the exclusion for employer-sponsored health benefits, the exclusion of state and local bond interest, education credits, and the deduction for student loan interest. Revenue estimates include micro-dynamic responses, but distributional estimates are static. Because the proposal on balance reduces marginal tax rates and therefore has positive revenue feedback, aggregate tax burdens decline with revenue held constant. *Source:* Urban-Brookings Tax Policy Center Microsimulation Model (version 0515-2).

Table 5.4b Revenue neutral repeal of selected tax expenditures except charitable deduction: Change in average tax rates, calendar year 2016

Income Group	*Reduce All Marginal Tax Rates by 20.6% (%)*	*Reduce All Marginal Tax Rates by 4.28% of Income (%)*	*Reduce All Marginal Rates 25% and Above to 21.1% (%)*
Lowest quintile	0.38	0.20	0.55
Second quintile	0.74	0.24	1.44
Middle quintile	0.84	0.16	2.13
Fourth quintile	0.47	−0.13	2.03
80–90 percentiles	0.37	0.10	1.79
90–95 percentiles	−0.23	−0.15	0.71
95–99 percentiles	−1.43	−0.66	−2.19
Top 1%	−2.90	−0.90	−7.88
All	−0.34	−0.21	−0.42

Note: Proposal repeals all itemized deductions except the deduction for charitable contribution and also repeals the exclusion for employer-sponsored health benefits, the exclusion of state and local bond interest, education credits, and the deduction for student loan interest. Revenue estimates include micro-dynamic responses, but distributional estimates are static. Because the proposal on balance reduces marginal tax rates and therefore has positive revenue feedback, aggregate tax burdens decline with revenue held constant. *Source:* Urban-Brookings Tax Policy Center Microsimulation Model (version 0515-2).

Table 5.4c Revenue neutral repeal of AMT, the limitation on itemized deductions and selected tax expenditures except charitable and mortgage interest deductions: Change in average tax rates, calendar year 2016

Income Group	*Reduce All Marginal Tax Rates by 18.3% (%)*	*Reduce All Marginal Tax Rates by 3.79% of Income (%)*	*Reduce All Marginal Rates 25% and Above to 22.1% (%)*
Lowest quintile	0.39	0.24	0.54
Second quintile	0.78	0.34	1.40
Middle quintile	0.85	0.25	2.00
Fourth quintile	0.39	−0.14	1.81
80–90 percentiles	0.25	0.00	1.65
90–95 percentiles	−0.32	−0.26	0.73
95–99 percentiles	−1.48	−0.84	−2.00
Top 1%	−2.56	−0.79	−7.40
All	−0.33	−0.22	−0.40

Note: Proposal repeals all itemized deductions except the deductions for charitable contributions and mortgage interest and also repeals the exclusion for employer-sponsored health benefits, the exclusion of state and local bond interest, education credits, and the deduction for student loan interest. Revenue estimates include micro-dynamic responses, but distributional estimates are static. Because the proposal on balance reduces marginal tax rates and therefore has positive revenue feedback, aggregate tax burdens decline with revenue held constant. *Source:* Urban-Brookings Tax Policy Center Microsimulation Model (version 0515-2).

5.4.4 Distributional Effects of Alternative Ways of Limiting Tax Expenditures, Combined with a Constant Percentage Cut in Marginal Tax Rates

We now turn to a comparison of the distributional effects of different ways of limiting tax expenditures. This comparison is most meaningful if we compare options with the same effects on federal receipts.

First, however, we show the distributional effects of replacing the AMT and the limitation on itemized deductions with two ways of limiting tax expenditures—the Obama approach of limiting the benefit per dollar of exemption or deduction and the Feldstein et al. approach of limiting the tax saving to a fixed percentage of AGI. The Obama approach with a 28% limit and the tax expenditures we select for inclusion loses revenue and reduces tax burdens on average (table 5.5), while the Feldstein approach with the same tax expenditures limited to 2% of modified adjusted gross income raises revenue.[18] The 28% limit option provides the largest net tax cut as a share

[18] The actual Obama budget proposal raised considerable revenue because it retained the AMT and the limitation on itemized deductions and included some tax expenditures (primarily contributions to qualified retirement saving plans) that are not included in our simulations.

Table 5.5 Distributional effects of alternative limits on tax expenditures repeal AMT and the limitation on itemized deductions; limit benefits of tax expenditures: Change in average tax rates, calendar year 2016

Income Group	*Limit Benefit of Certain Tax Expenditures to 28% Rate*[a] *(%)*	*Limit Benefit of Certain Tax Expenditures to 2% of Modified AGI*[b] *(%)*	*Limit Benefit of Entire Group Except Charitable to 2% of Modified AGI (%)*	*Limit Benefit of All Except Charitable and Mortgage Interest to 2% of Modified AGI (%)*
Lowest quintile	0.00	0.16	0.16	0.15
Second quintile	0.00	0.56	0.55	0.50
Middle quintile	0.00	1.16	1.13	0.98
Fourth quintile	−0.01	1.63	1.55	1.27
80–90 percentiles	−0.05	1.94	1.82	1.43
90–95 percentiles	−0.16	1.91	1.73	1.19
95–99 percentiles	−0.42	1.58	1.24	0.51
Top 1%	−0.09	1.60	0.71	0.49
All	−0.09	1.48	1.23	0.91

Note: Proposal limits the benefits of all itemized deductions except where otherwise noted and also limits tax benefits from the exclusion for employer-sponsored health benefits, the exclusion of state and local bond interest, education credits, and the deduction for student loan interest. Modified AGI is AGI plus employer-sponsored health benefits plus state and local bond interest income. [a] Limits the tax saving from selected deductions and exclusions to 28% of amount deducted or excluded, as described in president's budget for fiscal year 2016; [b] Limits the tax saving from certain tax preferences to 2% of modified AGI, based on proposal by Feldstein, Feenberg, and MacGuineas (2011). *Source:* Urban-Brookings Tax Policy Center Microsimulation Model (version 0515-2).

of income to taxpayers in the 95–99 percentiles because this group benefits much more than others from elimination of the individual AMT and because the 28% limit does not raise their taxes enough to offset that benefit. The constant percentage of AGI limit, in contrast, is generally progressive although the average tax increase is somewhat higher for taxpayers in the 80–95 percentiles of the distribution than for those in the top 5%. Tax burdens at the very top, however, fall substantially if the charitable deduction is not subject to the 2% of AGI limit. And if both charitable and mortgage deductions are excluded from the limit, the tax rate increase is largest for taxpayers in the 80–90 percentiles, with both lower and higher income groups experiencing smaller increases in average tax rates.

If revenue from the 2% of modified AGI limit on tax expenditures were used to reduce marginal tax rates, the net distributional effects depend on how rates are cut (table 5.6a). With all selected tax expenditures subject to the limit, using the revenue to reduce marginal tax rates across the board by 12.8% (setting the maximum rate at 34.5% instead of

Table 5.6a Repeal AMT and the limitation on itemized deductions; limit benefits of selected tax expenditures to 2% of modified AGI with alternative revenue offsets: Change in average tax rates, calendar year 2016

Income Group	*No Offset (%)*	*Reduce All Individual Income Tax Rates by 12.8% (%)*	*Reduce All Individual Income Tax Rates by 2.7 Percentage Points (%)*	*Reduce 25% and Higher Individual Rates to 24.8% (%)*
Lowest quintile	0.16	0.06	−0.05	0.16
Second quintile	0.56	0.13	−0.19	0.56
Middle quintile	1.16	0.25	−0.19	1.15
Fourth quintile	1.63	0.30	−0.10	1.57
80–90 percentiles	1.94	0.27	0.06	1.76
90–95 percentiles	1.91	−0.04	−0.03	1.30
95–99 percentiles	1.58	−0.87	−0.42	−1.06
Top 1%	1.60	−1.45	−0.18	−6.23
All	1.48	−0.21	−0.07	−0.27

Note: Limits the tax saving from certain tax preferences to 2% of modified AGI. Tax preferences subject to limit are all itemized deductions, exclusions for employer-sponsored health benefits and exclusion of state and local bond interest, education credits, and the deduction for student loan interest. Modified AGI is AGI plus employer-sponsored health benefits and state and local bond interest income. Revenue estimates include micro-dynamic responses, but distributional estimates are static. Because revenue-neutral variants of the proposal on balance reduce marginal tax rates and therefore have positive revenue feedback, aggregate tax burdens decline with revenue held constant. *Source:* Urban-Brookings Tax Policy Center Microsimulation Model (version 0515-2).

39.6% and the bottom rate at 8.7% instead of 10%) results in a net tax increase for groups in the bottom 90% of the distribution and a net tax cut for groups in the top 10%, with the biggest tax rate cut going to the top 1% (1.45% of income). If the revenue is used to reduce marginal tax rates by 2.7 percentage points (lowering the top rate from 39.6 to 36.9% and the bottom rate from 10% to 7.3%), taxpayers in the bottom four quintiles and the top 10% are net winners, with only tax units in the 80–90 percentiles seeing a very small tax increase. All groups see a tax change of no more than 0.4% of income. Finally, if the revenue is used to reduce all rates that are currently 25% or higher to a maximum rate of 24.8% (with no changes in the lower brackets), then only taxpayers in the top 5% see tax cuts, with the top 1% receiving an average cut in tax burdens of 6.2% of income. Retaining the charitable and mortgage interest deductions does not change the pattern of winners and losers for the scenarios where the revenue is used to cut marginal rates across the board or only reduce the top rate (tables 5.6b and 5.6c), but does change the pattern when marginal rates are reduced by a constant number of percentage points. In that scenario, average tax rates increase in the middle of the distribution, but decline more for the top 5% than when all the selected tax expenditures are included in the limitation.

Table 5.6b Repeal AMT and the limitation on itemized deductions; limit benefits of selected tax expenditures excluding the charitable deduction to 2% of modified AGI with alternative revenue offsets: Change in average tax rates, calendar year 2016

Income Group	*No Offset (%)*	*Reduce All Individual Income Tax Rates by 10.9% (%)*	*Reduce All Individual Income Tax Rates by 2.2 Percentage Points (%)*	*Reduce 28% and Higher Individual Rates to 25.9% (%)*
Lowest quintile	0.16	0.07	−0.02	0.16
Second quintile	0.55	0.18	−0.08	0.55
Middle quintile	1.13	0.35	0.01	1.13
Fourth quintile	1.55	0.42	0.12	1.53
80–90 percentiles	1.82	0.39	0.26	1.74
90–95 percentiles	1.73	0.07	0.12	1.36
95–99 percentiles	1.24	−0.83	−0.41	−0.86
Top 1%	0.71	−1.79	−0.71	−6.12
All	1.23	−0.19	−0.10	−0.23

Note: Limits the tax saving from certain tax preferences to 2% of modified AGI. Tax preferences subject to limit are all itemized deductions except the deductions for charitable contributions and home mortgage interest, exclusions for employer-sponsored health benefits and exclusion of state and local bond interest, education credits, and the deduction for student loan interest. Modified AGI equals AGI plus employer-sponsored health benefits and state and local interest income. Revenue estimates include micro-dynamic responses, but distributional estimates are static. Because revenue-neutral variants of the proposal on balance reduce marginal tax rates and therefore have positive revenue feedback, aggregate tax burdens decline with revenue held constant. *Source:* Urban-Brookings Tax Policy Center Microsimulation Model (version 0515-2).

To compare the 2% of AGI limit with alternative ways of limiting tax expenditures, we set the parameters of the other tax expenditure limitation approaches so that all three methods would be revenue neutral if combined with elimination of the AMT and the limitation on itemized deductions and a 12.8% across the board cut in marginal tax rates (table 5.7). We substitute a surtax on AGI for high income taxpayers for the Obama limit on the rate at which tax expenditures can be claimed. The base of the surtax is modified AGI, as defined earlier, but excluding long-term capital gains and qualified dividends. The surtax proposal, similar to the other limitations, does not change the marginal tax rate on long-term capital gains and dividends because the rate cuts that the tax expenditure limits finance apply only to ordinary income, not to the preferential rates on gains and dividends.[19]

[19] All the revenue-neutral tax expenditure limitation proposals, however, indirectly reduce the tax expenditure for capital gains and dividends. By reducing marginal tax rates on ordinary income only, they reduce the differential between the rates on ordinary income and the rates on tax-preferred gains and dividends.

Table 5.6c Repeal AMT and the limitation on itemized deductions; limit benefits of selected tax expenditures excluding the charitable and mortgage interest deductions to 2% of modified AGI with alternative revenue offsets: Change in average tax rates, calendar year 2016

Income Group	*No Offset (%)*	*Reduce All Individual Income Tax Rates by 8.4% (%)*	*Reduce All Individual Income Tax Rates by 1.7 Percentage Points (%)*	*Reduce 28% and Higher Individual Rates to 27.9% (%)*
Lowest quintile	0.15	0.08	0.02	0.15
Second quintile	0.50	0.22	0.02	0.50
Middle quintile	0.98	0.39	0.12	0.98
Fourth quintile	1.27	0.41	0.17	1.27
80–90 percentiles	1.43	0.34	0.23	1.42
90–95 percentiles	1.19	−0.06	−0.03	1.14
95–99 percentiles	0.51	−1.04	−0.74	−0.70
Top 1%	0.49	−1.42	−0.61	−5.16
All	0.91	−0.17	−0.11	−0.20

Note: Limits the tax saving from certain tax preferences to 2% of modified AGI. Tax preferences subject to the limit are all itemized deductions except the deduction for charitable contributions, exclusions for employer-sponsored health benefits and exclusion of state and local bond interest, education credits, and the deduction for student loan interest. Modified AGI is AGI plus employer-sponsored health benefits and the exclusion of state and local bond interest. Revenue estimates include micro-dynamic responses, but distributional estimates are static. Because revenue-neutral variants of the proposal on balance reduce marginal tax rates and therefore have positive revenue feedback, aggregate tax burdens decline with revenue held constant. *Source:* Urban-Brookings Tax Policy Center Microsimulation Model (version 0515-2).

Among the three approaches, not surprisingly the most progressive one is the surtax on modified AGI. An 11.4% surtax on modified AGI in excess of the income for the current law 33% rate bracket, combined with a 12.8% cut in marginal tax rates, would raise taxes on average by 2.8% of income for taxpayers in the top 1% of the income distribution, while cutting tax rates for all groups below the top 5%. The least progressive is the percentage of AGI limit; it would reduce tax rates by 1.5% for the top 1%, while raising tax rates for all groups in the bottom 90% of the distribution. The cap on tax expenditures falls in between, it would reduce tax rates slightly in the bottom four quintiles, increase them by an even smaller percentage of income in the 80–95 percentiles and cut the average tax rate the most (but even then by less than 0.6% of income) for taxpayers in the 95–99 percentiles. This relatively large (though still modest) tax cut reflects the benefit taxpayers in the 95–99 percentiles receive from elimination of the individual AMT.

Table 5.7 Comparison of alternative revenue-neutral ways of limiting tax expenditures repeal AMT and the limitation on itemized deductions, limit tax expenditures, and reduce all marginal individual income tax rates by 12.8%: Change in average tax rates, calendar year 2016

Income Group	*Limit Benefit of Certain Tax Expenditures to 2% of Modified AGI*[a] *(%)*	*Cap Certain Tax Expenditures at $16,300*[b] *(%)*	*Impose 11.4% Surtax on Modified AGI Excluding Capital Gains and Dividends*[c] *(%)*
Lowest quintile	0.06	−0.07	−0.07
Second quintile	0.13	−0.29	−0.33
Middle quintile	0.25	−0.36	−0.68
Fourth quintile	0.30	−0.16	−1.03
80–90 percentiles	0.27	0.09	−1.34
90–95 percentiles	−0.04	0.01	−1.49
95–99 percentiles	−0.87	−0.55	0.14
Top 1%	−1.45	−0.26	2.82
All	−0.21	0.01	−0.18

Note: Tax preferences subject to the limit are all itemized deductions, exclusions for employer-sponsored health benefits and state and local bond interest, education credits, and the deduction for student loan interest. [a] Limit tax saving from selected tax preferences to 2% of AGI plus employer-sponsored health benefits and state and local bond interest; [b] Limit the sum of the dollar amounts of itemized deductions and selected exclusions to $16,300; [c] Impose a 11.4% surtax on adjusted gross income plus employer-sponsored health benefits and state and local bond interest, excluding long-term capital gains and qualified dividends. The tax only applies to income in excess of the threshold for the 33% rate under current law. *Source:* Urban-Brookings Tax Policy Center Microsimulation Model (version 0515-2).

5.4.5 Effects of Alternative Ways of Limiting Tax Expenditures on Marginal Tax Rates on Income and on the Incentive for Charitable Contributions

The three ways of limiting tax expenditures also have different effects on incentives to work, save, realize capital gains, and engage in activities eligible for deductions and exemptions (table 5.8). We represent the latter as the effect on the incentive for charitable contributions because it is much easier for taxpayers to change their charitable deductions in the short run in response to altered incentives than it is for them to change their state of residence (and thus their net expenses for state and local taxes) or the size of house they live in (and thus their net mortgage expenses).

The percentage of AGI limit and the dollar cap on deductions and exclusions have little effect on the incentive to realize capital gains, lowering the marginal rate on gains slightly (table 5.8a). The main source of change is the elimination of the limitation on

Table 5.8a Effective marginal tax rates on long-term capital gains under current law and alternative revenue-tax expenditure limits combined with 12.8% cut in all marginal income tax rates, calendar year 2016

Income Group	*Current Law (%)*	*Limit Benefit of Certain Tax Expenditures to 2% of Modified AGI[a] (%)*	*Impose Cap of $16,300 on Certain Tax Expenditures[b] (%)*	*Impose 11.4% High Income Surtax on Modified AGI Excluding Capital Gains and Dividends[c] (%)*
Lowest quintile	0.8	0.7	0.7	0.7
Second quintile	1.3	1.2	1.0	1.0
Middle quintile	6.0	7.4	6.5	5.7
Fourth quintile	9.5	10.3	10.2	9.2
80–90 percentiles	12.1	12.4	13.2	11.8
90–95 percentiles	13.4	12.1	12.9	12.5
95–99 percentiles	19.3	16.2	17.1	16.7
Top 1%	23.9	22.4	23.5	23.4
All	20.6	19.3	20.3	20.0

Note: Tax preferences subject to the limit are all itemized deductions, exclusions for employer-sponsored health benefits and state and local bond interest, education credits, and the deduction for student loan interest. [a] Limit the tax saving from selected tax preferences to 2% of AGI plus employer-sponsored health benefits and state and local bond interest; [b] Limit the sum of the dollar amounts of itemized deductions and selected exclusions to $16,300; [c] Impose a 11.4% surtax on AGI plus employer-sponsored health benefits and state and local bond interest, excluding long-term capital gains and qualified dividends. The tax only applies to income in excess of the threshold for the 33% rate under current law. *Source:* Urban-Brookings Tax Policy Center Microsimulation Model (version 0515-2).

itemized deductions and the individual AMT, which reduces the marginal tax rate on gains for many higher-income taxpayers. The effects of the three limitations on the marginal tax rate on dividends are similar to the effects on marginal tax rates on gains (table 5.8b).

The 2% of AGI limit and the cap on tax deductions and exclusions reduce the marginal tax rate on interest income, when combined with elimination of the AMT and the limitation on itemized deductions and cut in marginal income tax rates (table 5.8c). The option with the 11.4% of AGI surtax also reduces the marginal tax rate on interest income for the bottom 95% of the income distribution, but raises it for the top 5%. Because of the concentration of taxable interest income at the top of the distribution, the overall marginal tax rate on interest income increases with the surtax proposal.

Marginal income tax rates on wages also decline for the revenue-neutral changes that impose a percentage of AGI limit on tax expenditures or a fixed dollar limit on

Table 5.8b Effective marginal tax rates on qualified dividends under current law and alternative revenue-neutral tax expenditure limits combined with 12.8% cut in all marginal income tax rates, calendar year 2016

Income Group	*Current Law (%)*	*Limit Benefit of Certain Tax Expenditures to 2% of Modified AGI[a] (%)*	*Impose Cap of $16,300 on Certain Tax Expenditures[b] (%)*	*Impose 11.4 Percent High Income Surtax on Modified AGI Less Capital Gains and Dividends[c] (%)*
Lowest quintile	0.3	0.3	0.3	0.3
Second quintile	0.9	0.8	0.8	0.8
Middle quintile	6.6	7.6	6.9	6.3
Fourth quintile	10.8	11.4	11.4	10.6
80–90 percentiles	14.1	14.0	15.0	13.7
90–95 percentiles	16.1	14.4	15.4	15.0
95–99 percentiles	22.3	18.1	19.4	18.2
Top 1%	24.0	22.1	23.6	23.2
All	18.7	17.2	18.3	17.7

Note: Tax preferences subject to the limit are all itemized deductions, exclusions for employer-sponsored health benefits and state and local bond interest, education credits, and the deduction for student loan interest. [a] Limit the tax saving from selected tax preferences to 2% of AGI plus employer-sponsored health benefits and state and local bond interest. [b] Limit the sum of the dollar amounts of itemized deductions and selected exclusions to $16,300; [c] Impose a 11.4% surtax on AGI plus employer-sponsored health benefits and state and local bond interest, excluding long-term capital gains and qualified dividends. The tax only applies to income in excess of the threshold for the 33% rate under current law. *Source:* Urban-Brookings Tax Policy Center Microsimulation Model (version 0515-2).

deductions and exclusions (table 5.8d). They increase at the top of the distribution for the high-income AGI surtax, but the average marginal tax on wages for all taxpayers is slightly reduced compared with current law.

The various limits differ in how they affect the incentives to participate in tax-subsidized activities. Removing incentives that distort taxpayer choices increase economic efficiency and therefore may be one reason policymakers may want to limit tax expenditures. Policymakers may, however, instead want to reduce the incentives without removing them entirely in order to mute political opposition by groups that benefit from taxpayer or voter responses to federal subsidies, such as charities, home builders, or states and localities.

Assuming that charitable contributions are most responsive in the short run to changes in tax incentives, we simulate how the various limitations affect the tax incentive to contribute to charities (tables 5.8e and 5.8f). We define the tax price of giving as one minus marginal rate at which contributions can be deducted. A taxpayer

Table 5.8c Effective marginal tax rates on interest income under current law and alternative revenue-neutral tax expenditure limits combined with 12.8% cut in all marginal income tax rates, calendar year 2016

Income Group	*Current Law (%)*	*Limit Benefit of Certain Tax Expenditures to 2% of Modified AGI[a] (%)*	*Impose Cap of $16,300 on Certain Tax Expenditures[b] (%)*	*Impose 11.4% High Income Surtax on Modified AGI Excluding Capital Gains and Dividends[c] (%)*
Lowest quintile	2.0	2.2	1.8	1.8
Second quintile	5.6	6.2	5.3	5.0
Middle quintile	17.1	16.2	15.8	14.9
Fourth quintile	21.6	20.6	20.4	18.9
80–90 percentiles	25.0	22.1	22.9	21.4
90–95 percentiles	28.1	23.9	24.3	25.7
95–99 percentiles	35.0	31.0	32.1	37.9
Top 1%	37.3	34.8	36.5	42.3
All	26.9	24.9	25.7	28.1

Note: Tax preferences subject to the limit are all itemized deductions, exclusions for employer-sponsored health benefits and state and local bond interest, education credits, and the deduction for student loan interest. [a] Limit the tax saving from selected tax preferences to 2% of AGI plus employer-sponsored health benefits and state and local bond interest; [b] Limit the sum of the dollar amounts of itemized deductions and selected exclusions to $16,300; [c] Impose a 11.4% surtax on AGI plus employer-sponsored health benefits and state and local bond interest, excluding long-term capital gains and qualified dividends. The tax only applies to income in excess of the threshold for the 33% rate under current law. *Source:* Urban-Brookings Tax Policy Center Microsimulation Model (version 0515-2).

in the 28% bracket who itemizes faces a tax price of 72 cents of per dollar of additional contribution amounts because every dollar of giving reduces her tax liability by 28 cents.

The simulated results depend on whether we are examining the incentive to give an extra dollar above what is contributed under current law (the last dollar marginal rate, shown in table 5.8e) or the incentive to give the first dollar, assuming all other deductions and exemptions are unchanged (the first dollar marginal rate, shown in table 5.8f). The former governs the incentive to increase or reduce giving from current levels (i.e., the intensive margin), whereas the latter is more relevant to the incentive to make any donations (i.e., the extensive margin).

Under current law, the average last dollar marginal price of giving is 79 cents, with tax returns weighted by their amount of contributions. The price of giving is almost a dollar in the lowest quintile where very few taxpayers itemize, falling to 68 cents for the top 1%.

Table 5.8d Effective marginal income tax rates on wages under current law and alternative revenue-neutral tax expenditure limits combined with 12.8% cut in all marginal income tax rates, calendar year 2016

Income Group	*Current Law (%)*	*Limit Benefit of Certain Tax Expenditures to 2% of Modified AGI[a] (%)*	*Impose Cap of $16,300 on Certain Tax Expenditures[b] (%)*	*Impose 11.4% High Income Surtax on Modified AGI Excluding Capital Gains and Dividends[c] (%)*
Lowest quintile	1.6	1.7	1.0	1.0
Second quintile	15.5	14.8	14.2	14.1
Middle quintile	19.0	17.8	17.4	16.9
Fourth quintile	19.8	18.1	18.1	17.3
80–90 percentiles	25.4	22.1	23.1	22.3
90–95 percentiles	27.2	23.3	23.9	25.3
95–99 percentiles	33.1	28.5	29.5	38.4
Top 1%	38.9	32.3	33.9	45.0
All	24.4	21.4	21.9	24.2

Note: Tax preferences subject to the limit are all itemized deductions, exclusions for employer-sponsored health benefits and state and local bond interest, education credits, and the deduction for student loan interest. [a] Limit the tax saving from selected tax preferences to 2% of AGI plus employer-sponsored health benefits and state and local bond interest; [b] Limit the sum of the dollar amounts of itemized deductions and selected exclusions to $16,300; [c] Impose a 11.4% surtax on AGI plus employer-sponsored health benefits and state and local bond interest, excluding long-term capital gains and qualified dividends. The tax only applies to income in excess of the threshold for the 33% rate under current law. *Source:* Urban-Brookings Tax Policy Center Microsimulation Model (version 0515-2).

The 2% of AGI limit and dollar cap on tax expenditures both virtually eliminate the tax incentive to give an additional dollar to charity for all income groups. The tax price ranges from 0.98 to 1.00. This occurs because the large givers who have high weights in the calculation almost all make contributions in excess of the limitations and so get no deduction for additional contributions. The high-income surtax option also raises the tax pricing of giving by reducing ordinary marginal income rates, but the increase is relatively modest, rising on average for all taxpayers from 0.79 to 0.82.

The results for the percentage of AGI limitation differ somewhat when one looks at the incentives to give the first dollar to charity. The tax price still increases substantially but a 10% subsidy remains in place for the highest income taxpayers. This occurs because, as AGI increases, the limit of the benefit from tax expenditures also increases, so that some very high-income taxpayers remain below the limitation on their first

Table 5.8e Tax price of last dollar of charitable giving under current law and alternative revenue-neutral tax expenditure limits combined with 12.8% cut in all marginal income tax rates, calendar year 2016

Income Group	*Current Law*	*Limit Benefit of Certain Tax Expenditures to 2% of Modified AGI*[a]	*Impose Cap of $16,300 on Certain Tax Expenditures*[b]	*Impose 11.4% High Income Surtax on Modified AGI Less Capital Gains and Dividends*[c]
Lowest quintile	0.99	1.00	0.99	0.99
Second quintile	0.96	1.00	0.98	0.97
Middle quintile	0.92	1.00	0.98	0.93
Fourth quintile	0.88	1.00	0.99	0.89
80–90 percentiles	0.81	1.00	1.00	0.84
90–95 percentiles	0.77	1.0-	1.00	0.80
95–99 percentiles	0.70	0.99	1.00	0.75
Top 1%	0.68	0.99	1.00	0.71
All	0.79	1.00	0.99	0.82

Note: Tax price of giving an extra dollar to charitable organizations above current law contribution levels, which equals one minus the marginal tax rate at which contributions can be deducted. [a] Limit the tax saving from selected tax preferences to 2% of AGI plus employer-sponsored health benefits and state and local bond interest; [b] Limit the sum of the dollar amounts of itemized deductions and selected exclusions to $16,300; [c] Impose a 11.4% surtax on AGI plus employer-sponsored health benefits and state and local bond interest, excluding long-term capital gains and qualified dividends. The tax only applies to income in excess of the threshold for the 33% rate under current law. *Source:* Urban-Brookings Tax Policy Center Microsimulation Model (version 0515-2).

dollar of charitable contributions. The absolute dollar cap, however, still eliminates the incentive to give for most taxpayers because high-income taxpayers almost all have tax expenditures other than charity above the absolute dollar limit on tax deductions and exclusions.

These calculations of incentive effects are only illustrative. The calculations take account of factors other than statutory rates that help determine effective marginal rates, such as phase-outs of certain preferences among income limits and the phase-out of the taxpayer exemption and first-rate bracket under the individual AMT. They do not, however, account for the beneficial effect on incentives to work and save that those tax incentives provide by lowering the cost of the increased amounts of tax-favored goods and services (such as more housing services) that taxpayers would consume with additional labor or capital income. They therefore fail to account for the disincentive to work and save produced by eliminating tax incentives for goods whose consumption rises with income.

Table 5.8f Tax price of first dollar of charitable giving under current law and alternative revenue-neutral tax expenditure limits combined with 12.8% cut in all marginal income tax rates, calendar year 2016

Income Group	*Current Law*	*Limit Benefit of Certain Tax Expenditures to 2% of Modified AGI*[a]	*Impose Cap of $16,300 on Certain Tax Expenditures*[b]	*Impose 11.4% High Income Surtax on Modified AGI Excluding Capital Gains and Dividends*[c]
Lowest quintile	0.99	1.00	0.99	0.99
Second quintile	0.96	1.00	0.98	0.98
Middle quintile	0.92	1.00	0.98	0.96
Fourth quintile	0.88	1.00	0.99	0.93
80–90 percentiles	0.81	1.00	0.99	0.88
90–95 percentiles	0.77	0.99	1.00	0.83
95–99 percentiles	0.70	0.99	1.00	0.76
Top 1%	0.68	0.90	1.00	0.69
All	0.79	0.97	0.99	0.84

Note: Tax price of giving the first dollar to charitable organizations at current law levels of other itemized deductions, which equals one minus the marginal tax rate at which contributions can be deducted. [a] Limit the tax saving from selected tax preferences to 2% of AGI plus employer-sponsored health benefits and state and local bond interest; [b] Limit the sum of the dollar amounts of itemized deductions and selected exclusions to $16,300; [c] Impose an 11.4% surtax on AGI plus employer-sponsored health benefits and state and local bond interest, excluding long-term capital gains and qualified dividends. The tax only applies to income in excess of the threshold for the 33% rate under current law. *Source:* Urban-Brookings Tax Policy Center Microsimulation Model (version 0515-2).

5.5 CONCLUSIONS

Tax expenditures have been growing over time. All told, they add up to about $1.4 trillion or about 7.5% of GDP in 2016.

They represent a tempting target for tax reform. Many tax expenditures are poorly targeted, providing the largest benefits to high-income households. Sometimes, taxpayers may not even understand how the subsidies work, undermining their effectiveness. Many complicate the tax code and create a suspicion among taxpayers that they aren't getting their fair share of benefits, which may undermine voluntary compliance. They create opportunities for inefficient tax avoidance as taxpayers try to find creative ways use the tax preferences for unintended purposes. And, like direct spending programs, they require tax rates to be higher than they would otherwise be, which exacerbates the efficiency cost of taxation.

Tax expenditures, however, benefit many taxpayers and have the support of influential interest groups. Thus, policymakers and tax experts have looked to indirect ways to limit them as a group without singling out specific provisions. President Barack Obama has repeatedly proposed to limit the value of itemized deductions to 28%. Harvard economist Martin Feldstein and coauthors have proposed to limit the value of selected tax expenditures to 2% of adjusted gross income; 2012 presidential candidate Mitt Romney tweaked this proposal by suggesting a fixed dollar limit. Former House Ways and Means Committee Chairman Dave Camp (R-MI) proposed an innovative alternative to President Obama's limitation by combining rate reduction with a surtax on high-income taxpayers, which would also apply to certain income items that would otherwise be excluded from tax. The result is that the tax benefit per dollar of most exclusions, exemptions, and deductions would be limited to the highest tax rate excluding the surtax.

We find that repealing major individual income tax expenditures would raise substantial revenue—$282 to $366 billion in 2016 depending on the provisions. The 2% of AGI limit would raise on the order of half as much—$128 to $205 billion.

We examine the distribution of tax burdens under different assumptions about how the revenue from limiting tax expenditures would be returned to individual taxpayers. Among the options we examine, offsetting the limits with equal percentage point cuts in marginal tax rates would leave the distribution of tax burdens roughly unchanged. In contrast, offsetting them with equal percentage cuts in rates or by reducing the top rate or rates only would make the tax system generally less progressive. All the options are less progressive when the limitations exclude the deductions for charitable contributions and home mortgage interest.

We also examine the effects of three alternative methods of limiting tax expenditures, combined with an equal across the board percentage rate cut that keeps federal tax receipts constant. Among the three methods, we examine, the surtax approach has the most progressive distribution of the tax burden and the fixed percentage of AGI approach the least progressive, with the fixed dollar cap falling in between.

We conclude by looking at how revenue-neutral tax expenditure limits would affect marginal tax rates and incentives to realize capital gains, work, or donate to charity. We find that most of the limitations, if accompanied by reduced statutory marginal tax rates, would lower marginal effective tax rates on capital gains, dividends, interest, and wages. The high-income surtax approach, which indirectly caps the benefit of tax expenditures, would raise marginal tax rates on interest and wage income for upper-income taxpayers, who are the ones affected by the surtax.

We also examine the effect of limitations on incentives to donate to charity. We find that the high-income surtax reduces but does not eliminate the incentive to donate to charity as compared with current law because it lowers the marginal rate on deductible contributions without imposing a ceiling on them. The percentage of AGI caps or fixed dollar limitations, however, would eliminate the tax incentive to make additional donations to charity and sharply increase the first-dollar tax price for most filers. The exception is that the 2% of AGI limit retains a first-dollar incentive to donate for very high-income households because, absent charitable contributions, their tax savings from itemized deductions are often less than 2% of the expanded AGI measure we use in our policy options.

Overall we find that the effects of tax expenditure limits are very sensitive to what limitation method is used, what tax expenditures are subject to the limitation, and how the revenues they generate are returned to taxpayers. Tax expenditure limitations combined with rate reductions can be designed that make the tax system more progressive, reduce marginal tax rates on work and saving, and maintain some support for the activities the tax expenditures intend to promote. Not all options, however, would have these desired effects.

References

Batchelder, Lily L., Fred T. Goldberg, Jr., and Peter R. Orszag. 2006. "Efficiency and Tax Incentives: The Case for Refundable Tax Credits." *Stanford Law Review* 59 (1): 23–76.

Bipartisan Policy Center. 2010. "Restoring America's Future." http://bipartisanpolicy.org/sites/default/files/BPC%20FINAL%20REPORT%20FOR%20PRINTER%2002%2028%2011.pdf

Birnbaum, Jeffrey H., and Alan S. Murray. 1987. *Showdown at Gucci Gulch*. New York: Random House.

Bradford, David F. 2003. "Reforming Budgetary Language." In *Public Finance and Public Policy in the New Century*, edited by Sijbren Cnossen and Hans-Werner Sinn, 93–116. Cambridge, MA: MIT Press.

Buckley, John L. 2011. "Tax Expenditure Reform: Some Common Misconceptions." *Tax Notes*. July 19.

Burman, Leonard E. 2013. "Pathways to Tax Reform Revisited." *Public Finance Review* 41 (6): 755–90.

Burman, Leonard E., William G. Gale, and Jeffrey Rohaly. 2003. "Policy Watch: The Expanding Reach of the Individual Alternative Minimum Tax." *Journal of Economic Perspectives* 17 (2): 173–86.

Burman, Leonard E., William G. Gale, John Iselin, Jim Nunns, Jeff Rohaly, Joseph Rosenberg, and Roberton Williams. 2015. "An Analysis of Governor Bush's Tax Plan." http://www.taxpolicycenter.org/UploadedPDF/2000547-analysis-of-bush-tax-plan.pdf

Burman, Leonard E., and Marvin Phaup. 2012. "Tax Expenditures, the Size and Efficiency of Government, and Implications for Budget Reform." In *Tax Policy and the Economy*, vol. 26, edited by Jeffrey Brown, 93–124. Chicago: University of Chicago Press.

Committee on Ways and Means. 2014. "Tax Reform Act of 2014: Discussion Draft." February 26. http://waysandmeans.house.gov/UploadedFiles/Ways_and_Means_Section_by_Section_Summary_FINAL_022614.pdf

Congressional Budget Office. 2011. "Reducing the Deficit: Spending and Revenue Options." Washington, DC: Government Printing Office. http://www.cbo.gov/sites/default/files/cbofiles/ftpdocs/120xx/doc12085/03-10-reducingthedeficit.pdf

Ebeling, Ashlea. 2010. "IRS Okays Big Tax Break for Luxury Homeowners." Forbes.com, October 22. http://www.forbes.com/sites/ashleaebeling/2010/10/22/irs-okays-big-tax-break-for-luxury-homeowners/

Faricy, Christopher, and Christopher Ellis. 2013. "Public Attitudes toward Social Spending in the United States: The Differences between Direct Spending and Tax Expenditures." *Political Behavior* 2013 (1): 1–24.

Feldstein, Martin, Daniel Feenberg, and Maya MacGuineas. 2011. "Capping Individual Tax Expenditure Benefits." National Bureau of Economic Research Working Paper No. 16921. Cambridge, MA. http://www.nber.org/papers/w16921

Galper, Harvey, Joseph Rosenberg, Kim Rueben, and Eric Toder. 2014. "Who Benefits from Tax-Exempt Bonds? An Application of the Theory of Tax Incidence." *Municipal Finance Journal* 35 (2): 53–80.

Gravelle, Jane G., and Donald J. Marples. 2015. "The Effect of Base-Broadening Measures on Labor Supply and Investment: Considerations for Tax Reform." CRS Report R44242. Washington, DC: Congressional Research Service.

Howard, Christopher. 1997. *The Hidden Welfare State: Tax Expenditures and Social Policy in the United States*. Princeton, NJ: Princeton University Press.

Joint Committee on Taxation. 2015. "Estimating Changes in the Federal Individual Income Tax: Description of the Individual Tax Model." https://www.jct.gov/publications.html?func=startdown&id=4776

Marron, Donald. 2011. "How Large Are Tax Expenditures." *Tax Notes*, March 28.

Marron, Donald, and Eric Toder. 2012. "How Big Is the Federal Government?" Research Report. Tax Policy Center. March 26.

Mettler, Suzanne. 2011. *The Submerged State*. Chicago: University of Chicago Press.

National Commission on Fiscal Responsibility and Reform. 2010. "The Moment of Truth." http://www.fiscalcommission.gov/sites/fiscalcommission.gov/files/documents/TheMomentofTruth12_1_2010.pdf

President's Advisory Panel on Federal Tax Reform. 2005. "Simple, Fair, and Pro-Growth: Proposals to Fix America's Tax System." http://www.treasury.gov/resource-center/tax-policy/Documents/Simple-Fair-and-Pro-Growth-Proposals-to-Fix-Americas-Tax-System-11-2005.pdf

President's Economic Recovery Advisory Board. 2010. "The Report on Tax Reform Options: Simplification, Compliance, and Corporate Taxation." http://www.whitehouse.gov/sites/default/files/microsites/PERAB_Tax_Reform_Report_for_final_vote.pdf

Saez, Emmanuel, Joel Slemrod, and Seth H. Giertz. 2012. "The Elasticity of Taxable Income with Respect to Marginal Tax Rates: A Critical Review." *Journal of Economic Literature* 50 (1): 3–50.

Surrey, Stanley S. 1973. *Pathways to Tax Reform: The Concept of Tax Expenditures*. Cambridge, MA: Harvard University Press.

Surrey, Stanley S., and Paul McDaniel. 1985. *Tax Expenditures*. Cambridge, MA: Harvard University Press.

US Treasury. 2015. "Tax Expenditures, FY 2017." Update. November. https://www.treasury.gov/resource-center/tax-policy/Documents/Tax-Expenditures-FY2017-11132015.pdf

US Treasury. 2016. "General Explanations of the Administration's Fiscal Year 2017 Revenue Proposals." https://www.treasury.gov/resource-center/tax-policy/Documents/General-Explanations-FY2017.pdf

Wyden, Ron, and Dan Coats. 2011. "Bipartisan Tax Fairness and Simplification Act of 2011." http://www.gpo.gov/fdsys/pkg/BILLS-112s727is/pdf/BILLS-112s727is.pdf. Summary is at http://www.wyden.senate.gov/imo/media/doc/Wyden-Coats%20Two%20Pager%20FINAL1.pdf

APPENDIX: ESTIMATING ECONOMIC INCIDENCE, REVENUE, AND MARGINAL TAX RATES IN THE TAX POLICY CENTER MODEL

We used the Urban-Brookings Tax Policy Center's (TPC) large-scale microsimulation model to estimate revenue, distributional, and marginal tax rates of the various policy options. The model is similar to those used by the Congressional Budget Office (CBO), the Joint Committee on Taxation (JCT), and the Treasury's Office of Tax Analysis (OTA). It is based on the large public use file of individual income tax returns produced by the IRS augmented by statistically matched data from the Current Population Survey (CPS) of the U.S. Bureau of the Census and other sources.

5A.1 INCIDENCE OF INDIVIDUAL INCOME AND PAYROLL TAXES

Here are the relevant incidence assumptions as well as a brief description of the income classifier we use.

5A.1.1 Individual Income Taxes

TPC allocates the burden of changes in individual income taxes to individual income taxpayers in proportion to their changes in tax liability. Assuming the incidence of broad changes in income taxes falls on the payers themselves is correct to the extent that the tax changes are broad-based and taxpayers' labor supply and their supply of savings is relatively inelastic, so that taxes on work effort and saving fall mostly on suppliers of these factor inputs. This is the same assumption TPC uses in allocating the burden of payroll taxes to employees, regardless of whether the formal tax liability is placed on employers or employees.

This incidence assumption is not strictly correct in some circumstances, however. To the extent income tax benefits differentiate among taxpayers depending how they earn or spend their income, the incidence can shift among both different groups of income recipients (the sources side effect) and different groups of consumers (the uses side effect). An example is the provision that allows a tax exemption for interest on municipal bonds. Allocating the benefit of this tax exemption to holders of municipal bonds creates two sources of error. First, the measurement of the "sources side" benefit needs to be adjusted because as taxpayers shift their portfolios from taxable to tax-exempt holdings, the pretax return on tax-exempt bonds will fall and the pretax return on taxable bonds will rise. This change in relative pretax yields will shift the benefit from tax-exempt bondholders only to all recipients of capital income. Second, by driving down the cost of tax-exempt financing and raising the cost of taxable financing, the preference will lower the relative price of goods and services supplied by state and local governments and raise the relative price of private sector goods and services. The net effect of this "uses-side" change on different income groups will depend on how states react to their improved fiscal position and on how the distributional effects of higher prices of private goods compares with the distributional benefits households receive from lower state and local taxes or higher state and local public spending.

Galper et al. (2014) find that the exemption continues to primarily benefit higher-income individuals when one takes account of how the exemption affects relatively rates of return because the distribution of capital income is only slightly less tilted to the upper end of the distribution than the income from tax-exempt bonds. They also find that what one assumes about how state and local governments react determines which households benefit from the exemption. High-income households still receive a large share of the benefits, but low-income households may gain also to the extent that public spending increases instead of taxes falling and the benefits from state and local expenditures are distributed progressively.

5A.1.2 Payroll Taxes

In our distribution tables, we assume that the worker bears the burden of both the employer and employee portions of payroll taxes. This premise is widely accepted among economists. CBO, JCT, and Treasury all make the same assumption for their distributional analyses.

5A.1.3 Income Classifier

TPC uses an income concept called "expanded cash income"(ECI), a broad measure of pretax income, to rank tax units in distribution tables and to calculate effective tax rates. We define ECI as adjusted gross income (AGI) plus: above-the-line adjustments (e.g., IRA deductions, student loan interest, self-employed health insurance deduction, etc.), employer-paid health insurance and other nontaxable fringe benefits, employee and employer contributions to tax-deferred retirement savings plans, tax-exempt interest, nontaxable Social Security benefits, nontaxable pension and retirement income, accruals within defined benefit pension plans, inside buildup within defined contribution retirement accounts, cash and cash-like (e.g., SNAP) transfer income, employer's share of payroll taxes, and imputed corporate income tax liability.

5A.2 REVENUE ESTIMATES

TPC incorporates several forms of behavioral responses in its revenue estimates. First, we assume that reported taxable income on individual tax returns responds to changes in the statutory marginal income tax rate. Based on estimates in the academic literature, we generally assume an elasticity of taxable income (with respect to the net of tax rate) equal to 0.25.[20] For proposals that expand the tax base significantly—such as proposals that repeal, or significantly limit, itemized deductions—we adjust the elasticity downward. Second, we assume that sales of capital assets

[20] For a summary of the academic literature, see Saez, Slemrod, and Giertz (2012).

respond to changes in the tax rate on capital gains. For long-term capital gains realizations, our elasticity varies with the tax rate and is approximately −0.7 at a tax rate of 20%. We use a higher elasticity for the first two years after a change in the capital gains rate; the short-term elasticity is approximately −1.1 at a tax rate of 20%. These elasticities match those that Joint Committee on Taxation (JCT) describes in an early publication (Joint Committee on Taxation 2015) outlining its estimating methodology. Although JCT has not published the specific taxable income or capital gains elasticities that it now uses, TPC's behavioral assumptions appear broadly similar to those that JCT currently uses. In the case of certain policy proposals, different behavioral assumptions would be a source of difference between TPC and JCT revenue estimates.

5A.3 ESTIMATING EFFECTIVE MARGINAL TAX RATES (EMTR)

TPC estimates the EMTR on an income source (e.g., wages and salaries) by first calculating the household's individual income tax based on the household's actual income. We then add $1,000 to the income source and recalculate the household's individual income tax liability. We calculate the effective marginal tax rate as the change in tax divided by the $1,000 increase in income. These estimates are static in the sense that we do not allow the higher wages to affect any other form of reported income or deduction. When we calculate the average effective marginal tax rate across income classes, we weight each household's EMTR by the original amount of the income source that the household reported.

ACKNOWLEDGMENTS

Prepared for "The Economics of Tax Policy," Brookings Institution Conference, December 3–4, 2015. We thank Alan Auerbach, Louis Kaplow, and other participants in the conference, for helpful comments. Views expressed are those of the authors and should not be attributed to our funders or the institutions with which we are affiliated. Comments are welcome. Contact lburman@urban.org, etoder@urban.org.

COMMENTARY ON CHAPTER 5

Louis Kaplow

The tax expenditure limitation proposals that Burman, Toder, Berger, and Rohaly (BTBR) examine in chapter 5 are advanced not only because they reduce distortions induced by the relative preference for some types of expenditures over others but also for other reasons: efficiency gains from enabling lower marginal tax rates on account of the broader tax base; improvements in the distribution of income on account of overturning the "upside down" effect of deductions and exclusions; and enhanced revenue.[1] This commentary aims to cast a different light on BTBR and the proposals they analyze by application of modern extensions to the optimal taxation framework that employ a distribution-neutral methodology for assessing tax reforms. (For a more extensive assessment of how this framework applies to tax expenditure limitation proposals, see Kaplow, forthcoming.)

Section 5C.1 states this methodology, which begins with the Mirrlees (1971) optimal taxation model as augmented by Atkinson and Stiglitz (1976) to incorporate commodity taxation. Tax expenditures provide subsidies to different commodities and hence are encompassed by this model. Next is a sketch of the distribution-neutral framework (e.g., Kaplow 2004, 2008).

Section 5C.2 uses this methodology to disentangle the distinctive efficiency consequences due to the reform of tax expenditures from the efficiency, distribution, and revenue consequences of changing overall features of the tax system—changes that can be made independently of whether tax expenditures are reformed. The analysis provides a clearer positive and normative understanding of tax expenditure reform and reveals how a number of commonly held views are misleading. Prominent analysts argue that limiting tax expenditures enables one to enjoy a free lunch: raising revenue without raising tax rates, reducing the distortion due to high marginal tax rates, or generating enhanced progressivity without raising the distortion ordinarily associated with redistributive taxation.[2] Unfortunately, these lunches are not free and, as often served, are not even available at a discount.

[1] For proposals and related analyses, see also Feldstein (2015), Schizer (2015), and Toder, Rosenberg, and Eng (2013).

[2] Consider BTBR: Tax expenditures "require tax rates to be higher than they would otherwise be, which exacerbates the efficiency cost of taxation" (138); "Tax expenditure limitations combined with rate reductions can be designed that make the tax system more progressive [and] reduce marginal tax rates on work and saving. . . ." (140) And Feldstein (2015): "Limiting tax expenditures would

5C.1 FRAMEWORK

5C.1.1 Optimal Income and Commodity Taxation

Mirrlees (1971) launched the modern study of optimal income taxation (which includes transfers to the poor), and his approach has provided the backbone for much subsequent work in public economics that seeks to ground policy analysis in first principles. Atkinson and Stiglitz's (1976) important extension combines the Mirrlees optimal income tax problem with commodity taxation. Note that differential commodity taxation includes the case of relative subsidies (the commodity taxes may be negative, and it includes systems such as a VAT that provides preferential rates or exclusions). Moreover, the notion of "commodities" is understood broadly as encompassing all forms of expenditures and hence, combined with the first point, readily incorporates tax expenditures. Indeed, this application does not extend the commodity tax framework but merely recognizes that tax expenditures are in fact a means of differential commodity taxation.

Atkinson and Stiglitz's central result was that, when individuals' (taken to be common) utility function is weakly separable in labor, then it is optimal to employ uniform commodity taxation. The basic intuition comes from principles of second best analysis. Here, the preexisting distortion is of the labor-leisure choice. Hence, with weak separability—meaning that relative changes in an individual's consumption bundle do not affect labor supply directly—there is nothing to be gained by any distortion of consumption allocations. All that remains is the simple efficiency cost of consumption distortion from any differential commodity taxation.

5C.1.2 Distribution-Neutral Approach

There is a long-standing tradition in public economics of employing a *revenue*-neutral approach when assessing reform proposals (other than those aimed at raising or reducing revenue). In a similar spirit, some work—and much of my own writing over the past two decades—has advanced a complementary, *distribution*-neutral approach. See, for example, Kaplow (1996, 2004, 2006, 2008, 2012). In a nutshell, the distribution-neutral approach combines a reform proposal with an adjustment to the income tax schedule that is designed to be distributively offsetting at all income levels.

When two different studies employ this methodology to evaluate the same reform, any differences in conclusions will correspondingly reflect differences in the assessment of the distinctive features of the core reform, rather than different choices in how to balance the budget. As BTBR amply demonstrate, distributive and distortionary consequences of a given tax expenditure limitation proposal depend on how the revenue is rebated. (The same is true of environmental reforms and many other policies considered in this conference volume.) Even with revenue-neutrality, there is an

raise revenue without increasing marginal tax rates" (1); "The two percent cap would also lower the marginal tax rate of all the affected taxpayers" (5).

infinite variety of ways to balance the budget, with all manner of consequences for distribution and distortion (although, as will be explained, the two are tightly related). Hence, the gains from disentangling the analysis of particular reforms from broader fiscal issues are immense.

Consider some contemplated reform. As stated, distribution-neutral implementation involves adjustment of the income tax schedule so as to offset the reform's distributive effects on utility for all levels of before-tax income. This income tax adjustment has two components. First, it washes out any effects on taxes paid (or transfers received) as a mechanical consequence of the reform. For a tax expenditure limitation, one simply computes how much taxes paid rise at each level of income and adjusts (reduces) income tax rates accordingly. Second, because the income tax adjustment is, in principle, designed to hold individuals' *utility* constant, the full income tax adjustment must also offset any other effects of the core reform on utility. Suppose, for example, that a tax expenditure proposal reduces only inefficient subsidies on certain forms of consumption. In that case, the utility consequence of reducing consumption distortion is to raise utility. Hence, the complete adjustment would involve somewhat higher income tax rates than those described in step one.

Having described what the distribution-neutral experiment *is*, let us now examine its consequences. Regarding distribution, it is obvious that there is no effect, by construction.

Next, consider labor supply, which is usually taken to be a first-order factor for many policies, including significant reforms of tax expenditures. Under a distribution-neutral approach, labor supply effects recede. More precisely, if one assumes that labor effort is weakly separable in individuals' utility functions, as in Atkinson and Stiglitz's (1976) demonstration of when uniform commodity taxation is optimal, then labor supply effects are nil. Because distribution-neutral implementation holds utility constant for each level of earnings and hence for every level of labor effort that individuals might choose, the same level of labor effort will continue to maximize utility. See Kaplow (2004, 2006, 2008).

Finally, what is the effect of the reform on revenue? The answer is immediate from examination of the two components of the distribution-offsetting adjustment to the income tax schedule. The first component is a wash: at each level of income, we adjust income tax rates to offset the mechanical effects of the core reform on taxes paid. For proposals that reduce the availability of tax expenditures, revenues rise as a direct consequence, so income tax rates are accordingly reduced to, in essence, rebate the proceeds. The second component of the income tax adjustment absorbs the utility consequences of the reform (aside from the aforementioned mechanical effect of the change in tax payments). Because tax expenditure limitations reduce consumption distortions, they raise utility, so the second component of the income tax adjustment involves raising the income tax schedule to absorb this utility gain at each level of income. Combining these two components, we have an unambiguous increase in revenue.

In sum, the net revenue effect of the distribution-neutral reform package is the *only* effect of the overall reform, and it corresponds to the efficiency gain or loss produced.

How this revenue change is dealt with is, strictly speaking, outside the distribution-neutral experiment. For efficient reforms, which raise revenue, one might choose to distribute the surplus pro rata, generating a Pareto improvement.

5C.2 APPLICATION

5C.2.1 Different Types of Tax Expenditures

At the risk of oversimplification, it is helpful to distinguish three categories of purported tax expenditures. First are those income tax provisions that are best understood not as true tax expenditures but rather as refinements to income measurement. Classification is controversial, most notably because of disagreement about the proper normative baseline. Such questions are set to the side here.[3]

Second—and the focus here—are provisions that provide inefficient subsidies to certain forms of consumption. Application of section 5C.1's framework to reforms that eliminate such tax expenditures is straightforward. As explained, the distribution-neutral approach involves an adjustment to the income tax schedule that has two components. First, tax rates are reduced sufficiently at each income level to leave taxpayers with as much disposable income as before their tax expenditures were limited. Second, tax rates are increased sufficiently at each income level to absorb the utility gain from eliminating the distortion to individuals' expenditure decisions. Distribution-neutrality holds by construction. With regard to revenue, the first component alone entails revenue neutrality, and the second component results in a revenue gain that equals (in dollars) individuals' aggregate utility gains from the reduction in expenditure distortion.

A third category of tax expenditures includes those that correct otherwise distorted behavior. For example, the charitable contribution deduction may be seen as a Pigouvian subsidy on a class of expenditures that generates positive externalities. Analysis of this case involves a modest extension of section 1's basic framework. See Kaplow (2004, 2012). The core idea is that the subsidies should be moved toward the optimal Pigouvian correction (which is zero when there is no externality). If the charitable deduction is too generous in this regard, then limiting it would produce a gain, whereas if the deduction provided too little benefit, then further limitation would generate a loss.[4]

[3] Under a more rigorous optimal income tax analysis, such taxonomic questions have no direct role; the optimal treatment of any item is whatever comes out of the mechanism design exercise. Relatedly, because BTBR largely exclude capital taxation from their analysis, the proper way to incorporate that subject is less important for this commentary. For further exploration, see Kaplow (2008: ch. 9).

[4] As an aside, for atmospheric externalities, the optimal Pigouvian subsidy, when administered through the income tax, would take the form of a refundable credit (with no limit). One can also extend the analysis to the correction of so-called internalities. For further discussion, see Schizer (2015).

5C.2.2 Non-Distribution-Neutral Reforms

To many, one of the most apparent and disturbing features of tax expenditures is what Surrey (1973) referred to as their "upside-down" effect. Because exclusions and deductions have a value determined by individuals' marginal tax rates (MTRs)—and for other reasons—many tax expenditures are significantly more favorable to higher-income taxpayers. Accordingly, many favor tax expenditure limitations in order to augment progressivity.

As emphasized by Griffith (1989), however, this perspective is overly simplistic. After all, the existing regime did not take some tax rate schedule from Plato or Pluto, set it in stone, and then have someone else (Congress) superimpose tax expenditures. Rather, a single political process generated all the features of the existing regime. Moreover, this regime is reformed from time to time: sometimes the tax rate schedule, sometimes various of the tax expenditures, and sometimes a combination. An example of particular note is the Tax Reform Act of 1986, which (speaking roughly) broadened the base by reducing tax expenditures and simultaneously lowered rates, and in a manner that linked the two together, specifically, to achieve distribution neutrality (as well as revenue neutrality). In such a case, there is by construction no relationship between the level of tax expenditures and progressivity.

Suppose, however, that one wishes to understand and assess non-distribution-neutral reform packages, perhaps of the sort that some reformers envision under which tax expenditures would be significantly limited but the tax rate adjustments would result in an overall greater degree of redistribution. One can augment the distribution-neutral methodology using a simple two-step decomposition. See Kaplow (1996, 2004, 2008).

1. *Distribution-neutral implementation*: Combine the tax expenditure limitation component with a distribution-neutral income tax schedule adjustment of the sort examined throughout.

Then, an instant after this is to be enacted, and with the same effective date, do the following:

2. *Pure redistribution*: Implement an adjustment to the income tax schedule that moves from the distribution-neutral schedule to the actual schedule in the overall proposal under consideration.

To analyze any non-distribution-neutral reform, one can simply combine the analysis of these two steps.

Analysis of the first step is straightforward from the previous discussion. It is distribution neutral by construction. It does not affect labor supply. Its only consequence is the pure efficiency effect of the tax expenditure limitation with regard to reducing individuals' consumption distortions.

Analysis of the second step is readily understood once one appreciates what it is: a purely redistributive change to the income tax system. Accordingly, the correct analysis is generic: it is that from the standard optimal income tax problem. We know that if step two involves an increase in redistribution, for example, we have whatever social gains are deemed to be associated with that change and the social cost of increased distortion. A related point, to be elaborated in subsection 5C.2.4, is that if effective MTRs fall and hence distortion falls, then we know that we have less redistribution.

Note further that, being generic, this second step could be achieved in a variety of ways, including without regard to tax expenditure limitations. That is, step two—some particular reform to the income tax schedule that involves purely a change in redistribution—could be implemented by itself. It could also be combined instead with a change in the military budget, spending on highways, or the regulation of greenhouse gas emissions.

The distribution-neutral framework, even when one is not examining an actually distribution-neutral reform package, facilitates specialization and clarifies communication. If a single study aims to analyze the total effects of a non-distribution-neutral package—whether of tax expenditure limitations, road construction, or a gasoline tax—it must take on all the burdens of those who analyze optimal income taxation: making assumptions about elasticities, choosing a social welfare function, and so forth. If it instead analyzes the distribution-neutral version, it can focus on the distinctive features of the subject at hand. (Any distributive effects of the overall package might be displayed, but left for others to analyze.)

Closely related, it can be very difficult to compare two studies of the same subject if distribution-neutral implementation is not employed. As BTBR explain, there are many (indeed an infinite number of) ways to achieve revenue neutrality. And even if the two studies make the same assumption about redistribution (they are analyzing the same overall package), it may be difficult to disentangle whether, say, the first study's more favorable bottom line is due to its more positive assessment of the distinctive features of the reform or perhaps a more negative assessment of those but a more positive view of the resulting change in redistribution. By contrast, the use of distribution-neutral implementation provides a common metric that enables apples-to-apples comparisons.

5C.2.3 The Relationship between Tax Expenditure Limitations and Marginal Tax Rates

Whereas the previous subsection elaborated on distribution, this one will focus on the distortion side of the familiar distribution-distortion trade-off. The two-step decomposition makes clear that changes in both distribution and labor supply distortion will be located in the second, purely redistributive step of a reform. Unfortunately, this linkage is often forgotten. Some proponents of tax expenditure limitations believe that they can have their cake and eat it too—in economists' parlance, a free lunch (rather than dessert). We should not be surprised to discover that such is not the case.

Consider a linear income tax with marginal tax rate t. Furthermore, there are deductions or exclusions for tax expenditures that in aggregate are the fraction a of individuals' gross labor earnings y. Tax due is $t(1-\alpha)y$.

Now, examine a global tax expenditure limitation that allows only the fraction θ of tax expenditures to remain exempt. If the revenue is all used to reduce t, the new statutory tax rate becomes $\frac{1-\alpha}{1-\theta\alpha}t$. However, simple algebra shows that the tax due after the reform remains $t(1-\alpha)y$. Therefore, the following are true: (1) Individuals at all income levels pay the same amount of tax that they did before; this implies both revenue- and distribution-neutrality. (2) The *statutory* MTR falls from t to $\frac{1-\alpha}{1-\theta\alpha}t$, which is a lower rate because we are assuming that $\theta<1$. (3) The *effective* MTR stays the same, at $(1-\alpha)t$. This latter point is key. Note that the statutory MTR of t was not the effective MTR to begin with. After the reform, the effective MTR is unchanged: the new statutory MTR is $\frac{1-\alpha}{1-\theta\alpha}t$, which is applied to the fraction of income $1-\theta\alpha$, giving the same effective MTR of $(1-\alpha)t$.

Suggestions that broadening the tax base through tax expenditure reform enables lower MTRs are either misleading or incorrect. If interpreted as reductions of the statutory MTR, they are accurate but convey the misleading impression that the effective MTR and hence the distortion of the labor-leisure margin are lower. If interpreted as reductions in the effective MTR, they are incorrect.

5C.2.4 Progressivity and Distortion

A recurring theme of this commentary is that neither black magic nor tax expenditure limitations enable us to escape the distribution-distortion trade-off inherent in redistributive taxation. Distribution-neutral implementation leaves both distribution and labor supply distortion unchanged, features shared by the example in the preceding subsection. The two-step decomposition makes clear how deviations from distribution-neutrality can be isolated, leaving (as step two) a purely redistributive change to the tax system. And that is where our familiar distribution-distortion trade-off resides. Because some proponents of tax expenditure limitations present a rosier picture of the possibilities—suggesting that one can enhance progressivity, for example, without raising or even while lowering the core distortion of the income tax—some elaboration is useful.

For concreteness, let us employ a standard definition of progressivity (PROG): rising average tax rates (ATRs). That is, PROG(y) = dATR(y)/dy. Taking that simple derivative, we have PROG(y) = [MTR(y) – ATR(y)]/y. In the present discussion, MTR(y) and ATR(y) are both taken to be *effective* rates, in the spirit of the preceding subsection's analysis.

This expression teaches a straightforward lesson: the only way to increase the level of progressivity at a given income level—which is to say, to increase ATR(y) faster than before—is to push MTR(y) higher than before. Hence, the suggestion that we can increase progressivity while maintaining or reducing MTRs has to be mistaken. As subsection 5C.2.3 just explained, a significant part of the problem may involve confusing statutory and effective MTRs.

The only remaining wrinkle is how the efficiency gain from eliminating consumption-distorting tax expenditures might be distributed to the population—which is taken to be a choice that lies outside the distribution-neutral experiment. Note that if it was rebated pro rata, effective MTRs are unchanged but, actually, PROG rises because, like the lump-sum component of any tax schedule, an additional dollar is a greater percentage of income the lower is one's income. Hence, the core efficiency gain from tax expenditure reform does enable a free lunch. But that, indeed, is the entire point of basic efficiency analysis.

5C.2.5 Raising Revenue

Raising revenue is another often-advanced goal of tax expenditure limitation proposals. This too is best understood by applying the distribution-neutral framework. With distribution-neutral implementation, as we were just reminded, revenue effects arise entirely on account of correcting distortions caused by tax expenditures. Most who advance tax expenditure limitations on revenue-raising grounds, however, are not referring to this aspect, but instead have in mind retaining some or all of the revenue mechanically raised by the tax expenditure limitations in order to fund programs or reduce the deficit.

To analyze this further, consider the following variant of the two-step decomposition from subsection 5C.2.2:

1. *Distribution-neutral implementation*: Combine the tax expenditure limitation component with a distribution-neutral income tax schedule adjustment of the sort examined throughout.

Then, an instant after this is to be enacted, and with the same effective date, do the following:

2. *Pure revenue-raising*: Implement an adjustment to the income tax schedule that moves from the distribution-neutral schedule to the actual schedule in the overall proposal under consideration.

The only difference from the description of the original two-step decomposition is that the label "pure redistribution" is now changed to "pure revenue-raising." Again, the second step—here, a pure increase in (effective) tax rates to fund whatever—can be analyzed generically. That is, the analysis would be essentially the same if policymakers implemented step two without regard to whether it had anything to do with a tax expenditure limitation proposal. Higher taxes may be a good thing. Or they may not. But the answer does not depend on whether taxes are raised in isolation, as part of a tax expenditure limitation, as part of the use of proceeds from a carbon tax, or in some other manner.

It might be thought that revenue-raising is less distortionary, all else equal, after a tax expenditure limitation is implemented because one starts with lower MTRs. However, as explained in subsection 5C.2.3, this view confuses statutory and effective MTRs. If one enacted the tax expenditure limitation and did not use the proceeds to reduce tax rates, as in the prior illustration, then effective MTRs would rise rather than be constant. The only way to keep effective MTRs the same is to rebate the proceeds in a distribution-neutral fashion, leaving no revenue.

There is, however, an important respect in which revenue-raising (and redistribution, if one so chooses) may become more economically efficient as a consequence of tax expenditure limitations. Even though the benchmark effective MTR on labor income is unchanged—no free lunch there—it is the case that when a tax system has a broader base, it may well be less distortionary to raise MTRs. In a pure labor income tax regime, raising the MTR distorts labor supply and nothing more. In an income tax littered with distortionary tax expenditures—specifically ones that are in the form of exclusions and deductions and hence a function of statutory MTRs—raising statutory MTRs causes additional consumption distortions as well as labor supply distortion. For further analysis, see Kopczuk (2005) and Kopczuk and Slemrod (2002).

5C.2.6 Distribution Neutrality as a Descriptive Benchmark

BTBR do an impressive job not only in modeling the effects of tax expenditures on revenue and tax burdens at various levels of income but also in displaying the results of their analysis. The greatest challenge they face in this respect is that different formulations of tax expenditure limitations and different ways of rebating the revenue raised from such limitations have important effects on the resulting distributive outcomes. Moreover, we must intersect each limitation proposal with each method of using the revenue to cut tax rates (and there is an infinity of ways to do the latter).

A distribution-neutral benchmark can help. One simple way to display a tax expenditure limitation's consequences is to compare statutory MTRs under it to those under distribution-neutral implementation. The pattern of differences would show the distributive effect of the limitation proposal, setting aside how the proceeds are used. Alternatively, one might graph total taxes paid as a function of income for each of the three tax expenditure limitation proposals that BTBR examine and for distribution-neutral implementation (which is equivalent in this respect to the status quo). This single graph would clearly depict the differing distributive effects. A picture is worth (at least) a thousand words, and they can be absorbed more readily than if the thousand words (numbers) appear in one or more dense tables.

One can proceed similarly in order to compare the effect of various ways of reducing tax rates in order to rebate the revenues raised by a tax expenditure limitation proposal. That is, one can present taxes paid as a function of income under distribution-neutral implementation and compare it to the schedule under each alternative. Likewise, one could present the distribution-neutral schedule and the schedules for each of the posited alternative means of returning the revenue on a single graph, making clear all the differences.

BTBR also consider how various packages might affect incentives, and here I will focus on labor effort. The aforementioned graphs provide this information as well. We know that, in the benchmark case, the distribution-neutral version leaves labor effort unchanged. Hence, wherever the slope of the tax schedule under an alternative scheme is higher (lower) than under distribution-neutral implementation, work incentives are reduced (increased).[5] Or, more directly, by graphing the effective MTRs under the distribution-neutral version and any other, one can immediately see how labor incentives change.

Note that each of these comparisons between tax schedules under various combinations of expenditure limitation and tax rate reduction and tax schedules under distribution-neutral implementation of the corresponding tax expenditure limitation is simply a depiction of the two-step decomposition introduced previously. Step one is the distribution-neutral curve. Each of the other curves combines steps one and two. Hence, the difference between the distribution-neutral curve and another curve will depict step two—the purely redistributive component—in isolation.

5C.3 CONCLUSION

The distribution-neutral framework for policy analysis that is developed in a body of work over the last two decades is an extremely powerful tool for the analysis of tax expenditure limitations. And the two-step decomposition allows one to isolate the distinctive effect of tax expenditure reform—the reduction in distortions of expenditure choices—from effects on distribution, labor supply distortion, and revenue. The analysis shows how a number of commonly advanced beliefs about the benefits of tax expenditure limitation proposals—including the view that there exists a free lunch wherein one can reduce MTRs and simultaneously enhance revenue or redistribution—are largely illusory.

Although outside the scope of this commentary, a distribution-neutral approach may also have some bearing on the construction of politically feasible reform packages. The Tax Reform Act of 1986 ostensibly broadened the tax base via the reduction of tax expenditures in a manner that was not only revenue neutral but also distribution neutral. As explained, distribution-neutral packages result in Pareto improvements (more realistically, gains on average to every slice of the income distribution) when the underlying reforms are efficient. Such a package may be politically feasible.

ACKNOWLEDGMENTS

I am grateful to Alan Auerbach for comments, Jonathan Westreich for research assistance, and the John M. Olin Center for Law, Economics, and Business at Harvard

[5] The text refers to the substitution effect because it is MTRs that are being compared. To capture the uncompensated change, one would also have to integrate the effects, or examine the schedules for total taxes paid, to extract the income change and then determine the income effect.

University for financial support. The analysis here is applicable to many of the policies examined elsewhere in this conference volume—specifically, Williams; Dynarksi and Scott-Clayton; Hoynes and Rothstein; and Friedman—and casts a different light on a number of their points relating to distribution, distortion, and the purportedly wasteful use of government revenue. Disclaimer: I occasionally consult on antitrust cases, and my spouse is in the legal department of a financial services firm.

REFERENCES

Atkinson, Anthony B., and Joseph E. Stiglitz. 1976. "The Design of Tax Structure: Direct versus Indirect Taxation." *Journal of Public Economics* 6: 55–75.

Feldstein, Martin S. 2015. "Raising Revenue by Limiting Tax Expenditures." In *Tax Policy and the Economy*, vol. 29, edited by Jeffrey R. Brown, 1–11. Chicago: University of Chicago Press.

Griffith, Thomas D. 1989. "Theories of Personal Deductions in the Income Tax." *Hastings Law Journal* 40 (2): 343–95.

Kaplow, Louis. 1996. "The Optimal Supply of Public Goods and the Distortionary Cost of Taxation." *National Tax Journal* 49 (4): 513–33.

Kaplow, Louis. 2004. "On the (Ir)Relevance of Distribution and Labor Supply Distortion to Government Policy." *Journal of Economic Perspectives* 18 (4): 159–75.

Kaplow, Louis. 2006. "On the Undesirability of Commodity Taxation Even When Income Taxation Is Not Optimal." *Journal of Public Economics* 90 (6–7): 1235–50.

Kaplow, Louis. 2008. *The Theory of Taxation and Public Economics*. Princeton, NJ: Princeton University Press.

Kaplow, Louis. 2012. "Optimal Control of Externalities in the Presence of an Income Tax." *International Economic Review* 53 (2): 487–509.

Kaplow, Louis. Forthcoming. "A Distribution-Neutral Perspective on Tax Expenditure Limitations." In *Tax Policy and the Economy*, vol. 31, edited by Robert Moffitt. Chicago: University of Chicago Press.

Kopczuk, Wojciech. 2005. "Tax Bases, Tax Rates and the Elasticity of Reported Income." *Journal of Public Economics* 89 (11–12): 2093–2119.

Kopczuk, Wojciech, and Joel Slemrod. 2002. "The Optimal Elasticity of Taxable Income." *Journal of Public Economics* 84 (1): 91–112.

Mirrlees, James A. 1971. "An Exploration in the Theory of Optimum Income Taxation." *Review of Economic Studies* 38 (2): 175–208.

Schizer, David M. 2015. "Limiting Tax Expenditures." *Tax Law Review* 68 (2): 275–354.

Surrey, Stanley S. 1973. *Pathways to Tax Reform: The Concept of Tax Expenditures*. Cambridge, MA: Harvard University Press.

Toder, Eric J., Joseph Rosenberg, and Amanda Eng. 2013. "Evaluating Broad-Based Approaches for Limiting Tax Expenditures." *National Tax Journal* 66 (4): 807–32.

6

TAX BENEFITS FOR COLLEGE ATTENDANCE

Susan Dynarski and Judith Scott-Clayton

6.1 INTRODUCTION

There are many ways a society can finance college, and over time the United States has tried almost all of them. Starting in the nineteenth century, state taxpayers funded college education by establishing public universities, which are now attended by 80% of undergraduates. Through the Morrill Act, the federal government provided each state with a large parcel of land, which states then sold to raise money for building their colleges. State tax revenues paid for the bulk of operating expenses of these colleges, allowing them to charge artificially low prices.

In the 1960s, portable grants and loans emerged as a new source of government funding for college (table 6.2 provides a brief description of key federal programs for postsecondary education.). With the Higher Education Act of 1965, the federal government established new loans and grants for college students. Unlike the state subsidies, which are delivered to institutions, these funds travel with the students, as vouchers, and can be used at any accredited college—including private colleges. The Pell Grant, introduced in the early 1970s further expanded federal grants for students; still the largest source of grants for college, the Pell Grant targets funds on low-income students.

In recent decades, federal grants and loans have grown even more important, as states have scaled back on their subsidies to public colleges, which have, in turn, raised tuition prices.[1] Political pressure mounted on politicians to relieve the burden of rising costs, especially among middle- and upper-income families who were not eligible for the Pell Grant.

In this context, presidential candidate Bill Clinton proposed major new tax benefits for college attendance during his 1996 campaign. Since then, the role of the federal tax code in subsidizing college has expanded rapidly. In 2015, households received $19.7 billion in tax credits for education (Joint Committee on Taxation 2015a). The growth has been sharp and rapid: in 1998, the figure was $4.9 billion (Bulman and Hoxby 2015a).[2] And the tax credits are just one of more than a dozen different tax subsidies for education. Table 6.1 shows that these tax subsidies together now provide nearly as much support for postsecondary education as does the Pell Grant program.

[1] Private colleges have also rapidly increased tuition prices, for reasons debated by economists.

[2] Dollars adjusted to 2015 real values unless otherwise noted.

Table 6.1 Federal support for postsecondary students by source, 2013 (in billions of dollars)

Tax Credits/Deductions/Exclusions	**31.8**
Grants	**48.9**
Pell	33.7
Veterans/Military	13.8
Supplemental Educational Opportunity	0.7
Other	0.7
Loans	**95.9**
Unsubsidized Stafford	51.9
Subsidized Stafford	25.4
PLUS	17.5
Perkins	1.0
Other	0.1
Work-Study	**1.0**
Total Federal Support	**182.9**

Notes: Grants, loans, and work study information for 2013–14; tax benefits information for 2013. Loan amounts represent total amounts disbursed (rather than net costs to the government). Table adapted from College Board (2014) for grants, loans, and work study, and Crandall-Hollick (2014a) for tax benefits. All values in 2013 constant dollars.

In this chapter, we describe the federal tax subsidies for higher education, their history, their incidence, and their behavioral effects. The federal tax system also includes benefits for other levels of education, but more than three-quarters of all federal tax expenditures for education are for college. The tax system subsidizes the families of *future* college students through the Coverdell and 529 programs, tax-advantaged savings plans authorized by the federal and state governments, respectively. The federal and state tax systems subsidize *current* college students and their families through tax credits, a deduction for tuition costs and loan interest, an exclusion of scholarships, grants, and tuition reductions from taxable income, and a dependent exemption for students aged 19 to 23. Finally, the tax code subsidizes *former* college students with a deduction for interest paid on student loans.

The tax subsidies for education are now extensive, complicated, and expensive. Compelling evidence, using rigorous empirical methods, indicates that the tax credits and tuition tax deduction (which account for the bulk of the tax expenditures for education) have precisely zero effect on human capital accumulation. If their intent is to increase schooling, they are a failure.

An alternative goal of the tax benefits for education is a transfer to middle-income families. If so, they are a very leaky bucket, since they impose extensive administrative burdens on households, colleges, and government. Reducing the tax rates applied to these families would be a more transparent and less expensive approach to achieving this goal.

Table 6.2 Description of key federal programs for postsecondary students

	Federal Tax Credits and Deductions
Hope Credit	Provided a maximum credit of $1,800 for qualifying expenses relating to tuition and fees, only for students in their first two years of college, and only for families with tax liability. The American Opportunity Tax Credit replaced the Hope credit in 2009.
Lifetime Learning Credit (LLC)	Eligible tax filers are able to receive a maximum credit of $2,000 for tuition and fees expenses.
American Opportunity Tax Credit (AOTC)	AOTC replaced the Hope the credit in 2009 and allows for a credit up to $2,500 for expenses relating to tuition and fees and course materials. The credit rate is 100 percent for the first $2,000 of expenses and 25 percent on the next $2,000. Up to $1,000 of the credit is refundable for families with limited or no tax liability.
Tuition and Loan Interest Deductions	These deductions offer filers a maximum deduction of $4,000 for expenses relating to tuition and fees. To date, this deduction only extends through 2016.
Saving Incentives	Interest accumulates tax-free when families save for college using Federal Coverdell accounts and state 529 savings plans. Withdrawals from these accounts are not taxed unless the amount withdrawn is greater than the student's education expenses.
Dependent Exemption	A parent or guardian has the ability to claim an exemption for a dependent who is between the ages of 19 and 23 and is a full-time student. The filer is allowed an exemption of $3,950 per dependent.
	Federal Student Aid Programs
Pell Grant	The largest funded need-based aid program in the United States. Currently, students can receive a grant amount up to $5,500. The size of the Pell award depends primarily upon family income and enrollment intensity.
Unsubsidized and Subsidized Stafford Loans	Subsidized and unsubsidized loans, also known as Stafford Loans, are administered by the federal government through the Federal Direct Loan Program (FDLP). Unsubsidized loans are available to all students regardless of need. With subsidized loans, eligibility is based on need and the federal government pays the interest on these loans while the student is in college. The maximum amount a dependent student can borrow for an undergraduate degree under the Stafford Loan programs is currently $31,000.

Sources: US Government Accountability Office (2012) and Crandall-Hollick (2014a).

Streamlining the tax benefits for education could potentially enhance their efficiency. At a minimum, a simpler system of education tax benefits would decrease the administrative and time costs of transferring funds to households with postsecondary expenses. At best, simplification would clarify incentives and increase investments in human capital.

6.2 OVERVIEW OF TAX BENEFITS FOR HIGHER EDUCATION

6.2.1 Rationale and History

The economic efficiency argument for subsidizing education rests upon the belief that students, facing market prices for college, will purchase less than the socially optimal level of college. These suboptimal decisions can result from several factors (see Page and Scott-Clayton 2016, for a review). First is the presence of social externalities: a college-educated population may generate benefits to society above and beyond the benefits reaped by individuals, including improved infant health, reduced reliance on social welfare programs, and increased civic participation (Dee 2004; Oreopoulos and Petronijevic 2013).[3] Second, education may also involve internalities, or private costs and benefits that are not fully realized at the time of the decision. For example, individuals may make suboptimal investments because they underestimate their own return to attending or overestimate the cost. Third, common foibles of human behavior may result in procrastination, decision avoidance, and default bias in college planning and decision-making (Lavecchia, Liu, and Oreopoulos 2014). Finally, if prospective students face credit constraints, they may not be able to borrow enough to make optimal investments in college. Along with direct institutional subsidies and financial aid, tax benefits are a policy tool that can lower the effective price of college, and thus encourage families to invest more in college than they would have otherwise.

Of course, in practice, tax expenditures may serve other motivations beyond economic efficiency, including a desire to redistribute income. Beyond promoting college attendance, policy discussions around the higher education tax benefits have also reflected a desire to provide assistance to middle-class families (Crandall-Hollick 2014b; Lederman 1997). While targeted tax expenditures may be an economically inefficient means of transferring income to the middle class (as opposed to altering the underlying tax brackets and tax rates directly), they have proved more popular and easier to implement than fundamental tax reforms. Thus, even if these tax benefits do little to promote college enrollment, they may nonetheless serve a transfer purpose.

[3] Price subsidies may also be justified if families underestimate the value of college or are unable to make optimal investments due to borrowing constraints. Note that these latter two concerns, however, are more commonly cited as justifications for need-based financial aid than as justifications for the tax benefits, which are not particularly targeted by income.

Policymakers have a variety of tools at their disposal for subsidizing education: they can directly subsidize educational institutions through expenditures, they can directly subsidize students through student aid or voucher programs, and/or they can implement targeted tax credits and deductions. At the state and local level, subsidies for both K–12 and postsecondary education have predominantly taken the form of direct expenditures to public institutions, while at the federal level, subsidies have predominantly taken the form of direct aid to students.

The proper role of tax breaks for private spending on education has been a contentious topic for decades (Moynihan 1978). Private school associations and parents of children in private schools have long lobbied for tax deductions for private school tuition (for an analysis of one such proposal, see Samwick 2013). Opponents have viewed such a deduction as a back door to government funding to religious schools. While a number of states eventually implemented tax credits for tuition paid at private elementary and secondary schools, federal tuition deductions and credits for private elementary and secondary schooling were repeatedly proposed and repeatedly defeated over the years.

Nonetheless, these early efforts to push for tax benefits for private schooling may have sown the seeds for the recent expansion of these subsidies in federal postsecondary policy. At least two major expansions of the federal role in postsecondary finance were conceived as political responses to pressure to institute a private school tax break for middle-income constituents: both the Guaranteed Student Loan (introduced in 1965, as part of the Higher Education Act) and the Middle Income Student Assistance Act (1978), which extended federal financial aid to middle- and upper-income families, emerged as compromise policies during battles over a tuition tax credit (Hearn 2001).

From the mid-1960s through the mid-1990s, federal subsidies for higher education continued to predominantly take the form of student grants and loans. That began to change with the introduction of the Hope and Lifetime Learning tax credits for postsecondary education in 1997. Since then, the magnitude and scope of federal tax benefits has expanded dramatically, driven largely by tax credits. As shown in table 6.3, the federal government annually spends over $30 billion dollars on an array of tax benefits for higher education, about two-thirds the amount provided in federal grants to undergraduates, and more than half the magnitude of all types of federal expenditures on elementary and secondary education.[4] For context, table 6.3 also provides information on federal tax benefits for other levels of education (the largest of these, the deduction for charitable contributions to educational institutions, may apply to any level of education).

[4] The Joint Committee on Taxation (JCT) estimates $32 billion in tax benefits for postsecondary education in 2015 (see table 6.1). The College Board (2015) estimates $45 billion in federal grants for postsecondary education in 2013–14. Note that the JCT estimate includes both undergraduate and graduate benefits. US Department of Education estimates total federal expenditures of $57 billion on elementary and secondary education in 2012–13 (NCES Digest of Education Statistics, table 235.10, "Revenues for Public Elementary and Secondary Schools, by Source of Funds: Selected Years, 1919–20 through 2012–13," https://nces.ed.gov/programs/digest/d15/tables/dt15_235.10.asp?current=yes).

Table 6.3 Estimated tax expenditures on tax benefits for education (in billions of dollars)

Tax Benefit	*2015*	*2016*	*2017*	*2018*	*2019*
Benefits exclusively for higher education:					
Credits for tuition for post-secondary education	19.7	21.0	21.1	14.8	21.3
Parental personal exemption for students aged 19 to 23	4.5	4.7	4.9	5.2	5.5
Exclusion of scholarship and fellowship income	2.7	2.9	3.0	3.2	3.4
Deduction for interest on student loans	2.0	2.1	2.2	2.3	2.4
Exclusion of employer-provided education assistance	1.2	1.2	1.2	1.3	1.3
Exclusion of tax on earnings of qualified tuition programs:	0.7	0.9	1.2	1.4	1.5
Exclusion of employer-provided tuition reduction benefits	0.3	0.3	0.3	0.3	0.3
Deduction for tuition and fees	0.3	0.4	0.2	0.0	0.0
Exclusion of certain discharged student loans from income	0.2	0.2	0.2	0.2	0.2
Exclusion of earnings of Coverdell education savings accounts	0.1	0.1	0.1	0.1	0.1
Subtotal	**31.7**	**33.8**	**34.5**	**28.8**	**36.0**
Other tax benefits for education:					
Deduction for charitable contributions to educational institutions	6.2	6.4	6.6	6.8	7.1
Exclusion of interest on state/local government bonds for educational facilities	2.6	2.6	2.8	2.9	3.1
Qualified school construction bonds	1.0	1.1	1.2	1.3	1.4
Exclusion of interest on state/local government bonds for student loans	0.4	0.4	0.4	0.5	0.5
Deduction for expenses of elementary/secondary school teachers	n/a	0.3	0.2	0.2	0.3
Credit for holders of qualified zone academy bonds	0.1	0.1	0.1	0.1	0.1
Grand Total	**42.0**	**44.6**	**45.8**	**40.7**	**48.5**

Source: Joint Committee on Taxation (2015a). To adjust reported amounts for recent changes as a result of the Protecting Americans from Tax Hikes (PATH) Act of 2015, budget impact estimates from the Joint Committee on Taxation (2015b) are also incorporated. See Crandall-Hollick (2016) for additional notes on the higher education tax benefits.

In the following sections, we discuss each of the major existing federal tax benefits for college enrollment in more detail, along with a brief summary of related benefits that we place outside the scope of this discussion.[5]

6.2.2 Federal Tax Credits and Deductions for Currently Enrolled Students

The most long-standing tax benefit for households with college students is the dependent deduction. While children are generally considered independent for tax purposes after age eighteen, the age limit is extended through twenty-three if the child is enrolled in school. This tax break allows families to save up to several thousand dollars a year for each child enrolled in college because parents can claim a dependent exemption for the student (thus reducing their taxable income), or qualify for the Earned Income Tax Credit (a refundable credit for low-income families). These provisions save households up to several thousand dollars a year for each child enrolled in college and were estimated to cost $4.5 billion in 2015 (Crandall-Hollick 2016).

In 1996 Bill Clinton, then a candidate for the presidency, proposed a tax credit for the first two years of college costs. After Clinton's election, this proposal took shape as the Hope and Lifetime Learning Credits, introduced in 1997. These allowed families of college students to offset their educational costs with tax credits of up to $1,500 a year.

The new credits remained largely unchanged for ten years, with minor tweaks to their maximum values and AGI phase-out ranges. But the number of households receiving the credits rose by more than half, from about 4.5 million filers in 1998 to 7.5 million in 2008. The credits totaled $7.6 billion in the 2008 tax year.

Responding to critiques that the existing programs were of limited benefit to low-income families, presidential candidate Barack Obama proposed a tax credit that would cover a broader range of educational expenses than the Hope Credit and would be partially refundable for families with zero tax liability. This proposal took form in 2009 as the American Opportunity Tax Credit (AOTC), a renamed and modified version of the Hope credit. AOTC was created as part of the American Recovery and Reinvestment Act of 2009 and temporarily replaced the HOPE Credit for 2009 and 2010. AOTC was extended through 2017 by the American Taxpayer Relief Act of 2012 and made permanent in late 2015 by the Protecting Americans from Tax Hikes (PATH) Act of 2015.

As of 2015, the maximum benefit for the AOTC is $2,500, with $1,000 refundable. All of the first $2,000 in qualifying expenses is eligible for the credit, and 25% of an additional $2,000. Eligible expenses include course-related books and supplies. This allows students attending low-tuition public institutions to access more of the

[5] The role of tax benefits for education has grown over time at the state level as well, particularly in recent years in the form of tax-advantaged college savings programs. We will not provide a survey of state programs, however, since they are dwarfed in magnitude by the federal subsidies.

credit. Students are allowed to claim the credit for four years of undergraduate education (unlike Hope, which was limited to two years). Like the former Hope Credit, the AOTC is available for all eligible students in the household; by contrast, only one Lifetime Learning Credit may be claimed per household (Department of the Treasury, Internal Revenue Service 2011).

With the introduction of the AOTC, the cost of the tax credits rose sharply. In 2010, spending on the AOTC was nearly $19 billion, comparable to annual spending on the Pell Grant program just a few years earlier (Crandall-Hollick 2014b; College Board 2011). Combined spending on the AOTC and the much smaller LLC was estimated at approximately $20 billion in 2015, compared with $30 billion for the Pell program (College Board 2015; Crandall-Hollick 2016). Since 2002, families not claiming one of the education tax credits have been able to deduct up to $4,000 in tuition fees from income (even if they do not itemize).The benefit has been repeatedly extended, most recently by the PATH Act of 2015, which extended the deduction through 2016.[6] Additionally, up to $2,500 in interest on student loans is deductible from taxable income, for households with incomes up to $80,000 (single) or $160,000 (married) (Crandall-Hollick 2014a).

6.2.3 Federal Savings Incentives for Prospective College Students

In parallel with the tax credits, a set of tax benefits intended to increase education saving has emerged. In 1997, the same legislation that established the tax credits created the Education IRA, now called the Coverdell Education Savings Account (ESA). The Coverdell is structured much like the Roth IRA, with after-tax dollars growing tax-free. Earnings are never taxed if Coverdell withdrawals are used for education expenses. The Coverdell can be used for elementary or secondary education, as well as for higher education. The Coverdell currently allows for annual, after-tax deposits of up to $2,000. The far more generous contribution limits for the 529 vary by state: cumulative contribution limits for a beneficiary range from $250,000 to $400,000 (Crandall-Hollick, 2015).

While the Coverdell is a product of federal legislation, 529 savings plans are an invention of the states. The 529 savings plans have their roots in prepaid tuition plans, the first of which was introduced by Michigan in 1986. Those who purchased shares in Michigan's plan were guaranteed that their investment would cover the cost of a certain number of semesters at Michigan schools. Michigan exempted investment returns in its prepaid plan from state taxes and argued to the Internal Revenue Service that returns should also be exempted from federal taxes. The IRS disagreed, but Michigan went forward with the plan and sued the IRS for a refund of taxes paid, winning its case in 1994.

[6] The benefit was originally set to expire in 2005, but in 2006 it was extended to cover 2006 and 2007; in 2008, it was extended to cover 2008 and 2009; and in 2010, it was extended to cover 2010 and 2011. For 2011, the income limit for this benefit was $80,000 for single filers or $160,000 for joint returns.

In 1997, Congress codified the federal tax treatment of the tuition plans in Internal Revenue Code Section 529. IRC 529 also contains language that recognized a variant on the prepaid plans that had been introduced by a handful of states: the tax-advantaged college savings plan. Like the Coverdell, these new savings plans allowed after-tax investments to grow free of federal and state taxes; however, withdrawals used for postsecondary costs were not exempt from federal taxation. With the passage of tax reform in 2001, the federal tax on withdrawals from 529 savings plans was eliminated. States that did not already have a savings plan quickly established one. The growth of the 529 savings plans has far outstripped that of the prepaid plans, likely because of their greater fungibility and potentially higher returns.

While these benefits may appear small from the lens of federal tax expenditures, this lens may understate the role of these programs, which are ultimately intended to use the tax benefit to leverage much larger private investments in education. Whether or not they actually do so is not straightforward to determine, as we will discuss in section 6.3.1. What is clear is that the volume of assets held in these accounts has grown substantially over time: 529 accounts include over $250 billion in assets under management nationally, up from about $10 billion in 2000 and $80 billion in 2005 (College Savings Plans Network 2015). In addition, Coverdell accounts held about $7 billion dollars in mutual funds in 2014 (Investment Company Institute 2016). As these accounts are drawn down in the coming decades, their revenue consequences will increase.

6.2.4 Other Tax Benefits for Postsecondary Education

Of the higher education tax benefits outlined in table 6.1, it is clear that the tax credits are by far the largest, representing more than two-thirds of the total. But additional benefits accrue to students after graduation, in the form of student loan interest deductions and student loan forgiveness. Up to $2,500 in interest on student loans is deductible from taxable income for households with incomes up to $80,000 (single) or $160,000 (married). This deduction is for interest on any student loans, not just federal loans. This deduction was estimated to cost $1.4 billion in tax revenue in 2014 (Crandall-Hollick 2014a). With rapid increases in the share of middle-income families carrying student loan debt (Simon and Barry 2012), this amount is projected to grow to $2.4 billion in 2019 (JCT 2015a).

The exclusion of some discharged student loans, in contrast, is estimated to cost only about $200 million each year and has remained flat over time. For those aware of the increasing generosity of income-based student loan repayment programs, which forgive remaining debt after twenty or twenty-five years depending on the program, this may come as a surprise. The reason for the limited tax expenditure on these exclusions is that only loans forgiven for working for a certain period of time in "certain professions" or "a broad class of employers" are excluded (IRS 2015). Thus, while balances discharged under the Public Service Loan Forgiveness or Teacher Loan Forgiveness programs are tax-exempt, those discharged under any of the income-driven repayment plans are taxable as income. Moreover, the primary cost of any type of loan forgiveness program is the loan balance itself, not the potential income tax foregone, but only the latter is a tax expenditure.

The biggest tax benefit for education outside of the higher education tax credits is the deduction for charitable contributions to educational institutions, estimated to cost $6.2 billion in 2015, rising to $7.1 billion in 2019. While it is not possible with the JCT data to separate how much of this tax expenditure is due to postsecondary giving, experts estimate that 60%–70% of all charitable giving in education is for higher education (Tyson 2014). The Council for Aid to Education, which conducts an annual institutional survey, estimates that postsecondary institutions received $40.3 billion in charitable contributions in 2015, the highest level since the survey began in 1957 (Council for Aid to Education 2016).

Allowing households to deduct their charitable donations provides an incentive for them to give more than they would have otherwise. The policy rationale for such an incentive is that it encourages support of institutions that provide broader social value (Randolph 2015). Critics have questioned, however, whether postsecondary charitable giving is always in the public interest given the unequal distribution of contributions across institutions. Of the $40 billion donated to postsecondary education, seventeen elite institutions accounted for more than $10 billion in donations received (Lederman 2016). Many of these same institutions also receive disproportionate benefits from the tax-exempt treatment of their endowment gains and land holdings (Woodhouse 2015).

6.3 THE INCIDENCE AND IMPACT OF TAX BENEFITS FOR HIGHER EDUCATION

6.3.1 Empirical Challenges

Understanding the economic incidence of these tax benefits is critical, whether the goal is to change behavior, redistribute resources, or both. Assessing incidence can be tricky, however, for at least three reasons. First, any individual tax benefit may interact with other provisions in the tax code (or federal financial aid system) in complex ways. Most obviously, who benefits most from a tax deduction depends not just on the parameters of the deduction itself but also on marginal tax rates. Claiming one tax credit also may affect eligibility for claiming another.

Second, take-up is never perfect: not all who qualify for a tax benefit will claim it. In some cases the decision not to claim may be a reasoned one; for example, a family may decide that the value of current consumption is greater than the value of saving for college. In other cases, confusion and bureaucratic hurdles may serve as barriers to take-up.

Finally, the incidence of a tax benefit may be affected by the responses of other people or firms. For example, schools could capture some of the benefits of the tax subsidies by increasing tuition or reducing aid.

A full assessment of incidence thus requires far more than a description of eligibility criteria, phase-in and phase-out regions, and benefit calculations. At a minimum, it requires detailed data on actual tax records for taxpayers of varying characteristics; it may also require information on possible institutional responses and an identification strategy for identify causal effects.

For those who do receive a benefit from these subsidies, is it a pure transfer, or do the tax benefits increase college enrollment, or increase the quality/intensity of college enrollment? A naïve comparison of college enrollments among those that received the tax benefit versus those that did not would be contaminated by reverse causality because those that do not enroll in college cannot claim the associated tax benefits. In other words, college enrollment may determine whether or not a person is "treated" by the tax benefit rather than the other way around.

To estimate the causal impact of the tax benefits requires comparing similar groups, one that is potentially eligible for the benefit and one that is not, for reasons that are unrelated to potential college enrollment. Since income largely determines eligibility for the tax benefits, and income has its own effects on college enrollment, it is difficult to isolate the effect of the tax benefits themselves. The most credible estimates of the impact of the education tax credits utilize quasi-experimental approaches. Several studies take advantage of changes over time in the availability or generosity of benefits for observably similar tax filers, while two studies utilize rich administrative data to compare families just above and just below discontinuities or kinks in the eligibility formula. These quasi-experimental analyses are described in more detail in section 6.3.3.

Estimating the impact of the education savings incentives and student loan interest deductions is yet more challenging because decades can separate college enrollment and the receipt of benefits. For example, families may benefit from education savings incentives for nearly two decades before children reach the age of college enrollment. A difference-in-difference analysis comparing families of, say, 10-year-olds, just before and after the introduction or expansion of savings benefits is unlikely to yield clear findings, since the "treated" group of families is eligible for the benefit for eight years prior to college-age while the "control" group is eligible for only one year less. Attempting to identify a completely unaffected group would require examining families at different points in time, during which other factors may intervene to contaminate the comparison. These challenges may explain why there is far more research on the impact of the tuition tax credits and deductions rather than on the college savings and student loan benefits.

6.3.2. Economic Incidence: Who Benefits?

6.3.2.1 Incidence of the Tax Credits

From their inception, the LLC and former HOPE credit have primarily benefited middle- and upper-income families. At very low AGIs (below $10,000), families did not qualify for the credits because they had insufficient tax liability (and the credits were not refundable). Even for those with higher AGIs, the value of the credits could be limited by the definition of allowable expenses, which consisted only of tuition and fees. A typical, low-income student attending a community college with average tuition and fees of $3,322 in 2012–13 (National Center for Education Statistics, 2013) and receiving the average Pell Grant of $3,678 (College Board 2014) would have had no expenses eligible for Hope or LLC. For a middle-income student attending a more expensive private college and not receiving any grant aid, allowable expenses would generate the maximum tax credit.

The AOTC reaches higher-income families than did the Hope credit. The AGI cap on the AOTC is considerably higher than that on the Hope Credit: $180,000 for a joint return. Before AOTC, 18% of the dollars devoted to the education tax credits and deductions went to families with incomes over $100,000; the figure for 2012 was 24% (College Board 2014). The AGI cap on the AOTC is higher than that on any of the other credits or deductions. High-income households that were once only eligible for the tuition tax deduction are now eligible for the more generous AOTC. As a result, the share of households claiming the deduction has dropped while the share claiming the credits has risen. There is no guarantee that households always choose the benefit of greatest value, however. Turner (2011a) finds that families often fail to optimize, likely due to the complexity of understanding the different eligibility rules and benefit calculations and how they interact with other elements in the tax calculation.

The AOTC also benefits low-income families more than the old HOPE credit, for two reasons. First, because the AOTC is partially refundable, families can benefit from the credit even if their income is too low to owe any income taxes. Second, unlike the original HOPE credit, the AOTC covers not just tuition and fees but also course-related books, supplies, and equipment. This allows low-income students to benefit even if their tuition and fees are already fully covered by financial aid. As a result, expenditures for low-AGI families have increased: pre-AOTC 5% of the credit and tuition deduction dollars went to filers with incomes under $25,000; in 2012 the share was 24%.

Another factor that affects incidence is how financial aid changes in response to the receipt of these tax credits. In the federal financial aid formula, taxes paid are deducted from income; thus in general anything that reduces taxes paid will increase ability to pay in the eyes of the aid formula. To avoid having the education tax credits unintentionally reduce financial aid eligibility, the FAFSA currently requires information on the amount of AOTC and LLC received. In practice, however, these and other tweaks to the basic aid formula—which depends most heavily on family income, family size, and number in college—have little effect on Pell Grant or student loan eligibility (Dynarski, Scott-Clayton, and Wiederspan 2013). Institutional aid may be more sensitive: Nicholas Turner (2012) finds evidence that some colleges may reduce grant assistance nearly dollar-for-dollar for students eligible for tax-based aid.

6.3.2.2 Incidence of Savings Incentives

The benefits of education savings accounts rise sharply with income, since those with the highest marginal tax rates benefit the most from sheltering capital income from taxation. These additional deductions have little to no value for low-income families, who often take the standard deduction rather than itemize and who face relatively low marginal tax rates. Further, the accounts are risky for families for whom the college attendance of children is uncertain, since account holders are penalized if the accounts are not used for schooling (Dynarski 2004). Finally, the financial aid system reduces aid disproportionately for those families that hold their assets in the 529 or ESA rather than conventional saving vehicles. Since the highest-income families are unaffected by the aid tax, this further intensifies the positive correlation between income and the advantages of the tax-advantaged college savings accounts.

6.3.3 Behavioral Impacts of the Tuition Tax Credits and Deduction

Long (2004) is the first to provide a quasi-experimental analysis of the impact of education tax credits on college enrollment. Using annual data from the October Current Population Survey (CPS) from 1990 to 2000, she identifies families potentially eligible for an education tax credit based on income and tax filing status (single or joint return). She uses a difference-in-difference approach to compare college enrollment rates for potentially eligible versus ineligible households, before and after the introduction of the Hope and Lifetime Learning Credits in 1998.

Long finds no evidence that college enrollments increased faster among eligible groups, and hypothesizes that this could be due to lack of awareness among families on the margin of college enrollment. She notes, however, that the CPS data are not ideally suited to the analysis: income is measured in ranges, making it difficult to precisely determine eligibility and potentially attenuating the effect estimates; moreover, for young adults, the availability of family income depends upon whether they are still part of their parents' household, which is itself potentially determined by college enrollment status.

Two later studies using smaller samples with more accurate information on family income and later years of data found some positive enrollment effects of the introduction of the tax credits. LaLumia (2012) uses an individual fixed-effects approach, comparing eligible individuals' enrollment status before and after the introduction of the tax credits and tuition deduction in 1998, with data from the National Longitudinal Survey of Youth 1979 (NLSY-79). The advantage of this analysis is more detailed data on family income and a window of data extending to 2006, giving the tax benefits more time to have an effect. The disadvantage is that, due to the age of the sample, effects can only be estimated for older individuals (33 to 50), a group for whom college enrollment is relatively rare. LaLumia finds no effect of the benefits on enrollment for the sample overall, though positive effects are found for adults whose educational attainment in 1998 fell below their expectations in 1979.

Turner (2011b) applies a difference-in-difference using data from the Survey of Income and Program Participation (SIPP) from 1996 to 2003. But unlike the prior papers, Turner (2011b) focuses not on comparing eligible versus ineligible groups around the introduction of the tax credits, but in changes in the generosity of tax-based aid (including the tuition deduction) for eligible groups over time. In particular, changes to the tuition deduction in 2002 and increases in the generosity of the LLC in 2003 created differential increases in potential aid among eligible groups. Turner (2011) focuses on 18- and 19-year-olds and finds that an extra $100 of tax-based aid increases college enrollment by 0.4 percentage points—an estimate in line with the magnitudes of enrollment effects found for grant aid (for a review of the impacts of financial aid, see Dynarski and Scott-Clayton 2013).

The positive findings in Turner (2011b) are surprising in light of other work by the same author (Turner 2011a, 2012) finding that families often fail to optimize their choice of tax benefit and that colleges reduce grant assistance nearly dollar-for-dollar for students eligible for tax-based aid. Turner (2011b) notes that these seemingly contradictory findings may be due to differences in the sample examined (Turner 2012 focuses on four-year institutions, which have the most grant aid to crowd out, while the enrollment effects in Turner 2011b may be driven by two-year enrollees, although the SIPP do not allow him to differentiate). An alternative concern, however, is that institutional aid may be increasing differentially for the same income groups affected by the increasing generosity of tax benefits over this time period, generating possibly spurious estimates of the impact of tax-based aid.

Two recent papers by Bulman and Hoxby (2015) and Hoxby and Bulman (2016) provide the most definitive evidence on the enrollment effects of tax-based aid. Both papers utilize rich, individual-level administrative data from the Internal Revenue Service (IRS) on the population of potential tax return filers. These data include income and tax data from income tax forms as well as W-2 data from non-filers; enrollment information is derived from Form 1098t data, which institutions use to directly report to the IRS information on individuals' enrollment intensity and tuition and fee payments. The precise data on income and extremely large number of observations enables them to utilize regression discontinuity and regression kink analyses around eligibility cutoffs and phase-out regions, in addition to using a difference-in-difference to examine the effect of the introduction of the AOTC in 2009.

Bulman and Hoxby (2015) use a regression kink design to examine the effect of the HTC and LLC for filers at the boundaries of the phase-out regions of each credit. The intuition behind the design is that in the absence of the "kink" in tax credit eligibility, we should expect the relationship between income and college enrollment to change smoothly. In many applications, however, data limitations make it quite challenging to distinguish a true "kink" from an abrupt but nonetheless smooth change in the outcome distribution. Given the vast data at their disposal, this is not a concern in their analysis. They show clear kinks in actual usage of the tax credits in the expected directions over these phase-out regions, but no corresponding kink in enrollment behavior.

In a second analysis, Bulman and Hoxby examine the introduction of the AOTC in 2009, using a difference-in-difference approach that makes use of the fact that the AOTC increased tax-based aid differentially for filers at various points in the income distribution. They find very precisely estimated zero effects on enrollment.

Finally, Hoxby and Bulman (2016) use a regression-discontinuity design to estimate the effects of the tuition tax deduction for families around the maximum income cutoff for eligibility. They find evidence that families manage income to fall just below the cutoff, but using an "optimal doughnut-hole" design that determines which observations are in the manipulable range around the cutoff and then discards these, they find no evidence that the deduction impacts college enrollment decisions (or other margins such as enrollment intensity, enrollment in a four-year college, tuition paid, or student loans taken).[7]

6.3.4 Behavioral Effects of the Savings Incentives

Descriptive research has found that family assets and savings are correlated with children's college enrollment and progress (see review by Elliott and Beverly 2011). But estimating the causal impact of the college savings plans on college enrollments is extremely challenging for the reasons already discussed. Still, research on other related programs may be at least somewhat informative regarding the likely effects of the program at least on more proximal outcomes such as college savings behavior.

For example, a recent randomized experiment examines the effect of additional incentives for educational savings. Part of a broader national initiative to promote Savings for Education, Entrepreneurship, and Downpayment (SEED) accounts, the SEED for Oklahoma Kids (SEED OK) program in 2008 automatically opened a 529 account for infants in the treatment group with an initial $1,000 deposit. The program additionally encouraged parents to open a second "participant-owned" 529 account by offering a $100 account-opening incentive and a savings match for low-income families.[8] Approximately a year and a half after treatment assignment, 16% of families in the treatment group had an individually owned 529 account, compared with only about 2% of families in the control group, though the treated families did not save significantly more overall (Nam, Kim, Clancy, Zager, and Sherraden 2012).[9] Although the children in the study families are very young, and impacts may grow over time, in some ways these results highlight how difficult it is to promote these accounts.

6.4 POLICY DISCUSSION

6.4.1 Increasing Complexity

With dozens of tax and aid programs available, two-thirds of students are now eligible for some sort of discount on their college costs. The increasing scope and diversity of subsidies for education implies increased complexity—both for students trying to estimate their college costs and for policymakers trying to ensure coherence across

[7] It is worth noting that because families may be eligible for both the AOTC and the deduction for tuition and fees, but can only take one or the other, the families who are most affected by the cutoff for the tuition and fees deduction are those who are not eligible for AOTC (e.g., beyond four years of undergraduate education or enrolled less than half time).

[8] The match was 1:1 for families with AGI below $29,000 and 0.5:1 for families with AGI between $29,000 and $43,000.

[9] Unsurprisingly, nearly 100% of the treatment group accepted the automatic account.

programs. The proliferation of programs, each well-intentioned, has created a system that makes it difficult for families—especially "first-generation" families in which neither parent has attended college—to know just how affordable college can be. Calculating the net price of college for a given family requires understanding their finances as well as the rules of the Pell Grant, student loans, the tuition tax credits, state grant programs, and aid offered by individual colleges. Evidence suggests that students are quite poor at estimating net prices.

A symptom of the general confusion is that some aid goes unclaimed: the Government Accountability Office recently calculated that 14% of families eligible for an education tax benefit failed to claim it. Forty percent of filers who used the tuition tax deduction would have been better off claiming one of the tax credits instead.

The Government Accountability Office has found that many families do not choose the tax advantage that would most benefit them. Families can choose among the AOTC, LLC, tuition tax deduction, or disbursement from a 529 or Coverdell to cover current expenses. Different types of expenditures (tuition, books, living expenses) qualify for some of these but not others. GAO found that about 15% percent of filers made a suboptimal choice, suggesting substantial confusion among filers and tax preparers (US Government Accountability Office 2012).

6.4.2 Suitability of Tax System for Delivering Subsidies to Schooling Costs

In 2011, the Treasury Inspector General for Tax Administration (TIGTA) released a report highly critical of the administration of the AOTC (Treasury Inspector General for Tax Administration 2011). TIGTA inspected the income tax returns that claimed in AOTC in 2009, the first year of the credit, and found ambiguities in two million returns qualifying for $3 billion in credits. Most of these flagged returns lacked a Form 1098-T by the IRS that support students' attendance at an eligible college. The same colleges that qualify for federal financial aid qualify for the tax credits, so this reflects a failure of coordination between the US Department of Education (hereinafter, ED), which has a constantly updated list of eligible institutions, and the IRS which failed to obtain it. The report pointedly referred IRS to a publicly available dataset of institutions in the Integrated Postsecondary Education Data System.

The report also noted that institutions inconsistently fill out the 1098-T, the information return that is used to report eligible postsecondary expenses to IRS. The intent of this form is to gather information about a student's costs net of any scholarship aid. The TIGTA concluded that some colleges fail to net out scholarships. TIGTA also identified 350,000 cases in which a household received a credit even though the information on the 1098-T indicated they did not fulfill at least one of the eligibility criteria (at least half-time, undergraduate). The report emphasized that reducing fraud and error in the education credits will require better gathering of information from taxpayers and postsecondary institutions.

IRS defended its performance in its response in the TIGTA report, indicating that fraud was not nearly as rampant as the report implied (Treasury Inspector General for Tax Administration 2011). In particular, IRS noted that while the TIGTA report correctly noted that millions of AOTC recipients had not had their postsecondary institutions confirmed, this was due not to fraudulent filings but to weaknesses in the IRS's databases of eligible institutions, which they pledged to improve.

In response to the TIGTA report, legislation was introduced to the House to tighten administration of the AOTC. The proposed legislation would require that taxpayers list the employer identification number of a student's postsecondary institution. In theory, this should be present on the 1098-T, but apparently some institutions listed incorrectly.

None of these administrative challenges are insurmountable. The TIGTA is holding IRS to a degree of oversight that ED has maintained over colleges for decades. However, while ED has all of the necessary lists and procedures and lines of communication in place, IRS is relatively new to the student aid game. Until the agency gets its procedures into place, the opportunities for error and fraud are widened. The TIGTA report warns, however, that improving these procedures may create additional paperwork burdens for families and colleges.

With the rapid growth of the tax credits, an increasing number of students now complete paperwork for both the IRS and the US Department of Education in order to obtain college funding. And there is more paperwork on the horizon for families and colleges, with the Treasury Inspector General putting pressure on the IRS to obtain more documentation from applicants and colleges regarding their eligibility for the tax credits. If carried through, these steps will largely duplicate the work that ED already does in administering the traditional aid programs and multiply paperwork burdens on households and colleges.

ED and IRS bring complementary strengths to the administration of aid for college. ED has long experience in delivering aid to students and communicating with colleges. IRS has a well-developed capacity for gathering and verifying income data from households. Conversely, IRS has little experience with verifying student enrollment and delivering aid when it is needed. And while ED has long experience in gathering income data from applicants, it does so by imposing substantial paperwork burdens upon households and colleges. Just one example: colleges are statutorily required to "verify" a minimum of 30% of their aid applications each year, an auditing process that requires applicants to submit extra supporting documentation, including copies of tax returns. Some colleges audit 100% of their aid applications. Were tax data alone used to calculate aid eligibility, the data underlying all applications would automatically be verified, since it would come from the IRS rather than the applicant.

6.4.3 Prospects for Reform

When choosing a path forward, it is critical to keep this in mind: the tax credits and tuition tax deduction apparently have no effect on human capital accumulation. Until this year, economists strongly suspected that this was the case, but recent evidence based on the universe of household tax records (Bulman and Hoxby 2015; Hoxby and Bulman 2016) is dispositive. The tax credits and tax deduction, which account for most of the tax expenditures for postsecondary education, do not affect schooling decisions. While part of the explanation may be that institutions capture some of these tax benefits via reductions in financial aid (Turner 2012), Hoxby and Bulman (2016) argue that the main explanation relates to how and when these benefits are received. In particular, tax benefits may not be realized until nearly a year after an enrollment decision is first made, and because the benefits are delivered as part of the income tax filing process, the authors argue that they are more likely to be perceived simply as a windfall rather than as an incentive for educational investment.

To achieve the goal of increasing human capital investments, the tax incentives would have to be restructured so that they are targeted at households whose investments are plausibly sensitive to price, and delivered when schooling expenses are being paid. One proposal suggested by Hoxby and Bulman (2016) would be to compute eligibility for the credits automatically using income tax information in the year an individual turns 17, rather than the year of enrollment, and proactively notify prospective students of their eligibility. In addition, they propose that institutions could file to receive the benefits directly from the IRS, so that a student would only need to present evidence of eligibility in order to have the institution credit their account immediately upon enrollment.

An even more comprehensive approach would be to consolidate the credits with the Pell Grant program, creating a single grant program that subsidizes, at the time that tuition is due, the postsecondary expenses of low- and middle-income families. Eligibility for this program could automatically be determined using tax data, with funds delivered by the Department of Education. As described in Dynarski and Scott-Clayton (2007), families could apply for a consolidated grant by simply checking off a box on their income tax forms. While IRS has all the data needed to determine grant eligibility, the Department of Education has the infrastructure in place to deliver funds to schools. We therefore suggest that the role of the IRS be limited to forwarding applicants' adjusted gross income, dependency status, and number of dependents to the Department of Education, which will calculate aid eligibility and send vouchers directly to the institutions at which students are enrolled. This consolidation would eliminate the duplicative administrative burdens now placed upon colleges and households by Treasury and ED. Treasury has a comparative advantage in calculating ability to pay, given it already serves this function for the income tax system. ED has a comparative advantage in delivering funds to schools and colleges, given it already serves this function with the Pell and Stafford loan programs. Dynarski and Scott-Clayton (2007) show that the existing combined distribution of Pell awards and tax credits could be replicated using only information available from income tax records. While a natural concern is that lots of wealthy families may suddenly qualify for aid if assets are not considered (as they are in the current federal student aid application), Dynarski and Scott-Clayton (2007) show that vanishingly few families with incomes low enough to qualify for Pell Grants have assets that would disqualify them for an award.[10]

[10] This is due both to low levels of assets in general, as well as the fact that most assets are in the form of primary housing or retirement accounts, both of which are excluded in the federal financial aid formula.

The goal of the education tax incentives could instead be redefined as explicitly redistributive: the transfer of income to households with postsecondary expenses. In this case, the transfer should be achieved at the lowest cost possible to households, government, and colleges. A relatively straightforward subsidy to postsecondary education is already embedded in the dependent deduction, which applies to children up to age 24 if they are enrolled in college. This provision also extends eligibility for the EITC. A single, refundable credit could be created to make the subsidy more generous. Currently, the AOTC is calculated as 100% of the first $2,000 in expenses and 25% of the next $2,000, but just 40% of this total is refundable. A simplified credit could be equal to 100% of eligible expenses (up to a limit) and fully refundable.

The tax benefits for education are a costly way to reduce the tax burden on middle-income families, imposing extensive administrative costs on households, colleges, and government. Reducing the tax rates applied to these families would be a more transparent and less expensive approach to achieving this goal. At a minimum, a simpler system of education tax benefits would decrease the administrative and time costs of transferring funds to households with postsecondary expenses. At best, simplification would clarify incentives and increase investments in human capital.

REFERENCES

Bulman, George, and Caroline Hoxby. 2015. "The Returns to the Federal Tax Credits for Higher Education." National Bureau of Economic Research Working Paper 20833.

College Board. 2013. "Trends in Student Aid." Trends in Higher Education Series. http://trends.collegeboard.org/sites/default/files/student-aid-2013-full-report.pdf

College Savings Plan Network. 2015. "529 Plan Data (Reporting Date: December 31, 2015)." http://www.collegesavings.org/wp-content/uploads/2015/09/Dec-2015.pdf

Council for Aid to Education. 2016. "Colleges and Universities Raise Record $40.30 Billion in 2015." Press release, January 27. http://cae.org/fundraising-in-education/survey-results-other-research/annual-press-release/

Crandall-Hollick, Margot. 2014a. "Higher Education Tax Benefits: Brief Overview and Budgetary Effects." Congressional Research Service Report 41967.

Crandall-Hollick, Margot. 2014b. "The American Opportunity Tax Credit: Overview, Analysis, and Policy Options." Congressional Research Service Report 42561.

Crandall-Hollick, Margot. 2015. "Tax-Preferred College Savings Plans: An Introduction to 529 Plans." Congressional Research Service Report 42807.

Crandall-Hollick, Margot. 2016. "Higher Education Tax Benefits: Brief Overview and Budgetary Effects." Congressional Research Service Report 41967.

Dynarski, Susan. 2004. "Who Benefits from the Education Saving Incentives? Income, Educational Expectations and the Value of the 529 and Coverdell." *National Tax Journal* 57 (2): 359–83.

Dynarski, Susan, and Judith Scott-Clayton. 2007. "College Grants on a Postcard: A Proposal for Simple and Predictable Federal Student Aid." Hamilton Project Discussion Paper 2007-01. Washington, DC: Brookings Institution.

Dynarski, Susan, and Judith Scott-Clayton. 2013. "Financial Aid Policy: Lessons from Research." *Future of Children* 23 (1): 67–91.

Dynarski, Susan, Judith Scott-Clayton, and Mark Wiederspan. 2013. "Simplifying Tax Incentives and Aid for College: Progress and Prospects." In *Tax Policy and the Economy*, vol. 27, edited by Jeffrey Brown, 161–201. Chicago: University of Chicago.

Elliott, William, and Sondra Beverly. 2011. "Staying on Course: The Effects of Savings and Assets on the College Progress of Young Adults." *American Journal of Education* 117 (3): 343–74.

Hearn, James C. 2001. "The Paradox of Growth in Federal Aid for College Students, 1960–1990." In *The Finance of Higher Education: Theory, Research, Policy, and Practice*, edited by Michael B. Paulsen and John C. Smart, 267–320. New York: Agathon Press.

Hoxby, Caroline, and George Bulman. 2015. "The Returns to the Federal Tax Credits for Higher Education." National Bureau of Economic Research Working Paper 21554.

Hoxby, Caroline, and George Bulman. 2016. "The Effects of the Tax Deduction for Postsecondary Tuition: Implications for Structuring Tax-Based Aid." *Economics of Education Review* 51:23–60.

Investment Company Institute. 2016. "Frequently Asked Questions about Coverdell Education Savings Accounts." https://www.ici.org/pubs/faqs/faqs_coverdell

Joint Committee on Taxation. 2014. "Background and Present Law Related to Tax Benefits for Education." JCX-70-14. June 24.

Joint Committee on Taxation. 2015a. "Estimates of Federal Tax Expenditures for Fiscal Years 2015–2019." JCX-141R-15. December 7.

Joint Committee on Taxation. 2015b. "Estimated Budget Effects of Division Q of Amendment #2 to the Senate Amendment to H.R. 2029 (Rules committee print 114-40), the 'Protecting Americans from Tax Hikes Act of 2015.'" JCX-143-15. December 16.

LaLumia, Sara. 2012. "Tax Preferences for Higher Education and Adult College Enrollment." *National Tax Journal* 65 (1): 59–90.

Lavecchia, Adam M., Heidi Liu, and Philip Oreopoulos. 2014. "Behavioral Economics of Education: Progress and Possibilities." National Bureau of Economic Research Working Paper 20609.

Lederman, Doug. 1997. "The Politicking and Policy Making Behind a $40-Billion Windfall." *Chronicle of Higher Education* 44 (14) (November): A28–A32.

Lederman, Doug. 2016. "In Giving to Colleges, the One Percenters Gain." *Inside Higher Ed*, January 27. https://www.insidehighered.com/news/2016/01/27/giving-colleges-hits-another-record-high-wealthy-institutions-get-most

Long, Bridget T. 2004. "The Impact of Federal Tax Credits for Higher Education Expenses." In *College Choices: The Economics of Where to Go, When to Go, and How to Pay for It*, edited by Caroline Hoxby, 101–68. Chicago: University of Chicago Press.

Moynihan, Daniel P. 1978. "Why Private Schools Merit Public Aid: The Constitutional Case for Tuition Tax Credits." Address to the National Association of Independent Schools Annual Conference, New York City, New York.

Nam, Yunju, Youngmi Kim, Margaret Clancy, Robert Zager, and Michael Sherraden. 2013. "Do Child Development Accounts Promote Account Holding, Saving, and Asset Accumulation for Children's Future? Evidence from a Statewide Randomized Experiment." *Journal of Policy Analysis and Management* 32 (1): 6–33.

National Center for Education Statistics. 2013. "Average Undergraduate Tuition and Fees and Room and Board Rates Charged for Full-time Students in Degree-Granting Postsecondary Institutions, by Level and Control of Institution: 1963–64 through 2012–13." Institute of Education Sciences. http://nces.ed.gov/programs/digest/d13/tables/dt13_330.10.asp

Oreopoulos, Philip, and Uros Petronijevic. 2016. "Making College Worth It: A Review of the Returns to Higher Education." *The Future of Children* 23 (1): 41–65.

Page, Lindsay, and Judith Scott-Clayton. 2016. "Improving College Access in the United States: Barriers and Policy Responses." *Economics of Education Review* 51:4–22.

Randolph, William C. 2015. "Tax Topics: Charitable Deductions." Tax Policy Center: A joint project of the Urban Institute and Brookings Institution. http://www.taxpolicycenter.org/taxtopics/encyclopedia/Charitable-Deductions.cfm

Samwick, Andrew A. 2013. "Donating the Voucher: An Alternative Tax Treatment of Private School Enrollment." In *Tax Policy and the Economy*, vol. 27, edited by Jeffrey R. Brown, 125–60. Chicago: University of Chicago Press.

Silliman, Benjamin R. 2011. "College Tuition Tax Credits: An Examination of the Impact of the American Opportunity, HOPE, and Lifetime Learning Tax Credits Since 1998." *Proceedings of American Society of Business and Behavioral Sciences* 18:279–88.

Simon, Ruth, and Rob Barry. 2012. "College Debt Hits Well-Off." *Wall Street Journal*, August 9. http://www.wsj.com/articles/SB10000872396390444246904577575382576303876

Tax Policy Center. 2016. "The Tax Policy Briefing Book: A Citizens' Guide for the 2016 Election and Beyond." Washington, DC: Urban Institute. http://www.taxpolicycenter.org/briefing-book

Treasury Inspector General for Tax Administration. 2011. "Billions of Dollars in Education Credits Appear to Be Erroneous." Reference Number: 2011-41-083.

Turner, Nicholas. 2011a. "Why Don't Taxpayers Maximize their Tax-Based Student Aid? Salience and Inertia in Program Selection." *B.E. Journal of Economic Analysis and Policy* 11 (1): 1–24.

Turner, Nicholas. 2011b. "The Effect of Tax-Based Federal Student Aid on College Enrollment." *National Tax Journal* 64 (3): 839–62.

Turner, Nicholas. 2012. "Who Benefits from Student Aid? The Economic Incidence of Tax-Based Federal Student Aid." *Economics of Education Review* 31 (4): 463–81.

Tyson, Charlie. 2014. "Still a Charity Case." *Inside Higher Ed*, June 17. https://www.insidehighered.com/news/2014/06/17/charitable-giving-higher-education-restored-pre-recession-levels-report-indicates

US Government Accountability Office. 2012. "Higher Education: Improved Tax Information Could Help Families Pay for College." GAO-12-560.

Woodhouse, Kellie. 2015. "Widening Wealth Gap." *Inside Higher Ed*, May 21. https://www.insidehighered.com/news/2015/05/21/rich-universities-get-richer-are-poor-students-being-left-behind

COMMENTARY ON CHAPTER 6

David Figlio

It is particularly difficult to discuss "Tax Benefits for College Attendance" by Susan Dynarski and Judith Scott-Clayton because I heartily agree with my take on the authors' three principal conclusions: First, the tax system is an extraordinarily inefficient mechanism for subsidizing access to college. Second, the best mechanism for subsidizing access are outside of the tax system; for a more efficient and, arguably, equitable approach, it would be better to put the resources spent on tax incentives into grants paid when tuition is due. And third, the principal benefit of the tax system in this realm involves facilitating the delivery of financial aid. Dynarski and Scott-Clayton make all three points clearly and compellingly in their chapter. Moreover, they were extremely responsive to my initial suggestions, leaving very little to critique.

It is, however, still worthwhile to discuss some remaining distributional considerations regarding both the authors' proposals for simplifying college access as well through other ways in which US government implicitly subsidizes higher education.

As the authors point out, at present the Internal Revenue Service and the US Department of Education each maintain a complicated, burdensome, and highly duplicative set of systems to collect information that could be used to determine aid eligibility. The authors wisely propose that the two agencies streamline their processes—with the IRS collecting and verifying income data from households and the Department of Education collaborating with higher education institutions and delivering financial aid to students—with the current tax credits being consolidated within the Pell Grant program. The IRS, under their proposal, would collect and forward applicants' adjusted gross income, dependency status, and number of dependents to the Department of Education, and the Department would determine the degree of aid eligibility and make direct payments to the institutions where the students are enrolled.

This type of system has considerable advantages, as clearly articulated by the authors, but there are potential social costs associated with this approach. Currently, the Department of Education heavily considers aspects of family wealth when determining a family's ability to pay for college. Families are expected to make use of their assets to assist students in affording college. But asset measures are not collected by the IRS, leaving current household income as the method of determining aid eligibility. This is not an issue per se regarding low-income families, as extremely few families with incomes low enough to qualify for Pell Grants would be disqualified due to their assets (Dynarski and Scott-Clayton 2007). On the other hand, the higher we go up the income distribution, the more likely it is that treatment of wealth will determine the degree of financial aid eligibility. Eliminating the wealth adjustment in aid calculations will surely increase aid recipiency to more wealthy families. This need not be a first-order cause for concern from an equity perspective if financial aid is treated as a fixed entitlement, in which all eligible students receive their full aid amount regardless of the total bill of the financial aid program. But to the degree to which the government appropriates a limited amount to fund the full financial aid program and either proportionately funds student subsidies or allocates financial aid on a first come-first served basis, the elimination of the wealth factor in determining aid eligibility will likely transfer aid from comparatively needy students to comparatively wealthy students.

Moreover, this transfer, should it exist, would tend to privilege white families at the expense of black and Hispanic families. Thompson and Suarez (2015), investigating the 2013 Survey of Consumer Finances, demonstrate that at all levels of the income distribution, or across the education distribution, white households are dramatically wealthier than are their black and Hispanic counterparts. Therefore, in the event of a policy change in favor of basing aid eligibility solely on IRS-collected data, the decision to guarantee a given amount of financial aid to eligible recipients versus appropriating a fixed amount to be shared among all eligible recipients would likely have welfare implications, with the latter tending to favor higher wealth, and disproportionately white, families at the expense of lower wealth, and disproportionately minority, families. The design of the revised program will determine the degree to which this transfer occurs, should it occur at all.

The authors spend most of the chapter discussing the most visible tax system-related benefits to higher education, but there are also potential distributional consequences to the second-largest federal subsidy of higher education in the United States—the tax treatment of charitable contributions to higher education institutions, and of those institutions' endowments. Endowments are either tax-exempt because they are independent 501(c)(3) organizations, operated exclusively for charitable and educational purposes, or because they are part of a higher education institution that is itself a 501(c)(3) organization or public entity. As a consequence, the endowment's investment earnings are tax-free and a contributor's contributions to the endowment are usually tax-exempt as well. Sherlock et al. (2015) estimate that the value to higher education institutions of the tax-free status of endowment returns was $16 billion in fiscal year 2014, or $11 billion for private colleges and universities alone. In addition, the tax deduction for charitable contributions to higher education institutions, private activity tax-exempt bonds for nonprofit institutions, and the share of general obligation tax-exempt bonds accruing to public universities and colleges together total around another $11 billion (Sherlock et al. 2015). In sum, favorable federal tax treatment of colleges and universities leads to a considerable subsidy to these institutions' activities.

Higher education institutions have very substantial educational and research purposes that certainly dramatically benefit society. These colleges and universities are engines of economic growth and offer many opportunities for social advancement. Many of these institutions, including Northwestern University, where I work, use large shares of their endowment income to heavily subsidize access and attendance by low- and moderate-income families. In my mind, there is no question that the vast majority of the American colleges and universities that are tax-exempt organizations fulfill this mission.

That said, the lion's share of the federal tax subsidies that accrue to higher education institutions by virtue of their tax-exempt status are enjoyed by a relatively small share of institutions. Three-quarters (75.8% in fiscal year 2014) of all university endowments are concentrated in institutions with the 100 largest endowments, while nearly half (48.5%) are shared by the top twenty university endowments (Sherlock et al. 2015). One-quarter (24.7%) of the total endowments are represented by Harvard University, the University of Texas, Yale University, Stanford University, and Princeton University, and 7% by Harvard University alone. While the median private, nonprofit doctoral institution has $70,900 in endowment assets per student and the median public doctoral institution has $16,600 in endowment assets per student, the means are $214,300 and $28,000, respectively, driven by the wealth concentration in the hands of a small number of institutions (Sherlock et al. 2015)—Princeton, Yale, Harvard, and Stanford, respectively, have per student endowments of $2.6 million, $2.0 million, $1.3 million, and $1.2 million.

The concentration of these tax subsidies at a small number of institutions may be justified, but doing so has some social costs, where the students whose educations are disproportionately subsidized are drawn from a particular portion of the distribution of students. The nineteen extraordinarily selective private institutions among the *U.S. News and World Report* top twenty national universities account for 39.3% of all university endowments and 57.5% of all private endowment assets. Of the twenty-seven private colleges and universities with endowments over $2 billion, twenty-six are classified as "most selective" by *U.S. News and World Report*, with the other (University of Richmond, classified as "more selective") while among the fifty-three private colleges and universities with endowments over $1 billion, forty-one are classified as "most selective" with the remaining twelve classified as "more selective." Few institutions, public or private, that serve relatively less rarefied sets of students have particularly large endowments.

There are possible tax treatments that could maintain the substantial endowment subsidies for the well-endowed, largely elite universities while transferring a portion of that subsidy to institutions serving a broader sweep of the American student population. For instance, the Tax Reform Act of 2014 (H.R. 1) included a proposal to impose a 1% flat excise tax on private college and university endowments that exceed $100,000 per full-time student, with part-time students measured as full-time student equivalents. The specific features of this proposal, such as the excise tax rate and the threshold for inclusion in the excise tax, are arbitrary, and the presence of a sharp "all-or-nothing" threshold could lead to unintended manipulation of either the numerator or denominator by institutions near the margin of exposure to the new excise tax. Nonetheless, such a measure (or, alternatively, a tax on endowment earnings), coupled with earmarking revenues to further support financial aid at less competitive colleges and universities, could provide an opportunity to ensure that a portion of the tax subsidies to the mission of higher education institutions that come through the favorable tax treatment of endowment income and charitable contributions are shared with a wider range of higher education institutions and students. Of course, a detailed assessment of the benefits and costs of such a proposal, along with a discussion of the potential distortionary incentive effects that would unquestionably accompany it, is beyond the scope of this commentary.

In summary, the American system of providing tax benefits for college attendance is at present extremely inefficient. Dynarski and Scott-Clayton offer a clear-headed review of the waterfront of the direct subsidies to students and make thoughtful proposals for reform and improved system efficiency. When carrying out their sensible proposals, it is important to keep in mind potential unintended redistributive consequences, particularly as pertains to the elimination of the wealth criterion for financial aid award determination. Meanwhile, it makes sense to think about the other ways through which the federal government, by virtue of the tax system, subsidizes higher education institutions, and the potential distributional consequences of those actions.

REFERENCES

Dynarski, Susan, and Judith Scott-Clayton. 2007. "College Grants on a Postcard: A Proposal for Simple and Predictable Federal Student Aid." Hamilton Project Discussion Paper 2007-01. Washington, DC: Brookings Institution.

Sherlock, Molly F., Jane G. Gravelle, Margot L. Crandall-Hollick, and Jeffrey M. Stupak. 2015. "College and University Endowments: Overview and Tax Policy Options." Congressional Research Service Report. Washington, DC: Congressional Research Service.

Thompson, Jeffrey P., and Gustavo A. Suarez. 2015. "Exploring the Racial Wealth Gap Using the Survey of Consumer Finances." Finance and Economics Discussion Series 2015-076. Washington, DC: Board of Governors of the Federal Reserve System. http://dx.doi.org/10.17016/FEDS.2015.076

7

TAX POLICY TOWARD LOW-INCOME FAMILIES

Hilary Hoynes and Jesse Rothstein

7.1 INTRODUCTION

The tax code focuses on high-income families because that is where the money is. The bottom 40% of tax filing units—those with incomes below $39,370—earned just 14% of pretax income in 2013 (Tax Policy Center 2013). Under any even slightly progressive tax schedule this group would contribute very little revenue.

But the tax code is used to pursue purposes and objectives other than revenue collection. Today, the two most prominent provisions of the federal income tax code that target low-income tax filers, the Earned Income Tax Credit (EITC) and the less prominent but similar Child Tax Credit (CTC), are explicitly redistributive, designed to transfer money to families rather than tax it away from them.

The EITC is a tax credit available to lower-income families with positive earned income. Importantly, it is refundable: many recipients' incomes are too low to generate substantial tax obligations, so with the EITC their liabilities are negative, and they receive refund checks from the Internal Revenue Service. In 2013, 87% of the total tax expenditure of the EITC took the form of tax refunds (Internal Review Service 2015a).

Since its introduction in 1975, the EITC has grown to become a central element of the US social safety net (Bitler, Hoynes, and Kuka 2016). In 2013, the EITC reached 28.8 million tax filers at a total cost of $68 billion. Almost 20% of all tax filers and 44% of filers with children receive the credit. The maximum credit in 2015 was $6,242 for families with three children, $5,548 for those with two children, $3,359 for those with one child, and $503 for those without children—this can be as much as 45% of a family's pretax income. Overall, the average credit amount for families with children is a substantial $3,063 (Internal Review Service 2015a). The program dwarfs traditional cash welfare (Temporary Assistance for Needy Families, or TANF), which reached only 1.6 million families in 2013, an almost 70% decline since 1994.

The CTC is more recent, introduced in 1997. It is structurally similar to the EITC, but more universal in design and less targeted on lower-income families. In 2015, it was available to families with incomes as high as $150,000 for married couples ($115,000 for singles), with the maximum credit available at incomes as high as $110,000 for married couples ($75,000 for singles). The CTC is not inflation adjusted, so these parameters are generally fixed in nominal terms from one year to the next; the nominal maximum credit has been unchanged at $1,000 per child since 2003. Although this is much smaller than the maximum EITC, the CTC's broader reach across the income distribution means that total expenditures are comparable ($56 billion for the CTC vs. $68 billion for the EITC in 2013).

The CTC, unlike the EITC, is not fully refundable. This has limited its value to low-income families. But in 2009, the American Recovery and Reinvestment Act greatly expanded the refundability of the CTC, making the schedule similar to the EITC's. This expansion was originally a temporary one, but has recently been made permanent.

In this chapter, we review the roles of the EITC and CTC, what is known about their impacts and distributional consequences, and the possibilities for reform. We begin in section 7.2 by discussing the goals of the programs, and in section 7.3 we review their structure and history. Section 7.4 discusses the economics of in-work tax credits like the EITC and CTC. Section 7.5 evaluates what we know about how the programs affect these objectives. In section 7.6, we discuss possible reforms that might help further the program goals set out in section 7.2. In section 7.7, we conclude.

7.2 FRAMING: WHAT ARE THE OBJECTIVES OF THESE TAX PROVISIONS?

The EITC and CTC are best seen not as taxes but as transfer programs that happen to be administered through the tax code. As we see it, they have three primary goals. First, all means-tested transfer programs are designed in part to achieve distributional objectives. In the case of the EITC, these are to transfer funds to low- and moderate-income families, and particularly to those with children. The CTC's distributional aims are less clear, given its high phase-out point—the target is clearly the broad middle class rather than just the lowest-income families. It may be better thought of as a "universal child benefit," aimed at horizontal equity between families with and without children. Differing schedules by family type are a long-standing feature of the US tax system, and distinguishing by the number of children may make sense if, for example, the marginal utility of consumption declines more slowly the larger the family is.[1]

The two other main goals are what distinguish the EITC and CTC from other transfer programs. Each aims to encourage work (though as we discuss in section 7.4 this is not true for all families) and to limit the high administrative costs associated with other transfer programs that require very labor-intensive eligibility screening.

The EITC is quite successful at all three goals. Almost three-quarters of its benefits go to families with annual incomes below $25,000, roughly the 24th percentile of the income distribution (DeNavas et al. 2015; Internal Review Service 2015a), and EITC

[1] The dependent exemption would seem to be able to accomplish this, without need for the CTC. Like the CTC, the dependent exemption phases out as income rises. The primary differences between the two are that the CTC is (partially) refundable and that it distinguishes between children and other dependents.

payments lift millions of families out of poverty each year. The evidence indicates that the program has substantially raised the labor force participation rates of single mothers, by perhaps 5 to 8 percentage points (though there is also evidence of smaller negative effects on married women's participation and on the intensive margin). Finally, the tax system has many administrative advantages over a welfare bureaucracy and has proved to be an efficient means of distributing the EITC. As we discuss in section 7.5, however, there are nontrivial rates of noncompliance with the EITC, particularly on dimensions that are not well tracked by existing third-party reporting).[2]

The CTC is much less studied. It performs much less well at transferring income to the neediest families and is likely less effective at encouraging work as well. But like the EITC, it is quite inexpensive to administer, and its redistribution to the middle and upper middle parts of the income distribution is apparently also valued by policymakers.

Nevertheless, although these provisions generally do a good job of meeting their objectives, neither is perfect. In section 7.4, we discuss some options for reforming the programs that might be considered.

7.3 CURRENT POLICIES AND RECENT REFORMS

To be eligible for the EITC, a taxpayer—or tax filing unit—must have earned income during the tax year.[3] The value of the credit is determined by a benefit schedule with three regions, known as the "phase-in," "flat" (or "plateau"), and "phase-out." In the phase-in region, the credit increases by a share of each additional dollar earned. Once the credit reaches its maximum value, the taxpayer is in the second, "flat" region, where additional earnings do not affect the credit value. In the final region, the credit declines with each additional dollar of earnings (or, adjusted gross income, or AGI, if that is higher) until it is zero.

The exact parameters of the schedule vary by filing status and by the number of qualifying children, but the basic shape is the same. Figure 7.1 displays the schedule in 2015 as a function of earned income for single taxpayers with no, one, two, and three or more children. The figure makes clear that the credit for families with children is much different than that for childless families, and we start with the former. The phase-in or subsidy rate is substantial at 34% (or 40% or 45%) for those with one (or two or three) children, while the phase-out rate is much lower, at 15.98% (21.06%)

[2] There are also drawbacks to tax-based administration, however. Two are that tax refunds are generally paid only once a year and relatively easily captured by for-profit firms via fees for tax preparation or high interest rates on tax refund anticipation loans. The now-defunct Advance EITC program allowed for more gradual payment, but take-up was extremely low (even in experiments designed to target information and default effects; see IRS and US Department of the Treasury 1999; Jones 2010; US Government Accountability Office 2007). Recent reforms have dramatically reduced the prevalence of tax refund anticipation loans

[3] Earned income is the sum of wages, tips, salary, union strike benefits, some disability payments, and net self-employment earnings (IRS and US Department of the Treasury 2013).

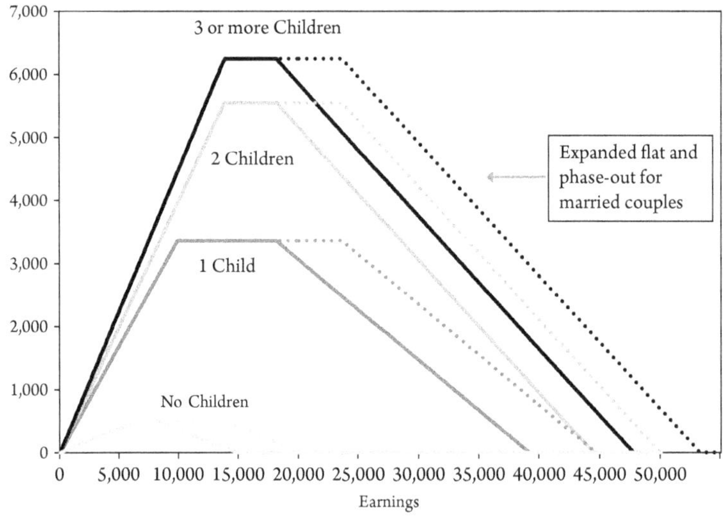

Figure 7.1 EITC schedule, by number of children and marital status (2015 tax year). *Source:* Based on data from Internal Revenue Service (2014b).

for those with one (two or more) children. Maximum benefits range from $3,359 for families with one child to $6,242 for those with three or more. Single taxpayers with incomes above $39,131 (with one child), $44,454 (with two children), or $47,747 (with three or more children) are ineligible for the credit.[4] The credit for families without children is much less generous, with phase-in rate of 7.65%, a maximum credit of $503 and a maximum allowable income of $14,820.

Importantly, the EITC is refundable: if the credit exceeds a taxpayer's tax liability, he or she receives the difference as a refund. Typically, families with earnings below $20,000–$25,000 will owe very little income tax, so the bulk of the EITC will arrive as a refund even when withholding is zero.[5]

As elsewhere in the tax code, there are many complexities and special cases, not all illustrated in figure 7.1. Married couples, for example, have slightly different schedules—with longer "plateau" segments and higher phase-out points—than do single filers with the same number of children (as illustrated by the dotted lines in figure 7.1). Defining qualifying children is also difficult, and qualification for the EITC differs from that for the dependent exemption.[6] Finally, the schedule is slightly more

[4] Unmarried taxpayers with dependents are termed head of household filers. In this chapter, we typically refer to this group as "single filers with children" or "single parents with children."

[5] For example, a single parent with two children enters the first bracket (with a 10% marginal tax rate) at gross earnings of $22,000.

[6] A qualifying child for the EITC is younger than 19 (or younger than 24 and a full-time student), lives with the taxpayer for more than half the year, has a valid social security number, and is not claimed as a dependent by another taxpayer (IRS and US Department of the Treasury 2013). In some circumstances, a grandchild can qualify.

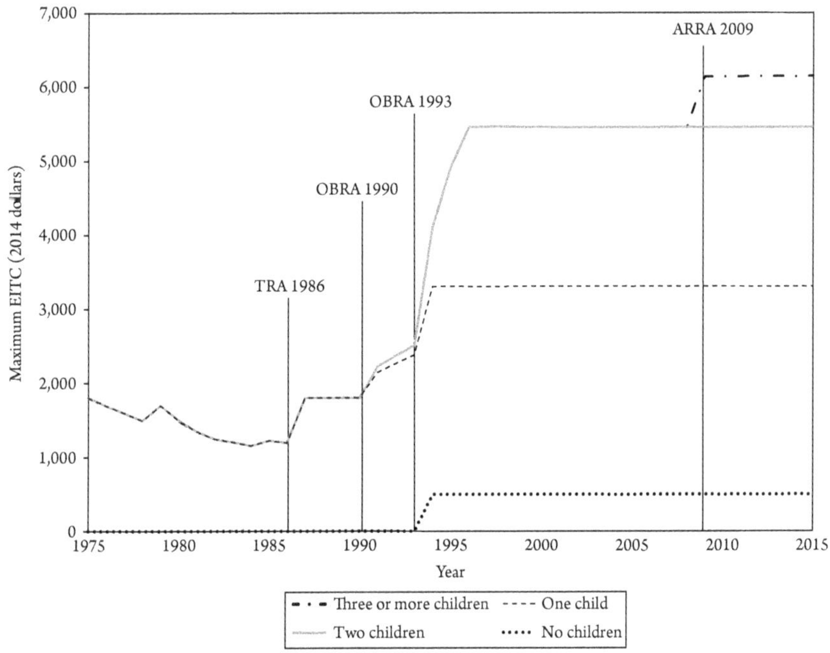

Figure 7.2 Real maximum EITC credit over time, by number of children. *Source:* Based on data from Tax Policy Center (2015b).

complex for families with unearned income. When earnings place the family in the plateau or phase-out ranges and adjusted gross income (including unearned income) exceeds earned income, the credit is based on the latter.

The current EITC schedule reflects substantial growth over time. Figure 7.2 shows how the maximum credit has evolved for families of different sizes. After the program's introduction in 1975, inflation gradually eroded the real maximum benefit. The 1987 expansion of the EITC, passed as part of the Tax Reform Act of 1986, increased the generosity of the credit and indexed the credit schedule to inflation. The most prominent change was the 1993 expansion, enacted as one of President Bill Clinton's signature initiatives—it introduced a credit for families without children for the first time, and greatly increased the credit for families with two or more children. Elsewhere in figure 7.2, one can see smaller expansions in the early 1990s, as well as the introduction of a separate three-child schedule in 2009. This last change was part of the 2009 American Recovery and Reinvestment Act (ARRA) and was originally set to expire at the end of 2010 but has since been extended through 2017. Table 7.1 shows the specific credit parameters for selected years.

The Child Tax Credit (CTC) has a similar form to the EITC, with a phase-in, flat and phase-out structure, and a schedule that differs somewhat across family types.[7]

[7] The relevant family type distinctions differ somewhat from the EITC: only children 16 and under (at the end of the tax year) qualify for the CTC, and it is available to married taxpayers who file separately (who cannot receive the EITC).

Table 7.1 Earned Income Tax Credit parameters, 1975–2015 (selected years), in 2014 dollars

					Phaseout Range	
Calendar Year	*Credit Rate (%)*	*Minimum Income for Maximum Credit*	*Maximum Credit*	*Phaseout Rate (%)*	*Beginning Income*	*Ending Income*
2015						
No children	7.65	6,580	503	7.65	8,240	14,820
One child	34.00	9,880	3,359	15.98	18,110	39,131
Two children	40.00	13,870	5,548	21.06	18,110	44,454
Three children	45.00	13,870	6,242	21.06	18,110	47,747
2014						
No children	7.65	6,582	504	7.65	8,238	14,821
One child	34.00	9,874	3,357	15.98	18,112	39,120
Two children	40.00	13,866	5,546	21.06	18,112	44,448
Three children	45.00	13,866	6,240	21.06	18,112	47,740
2009						
No children	8.44	6,587	504	7.65	8,242	14,829
One child	37.51	9,875	3,358	15.98	18,117	39,129
Two children	44.13	13,869	5,548	21.06	18,117	44,460
Three children	49.65	13,869	6,242	21.06	18,117	47,753
2003						
No children	10.09	6,582	504	7.65	8,231	14,813
One child	44.85	9,880	3,360	15.98	18,111	39,132
Two children	52.76	13,863	5,545	21.06	18,111	44,442
1996						
No children	7.65	6,583	504	7.65	8,237	14,821
One child	34.00	9,875	3,357	15.98	18,112	39,123
Two children	40.00	13,869	5,548	21.06	18,112	44,454
1995						
No children	7.65	6,578	504	7.65	8,231	14,809
One child	34.00	9,883	3,360	15.98	18,114	39,141
Two children	36.00	13,862	4,990	20.22	18,114	42,794
1994						
No children	7.65	6,585	504	7.65	8,231	14,815
One child	26.30	12,758	3,355	15.98	18,107	39,104
Two children	30.00	13,869	4,161	17.68	18,107	41,641
1993						
One child	18.50	13,148	2,433	13.21	20,697	39,104
Two children	19.50	13,148	2,563	13.93	20,697	39,104

Table 7.1 Continued

Calendar Year	*Credit Rate (%)*	*Minimum Income for Maximum Credit*	*Maximum Credit*	*Phaseout Rate (%)*	*Phaseout Range*	
					Beginning Income	*Ending Income*
1992						
One child	17.60	13,146	2,315	12.57	20,699	39,107
Two children	18.40	13,146	2,419	13.14	20,699	39,107
1991						
One child	16.70	13,141	2,194	11.93	20,705	39,110
Two children	17.30	13,141	2,273	12.36	20,705	39,110
1990	14.00	13,140	1,839	10	20,703	39,099
1989	14.00	13,137	1,839	10	20,695	39,087
1988	14.00	13,133	1,839	10	19,887	37,543
1987	14.00	13,134	1,838	10	14,949	33,337
1985–86	11.00	11,288	1,242	12.22	14,675	24,834
1979–84	10.00	14,679	1,468	12.5	17,615	29,358
1975–78	10.00	17,635	1,764	10	17,635	35,270

Notes: Beginning in 2002, the values of the beginning and ending points of the phase-out range were increased for married taxpayers filing jointly. The values for these taxpayers were $1,000 higher than the listed values from 2002 to 2004, $2,000 higher from 2005 to 2007, $3,000 higher in 2008, $5,000 higher in 2009, $5,010 higher in 2010, $5,080 higher in 2011, $5,210 higher in 2012, $5,340 higher in 2013, $5,430 higher in 2014, and $5,520 higher in 2015. *Source:* Based on data from Tax Policy Center (2015b) and US Bureau of Labor Statistics (2014).

However, the structure of the two programs is otherwise different. The CTC depends only on adjusted gross income (AGI), not on earnings. The phase-in and phase-out rates are 15% and 5%, much smaller in magnitude than the EITC. The maximum credit is $1,000 per qualifying child and unlike the EITC the credit is fixed nominally and does not change each year with prices. Importantly, the CTC schedule has an extremely large flat (plateau) range. For two-child tax units, it ranges from $13,333 to $75,000 if single and to $110,000 if married. As a consequence, families with quite high incomes can receive positive CTCs. For example, married couples with three children (who face the most generous schedules) are ineligible for the EITC if their earnings exceed $53,267, but can receive the CTC with incomes as high as $170,000. Table 7.2 shows specific CTC parameters for different family types.

Another major difference is that the CTC, unlike the EITC, is not fully refundable. The refundable portion of the CTC is known as the Additional Child Tax Credit (ACTC) and is limited to 15% of earned income above a fixed threshold. This threshold was $11,500 (in nominal dollars) in 2007, preventing most low income families from receiving meaningful CTCs. But in 2009, ARRA reduced the threshold

Table 7.2 Child Tax Credit parameters, 1997–2015, in 2015 dollars

Non-Time-Varying Parameters (in Nominal Dollars)			
Phase-in rate	15%		
Phase-out rate	5%		
Beginning of phase-out range			
Head of Household	75,000		
Married, Filing Separately	55,000		
Married, Filing Jointly	110,000		
End of phase-out range	1 child	2 children	3 children
Head of Household	95,000	115,000	135,000
Married, Filing Separately	75,000	95,000	115,000
Married, Filing Jointly	130,000	150,000	170,000

Time-Varying Parameters (in 2015 Dollars)

Year	*Maximum Credit per Child*		*Refundable Component*		
	($ Nominal)	*($ 2015)*	*Threshold ($ Nominal)*	*Threshold ($ 2015)*	*Rate above Threshold*
1997	500	742	n/a	n/a	n/a
1998	400	584	n/a	n/a	n/a
1999	500	717	n/a	n/a	n/a
2000	500	695	n/a	n/a	n/a
2001	600	808	10,000	13,461	0.1
2002	600	795	10,350	13,714	0.1
2003	1,000	1,295	10,500	13,603	0.1
2004	1,000	1,266	10,750	13,613	0.15

2005	1,000	1,228	11,000	13,510	0.15
2006	1,000	1,182	11,300	13,357	0.15
2007	1,000	1,156	11,750	13,578	0.15
2008	1,000	1,108	8,500	9,421	0.15
2009	1,000	1,106	3,000	3,319	0.15
2010	1,000	1,090	3,000	3,271	0.15
2011	1,000	1,064	3,000	3,193	0.15
2012	1,000	1,038	3,000	3,113	0.15
2013	1,000	1,020	3,000	3,061	0.15
2014	1,000	1,005	3,000	3,014	0.15
2015	1,000	1,000	3,000	3,000	0.15

Sources: Based on Congressional Research Service (2014) and US Bureau of Labor Statistics (2014).

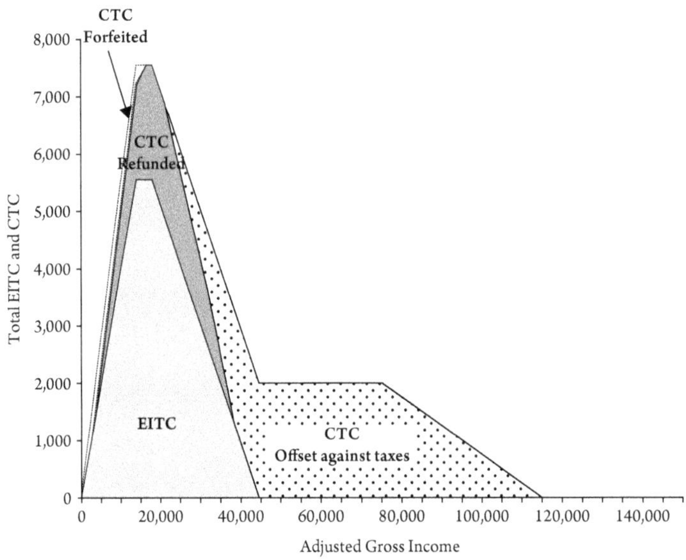

Figure 7.3 Combined EITC and CTC schedules for heads of households with 2 children. *Notes:* Figures reflect a head-of-household filer with two children who qualify under dependent exemption, EITC, and CTC rules but zero Child and Dependent Care Tax credit eligibility. The "CTC Forfeited" area reflects the family's CTC eligibility that cannot be received due to the limit on the portion of the CTC that is refundable. *Sources:* Based on data from GPO (2011), Pomerleau (2014), Steuerle and Quakenbush (2015), and Tax Policy Center (2015b).

to $3,000 (again nominal). This allowed more taxpayers to claim the Additional Child Tax Credit and increased the amount of refundable credits, making the low-income portion of the schedule more similar to the EITC. Like the three-child EITC provision of ARRA, the reduced CTC threshold was originally set to expire at the end of 2010, but it was made permanent in late 2015.

Figure 7.3 augments the EITC schedule for single (head-of-household) taxpayers with two children, as illustrated in figure 7.1, with additional areas representing the portions of the CTC that are used to offset other taxes and refunded under the 2014 schedule.[8] The figure also shows (in an area labeled as "CTC Forfeited") the portion of the credit that is forgone by very low income families for whom the refundability limit is binding. This makes clear that the refundable portion of the CTC serves in large part to expand the EITC, serving approximately the same income range but increasing the benefit. By contrast, the portion of the CTC that offsets other tax liabilities rises much higher in the income distribution, not even beginning to phase out until income is double or more of the maximum value under the EITC.

Figure 7.4 shows tax expenditures on the EITC and CTC over time, in real 2014 dollars and including both tax refunds and foregone tax revenues. The EITC expanded from about $5 billion per year in the 1980s to nearly $50 billion in the mid-1990s and has grown gradually since then. EITC expenditures were just shy of $70 billion

[8] The calculations are for a family with no unearned income or itemized deductions that does not receive the Child and Dependent Care Credit.

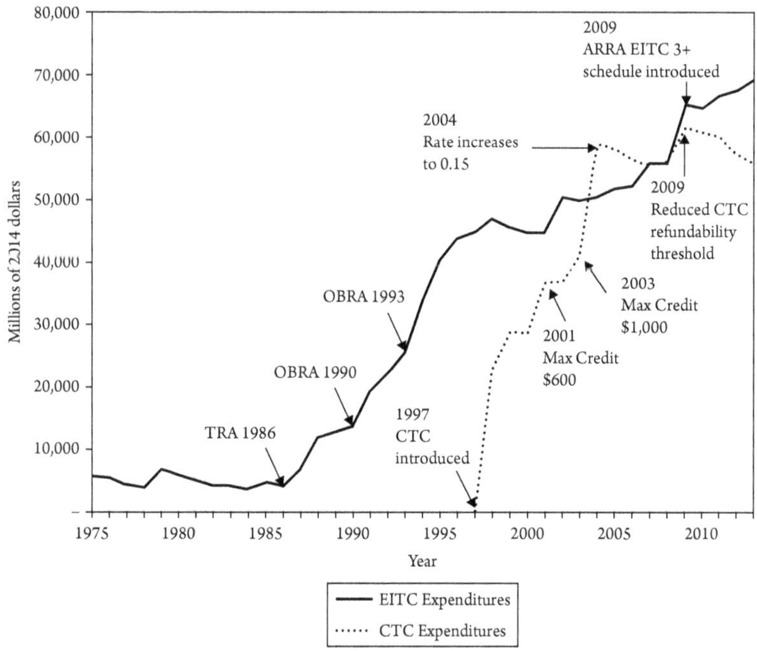

Figure 7.4 Annual cost of the EITC and CTC (Millions of 2014 dollars). *Note*: Each series includes both tax refunds and credits that offset tax liabilities. *Sources*: Based on data from Internal Revenue Service (2014c, 2014d, 2015b), Tax Policy Center (2014, 2015a), and US Bureau of Labor Statistics (2014).

in 2013. The CTC was introduced in 1997, but has grown extremely rapidly since then—since 2003, its total cost has been comparable to the EITC.

An often-voiced concern about means-tested transfer programs is that they can create high effective marginal tax rates (MTRs) as they phase out, and that the constellation of overlapping programs can create an extremely complex budget constraint. Figure 7.5, taken from Steuerle and Quakenbush (2015), shows the combined value of the EITC, the CTC, and other tax- and universally available benefit provisions affecting low-income families (the Child and Dependent Care tax credit; the Supplemental Nutrition Assistance Program, SNAP; Medicaid; the Children's Health Insurance Program, CHIP; and health insurance premium assistance under the Affordable Care Act).[9] We assume here that families participate in all of the available programs, where in fact there is substantial non-participation in each. The tax provisions are at the bottom, with transfers and health programs above them. Three things are of note here. First, the cash value of Medicaid and SNAP benefits (formerly known as food stamps) is much larger than that of the EITC for a family with income below $25,000 (though families may not value health insurance at its full cost). Second, despite this, the overall trapezoid shape created by the EITC schedule, with negative marginal tax rates (i.e., a positive slope in figure 7.5)

[9] The figure shows the programs in Colorado. It would be qualitatively similar in other states, but Medicaid differs across states both in its value and in its reach into the income distribution (for states that did not take up the Affordable Care Act Medicaid expansion).

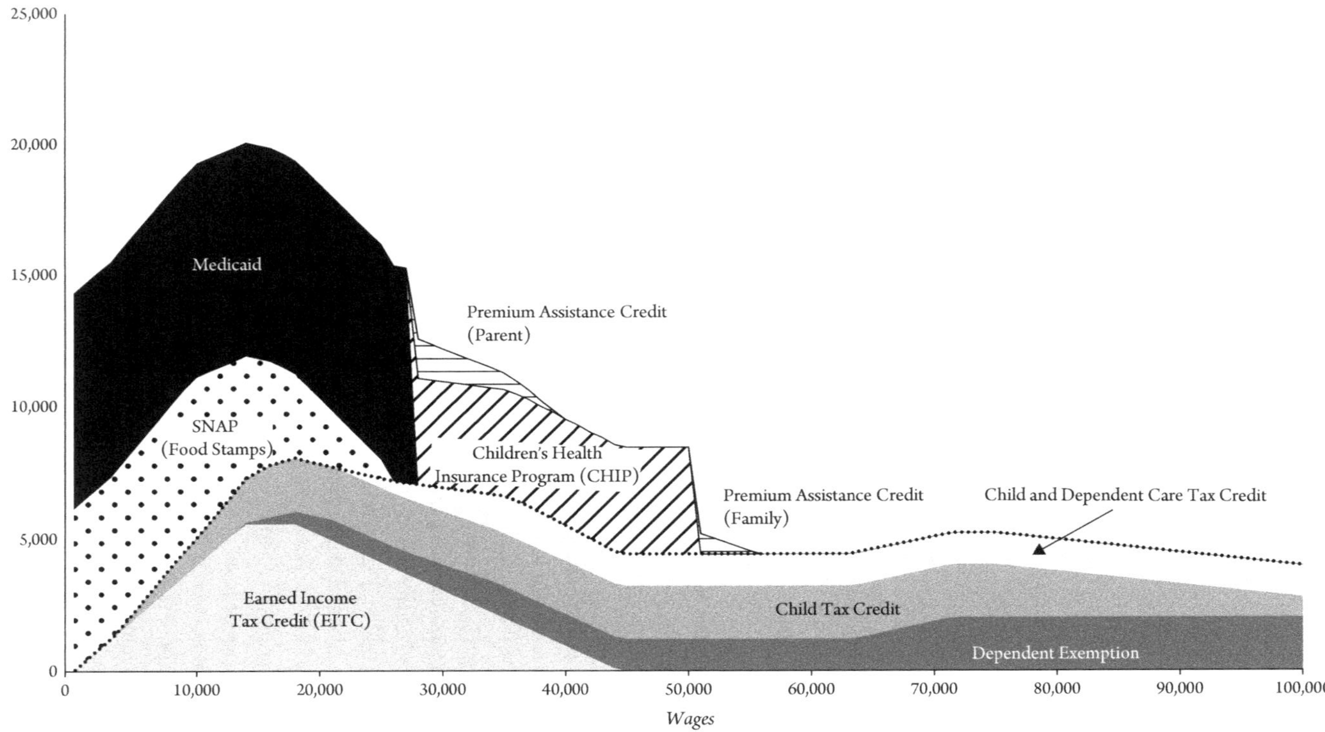

Figure 7.5 Tax and transfer benefits for universally available programs, by income (single adult with 2 children, 2015). *Notes:* Estimated value of tax and transfer benefits for a single parent with two children living in Colorado. Calculations assume that both children qualify for dependent exemptions, the EITC, the CTC, and the Child and Dependent Care Tax Credit. Premium assistance credit excludes the value of penalties paid by employers on the beneficiaries' behalf and the value of additional cost-sharing subsidies. Health coverage and quality of services provided varies by source: Medicaid and CHIP benefits are more comprehensive and have less cost-sharing than those in the exchange. Medicaid and CHIP also pay providers for services at lower rates than private insurers. *Source:* Based on data from Steuerle and Quakenbush (2015).

at low incomes and positive marginal tax rates (a negative slope) at higher levels, shows through despite all of the other programs that are layered on top of it. Third, the EITC serves a population that is also targeted by other means-tested transfers, where the CTC serves a much higher-income population that is unlikely to be receiving other transfers.

Figure 7.6 provides another look at the interaction among programs. Here, we plot the net effective marginal tax rate (EMTR), again assuming 100% take-up of the tax and transfer programs. In the figure, the solid line shows the EMTR for all tax and benefit programs, the dashed line shows the EMTR generated by federal income taxes (EITC, CTC, and the ordinary income tax), and the dotted line shows the EMTR for the EITC and CTC alone. (This figure is also taken from Steuerle and Quakenbush [2015], but we modify it by adding the third series.) Again, we see that other programs shift the marginal tax rate schedule around, but that the basic pattern of negative, zero, then positive MTRs created by the EITC and CTC carries through to the overall schedule.[10]

The US EITC has parallels in programs in place in many other developed countries (OECD 2011). One that is often discussed is the United Kingdom's Working Families Tax Credit (WFTC; see, e.g., Blundell and Hoynes 2004). Like the EITC, it is available only to those who work. A key design difference is that the WFTC does not have a phase-in negative marginal tax rate; rather, it is available only to those who meet minimum weekly hours requirements.

Enumerating the universe of EITC-like programs (often referred to as "In-Work Tax Credits") in other countries is difficult, as similar tax structures can appear quite different depending on how the different portions are labeled. (Consider, for example, the "program" consisting of the combination of payroll taxes, the EITC, and the TANF and food stamps benefit phase-outs.) There is a great deal of heterogeneity in implementation (see Nichols and Rothstein 2015; OECD 2011), in part reflecting different weights placed on the three goals we have outlined. The OECD (2011) classifies programs into those that are more targeted (this group includes the United States, United Kingdom, and France) and those that are more universal with low or no phase-out (this group includes Denmark, Sweden, and The Netherlands). The US program stands out as more generous and as having one of the largest phase-in rates.

7.4 THE ECONOMICS OF IN-WORK TAX CREDITS

We discuss labor-supply incentives under the EITC; those created by the CTC are generally similar, though we also discuss a few relevant differences.

The EITC generates labor-supply incentives on the intensive and extensive margins that differ depending on marital status.[11] Among single parents, who represent 60% of

[10] The figure shows average MTRs over $5,000 income ranges to smooth over spikes in MTRs when taxes and benefits change discretely. This smoothing obscures the zero MTR in the plateau region of the combined EITC and CTC schedule—the $15,000 to $20,000 range includes a portion of the phase-out range as well.

[11] This discussion draws from our prior work including Eissa and Hoynes (2006a), Hoynes and Patel (2015), and Nichols and Rothstein (2015).

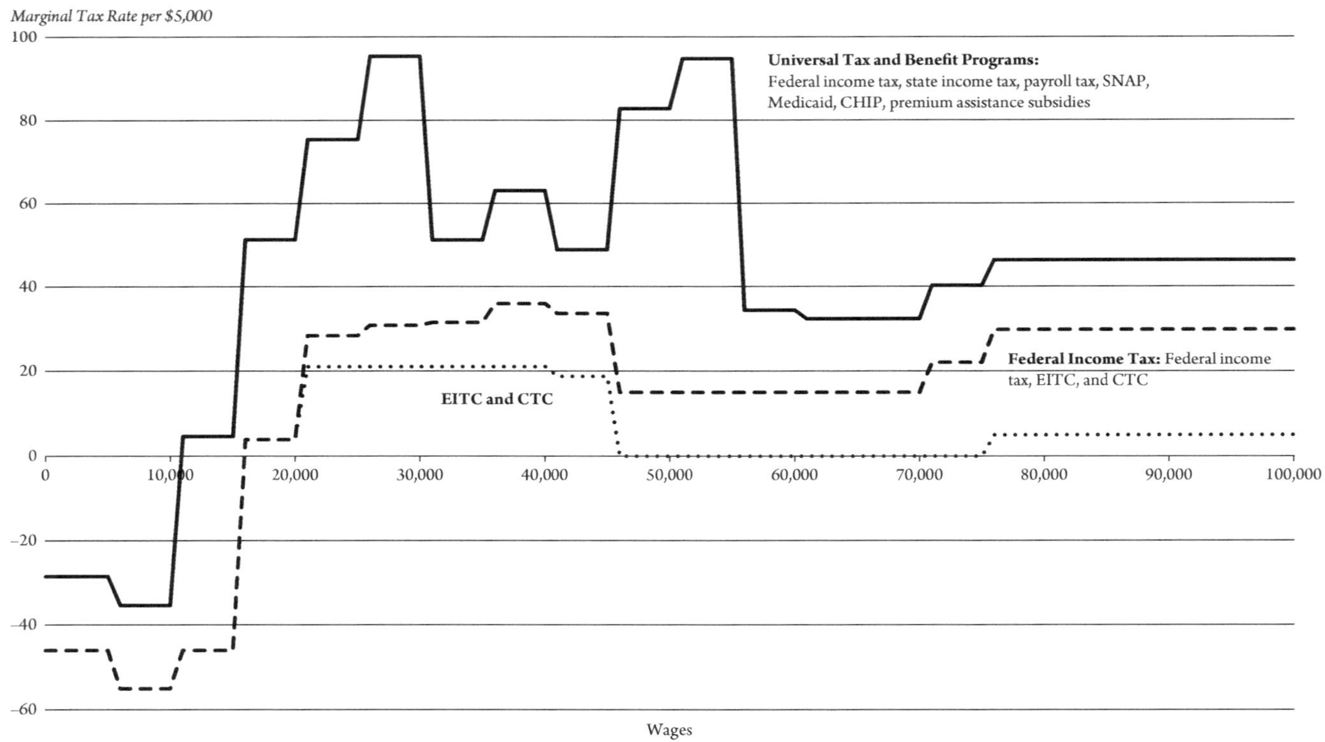

Figure 7.6 Effective marginal tax rates, by income (single adult with 2 children). *Notes:* Average effective marginal tax rates facing a single parent with two children living in Colorado. See notes to figure 7.5. The effective marginal tax rate is averaged over $5,000 income bins and is calculated using changes in net income after taxes and transfers given changes in total compensation (including employer share of payroll taxes). *Source:* Based on data from Steuerle and Quakenbush (2015).

EITC filers and 74% of total EITC tax expenditures, the EITC increases the returns to entering employment for those outside of the labor force, leading to an increase in labor supply on the extensive margin. The phase-in marginal tax rates are large in magnitude, currently −34% for those with one child, −40% for those with two children, and −45% for those with three or more children. This leads to sizable increases in the first-hour net-of-tax wage (though a small portion of this is offset by other taxes, most notably payroll taxes, and by phase-outs in other transfer program schedules), and thus to large incentives to enter work. Even for those whose potential earnings are beyond the phase-in, the EITC increases the net-of-tax wage for entering work so long as potential earnings are below the end of the phase-out range. Figure 7.7 illustrates the canonical budget constraint and income–leisure trade-off under the EITC.

The effects of the EITC on the intensive margin, for those already in the labor market, are less unambiguously work-promoting. In the phase-in region, the EITC increases the net-of-tax wage; the effect on the intensive margin is ambiguous due to a positive substitution effect and a negative income effect. On the other hand, in the phase-out region, both substitution and income effects create a consistent incentive to reduce labor supply, while in the flat region the substitution effect is zero but the pure income effect also is predicted to reduce labor supply.

Because the EITC is based on family income, the credit leads to a somewhat different set of incentives for married taxpayers. Overall, as with singles, we would expect higher rates of "family" employment (participation by at least one family member) for married couples, as a result of the credit being tied to work. But individual participation incentives can be more complex, particularly for secondary earners. Consider

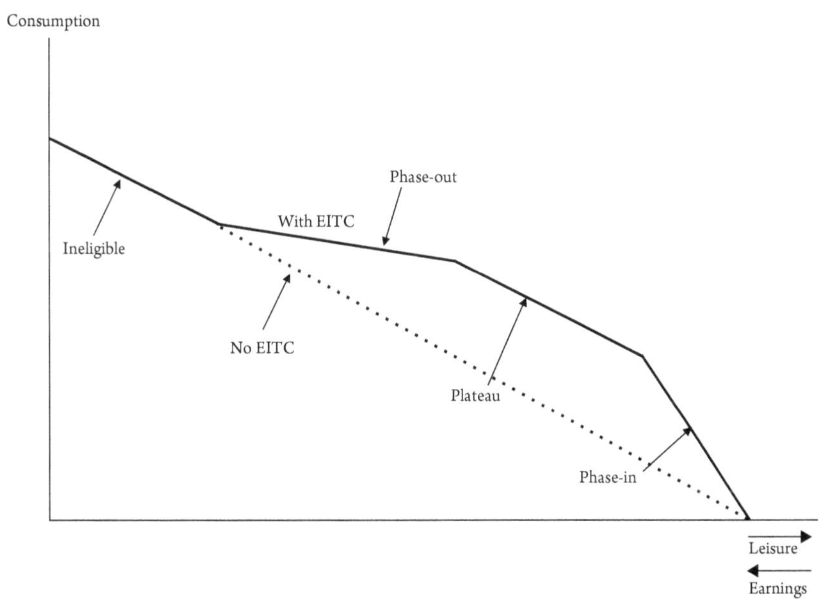

Figure 7.7 EITC budget constraint

a sequential labor-supply decision, where one spouse chooses his/her labor supply (non-strategically) before the other. The primary earner faces the same labor-supply incentives as does a single filer. However, suppose the primary earner earns enough to take the family into the phase-out range on his/her own. In this case, the second mover can only reduce the family's credit by working, and the EITC thus reduces net returns to labor market participation. Importantly, though, the effective positive tax rate here is smaller in magnitude than the negative rate faced by single parents: it can never be bigger than the EITC phase-out rate (currently maxing out at 21.06%) and will often be much smaller.

As this makes clear, there are two unambiguous pro-work incentives in the EITC: single parents and married couples (jointly) are encouraged to work rather than to remain out of the labor force. This is perhaps not surprising, as it is exactly this intended response that motivated the design of the program. But for other groups (secondary earners) and at other margins (hours of work rather than annual participation) the incentives can work in the opposite direction, discouraging rather than encouraging work.

The broad EITC structure can be seen as an efficient way to redistribute income and encourage work. Saez (2002) shows that the optimal income tax schedule can take an EITC-like form when labor supply is more elastic at the extensive than at the intensive margin. However, Saez's model, like most other optimal tax models, abstracts from the United States' family-based tax system. It is difficult to understand the positive tax rate that secondary earners face on the first dollar of earnings as anything other than a necessary consequence of implementing the EITC within such a system.[12] (Other countries typically tax at the individual level.)

The self-employed face additional incentives not captured by this discussion. These mostly relate to reporting—where wage and salary earnings are reported to the IRS by the employer (on the Form W-2 earnings report), self-employed workers report their own earnings with limited third-party verification, and they may be able to change the amount of earnings reported without changing their actual labor supply. Additionally, many self-employed workers make accounting decisions about how to allocate business income between earnings and profits and may have some latitude about the costs they deduct from business earnings. Those in the phase-out range of the EITC schedule and even some with earnings above the end of that range can face an incentive to hide or reclassify some earnings in order to maximize their credit (this would also reduce federal income taxes).

By contrast, those in the phase-in range face incentives to *raise* their reported earnings. This is because the EITC phase-in rate is higher, in absolute value, than the additional payroll (and ordinary income) taxes that would need to be paid on additional reported earnings. Similar incentives apply to those choosing between formal and informal (i.e., under the table) work—the EITC raises the return to being paid

[12] Berlin (2007) and Kearney and Turner (2013) propose reforms that would move toward an individual-based system.

formally, though it can also incentivize shifting a portion of compensation under the table for those in the phase-out range. Most IRS enforcement efforts are focused on identifying under-reporting, and a taxpayer who over-reported her self-employment income in order to increase her EITC may be hard to detect.[13]

Labor-supply predictions under the CTC are similar, but more muted given the smaller credit amount. The general shapes of the two credits are similar, each with phase-in, flat, and phase-out regions. However, the "flat" portion of the CTC is very large and the phase-out rate is low, only 5%, and comes in at relatively high income levels—among families with two children the phase-out region starts at $110,000 for married couples and $75,000 for single parents and ends at $150,000 and $115,000, respectively.

The incentive to participate in the labor market under both the EITC and the CTC is based on the (negative) average tax rate at potential earnings. The CTC never creates an average tax rate (ATR) smaller than −13.04% (this is for three-child families), and for most potential workers it is larger than this. (The combined ATR of the two programs in combination can be much more negative, but this is driven by the EITC.) Thus, while the CTC shares the EITC's pro-participation incentive, the CTC's contribution is likely to be small. The secondary earner and intensive margin incentives are less important as well, given the long reach of the program.

The EITC and CTC also create incentives surrounding other decisions that would affect the tax credit, most notably marriage and fertility. These are not explicit goals of the programs, and indeed the incentivized behavior is often counter to what we might hope to promote, but are inherent in a credit administered through the family-based tax system and tied to the presence and number of children. In particular, the EITC creates incentives for low-income one-earner couples to legally marry, while for low-income two-earner couples the incentive is to avoid marriage or separate. The substitution effects are fairly clear here, but there may also be income effects at work, possibly in the opposite direction: increased financial resources due to the EITC and CTC may free some women from the pressure to enter into unpromising marriages. On net then, the EITC and CTC, like ordinary income taxes, create marriage penalties for some and marriages bonuses for others. Additionally, because the credits increase with the number of children, they may incentivize additional births.

Given the distributional goal of the credits, it is useful to consider their expected effects on the distribution of income. We distinguish two types of effects: the *direct* and *indirect* effects of the programs on net disposable income. The direct effect is simply the EITC or CTC payment, which, of course, raises after-tax and transfer income. The indirect effect comes from any induced change in pretax earnings and other family income. For those induced to enter the labor market, increases in earnings increase family income (a positive indirect effect), but this may be partly offset by reductions

[13] Consider, for example, a self-employed individual in the phase-in range who chooses not to claim a business expense deduction to which she would otherwise be entitled, as doing so would reduce her net earnings and thus her EITC. It is not clear that this would be preventable even if detected.

in other income sources, such as cash welfare and SNAP. For those already in the workforce, the indirect effect is likely to be negative, but, for plausible elasticities, much smaller than the positive direct effect.

There is another indirect effect as well, not yet discussed. Specifically, the EITC may affect *pretax* wages. Since the negative effective tax rate encourages increased labor force participation, standard tax incidence models suggest that the credit will be shared between the buyers and sellers of labor (Leigh 2010; Rothstein 2008, 2010). This occurs through a reduced pretax wage, allowing employers of EITC recipients to capture a portion of the money spent on the EITC (and, as a side effect, creating a transfer from non-EITC workers competing in the same labor markets as the recipients to their employers). This fact was not prominent in early discussions of the EITC, but concerns about incidence have become more prominent as the EITC has expanded in the presence of relatively low minimum wages.

It is useful to relate back to the credit schedule to consider where in the income distribution we expect to see these direct and indirect gains. Figure 7.8 provides some of this information by illustrating the 2015 EITC in income/poverty space for six groups defined by marital status and number of children. In each figure, the x-axis is pretax earnings (or AGI), and the y-axis is after tax income (earnings plus the EITC), expressed as a percentage of the poverty threshold. Consider a single parent with two children working full-time at the federal minimum wage (this group is in figure 7.8e). Pretax earnings would be $15,080, or about 75% of the federal poverty line (FPL). But this family would be in the plateau region of the EITC, with a credit of $5,548 that would bring post-EITC income to 103% of the FPL. Seen somewhat differently, a family with earnings as low as $14,542—placing it just above the top of the EITC phase-in region—would be at 72% of the FPL without the EITC but would be lifted to the FPL by the EITC. Figure 7.8f shows that a married couple with two children with earnings of $18,702 (in the flat region) would be at 77% of the FPL without the EITC but would be lifted out of poverty by the EITC. By contrast, the credit for the childless (panels a and b) is sufficiently ungenerous that all recipients remain in poverty even when their credits are counted as income.

7.5 WHAT DO WE KNOW ABOUT HOW WELL THE PROGRAMS ACCOMPLISH THEIR OBJECTIVES?

We organize our assessment of the available evidence around the three goals: distributional, encouragement of work, and limiting of noncompliance and administrative costs. We begin in section 7.5.1 by presenting empirical estimates of the distributional effects, neglecting behavioral adjustments. We then review the empirical literatures measuring behavioral effects on labor supply (and other outcomes) in section 7.5.2 and noncompliance in section 7.5.3. There is much more direct evidence regarding the EITC, which has a much higher public profile, than about the CTC, so our discussion focuses on the former. In the final subsection, 7.5.4, we present the available evidence on what is missed by the static perspective—on the distributional impacts of

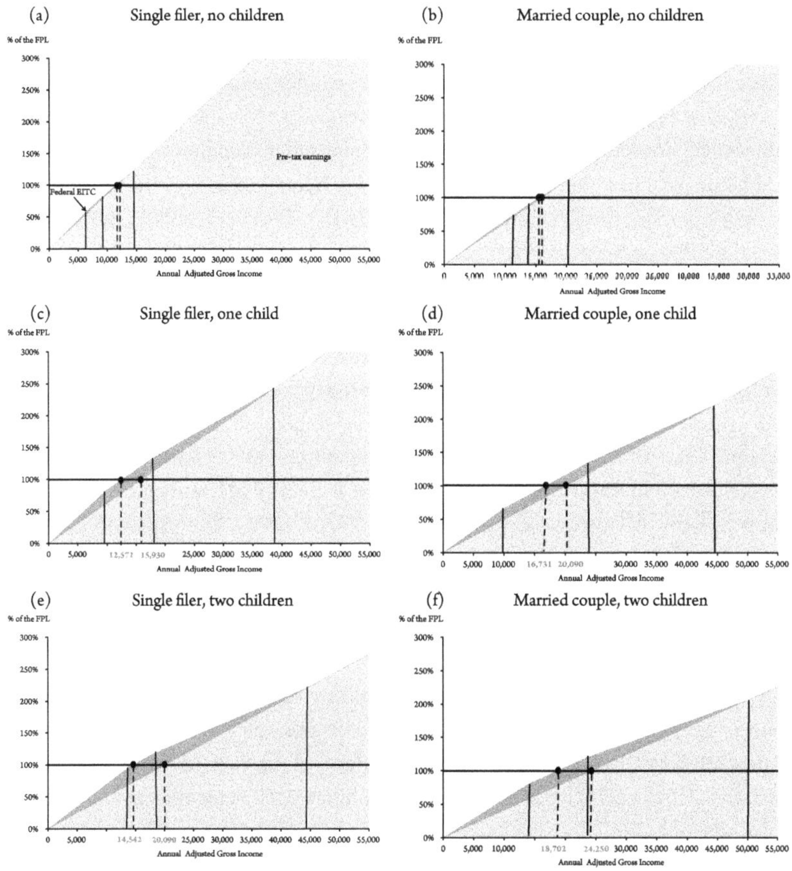

Figure 7.8 Pre-EITC and post-EITC income and poverty, 2015 tax year. *Notes:* Solid vertical lines indicate the location of EITC kink points; see table 7.1 for exact values. Dashed vertical lines indicate the pre-tax income at which a family reaches the poverty line, with or without the EITC. In panel a, these are at pre-tax earnings of $11,770 without EITC or $11,518 with EITC; in panel b, they are at $15,930 and $15,565, respectively. *Sources*: Based on California Department of Health Care Services (2015), California State Legislature (2015), and Tax Policy Center (2015b).

the programs once indirect effects operating through labor supply and other changes that influence pretax income are included.

7.5.1 Static Distributional Effects

Median family income in 2014 was $53,657, the 20th percentile was $21,432, and the 40th percentile was $41,186 (DeNavas-Walt and Proctor 2015). Comparing these figures to figure 7.8 shows that a large fraction of families have incomes that are both (a) not too far from the FPL and (b) in the range where the EITC can have a substantial effect. This suggests that the EITC has the potential to have important effects on after-tax poverty and income distributions, even before considering any indirect effects operating through labor-supply channels.

We rely on two sources in assessing the static distributional effects of the EITC and CTC. The first is the Census Bureau's calculations for the new Supplemental Poverty Measure (SPM).[14] The SPM resource measure includes taxes and both cash and non-cash benefits, allowing for a simple static calculation as to the anti-poverty effects of the EITC and CTC covering the whole population of tax filers and non-filers alike. In 2014, the SPM poverty rate was 15.3%, but the Census Bureau calculates that it would have been 18.4% without the EITC and CTC (Short 2015). The effect on child poverty is even larger: the SPM poverty rate for those under 18 years of age was 16.7% but would have been 23.8% without the refundable tax credits. Based on these numbers, the EITC and CTC can be credited with lifting 9.8 million people, including 5.2 million children, out of poverty. The effects on total poverty are far larger than those of any other single program except Social Security, and the effects on child poverty are the largest without exception.

Of course to gain these benefits, a family has to take-up EITC benefits (file taxes and request the EITC). In the past decades, take-up rates for families with children have been steady at 80% or more (Plueger 2009; Scholz 1994), fairly high compared to other programs serving low-income families (Currie 2006). The expansions to childless taxpayers, who have lower take-up rates, has led to a decline in the overall take-up rate estimated to be 75% in 2005 (Plueger 2009).

The second approach limits attention to tax filers, as represented in the Statistics of Income Public Use File distributed by the IRS. We begin by illustrating the *potential reach* of the two programs. Figures 7.9 and 7.10 show the pretax income distribution of tax filers in 2009 (the most recent year available), inflated to 2014 dollars and presented by marital status (married, single) and number of children (zero, 1, 2, 3 or more).[15] Figure 7.9 is for single filers and figure 7.10 is for married. The income tabulations include all tax filers, not just EITC or CTC recipients.[16] Overlaid on each figure are the EITC and CTC schedules. Several observations can be drawn from these figures. First, they illustrate the variation in the generosity of the schedule across the eight groups. The credits are substantially larger for families with children than for those without children, and the credits are larger for families with more children. Second, they show that the potential reach of the EITC, particularly among single parents, is very high. Only 30% of singles with one child and 18% of singles with two children have earnings higher than the top of the phase-out range (compared to 75% and 76% for married families with one and two children, respectively). Third, they show that the CTC extends to very high income levels, and the majority of both single and married parents qualify for substantial benefits.

[14] Official poverty is based on pretax cash income. Thus, the direct (or static) impact of the EITC on official poverty is zero by construction. The SPM is designed, in part, to capture the effects of tax and other policies on poverty that are missed by the official poverty measure.

[15] In these and future figures, tax filers are divided by the number of children claimed as exemptions. This generally corresponds to the number of qualifying children for the EITC and CTC, though there are exceptions.

[16] We limit the sample in each case to those returns with earned income between $1 and $200,000 and indicate in figure notes the share of total filers for that demographic group that are excluded from the histogram (those filers with earned income that is < = 0 or > $200,000).

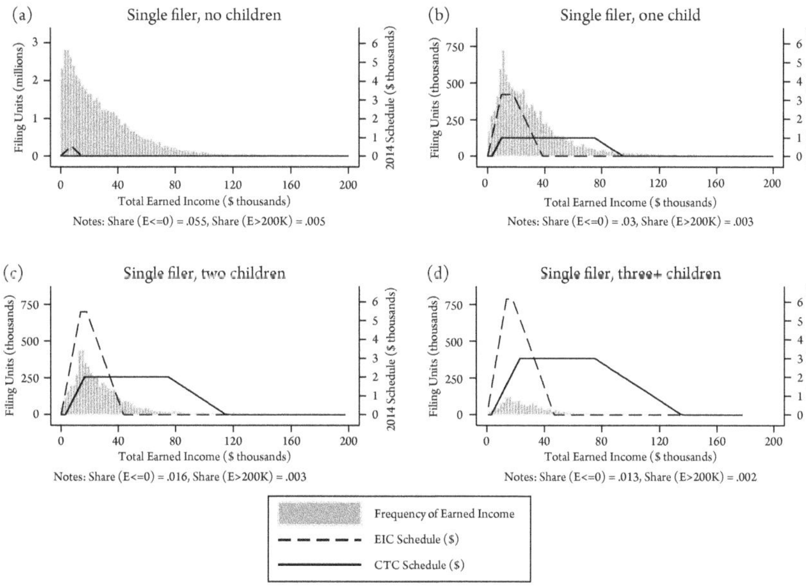

Figure 7.9 Distribution of earnings by filing status and number of children. *Notes*: Graph displays EITC and CTC schedules from 2014, along with 2009 income distributions adjusted to 2014 dollars. Incomes less than or equal to zero or above $200,000 are not shown; notes under each panel indicate the share of filers in each category. The sample excludes filing units receiving social security but without children, and those filing late. The left y-axis in panel (a) differs from the left y-axis in panels b-d. Panels a, b, c, and d represent 47%, 8%, 4%, and 1% of all filing units, respectively. *Source*: Authors' calculations from 2009 Tax Model files created by the Statistics of Income Division of the IRS.

Next, we move from the potential reach to the actual use of the programs—not all families are eligible, and while take-up rates are high they are not complete. We use the Tax Policy Center's (TPC) microsimulation model, applied to the same Statistics of Income file, to measure the distribution of EITC and CTC benefits under current law. We discuss these current law findings in the next paragraphs. In a later section, we use the same approach to examine the distributional impacts of alternative policies.[17]

To illustrate the benefits of current law EITC and CTC, we use the TPC simulations to zero each out in turn. By comparing the resulting estimates to those obtained using the actual policies, we can estimate the distribution of the benefits from each. By design, the TPC simulations assume that pretax income and earnings, as well as all other characteristics (e.g., number of children) are unaffected by counterfactual tax rules and thus only capture the *static* effects of the current policies. We discuss the implications for the full dynamics effects in section 7.5.4.

Figure 7.11 summarizes the EITC and CTC in terms of their distribution across family types (as well as also showing the distribution of total tax filers across these

[17] We thank Elaine Maag and the TPC tax model team for providing us with these simulations.

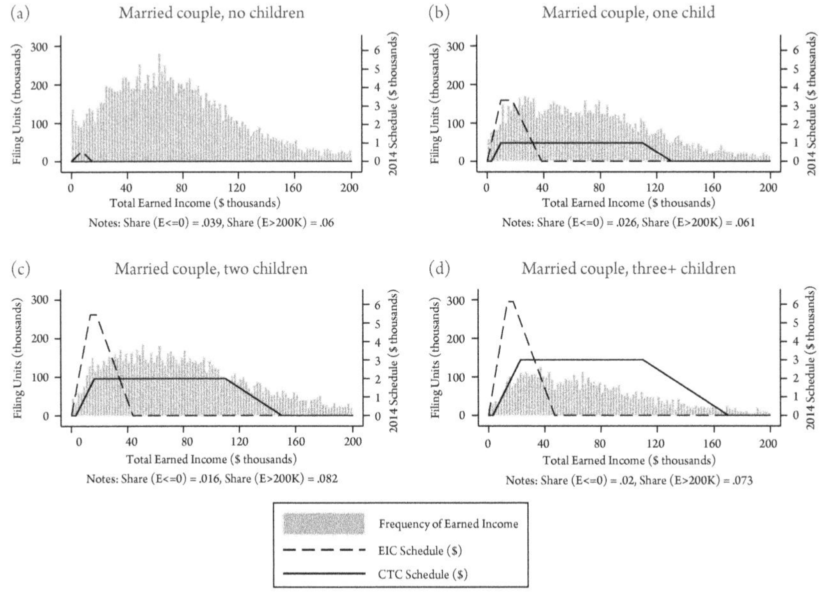

Figure 7.10 Distribution of earnings by filing status and number of children. *Notes:* Graph displays EITC and CTC schedules from 2014, along with 2009 income distributions adjusted to 2014 dollars. Incomes less than or equal to zero or above $200,000 are not shown; notes under each panel indicate the share of filers in each category. The sample excludes married couples filing separately, filing units receiving social security but without children, and those filing late. Panels a, b, c, and d correspond to 18%, 7%, 8%, and 5% of all filing units, respectively. *Source:* Authors' calculations from 2009 Tax Model files created by the Statistics of Income Division of the IRS.

groups). Over 60% of EITC benefits go to head-of-household filers (i.e., to single parents), but this group receives only 40% of CTC benefits. This is due to the CTC's high income limits, which allow over half of the benefits to flow to married couples (many dual-earners); this group gets less than one-quarter of EITC benefits. Not surprisingly, childless single and married filers get few benefits under either policy.[18]

Figure 7.12a plots the distribution of EITC and CTC benefits across the income distribution, pooling tax filers of all different family types. The *x*-axis shows bins of 2015 filing-unit income. There are three sets of bars: The first plots the share of total tax units in each income group; the second the share of total EITC benefits that accrue to each income group; and the third the share of total CTC benefits received by each income group. As context for these shares, note that the total cost of the EITC in 2015 is estimated by the TPC model at $69 billion, while the CTC is $55 billion.[19] The line graph illustrates the share of total income accounted for by each income group—not

[18] Both CTC and EITC bars are non-zero for the "single" and "joint no children" groups. There are some circumstances in which a filer can receive the EITC or CTC while not claiming child exemptions.

[19] The CTC series here includes both credits that are used to offset income tax liabilities and credits issued as refunds, but not those that are forfeited because they exceed the refundability limit.

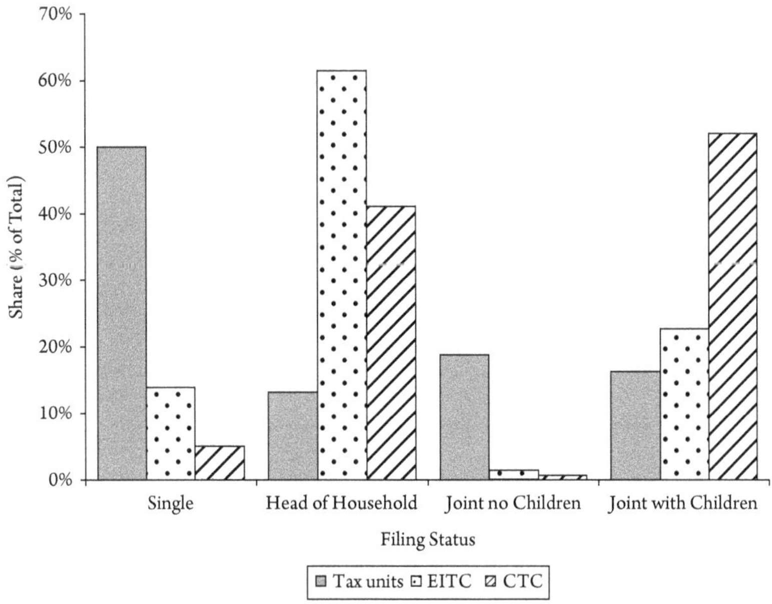

Figure 7.11 Distribution of 2015 EITC and CTC benefits across filing types. *Note:* Filers are classified as with or without children based on the presence or absence of child exemptions, which may not correspond to qualifying children under the EITC and/or CTC. Married filing separately returns (1.7% of the total) are not shown. *Source:* Based on data from Urban-Brookings Tax Policy Center Microsimulation Model (version 0515-1).

surprisingly, the highest income categories account for a much larger share of income than of filing units or of program benefits.

The EITC series in figure 7.12a shows the distributional goal of the program is well met—nearly 60% of the benefits go to filers with income below $30,000. The CTC is less successful in this regard—only one-fifth of benefits go to families with incomes below $30,000. At the other end of the spectrum, 57% of CTC benefits but only 11% of EITC benefits go to filers with incomes over $50,000; over 20% of CTC benefits go to families with incomes above $100,000.

The remaining panels in figure 7.12 show the distribution across both family type and income, distinguishing among married couples with children (figure 7.12b), married couples without children (figure 7.12d), single filers with children (figure 7.12c), and single filers without children (figure 7.12e). For each subgroup, we display the relevant series (tax units, pretax income, EITC benefits, and CTC benefits) as shares of the total (all filers) amount. Comparing the EITC bars to the tax unit bars in these figures, it is clear that much of the variation in EITC benefits across married- and single-parent families, as seen in figure 7.11, is a reflection of income distributions within each group. There are roughly 15% more married-with-children returns as head-of-household returns, but the latter are 3.7 times as likely to have incomes below $40,000. CTC payments are much less sensitive to income, so are more concentrated in married-couple families.

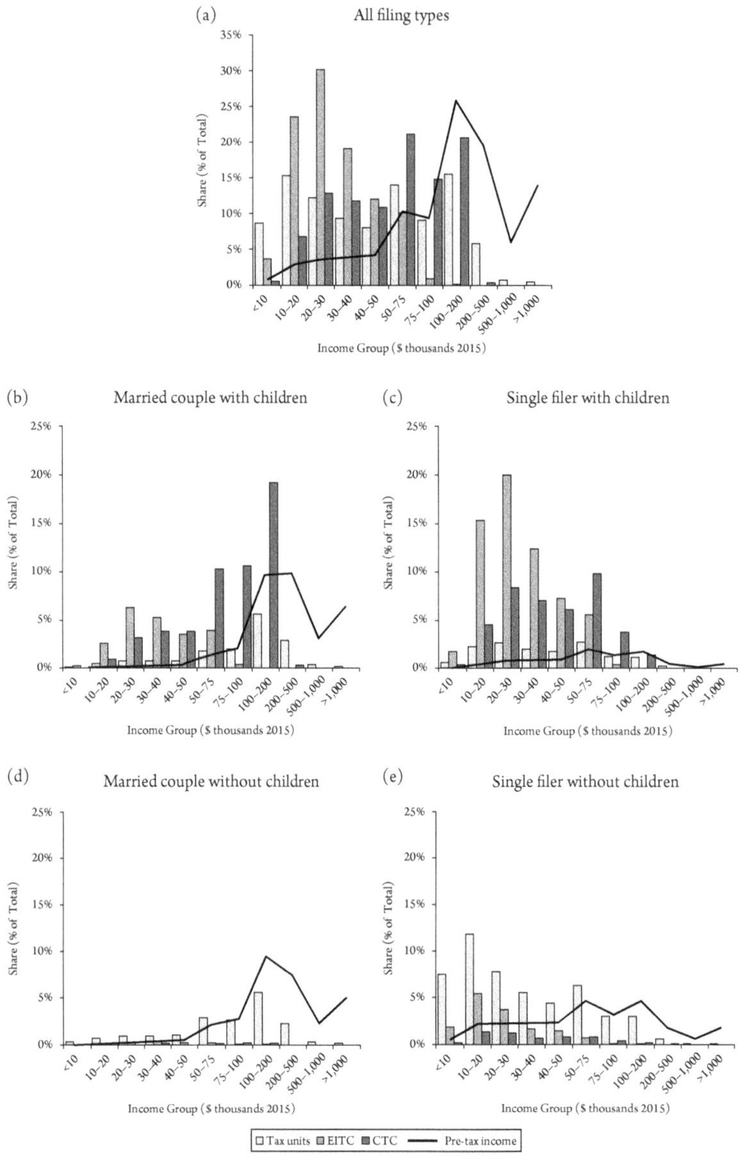

Figure 7.12 Distributional benefits of 2015 EITC and CTC and total pre-tax income across filing types and income group. *Notes:* Tax units, pre-tax income, and EITC benefits are each expressed as shares of their respective total overall tax filing units, across all filing statuses and income levels. Filers are classified as with or without children based on the presence or absence of child exemptions, which may not correspond to qualifying children under the EITC and/or CTC. Married filing separately returns (1.7% of the total) are not shown separately but are included in panel (a). *Source:* Based on data from Urban-Brookings Tax Policy Center Microsimulation Model (version 0515-1).

One limit to the redistributive power of the EITC is not reflected in figure 7.12: most of the benefits are distributed as tax refunds in the spring. If families are credit constrained—as many EITC recipients likely are—then an annual lump-sum payment has a smaller effect on the household's welfare than would one that is more evenly distributed, and thus the EITC is a less effective redistribution policy than it appears based on annual income distributions. The Advance EITC program allowed recipients to receive their credits throughout the year, but take-up was extremely low (under 1%) and the IRS eventually cancelled the program. Its failure does not seem to be due to lack of information or even default effects: experiments that inform recipients about the program and to overcome default behavior had only minor impacts on take-up (IRS 1999; Jones 2010). This could indicate that recipients prefer their EITC payments as lump-sums, perhaps seeing the program as a form of forced saving (see the discussion in Nichols and Rothstein 2015). But the preferences of EITC recipients in this regard are not well understood.

7.5.2 Behavioral Effects

A significant body of research examines the behavioral effects of the EITC, much of it exploiting significant expansions in the tax acts of 1986, 1990, 1993, and 2009. There have even been several comprehensive reviews of the literature (e.g., see Eissa and Hoynes 2006a; Hotz and Scholz 2003; Nichols and Rothstein 2015). Rather than recapitulate those reviews, here we provide only a brief summary of the main findings in the literature.

The main focus of the empirical literature regarding the EITC, particularly in the early years, was to quantify and explore the main pro-work aspect of the program: the incentive it creates for single parents to participate in the labor force. In practice, this meant analyses of employment decisions (at the extensive margin) of less-educated single mothers. Most studies take a quasi-experimental approach leveraging the variation across tax year and family size in the federal credit, essentially using women with no children or women with just a single child as controls. (A smaller set of papers uses variation in state EITCs, which add on to the federal credit.) The 1993 expansion provides a particularly attractive policy reform because it represents the largest expansion of the credit in its history (see figures 7.2 and 7.4) and the expansion for women with two or more children was much larger than the expansion for women with one child (thus allowing for a comparison among single women with children, comparing those with two or more children to those with one child).

Across all of the different types of comparisons, the evidence nearly universally points to a significant positive effect of the EITC on the labor force participation (or employment) of single women with children. For example, Eissa and Liebman (1996) find labor force participation increased by 2.8 percentage points for single women with children, relative to single women without children, after the EITC expansion of 1986. Over a longer period, Meyer and Rosenbaum (2001) find that the EITC raised labor force participation by 7.2 percentage points for single women with children

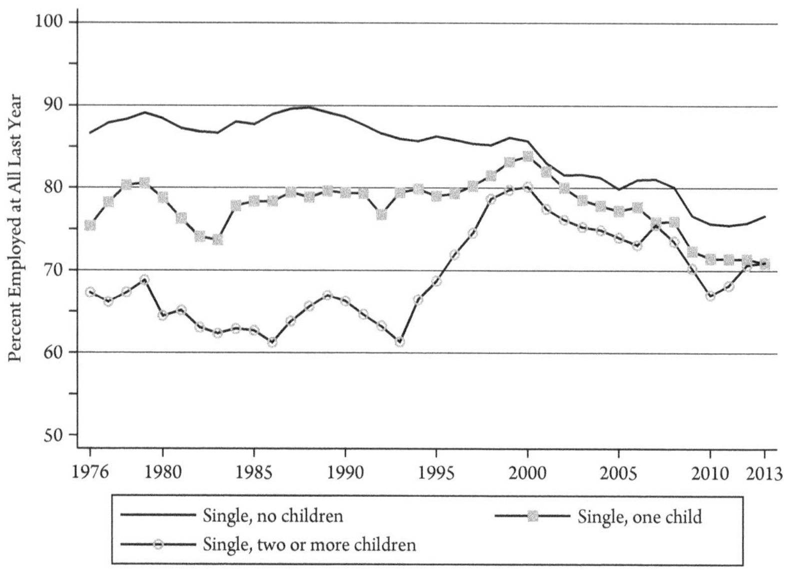

Figure 7.13 Employment rates of unmarried women over time, by number of children. *Note:* Sample consists of unmarried women aged 19–44. *Source:* Authors' analysis of the Current Population Survey Annual Social and Economic Supplement (US Census Bureau 2015).

relative to those without children between 1984 and 1996. Hoynes and Patel (2015) find that the 1993 expansion increased employment by 6.1 percentage points, with larger effects for women with two or more children. Using the approach in Chetty et al. (2013), the extensive margin elasticities for these studies range from 0.30 to 0.45 (Hoynes and Patel 2015).[20]

The changes in employment, particularly for the 1993 expansion, are evident in the basic unconditional trends. This is illustrated in figure 7.13 (based on Nichols and Rothstein 2015: figure 8b), where we use the March Current Population Survey and plot the percentage of single women (those with zero, one, two, or more children) working at all during the year for each year from 1976 to 2013. The figure illustrates that for the two decades before 1993, the annual employment rate for unmarried women with children was substantially below that for single women without children. By 2000, the gap narrowed substantially, with an especially dramatic increase for single women with two or more children (who experienced a larger EITC expansion). Since then, employment rates show a decline for all groups, likely reflecting adverse macroeconomic conditions.

Figure 7.14, taken from figure 7 in Hoynes and Patel (2015), illustrates the quasi-experimental estimates of the EITC from the 1993 expansion, controlling for other

[20] These elasticities are with respect to the net of tax wage, taking account of other taxes. It is more common in the EITC literature to report elasticities with respect to gross earnings plus the EITC (or, equivalently, with respect to the EITC average tax rate). These are higher, in the 0.7–1.0 range. See Chetty et al. (2013: appendix B).

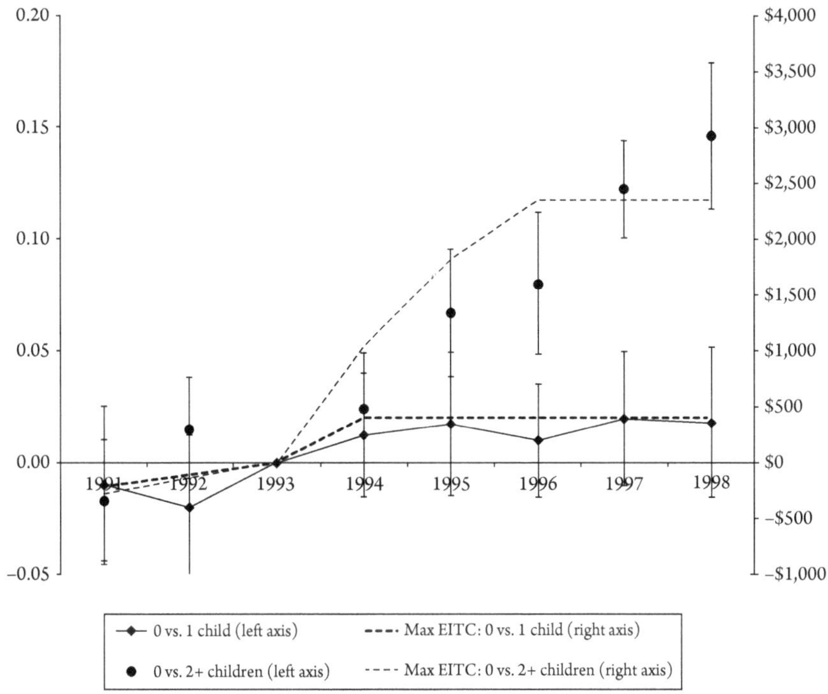

Figure 7.14 Event time estimates of the effect of the 1993 EITC expansion on the employment of single women with children. *Notes:* The sample includes single women, ages 24 through 48 with some college education or less from the 1992 through 1999 Current Population Survey Annual Social and Economic Supplement. Coefficients are estimates from an event study model with single women without children as the control group and 1993 as the omitted year. The dashed lines show the change in maximum EITC benefits for the treatment minus the control for each year. Vertical bars show 95% confidence intervals, adjusted for clustering at the state level. *Source:* Figure 7 from Hoynes and Patel (2015).

contemporaneous effects such as welfare reform and the strong labor market (Blank 2001). The figure plots event time coefficients and 95% confidence intervals for single women with two more children and with one child, both compared to single women without children. The omitted year is 1993 (the year prior to the policy expansion). The graph also displays the change in the real average maximum credit across the groups (dashed line, right axis) to give some guidance as to how the EITC is changing over time and across groups. The figure shows that differential labor supply increases after 1993 closely follow the pattern of EITC expansions—women with children increase their employment relative to women without children, with larger effects for women with two or more children.[21]

This graph makes quite clear that the EITC has a large positive effect on single mothers' labor force participation. This conclusion is consistent across studies: estimated

[21] It also shows that in the years prior to the expansion, employment was trending similarly across the groups, validating the use of women without children as controls.

extensive margin effects are quite robust across different time periods (including studies identified from pre-1993 expansions) and using different identification approaches (including more structural approaches or using state EITC expansions). There are fewer studies of married couples, but the available evidence shows that the EITC leads to small reductions in the employment of married women, consistent with the predictions above, and there is little evidence of any effects on men (Eissa and Hoynes 2004, 2006b).

A second question concerns the EITC's effect on the intensive margin. Estimates based on quasi-experimental approaches like that illustrated in figure 7.14 show little sign of meaningful effects (Hotz and Scholz 2003; Nichols and Rothstein 2015). However, standard difference-in-differences research designs are not ideally suited to this question due to the confounding effects of composition—the large extensive margin effects mean that the composition of the working population is different between the pre- and post-EITC periods.

In the past decade, the EITC literature has refocused on the intensive margin using other methods. Saez (2010), which looks for "bunching" in the income distribution around the kinks in the EITC schedule, was one of the first in this vein. Like other bunching studies that have followed, Saez found little sign that families in the phase-out range reduce their labor supply to maximize their credits, but did find evidence that workers in the phase-in range adjust to increase their credits (Saez 2010; see also Chetty, Friedman, and Saez 2013; Chetty and Saez 2013; Mortenson and Whitten 2015). Most of this effect derives from self-employed workers, who generally self-report their earnings without independent verification on the part of the IRS. It is thus difficult to determine whether it is a real behavioral effect or a change in reporting. Chetty, Friedman, and Saez (2013) use earnings distributions of families in the year after the birth of a child to look for intensive margin responses. They find that the intensive margin elasticity is small on average, around 0.14, though they argue that this is attenuated due to a lack of information about the incentives that families face.

There are a handful of studies that examine the effect of the EITC on marriage (e.g., Ellwood 2000; Herbst 2011; Michelmore 2014; Rosenbaum 2000). The empirical evidence is largely inconclusive, though it generally points to small effects. There is less evidence on the effects of the EITC on fertility (Baughman and Dickert-Conlin 2009), but again the results suggest small effects. Finally, though somewhat outside the scope of this chapter, there is a recent and growing literature that uses the increase in after-tax income generated by the EITC to examine impacts on downstream outcomes. The credit has been found to lead to increases in infant health (Baker 2008; Baughman 2012; Hoynes, Miller, and Simon 2015; Strully et al. 2010), maternal health (Evans and Garthwaite 2014), children's cognitive outcomes (Chetty, Friedman, and Rockoff 2011; Dahl and Lochner 2012), and educational attainment (Manoli and Turner 2014; Michelmore 2013). These are generally interpreted as income effects, though it is possible that a portion of each effect is directly related to increased maternal employment.

In sum, the evidence on behavioral effects shows that the EITC leads to substantial increases in employment for single mothers, concentrated among less-skilled women and among those with more than one child. There is also evidence of small reductions in employment for secondary earners in married couples but little evidence of any induced changes in male labor supply. Although there is less evidence on the intensive margin of labor supply, the available evidence suggest at most small responses. There is little evidence that the EITC has much of an effect on marriage or fertility.

7.5.3 Compliance

Overclaiming of the EITC has been a persistent concern with the program. The most recent IRS study (Internal Revenue Service 2014a), based on audited 2006–2008 returns, found an overclaiming rate between 28.5% and 39.1% of all EITC dollars claimed (the range derives from assumptions about taxpayers who did not participate in the audit).[22] There are two primary sources of noncompliance—misclaiming of qualifying children and income misreporting.

Qualifying child violations occur in 30% of returns with overclaims, but represent over half of overclaimed dollars. The EITC's qualifying child rules are complex, and—despite recent changes aimed at harmonization—differ from those for child exemptions. IRS Publication 596 lists a multitude of examples in which many economists would have trouble identifying who was eligible to claim the credit and many situations in which multiple filers could claim different credits with choices over who claims qualifying children.[23] The optimal choice is often hard to determine. Greenstein and Wancheck (2011) conclude that "EITC overpayments most commonly result from misunderstanding of how to apply the EITC's intricate rules regarding who may claim a child, especially in changing family situations involving separated, divorced, or three-generation families." Although definitions have been changed to better align with those used elsewhere in the tax code and the IRS has increased its efforts to verify children's identities (by, e.g., requiring reporting of the child's social security number on the tax form), misreporting of qualifying children remains high.

The other major category of overclaiming, income misreporting, is more common but results in smaller overpayments, on average. About two-thirds of returns with overclaims misreport income. Incorrect reporting of self-employment income is the primary source of income misreporting (in part reflecting the lack of second party verification that is available for wage and salary income).

[22] The IRS is able to disallow some overclaims, so the overpayment rate is lower—around 24% in recent years. Moreover, the rates of overclaiming may be overstated in the administrative data, as filers who request reconsideration of credit denials succeed in overturning nearly half of IRS rulings (National Taxpayer Advocate 2004).

[23] Residency test failures are the most common in the overclaiming audits, suggesting that many non-custodial parents claim a child who should have been claimable only by the custodial parent. Enforcement is challenging for the IRS, as many components of the qualifying child definition are not readily observed.

Another source of evidence related to reporting or noncompliance comes from the "bunching" studies discussed above. In the original Saez study (Saez 2010), since replicated by others (e.g., Chetty et al. 2013), there is substantial evidence of bunching at the end of the phase-in region, at the first EITC kink. Chetty and Saez (2013) found something similar as the result of an information treatment at H&R Block: the provision of information about the tax schedule led families to move toward the first kink point. There is no sign of bunching at the second kink point (between the plateau and the phase-out range), nor of a hollowing out of the density at the third (at the end of the phase-out range), though the standard model would predict all three.

As Saez points out, the total marginal tax rate, combining the EITC and other taxes (e.g., payroll taxes), is generally negative in the phase-in range, implying that a filer with earnings below the first kink point would come out ahead by reporting to the IRS *higher* earnings than he/she actually had. Saez (2010) and others find that the bunching at the first kink point is entirely driven by the self-employed, who likely have a fair amount of latitude over how much income to report. Thus, Saez suggests that the bunching he observes likely reflects decisions to report casual earnings (from, e.g., babysitting) that would not have been reported to the IRS in the absence of the EITC, though it is also possible that some of it reflects a true intensive margin response or reporting income that was not actually received in order to maximize the value of the EITC.

7.5.4 Dynamic Distributional Effects

The evidence suggests that the labor-supply impacts of the EITC are large, particularly on the participation decisions of single parents, and may have important implications for the distributional impacts of the policy. Unfortunately, there is little evidence that quantifies the distributional effects of the EITC taking account of the full behavioral responses.

A handful of studies estimate the effect of the EITC on income or poverty (Bollinger, Gonzalez, and Ziliak 2009; Grogger 2003; Gunderson and Ziliak 2004; Hoynes and Patel 2015). This literature shows that the *direct* (EITC payment) and *indirect* (through earnings net of changes in other income) channels combine to lead to large effects of EITC on income. For example, Hoynes and Patel (2015) use difference-in-difference (DD) and parameterized DD models to estimate the effects of the EITC on the distribution of after tax and transfer income relative to poverty among single mothers with less than a college education. They find that the 1993 expansion led to a 7.9 percentage point increase in the percent of families with children with after-tax and transfer income above poverty. They estimate similar models for the propensity to have after-tax and transfer income above various income to poverty thresholds. Figure 7.15 (taken from figure 11 in Hoynes and Patel 2015) provides their core results. They find that the EITC has little effect on the very lowest income groups (below 75% of poverty), likely reflecting low labor market attachment of families in this range. Between 75% and 150% of the FPL, the effects of the EITC are large and statistically significant; they then fall to zero by 250% poverty.

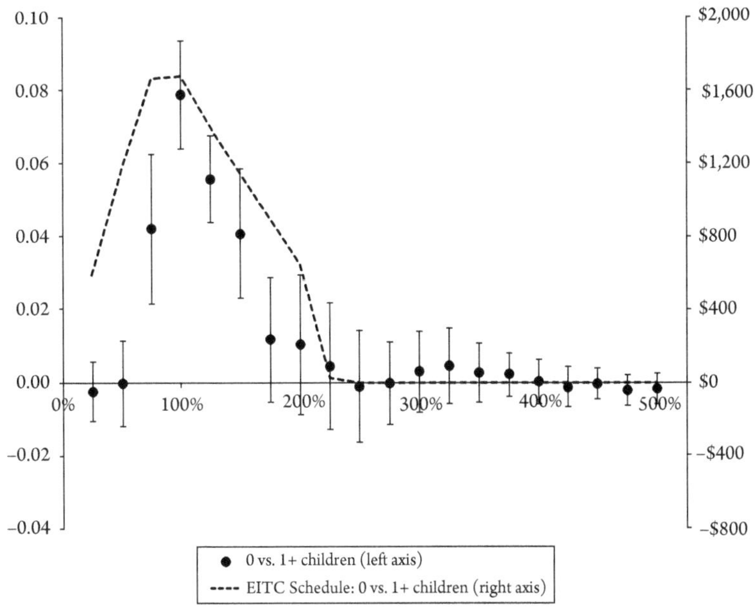

Figure 7.15 Difference-in-difference estimates of the effect of the 1993 EITC expansion on the distribution of after-tax and transfer income as a share of the federal poverty threshold. *Notes:* The sample includes single women, ages 24 through 48 with some college education or less from the 1992 through 1999 Current Population Survey Annual Social and Economic Supplement. Each dot and whisker represents a single regression estimate and 95% confidence interval (adjusted for clustering at the state level). Each model is a difference-in-difference model comparing women with children to women without children, before and after 1993. The dashed line is the weighted change in EITC benefits for families with children versus those without children across the 1993 EITC expansion. *Source:* Figure 11 from Hoynes and Patel (2015).

Hoynes and Patel then use these results to compare the static distributional effects of the EITC (direct effect only) to the dynamic distributional effects (direct and indirect effects). They find that, for their sample of single mothers with children, ignoring the indirect effects of the EITC (increased earnings net of changes in other income) leads to significant underestimates of the distributional effects. For example, they find that the total effect of the EITC removes 2.4 million children from poverty compared to 1.2 million when considering only the direct effect.

Another dimension of dynamic effects has to do with tax incidence, the effect of the EITC on pretax wages. As we discussed in section 7.4, the standard incidence model predicts that the EITC should, to some degree, reduce pretax wages. These effects would be felt by EITC-eligible and non-eligible workers (who mix in the workplace) alike. Such general equilibrium effects are difficult to estimate using credible research designs, especially given the widespread use of the variation by tax year and number of children (e.g., OBRA 93), as wage effects would be common to all family types in the same year. Leigh (2010) exploits the introduction of state level EITCs in a DD framework, essentially relying on the assumption that employers do little substitution of workers across states. He finds that a 10% increase in the EITC leads to a 5% (2%) reduction in pretax wages for high school dropouts (high school graduates) and no effect on the wages of college graduates. Rothstein (2010; see also Rothstein 2008) takes a simulation approach by relying on previous estimates of demand and supply elasticities to calibrate a calculation of the distributional effects of the EITC. He finds that $1 in EITC payments leads to $0.09 worth of increased labor supply but a $0.27 decline in worker pretax incomes—the difference, $0.36, is transferred to employers through reduced pretax wages. As a consequence, after-tax income rises by only $0.73.

Although none of the evidence is airtight, it appears that employers of low-wage labor capture a meaningful share of the credit through reduced wages and that this comes to some extent at the expense of low-skill workers who are not eligible for the credit (due, e.g., to not having children). The implied effects are large enough to have quantitatively important implications for the EITC's distributional impacts—a crude calculation based on Rothstein's (2010) results suggests that static calculations could overstate the transfer to recipients by as much as one-third, and that dynamic calculations like Hoynes and Patel's (2015) overstate it by as much as one-half (based on the ratio of Rothstein's (2010) wage-constant effect on after-tax income, $1.09, to the net effect inclusive of wage responses, $0.73). But this remains an under-studied topic, and the effective confidence intervals around these estimates are large.

7.6 POTENTIAL REFORMS

The evidence indicates that the EITC is doing a good job of meeting its objectives. It successfully targets low-income working families, bringing many of them out of poverty; it has meaningful positive effects on labor force participation, with small or zero negative effects on the intensive margin and for secondary earners; and, while there is evidence of substantial overclaiming, the dollar amounts are not that large, and errors seem to relate in large part to qualifying child definitions. The CTC, while less studied, is clearly less effective on at least the distributive and labor-supply dimensions.

But although the EITC is doing well on all three margins, it would be possible to improve. The concern most commonly voiced about the EITC is that it largely fails to reach childless workers (including non-custodial parents). For the CTC, an important concern is that it misses too many low-income families, certainly before but even after the 2009 expansion to its refundability (West, Boteach, and Vallas 2015).

To illustrate the possibilities for reform, we consider potential changes aimed at addressing these concerns. First, we examine expansions of the childless EITC, both President Obama's proposal to double this credit and a more ambitious expansion designed to bring the childless EITC to rough parity (in family-need-adjusted terms) with that available to families with children. Second, we assess the impact of the recent reduction of the earnings threshold for refundability of the CTC and consider reducing it further.

7.6.1 The Childless EITC

Because historically the EITC was seen (at least by some) as an alternative to cash welfare for families with children, it was initially unavailable to childless adults and remains comparatively limited for them. But views of the purpose of the EITC have evolved, and it is now seen, at least in part, as a way of compensating for the erosion of real wages paid to low-income workers. This does not provide much rationale for excluding childless workers, and so there is increasing interest in expanding this portion of the credit. In 2015, President Obama proposed a substantial expansion—roughly doubling the generosity of the childless credit, as well as extending the plateau and phase-out ranges to higher income levels. But even this proposal, if enacted, would leave the childless credit much smaller than that available to families with children.

We compare three versions of the childless EITC: current law, the Obama administration proposal, and a more aggressive proposal of our own invention. The latter is designed to set the maximum credit for a single childless adult to the same level as for a single adult with one child, after adjusting for the different needs of one- and two-person families using a standard equivalence scale. We keep the phase-in range the same as in current law and solve for the needed phase-in rate; this turns out to be nearly identical (33.8% vs. 34%) to that for one-child families under current law. We set the plateau for single adults to have a width of $5,000, very similar to its width under Obama's proposal and to the plateau for multiple-child families under current law. Following the schedule for families with children, we extend the plateau range by $5,500 for married couples. We set the phase-out rate to match the current one-child schedule (15.98%).

Figure 7.16 illustrates the schedules under the three alternatives, with the one-child single schedule shown as well for comparison. Either of the alternatives to current policy would better serve the purpose of redistributing more money to low-income families, and would do more to encourage labor force participation, than does the current schedule. They would likely reduce overclaiming: although childless individuals and couples would face the same incentives as do those with children to over-report self-employment income, the great incentive that families currently face to misclaim qualifying children would be much reduced and, in many cases, nearly eliminated. The expanded credit would also lead to changes in incentives for marriage. Couples without children would face similar incentives as those for couples with children (marriage penalties for two earners and marriage subsidies for one earners), and marriage penalties for two-earner couples with children would increase. The existing research, however, suggests these changes in marriage penalties (and subsidies) will not translate to meaningful changes in marriage.

We use the Urban-Brookings TPC Microsimulation model to quantify the cost of these changes. Table 7.3 shows the results. The Obama proposal would increase the number of recipients of the childless credit by over 60%, reaching higher into the income distribution, and more than double the average credit. The

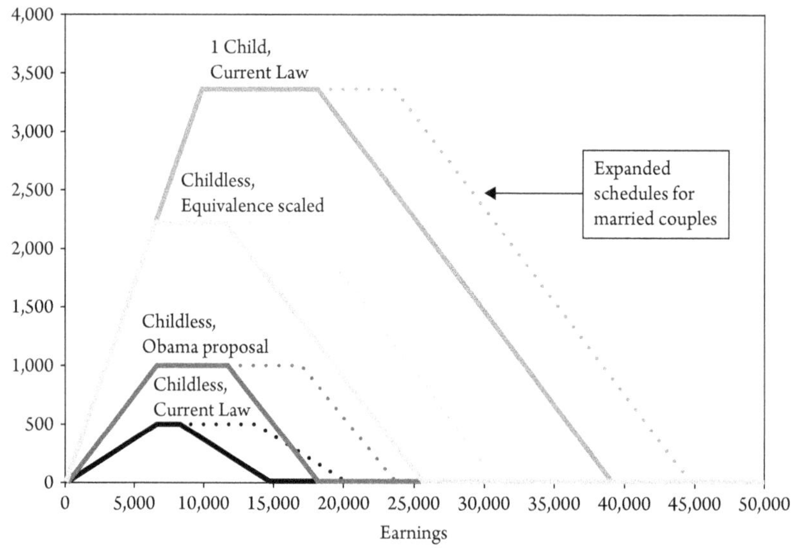

Figure 7.16 Childless EITC schedules under current law and proposed alternatives. *Notes:* Solid lines show the schedule for single and head-of-household filers; dotted lines for married filers. Dollar values expressed in 2015 dollars. *Source:* Based on Executive Office of the President and US Treasury Department (2014), updated to 2015, and authors' tabulations.

more generous, equivalence-scaled expansion would raise the number of recipients by 127% and nearly quintuple the average credit. Clearly, each of these represents a dramatic expansion of the program: the Obama expansion would transfer an additional \$4.6 billion to low-income childless families, more than tripling the cost of the childless EITC, while the more generous expansion would transfer an additional \$18.3 billion (each on top of the \$68.5 billion cost of the EITC under current law).[24] To reiterate, this is a static simulation and there is no response of labor supply modelled here, either on the extensive (we would expect more filers) or intensive margin. Such responses would increase the cost of each alternative, though likely not dramatically.

Of course, these schedules are not the only option for expanding the EITC for taxpayers without children. One alternative that has received some attention is an expansion of eligibility for non-custodial parents, conditioned on the payment of child support and designed to create incentives to do so (Primus 2006). New York and Washington, DC, have implemented non-custodial parent credits, and a regression discontinuity evaluation of the New York program shows positive effects on both employment and child support payment (Nichols, Sorenson, and Lippold 2012).

[24] The Obama administration estimates the cost of the Obama proposal to be \$60 billion over ten years (Executive Office of the President and US Treasury Department 2014).

Table 7.3 Childless filer proposals

Parameters	*Current Law*		*Expanded Proposal*		*Equivalence Scaled*	
Eligible ages	25–64		21–66		21–64	
Recipient filing units (millions)	6.6		10.9		15.1	
	Fraction Receiving	*Avg. Credit Among Recipients*	*Fraction Receiving*	*Avg. Credit Among Recipients*	*Fraction Receiving*	*Avg. Credit Among Recipients*
By income (in $1,000s)						
Less than 10	19%	$322	24%	$594	24%	$1,402
10–20	13%	$281	22%	$667	23%	$1,778
20–30	5%	$238	12%	$488	29%	$1,058
30–40	2%	$303	4%	$539	15%	$764
40–50	2%	$339	3%	$659	4%	$1,176
50–75	1%	—	1%	—	2%	$1,111
75–100	0%	—	0%	—	0%	—
All	6%	$284	9%	$597	13%	$1,339
Total cost for childless families (billions of $)	$1.9		$6.5		$20.2	
Incremental cost over current law (billions of $)	–		$4.6		$18.3	

Notes: "Fraction receiving" columns represent the number of recipients of the childless credit divided by the number of tax filers without child exemptions. Average credits not reported for cells where 1% or fewer of filers receive the credit. *Sources*: Based on data from Urban-Brookings Tax Policy Center Microsimulation Model (version 0515-1). Cols 3-4 based on data from Executive Office of the President and US Treasury Department (2014), updated to 2015.

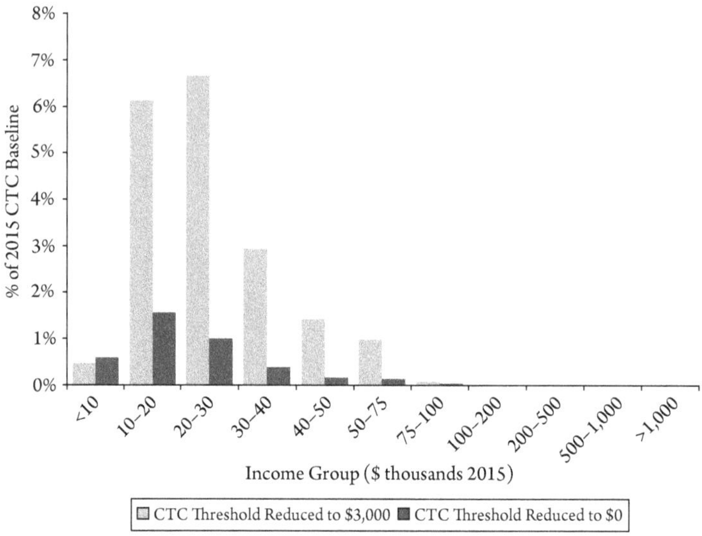

Figure 7.17 Distributional effect of changes to CTC refundability thresholds. *Notes:* Distribution of tax benefits for each change are expressed as shares of total CTC expenditures in 2015. *Source:* Urban-Brookings Tax Policy Center Microsimulation Model (version 0515-1).

7.6.2 CTC Refundability Threshold

Prior to 2009, the lowest income filers were effectively ineligible for the CTC, as they had no income tax liability and CTC refunds were limited to 15% of earnings in excess of $11,500 (in 2007). The refundability threshold was reduced to $3,000 in 2009, a provision that was made permanent in late 2015. We use the TPC microsimulation model to illustrate the importance of this expansion in the credit. The first set of bars in figure 7.17 show the distribution of the additional $10.4 billion in 2015 CTC payments that resulted from the 2009 reduction of the threshold, large relative to the total cost of $56 billion.[25] (Once again, this is a static analysis that does not account for changes in labor-supply behavior.) As shown in figure 7.17, nearly all—over 70%—of the additional benefits flow to families with incomes below $30,000. This shows that the increase in the CTC's refundability dramatically changed the program, making it much more progressive.

One might be interested in further increasing the progressivity of the CTC, which remains much more regressive than the EITC. The second series in figure 7.17 explores a further expansion of CTC refundability, obtained by reducing the threshold all the way to zero (from $3,000). This would make the CTC structure nearly identical to the EITC's (albeit with a much longer plateau region). Using the TPC simulation, we find that this policy (proposed by West, Boteach, and Vallas 2015) would cost $2.2 billion

[25] This simulation, along with the others, is for tax year 2015. We set the threshold for refundability under the pre-2007 policy at $13,850 (2015 dollars), adjusted for inflation from the 2001 threshold of $10,000 (nominal).

(a 4% increase over current law), and again nearly all benefits would flow to the lowest-income families.[26]

7.6.3 Other Reforms: Labor Supply, Compliance, and Timing

Neither of the proposals are designed primarily to improve the EITC's labor-supply impacts, though here too there are reasons to be dissatisfied with the status quo. The EITC has large positive effects on labor force participation among single parents, with little if any negative effect on hours of work of those who would work in any case. But for married couples the labor-supply impacts are not so positive: Eissa and Hoynes (2004) document a negative effect on the labor supply of married women, many of whom are secondary earners and who therefore would qualify for a larger EITC if they did not work than if they did.

Unfortunately, there are few good options for avoiding this problem. It is merely an example of the marriage penalties that are inherent in any progressive, family-based tax system and, like other marriage penalties, is quite difficult to avoid. Berlin (2007) proposes making the EITC depend on individual rather than family earnings. Holt and Maag (2009) propose replacing the EITC and CTC with a worker credit, based on individual earnings, and a child credit based on family earnings. This would eliminate the second worker penalty, but would represent an enormous change in the US tax system and would cost tens of billions of dollars. A more incremental proposal comes from Kearney and Turner (2013), who would create a secondary earner deduction that would reduce the second worker penalty and effectively extend the EITC schedule for two-earner families.

In terms of compliance, the major issues concern overclaiming of qualifying children and misreporting of self-employment income. The first would be addressed by the expansion of the childless credit. The second is more difficult. California, which introduced its own EITC in 2015, disallows self-employment income from EITC calculations. TPC's model indicates that the total effect of adopting a similar rule at the federal level would be to reduce EITC expenditures by $11 billion. As this is far in excess of any plausible estimate of the amount of overpayment due to income misreporting, it is clear that the primary effect would be to deny the credit to many of the intended recipients. It might be better to tighten up enforcement around self-employment income, while recognizing that not all misreporting can be prevented.

Another way to improve the performance of the EITC vis-à-vis our three objectives is to increase the take-up rate. The estimated 75% take-up rate, while high relative to other parts of the social safety net, still leaves room for improvement. We know that take-up is lower among those eligible for smaller credits, notably childless taxpayers and those with very low earning levels (Plueger 2009). A challenge with increasing take-up for this group is that it disproportionately includes those not filing a tax return (and often not legally required to). Recent evidence based on experimental designs and IRS partnerships shows that informational mailers can lead to significant increases in take-up (Bhargava and Manoli 2015; Guyton et al. 2016).

[26] Maag (2015) explores the implications of changes in the CTC refundability threshold, as well as other potential changes to the program, in more detail.

A final type of change to consider would be one aimed at distributing EITC and CTC payments more gradually rather than as annual lump sums, as this is a persistent limitation of the EITC as an anti-poverty program. Unfortunately, in the wake of the failure of the Advance EITC program, we are not aware of good proposals to do so. Much more needs to be understood about the role that EITC payments play in their recipients' lives (see, e.g., Halpern-Meekin et al. 2015) in order to inform welfare-improving changes of this type.

7.7 CONCLUSION

In this chapter, we examine the state of tax policy for families with children. We focus on the two most important provisions, the EITC and the CTC. We discuss these two programs within the lens of the three presumed goals of the programs: distributional, encouragement of work, and limiting of administrative costs and noncompliance. To discuss these three goals, we use tax data and quantify the static distributional features of the programs. We also summarize the existing research to assess how the programs meet the other two goals.

We conclude that the EITC well meets all three of these goals. The policy provides substantial increases to income for low to moderate income families. A large body of research shows that the first-order behavioral effect of the policy is to increase employment among single mothers with children. Married couples also benefit from the program, though the policy does induce modest reductions in secondary earner employment. Administrative costs are low, particularly compared to the public assistance alternatives to the EITC. Compliance remains an issue, with complicated rules for claiming children and incentives to overreport self-employment income (though it is not clear that noncompliance is any worse than for other redistribution programs). The CTC looks much less favorable within this lens. The credit is not targeted, with a large share of the expenditures extending way above median income groups. However, the 2009 expansion of the credit, making the CTC refundable at low earnings levels, is highly targeted and effectively represents an expansion of the EITC.

We also discuss and simulate proposals to reform the EITC that would improve one or more of the three program goals. Expansions of the childless EITC would be quite progressive but also expensive. Limitation of the use of self-employment income to qualify for the EITC would reduce the program's cost but would also exclude a group that is likely as deserving as traditional employees. Finally, the recent reduction of the refundability threshold for the CTC dramatically improved the program's redistributive value. A further reduction all the way to zero would be less costly, with equally progressive distributional impacts.

ACKNOWLEDGMENTS

We are very grateful to staff at the Tax Policy Center and particularly Elaine Maag for providing us with simulations of the Urban Brookings Tax Policy Center Microsimulation model. We thank Claire Montialoux, Audrey Tiew, and Darian Woods for excellent research assistance. Portions of this chapter draw heavily on Nichols and Rothstein (2015) and Hoynes and Patel (2015). We are grateful for helpful comments from Alan Auerbach, Louis Kaplow, Jim Hines, Len Berman, Diane Schanzenbach, Bob Greenstein, Chye-Ching Huang, and participants in the "Economics of Tax Policy" conference held in Washington, DC, on December 3–4, 2015.

REFERENCES

Baker, Kevin. 2008. "Do Cash Transfer Programs Improve Infant Health: Evidence from the 1993 Expansion of the Earned Income Tax Credit." https://economics.nd.edu/assets/24011/baker_paper.pdf

Baughman, Reagan A. 2012. "The Effects of State EITC Expansion on Children's Health." The Carsey Institute at the Scholars' Repository Paper 168.

Baughman, Reagan A., and Stacy Dickert-Conlin. 2009. "The Earned Income Tax Credit and Fertility." *Journal of Population Economics* 22 (3): 537–63.

Berlin, Gordon L. 2007. "Rewarding the Work of Individuals: A Counterintuitive Approach to Reducing Poverty and Strengthening Families." *The Future of Children* 17 (2): 17–42.

Bhargava, Saurabh, and Dayanand Manoli. 2015. "Psychological Frictions and the Incomplete Take-Up of Social Benefits: Evidence from an IRS Field Experiment." *American Economic Review* 105 (11): 3489–529.

Bitler, Marianne P., Hilary Hoynes, and Elira Kuka. 2016. "Do In-Work Tax Credits Serve as a Safety Net?" *Journal of Human Resources*, forthcoming. doi:10.3368/jhr.52.2.0614-6433R1.

Blank, Rebecca. 2001. "Declining Caseloads Increased Work: What Can We Conclude about the Effects of Welfare Reform?" *Economic Policy Review* 7 (2): 25–36.

Blundell, Richard, and Hilary W. Hoynes. 2004. "Has 'In-Work' Benefit Reform Helped the Labor Market?" In *Seeking a Premier Economy: The Economic Effects of British Economic Reforms, 1980–2000*, edited by David Card, Richard Blundell, and Richard B. Freeman, 411–59. Chicago: University of Chicago Press.

Bollinger, Christopher, Luis Gonzalez, and James P. Ziliak. 2009. "Welfare Reform and the Level and Composition of Income." In *Welfare Reform and Its Long-Term Consequences for America's Poor*, edited by James P. Ziliak, 59–103. Cambridge: Cambridge University Press.

California Department of Health Care Services. 2015. *Federal Poverty Levels*. Sacramento: Medi-Cal Eligibility Division. http://www.dhcs.ca.gov/services/medi-cal/eligibility/Documents/ACWDL2015/ACWDL15-14.pdf

California State Legislature. 2015. Assembly Bill No. 43. 2015-2016 Regular Session. http://www.leginfo.ca.gov/pub/15-16/bill/asm/ab_0001-0050/ab_43_bill_20150212_amended_asm_v97.pdf

Chetty, Raj, John Friedman, and John Rockoff. 2011. *New Evidence on the Long-Term Impacts of Tax Credits*. Washington, DC: US Internal Revenue Service.

Chetty, Raj, John N. Friedman, and Emmanuel Saez. 2013. "Using Differences in Knowledge across Neighborhoods to Uncover the Impacts of the EITC on Earnings." *American Economic Review* 103 (7): 2683–721.

Chetty, Raj, Adam Guren, Day Manoli, and Andrea Weber. 2013. "Does Indivisible Labor Explain the Difference between Micro and Macro Elasticities? A Meta-Analysis of Extensive Margin Elasticities." *NBER Macroeconomics Annual 2012* 27:1–56.

Chetty, Raj, and Emmanuel Saez. 2013. "Teaching the Tax Code: Earnings Responses to an Experiment with EITC Recipients." *American Economic Journal: Applied Economics* 5 (1): 1–31.

Congressional Research Service. 2014. "The Child Tax Credit Current Law and Legislative History." https://www.fas.org/sgp/crs/misc/R41873.pdf.

Currie, Janet. 2006. "The Take-up of Social Benefits." In *Poverty, the Distribution of Income, and Public Policy*, edited by Alan Auerbach, David Card, and John Quigley, 80–148. New York: Russell Sage.

Dahl, Gordon B., and Lance Lochner. 2012. "The Impact of Family Income on Child Achievement: Evidence from the Earned Income Tax Credit." *American Economic Review* 102 (5): 1927–56.

DeNavas-Walt, Carmen, and Bernadette D. Proctor. 2015. *Income and Poverty in the United States: 2014, Current Population Reports P60-252*. Washington, DC: US Census Bureau.

Eissa, Nada, and Hilary W. Hoynes. 2004. "Taxes and the Labor Market Participation of Married Couples: The Earned Income Tax Credit." *Journal of Public Economics* 88 (9): 1931–58.

Eissa, Nada, and Hilary W. Hoynes. 2006a. "Behavioral Responses to Taxes: Lessons from the EITC and Labor Supply." In *Tax Policy and the Economy*, vol. 20, edited by J. M. Poterba, 74–110. Cambridge, MA: MIT Press.

Eissa, Nada, and Hilary W. Hoynes. 2006b. "The Hours of Work Response of Married Couples: Taxes and the Earned Income Tax Credit." In *Tax Policy and Labor Market Performance*, edited by Jonas Agell and Peter Birch Sorensen, 187–207. Cambridge, MA: MIT Press.

Eissa, Nada, and Jeffrey B. Liebman. 1996. "Labor Supply Response to the Earned Income Tax Credit." *Quarterly Journal of Economics* 11 (2): 605–37.

Ellwood, David T. 2000. "The Impact of the Earned Income Tax Credit and Social Policy Reforms on Work, Marriage, and Living Arrangements." *National Tax Journal* 53 (4, part 2): 1063–105.

Evans, William N., and Craig L. Garthwaite. 2014. "Giving Mom a Break: The Impact of Higher EITC Payments on Maternal Health." *American Economic Journal: Economic Policy* 6 (2): 258–90.

Executive Office of the President and US Treasury Department. 2014. "The President's Proposal to Expand the Earned Income Tax Credit." https://www.whitehouse.gov/sites/default/files/docs/eitc_report.pdf

Greenstein, Robert, and John Wancheck. 2011. *Earned Income Tax Credit Overpayment and Error Issues*. Washington, DC: Center on Budget and Policy Priorities.

Grogger, Jeffrey. 2003. "The Effects of Time Limits, the EITC, and Other Policy Changes on Welfare Use, Work and Income among Female-Headed Families." *Review of Economics and Statistics* 85 (2): 394–408.

Gunderson, Craig, and James Ziliak. 2004. "Poverty and Macroeconomic Performance across Space, Race, and Family Structure." *Demography* 41 (1): 61–86.

Guyton, John, Day Manoli, Brenda Schafer, and Michael Sebastiani. 2016. "Reminders and Recidivism: Evidence from Tax Filing and EITC Participation among Low-Income Nonfilers." Working Paper, University of Texas.

Halpern-Meekin, Sarah, Kathryn Edin, Laura Tach, and Jennifer Sykes. 2015. *It's Not Like I'm Poor: How Working Families Make Ends Meet in a Post-Welfare World*. Berkeley: University of California Press.

Herbst, Chris M. 2011. "The Impact of the Earned Income Tax Credit on Marriage and Divorce: Evidence from Flow Data." *Population Research Policy Review* 30: 101–28.

Holt, Stephen, and Elaine Maag. 2009. "Considerations in Efforts to Restructure Refundable Work-Based Credits." Urban Institute Working Paper.

Hotz, V. Joseph, and John Karl Scholz. 2003. "The Earned Income Tax Credit." In *Means-Tested Transfer Programs in the United States*, edited by Robert A. Moffitt, 141–97. Chicago: University of Chicago Press.

Hoynes, Hilary W., Doug L. Miller, and David Simon. 2015. "Income, the Earned Income Tax Credit and Infant Health." *American Economic Journal: Economic Policy* 7 (1): 172–211.

Hoynes, Hilary W., and Ankur Patel. 2015. "Effective Policy for Reducing Inequality? The Earned Income Tax Credit and the Distribution of Income." National Bureau of Economic Research Working Paper No. 21340. July.

Internal Revenue Service (IRS). 2009. "2009 Tax Model File." Statistics of Income Division (SOI). http://users.nber.org/~taxsim/gdb/

Internal Revenue Service (IRS). 2014a. "Compliance Estimates for the Earned Income Tax Credit Claimed on 2006–2008 Returns." Research, Analysis & Statistics Report Publication 5162.

Internal Revenue Service (IRS). 2014b. "Revenue Procedure 14-61." https://www.irs.gov/pub/irs-drop/rp-14-61.pdf

Internal Revenue Service (IRS). 2014c. "Table 1: Individual income Tax Returns: Selected Income and Tax Items for Tax Years 1999–2012." http://www.irs.gov/uac/SOI-Tax-Stats-Historical-Table-1

Internal Revenue Service (IRS). 2014d. "Table 3.3 All Returns: Tax Liability, Tax Credits, and Tax Payments." Publication no. 1304. http://www.irs.gov/file_source/pub/irs-soi/12in33ar.xls

Internal Revenue Service (IRS). 2015a. "Individual Income Tax Returns, Preliminary Data, 2013." Statistics of Income Bulletin, Spring. https://www.irs.gov/pub/irs-soi/soi-a-inpd-id1505.pdf

Internal Revenue Service (IRS). 2015b. "Table 2.5." Statistics of Income Division Publication 1304. https://www.irs.gov/pub/irs-soi/14in25ic.xls

Internal Revenue Service (IRS) and US Department of the Treasury. 1999. "Advanced Earned Income Tax Credit: 1994 and 1997 Notice Study: A Report to Congress." Washington, DC: IRS.

Internal Revenue Service (IRS) and US Department of the Treasury. 2013. "2013 EITC Income Limits, Maximum Amounts and Tax Law Changes." http://www.irs.gov/Individuals/2013-EITC-Income-Limits,-Maximum-Credit—Amounts-And-Tax-Law-Changes

Jones, Damon. 2010. "Information, Preferences and Public Benefit Participation: Experimental Evidence from the Advance EITC and 401(k) Savings. *American Economic Journal* 2(2):147–63.

Kearney, Melissa S., and Lesley J. Turner. 2013. "Giving Secondary Earners a Tax Break: A Proposal to Help Low- and Middle-Income Families." Hamilton Project Discussion Paper 2013-07. December.

Leigh, Andrew. 2010. "Who Benefits from the Earned Income Tax Credit? Incidence among Recipients, Coworkers and Firms." *B.E. Journal of Economic Analysis & Policy* 10 (1). http://www.degruyter.com/view/j/bejeap.2010.10.1/bejeap.2010.10.1.1994/bejeap.2010.10.1.1994.xml

Maag, Elaine. 2015. "Reforming the Child Tax Credit How Different Proposals Change Who Benefits." Urban Institute.

Manoli, Day, and Nick Turner. 2014. "Cash-on-Hand and College Enrollment: Evidence from Population Tax Data and Policy Nonlinearities." NBER Working Paper 19836.

Meyer, Bruce D., and Dan T. Rosenbaum. 2001. "Welfare, the Earned Income Tax Credit, and the Labor Supply of Single Mothers." *Quarterly Journal of Economics* 116 (3): 1063–114.

Michelmore, Katherine. 2013. "The Effect of Income on Educational Attainment: Evidence from State Earned Income Tax Credit Expansions." SSRN Working Paper 2356444.

Michelmore, Katherine. 2014. "EITC and Union Formation: The Impact of Expected Spouse Earnings." Cornell University Working Paper.

Mortenson, Jacob A., and Andrew Whitten. 2015. "How Sensitive Are Taxpayers to Marginal Tax Rates? Evidence from Income Bunching in the United States." http://papers.ssrn.com/sol3/Papers.cfm?abstract_id=2719859

National Taxpayer Advocate. 2004. *National Taxpayer Advocate 2004 Annual Report to Congress*. Vol. 2. *Earned Income Tax Credit (EITC) Audit Reconsideration Study*. Washington, DC: Internal Revenue Service.

Nichols, Austin, and Jesse Rothstein. 2015. "The Earned Income Tax Credit." http://eml.berkeley.edu/~jrothst/workingpapers/nichols-rothstein-Sep2015.pdf

Nichols, Austin, Elaine Sorensen, and Kye Lippold. 2012. *The New York Noncustodial Parent EITC: Its Impact on Child Support Payments and Employment*. Washington, DC: Urban Institute.

OECD. 2011. "Taxation and Employment 2011." OECD Tax Policy Studies No. 21.

Plueger, Dean, 2009. "Earned Income Tax Credit Participation Rate for Tax Year 2005." Washington, DC: Internal Revenue Service.

Pomerleau, Kyle. 2014. "2015 Tax Brackets." *Tax Foundation*, October 2. http://taxfoundation.org/article/2015-tax-brackets

Primus, Wendell. 2006. "Improving Public Policies to Increase the Income and Employment of Low-Income Nonresident Fathers." In *Black Males Left Behind*, edited by Ronald B. Mincy, 211–48. Washington, DC: Urban Institute Press.

Rosenbaum, Dan T. 2000. "Taxes, the Earned Income Tax Credit, and Marital Status." 1999–2000 ASPE Census Bureau Small Grants Sponsored Research Conference.

Rothstein, Jesse. 2008. "The Unintended Consequences of Encouraging Work: Tax Incidence and the EITC." Princeton University Working Paper.

Rothstein, Jesse. 2010. "Is the EITC as Good as an NIT? Conditional Cash Transfers and Tax Incidence." *American Economic Journal: Economic Policy* 2 (1): 177–208.

Saez, Emmanuel. 2002. "Optimal Income Transfer Programs: Intensive Versus Extensive Labor Supply Responses." *Quarterly Journal of Economics* 107 (3):1039–73.

Saez, Emmanuel. 2010. "Do Taxpayers Bunch at Kink Points?" *American Economic Journal: Economic Policy* 2 (3): 180–212.

Scholz, John Karl. 1994. "The Earned Income Tax Credit: Participation, Compliance, and Antipoverty Effectiveness." *National Tax Journal* 47 (1): 64–87.

Short, Kathleen. 2015. "The Research Supplemental Poverty Measure: 2014." US Census Bureau Current Population Report P60–254.

Steuerle, Eugene, and Caleb Quakenbush. 2015. *Marginal Tax Rates and 21st Century Welfare Reform*. Washington, DC: Urban Institute.

Strully, Kate W., David H. Rehkopf, and Ziming Xuan. 2010. "Aspects of Prenatal Poverty on Infant Health: State Earned Income Tax Credits and Birth Weight." *American Sociological Review* 75 (4): 534–62.

Tax Policy Center. 2013. "Baseline Share of Federal Taxes by Filing Status; by Cash Income Percentile, 2013." http://www.taxpolicycenter.org/numbers/displayatab.cfm?DocID=3806

Tax Policy Center. 2014. "Real Federal Spending on EITC, CTC and Welfare: FY1975–2011." http://www.taxpolicycenter.org/taxfacts/displayafact.cfm?Docid=266

Tax Policy Center. 2015a. "Earned Income Tax Credit: Number of Recipients and Amounts of Credit, 1975–2012." http://www.taxpolicycenter.org/taxfacts/displayafact.cfm?Docid=37

Tax Policy Center. 2015b. "Earned Income Tax Credit Parameters, 1975–2015." http://taxpolicycenter.org/taxfacts/displayafact.cfm?Docid=36

Urban-Brookings Tax Policy Center. 2015. *Microsimulation Model (version 0515-1)*. http://www.urban.org/research/data-methods/data-analysis/quantitative-data-analysis/microsimulation/tax-policy-center-microsimulation-model

US Bureau of Labor Statistics (BLS). 2014. "Table 24. Historical Consumer Price Index for All Urban Consumers (CPI-U), 74. December to December Changes." *CPI Detailed Report December 2014*. http://www.bls.gov/cpi/cpid1412.pdf

US Census Bureau. 2015. "CPS 2015 Annual Social and Economic Supplement (ASEC)." https://www.census.gov/cps/data/

US Government Accountability Office (GAO). 2007. *Advanced Earned Income Tax Credit: Low Use and Small Dollars Paid Impeded IRS's Efforts to Reduce High Noncompliance, Report No. GAO-07-1110*. Washington, DC: US GAO.

US Government Publishing Office (GPO). 2011. 26 U.S.C. 24—Child Tax Credit.

West, Rachel, Melissa Boteach, and Rebecca Vallas. 2015. *Harnessing the Child Tax Credit as a Tool to Invest in the Next Generation*. Washington, DC: Center for American Progress.

COMMENTARY ON CHAPTER 7

Diane Whitmore Schanzenbach

The chapter by Hoynes and Rothstein provides a clear and useful overview of the Earned Income Tax Credit (EITC) and the Child Tax Credits (CTCs). The EITC, along with the Supplemental Nutrition Assistance Program, is among the US's most powerful antipoverty programs, lifting over 10 million people—including 5 million children—out of poverty in 2014 (Sherman and Trisi 2015). The CTC, on the other hand, while structurally similar to the EITC is less targeted, providing tax payments to families with incomes up to $150,000 for married couples and with limited refundability to low-income families. The chapter highlights the importance of the EITC, and to a lesser extent the CTC, in the broader safety net and its complex suite of tax and transfer programs.

At this point, the literature on the EITC is quite developed, and Hoynes and Rothstein provide a concise and theoretically motivated literature review. (On the other hand, less is known about the CTC and that is a clear hole in the literature.) The structure of the EITC—with its phase-in range, a flat range, and a phase-out range—yields predictions about how recipients will alter their work effort in response to the incentive. Many of us use this example to teach undergraduates about income and substitution effects, noting that in two of the three ranges the EITC is predicted to *reduce* work effort.

I find that my undergraduates are then disappointed, newly armed with their understanding of income and substitution effects, that (as Hoynes and Rothstein describe) the empirical results do not line up well with the simple theory predictions. On one hand, the literature generally finds large increases in employment in response to the EITC—especially among single mothers. In addition, the literature finds that the EITC has large impact on earnings both through the effect of the EITC payment itself and also through the individual's earnings (net of other changes in income). Both of these findings emerge across studies using a variety research designs. On the other hand, studies that examine the impact of the EITC on the intensive margin do not find the predicted decrease in work effort. Some work has been done trying to understand this, but more work would be useful to help us better understand why there is such a difference between the simple theoretical predictions and the empirical results. For example, is the elasticity of hours worked small, so that the predicted negative impact in the flat and phase-out ranges is negligible? Or would workers prefer to reduce their hours, but there are institutional barriers that limit their ability to choose hours worked?

Particular strengths of this chapter, and what sets it apart from other recent literature reviews, are the authors' inclusion of policy simulations, provided by the Tax Policy Center (TPC). For example, there is great interest in expanding the EITC for (low-skilled) childless workers, a group that does not have much other access to the safety net, and has suffered greatly in recent years from declines in both wage and participation rates. The more modest of the proposed expansions is the current Obama proposal, which is predicted to increase the number of recipients of the childless credit by over 60% and more than double the value of the average credit at a cost of an additional $4.6 billion (on top of the $68.5 billion EITC cost under current law). An important limitation is that the simulation—by TPC convention—is based on a static model and does not include predicted increases in participation or on intensive margins. Given the rest of the EITC literature, it seems reasonable to speculate that the response on the intensive margin likely will not be large; however, the potential impact on the extensive margin may be more important, particularly in the face of declining labor force participation among the targeted group. From a broader perspective, an increase in labor force participation among this group may turn out to be socially beneficial in a manner that eclipses the additional earnings and income gained. Recent literature finds important spillover impacts of job loss on health and well-being (Autor et al. 2016; Sullivan and von Wachter 2009). If the impact is symmetric for job gains, then we would expect the benefits of an EITC expansion for childless workers—and its commensurate impact increasing labor force participation—to be more beneficial than the increased earnings alone would imply.

The CTC policy simulations are also very interesting and will be useful to illustrate the importance of the refundability threshold for those of us that teach this topic to undergraduate tax students. The first simulation illustrates the cost and distributional impact of the 2009 policy that lowered the CTC's refundability threshold from $11,500 to $3,000. The additional $10 billion in payments (relative to a total cost of $56 billion) overwhelmingly went to low-income families, making the credit much more progressive. The simulation of a potential reform making the credit entirely refundable is also informative, increasing the total cost only a modest 4% with essentially all of the benefits flowing to very low-income families.

7C.1 FUTURE RESEARCH DIRECTIONS

Despite all of the work that has been done on the EITC, there are many additional questions in need of study, and the Hoynes and Rothstein chapter does a good job of teeing up important questions that should be addressed in further research. The next steps in the EITC literature should consider issues of optimal program design and of the interaction between programs. For example, since the literature has established the large impact the EITC has had on employment participation and earnings among low-skilled workers with children, it would be worthwhile knowing more about how earnings and labor force attachment evolve over the careers of workers who were induced to join the labor force because of the EITC. Do workers remain reliant on the EITC throughout their careers, or as they become more attached to the labor force (and perhaps gain additional skills) do their incomes rise such that they become ineligible for the credit?

There is some concern among policymakers that the marriage penalties in the EITC may discourage marriage or encourage unwed childbearing (e.g., Sawhill and Karpilow 2014). It would be useful to know how large this effect is empirically, and if it is has a meaningful impact what types of reforms could be used to address it. For example, Kearney and Turner (2013) propose a tax credit for secondary earners, while others propose taxing based on individual earnings instead of household earnings (Berlin 2007; Carasso et al. 2008).

Thinking more broadly about the range of tax and transfer programs aimed at low-income families, as documented in the chapter, the current set of income support programs is a complex web of tax expenditures and direct spending programs, with different programs in effect at various points across the income distribution. More work is needed into how the current mix of programs compares to an optimal mix of income supports, considering trade-offs between tax expenditures like the EITC and CTCs, direct spending on SNAP and Medicaid, and even considering the role of direct regulation such as minimum wage legislation. Special consideration should be made to the relative performance of the mix of programs during cyclical downturns as well. For example, during the Great Recession, EITC participation increased and EITC payments made up a modestly larger share of income compared to the pre-recession period (Anderson et al. 2015). Important questions remain, though, about whether different or additional programs may be more effective at stimulating employment among low-skilled workers during economic downturns, for example, employment subsidies paid directly to firms (Phelps 1994).

Related to these questions are issues regarding the timing of benefits payments, because each type of program comes with a different payment frequency. An increased minimum wage is seen in each paycheck, while SNAP benefits are paid monthly—similar frequency to required household expenditures such as housing payments, commuting costs, and food purchases. The EITC, on the other hand, comes in a relatively large lump-sum annual payment, typically in February or March. Previously, an advance monthly payment option was available, but it was discontinued after few households took up the program—apparently because they preferred to receive a larger lump-sum payment, even though economic theory would predict that credit-constrained households experience a welfare increase from a lump sum at the end of the year than a flow of benefits throughout the year. There is some evidence that EITC refunds are spent on durable goods, or to pay down debt, and that it is spent quickly (Barrow and McGranahan 2000; Goodman-Bacon and McGranahan 2008; Smeeding et al. 2000). Understanding the impacts of the timing of income receipt and how that impacts spending patterns and household well-being, drawing on insights from behavioral economics and the literature on consumption smoothing, is an area in need of additional study. Related to this are questions about low-income households regard what is the maximum share of income that can reasonably be received through an annual lump sum, and how that informs the desirability of further expansions of the EITC compared with other policy options.

Overall, the literature points to an ultimate question of whether we have pushed the EITC to its limits—at least among workers with children—or whether it is still desirable to further expand the credit. Would a further expanded credit still succeed in drawing even more workers into labor force (or otherwise improve the well-being of families)? If it is possible to expand the credit further, what type of expansion would most cost-effectively further policymakers' goals of promoting work and lifting families out of poverty? If, on the other hand, we have essentially expanded the EITC to its functional limits, we need to turn to the study of what other policies are needed to achieve these ends.

REFERENCES

Anderson, Patricia, Kristin F. Butcher, and Diane Whitmore Schanzenbach. 2015. "Changes in Safety Net Use during the Great Recession." *American Economic Review: Papers & Proceedings* 105 (5): 161–65.

Autor, David H., David Dorn, and Gordon H. Hanson. 2016. "The China Shock: Learning from Labor Market Adjustment to Large Changes in Trade." NBER Working Paper #21906.

Barrow, Lisa, and Leslie McGranahan. 2000. "The Effects of the Earned Income Credit on the Seasonality of Household Expenditures." *National Tax Journal* 53 (4): 1211–43.

Berlin, Gordon L. 2007. "Rewarding the Work of Individuals: A Counterintuitive Approach to Reducing Poverty and Strengthening Families." *The Future of Children* 17 (2): 17–42.

Carasso, Adam, Harry Holzer, Elaine Maag, and C. Eugene Steurle. 2008. "The Next Stage for Social Policy: Encouraging Work and Family Formation among Low-Income Men." Washington, DC: Urban Institute.

Goodman-Bacon, Andrew, and Leslie McGranahan. 2008. "How Do EITC Recipients Spend Their Refunds?." *Economic Perspectives* 32 (2): 00–00.

Sawhill, Isabel, and Quentin Karpilow. 2014. "Raising the Minimum Wage and Redesigning the EITC." Washington, DC: Brookings Institution.

Sherman, Arloc, and Danilo Trisi. 2015. "Safety Net More Effective Against Poverty Than Previously Thought: Correcting for Underreporting of Benefits Reveals Stronger Reductions in Poverty and Deep Poverty in All States." Center on Budget and Policy Priorities, Washington, DC.

Smeeding, Timothy M., Katherin Ross, and Michael O'Connor. 2000. "The EITC: Expectation, Knowledge, Use, and Economic and Social Mobility." *National Tax Journal* 53 (4): 1187–209.

Sullivan, Daniel, and Till Von Wachter. 2009. "Job Displacement and Mortality: An Analysis Using Administrative Data." *Quarterly Journal of Economics* 124 (3): 1265–306.

8

THE ECONOMICS OF CORPORATE AND BUSINESS TAX REFORM

Dhammika Dharmapala

8.1 INTRODUCTION

Discussion of business tax reform in the United States has grown in recent years, to the point where it has now reached a crescendo. An emerging consensus on the need for reform has been built around the anomalous status of the United States as the only remaining major economy that imposes worldwide taxation on its resident multinational corporations (MNCs) and by the widespread acknowledgment that the US statutory corporate tax rate is much higher than that prevailing elsewhere. There also now appears to be a fairly broad consensus on the general shape of reforms of business taxation. The aim of this chapter is to review the lessons from current economic research for business tax reform. It develops a simple framework highlighting ten behavioral margins affected by corporate taxation that economic research has found to be important. It then assesses major current reform proposals in the light of this framework.

This review focuses on the economics, rather than the politics, of tax reform. The current political consensus rules out certain policy options. For instance, the Senate Finance Committee report on business tax reform (US Senate, Committee on Finance, 2014; known as the Hatch Report) describes a value-added tax (VAT) as a "bad" idea.[1] In contrast, this chapter reviews all possible options to the extent that they provide useful benchmarks or insights. The emphasis here is also not on specific legislative or policy proposals, but rather on presenting a more abstract set of principles that can guide policymaking over the longer term.

The scope of this review encompasses the taxation of both corporations and other business entities. As much business activity takes place within pass-through form, some consideration of personal taxation and how it interacts with corporate taxation is unavoidable. In view of the importance of the international aspects of business

[1] "Adoption of a VAT is a bad idea" (US Senate, Committee on Finance 2014: 55). In the television comedy series *Yes, Prime Minister*, the fictional senior civil servant Sir Humphrey Appleby explains that " 'controversial' only means 'this will lose you votes.' 'Courageous' means 'this will lose you the election.' " The Hatch report, which uses a rather less subtle political lexicon, does not explain how many votes a "bad" idea would lose.

taxation, this chapter addresses both international and domestic reforms within a unified perspective. Despite the current policy interest in income inequality and ongoing concerns about public debt, this chapter focuses on issues of efficiency rather than distribution or revenue. In part, this is because the incidence of the corporate income tax remains controversial, with some evidence that much of it is borne by workers (e.g., Arulampalam, Devereux, and Maffini 2012). A focus on efficiency also highlights the distinctive contributions of economic research to tax policy. This is not, however, to downplay the importance of distribution and revenue.[2]

This chapter begins by identifying ten types of inefficiencies created by the current corporate tax regime. These include distortions to the amount and location of investment by firms, to the use of external debt, to payout and repatriation decisions, to the organizational form chosen by firms, to the ownership of assets and the market for corporate control, and to patterns of global portfolio investment. Particularly relevant to international tax reform are the "lockout effect" (the retention of cash by US MNCs within foreign affiliates) and deadweight costs created by the expenditure of resources by firms on tax planning. This review aims to clarify these efficiency consequences and to briefly describe the empirical evidence regarding the magnitude of these distortions.

The chapter then discusses proposed reforms of US business taxation, focusing on three broad classes of reforms, and evaluates each of these in the light of the framework introduced earlier. This discussion is necessarily selective and does not seek to exhaustively catalog every reform proposal that has been suggested. The first category is a "consensus" approach that encompasses the proposals most widely discussed in the policy arena. This involves a corporate tax rate reduction (from the current 35% rate to somewhere between 20% and 28%) combined with dividend exemption and various other elements, such as a one-time levy on the foreign cash holdings of US MNCs and a minimum tax on their future foreign income. This type of reform would fully solve the lockout problem and mitigate several of the other distortions, but would leave many inefficiencies in place.

The second type of reform is a formula apportionment system. This would address about half of the efficiency issues identified here, but may create new types of efficiency costs. Its most attractive feature—its departure from the traditional international tax law concepts of source and residence—also characterizes many of the proposals within the third category. These include a destination-based VAT (which faces significant political obstacles, but is an important conceptual benchmark notwithstanding the aspersions cast on it by the Hatch Report), a destination-based cash flow tax (Auerbach 2010; Auerbach, Devereux, and Simpson 2010), and variants of a VAT such as the flat tax. These types of reforms would solve virtually all of the inefficiencies associated with the corporate tax.

[2] The current consensus on business tax reform often takes as a constraint that reform should be revenue-neutral within the business (or corporate) sector, which may indicate a desire to maintain the existing (albeit unknown) pattern of distributional burdens.

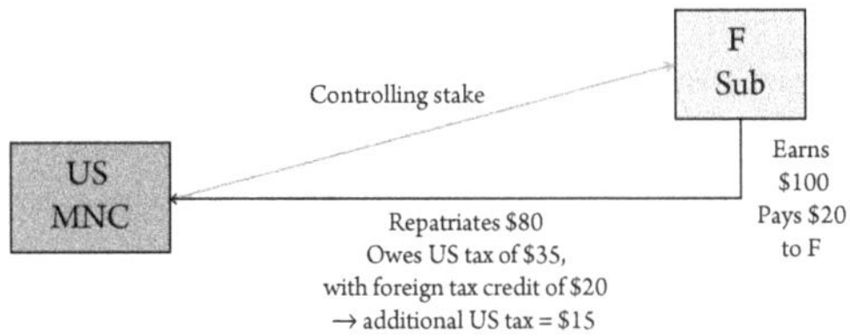

Figure 8.1 A simple characterization of the US international tax regime

This chapter proceeds as follows. Section 8.2 introduces a general framework for understanding the efficiency costs of corporate taxation. Section 8.3 analyzes the "consensus" reforms. Section 8.4 discusses proposals for a formula apportionment system. Section 8.5 analyzes consumption-type tax reforms, and section 8.6 concludes.

8.2 A GENERAL FRAMEWORK: THE EFFICIENCY COSTS OF CORPORATE TAXATION

The US corporate tax is now over a century old. First imposed in 1909 as an excise tax on the privilege of doing business in corporate form, and subsequently in the form of an income tax (Shaviro 2009), the corporate tax applies to business entities that are organized as "C corporations" (named for subchapter C of the tax code). Importantly, it does not apply to other types of business entities. Space constraints preclude a discussion of its history and the various arguments for and against its existence (see, e.g., Shaviro 2009). However, we briefly summarize the US international tax regime as it applies to MNCs.

Figure 8.1 depicts a simple scenario in which a US parent owns a controlling stake in a foreign affiliate, separately incorporated under the laws of a foreign country F. Suppose that the US tax rate is 35% and country F's tax rate is 20%. Assume that this foreign affiliate earns $100 of income, and therefore pays $20 of tax to the government of F. There are no immediate US tax consequences. However, when the affiliate pays a dividend to its US parent, the latter has $100 of income under US tax law, with a foreign tax credit for the tax paid to F. The payment of this dividend is often termed the "repatriation" of earnings. Because of the foreign tax credit, taxes due upon repatriation are generally equal to the difference between the foreign tax paid and the tax that would be due if earnings were taxed at the US rate. In our example, an additional $15 would be due in US tax when the earnings are repatriated. This additional US tax—and its deferral until repatriation—creates distortions that many reform proposals seek to address.[3]

In our example, the United States is the "residence" country (where the MNC parent is based) and F is the "source" country (where the affiliate's business operations

[3] The Hatch Report (US Senate, Committee on Finance 2014: 275) dismisses as "bad tax policy" reforms that would eliminate deferral and impose immediate worldwide taxation of US MNCs. Grubert and Altshuler (2008) analyze in detail a proposal of this type.

are located). The distinction between "residence" (or "home") countries and "source" (or "host") countries is fundamental to international taxation. The income generated by normal business operations in the source country is referred to as "active" business income, whereas income received from other sources unconnected to normal business operations (such as interest income) is referred to as "passive" income. Residence countries (such as the United States) with "worldwide" tax systems impose tax on the active foreign business income of resident MNCs (generally with a credit for taxes paid to the source country). It is far more common, however, for residence countries to use "territorial" (or "dividend exemption") systems, in which the "active" foreign income derived by resident MNCs from foreign business operations is exempt from residence country taxation (so that this income is taxed only by the source country). Even territorial residence countries may, however, tax the passive foreign income earned by their resident MNCs.

In order to provide a framework for understanding the efficiency consequences of corporate and international taxation, we distinguish among ten distinct behavioral margins. This is primarily for expositional purposes; there is no suggestion here that counting the number of margins addressed by a reform proposal is sufficient to evaluate the proposal's impact. Moreover, we do not intend to imply that each margin is of equal importance. Their relative importance is not fully settled, but some general impressions can be derived from the brief summaries of the empirical evidence regarding their magnitude. We thus use this framework merely as a heuristic guide that is useful in evaluating current reform proposals.

8.2.1 Distortions to the Location of Investment—Extensive and Intensive Margins

Perhaps the most straightforward inefficiencies associated with corporate and international taxation relate to the location of economic activity. Locational decisions—whether and how much to invest in a given jurisdiction—are sometimes made at the margin (e.g., how large a factory to build), but when there are large fixed costs they may also be discrete in nature. Discrete real investment choices depend on the effective average tax rate (EATR) on the returns from the investment, taking account of depreciation allowances and other provisions that affect the tax base (Devereux and Griffith 1998, 2003). On the other hand, how much real investment to undertake in a given location (conditional on operating in that location) depends on the effective marginal tax rate (EMTR)—the tax rate on an extra dollar of income generated by investment.

These extensive and intensive margins of investment constitute the first two of our ten potential distortions from corporate taxation. The efficiency cost from distortions to the location of economic activity can be illustrated as follows. Consider \$100 of investment that can be undertaken in either country A (which has a pretax return of \$10 and a tax rate of 10%) or country B (which has a pretax return of \$15 and a tax rate of 45%). Country A will be preferred even though the pretax return is higher in country B. This inefficiency arises from a divergence between the social and private returns—the (global) social return includes both the firm's after-tax return and governments' tax revenues, whereas the firm's private return includes only the after-tax return. As the firm is the decision-maker, it is unsurprising that it maximizes the private rather than social return.

There is a large empirical literature studying the effects of taxes on the location of investment. Particularly voluminous is the literature at the country level on taxes and foreign direct investment (FDI), which generally combines the effects of discrete locational choices and of the amount of investment. As reported in a meta-study by de Mooij and Ederveen (2003), the median tax rate elasticity found in this literature is around −3.3 (that is, a 1 percentage point reduction in the host-country tax rate raises inbound FDI by 3.3%), suggesting a quite substantial response of the location of investment to taxes. Devereux and Griffith (1998) are unusual in isolating the separate effect of the EATR. They use a sample of US firms operating in Europe and analyze the probability of these firms choosing to produce in particular European countries. For instance, they find that a 1 percentage point increase in the UK's EATR reduces the probability of a US firm producing in the United Kingdom by 1.3 percentage points, indicating a sizable effect on discrete location choices.

8.2.2 Income-Shifting

A particularly prominent issue relating to international taxation is the shifting of income by MNCs across jurisdictions in response to tax rate differentials. The OECD's Base Erosion and Profit Shifting (BEPS) initiative has directed global attention to this phenomenon (e.g., OECD 2013). The term "income-shifting" generally encompasses both strategic transfer pricing (for instance, charging relatively low prices for goods and services transferred from high-tax to low-tax affiliates) and the strategic use of inter-affiliate debt (for instance, financing the activities of high-tax affiliates using debt issued by low-tax affiliates); see Dharmapala (2008, 2014a) for a discussion.

There is a large body of empirical evidence on the magnitude of MNCs' income-shifting, as reviewed in Dharmapala (2014a). Among economists who have studied this topic, the most influential approach is that developed by Hines and Rice (1994).[4] The more recent literature in this tradition uses commercial databases that provide unconsolidated (i.e., affiliate-level rather than consolidated worldwide MNC-level) financial and ownership information for multinational affiliates, such as the Amadeus database compiled by the Bureau van Dijk. The basic premise is that the observed pretax income of an affiliate represents the sum of "true" income and income that is

[4] Other approaches to the measurement of income-shifting have been developed in the accounting literature, as reviewed in Dharmapala (2014a). In addition, Dharmapala and Riedel (2013) propose an alternative approach that relies not on variation in tax rates but on income shocks experienced by parents that are propagated differentially among low-tax and high-tax affiliates.

shifted in or out. Measures of the capital and labor inputs used by the affiliate are used to predict the counterfactual "true" level of income. Shifted income is determined by the tax incentive to move income in or out of the affiliate, proxied by the tax rate difference across affiliates of the MNC. The source of identification is from changes in the statutory tax rates of countries that generate variation in the tax incentive to shift income to and from the affiliate.

The consensus of the recent literature is a semi-elasticity of reported income with respect to the tax rate differential across countries of 0.8 (Dharmapala 2014a). This entails that a 10 percentage point increase in the tax rate difference between an affiliate and its parent (e.g., because the tax rate in the affiliate's country falls from 35% to 25%) would increase the pretax income reported by the affiliate by 8% (e.g., from $100,000 to $108,000).

This evidence pertains to the magnitude of income-shifting, rather than to its efficiency cost. The literature has generally not focused directly on the circumstances in which the magnitude of income-shifting is a sufficient statistic for its deadweight cost. Thus, we address this issue using a simple model of income-shifting based on the framework in Dharmapala and Riedel (2013). The approach resembles that of Chetty (2009), which analyzes the relationship between individuals' labor-supply decisions and their evasion and avoidance responses to taxes.

Consider an MNC that consists of affiliates in countries a and b. These affiliates earn exogenous pretax profits π_i and face corporate tax rates t_i, where $i \in \{a,b\}$.[5] Assume that country a (where the MNC is resident) is the higher-tax country (i.e., $t_a > t_b$), and has a territorial tax system that does not seek to tax the MNC's foreign profits. The MNC can shift reported income between the two affiliates; shifting an amount y entails incurring an increasing, convex cost $C(Y)$. The MNC's global after-tax profits are:

$$\Pi = (1-t_a)(\pi_a - y) + (1-t_b)(\pi_b + y) - C(y) \tag{1}$$

The MNC chooses y to maximize Π; the FOC is:

$$C'(y) = t_a - t_b \tag{2}$$

Suppose initially that $C(y)$ is entirely a pure resource cost. Then, the national welfare of country a can be defined as follows:

$$W_a = \Pi + t_a(\pi_a - y) \tag{3}$$

[5] While we assume exogenous profits here, it is important to note that there may be interactions between income-shifting and the "real" locational distortions discussed in section (8.2.1). The opportunity to engage in income-shifting may either mitigate or exacerbate real responses to tax differentials. There are also other potential distortions associated with income-shifting, such as an incentive to inefficiently use transactions with related parties rather than with arm's length parties.

Here, national welfare is the sum of the resident MNC's after-tax global profits and domestic tax revenue. Assuming t_b is fixed, the impact on country *a*'s welfare of a small change in t_a is then found by differentiating W_a with respect to t_a while holding t_b constant. Π in Equation (3) is the maximized value of the MNC's profits, so an envelope theorem argument (analogous to that used in Chetty 2009) implies that behavioral responses can be ignored when differentiating Π with respect to t_a. Thus, holding t_b constant:

$$\frac{dW_a}{dt_a} = t_a \frac{d(\pi_a - y)}{dt_a} \tag{4}$$

$\frac{d(\pi_a - y)}{dt_a}$ is a measure of the responsiveness of reported income to the tax rate, and under these circumstances Equation (4) shows that it is a sufficient statistic for the marginal deadweight loss experienced by country *a* from income-shifting.

Now suppose that $C(y)$ is not a resource cost, but a payment to tax planning professionals resident in country *a* (i.e., a transfer). Even in these circumstances, tax planning may still give rise to a social cost. Tax planners' output is not socially valuable, being merely a transfer from the fisc (i.e., other taxpayers) to the firm. However, their supply of tax planning services potentially results in foregone socially valuable output in their next-best occupation. This foregone output represents the deadweight cost of tax planning, which Dharmapala (2014b: 12) suggests "should be understood primarily as a misallocation of talent—for example, where someone who could have been another Mozart or could have found a cure for cancer instead toils away producing transfer pricing documentation."

Let $P(y)$ be an increasing, convex function that represents the output that would have been produced by tax planners in their counterfactual occupation.[6] The national welfare of country *a* can then be expressed as:

$$W_a = \Pi + t_a(\pi_a - y) + C(y) - P(y) \tag{5}$$

If $C(y) = P(y)$, which would represent a scenario in which tax planners operate in a highly competitive labor market and in which all of their counterfactual output is socially valuable, then Equation (5) is identical to Equation (3). The responsiveness of reported income to the tax rate is again a sufficient statistic for the marginal deadweight loss from income-shifting.

On the other hand, it may not be unreasonable to assume that $C(y) > P(y)$. This assumption entails either that tax planners enjoy some rents in their tax planning

[6] If $P(y) = 0$, then the social cost of income-shifting is zero, even if the estimated elasticity of reported income happens to be large. Note that in Equation (2), the MNC equates the marginal private cost, not the marginal social cost, with the tax differential.

occupation (i.e. their wages as tax planners are strictly higher than in their next-best occupation), or that some of the output that they would produce in their next-best occupation is not socially valuable. Under these conditions, an envelope theorem argument can be used to derive:

$$\frac{dW_a}{dt_a} = t_a \frac{d(\pi_a - y)}{dt_a} + \frac{dy}{dt_a}\left[(t_a - t_b) - \frac{dP}{dy}\right] \tag{6}$$

Here, the marginal deadweight cost depends not only on the responsiveness of reported income but also on other terms such as $\frac{dP}{dy}$, on which empirical evidence is scarce.[7] Thus, when $C(y) > P(y)$, the responsiveness of reported income is not a sufficient statistic for the marginal deadweight loss of income-shifting. It follows that even if a reduction in the tax rate leads to a substantial increase in reported income, the corresponding reduction in deadweight cost may be small if a substantial portion of the costs of income-shifting are transfers.[8]

8.2.3 The Location of Intellectual Property

In recent years, policymakers have become increasingly concerned with attracting income from patents and other forms of intellectual property to their jurisdictions. This is largely separate from the much more long-standing interest in promoting research and development (R&D) activity. In pursuit of the former aim, a number of European countries and China have adopted "patent box" regimes, involving favorable treatment of income derived from patents. There has been growing discussion as to whether the United States should follow suit.

The existing evidence suggests that MNCs are highly responsive to tax differences in deciding which of their affiliates applies for a patent (and consequently where intellectual property is formally held). Using the Amadeus database, Dischinger and Riedel (2011) find that intangible asset holdings are disproportionately concentrated among affiliates in low-tax jurisdictions: a decrease in the average tax difference to other affiliates of 1 percentage point raises the subsidiary's level of intangible assets by 2.2%. Karkinsky and Riedel (2012) test whether patent applications are more likely to be

[7] Although there is a large and growing literature on corporate tax avoidance (e.g., Desai and Dharmapala 2006, 2009a), there is very limited evidence on $C(y)$ and essentially no evidence on $P(y)$. A rare exception is Mills, Erickson, and Maydew (1998), who use data from a confidential survey about the tax planning practices of 365 large US firms to analyze how tax planning expenditures are related to firm characteristics.

[8] Even if the marginal deadweight cost is small, what is more relevant in assessing fundamental reforms such as the destination-based cash flow tax is the aggregate deadweight cost $P(y)$, which is not easily observable.

made by lower-tax affiliates, and find a semi-elasticity of −3.5: at the sample mean, this implies that an increase in the corporate tax rate of 1 percentage point reduces the number of patent applications by 3.5%. A more recent study by Alstadsæter et al. (2015) specifically examines patent boxes, isolating their impact from that of the general corporate tax rate, and also finds a quantitatively large effect.

The efficiency implications of where patents are formally held are likely to be minimal, unless some real R&D activity is required in the jurisdictions where patents are held in order to enjoy the tax benefit (which may distort the location of R&D across countries). Of course, there is a general argument for subsidizing R&D activity because firms cannot appropriate the social returns from their investment. However, R&D is directly subsidized through tax credits, and patents are protected by intellectual property law, allowing patentholders to earn rents that incentivize innovation. Unless these instruments are for some reason not being used optimally, it is difficult to envisage any additional role for patent boxes in subsidizing R&D activity.

The strongest argument for a patent box seems to be that this type of income is particularly mobile, and so countries should lower its tax burden as part of a process of engaging in tax competition. This bears some resemblance to "defecting" in a prisoner's dilemma game, but it should not be forgotten that this strategy is privately optimal (assuming that there is no available multilateral process to constrain tax competition). The main efficiency cost (apart from the potential distortion to the location of R&D) is likely to be an increase in the deadweight cost of tax planning, as patent box regimes create additional complexity.

8.2.4 Distortions to the Use of External Debt

A corporation's interest payments on debt are deductible, unlike its payment of returns to equityholders.[9] This tax treatment gives rise to an incentive for corporations to use more debt finance than they would otherwise choose. It is important to note that this incentive pertains to *external* debt—that is, borrowing at arm's length from lenders external to the corporation or affiliated group of companies to which it belongs—as distinct from income-shifting via the use of inter-affiliate debt. The latter does not entail the same type of "real" resource costs as external debt, though it does create deadweight costs of tax planning of the sort discussed in section 8.2.2.

The efficiency cost of the tax-induced excessive use of external debt is generally framed in terms of the resource costs of insolvency and corporate reorganization (e.g., Dharmapala 2009).[10] When firms use more external debt than they otherwise would

[9] This tax preference arguably has its origins in the accounting treatment of interest payments as an expense associated with earning income. It therefore appears natural for interest payments to be deductible. Historically, the asymmetric treatment of interest and equity returns appears to have its origins in the efforts of accounting rules to measure the income of a business from the perspective of the equityholders (e.g., de Mooij 2012; Desai and Dharmapala 2015).

[10] Desai and Dharmapala (2015) suggest that under some circumstances, differences among MNCs in the extent to which they can deduct interest may lead to distortions in the pattern of ownership, similar to those discussed in section 8.2.7.

because of the tax deductibility of interest payments, the costs of insolvency and reorganization are incurred more frequently. These costs are not identical to the legal costs incurred in the bankruptcy process, which are primarily a transfer. Rather, deadweight costs arise because of a misallocation of labor—the returns to bankruptcy practice rise, drawing in more lawyers at the margin who would have produced more socially valuable output elsewhere (absent the tax incentive for firms to use too much debt). In addition, when leverage is high and agency costs of debt exist, equityholders may seek to transfer wealth to themselves from bondholders through greater risk-taking. There may be additional deadweight costs due to this behavior when leverage is higher due to the tax bias toward debt.

Framed in this way, the efficiency costs of debt bias seem somewhat attenuated. The consensus estimate of the literature on the magnitude of debt bias is that a 10 percentage point reduction in the corporate tax rate (e.g., from 35% to 25%) reduces the debt-to-asset ratio by 2.8 percentage points (e.g., from 50% to 47.2%) (see de Mooij 2012). The efficiency costs implied by the bankruptcy cost framework are very modest (Gordon 2010), amounting to less than 1% of US corporate tax revenue.

While the traditional view has been that the efficiency costs of debt bias are small, since the financial crisis of 2008 there has emerged a new focus on the role of tax-induced debt bias in affecting the likelihood of financial crises. De Mooij, Keen, and Orihara (2014) find that a higher degree of tax bias toward debt is associated with higher leverage among banks, which in turn is associated with a higher probability of a financial crisis among OECD countries. If the tax bias toward debt is indeed associated with financial instability, then its efficiency costs may be quite different in both nature and scale. For instance, they may include output losses from the effects of financial crises on the real economy. However, economists' understanding of the causes of the crisis and the role of taxation remain very much a work in progress.

8.2.5 Distortions to Payout and Repatriation Decisions

Corporations' choices of whether to pay dividends to equityholders, to repurchase shares, or to retain cash are influenced by the personal tax treatment of dividends and capital gains. Historically, dividends were taxed more heavily than capital gains—for instance, prior to the 2003 tax reform (the Jobs and Growth Tax Relief Reconciliation Act, or JGTRRA), the top rate on dividend income was 38.6%, while the tax rate on long-term capital gains was 20%. The 2003 tax reform reduced these rates to 15%. The top rate on both dividends and capital gains has risen to 20% since 2013, but these rates have remained equal to each other. Nonetheless, there is still some advantage to the retention of cash, as personal taxes are deferred until the realization of capital gains, and to repurchases when these represent a recovery of basis.

Evidence from the 2003 tax reform suggests that dividend payments are quite sensitive to the tax rate on dividends—Chetty and Saez (2005) find a 20% increase in dividend payments following the 2003 reform, with the response being stronger among firms where agency costs appear to be lower. To the extent that taxes induce firms to retain more cash, the primary inefficiency is likely to be from agency costs of free cash flow (i.e., negative-value investments). The bias toward retention also represents a distortion to the timing of payout. In principle, this may distort stockholders' intertemporal pattern of consumption if they are credit-constrained or otherwise prone to consuming more out of dividend income (for instance, due to placing dividend income in a different "mental account"). However, given that most stock is owned by households with higher incomes and reasonable access to credit, it is unlikely that this type of distortion is important.

The payment (or "repatriation") of dividends from foreign affiliates to their US parents raises a quite different set of issues. As previously discussed, the US tax is imposed only at the time of repatriation, enabling US MNCs to defer US taxes on active foreign income. When there are no profitable active investments abroad, deferral can be achieved by accumulating passive assets in low-tax affiliates, despite the Subpart F provisions that impose immediate US taxation of passive foreign income. Suppose that a foreign affiliate of a US MNC earns $100 of active income, delays repatriation, and invests in a portfolio of passive assets that earns a 10% annual return. Each year, it will be subject to immediate US tax at 35% on the $10 return (with a credit for any foreign tax paid). However, the US tax on the original $100 of active income is deferred until the time of repatriation (Weichenrieder 1996).

This incentive to delay payment of dividends to the parent has become widely known as the "lockout" effect (because cash held abroad is said to be "locked out" of the US parent). The issue is one of great practical significance, as indicated by the large amounts of cash held by US MNCs in their foreign affiliates, currently estimated to be about $2.1 trillion.[11] In 2004, Congress enacted the American Job Creation Act (AJCA), which contained a provision (known as the Homeland Investment Act) that enabled US MNCs to repatriate foreign cash at a drastically reduced tax rate of 5.25% during 2005. This was ostensibly a one-time repatriation holiday, but Congress has on several occasions considered repeating this exercise and it remains part of the policy debate today.

A primary efficiency cost of the lockout effect is the possibility of negative-value investments abroad by affiliates of US MNCs due to the tax costs of repatriating cash to the United States. For instance, Hanlon, Lester, and Verdi (2015) analyze the market responses to announcements of acquisitions. They find that market reactions are less positive for the announcement of foreign acquisitions by US MNCs that have particularly large tax-induced foreign cash holdings. In particular, "a one-standard-deviation increase in our proxies for tax-induced foreign cash is associated with a lower acquirer's abnormal return of 0.32–0.38%, representing roughly 5–6% of the transaction value, or approximately $5–$6 million per deal" (181).

In addition, there is a possibility of foregone profitable investments in the United States if the parent is cash-constrained. This appears unlikely to be a significant problem, based on the results of studies of the AJCA. For instance,

[11] See, e.g., the Citizens for Tax Justice report on "$2.1 Trillion in Corporate Profits Held Offshore: A Comparison of International Tax Proposals" at http://ctj.org/pdf/repatriation0715.pdf.

Dharmapala, Foley, and Forbes (2011) analyze the uses to which repatriated funds under the AJCA were put. The law ostensibly required that repatriated funds were to be used to increase US investment and employment in order to qualify for the tax benefit. Dharmapala, Foley, and Forbes (2011) use an instrumental variables strategy—based on ownership characteristics (such as the presence of tax haven affiliates and holding company structures) determined prior to the AJCA that increased the value of the tax holiday to firms—to identify the effects of exogenous increases in repatriations on a variety of outcome variables. They find no detectable impact on US investment or employment but find an effect on share repurchases, a pattern of responses that suggests that US MNC parents were not financially constrained.[12]

8.2.6 Distortions to the Choice of Organizational Form

The issue of "organizational form" refers to the choice on the part of a business entity of whether to incorporate or to operate in one of a number of possible noncorporate forms. The tax significance is that the income of noncorporate entities is "passed through" to the individual owners and taxed at the applicable personal tax rate. The existence of an entity-level tax on corporations, combined with the preferential personal tax rates on dividend and capital gains income distributed by corporations, can create incentives for an entity to either incorporate or avoid incorporation for tax reasons.

There is a substantial literature that seeks to measure the sensitivity of organizational form choices to tax rates (e.g., Gordon and MacKie-Mason 1994). For instance, Goolsbee (2004) uses cross-sectional data on the organizational form of firms across states with varying ratios of corporate to personal taxation. He finds that a 1 percentage point increase in the corporate income tax rate reduces the corporate share of firms by 2.5%, indicating that this choice is quite responsive to the relative tax burden on corporations and pass-through entities. However, the efficiency cost is quite difficult to quantify. Goolsbee (2004) finds no detectable impact of organizational form on a firm's business operations. Rather, the efficiency cost is likely to consist of higher transaction costs. For instance, the Delaware corporation is an entity that is well-known among lawyers, whereas other legal forms such as limited liability companies (LLCs) may be less familiar.

The United States is characterized by an extraordinarily large fraction of business activity being undertaken through noncorporate vehicles—in 2011, 54.2% of US

[12] There may, however, be other efficiency costs of lockout, such as increased agency costs of debt if the US parent borrows large amounts instead of repatriating. Early estimates of the overall deadweight cost of lockout were relatively modest—Desai, Foley, and Hines (2001) estimate this cost as being about 2.5% of repatriations, while Grubert and Mutti (2001) estimate that it is about 1% of foreign income. However, current conditions are quite different, in particular, with respect to the amount of cash held overseas.

business income was earned in pass-through entities (Cooper et al. 2015). However, some commentators have expressed concern that corporate tax reform may create a tax advantage to incorporation. Sanchirico (2016) highlights the irony of lowering corporate tax rates to address the lockout problem created by the availability of deferral for MNCs while at the same time creating opportunities for the deferral of taxation by domestic entities and individuals via incorporation. In the policy arena, there has also been a certain amount of resistance to lowering the corporate tax on the grounds that it would not benefit (and may adversely affect the competitiveness of) noncorporate business entities.

The central problem here can be characterized as one where the corporate tax rate is a single instrument that affects two very different kinds of behavior—the incorporation decisions of (typically small) business entities or individuals, and the location and investment decisions of large MNCs. Given the extensive array of inefficiencies attributable to the current corporate tax regime, it would seem inadvisable to forestall reform in order to prevent excessive incorporation by small entities. An alternative approach is to create different instruments to address the different behavioral margins. Currently, the US corporate tax has a graduated ("progressive") rate structure, with a 15% rate on the first $50,000.[13] One alternative may be to set the rate on the first $*x* of income at 35% (where *x* is chosen appropriately to reflect the likely upper bound on the income of the individuals and small business entities that may engage in excessive incorporation) and to set a 25% rate on corporate income above $*x*. In an admittedly rough way, this would subject the income of smaller corporations to a higher rate (which can be set to ensure neutrality with regard to organizational form) while giving larger corporations the benefit of a lower marginal rate.

There are also a number of other alternatives, such as increasing the tax rate on equity returns[14] (i.e., dividends and capital gains[15]). It may also be possible to create a special regime for closely held corporations, where retained cash is deemed to have been paid as dividends to limit the deferral advantage, or closely held corporations could simply be treated as pass-through entities, as proposed by Yin (1998).

[13] This graduated structure applies only for quite low levels of income, however, with a 34% rate for income above $335,000 and a 35% rate above $10 million—see, e.g., Internal Revenue Service, 2014 Instructions for Form 1120.

[14] The tax on equity returns has been set at a relatively low level to address concerns about the burden on corporations' cost of capital of taxation at both the corporate and personal levels. However, with increasingly globalized capital markets, the personal tax on US residents arguably plays less of a role in determining the cost of capital for US firms (e.g., Desai and Dharmapala 2011).

[15] There are some clear disadvantages of higher personal taxes, for instance, increasing the capital gains tax may exacerbate the lock-in problem. This could be mitigated by other changes to capital gains taxation, such as requiring taxpayers to pay interest to offset the deferral advantage associated with the realization doctrine.

8.2.7 Distortions to Asset Ownership and the Market for Corporate Control

The modern theory of the MNC emphasizes the central importance of the advantages of the common ownership of assets across countries in inducing (some) firms to become multinational. In particular, the widely used OLI (ownership, location, and internalization) framework stresses that the ownership of assets affects their productivity. When multinationality is viewed in this light, the importance of tax rules that do not distort the pattern of ownership of assets across locations—for instance, which affiliates are owned by which parents—becomes readily apparent (e.g., Desai and Hines 2003). The US worldwide tax system, it is often argued, potentially distorts these patterns of ownership by placing an extra burden on US MNCs.

To illustrate, consider a scenario where a US MNC is competing with an MNC based in country B to acquire an asset in a third country C. Suppose that B imposes a 35% tax rate and is territorial, the United States imposes a 35% rate on worldwide basis, and C imposes a 20% tax. If the affiliate in C is owned by the MNC from country B, then it faces a 20% local tax rate and no additional home country tax. If that same affiliate is owned by the US MNC, it faces the 35% US tax (with a foreign tax credit) in addition to the local tax, if repatriation is immediate. For instance, if the affiliate earns \$100 (pretax) under US ownership but only \$85 (pretax) under B ownership, the after-tax return is \$65 for the US MNC and \$68 for the country B MNC. The latter will acquire the asset even though it is the less productive owner.

The efficiency cost in this type of scenario is the lower productivity of assets (in pretax terms) as a result of ownership distortions. Measuring the effects of ownership on productivity directly is not straightforward. However, the disadvantages of US residence for MNCs have increasingly been reflected in the market for corporate control. In particular, corporate inversions have become a major issue in recent years. These are mergers and acquisitions (M&A) in which a US MNC is acquired by a foreign firm, with the combined entity subsequently establishing its tax domicile outside the United States.[16]

A growing body of evidence has used data on M&A to estimate the impact of taxes, and especially of residence-based taxes on foreign income, on the pattern and value of these transactions. For instance, Huizinga and Voget (2009) analyze a large sample of cross-border M&A transactions over the 1985–2004 period. They estimate that eliminating the US worldwide tax would have increased the fraction of post-merger entities with US domiciles from 53% to 58%. Voget (2011) analyzes instances in which MNCs relocated their headquarters or residence over the 1997–2007 period. He finds that a 10 percentage point increase in the repatriation tax increases such relocations by a third. Feld et al. (2013) estimate that a switch from the US worldwide system to a territorial system would increase the number of M&A transactions with US acquirers by 17%.

[16] Another potential response is for new US-headquartered startups to begin life incorporated in a foreign tax haven jurisdiction in order to escape future US taxation of foreign income—see e.g. Desai and Dharmapala (2010).

Using data on foreign acquisitions of US firms over the 1990–2010 period, Bird (2015) also finds large tax-induced distortions of the M&A market and estimates substantial welfare losses. Overall, this body of evidence suggests strongly that patterns of ownership among MNCs are quite substantially distorted by the US international tax regime.

8.2.8 Distortions to the Choices of Portfolio Investors

The discussion in section 8.2.7 focused on the acquisition of assets by different potential MNC acquirers. When such acquisitions are equity-financed, the funds are ultimately provided by portfolio investors. These portfolio investors can choose the firms in which they buy shares, to an increasing degree across national borders. Thus, to the extent that US MNCs are disadvantaged by the US tax system, they will be disfavored as vehicles for investment by portfolio investors. Desai and Dharmapala (2009b) construct a simple model in which US portfolio investors can achieve international diversification goals by either investing in US MNCs that operate abroad (engaging in FDI) or by buying stock in firms in foreign countries (i.e., engaging in foreign portfolio investment, or FPI). In this setting, the additional US tax on foreign income induces US portfolio investors to supply less capital to the US MNC and to invest instead in foreign firms.

Desai and Dharmapala (2009b) find evidence consistent with the importance of this phenomenon by combining data on US outbound FPI and US outbound FDI in fifty countries over the 1994–2005 period. First, as shown in figure 8.2, the ratio of FPI to aggregate US equity holdings (FPI plus FDI) is higher in countries with lower corporate tax rates (where the US residual tax is more burdensome). This pattern is confirmed in a regression analysis that controls for a variety of factors, including country-specific linear time trends. Their estimated coefficient of −0.033 implies an elasticity of FPI with respect to the local corporate tax rate of approximately −1. Thus, a 10% reduction in a country's corporate tax rate (e.g., from 35% to 31.5%) would be predicted to lead to a 10% increase in the value of equity held by US portfolio investors. This is another manifestation of the distortion of ownership patterns by worldwide taxation, albeit an ongoing process that lacks the drama of corporate inversion transactions.

8.3 "CONSENSUS" REFORMS: TERRITORIALISM WITH A REDUCTION IN THE CORPORATE TAX RATE

There appears to be an emerging consensus in policy circles on the general outlines of business and corporate tax reform, although there remains much uncertainty about its precise shape and the likelihood and timeframe of its enactment. The aim here is to briefly sketch the major features of this consensus, and to discuss the efficiency consequences of this type of reform in the light of the framework in section 8.2. The major impetus for reform appears to stem from the lockout problem and from the recognition that the US statutory corporate tax is out of step with those of other comparable countries. This tax rate differential has become increasingly

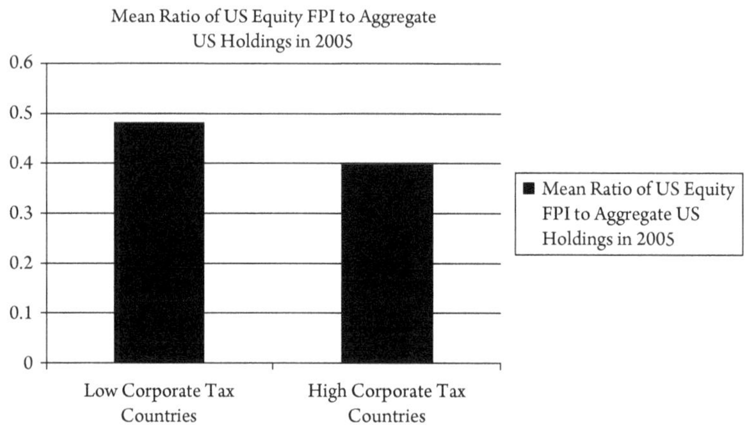

Figure 8.2 Portfolio investment abroad by US residents. *Notes:* This figure is drawn from Desai and Dharmapala (2009b: figure 2) and Desai and Dharmapala (2010: figure 5). It depicts the mean ratio of outbound US FPI to aggregate US holdings (where aggregate US holdings are defined as the sum of US FPI and US FDI) for two subsamples of countries. The bars represent ratios for subsamples divided at the median corporate tax rate. Data on corporate tax rates (specifically, the top statutory corporate tax rate) is obtained from the data provided by the accounting firm PricewaterhouseCoopers' worldwide summaries of corporate tax rates. The data on FPI by US investors are obtained from the US Treasury's Treasury International Capital (TIC) reporting system, available at http://www.treas.gov/tic/. The data on FDI are obtained from the Bureau of Economic Analysis (BEA), available at http://www.bea.gov.

difficult to ignore, as has the accumulation of cash held by the foreign affiliates of US MNCs and the growth of corporate inversions. Thus, the key elements of the emerging consensus are a reduction in the corporate tax rate to somewhere between 20% and 28% (we use 25% for concreteness in the discussion) and a shift from a worldwide to a territorial system (i.e., the exemption from US tax of dividends paid by foreign affiliates to their US parents). Broadly speaking, this is the type of reform envisaged by the Hatch Report and embodied in a number of current legislative proposals.

However, there is greater disagreement and uncertainty about various other elements of a possible reform package, especially the anti-avoidance rules that may be introduced as part of a reform. In particular, two quite novel ideas (analyzed in more detail in sections 8.3.2 and 8.3.3 have been widely discussed: (1) a one-time levy on the foreign cash holdings of US MNCs to be implemented at the time of the reform and (2) a minimum tax on foreign income.

8.3.1 Evaluating "Consensus" Reforms

Of the distortions catalogued in section 8.2, only one—the lockout effect—is unambiguously and fully addressed by this type of "consensus" reform. This is because a dividend exemption system implies that there is no advantage to delaying repatriations.[17] The evidence from two other major economies—the United Kingdom and Japan—that implemented territorial reforms in 2009 supports the idea that such a reform in the United States will solve the lockout problem. For instance, Egger et al. (2015) find that repatriations by foreign affiliates of UK MNCs increased following the UK reform. Moreover, investment by these affiliates declined after the reform, suggesting that they had previously been engaging in negative-value investments. These effects occurred even though (pre-reform) UK rules allowed greater scope for UK MNCs to return cash to the parent via mechanisms that avoided the repatriation tax than is the case for US MNCs. Hasegawa and Kiyota (2015) find similarly that repatriations from foreign affiliates with large amounts of retained earnings increased after the Japanese reform.

Ownership distortions relating to M&A activity and portfolio investment would be mitigated by a dividend exemption regime and by a lower corporate tax rate. Again, evidence from the UK and Japanese reforms is instructive. Liu (2015) finds that UK MNCs increased their activity in lower-tax foreign countries (where they were previously most burdened by the repatriation tax); this effect was not offset by reduced activity in higher-tax foreign countries or the United Kingdom. Feld et al. (2013) find that following the Japanese reform, the number of M&A transactions with a Japanese acquirer increased by about 32%. However, the extent to which these inefficiencies will be mitigated depends to a significant degree on the choice of a minimum tax.

Incentives for income-shifting out of the United States are likely to be mitigated by the lower corporate tax rate. On the other hand, it is often argued that moving to a territorial system may increase the gains from shifting income out of the United States. This is because under the current regime any income shifted out of the United States will eventually be subject to the repatriation tax upon repatriation to the United States. This would not be the case for active business income under a territorial system, thereby arguably creating a greater incentive for income-shifting. As was discussed in section 8.2.2, however, the efficiency gains from changes in income-shifting activity are not straightforward to assess. Some of the purely domestic distortions would also be mitigated, but not eliminated, by a reduction in the corporate tax rate.

In summary, a "consensus" reform would mark a significant advance that would address the most glaring problems of the US corporate tax—the high statutory rate and the lockout problem—and would also mitigate a range of other distortions, both international and domestic. However, it would leave many of the inefficiencies of corporate taxation largely untouched.

8.3.2 A One-Time Levy on Foreign Cash Holdings

A territorial reform would relieve US MNCs of the burden of future repatriation taxes. It might seem that a reasonable *quid pro quo* would be the payment of a one-time levy,

[17] This is true even with a minimum tax on foreign income set at a high rate, as the minimum tax would be applied on an immediate basis (without deferral).

calibrated to the effective tax burden of the pre-reform repatriation tax. This element of a potential tax reform has gained significant support. In addition to preventing a windfall gain from tax reform for MNCs, this one-time levy is also viewed as an efficient (i.e., nondistortionary) source of revenue. The latter claim raises a puzzle, however. If it is indeed true that this would (credibly) be a one-time levy, then on efficiency grounds it is not clear why a levy should be limited to the expected burden of the repatriation tax—it would be efficient to tax the foreign cash holdings of MNCs at 100% in order to reduce other distortionary taxes.

Of course, the efficiency of such a levy depends crucially on the credibility of the promise that the levy will not be repeated. Once the administrative apparatus for taxing foreign cash is established, it will be tempting for Congress to repeat the ostensibly "one-time" levy. Past experience with other "one-time" policies in the international tax arena may be instructive. As discussed earlier, in 2004 Congress enacted the AJCA, one component of which was a "one-time" repatriation tax holiday. In 2009 and 2011, members of Congress sought several times to repeat the "one-time" holiday and came fairly close to succeeding on some occasions. Indeed, a repatriation tax holiday is still discussed as a possibility in some policy circles today. This experience engenders little confidence in the one-time nature of the levy on foreign cash.

If the "one-time" levy on foreign cash is anticipated to recur, it may lead to a new type of inefficiency: excessive future repatriations. Suppose that a US MNC generates \$1 abroad (following a tax reform that eliminates taxation upon repatriation). Repatriating immediately ensures that this cash will escape any future US levy, whereas keeping the cash abroad entails some possibility of the recurrence of the "one-time" levy. Other things equal, this will encourage repatriation. In a frictionless world, this would not matter for efficiency, as cash can be borrowed as needed for profitable investment projects. Even in a situation where the MNC faces a higher cost of external relative to internal cash (and hence the use of internal capital markets is valuable), there would be no efficiency cost if the MNC can hold cash within the US parent and redeploy it to affiliates when profitable investment opportunities emerge. However, in the presence of agency costs among affiliates, repatriation to the US parent may create pressure to either use the funds for US investment or to pay out dividends to common stockholders, foregoing more valuable investment opportunities abroad.[18]

8.3.3 A Minimum Tax on Foreign Income

Proposals for a minimum tax on the foreign income of US MNCs take many forms (Grubert and Altshuler 2013). For instance, the tax may be applied on a uniform basis (to all foreign income) or on a per-country basis. It may contain a "cliff" (where foreign income not subject to a sufficiently high foreign tax rate is subject to the full US

[18] The expected burden of future levies may also create ownership distortions by adversely affecting the ability of US MNCs to compete for the purchase of foreign assets, relative to non-US MNCs that do not face the possibility of a levy on overseas cash holdings.

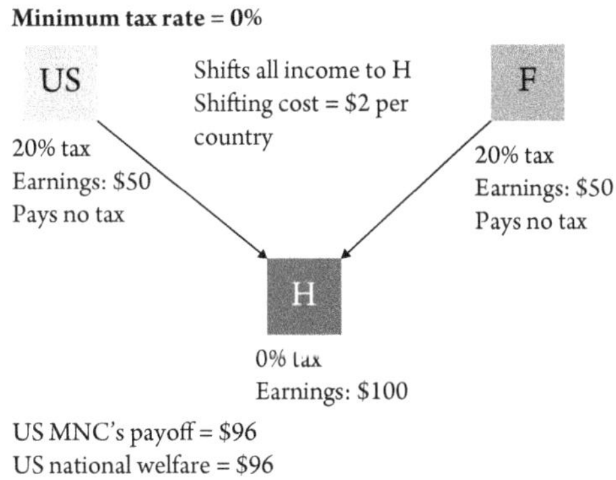

Figure 8.3 US national welfare without a minimum tax

rate) or may be applied at a rate that is substantially lower than the regular US rate. It may in some versions include an exemption for active business income or an exemption for a normal return to capital. Here, we ignore these complexities, and focus on the most straightforward version, assuming that it applies broadly to foreign-source income as that concept is currently defined.[19]

The main point that we make through a simple numerical example is that if the minimum tax rate is set relatively high, it will reduce foreign-to-foreign income-shifting by US MNCs. While this reduces the deadweight costs of tax planning, it may reduce US national welfare by increasing the amount of foreign tax paid by US MNCs. On the other hand, if the minimum tax rate is low, then it will not have much impact on foreign-to-foreign income-shifting. While US national welfare will not be reduced by increased payment of foreign taxes, the deadweight cost of tax planning will also not change substantially. To be sure, a minimum tax can generate a certain amount of additional US tax revenue. However, the aim of reform should arguably be to increase social welfare rather than to increase revenue.

To illustrate these points, consider a world with three countries (as illustrated in figure 8.3)—the United States, a high-tax foreign country F, and a zero-tax haven H. Suppose that the United States has enacted a territorial tax reform that involves dividend exemption with a corporate tax rate of 20%. Suppose that country F also imposes a corporate tax of 20%. Assume that the US MNC earns $50 in the United States and $50 in country F. It can choose to engage in tax planning to shift all $50 from the United States to H at a fixed cost of $2.[20] Similarly, the US MNC can choose to engage in tax planning to shift all $50 from country F to H, also at a fixed cost of $2.

[19] Grubert and Altshuler (2013) carefully define alternative versions of the minimum tax and conduct numerical simulations of the impact on US and foreign tax revenues and other relevant outcomes. Ultimately, they argue for a per-country minimum tax, which they argue would reduce the incentives for income–shifting.

[20] This tax planning cost is assumed to not be tax-deductible, though this is not crucial for the conclusions.

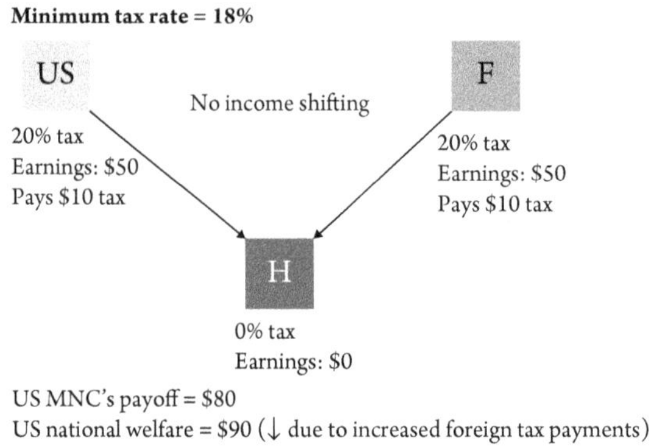

Figure 8.4 The effects of the minimum tax on US national welfare

As in Equation (3), US national welfare is the sum of the after-tax profits of the US-resident MNC and US tax revenue.

Suppose initially that there is no minimum tax. Then, the US MNC will shift all income to H. Its payoff is its pretax worldwide income, minus its tax planning costs (i.e. $96) and US national welfare is therefore also $96 (see figure 8.3).[21] Now, suppose we introduce a minimum tax of 18%. In this scenario with a relatively high minimum tax, US MNCs are deterred from income-shifting.[22] This implies that the deadweight cost of tax planning is saved, but US national welfare is now lower than without a minimum tax (specifically, it is $90 < $96; see figure 8.4). Thus, the minimum tax can lower US national welfare by deterring foreign-to-foreign shifting and increasing tax payments to foreign governments by US MNCs.[23]

This reduction in US national welfare will not occur when the minimum tax rate is set relatively low. For instance, suppose it is 10%. Then, the US MNC will shift all its income to H and US national welfare will again be $96.[24] This is, of course, no

[21] The US MNC can avoid $10 of tax in each of the United States and country F at a cost of $2 per country of undertaking tax planning. Thus, the US MNC will shift all income to H. Its payoff is then $100 – $2 – $2 = $96.

[22] If the US MNC shifts its income from the United States and country F to H, its payoff is now 50 – 2 – 9 + 50 – 2 – 9 = $78. That is, it incurs the $2 tax planning cost per country and also pays a $9 minimum tax to the United States as the tax rate in H is zero. If it were to refrain from tax planning, it would shift no income to H and would pay $10 of tax to the United States and $10 of tax to the government of country F, and its payoff would be 50 – 10 + 50 – 10 = $80.

[23] This type of outcome may be less likely if current income-shifting is primarily from the United States to H, rather than from country F to H. However, the (limited) existing evidence suggests that income-shifting out of the parent tends to be smaller in magnitude than foreign-to-foreign shifting (Dischinger, Knoll, and Riedel 2014), possibly due to agency costs between the managers of the parent and managers of affiliates.

[24] The US MNC faces a minimum tax of $5 if it shifts to H. It will thus be willing to incur the $2 per country tax planning cost. The US MNC's payoff = 50 – 2 – 5 + 50 – 2 – 5 = $86 from shifting income, whereas it would be $80 if it chose not to engage in income-shifting.

lower than without a minimum tax, but also no higher, so the minimum tax does not enhance US national welfare. Of course, Equation (3) may be overly simplistic in that national welfare may place greater weight on tax revenue than on the MNC's profits. Then, a 10% minimum tax makes the United States better off due to increased revenue. However, this effect is likely to be modest in magnitude. More important, even if additional tax revenue is socially desirable, it is not clear why the foreign-source income of US MNCs is the least distortionary source of such revenue, when one could instead increase personal tax rates (or introduce a VAT).

8.4 FORMULA APPORTIONMENT

The current system of international taxation is based on separate accounting (SA) for each affiliate of an MNC. Proposals for formula apportionment (FA) are premised on the idea that it is impossible to separate out the activities of different legal entities within the same economic firm. Implementing FA requires first defining a consolidated worldwide entity to which FA is to be applied. Its aggregate worldwide income is then apportioned based on a formula (such as the fraction of its worldwide sales that take place in the relevant jurisdiction).[25] Thus, FA dispenses with both of the traditional international tax law concepts of source and residence, and replaces them with a formula that allocates tax base among countries based typically on the location of consumers.

It is most natural to envisage FA being implemented on a multilateral basis, with some agreement among governments on the formula. However, in principle it is possible to imagine unilateral US implementation of FA, although this creates a possibility of double taxation or nontaxation. Indeed, the United States would then become a haven for inward income-shifting—income reported in the United States does not increase US tax liability, while shifting income out of jurisdictions that continue to use the source principle would reduce tax liability there. This effect may create pressure on foreign countries to follow suit and adopt FA themselves.

By abandoning the source and residence principles, FA would solve many of the international distortions associated with corporate taxation. There would no longer be any incentive to engage in the currently prevalent forms of income-shifting, as tax liability would be based on the location of sales and not the source of income. Repatriation decisions would have no tax consequences, so the lockout effect and ownership distortions due to the residual tax would disappear. However, distortions that are primarily domestic—such as the bias toward external debt, the bias toward retaining cash, and distortions to the choice of organizational form—would be essentially unaffected by FA. Thus, FA can be expected to directly address about half of the distortions identified in section 8.2, while doing very little to mitigate the remainder.

[25] For instance, an MNC that generates $100 of worldwide income and generates 20% of its worldwide sales revenue in the United States would be deemed to have taxable income of $20 in the United States.

Moreover, it is possible that FA may give rise to new kinds of efficiency costs that are unknown under the current SA system. For instance, firms may sell their products to arm's length wholesalers in low-tax jurisdictions who then resell in high-tax countries. Proponents have suggested look-through provisions to address such "reselling" strategies, but it is unclear how they would apply if the reseller modifies and adds some value to the product before reselling.

MNCs may also respond to an FA system by altering their patterns of asset ownership. For instance, MNCs would have an incentive to acquire businesses earning modest rates of return (such as restaurants) in low-tax countries, thereby increasing the fraction of their sales that are allocated to low-tax countries (e.g., Altshuler and Grubert 2010). Conversely, routine activities would no longer be conducted in-house in high-tax countries. Such changes to ownership patterns may have significant efficiency costs.[26] Avi Yonah, Clausing, and Durst (2008) propose an FA system that would impute a fixed "normal" return to routine activities and use a sales-based formula to allocate only the returns to nonroutine activities. This would address the "restaurant" problem to the extent that the restaurant's returns would be classified as a "routine" activity and allocated fully to the low-tax country. However, it would place considerable pressure on the distinction between routine and nonroutine activities, a distinction that is far from self-evident.[27]

FA is in many respects an important idea. Even in the rosiest scenario, however, it would only address about half of the distortions associated with the corporate tax, and it may give rise to new distortions from which we are currently spared. However, FA's most attractive feature—of moving away from the source and residence principles—also characterizes the destination-based corporate tax, to which we turn next.

8.5 THE DESTINATION-BASED CASH FLOW TAX AND VAT-TYPE OPTIONS

A rather more fundamental type of reform than we have considered so far would involve moving from the income-type taxation of businesses toward a consumption-type tax system. Consumption-type taxes—such as cash flow taxes and various forms of a VAT—all share some fundamental commonalities. A cash flow tax takes as its base the net cash flows of a firm (its cash receipts minus its cash outlays). As investment is fully deductible at the time it is undertaken (i.e., fully "expensed"), a cash flow tax is a tax on economic rents, exempting the normal return to capital. The destination-based cash flow tax (DBCFT) builds on this idea by adding a destination principle that

[26] Altshuler and Grubert (2010) develop a model that analyzes the consequences of FA and SA systems in a unified framework and conclude that FA offers little overall advantage once MNCs' strategic responses to the FA system are taken into account.

[27] There are also a number of other difficult issues related to the implementation of FA, such as the definition of unitary entities for tax purposes.

addresses many of the cross-jurisdictional distortions of corporate taxation (Auerbach 2010; Auerbach, Devereux, and Simpson 2010).[28]

Moving to a DBCFT from the existing corporate income tax involves two major steps. The first is to transform the tax base from income to cash flow. This is accomplished by allowing deductions for all cash outflows (including the full cost of investment expenditures). The full expensing of investment eliminates distortions to the amount of investment. All cash receipts (apart from cash generated by the issuance of equity) are included in the tax base. Borrowed funds are included in the tax base, while interest payments are deductible as they constitute cash outflows. The symmetric treatment of borrowed funds and interest payments eliminates debt bias.

The second step is the introduction of the destination principle. A cash flow tax that uses a source principle may distort discrete investment and location choices, even though it fully expenses investment, because the EATR may differ across locations. In contrast, the destination principle is based on the location of consumption. It is implemented by ensuring that the DBCFT does not apply to any form of cross-border activity. Income from abroad—whether earned by a foreign affiliate or from exports—is excluded. This exclusion of foreign-related cash receipts goes considerably beyond what territorial income tax systems seek to achieve, and its conceptual basis is quite different. For a territorial income tax system, the key principle is source, and foreign-source income is exempt under certain conditions; however, income from abroad that is attributable to domestic economic activity is taxable. Under a DBCFT, the guiding principle is destination rather than source, and so what matters is the location of consumption, not the source of income. Thus, there is also no deduction for the cost of purchases made abroad. The DBCFT's stance of ignoring foreign transactions is essentially equivalent to the border adjustments made under a destination-based VAT, which ensure that the base of the VAT includes only domestic consumption.

The DBCFT would solve virtually all distortions from the corporate tax. It was noted earlier that it would not affect the amount or location of investment and that it would eliminate debt bias. There is no gain from income-shifting because the source principle has been jettisoned. Under a DBCFT, there are no tax consequences associated with repatriation. Thus, lockout will not occur, and there will be no ownership distortions. Notwithstanding the caveats raised by the analysis in section 8.2.2, it is reasonable to expect that there would be a substantial efficiency gain from the elimination of the deadweight costs associated with the (mis)allocation of workers to tax planning activity.

The only possible exceptions to this rosy scenario relate to areas where the DBCFT interacts with the personal tax system. In particular, the distortion to payout depends on the personal tax treatment of dividends and capital gains, while the distortion to the choice of organizational form depends on the personal tax treatment of pass-through

[28] Devereux and de la Feria (2014) address issues relating to the implementation of a DBCFT. Note that the DBCFT proposal formulated by Auerbach (2010) applies to financial as well as nonfinancial firms.

business income. The adoption of a DBCFT does not, by itself, settle these issues, and the consequences with respect to these margins depend on the personal tax system with which the DBCFT is paired.

One possibility is that the current personal income tax system continues to operate. Then, some distortions, for instance to organizational form, may persist. To address issues of organizational form, Auerbach (2010) proposes extending the DBCFT to S corporations (pass-through entities that are close substitutes for C corporations), based on the number of shareholders rather than on legal form. This would reduce the distortion, and while there may be some inefficiency at the margin (for instance, firms keeping the number of shareholders above or below the threshold for application of the DBCFT), it might reasonably be expected to be localized and small.

An alternative perspective emphasizes the commonalities between the DBCFT and the VAT. The DBCFT is equivalent to a destination-based subtraction-method VAT with a deduction for payroll (Auerbach, Devereux, and Simpson 2010).[29] Thus, the DBCFT could be viewed as the business component of a subtraction-method VAT (with a deduction at the business level for wages). Value-added due to labor inputs could then be taxed at the individual level, with this individual wage tax replacing the current personal income tax. The individual tax on value-added due to labor would resemble the individual component of other subtraction-method VAT-type proposals, such as the well-known Hall and Rabushka (1995) flat tax. When paired with an individual-level tax on value-added due to labor, the DBCFT would eliminate all the distortions catalogued in section 8.2. In particular, organizational form distortions of the type discussed in section 8.2.6 will not occur because there is no personal income tax, and payout to common stockholders will also be unaffected by this tax system as there would be no personal tax on dividends or capital gains.

The DBCFT is thus clearly very attractive, in that it can solve essentially all of the inefficiencies described in section 8.2. It should be remembered, however, that this virtue is shared by VAT-type proposals such as the flat tax and by a VAT (especially a "full-replacement" VAT under which personal and corporate income taxes would be eliminated).[30] Moreover, implementing a DBCFT would raise new issues of administration and law, whereas the implementation of a VAT could draw on the extensive body of law and experience developed by about 150 countries over several decades. Thus, the introduction of a VAT or one of its variants would seem to be a policy that

[29] VAT systems generally use either the subtraction method—which involves computing the value of sales, subtracting the costs of inputs, and then applying the VAT rate to the result—or the credit-invoice method, which involves computing the value of sales, applying the VAT rate to the result, and then subtracting the VAT paid on inputs (which are established using the invoices provided by suppliers). These approaches are fundamentally equivalent, and tax the same base (namely, consumption). However, the credit-invoice method predominates around the world and is thought to have various administrative advantages (Grinberg 2010).

[30] Note, however, that while legal form as such does not matter for VAT liability, there may be a different distortion to firm size around the VAT threshold. Most countries apply VAT only above a threshold, typically defined in terms of turnover (e.g., Liu and Lockwood 2015), and firms may "bunch" below such a threshold.

is worthy of serious consideration, notwithstanding its lack of political popularity and the opprobrium it attracts in the Hatch Report.[31] However, a full consideration of the ramifications of such a fundamental reform is beyond the scope of this chapter.

8.6 CONCLUSION

This chapter has reviewed lessons from economic research for the current debate on business tax reform in the United States. It began by presenting a simple framework highlighting ten behavioral margins affected by corporate taxation. Three broad categories of reforms were then analyzed in the light of this framework. The major general lesson to be drawn is that the relatively modest reforms (involving lower corporate tax rates and dividend exemption) that are under discussion are likely to generate only modest gains, while leaving many of the inefficiencies of corporate taxation unaddressed. More fundamental reforms, however, have the potential to eliminate all or most of the inefficiencies of corporate taxation.

While arguments for fundamental reform may seem utopian, a combination of domestic and international factors arguably create a unique opportunity for policymakers. In particular, there is widespread agreement within the United States on the need for business tax reform. At the same time, global dissatisfaction with the current international tax regime—based on source and residence principles—has grown, as evidenced by the BEPS initiative. All of these concerns can be addressed through business tax reforms that move beyond the source and residence principles, for instance, by implementing the destination-based consumption-type taxes described in section 8.5.

ACKNOWLEDGMENTS

I wish to thank participants at the conference on "The Economics of Tax Policy" held at the Brookings Institution (especially Alan Auerbach and my discussant Rosanne Altshuler) for valuable comments and suggestions. I also thank Mihir Desai, Daniel Hemel, Nathaniel Hendren, Jim Hines, Damon Jones, David Weisbach, and Eric Zwick for helpful discussions on topics related to this chapter. I also acknowledge the financial support of the Lee and Brena Freeman Faculty Research Fund at the University of Chicago Law School. Any remaining errors or omissions are, of course, my own.

REFERENCES

Alstadsæter, Annette, Salvador Barrios, Gaetan Nicodème, G. J., Agnieszka Maria Skonieczna, and Antonio Vezzani. 2015. "Patent Boxes Design, Patents Location and Local R&D." CESifo Working Paper No. 5416.

[31] In the US political arena, a VAT is criticized primarily for two reasons—its "regressivity" relative to the current personal income tax and its reputation as a "money machine" that is "too" efficient at raising revenue. The distributional issues are important, though it should be remembered that redistribution can be achieved via expenditures as well as revenues.

Altshuler, Rosanne, and Harry Grubert. 2010. "Formula Apportionment: Is It Better Than the Current System and Are There Better Alternatives?." *National Tax Journal* 63 (4): 1145–84.

Arulampalam, Wiji, Michael P. Devereux, and Giorgia Maffini. 2012. "The Direct Incidence of Corporate Income Tax on Wages." *European Economic Review* 56 (6): 1038–54.

Auerbach, Alan J. 2010. *A Modern Corporate Tax*. Washington, DC: Center for American Progress and the Hamilton Project.

Auerbach, Alan J., Michael P. Devereux, and Helen Simpson. 2010. "Taxing Corporate Income." In *Dimensions of Tax Design: The Mirrlees Review*, edited by James A. Mirrlees, Stuart Adam, Tim Besley, Richard Blundell, Steve Bond, Robert Chote, Malcolm Gammie, Paul Johnson, Gareth Myles, and James Poterba, 837–93. Oxford: Oxford University Press.

Avi-Yonah, Reuven S., Kimberly A. Clausing, and Michael C. Durst. 2008. "Allocating Business Profits for Tax Purposes: A Proposal to Adopt a Formulary Profit Split." *Florida Tax Review* 9 (5): 497–553.

Bird, Andrew. 2015. "Domestic Taxes and Inbound Acquisitions." http://www.andrew.cmu.edu/user/apmb/Bird_TaxMA.pdf.

Chetty, Raj. 2009. "Is the Taxable Income Elasticity Sufficient to Calculate Deadweight Loss? The Implications of Evasion and Avoidance." *American Economic Journal: Economic Policy* 1 (2): 31–52.

Chetty, Raj, and Emmanuel Saez. 2005. "Dividend Taxes and Corporate Behavior: Evidence from the 2003 Dividend Tax Cut." *Quarterly Journal of Economics* 120 (3): 791–833.

Cooper, Michael, John McClelland, James Pearce, Richard Prisinzano, Joseph Sullivan, Danny Yagan, Owen Zidar, and Eric Zwick. 2015. "Business in the United States: Who Owns it and How Much Tax Do They Pay?." *Tax Policy and the Economy* 30:91–128.

De Mooij, Ruud A. 2012. "Tax Biases to Debt Finance: Assessing the Problem, Finding Solutions." *Fiscal Studies* 33 (4): 489–512.

De Mooij, Ruud A., and Sjef Ederveen. 2003. "Taxation and Foreign Direct Investment: A Synthesis of Empirical Research." *International Tax and Public Finance* 10 (6): 673–93.

De Mooij, Ruud A., Michael Keen, and Masanori Orihara. 2014. "Taxation, Bank Leverage, and Financial Crises." In *Taxation and Regulation of the Financial Sector*, edited by Ruud A. de Mooij and Gaëtan Nicodème, 229–52. Cambridge, MA: MIT Press.

Desai, Mihir A., and Dhammika Dharmapala. 2006. "Corporate Tax Avoidance and High-Powered Incentives." *Journal of Financial Economics* 79 (1): 145–79.

Desai, Mihir A., and Dhammika Dharmapala. 2009a. "Corporate Tax Avoidance and Firm Value." *Review of Economics and Statistics* 91 (3): 537–46.

Desai, Mihir A., and Dhammika Dharmapala. 2009b. "Taxes, Institutions and Foreign Diversification Opportunities." *Journal of Public Economics* 93 (5): 703–14.

Desai, Mihir A., and Dhammika Dharmapala. 2010. "Do Strong Fences Make Strong Neighbors?" *National Tax Journal* 63 (4): 723–40.

Desai, Mihir A., and Dhammika Dharmapala. 2011. "Dividend Taxes and International Portfolio Choice." *Review of Economics and Statistics* 93 (1): 266–84.

Desai, Mihir A., and Dhammika Dharmapala. 2015. "Interest Deductions in a Multijurisdictional World." *National Tax Journal* 68 (3): 653–80.

Desai, Mihir A., C. Fritz Foley, and James R. Hines, Jr. 2001. "Repatriation Taxes and Dividend Distortions." *National Tax Journal* 54 (4): 829–51.

Desai, Mihir A., and James R. Hines, Jr. 2003. "Evaluating International Tax Reform." *National Tax Journal* 56 (3): 487–502.

Devereux, Michael P., and Rita de la Feria. 2014. "Designing and Implementing a Destination-Based Corporate Tax." Oxford University Centre for Business Taxation Working Paper No. 14/07.

Devereux, Michael P., and Rachel Griffith. 1998. "Taxes and the Location of Production: Evidence from a Panel of US Multinationals." *Journal of Public Economics* 68 (3): 335–67.

Devereux, Michael P., and Rachel Griffith. 2003. "Evaluating Tax Policy for Location Decisions." *International Tax and Public Finance* 10 (2): 107–26.

Dharmapala, Dhammika. 2008. "What Problems and Opportunities Are Created by Tax Havens?." *Oxford Review of Economic Policy* 24 (4): 661–79.

Dharmapala, Dhammika. 2009. "The Impact of Taxes on Dividends and Corporate Financial Policy: Lessons from the 2000's." In *Tax Policy Lessons from the 2000s*, edited by Alan D. Viard, 199–233. Washington, DC: American Enterprise Institute Press.

Dharmapala, Dhammika. 2014a. "What Do We Know about Base Erosion and Profit Shifting? A Review of the Empirical Literature." *Fiscal Studies* 35 (4): 421–48.

Dharmapala, Dhammika. 2014b. "Base Erosion and Profit Shifting: A Simple Conceptual Framework." *CESifo DICE Report* 12 (4): 8–14.

Dharmapala, Dhammika, C. Fritz Foley, and Kristin J. Forbes. 2011. "Watch What I Do, Not What I Say: The Unintended Consequences of the Homeland Investment Act." *Journal of Finance* 66 (3): 753–87.

Dharmapala, Dhammika, and Nadine Riedel. 2013. "Earnings Shocks and Tax-Motivated Income Shifting: Evidence from European Multinationals." *Journal of Public Economics* 97 (1): 95–107.

Dischinger, Matthias, Bodo Knoll, and Nadine Riedel. 2014. "The Role of Headquarters in Multinational Profit Shifting Strategies." *International Tax and Public Finance* 21 (2): 248–71.

Dischinger, Matthias, and Nadine Riedel. 2011. "Corporate Taxes and the Location of Intangible Assets within Multinational Firms" *Journal of Public Economics* 95 (7–8): 691–707.

Egger, Peter, Valeria Merlo, Martin Ruf, and Georg Wamser. 2015. "Consequences of the New UK Tax Exemption System: Evidence from Micro-level Data." *Economic Journal* 125 (589): 1764–89.

Feld, Lars P., Martin Ruf, Uwe Scheuering, Ulrich Schreiber, and Johannes Voget. 2013. "Effects of Territorial and Worldwide Corporation Tax Systems on Outbound M&As." ZEW-Centre for European Economic Research Discussion Paper 13-088.

Goolsbee, Austan. 2004. "The Impact of the Corporate Income Tax: Evidence from State Organizational Form Data." *Journal of Public Economics* 88 (11): 2283–99.

Gordon, Roger H. 2010. "Taxation and Corporate Use of Debt: Implications for Tax Policy." *National Tax Journal* 63 (1): 151–74.

Gordon, Roger H., and Jeffrey K. MacKie-Mason. 1994. "Tax Distortions to the Choice of Organizational Form." *Journal of Public Economics* 55 (2): 279–306.

Grinberg, Itai. 2010. "Where Credit Is Due: Advantages of the Credit-Invoice Method for a Partial Replacement VAT." *Tax Law Review* 63 (2): 309–58.

Grubert, Harry, and Rosanne Altshuler. 2008. "Corporate Taxes in the World Economy: Reforming the Taxation of Cross-Border Income." In *Fundamental Tax Reform: Issues, Choices and Implications*, edited by John W. Diamond and George R. Zodrow, 319–54. Cambridge, MA: MIT Press.

Grubert, Harry, and Rosanne Altshuler. 2013. "Fixing the System: An Analysis of Alternative Proposals for the Reform of International Tax." *National Tax Journal* 66 (3): 671–712.

Grubert, Harry, and John Mutti. 2001. *Taxing International Business Income: Dividend Exemption versus the Current System*. Washington, DC: American Enterprise Institute Press.

Hall, Robert E., and Alvin Rabushka. 1995. *The Flat Tax*. Stanford, CA: Hoover Institution Press.

Hanlon, Michelle, Rebecca Lester, and Rodrigo Verdi. 2015. "The Effect of Repatriation Tax Costs on US Multinational Investment." *Journal of Financial Economics* 116 (1): 179–96.

Hasegawa, Makoto, and Kozo Kiyota. 2015. "The Effect of Moving to a Territorial Tax System on Profit Repatriations: Evidence from Japan." GRIPS Discussion Paper 15-09.

Hines, James R., Jr., and Eric M. Rice. 1994. "Fiscal Paradise: Foreign Tax Havens and American Business" *Quarterly Journal of Economics* 109 (1): 149–82.

Huizinga, Harry P., and Johannes Voget. 2009. "International Taxation and the Direction and Volume of Cross-Border M&As." *Journal of Finance* 64 (3): 1217–49.

Karkinsky, Tom, and Nadine Riedel. 2012. "Corporate Taxation and the Choice of Patent Location within Multinational Firms." *Journal of International Economics* 88 (1): 176–85.

Liu, Li. 2015. "International Taxation and MNE Investment: Evidence from the UK Change to Territoriality." http://www.sbs.ox.ac.uk/sites/default/files/Business_Taxation/Events/conferences/symposia/2015/liu-paper3.pdf

Liu, Li, and Ben Lockwood. 2015. "VAT Notches." CEPR Discussion Paper No. DP10606.

Mills, Lillian F., Merle Erickson, and Eric L. Maydew. 1998. "Investments in Tax Planning." *Journal of the American Taxation Association* 20 (1): 1–20.

OECD (2013). *Action Plan on Base Erosion and Profit Shifting*. Paris: OECD.

Sanchirico, Chris William. 2016. "Tax Inertia: A General Framework with Specific Application to Business Tax Reform." *Tax Law Review* 69 (2): 135–230.

Shaviro, Daniel N. 2009. *Decoding the US Corporate Tax*. Washington, DC: Urban Institute Press.

US Senate, Committee on Finance. 2014. "Comprehensive Tax Reform for 2015 and Beyond." Washington, DC.

Voget, Johannes. 2011. "Relocation of Headquarters and International Taxation." *Journal of Public Economics* 95 (9): 1067–81.

Weichenrieder, Alfons J. 1996. "Anti-Tax-Avoidance Provisions and the Size of Foreign Direct Investment." *International Tax and Public Finance* 3 (1): 67–81.

Yin, George K. 1998. "Future Taxation of Private Business Firms." *Florida Tax Review* 4 (3): 141–248.

COMMENTARY ON CHAPTER 8

Rosanne Altshuler

8C.1 INTRODUCTION

Competitive businesses and competitive governments have put tremendous pressure on the US corporate income tax. The United States is now the only major country with a worldwide system for taxing cross-border corporate income and has the distinction of imposing the highest federal statutory corporate tax rate among developed countries. The US system of taxing international income has been painted as the villain driving US corporations to move their headquarters to countries with more favorable tax regimes. The corporate base has been eroded by tax preferences, income-shifting by US- and foreign-headquartered firms, and the ability of US businesses to avoid the corporate tax entirely by operating in the non-corporate form. While policymakers and business leaders agree that the corporate tax is in desperate need for reform, controversy exists over what form any new system should take. Public finance economists can play an important role by providing information that can help guide the debate over the benefits and costs of different reforms. In chapter 8, Dhammika Dharmapala does just that by masterfully synthesizing information from recent economic (and accounting) research and offering a framework to evaluate corporate tax reforms.

8C.2 THE FRAMEWORK: THE EFFICIENCY COSTS OF CORPORATION TAXATION

Dharmapala's framework for assessing tax systems is quite simple: identify the most important sources of inefficiency in the current corporate tax code and consider how those distortions may change under any reform. The starting point for this approach is an assumption that one can contribute to the debate by focusing only on the efficiency costs of different tax systems. He argues that uncertainty in the economics literature regarding who bears the burden of the corporate tax makes it difficult to include distributional consequences in an analysis of reforms. While there is something to be said for this view, I believe readers would benefit from a short discussion of how different reforms impact the distribution of tax burdens across the income distribution. A recent set of proposals, for example, would significantly shift the burden of the taxation of capital income from the corporate to the personal level (see, e.g., Graetz and Warren 2016; Grubert and Altshuler 2016; and Toder and Viard 2016). These types of reforms, as well as the ones considered in chapter 8, have distributional consequences that would certainly be part of any debate over their desirability.

Dharmapala's framework also puts aside consideration of the revenue consequences of alternative reforms. While one could argue that revenue goals should not guide reform, if there is a revenue constraint in play (and there almost always is!) one must balance the efficiency gains of any reform against the losses associated with the new tax instruments adopted to make up revenue shortfalls. There are also other important dimensions of evaluating reforms that this simple framework ignores including complexity, administration costs, transition, and the reaction of foreign governments to any US tax change. With these shortcomings on the table, I must admit I agree with Dharmapala that a focus purely on efficiency is useful. Further, as he points out, research in this arena offers essential information to policymakers. In fact, chapter 8 provides readers with key insight into the magnitude and significance of the myriad inefficiencies associated with the corporate tax.

As Dharmapala acknowledges, one cannot identify the tax system that would raise a given amount of revenue at the lowest efficiency cost by simply counting distortions. To "get it right" requires a model that allows for interactions between economic decisions (removing the lock-in effect of the repatriation tax, e.g., can increase or decrease income-shifting incentives) and, further, specifies a welfare function for a social planner to maximize. This monumental exercise is well beyond the scope of the chapter. That said, it would be helpful to understand what efficiency criteria is being used to evaluate distortions. Is the standard capital export neutrality? This seems to be the case in the discussion of location distortions. At the same time, capital ownership neutrality seems to be the criteria applied in the discussion of distortions to asset ownership and the market for corporate control. While none of these efficiency standards are compelling—they are based on simple models that ignore income-shifting and require special assumptions regarding capital markets—some discussion seems appropriate.

Grubert and Altshuler (2013) argue that a useful approach to evaluating the efficiency consequences of different reforms is to focus on whether they move the system away from results that likely would not be optimal under any criteria. An example would be a reform that reduces (or eliminates) the ability to generate large negative effective tax rates on investments abroad. Dharmapala's evaluation of a "consensual reform" that lowers the corporate tax rate and moves to a dividend exemption system would be more informative if he were to adopt this approach. As discussed further below, the ability to shift income out of the United States and from high-tax foreign affiliates to low-tax affiliates (and tax havens) under the current system can substantially lower the effective tax cost of investing. Grubert and Altshuler simulate effective tax rates on investments by US multinationals in low tax locations abroad under the current system and alternative reforms. These simulations demonstrate that combining a minimum tax with dividend exemption removes the subsidy to foreign investment in low-tax locations that exists in the current US system and would be accentuated under dividend exemption. This benefit of the minimum tax is missing from Dharmapala's discussion.

Dharmapala identifies ten important inefficiencies created by the US corporate income tax and provides an overview of what we know regarding the various behavioral elasticities necessary to measure the efficiency cost of the current system (under any efficiency criteria) and evaluate reforms. In my view, two key distortions created by current US international tax system deserve a bit more discussion: the lockout effect and incentives for income-shifting.

8C.2.1 The Efficiency Cost of Lockout

The deferral feature of the US worldwide tax system allows foreign business income of US multinational corporations to be taxed at a lower effective rate than it would be if it were earned in the United States. When combined with financial accounting rules that effectively treat deferred earnings as permanently exempt, deferral creates a "lockout" effect with associated efficiency costs. As Dharmapala notes, corporations will engage in inefficient behavior to avoid the tax due upon repatriation and the associated reduction in after-tax book income. For example, a parent corporation that wants to invest in a project in the United States, distribute dividends to shareholders, or buy back its shares may borrow at home instead of remitting foreign profits in order to extend the deferral of US tax on foreign earnings. This maneuver allows the US parent to defer the US corporate tax, but raises the cost of capital for domestic uses.

The burden of the tax on foreign subsidiary dividends is a key issue for understanding both the benefits and detriments of moving to a dividend exemption system (the "consensus" reform considered in the final part of chapter 8) and how the current system differs from dividend exemption. The burden of the tax includes both the actual tax paid upon repatriation and the implicit costs of deferring income. These implicit costs include, for example, the cost of using parent debt to finance domestic projects as a substitute for foreign profits (which will increase as debt on the parent's balance sheet expands), payments to tax planners, foregone domestic investment opportunities and foreign acquisitions that may not have been undertaken in the absence of the tax.

Dharmapala briefly discusses estimates of the efficiency cost of deferral from work by Grubert and Mutti (2001) and Desai, Foley, and Hines (2001) in note 12. These estimates suggest a relatively modest efficiency cost of about 1% of foreign income. Dharmapala posits that the large stock of profits held abroad may have increased the marginal cost of deferral. Grubert and Altshuler (2013) use data from US Treasury corporate tax files to derive an estimate of the cost of deferring foreign income that takes the growing stock of profits retained abroad into account. Their work suggests that the efficiency cost of the tax on foreign profits for a highly profitable company is about 5 to 7 percentage points today. This efficiency cost is a key parameter for evaluating how US multinational corporations will respond to a move toward a territorial tax system.

8C.2.2 The Efficiency Cost of Income-Shifting

Dharmapala's discussion of the efficiency cost of income-shifting is particularly interesting as it includes a simple model to determine whether the responsiveness of reported income to tax differences (for which there is evidence from the literature) is a sufficient statistic for the deadweight cost of income-shifting. The conclusion is that the responsiveness of reported income to the home country tax rate is a sufficient statistic for the marginal deadweight loss experienced by the country from income-shifting if the cost of income-shifting is a pure resource cost but may not be if is simply a transfer (a payment to tax planning professionals in the country). I am not convinced that this model considers all of the costs of income-shifting, however. In particular, Dharmapala does not take into account that opportunities for income-shifting can significantly lower the tax costs of investing in a particular location.

Income-shifting alters the effective tax rate on new investment because added investment in a location increases the opportunity for additional income-shifting. The new investment creates opportunities for more transactions with related parties and provides a greater ability to use intangibles developed in the United States. In addition, if hybrid entities in tax havens can be used, investment incentives are the same as if the host countries for operating subsidiaries had lowered their tax rates. The conclusion is that income-shifting distorts the decision of where to place both tangible and intangible assets. This effect of income-shifting should be included in any measure of its efficiency cost.

8C.3 CONCLUSION

While I have highlighted some omissions from the analysis which could easily be viewed as quibbles, overall chapter 8 offers an essential review of the efficiency costs of corporate taxation. Dharmapala has made a significant contribution by showing us how lessons from the current research on corporate taxation can be used to evaluate reforms. His discussion of territorial taxation with a lower statutory corporate tax rate, formulary apportionment, and destination-based cash flow taxes demonstrates clearly that partial reforms of the current system offer less in terms of efficiency gains than fundamental reforms that move away from income taxation altogether. This is an important lesson in itself.

REFERENCES

Desai, Mihir A., C. Fritz Foley, and James R. Hines, Jr. 2001. "Repatriation Taxes and Dividend Distortions." *National Tax Journal* 54 (4): 829–51.

Graetz, Michael J., and Alvin C. Warren, Jr. 2016. "Integration of Corporate and Shareholder Taxes." *National Tax Journal* 69 (3): 677–700.

Grubert, Harry, and Rosanne Altshuler. 2013. "Fixing the System: An Analysis of Alternative Proposals for the Reform of International Tax." *National Tax Journal* 66 (4): 671–712.

Grubert, Harry, and Rosanne Altshuler. 2016. "Shifting the Burden of Taxation from the Corporate to the Personal Level and Getting the Corporate Tax Rate Down to 15 Percent." *National Tax Journal* 69 (3): 643–76.

Grubert, Harry, and John Mutti. 2001. *Taxing International Business Income: Dividend Exemption versus the Current System.* Washington, DC: American Enterprise Institute.

Toder, Eric, and Alan D. Viard. 2016. "Replacing Corporate Tax Revenues with a Mark-To-Market Tax on Shareholder Income." *National Tax Journal* 69 (3): 701–32.

9

US CAPITAL GAINS AND ESTATE TAXATION

A STATUS REPORT AND DIRECTIONS FOR A REFORM

Wojciech Kopczuk

9.1 INTRODUCTION

The US estate taxation has undergone major changes since 2001 when a major volume devoted to economic research on the topic was published (Gale et al. 2001). Much has happened on the research front as well, although there is certainly still room for further rethinking. The objective of this chapter is to provide a policy-relevant overview of the current state of research and directions for a reform.

9.2 POLICY LANDSCAPE

The estate tax has evolved dramatically over the last fifteen years as figure 9.1 illustrates. As of 2001, the exemption stood at $675,000 and the top marginal tax rate was 55%, applying to estates over $3,000,000. As a result of changes introduced by the Economic Growth and Recovery Tax Act of 2001, the rate structure and exemption evolved over the next nine years. By 2009, the exemption increased to $3,500,000 and the top rate declined to 45%. In 2010, the tax was temporarily repealed (as I will describe in a bit more detail shortly). The estate tax provisions of the 2001 Act were scheduled to "sunset" as of 2011, at which point the tax would have returned to its 2001 structure. Instead, initially the top rate was set at 35% in 2011 and 2012, and the exemption at $5,000,000. Starting with 2013, the top rate stood at 40% and the exemption is automatically adjusted for inflation (it is $5,430,000 in 2015).

These changes resulted in a major decline in the number of tax returns filed, as well as a sizable reduction in revenue. Figure 9.2 shows the overall number of tax returns filed and the overall number of taxable returns.[1] The decline in the reach of the tax has been dramatic—the number of returns in 2014 is only about 10% of that in 2001. Figure 9.3 shows the overall gross estate reported on tax returns and net tax liability (in current dollars). Here the decline was less pronounced, although still important.

[1] Note that, because of data availability, these are year-of-filing numbers; the great majority of tax returns (over 80%) are filed between 9 and 18 months after the taxpayer's death, so that tax returns filed in a given year primarily but not exclusively reflect deaths in the prior year.

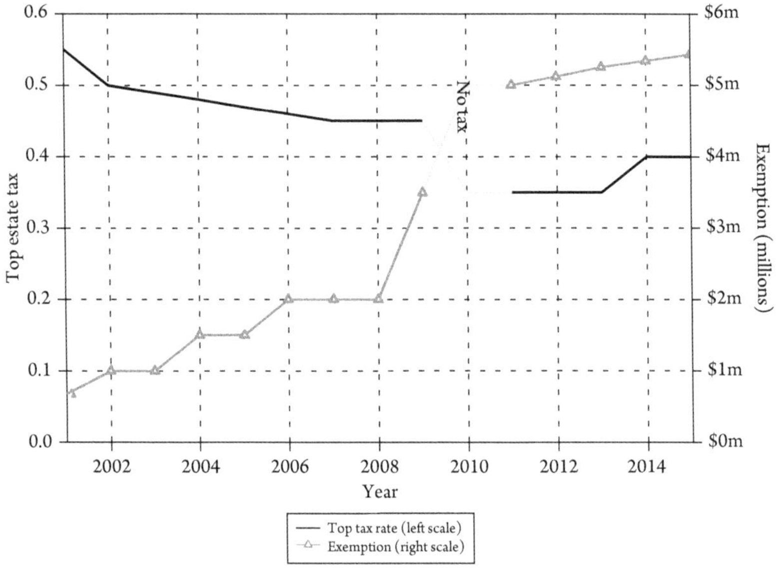

Figure 9.1 Top tax rate and exemption, 2001–2014

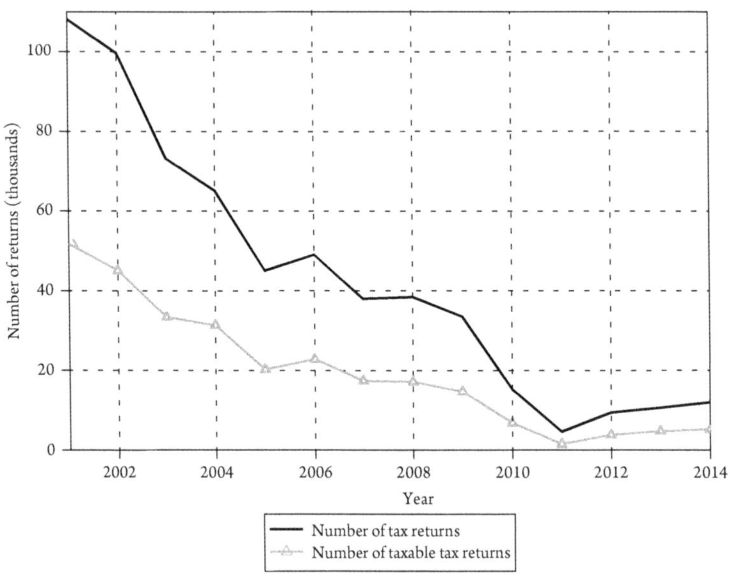

Figure 9.2 Number of tax returns, 2001–2014

Consistently with rate reductions, the overall revenue declined more than gross estates reported on the tax returns. Finally, figure 9.4 shows the number of estates (overall and taxable) with gross value of assets above $10 million (this is the largest group that is consistently taxable over the period that is broken down in the IRS Statistics of Income publications). Except for the 2011 dip that was due to the repeal, the number of returns appears to primarily change with the state of the economy.

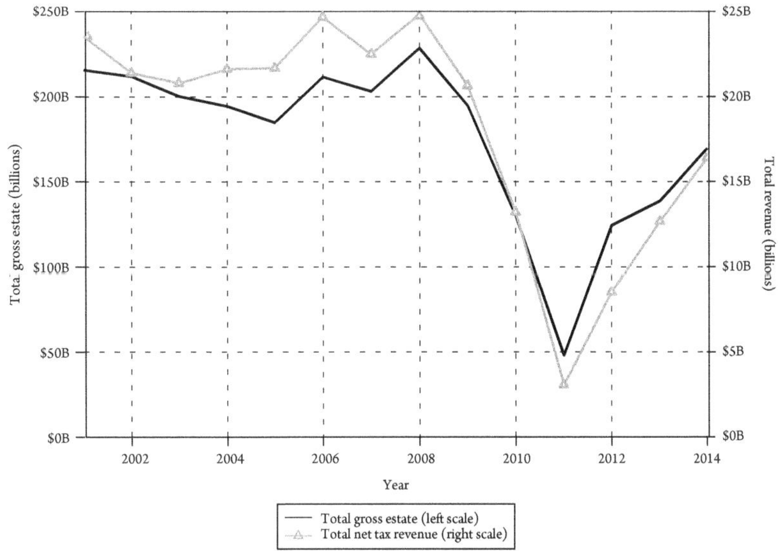

Figure 9.3 Total gross estate and revenue, 2001–2014

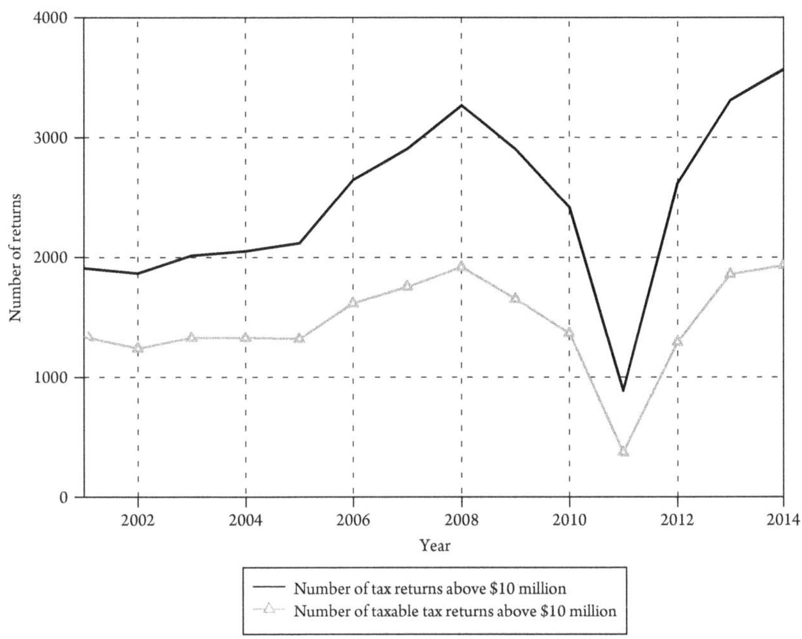

Figure 9.4 Number of tax returns above $10 million, 2001–2014

The repeal of the tax in 2010 required specifying implications for the rest of the tax system in the world without estate taxation. The key consideration here has to do with the step up in basis at death. Appreciated assets that were not sold before the death of the taxpayer (and hence contain capital gains not realized before death) have their tax base reset to the date of death value and thus escape capital gains taxation (though they are naturally subject to the estate tax if the estate is taxable). As part of the repeal, the law in effect for 2010 specified an alternative approach to treating capital gains at death. Instead of allowing for step up, the approach was to implement the carryover basis: the basis for capital gains was not stepped up but instead the original basis carried over to the recipient (though with allowance for an increase in basis of $1,300,000 and an additional allowance of $3,000,000 for the spouse). This is the approach that mimics the current gift tax treatment of capital gains and an approach that was previously enacted in 1976 but repealed before it went into effect.

To complicate matters somewhat, this new treatment of capital gains at death in 2010 was made elective: taxpayers could opt into it or they could instead choose to be subject to the estate tax in its 2011 form. Even when all estate consisted of unrealized capital gains, marginal tax rate differences might seem to favor capital gains treatment. Still, some estate tax returns were filed in this new tax regime. Taxpayers that opted for carry-over capital gains tax treatment had to file information Form 8898. Just over 8,000 of such returns were filed (Office of Tax Analysis 2014). For comparison, there were 7,510 estate tax returns filed for taxpayers with gross estates above $5 million who died in 2009 ($5 million was also the threshold for elective 2010 estate tax treatment) and 9,447 in 2011. While SOI makes year-of-death summary statistics available only in some years (the data is available for 2009 and 2011, in particular, but not for 2010), Office of Tax Analysis (2014) reports based on unpublished data made available to them that 2,832 estate tax returns with gross values above $5 million were filed for 2010 decedents, so that there were about 11,000 of forms 8898 and over $5 million estate tax returns combined that were filed. Given the fairly flat stock market in 2011, it suggests that there were some estates that would otherwise be nontaxable and whose executors selected the carryover treatment (though, perhaps, capital gains in these estates may have already been below the exempt capital gain allowance amount). On the other hand, the fact that some estate tax returns were filed indicates that in some cases the estate tax treatment was beneficial to taxpayers when compared to capital gains tax treatment. Only 352 of these estates had tax liability so, naturally, this preference is likely there only for relatively small estates, tax returns with a lot of deductions and those with relatively high share of capital gains. Finally, Office of Tax Analysis (2014) also reports that there were 4,559 estate tax returns filed for 2010 deaths that fell under the $5,000,000 threshold. While the IRS does not explicitly report tax returns under the filing threshold in its year-of-death summary statistics, it does so in the year-of-filing data—for 2011–2014, the number of such returns was between 1,000 and 1,500 (with a small number of them likely corresponding to deaths before 2010 when the threshold was lower) so that the number of such small filings for 2010 deaths appears unusually large. This is perhaps indicating that some small returns were filed unnecessarily to explicitly opt against carryover capital gains treatment.

The estate tax and gift taxes are naturally related and, since 1977, they have been directly connected through the existence of the unified tax credit that applies jointly to both estate and gift taxes. Changes in the 2000s temporarily modified this link. While the unified credit had increased from $675,000 in 2001 to $3.5million between 1999 and 2009, the portion of it that could have been used toward gifts was only lifted to $1 million as of 2002 (in step with the estate tax) and kept at that level for the rest of the 2000s. With the reinstatement of the estate tax in 2011, the joint unified credit feature has been brought back, so that again the full lifetime exemption can be used for either gifts or estates.

The rate structure under the gift tax has always been the same as for the estate tax. However, while the estate tax applies to the tax inclusive basis, the gift tax applies in a tax exclusive fashion. Hence, the marginal tax rate of t results in the taxpayer retaining $1- t$ net-of-tax in the case of estate, while the marginal tax rate for gifts as a share of gift-plus-tax basis is $t/(1 + t)$. In particular, it implies that—despite nominal unification—the marginal tax rate on gifts is lower than the marginal tax rate on estates. Furthermore, small gifts are tax-exempt—as of 2014, a taxpayer may give up to $14,000 per donee tax free. On the other hand, the step-up preference for capital gains does not apply in the case of gifts, thereby reducing the gift tax treatment advantage for appreciated assets.

It is interesting to note that the gift tax was left in place in 2010 despite removal of the estate tax. While that might seem internally inconsistent, it is not necessarily so both from the short- and the long-run point of view. In the short run, most of the observers and—likely—the policymakers expected the repeal to be temporary so that lack of gift taxation would lead to an erosion of the future tax base. From the longer-term policy-design perspective, the gift tax plays an important role in reducing tax avoidance possibilities not just for the estate tax but also in the case of the income tax where a transfer of an income-generating asset to another person (e.g., a child) in a lower tax bracket is a potential tax avoidance approach.

The final component of the estate tax system is the Generation Skipping Tax (GST) that applies to transfers that pass a generation and avoid corresponding layer of taxation (e.g. direct transfers to grandchildren). This tax has followed the same modifications as the basic estate tax: first, gradual increases in exemption and reductions of tax rates, then repeal, and—finally—reinstatement.

The estate tax has been in place in the United States since 1916.[2] The basic structure of the current system of estate/gift/GST taxes originated in the 1976 Act that overhauled the whole system. The main component of that reform was unification of the estate and gift tax systems via unified credit. There were other major tax provisions over the years that are of continuing interest and highlight various problems in implementing the effective estate tax regime. The introduction of the GST tax in 1976 was intended to eliminate a particular form of tax avoidance where a child could benefit

[2] See Luckey (2008) for a much more comprehensive overview of the history of estate, gift, and GST legislations.

from an asset during his or her lifetime but a grandchild would obtain the ownership at the child's death—this strategy was intended to avoid the tax for an intermediate generation. The estate tax treatment of marital transfers had been controversial since the tax was introduced. One of the issues was an effectively different treatment of taxpayers in community-property states where assets were split between spouses by default. Another one was a more general point about appropriateness of imposing a tax on individual rather than on household level. This issue was addressed in steps over time: first, through an introduction of marital deduction in 1948, then its expansion in 1976, implementation of unlimited deduction in 1981, and finally introduction of portability of the unified credit between spouses in 2011. The 1976 reforms also attempted to address the capital gains exemption via step-up in basis but it was a short-lived effort: the rule to introduce carryover basis was suspended in 1978 before it went into effect, and then it was repealed outright in 1980.

9.3 THEORETICAL LANDSCAPE

Modeling intergenerational transfers starts with assumptions about individual preferences and the economic environment that result in a motive to leave a bequest.[3] In principle, bequests may be intentional or not. Unintentional bequests may arise for a number of reasons: as the result of uncertainty about the lifespan ("accidental bequests"), when individuals have incorrect assessment of their mortality ("denial of death"), or when wealth enters preferences directly (e.g., with wealth as a measure of status or proxy for control). Alternatively, an individual may directly value bequests (joy-of-giving) or benefit from consequences of bequests (increased utility of a child in the case of altruism, specific services in the case of exchange). The motivation for bequests matters both for predicted behavioral response to taxation and for its welfare implications. The literature on these topics is vast and has not settled on a single motive. Work on understanding the shape of the wealth distribution and on bequest patterns and behavioral responses to taxation informs it by indicating the need for a mixed motive: precautionary considerations and "accidental" bequests are important, but some form of bequest motivation is necessary to explain the top tail of the distribution. Responsiveness to taxation indicates intentional motives, although altruism is not powerful enough to explain the tail; there is also evidence that control over wealth during life is important. When considering taxation at the very top of the distribution, the key considerations simplify similarly as in the work on the top marginal tax rates (Diamond 1998; Saez 2001): with marginal utility converging to zero, behavioral elasticities are important for understanding revenue implications, while welfare consequences of the tax remain important only to the extent that bequests influence overall welfare through channels other than utility of the wealthy donors or donees (in particular, when they generate externalities, including those of a fiscal nature).

[3] For a much more extensive overview of theoretical literature on estate taxation and additional references, see Kopczuk (2013b).

Theoretical analysis of desirability of estate taxation used to take as its departure point models of capital taxation. An estate tax is a form of a tax on capital, hence it is convenient to start with models of capital taxation more generally and extend them to consider specific features of the estate tax context: bequest motivations that may generate behavior different than that following from other reasons to save, interactions between parents and children and implications of wealth rather than capital income taxation. While this is an attractive line of thinking, the applicability of the long-standing Chamley-Judd theorem showing optimality of zero capital tax rate in the long run (Chamley 1986; Judd 1985) has recently been challenged by Straub and Werning (2015) who showed that it holds only under restrictive conditions. Furthermore, the Chamley-Judd result has always been a somewhat unrealistic departure point because of its unattractive assumptions about feasible instruments (no initial taxation) and, even with these assumptions, lack of robustness due to time inconsistency of the optimal policy. However, despite the unsettled status of capital income tax literature, recent research has illuminated a number of considerations that are relevant for thinking about estate taxation.

Farhi and Werning (2010) focused on implications of externality from giving: bequests benefit parents and children; even when parents internalize the effect on children, the policymaker may put stronger preference on a child's welfare recognizing that it benefits altruistic parents as well. This has a natural implication of pushing in the direction of subsidies to bequests and, interestingly, does so in a "progressive" fashion by calling for subsidies to bequests at the bottom of the distribution and the marginal subsidy disappearing at the top. Building on this model, Kopczuk (2013a) additionally incorporates a fiscal externality from bequests: transfers discourage labor supply of children due to income effect (one can also think of it as incorporating the Carnegie-hypothesis effect) with corresponding revenue consequences when children's income is taxed. This extension gives rise to an appealing structure of taxation: subsidies to giving toward the bottom of the distribution (consistent, e.g., with policies that encourage parental investment in human capital of their children) and taxes at the top where the motive for subsidy vanishes and only fiscal externality is of relevance. An interesting aspect of these papers is that the responsiveness of bequests/estates to taxation is not a relevant parameter for designing the estate tax. This may seem counterintuitive, since one would naturally expect that the distortionary effect on bequests determines the extent of deadweight loss. However, in these models the role of estate taxation is corrective: it is supposed to address externalities from giving and from fiscal consequences of transfers. As is the case with Pigouvian taxation more generally, the correction depends on the gap between private and socially desirable incentives rather than responsiveness. Excess burden does matter, but it is the marginal excess burden of the overall tax system (the Marginal Cost of Funds or, more technically, Lagrangian multiplier on the budget constraint) rather than that of the estate tax in isolation.

A different direction has been pursued by Piketty and Saez (2013), who explicitly incorporate imperfect correlation of abilities across generations in an infinite horizon model and study long-run optimal income and inheritance taxation. Their main conclusion is that optimal inheritance tax is nonzero in the steady state. The two main limitations of this analysis is the lack of modeling of the policy along the transition path to the steady state (so that it is potentially subject to caveats identified by Straub and Werning 2015), and analysis of linear taxes only so that the results are not necessarily a guide for policy at the top of the distribution. The paper is also better thought of as modeling the overall lifetime capital income and estate tax rate, rather than the estate tax alone. The results are expressed in terms of behavioral elasticities that incorporate steady-state adjustments and, hence, are hard to relate to feasible empirical estimates: the required behavioral elasticities correspond to moving across long-run equilibria corresponding to different policies and estimating such elasticities is a daunting task.

Three other theoretical points are worth mentioning.

First, behavioral implications of taxation on bequests may influence aggregate capital stock. This point is part of the Chamley-Judd result, but by itself it does not necessarily imply that capital tax is undesirable. Aiyagari (1995) showed that capital tax may in fact be necessary to address dynamic inefficiency that naturally arises due to overaccumulation driven by precautionary saving. Saez (2002) makes an important point that increased rate of return caused by reduced accumulation of the rich due to progressive estate tax should stimulate saving by those unaffected by the tax. In the special case that he considers, there is in fact no effect of progressive estate taxation on the aggregate capital stock.

Second, understanding the process and implications of wealth accumulation at the top of the distribution is bound to matter. A few recent papers have considered optimal income tax implications of superstar effects and rents; extension to the estate tax is of interest. Implications of the motive for control over wealth and relative status implications of wealth have not been analyzed, but are bound to interact with welfare implications of the tax and its revenue implications.

Finally, any potential externalities from wealth concentration are potentially important. This includes effects that might flow through the political system or economic influence. It also includes any value that might be placed on equality of opportunities and would thus go beyond the welfarist framework.

9.4 EMPIRICAL EVIDENCE

One of the natural questions to ask regarding behavioral responses to estate taxation is about its effect on wealth accumulation. This is a question that is hard to compellingly answer empirically. A number of papers in the United States attempted to shed light on it. Kopczuk and Slemrod (2001) relied on repeated cross-section of estate tax returns and variation over time and taxpayers' age at death (which corresponds to different tax regimes in place at any particular stage of life). Holtz-Eakin and Marples (2001) exploited cross-sectional wealth information and variation in state tax rates. Joulfaian (2006) resorted to using estate tax series. While none of these strategies is particularly appealing by the post-"credibility revolution" standards of what constitutes a convincing empirical design, interestingly they produce fairly similar estimates of the elasticity of estate to net-of-tax rate of between 0.1 and 0.2. Similarity of the estimates based on wealth during life and estate at death is also consistent with the responsiveness on the real rather than avoidance margin.

A recent paper by Goupille-Lebret and Infante (2015) uses unusual data from France to estimate responsiveness of wealth accumulation to tax considerations based on a much stronger research design. Life insurance in France is about a quarter of the overall bequest flows. Despite its name, it need not necessarily have insurance features and instead is used as a vehicle for wealth accumulation (similar to whole life insurance). Importantly, it is preferentially treated for both income tax and inheritance tax purposes (it is comparable to Roth IRA treatment over the lifetime coupled with preferential treatment at death). Changes over the years reduced the tax advantage (while grandfathering some old policies) and introduced discontinuous treatment of contributions made before turning 70. This context gives rise to age and time discontinuities and allows for identifying accumulation of assets intended for bequest as it accrues over a lifetime rather than relying solely on observations at death. While the analysis has important limitations (most importantly, inability to observe other types of assets), it convincingly indicates the presence of an important but relatively small response. The estimated magnitude of the tax effect is in line with that obtained from less compellingly identified US studies.

The United States does not have an annual wealth tax, although there are occasional suggestions for it to be considered and Piketty (2014) has suggested an internationally coordinated wealth tax as a prescription for addressing wealth inequality (see Mintz 1991; Auerbach 2008, for an overview of different forms that wealth taxation can take). The evidence on the impact of wealth taxation is scant. An important recent exception is the paper by Seim (2015) who analyzes the response to the Swedish wealth tax and finds strong evidence of tax avoidance using bunching design—remarkable, given that one might think that wealth (stock) is harder to control than income (flow) and given that empirical studies of income responsiveness using bunching design usually yield very small behavioral elasticity. The presence of strong avoidance response in Sweden may reflect poor design of the tax that had trouble targeting a comprehensive measure of wealth. Underreporting of cars (that at the time were not observable to tax authorities) was the main empirically observable source of response and preferential treatment of business assets reflected difficulty in valuing these types of wealth holdings. However, poor design of wealth taxation is likely to be a norm rather than exception. Brown (1991) analyzed practical administrative difficulties in imposing wealth taxation and concluded that they are insurmountable.

Adam et al. (2011) also conclude that experience with attempts to implement wealth taxation has been discouraging in practice. They additionally make an important point that this form of taxation falls disproportionately on normal return rather than excess return, and hence that it is unappealing on both efficiency and normative grounds. In the simplest context, wealth and capital income taxes may be equivalent: normalizing initial investment to \$1 and denoting the rate of return by r, the wealth tax is imposed on $1 + r$, while a capital income tax is imposed on r. Ceteris paribus, a capital income tax at the rate of t would then collect as much revenue as the wealth tax of $t^w = t \cdot E[r]/(1 + E[r])$ where $E[r]$ is the expected return. Naturally, $t^w \ll t$ because the wealth tax is imposed on a much broader base. This equivalence breaks though when considering different components of the return. One of the strongest arguments for taxing wealth or capital income rests on the possibility of rents. Because the marginal increase in rate of return under wealth tax is taxed at a much lower rate than the marginal increase in capital income, wealth tax effectively taxes rents much more lightly than capital income tax does. Conversely, by taxing principal, wealth taxation effectively imposes heavy burden on the normal rate of return. This is most starkly visible in the (close to) zero interest rate world, $r \approx 0$. In that case, the tax-adjusted normal rate of return under the wealth tax is negative, while capital income tax does not have an effect. Hence, the wealth tax imposes burden precisely on the wrong components of the rate of return.[4]

A number of papers study the responsiveness of inter-vivos gifts to changes in the gift tax rates. Joulfaian (2014) documents large temporal responses of large taxable gifts associated with changes and (possibly) expectations about future tax rates around 2010. In older work (Joulfaian 2004), he also provides systematic evidence of responsiveness of aggregate gift flows over much of the twentieth century, in particular, very strong response in 1976 when unification of gift and estate taxation (and, hence, increased tax cost of making lifetime gifts due to offset of exemption on estate tax return) was announced. Ohlsson (2011) provides evidence of similar kind for Sweden. Time-series evidence indicating strong tax sensitivity of large taxable gifts is very compelling.

Page (2003) and Bernheim et al. (2004) use data from the Survey of Consumer Finances (SCF) and show responsiveness of gifts to estate taxation using cross-sectional variation in state tax rates and difference-in-difference design leveraging estate tax exemption increases, respectively. This evidence applies to people with moderate wealth (effectively, those captured by the SCF and not far from the tax threshold in the 1990s; i.e., net worth in the neighborhood of $1 million). Arrondel and Laferrère (2001) provide similar evidence for France. A number of papers (Joulfaian and McGarry 2004; McGarry 2000, 2001; Poterba 2001) focus on studying whether taxpayers take advantage of an annual gift tax exclusion ($14,000 as of 2015) that allows for tax-free transfers to anyone and is the simplest estate tax planning technique. They conclude that this strategy is underutilized, thereby suggesting that potential estate taxpayers do not act as tax minimizers (that does not mean that these gifts are not extensively used, just that they are not used sufficiently from tax minimization point of view). Joulfaian and McGarry (2004) further find that only about one-third of ultimate estate taxpayers make taxable gifts over their lifetime despite apparent significant tax advantage of inter-vivos gifts. Part of the explanation here may be different tax treatment of capital gains under gift and estate regimes (carryover basis vs. step-up). Joulfaian (2005) analyzes tax incentives while accounting for capital gains treatment,

[4] A capital income tax is also in principle more amenable to exempting normal rate of return altogether.

concludes that gifts are usually but not universally tax advantaged, and estimates tax responsiveness of gifts while properly accounting for these considerations. Kopczuk (2007) shows that large estates strongly decline following the onset of a terminal illness, with avoidance being the most plausible channel.

Overall, the empirical evidence suggests that bequests and gifts respond to taxation, with large gifts, in particular, exhibiting very strong temporal responsiveness around tax changes. At the same time, tax minimization does not appear to be the right approach to modeling taxpayer responsiveness both because lifetime gifts are too small to be consistent with it and because large responses shortly before death indicate insufficient planning before. The importance of retaining control over assets is a leading explanation that allows for reconciling these patterns (Kopczuk 2007; Schmalbeck 2001).

The responsiveness of gifts indicates some tax planning, but the overall extent of tax avoidance is harder to evaluate. One approach is to compare the actual estate tax liability to expected tax liability using cross-sectional survey-based information about wealth distribution and assumptions about mortality rates. Unfortunately, estimates using this approach are very sensitive to assumptions and the literature has not reached clear conclusions (Eller et al. 2001; Poterba 2000b; Wolff 1996). Audit-based studies (Eller and Johnson 1999; Eller et al. 2001; Erard 1999) estimate the extent of noncompliance at between 8% and 13% but, naturally, these estimates only reflect what is discovered during tax audits—either tax evasion or unsuccessful tax avoidance—and cannot be interpreted as the overall estimate of tax avoidance activity. An example of a successful form of tax avoidance is the use of marketability and minority discounts (Johnson et al. 2001; Poterba and Weisbenner 2003).

The direct evidence of implications of step up in basis is limited. Poterba (2001) provides evidence that the presence of unrealized capital gains discourage inter-vivos gifts because it would amount to foregoing the step-up benefit which does not apply to gifts. On the other hand, Auten and Joulfaian (2001) show that in the presence of step up higher estate tax weakens the lock-in effect by leading to earlier capital gains realizations. Poterba and Weisbenner (2001) estimate the effect of replacing the estate tax by constructive realization of capital gains and highlight distributional consequences of such a switch.

As discussed in the brief overview of theory in section 9.3, the effect of bequests on labor supply or income of recipients is one of the key determinants of desirability of estate taxation (Kopczuk 2013a). The early work on this topic framed the question as the "Carnegie hypothesis" (Holtz-Eakin et al. 1993; Joulfaian and Wilhelm 1994) and showed the negative effect of inheritances on labor force participation both using linked income and estate tax data and using data from the Panel Study of Income Dynamics (PSID). Brown et al. (2010) confirm this finding using an older Health and Retirement Study (HRS) sample. They study the effect on retirement while further controlling for bequest expectations, so that the response is identified off the unexpected component of bequest. Using Swedish data, Elinder et al. (2011) show that overall labor income declines following receipt of inheritance. Evidence from other shocks to wealth (Imbens et al. 2001; Kuhn et al. 2011; Poterba 2000a) is somewhat mixed though on balance also supportive of the presence of labor supply response.

Evidence suggests that there is a negative effect of inheritances on labor supply overall, but the effect on a particular class of donees—(actual or potential) entrepreneurs received separate attention. Holtz-Eakin et al. (1994a, b) find support for the hypothesis that inheritances matter for survival of small businesses; Brunetti (2006) finds suggestive evidence (using probate records and relying on the repeal of inheritance tax in California for identification) that the estate tax increases the likelihood of selling small businesses; and Tsoutsoura (2011) finds that the repeal of inheritance tax in Greece led to increased investment in transferred firms. All these papers therefore indicate potential importance of liquidity and financing constraints in inherited businesses. At the same time, a different strand of the literature (Bloom and Van Reenen 2007; Pérez-González 2006; Villalonga and Amit 2006) finds that inheritance of control within the family appears to be associated with reduced performance, so that the overall welfare implications of taxing transfers of business assets are mixed.

Finally, the work of Piketty (2011, 2014) has recently revisited the question of the role of inheritances in overall wealth accumulation and wealth concentration in particular. Older literature (Kotlikoff and Summers 1981; Modigliani 1988) focused on the question of the aggregate contribution of bequests to wealth accumulation. See Davies and Shorrocks (2000) for a review, with the bottom-line conclusion that bequests are responsible for roughly a half of the stock of wealth, although recent work of Piketty (2014) suggests important heterogeneity both over time and across countries. Cagetti and De Nardi (2008) review work on modeling wealth distribution and conclude that explaining the upper tail requires an introduction of some form of a bequest motive (see also De Nardi 2004; Dynan et al. 2004, 2002; Gale and Scholz 1994). Two recent papers (Boserup et al. 2016; Elinder et al. 2015) explore administrative data from Denmark and Sweden that allows for linking wealth holdings across generations to trace direct implications of inheritances for determining the shape of wealth distribution and the extent of inequality.

9.5 BEST PRACTICES AND REFORM

The empirical evidence provides support for the notion that estate and gift taxation leads to behavioral responses, although it is certainly not precise enough to definitively pin down its magnitude. It also points to the importance of tax avoidance, although it does not necessarily indicate that tax avoidance is the main source of responsiveness on the margin. Recent theoretical work opens up the possibility that some form of inheritance taxation may be a part of the optimal tax system and it does so in a way that is broadly consistent with the current structure of taxation: a tax that applies at the top of the distribution and potential arguments for preferences/subsidies elsewhere. In my view, the most convincing normative arguments for taxation of high estates have to do with their potential externalities—either reflecting fiscal effect due to reduced labor supply of recipients (with reasonable empirical support), or due to reduced equality of opportunities or potential externalities from wealth concentration (with speculative and anecdotal empirical support, in need of further work). There is also work that suggests the role of inheritance taxation as a redistributive instrument (Piketty and Saez 2013), but it is based on linear taxation and steady-state comparative statics, so that it is difficult to relate to the actual structure of the tax system.

Overall, the general question of whether a limited estate tax of the kind currently in place in the United States should be a part of the tax system deserves the firm answer of "it depends"—it depends on the weight that one puts on labor supply impact on recipients (with a tax applying only at the very top, such effects are not likely to be too important quantitatively even if they justify positive taxation) and the presence of externalities from wealth concentration on which evidence is scant and reasonable people might disagree. A more practical consideration are revenue consequences of any modification in rate structure and past experience suggests that they are important enough to make it difficult to eliminate this instrument even by positively predisposed majority. It is also worth noting that in the past estate taxation has been introduced or expanded during times when major resource mobilization was necessary, war financing in particular (Scheve and Stasavage 2012), so that there is an option value of having administration in place to use this form of taxation if necessary.

In what follows, I am going to focus on the design of the tax and its interaction with other components of the tax system.

9.5.1 Capital Gains

As the 2010 experience demonstrated, a repeal of the tax is likely to be associated with a modification of treatment of capital gains at death in order to reduce revenue consequences and also because it is difficult to simultaneously justify retaining taxation of realized capital gains during life and the lack of any tax liability if unrealized until death. Importantly though, it is difficult to find a rational argument for step up in the first place whether the estate tax is in place or not. The presence of step up creates a strong incentive not to realize capital gains. While any realization-based tax has incentives for deferral built into it by design, the ability to avoid the tax by holding assets until death creates particularly strong incentive for an obvious tax avoidance strategy and generates distortions due to lock-in or due to any costly attempts to tap into assets without triggering realization. It also introduces inequity between life-cycle and bequest-motivated savers.

Constructive realization (taxing unrealized capital gains at death) is a natural approach to modify the current treatment of capital gains. This approach is in place in Canada (referred to there as "deemed disposition") and it was proposed by President Obama in the 2015 State of the Union address. It arguably imposes lower compliance costs than the carry-over basis which has been attempted in the United States in 1976 and 2010, because it limits record-keeping to the lifetime of a taxpayer. It also effectively "unlocks" the gain, while the carry-over basis perpetuates lock-in of gains past death of the taxpayer. Because deferral advantage grows with the expected holding period, introducing a certain realization event at the death of a taxpayer would encourage lifetime realizations. A comprehensive application of this approach to any transfers either through gifts or at death would lead to overall simplification of the tax system, increased efficiency due to reduction in lock-in, and interestingly (given fiscal pressure) acceleration of tax revenue.

Introducing carryover approach at death would still be a significant improvement over the current system by eliminating the strong advantage of holding assets until death, although—naturally—it retains the standard lock-in incentive. The main advantage of carryover treatment over constructive realization regime has to do with liquidity constraints. This is usually not a concern with regular capital gains that are the result of arm's length transactions. It is a potential consideration though when transfer takes place without sale of the underlying asset (and, in particular, when there are plausible distortions that might be associated with sale—e.g., due to thinness of the market or disruptions to a business). As discussed in section 9.4, there is empirical evidence both to support the notion that these effects are sometimes important and against treating preserving continuity of family ownership as a desirable policy objective. Nevertheless, one can certainly imagine a system of constructive realization with similar preference for transfers of business assets as those existing under the estate tax (discounting value to reflect marketability or minority ownership, evaluating the value of a business at current rather than best use, paying tax in installments). One could also envision having a constructive realization system in general, but applying carryover basis for particular categories of assets where liquidity constraints are important. Another possibility would be to assess the tax at death and delay payment until the asset is sold.

The step up applies to all assets and not just to those that are subject to the estate tax. As the result, modification of tax treatment of capital gains at death has consequences for individuals across the distribution. For that reason, the 2010 repeal provided for allowance of $1,300,000 to increase basis in transferred assets (effectively, exempt part of the unrealized capital gain from taxation). Under the proposal outlined in the 2015 State of the Union address, the exemption would be much lower at $100,000. Naturally, the 2010 approach effectively exempted the great majority of estates from worrying about capital gains consequences, but at the same time it also retained the step-up advantage and hence incentives for deferral. While it seems like a logical continuation of a system in which small estates are not taxed, it is a puzzling approach from the point of view of thinking about the income tax. Certainly, small capital gains are not exempt if realized during the lifetime so why should they be exempt at death? Alternatively, if there is a reason to exempt them, why not extend that treatment to capital gains realized during the lifetime?

For example, imagine converting the $1,300,000 exemption at death to an "equivalent" annual exemption, say of $8,000 for concreteness.[5] A taxpayer could be offered an annual allowance in that amount to adjust basis, effectively exempting the first $8,000 of capital gains with the present value of the preference equivalent to exemption at death. Better yet, taxpayers could be allowed to either accumulate the unused

[5] Consider annual exemption of E, lifespan of 60 (adult) years and rate of return $r = 0.03$. Annuitized exemption E in text is obtained to equate discounted value at the time of death to $1,300,000: $1300000 = \Sigma_{t=0}^{60}(1 + r)^t E = E((1 + r)^{60} - 1)/r = E(1.03^{60} - 1)/0.03$ implying E = $7,972.85.

allowances or be given a lifetime allowance to be used as they wish. Alternatively, one could also consider income-related limits. The advantage of a system like this would be eliminating the deferral advantage by not introducing a point when capital gains are forgiven. I do not see a good reason for having a generous capital gains exemption in the first place (which would be on top of already existing preferential tax treatment of capital gains relative to other forms of capital income). Should one decide to have such an exemption though, there is little economic case for having the exemption granted at death rather than designing it in a way that would be (closer to) neutral with regard to timing of realization.

A modification of the capital gains tax treatment at death has budgetary repercussions. In order to evaluate these consequences, I implement a revenue estimation procedure. My objective here is not to have a fully definitive statement about the revenue implications, but rather to have a realistic starting point that highlights the important (in terms of revenue consequences) trade-offs and issues. In particular, this is a static estimation procedure that does not incorporate any behavioral responses.

I rely on the 2013 Survey of Consumer Finances to obtain the data on the distribution of assets, debt, and unrealized capital gains of households. Following Poterba and Weisbenner (2001), I apply mortality rates (adjusted to reflect lower mortality of the wealthy household) to heads of households to obtain the distribution of decedents. The two difficult steps in comparison of the SCF to the actual estate tax data have to do with (1) comparing *household* information in the SCF with *individual* tax returns in the estate tax data and (2) accounting for the difference in assets during life and those that are observed on tax returns at death. I focus on taxable estate tax returns only and assume the use of marital deduction by married estate taxpayers by wealth category that matches that observed in aggregate estate tax statistics. I also apply an ad hoc 25% discount to assets observed in the SCF in order to incorporate the evidence of estate tax planning and avoidance discussed before. Complete details of this procedure are in the Appendix.

Table 9.1 compares the 2013 estate tax data and the outcome of the calibration procedure based on the SCF. The calibration matches the number of taxpayers and generates gross estate, net estate, and tax revenue that are within 10% of the actual values. It is imperfect in terms of the distribution of taxpayers—it results in too many estate taxpayers with estates above $50 million, primarily reflecting the uncertain assumptions about the use of marital deduction. Since all the following counterfactual analysis relies on the same SCF data and the same baseline assumptions, I use the SCF estimate of the $16.8 billion of revenue as my baseline.

The SCF contains information about capital gains at death. Evaluating tax treatment of those gains requires taking a stand on the treatment of marital couples: Should capital gains transferred to a surviving spouse be subject to a tax or preferentially treated? I assume as my baseline that the treatment of capital gains at death is going to mimic the current estate tax treatment with unlimited spousal deduction and a portable exemption. As the result, I assume that the only taxable individuals are going to be the same categories that could be subject to the tax under the estate tax treatment: single individuals and married heads of households in the high net worth categories who choose not to utilize the full marital deduction. This procedure results

Table 9.1 Estates tax aggregates and revenue: Comparison of IRS data and SCF calibration

	Estate Tax (IRS)				*Estate Tax (SCF)*			
Asset category (m)	*Number of Returns*	*Gross Estates*	*Estates After Deductions*	*Tax Liability*	*Number of Returns*	*Gross Estates*	*Estates After Deductions*	*Tax Liability*
\$5–\$10	2,429	17.290	15.452	2.021	2,095	13.932	12.875	0.749
\$10–\$20	1,132	15.500	12.554	3.261	1,092	14.122	12.031	2.519
\$20–\$50	578	17.295	11.902	4.022	624	16.545	12.279	3.600
\$50+	223	37.510	17.827	6.675	526	49.183	27.644	9.953
Total	4,362	87.597	57.735	15.981	4,338	93.783	64.830	16.823

Note: See the Appendix for description of methodology. Comparison of the IRS estate tax information (based on taxable returns only) and the calibrated SCF data. All figures (other than the number of returns) in billions of dollars.

Table 9.2 Taxation of capital gains at death: Allowing for spousal preference

Asset Category (m)	*Number of Deaths*	*Total Capital Gains*	*Non-Housing Gains*	*Revenue, No Exemption*	*Revenue, \$500K Exemption*	*Revenue, \$1 Million Exemption*	*Revenue, \$2 Million Exemption*
< \$1	790,978	48.509	7.861	2.007	0.017	0.000	0.000
\$1–\$5	19,063	10.763	7.751	2.028	1.099	0.698	0.394
\$5–\$10	2,360	4.284	3.366	0.858	0.613	0.506	0.332
\$10–\$20	1,092	6.470	5.745	1.464	1.347	1.232	1.020
\$20–\$50	627	10.388	9.783	2.437	2.371	2.299	2.157
\$50+	526	25.240	24.848	5.996	5.952	5.890	5.769
Total	814,645	105.657	59.357	14.793	11.400	10.628	9.674

Note: See the Appendix for a description of methodology. The estimation procedure assumes the possibility of tax-free capital gains transfers to a surviving spouse utilized at the same proportion and by the same groups as is the case with the estate tax. All figures (other than the number of returns) in billions of dollars.

(table 9.2) in just over 800,000 (potentially) taxable individuals who hold approximately \$106 billion of unrealized capital gains, \$59 billion of which are non-housing related. Naturally, these gains are highly skewed: the 4,300 individuals in the estate tax paying categories account for 45% of all unrealized gains and 75% of non-housing gains. I assume that primary residence capital gains retain their current exemption of \$500,000 and apply the current maximum capital gains tax rate of 23.8% to everyone.

This approach results in almost \$15 billion of revenue—\$2 billion less than collected using the estate tax. Naturally, the burden of this tax is spread out over the full distribution; in particular \$4 billion is paid by individuals who would otherwise not be subject to the estate tax. The natural approach discussed before is to introduce an exemption. The following three columns show the revenue consequences of exemptions of \$500,000, \$1 million, and \$2 million: higher exemption has small revenue impact for the over $10 million group but it dramatically reduces the revenue from lower categories. A $1 million exemption “loses” $4 billion of revenue, $3.3 of which is accounted for by non-estate taxpayers.

Recent analysis of the Office of Tax Analysis (2014) and that of Gordon et al. (2015) concluded based on the form 8939 filings for 2010 taxpayers that capital gains constituted about 40% of estates of the form 8939 filers. In my calculations, the unrealized capital gains tax share in 2013 SCF for the population that gives rise to taxable estates is 37% of their net worth and 48% of gross estates after allowing for 25% tax avoidance reduction. These numbers are not inconsistent, but there are still many possible reasons for the difference between form 8939 filings and the SCF, including different definition of the sample (the 8939 data includes non-taxable taxpayers, in particular, married ones who would otherwise claim marital deduction) and non-representativeness of the SCF. To rudimentarily evaluate consequences of a higher capital gains share in overall assets, I inflate all capital gains by 20%. The results are shown in the first two columns of table 9.3. This scenario yields an additional $3 billion of revenue when no exemption is allowed and $2.4 billion revenue when the exemption is $1 million.

The additional revenue from eliminating the step up can be used to finance estate tax reduction. The third and fourth columns of table 9.3 show the implications of increasing the estate tax threshold to $10 million or reducing the estate tax rate from 40% to 30%. Both of these scenarios lead to a loss of $4.8 and $4.2 billion, respectively—still significantly less than the revenue collected from taxing step up in basis at death under any of the exemption scenarios considered in table 9.2. In particular, an increase in the estate tax threshold to $10 million coupled with eliminating step up in basis with a generous exemption (say of $2 million) would effectively shift the burden of the tax toward very high net worth individuals while benefiting individuals

Table 9.3 Modified assumptions about capital gains and estate tax rate structure

	Capital Gains ↑ 20%		*Estate Tax*	
Asset Category (m)	*No Exemption*	*$1 Million Exemption*	*Threshold at $10 Million*	*Rate to 30%*
<$1	2.550	0.000	0.000	0.000
$1–$5	2.491	0.989	0.000	0.000
$5–$10	1.047	0.654	0.000	0.562
$10–$20	1.769	1.536	0.644	1.889
$20–$50	2.931	2.794	2.414	2.700
$50+	7.199	7.096	8.954	7.464
Total	17.990	13.071	12.013	12.617

Note: See the Appendix for a description of methodology. The two capital gains scenarios assume an increase in capital gains by 20%. The estate tax scenarios assume a change in the threshold to $10 million or a decline in rate to 30%. All figures (other than the number of returns) in billions of dollars.

with currently taxable estates below $20 million. This suggests that there is room here for reforms that would eliminate the inefficiency of step up, would not lose revenue, and could benefit smaller taxable estates at the expense of the large ones.

As an aside, to the extent that the estate tax remains and step up is eliminated, one might worry that it effectively increases the tax burden of estate taxpayers. The solution that has been sometimes proposed is to provide credit for capital gains tax against estate tax liability. This is, of course, an approach with distributional consequences, but it also has incentive effects. In particular, a credit for capital gains tax liability at death would retain the deferral realization incentive unless it is also available for capital gains taxes paid before death. As before, introducing capital gains exemption (to the extent that one wants to have one in the first place) that is not conditional on death—perhaps a lifetime one—is a preferred approach.

All this discussion of capital gains treatment assumed that the new capital gains tax regime would continue to preserve spousal preference. The tax expenditures calculations of the cost of the step up in Office of Tax Analysis (2014) evaluate the revenue loss against the baseline of all capital gains being taxed at death and hence arrives at a much larger estimate than the $14.8 billion obtained from taxing capital gains with no exemption shown in column 4 of table 9.2. In table 9.4, I consider a somewhat different scenario where all capital gains held by heads of households are taxed at the time of their death. This scenario assumes no spousal preference and it also assumes that all capital gains are held by the head of household—while it is a strong assumption for married individuals, it allows me to abstract from the thorny issue of allocating ownership of assets to spouses. This approach makes a big difference: now the tax expenditure (imposing the tax with no exemption) is $36.4 billion—much larger than the previous estimate of $14.8 billion, reflecting the fact that most of the capital gains are held by married households. Correspondingly, the revenue losses from allowing for exemption are much larger too. I view these calculations primarily as an illustration of the importance of the spousal treatment—I expect that any reform of the step up

Table 9.4 Taxation of capital gains at death: Disallowing spousal preference

Asset Category (m)	*Number of Deaths*	*Total Capital Gains*	*Non-Housing Gains*	*Revenue, No Exemption*	*Revenue, $500,000 Exemption*	*Revenue, $1 Million Exemption*	*Revenue, $2 Million Exemption*
<$1	1,461,069	103.316	20.674	5.090	0.084	0.000	0.000
$1–$5	74,607	43.679	27.685	7.641	3.554	1.969	0.783
$5–$10	10,908	27.071	22.613	5.737	4.595	3.731	2.373
$10–$20	4,048	20.692	17.580	4.646	4.223	3.809	3.046
$20–$50	1,327	20.574	19.247	4.821	4.687	4.534	4.234
$50+	862	35.551	34.958	8.443	8.377	8.277	8.080
Total	1,552,821	250.887	142.759	36.380	25.523	22.323	18.517

Note: See the Appendix for a description of methodology. The estimation procedure assumes no tax preference for a surviving spouse. All figures (other than the number of returns) in billions of dollars.

would allow for generous preference for spousal transfers so that the results in table 9.2 are a much more realistic scenario to consider.

Concluding, it seems that the elimination of the step up at death is not sufficient to replace the revenue from the estate tax unless one is willing to part (at least partially) with spousal preference. Still, the tax on capital gains at death would allow for a significant reduction in estate tax burden if this is what the extra revenue is earmarked for.

9.5.2 The Role of Estate Taxation

This long discussion of capital gains taxation touched on the interaction between capital gains and estate tax. This interaction is an artifact of a problem with implementing capital gains taxes (they are based on realization rather than accrual). Capital gains taxation is a part of the system of taxing capital income. Estate tax is a tax on transfers. These two issues are conceptually separate—the design of the income tax and the appropriate burden on capital income within that system should govern decisions about capital gains taxation.

The estate tax, especially the type of tax that is in existence in the United States, serves a different objective. What is that objective? As discussed, the case for taxing estates arises at the top of the distribution (there actually may be reasons to subsidize rather than tax transfers at lower wealth levels) and has to do with addressing externalities through effects on behavior of the next generation, any aggregate implications of the concentration of wealth and its impact on equality of opportunities. From that point of view, the current estate tax is in a good place. It applies to a very small number of individuals with large net worth. When the exemption is at the current $5+ million level (and, with proper planning through the use of marital deduction and nontaxable gifts estates needn't be taxable way above that level), many of the considerations that were important in the past lost their bite. In particular, issues of small businesses being subject to taxation, liquidity constraints, and so on are no longer an appealing argument when just about 5,000 of 2 million decedents are subject to the tax. Portability of marital deduction addressed the remaining concern about treatment of spouses. While reasonable people might disagree about the appropriate tax rate and exemption, economic evidence leaves enough room to accommodate a range of views. For the estate tax as such, the standard advice of simplification and base broadening (via addressing existing avoidance opportunities and curtailing some of the abusive valuation strategies) perhaps coupled with compensating rate reduction is prudent.

One of the arguments that has been used to justify the presence of estate taxation since its onset was its role as a backstop to avoidance of other forms of taxation. The discussion of interaction with capital gains tax suggests that this is the role that the estate tax plays in that case, although it is the self-inflicted damage resulting from granting step-up benefits. More generally though, in the world where income is hard to observe or where people do not realize their income, a tax on wealth or estates may serve as a substitute for income tax. This is not an unreasonable view of the United States in the past. When much of wealth is held in a corporate form, with earnings retained rather than paid out as dividends or realized as capital gains (e.g., because a closely held firm is retained until death of the taxpayer), individual income tax is effectively avoided for extended periods of time. Before 1986, when individual income tax rates were high, the incentives to realize income were weak. This pre-1986 incentive not to realize is visible in the influential Piketty and Saez (2003) series of top income shares that shows 4.1 percentage point increase (from the base of 9.1%) in the share of income going to the top 1% between 1986 and 1988 when the relative incentives for corporate versus pass-through treatment changed and motivated conversions from C- to S-corporations (Gordon and Slemrod 2000). My recent work using data from Norway (Alstadsæter et al. 2015) that allows the allocation of business profits to shareholders as they accrue rather than when they are realized, documents that a tax reform that resulted in heavier taxation of capital gains and dividends led to an increase in retention of earnings within firms and massive decrease in visibility of income on individual income tax returns: top income shares are understated by 50% as the result (in contrast, accounting for accrual of business profits made little difference when taxation of dividends was light). While international tax avoidance issues remain important, it seems likely that as the result of a general shift toward pass-through entities, the United States has gotten much better in taxing income after 1986 so that the backstop to avoidance role of estate taxation is no longer a first order argument.

9.5.3 Gift Tax

Taxation of inter-vivos gifts is necessary to support an effective system of estate taxation. Integration of gift and estate taxation via unified credit is imperfect though and leaves much room for tax planning. First, gift tax rates are effectively lower than estate rates due to the difference in tax-exclusive versus tax-inclusive base. The lower rate was apparently an intentional decision of the Congress at the time the gift tax was introduced in 1932 that was intended to stimulate pre-payment of tax liability by making gifts rather than bequests. Be as it may, this is not an appealing argument for this disparity. There is no clear reason why the tax should distort the decision whether to give inter vivos or at death, and there are good reasons not to distort, since it creates opportunities for tax planning. Furthermore, the unified credit itself encourages gifts because the value of past transfers is not adjusted to reflect inflation or the return on them so that giving an asset before it appreciates uses up a smaller part of the credit. Accumulating transfers to reflect their present value using some assumed safe rate of return (e.g., on 10-year Treasuries) would reduce the magnitude of this distortion. In the discussion of capital gains, it was noted that the current treatment of capital gains under gift and estate tax is different. Harmonizing this treatment would eliminate yet another margin of distortions (and it is pretty intuitive that granting step up to inter-vivos gifts is not an appealing approach so that harmonizing would need to go in the direction of some form of taxing capital gains at death).

9.5.4 Integration with Income Tax

As mentioned, Canada taxes capital gains at death and it does so by including them in the income tax base for the terminal return. The short-lived income-inheritance tax introduced in the United States in 1894 (and later deemed unconstitutional) included inheritance in the income tax base. Some countries include gifts in the income tax base. One can tax estates or inheritance separately or one can integrate this form of taxation with income tax (Batchelder 2009). The appealing feature of such an approach is that, if integration takes place on the donee side, it allows for employing the progressive income tax structure to adjust tax liability according to the ultimate recipient's circumstances. This would be a dramatic change from the current system, but it is a coherent alternative possibility.

9.6 CONCLUSIONS

After years of changes, the estate tax is nowadays very different than it was fifteen years ago. It applies to one-tenth of the population that it used to, although the decline in revenue has been somewhat less dramatic. The increase in exemption and the fact that it is now indexed for inflation make many of the concerns that were raised in the past much less relevant. For example, when a couple with just basic planning involving the use of available exemption and the portable marital deduction can shelter $10 million from taxation, few small illiquid businesses are likely to be affected. Some of the preferences in the estate tax have been designed for a different population and could be reformed to broaden the base and possibly finance lower rates. Seen in isolation, this tax collects revenue in a way that does not appear grossly inefficient and plays, an arguably useful, role in targeting wealth concentration. Its most glaring inefficiencies have to do with its interactions with other components of the tax system: capital gains most importantly but also to some extent with gift taxation. Elimination of step up in basis at death should be high on the policy agenda and the preferred approach to replacing it is constructive realization rather than the usually proposed carryover basis. There is no clear justification for exempting any capital gains at death but to the extent that this approach is pursued, it would again result in similar distortions as step up. The preferred approach to exempting some capital gains, if one needs to do that for distributional reasons, would be to introduce a lifetime exemption. Such an approach could be implemented in a similar way in which the unified credit integrates exemptions for gift and estate tax purposes.

ACKNOWLEDGMENTS

I am grateful for helpful comments from Alan Auerbach, Jim Hines, Jim Poterba, and from participants in the Burch Center/Wharton/Urban-Brookings Tax Policy Center conference on Economics of Tax Policy reform. All errors are mine.

REFERENCES

Adam, Stuart, Timothy Besley, Richard Blundell, Stephen Bond, Robert Chote, Malcolm Gammie, Paul Johnson, Gareth Myles, and James Poterba. 2011. "Taxes on Wealth Transfers." In *Tax by Design: The Mirrlees Review*, edited by Institute for Fiscal Studies (IFS) and James Mirrlees, 347–67. Oxford: Oxford University Press.

Aiyagari, S. Rao. 1995. "Optimal Capital Income Taxation with Incomplete Markets, Borrowing Constraints and Constant Discounting." *Quarterly Journal of Economics* 103 (6): 1158–75.

Alstadsæter, Annette, Martin Jacob, Wojciech Kopczuk, and Kjetil Telle. 2015. "Accounting for Business Income in Measuring Top Income Shares: Integrated Accrual Approach Using Individual and Firm Data from Norway." University of Oslo, WHU, Columbia University and Statistics Norway, mimeo.

Arrondel, Luc, and Anne Laferrère. 2001. "Taxation and Wealth Transmission in France." *Journal of Public Economics* 79 (1): 3–33. ISPE 1998: Bequests and Wealth Taxation.

Auerbach, Alan J. 2008. "Taxation of Wealth." In *The New Palgrave Dictionary of Economics*, edited by Steven N. Durlauf and Lawrence E. Blume. Palgrave Macmillan.

Auten, Gerald, and David Joulfaian. 2001. "Bequest Taxes and Capital Gains Realizations." *Journal of Public Economics* 81 (2): 213–29.

Batchelder, Lily L. 2009. "What Should Society Expect from Heirs? A Proposal for a Comprehensive Inheritance Tax." *Tax Law Review* 63 (1): 1–111.

Bernheim, B. Douglas, Robert J. Lemke, and John Karl Scholz. 2004. "Do Estate and Gift Taxes Affect the Timing of Private Transfers?." *Journal of Public Economics* 88 (12): 2617–34.

Bloom, Nicholas, and John Van Reenen. 2007. "Measuring and Explaining Management Practices across Firms and Countries." *Quarterly Journal of Economics* 122 (4): 1351–408.

Boserup, Simon Halphen, Wojciech Kopczuk, and Claus Thustrup Kreiner. 2016. "The Role of Bequests in Shaping Wealth Inequality: Evidence from Danish Wealth Records." *American Economic Review Papers and Proceedings* 106 (5): 656–61.

Bricker, Jesse, Lisa J. Dettling, Alice Henriques, Joanne W. Hsu, Kevin B. Moore, John Sabelhaus, Jeffrey Thompson, and Richard A. Windle. 2014. "Changes in U.S. Family Finances from 2010 to 2013: Evidence from the Survey of Consumer Finances." *Federal Reserve Bulletin* 100 (4): 1–40.

Brown, Jeffrey R., Courtney C. Coile, and Scott J. Weisbenner. 2010. "The Effect of Inheritance Receipt on Retirement." *Review of Economics and Statistics* 92 (2): 425–34.

Brown, Robert D. 1991. "A Primer on the Implementation of Wealth Taxes." *Canadian Public Policy / Analyse de Politiques* 17 (3): 335–50.

Brunetti, Michael J. 2006. "The Estate Tax and the Demise of the Family Business." *Journal of Public Economics* 90 (10–11): 1975–93.

Cagetti, Marco, and Mariacristina De Nardi. 2008. "Wealth Inequality: Data and Models." *Macroeconomic Dynamics* 12 (S2): 285–313.

Chamley, Christophe. 1986. "Optimal Taxation of Capital Income in General Equilibrium with Infinite Lives." *Econometrica* 54 (3): 607–22.

Davies, James B., and Anthony F. Shorrocks. 2000. "The Distribution of Wealth." In *Handbook of Income Distribution*, edited by Anthony B. Atkinson and François Bourguignon, 605–75. North Holland: Elsevier.

De Nardi, Mariacristina. 2004. "Wealth Inequality and Intergenerational Links", *Review of Economic Studies* 71:743–68.

Diamond, Peter. 1998. "Optimal Income Taxation: An Example with U-Shaped Pattern of Optimal Tax Rates", *American Economic Review* 88 (1): 83–95.

Dynan, Karen E., Jonathan Skinner, Stephen P. Zeldes. 2002. "The Importance of Bequests and Life-Cycle Saving in Capital Accumulation: A New Answer." *American Economic Review* 92 (2): 274–78.

Dynan, Karen E., Jonathan Skinner, and Stephen P. Zeldes. 2004. "Do the Rich Save More?." *Journal of Political Economy* 112 (2): 397–444.

Elinder, Mikael, Oscar Erixson, Henry Ohlsson. 2011. "Carnegie Visits Nobel: Do Inheritances Affect Labor and Capital Income?" Working Paper 2011:5.

Elinder, Mikael, Oscar Erixson, and Daniel Waldenström. 2015. "Inheritance and Wealth Inequality: Evidence from Population Registers." 2015. Working Paper 2015:3.

Eller, Martha, Brian Erard, and Chih-Chin Ho. 2000. "The Magnitude and Determinants of Federal Estate Tax Noncompliance." Working Paper 2000-6. http://www.bus.umich.edu/otpr/papers/2000-6.PDF

Eller, Martha, and Barry W. Johnson. 1999. "Using a Sample of Federal Estate Returns to Examine the Effects of Audit Revaluation on Pre-Audit Estimates." Proceedings of the 1999 Meeting of the American Statistical Association, Section on Government Statistics.

Erard, Brian. 1999. "Estate Tax Underreporting Gap Study: A Report Prepared for the Internal Revenue Service Economic Analysis and Modeling Group."

Farhi, Emmanuel, and Iván Werning. 2010. "Progressive Estate Taxation." *Quarterly Journal of Economics* 125 (2): 635–73.

Gale, William G., James R. HinesJr., and Joel Slemrod, eds. 2001. *Rethinking Estate and Gift Taxation*. Washington, DC: Brookings Institution Press.

Gale, William G., and John Karl Scholz. 1994. "Intergenerational Transfers and the Accumulation of Wealth." *Journal of Economic Perspectives* 8 (4): 145–60.

Gordon, Robert, David Joulfaian, and James Poterba. 2015. "Choosing between the Estate Tax and Basis Carryover Regime of 2010." MIT, mimeo.

Gordon, Roger H., and Joel Slemrod. 2000. "Are 'Real' Responses to Taxes Simply Income Shifting between Corporate and Personal Tax Bases?." In *Does Atlas Shrug? The Economic Consequences of Taxing the Rich*, edited by Joel Slemrod, 240–280. New York: Harvard University Press and Russell Sage Foundation.

Goupille-Lebret, Jonathan, and Jose Infante. 2015. "Behavioral Responses to Inheritance Tax: Evidence from Notches in France." Paris School of Economics, mimeo.

Holtz-Eakin, Douglas, David Joulfaian, and Harvey S. Rosen. 1993. "The Carnegie Conjecture: Some Empirical Evidence." *Quarterly Journal of Economics* 108 (2): 413–35.

Holtz-Eakin, Douglas, David Joulfaian, and Harvey S. Rosen. 1994a. "Entrepreneurial Decisions and Liquidity Constraints." *RAND Journal of Economics* 25 (2): 334–47.

Holtz-Eakin, Douglas, David Joulfaian, and Harvey S. Rosen. 1994b. "Sticking It Out: Entrepreneurial Survival and Liquidity Constraints." *Journal of Political Economy* 102 (1): 53–75.

Holtz-Eakin, Douglas, and Donald Marples. 2001. *Distortion Costs of Taxing Wealth Accumulation: Income versus Estate Taxes*. NBER Working Paper No. 8261.

Imbens, Guido W., Donald B. Rubin, and Bruce I. Sacerdote. 2001. "Estimating the Effect of Unearned Income on Labor Earnings, Savings, and Consumption: Evidence from a Survey of Lottery Players." *American Economic Review* 91 (4): 778–94.

Johnson, Barry W., Jacob M. Mikow, and Martha Britton Eller. 2001. "Elements of Federal Estate Taxation." In *Rethinking Estate and Gift Taxation*, edited by William G. Gale, James R. HinesJr., and Joel Slemrod, 65–107. Washington, DC: Brookings Institution Press.

Joulfaian, David. 2004. "Gift Taxes and Lifetime Transfers: Time Series Evidence." *Journal of Public Economics* 88 (9–10): 1917–29.

Joulfaian, David. 2005. "Choosing between Gifts and Bequests: How Taxes Affect the Timing of Wealth Transfers." *Journal of Public Economics* 89 (11–12): 2069–91.

Joulfaian, David. 2006. "The Behavioral Response of Wealth Accumulation to Estate Taxation: Time Series Evidence." *National Tax Journal* 59 (2): 253–68.

Joulfaian, David. 2014. "Intergenerational Transfers under an Uncertain Estate Tax." US Department of Treasury, mimeo. http://ssrn.com/abstract=2489245

Joulfaian, David, and Kathleen McGarry. 2004. "Estate and Gift Tax Incentives and Inter Vivos Giving." *National Tax Journal* 57 (2, part 2): 429–44.

Joulfaian, David, and Mark O. Wilhelm. 1994. "Inheritance and Labor Supply." *Journal of Human Resources* 29 (4): 1205–34.

Judd, Kenneth L. 1985. "Redistributive Taxation in a Simple Perfect Foresight Model." *Journal of Public Economics* 28 (1): 59–83.

Kopczuk, Wojciech. 2007. "Bequest and Tax Planning: Evidence from Estate Tax Returns." *Quarterly Journal of Economics* 122 (4): 1801–54.

Kopczuk, Wojciech. 2013a. "Incentive Effects of Inheritances and Optimal Estate Taxation." *American Economic Review Papers and Proceedings* 103 (3): 472–77.

Kopczuk, Wojciech. 2013b. "Taxation of Intergenerational Transfers and Wealth." In *Handbook of Public Economics*, edited by Alan J. Auerbach, Raj Chetty, Martin S. Feldstein, and Emmanuel Saez, 329–90. North Holland: Elsevier.

Kopczuk, Wojciech, and Joel Slemrod. 2001. "The Impact of the Estate Tax on the Wealth Accumulation and Avoidance Behavior of Donors." In *Rethinking Estate and Gift Taxation*, edited by William G. Gale, James R. HinesJr., and Joel Slemrod, 299–343. Washington, DC: Brookings Institution Press.

Kotlikoff, Laurence J., and Lawrence H. Summers. 1981. "The Role of Intergenerational Transfers in Aggregate Capital Accumulation." *Journal of Political Economy* 89 (4): 706–32.

Kuhn, Peter, Peter Kooreman, Adriaan Soetevent, and Arie Kapteyn. 2011. "The Effects of Lottery Prizes on Winners and Their Neighbors: Evidence from the Dutch Postcode Lottery." *American Economic Review* 101 (5): 2226–47.

Luckey, John R. 2008. "A History of Federal Estate, Gift and Generation-Skipping Taxes." CRS Report for Congress, 95–444. Congressional Research Service.

McGarry, Kathleen. 2000. "Inter Vivos Transfers or Bequests? Estate Taxes and the Timing of Parental Giving." *Tax Policy and the Economy* 14:93–121.

McGarry, Kathleen. 2001. "The Cost of Equality: Unequal Bequests and Tax Avoidance." *Journal of Public Economics* 79 (1): 179–204.

Mintz, Jack M. 1991. "The Role of Wealth Taxation in the Overall Tax System." *Canadian Public Policy /Analyse de Politiques* 17 (3): 248–63.

Modigliani, Franco. 1988. "The Role of Intergenerational Transfers and Life Cycle Saving in the Accumulation of Wealth." *Journal of Economic Perspectives* 2 (2): 15–40.

Office of Tax Analysis. 2014. "Tax Expenditure for Exclusion of Capital Gains at Death." Special Studies in Tax Analysis, U.S. Department of the Treasury.

Ohlsson, Henry. 2011. "The Legacy of the Swedish Gift and Inheritance Tax, 1884–2004." *European Review of Economic History* 15 (3): 539–69.

Page, Benjamin R. 2003. "Bequest Taxes, Inter Vivos Gifts, and the Bequest Motive." *Journal of Public Economics* 87 (5–6): 1219–29.

Pérez-González, Francisco. 2006. "Inherited Control and Firm Performance." *American Economic Review* 96 (5): 1559–88.

Piketty, Thomas. 2011. "On the Long-Run Evolution of Inheritance: France 1820–2050." *Quarterly Journal of Economics* 126 (3): 1071–131.

Piketty, Thomas. 2014. *Capital in the Twenty-First Century*. Cambridge, MA and London, UK: Belknap Press.

Piketty, Thomas, and Emmanuel Saez. 2003. "Income Inequality in the United States, 1913–1998." *Quarterly Journal of Economics* 118(1): 1 39.

Piketty, Thomas, and Emmanuel Saez. 2013. "A Theory of Optimal Inheritance Taxation." *Econometrica* 81 (5): 1851–85.

Poterba, James M. 2000a. "Stock Market Wealth and Consumption." *Journal of Economic Perspectives* 14 (2): 99–118.

Poterba, James M. 2000b. "The Estate Tax and After-Tax Investment Returns." In *Does Atlas Shrug? The Economic Consequences of Taxing the Rich*, edited by Joel Slemrod, 329–49. New York: Harvard University Press and Russell Sage Foundation.

Poterba, James M. 2001. "Estate and Gift Taxes and Incentives for Inter Vivos Giving in the US." *Journal of Public Economics* 79 (1): 237–64.

Poterba, James M., and Scott Weisbenner. 2003. "Inter-Asset Differences in Effective Estate-Tax Burdens." *American Economic Review* 93 (2): 360–65.

Poterba, James M., and Scott Weisbenner. 2001. "The Distributional Burden of Taxing Estates and Unrealized Capital Gains at the Time of Death." In *Rethinking Estate and Gift Taxation*, edited by William G. Gale, James R. HinesJr., and Joel Slemrod, 422–449. Washington, DC: Brookings Institution Press.

Saez, Emmanuel. 2001. "Using Elasticities to Derive Optimal Income Tax Rates." *Review of Economic Studies* 68 (1): 205–29.

Saez, Emmanuel. 2002. "Optimal Progressive Capital Income Taxes in the Infinite Horizon Model." NBER Working Paper No. 9046.

Scheve, Kenneth, and David Stasavage. 2012. "Democracy, War and Wealth: Evidence from Two Centuries of Inheritance Taxation." *American Political Science Review* 106 (1): 81–102.

Schmalbeck, Richard. 2001. "Avoiding Federal Wealth Transfer Taxes." In *Rethinking Estate and Gift Taxation*, edited by William G. Gale, James R. HinesJr., and Joel Slemrod, 113–158. Washington, DC: Brookings Institution Press.

Seim, David. 2015. "Behavioral Responses to Wealth Taxes: Evidence from Sweden." Stockholm University, mimeo.

Society of Actuaries. 2014a, "Supplement to The RP-2014 Mortality Tables Report. RPH-2014, Headcount-Weighted Mortality Tables." Technical Report. https://www.soa.org/Research/Experience-Study/Pension/research-2014-rp.aspx

Society of Actuaries. 2014b. "The RP-2014 Mortality Tables Report." Technical Report. https://www.soa.org/Research/Experience-Study/Pension/research-2014-rp.aspx

Straub, Ludwig, and Iván Werning. 2015. "Positive Long Run Capital Taxation: Chamley-Judd Revisited." MIT, mimeo.

Tsoutsoura, Margarita. 2011. "The Effect of Succession Taxes on Family Firm Investment: Evidence from a Natural Experiment." Chicago Booth, mimeo.

Villalonga, Belen, and Raphael Amit. 2006. "How Do Family Ownership, Control and Management Affect Firm Value?." *Journal of Financial Economics* 80 (2): 385–417.

Wolff, Edward N. 1996. "Discussant's Comments on Douglas Holtz-Eakin, 'The Uneasy Case for Abolishing the Estate Tax.'" *Tax Law Review* 51 (3): 517–22.

APPENDIX: PROCEDURE FOR CONSTRUCTING REVENUE ESTIMATES

In order to assess the revenue consequences of taxing capital gains at death, I pursue a simple calibration exercise that relies on the 2013 Survey of Consumer Finances (SCF). The SCF collects information about wealth, income, and demographic characteristics of a representative sample of the US population, while oversampling the high income and net worth individuals, thereby making it the default choice for evaluating policies that apply to the top of the distribution. See Bricker et al. (2014) for a description of the data set. Critically important for my purposes, the SCF includes questions about unrealized capital gains. My starting point is to calibrate the SCF to the estate tax collections. This is not straightforward because (1) the SCF collects information about living individuals, while the estate tax applies to individuals who have died; (2) the unit of observation in the SCF is a household and the unit of observation in the estate tax data is an individual; (3) wealth reported in a survey need not be equal to assets reported on tax returns for a number of reasons, including inter-vivos giving, tax avoidance, different valuation approaches, and so on; (4) the SCF explicitly excludes the Forbes 400 individuals (tiny number of deaths but large wealth); and (5) the most recent available estate tax statistics pertain to the 2014 year-of-filing data, which reflects not just 2013 tax returns but also returns from other years. Hence, one should not expect a perfect match between the two.

In order to compare to estate tax returns, I rely on the SOI 2014 year of filing tabulations (https://www.irs.gov/pub/irs-soi/14es01fy.xls).

Following Poterba and Weisbenner (2001), I construct at-death distribution of wealth by applying mortality rates to the SCF sample. This is by itself not a trivial step because the mortality rate of the wealthy is known to be higher than that of the general public. Hence, I proceed by applying different mortality rates to the general public than to higher net worth individuals. Specifically, I apply 2013 (age and gender-specific) population mortality rates to everyone with net worth up to $1,000,000 and—lower—high-socioeconomic status rates to those above that level. The population mortality rates originate from the National Center for Health Statistics' Mortality Detail File, and I use the version disseminated by the Human Mortality Database (http://www.mortality.org; The United States of America, Death rates (period 1x1), modified on 21-Jul-2015). For the high net worth group, I rely on the Society of Actuaries annuitant mortality tables, RP-2014. Society of Actuaries (2014b) provides the background and a detailed description of this data. These mortality tables are based on the mortality experience of private retirement plans in the United States from 2004 and 2008, with estimated mortality improvement factors provided to adjust the baseline-year rates (2006) to the following years. I use the headcount-weighted (rather than amount-weighted) mortality rates in my analysis (Society of Actuaries 2014a). Annuitants are a diverse population and the age- and gender-specific mortality rates are available for a number of subgroups (everyone, white- and blue-collar workers, top and bottom quartiles of earnings distribution). I use white-collar worker-specific mortality rates (the lowest mortality group) and blend the mortality series for "employees" (available up to age 80) and "healthy annuitants" (available above age 50) by using the employees series for younger individuals, weighted average of the two series between 65 and 80 (with weight linearly increasing from 0 to 1 over this age range) and the annuitant series for the older individuals. These socio-economic mortality adjustments are non-trivial, but they are necessary to better approximate the mortality experience of the high net worth population. For example, the estimated number of 2013 head-of-household deaths with net worth above $1 million is about 205,000 using population mortality rates and just 117,000 using adjusted mortality rates.

The SCF reports household wealth, while the estate tax data is individual. There is no sufficient information in the SCF to directly evaluate how assets would be allocated among spouses for estate tax purposes. The precise marital status information of estate taxpayers is not available for 2014. However, the estate tax currently provides for the unlimited marital deduction and a portable exemption so that, for married individuals, use of marital deduction is close to universal. Out of 11,931 estate tax returns filed in 2014, 6,773 were non-taxable and 5,175 claimed marital deduction. Among 5,198 taxable returns, just 726 claimed marital deduction. Hence, for the most part taxable estate tax returns correspond to single (widowed or divorced) filers with a relative small number corresponding to married individuals. I proceed by assuming that only death of a head of household could result in a taxable estate. A single individual is a head of household and if the estate is sufficiently large, it is taxable. For married individuals, I specify the likelihood of the estate being taxable as the sum of the probability of the other spouse also dying in the same year plus the conditional (on wealth) probability of the married-individual's estate being taxable if the spouse does not die. I obtain the conditional probability of the married-individual's estate being taxable by calculating the share of taxable tax returns among those claiming spousal deduction in available wealth categories. This yields 5.6% probability in the $5–$10 million category, 17.6% in the $10–$20 million category, 33.5% in the $20–$50 category and 48.1% in the $50+ million category.

There is no hard information on the extent of mismatch of the levels of wealth observed in estate tax and the SCF data. I discuss the evidence of tax avoidance in section 9.4. Furthermore, the SCF data pertains to 2013 while the estate tax data corresponds to returns filed in 2014—since the majority of returns (80%) are filed between nine and eighteen months after the death of the taxpayer, most of the returns are for 2013 deaths but a non-trivial minority is for 2014 deaths or for prior years. Without a precise number to calibrate tax avoidance and timing mismatch to, I simply implement an ad hoc adjustment by reducing the value of SCF assets reported for estate tax purposes by 25%. This adjustments allows for (approximately) matching the number of estate taxpayers and aggregate gross estate figures.

Finally, to compare tax collections, I compute the share of deductions (other than debt or marital deduction) by gross estate size category from estate tax statistics and apply it to different categories in the estate tax data. I pursue a corresponding adjustment for marital deduction computed specifically for estate tax returns claiming marital deduction. Debt is observable in the SCF so that I subtract it directly.

In all tables, categories are defined in terms of assets rather than net worth (the difference is debt) to match the gross estate concept in the estate tax return data.

COMMENTARY ON CHAPTER 9

James M. Poterba

Chapter 9 provides a careful and comprehensive summary of existing research on the incentive and distributional effects of the estate tax, emphasizing recent research advances, and it calls attention to the critical interaction between the estate tax and the capital gains tax in the current US tax system. It points out that the estate tax has been a more active subject of research than the key capital gains tax provision that applies to transfers at death—basis step-up—and suggests that understanding the behavioral consequences of basis step-up at death is an important research priority. After raising questions about whether there is any role for basis step-up in an optimal income tax system, the chapter presents informative calculations on the revenue consequences of replacing basis step-up with alternative rules regarding capital gains that are held at the time of death. This analysis should stimulate further research as well as policy analysis on the basis step-up provision.

My comments explore three issues that are raised in the chapter: the comparison of estate taxes, or wealth taxes more generally, and capital income taxes in the current financial environment with low safe rates of return, the limits of current empirical evidence on the behavioral consequences of estate taxation, and the challenges of measuring the efficiency cost of lock-in associated with basis step-up.

9C.1 ESTATE TAXES, WEALTH TAXES, AND CAPITAL INCOME TAXES

In reviewing past research, the chapter notes that the estate tax is both a component of the capital income tax structure in a lifecycle setting and a tax on interpersonal transfers at death. Different theoretical models explore the design of estate taxes in settings that emphasize one or the other of these considerations. The role of the estate tax relative to the income tax in the lifetime capital income tax framework has increased in recent years, as long-term safe rates of return have fallen to historically low levels. In this environment, the distinction between capital income taxes on the flow of capital income, and estate or other wealth taxes on the stock of capital is particularly stark. This can be illustrated by comparing a hypothetical investor facing similar tax rules, but different rate of return opportunities, in 2000 and 2016.

Consider a 55-year-old US investor who expects to leave a taxable estate when she dies at the age of 90, and who faces a 45% combined federal and state income tax rate on interest income, as well as a 40% marginal federal estate tax rate. If this investor could invest in riskless long-term Treasury inflation-linked bonds at the yields that were available in in 2000, approximately 3.5% per year, her net-of-tax interest rate would be 1.925%. A $1,000 bond investment at age 60 would grow, in constant purchasing-power dollars, to $1,772 at age 90, and the estate tax of .40*($1772) = $709 would leave $1,063 for her heirs net of estate tax. The net of tax rate of return she would earn on this investment would be 0.2% per year, making the effective tax rate on the 3.5% real pretax return 94.3%. This high rate is the result of the estate tax applying to principal as well as investment income over the next thirty years; a 40% estate tax rate applied to an investment with a thirty-year horizon resembles a 1.33% per year reduction in the after-tax rate of return.

An estate tax, or any other wealth tax, can translate to a very high effective tax rate on capital income when the expected return is low. The chapter presents the key equation relating the effective capital income tax rate, *tc*, and the equivalent wealth tax rate, *tw*:

$$tc = \frac{1+r}{r} tw,$$

where *r* is the expected rate of return and all taxes are levied each period (e.g., each year). For an estate tax *te*, which is only levied once per generation, the equivalent wealth tax is roughly *te*/*G*, where *G* is the length of a generation. This approximation is more accurate in low return environments than when returns are substantial.

The foregoing example illustrates how the estate or wealth tax can represent a large share of the net-of-income-tax capital return, even when the expected return is substantial. When the expected return falls, the effective burden of a wealth tax rises. In early 2016, Treasury inflation-protected securities were yielding about 0.80 percentage points, nearly 3 percentage points less than fifteen years earlier. If we assume a thirty-year real interest rate of 1.0% and repeat the foregoing calculation, a $1,000 investment would yield an after-tax real return of 0.60% and would rise in value to $1,197 (inflation-adjusted) in thirty years. With an estate tax of 40%, the amount that the investor's heirs would receive is $718. The combination of the estate tax and the income tax on interest income results in a negative rate of return from the standpoint of the investor.

If capital income was untaxed and there was no estate tax, the investor earning a 3.5% annual rate of return would have been able to leave $2,807 to her heirs. Determining the respective effects of the income and estate tax in reducing this amount reflects the usual challenges of choosing a "stacking rule" in evaluating tax provisions. Operating in isolation, the income tax at a rate of 40% would reduce this amount by 37% (1 – $1,772/$2,807). If there were an estate tax but no income tax, the estate tax would reduce the pretax accumulation of $2,807 by 40%. Because the estate tax applies after the income tax has been collected on returns each year, the reduction in after-tax bequest is 25% (($1,772 – $1,063)/$2,807). The relative magnitudes of the income tax and estate tax effects are very different in a low-return environment.

With a 1% annual real return, the value of a $1,000 investment after thirty years would be $1,348. With a 40% tax rate on the return, this investment would be worth $1,197, so the income tax would reduce the value of the potential estate by 11%. This reflects the more modest role of capital accumulation, versus principal, in determining the amount that can be bequeathed after thirty years. The estate tax, in isolation, would continue to reduce the value of the estate by 40%. In the low-return case, after income taxes this would reduce the after-tax estate by $479, or by 36% of the no-income-tax accumulation after thirty years. The relative burden of the estate tax, compared with the annual capital income tax, is much greater in a low-return environment.

Taxing intergenerational transfers at a given rate has a larger effect on the amount of wealth that can be transferred net-of-tax in a low-return than in a high return environment. Piketty (2014) has called attention to the important role of the rate of return on wealth in determining the dynamics of the wealth distribution. This return is also important in determining the relative burdens of the estate and capital income taxes.

9C.2 THE BEHAVIORAL EFFECTS OF ESTATE TAXATION

Chapter 9's elegant review of estate taxation research should be the starting point for anyone exploring this research field. The estate tax potentially affects many dimensions of taxpayer behavior, most importantly, the labor supply of those who may leave bequests, the labor supply of those who receive bequests, the saving decisions of those who contemplate leaving bequests, and the saving decisions of those who anticipate receiving bequests. There has been a growing body of empirical work on the estate tax. Some of the most careful work relies on data from countries in which wealth taxes apply to a substantial share of the population. An important caveat in applying these studies to the US context concerns the extent to which the behavior of the small fraction of US taxpayers who can expect to pay the current federal estate tax can be inferred from the behavior of broader population segments in other nations, such as France and Sweden, with very different wealth distributions, and many fewer individuals who have amassed large wealth holdings.

There is now an increasingly convincing body of evidence suggesting that those who receive inheritances reduce their labor supply, but evidence on how the anticipation of estate taxes affects the lifecycle behavior of those who accumulate wealth is limited. A key challenge is determining the extent to which reduced opportunities to transfer wealth across generations discourages labor supply and saving. Mankiw (2010) presents an illustrative calculation, in the form of a personal reflection, on the combined effect of income and estate taxes on the effective tax rate facing those whose primary objective in earning income is to make transfers to their children. Measuring the number of potential estate tax payers who are concerned with the net tax burden on this margin of behavior, and then assessing behavioral response, are important empirical challenges.

Heterogeneity of the population that may be subject to estate taxation needs to be recognized, even when it leads to the disappointing conclusion that sample sizes of high-wealth decedents are small and the information that is available on their estate plans is limited. The chapter observes that the US estate tax is now projected to collect revenue from roughly 5,000 decedents each year. Given the concentration of wealth holdings, a high fraction of the wealth held by prospective estate tax payers is likely held by families that are well-advised by tax and estate professionals. The behavior of this group is important for assessing the revenue consequences of potential estate tax reforms.

One issue that receives only brief discussion in the chapter is the incidence of estate taxation. There is evidence on the "legal incidence," on the incomes of the decedents who pay the estate tax and on the positions in the US wealth distribution of this group. Yet there is relatively little discussion of how changes in the estate tax might affect the rate of return to capital and the wage–rental ratio. In part this reflects the central tendency of recent research, which treats the rate of return as fixed.

Could changes in the US estate tax have a large enough impact on the aggregate capital stock to affect the wage–rental ratio? Only a small number of households are currently affected by the tax, but their wealth holdings represent a non-trivial share of the US capital stock. Potential effects on the rate of return therefore hinge on the magnitude of the saving response to the tax. An older literature, exemplified by Stiglitz (1978), raised the possibility that if the estate tax reduced the level of capital accumulation, it would raise the rate of return to capital and potentially alter the pretax distribution of incomes. One might reasonably argue that in an integrated global capital market, the effect of changes in the US estate tax regime are unlikely to have substantial effects on the pretax rate of return available to investors. A global tax on inheritances, such as that called for by Piketty (2014), might however affect the relative returns on capital and labor.

9C.3 THE WELFARE COST OF LOCK-IN

In addition to reviewing recent theoretical and empirical work on the estate tax, chapter 9 discusses the basis step-up provisions that currently apply when capital assets are transferred at death. The opportunity to eliminate potential capital gains tax liability if an asset is held until death represents a powerful incentive to delay realizing gains, particularly for those late in life. It has been recognized at least since Bailey's (1969) discussion that basis step-up reduces the effective capital gains tax rate as well as the revenues collected from capital gains taxation. Analysts who favor an income tax over a consumption tax view step-up at death as an important gap in the income tax system. Those who support a consumption tax might be less critical, since as long as income tax was collected on the earnings out of which investors saved, and which led to the future capital gains, step-up provides consumption-tax treatment of the investment income. Economists in both camps would agree that there are distortions associated with the current step-up structure, which creates "lock-in" for investors with accrued gains.

While there are many empirical studies suggesting the presence of lock-in behavior when investors can reduce their capital gains tax burdens by deferring the sale of an asset, the welfare consequences of lock-in are less clear. This is because the economic theory of trading behavior remains poorly developed. Balcer and Judd (1987) develop a lifecycle model in which consumption demands generate asset sales, and Kiefer (1990) constructs a model in which investors receive information about various securities, and consequently choose to sell particular holdings at particular times in order to pursue higher expected returns. Kovenock and Rothschild (1987) develop a related framework that permits welfare analysis, by recognizing that the returns on different securities are imperfectly correlated, and that a realization-based tax that leads investors to hold their gains will also result in less-diversified investment portfolios. This leads to a loss in expected utility for investors, who bear more risk, for a given expected return, than they would if they were able to rebalance their portfolios without the "tax friction" of a realization-based capital gains tax. An accrual capital gains tax would not create this distortion. Lock-in may also raise required returns if investors demand higher pretax returns as compensation for their less-diversified portfolio structure. Chapter 9 appropriately highlights the potential distortions associated with basis step-up, and it notes that there would be substantial revenue gains from eliminating this tax provision. Developing a framework that can be used for the empirical analysis of lock-in, and to calibrate its welfare effects, is an important research priority.

Recent US experience provides new data on the importance of basis step-up in reducing federal revenues. As chapter 9 explains, under the provisions of a 2001 tax bill, in 2010 the federal estate expired. Congress reinstated the estate tax late in that year, and allowed executors of estates for decedents who passed away in 2010 to choose between paying the estate tax and stepping up asset basis, or carrying over asset basis and not paying the estate tax. Those who chose the carryover basis regime were required to report the asset basis and the fair market value for any assets that were passed to beneficiaries. Those who chose to pay the estate tax were only required to report the fair market value of assets that were transferred.

Gordon, Joulfaian, and Poterba (GJP) (2016) and the Office of Tax Analysis (2014) analyze the information from returns filed for 2010 decedents whose executors chose the basis carry-over regime. GJP (2016) report that the ratio of unrealized gains to fair market value, aggregating across all carry-over basis filings, was 44%. This ratio cannot be applied to all assets transferred at death, because some executors filed estate tax returns on behalf of their decedents. The choice between the estate tax and basis carryover regimes was not random and was in all likelihood correlated with the share of unrealized capital gains in the estate. Even under the extreme assumption that the basis equaled the fair market value of the assets in all of the estates for which executors chose to file estate tax returns, the ratio of unrealized gains to fair market value for all 2010 decedents who were potentially affected by the estate tax would be 34%.

It is difficult to translate this estimate of unrealized gains into an estimate of how basis step-up affects the effective capital gains tax rate; that requires an estimate of the share of accruing gains that were realized prior to death by those who were subject to the estate tax.

The cost of lock-in associated with basis step-up depends on the investment environment confronting taxpayers. If it is easy to borrow against appreciated assets, and if investors can find ways to hedge the returns of assets that they are encouraged to hold until death for tax reasons, then the distortions to both lifetime consumption profiles and to return opportunity sets may be modest. If it is difficult or expensive to hedge, and if borrowing is costly, the distortions will be greater. These aspects of the financial environment may change over time, and any estimate of the efficiency cost of lock-in must recognize this. Stiglitz (1983) pointed out that if investors could engage in wash sales, hold long and short positions in perfectly- or nearly-perfectly-correlated securities, and choose which positions to realize each year, then the realization based capital gains tax could become a subsidy rather than a tax on securities investments. This underscores the need to carefully model the investment environment when considering the effects of potential changes in the basis step-up rules.

Potential reforms to the basis step-up provisions could be considered more generally in the context of reform to a realization-based system of capital gains taxation. Auerbach (1992) explains that there are various ways to design tax systems that are equivalent to accrual-based taxation of gains, but that only require payment when assets are sold. The discussion of "deemed disposition" in Canada suggests the value of empirical comparisons between the realization behavior of investors in the two nations.

For some taxpayers, capital gains may be realized in only a few years during their lifetime, and in substantial amount at those times. A small business owner who sells a business would be an example of such a taxpayer; a real estate investor might face a similar realization pattern. For such taxpayers the design choice between an annual capital gains exemption and a lifetime exemption could be very important. Golombek (2013) explains that Canadian investors receive a substantial lifetime exemption from capital gains liability, but that gains in excess of that threshold are taxed at a high rate. Chapter 9 does a valuable service by moving beyond the discussion of repealing basis step-up and suggesting potential reform options, such as the Canadian model.

9C.4 SUMMARY

Chapter 9 offers an outstanding review of the current state of research on the estate tax, the tax treatment of capital gains held until death, and the potential reforms that might be contemplated to the current basis step-up provisions. It provides a springboard for future researchers to explore all of these issues. While the state of research has advanced rapidly in the last two decades, there is still a great deal more to be learned if we are to provide a firm foundation for tax policy design.

REFERENCES

Auerbach, Alan. 1992. "On the Design and Reform of Capital Gains Taxes." *American Economic Review* 82 (May): 263–67.

Bailey, Martin J. 1969. "Capital Gains and Income Taxation." In *The Taxation of Income from Capital*, edited by Arnold C. Harberger and Martin J. Bailey, 11–49. Washington, DC: Brookings Institution.

Balcer, Yves, and Kenneth Judd. 1987. "Effects of Capital Gains Taxation on Life-Cycle Investment and Portfolio Management." *Journal of Finance* 42 (July): 743–61.

Golombek, Jamie. 2013. "Death and Taxes: Leave Your Assets to Your Heirs Instead of the CRA." *Financial Post*, October 25. http://business.financialpost.com/personal-finance/debt/death-and-taxes-heres-what-happens-to-your-assets-when-you-die

Gordon, Robert, David Joulfaian, and James Poterba. 2016. "The Revenue and Incentive Effects of Basis Step-Up at Death: Lessons from the 2010 'Voluntary' Estate Tax Regime." *American Economic Review: Papers and Proceedings* 106 (May): 662–67.

Kiefer, Donald W. 1990. "Lock-In Effect within a Simple Model of Corporate Stock Trading." *National Tax Journal* 43 (March): 75–94.

Kovenock, David, and Michael Rothschild. 1987. "Notes on the Effect of Capital Gains Taxation on Non-Austrian Assets." In *Economic Policy in Theory and Practice*, edited by A. Razin and E. Sadka, 309–39. New York: St. Martin's Press.

Mankiw, N. Gregory. 2010. "I Can Afford Higher Taxes. But They'll Make Me Work Less." *New York Times*, October 9. http://www.nytimes.com/2010/10/10/business/economy/10view.html?_r=0

Office of Tax Analysis, US Treasury Department. 2014. "Tax Expenditure for Exclusion of Capital Gains at Death." Memorandum, Washington, DC.

Piketty, Thomas. 2014. *Capital in the Twenty-First Century*. Cambridge, MA: Belknap Press.

Stiglitz, Joseph E. 1978. "Notes on Estate Taxes, Redistribution, and the Concept of Balanced Growth Path Incidence." *Journal of Political Economy* 86: S137–S150.

Stiglitz, Joseph E. 1983. "Some Aspects of the Taxation of Capital Gains." *Journal of Public Economics* 21:257–94.

10

TAX POLICY AND RETIREMENT SAVINGS

John N. Friedman

Tax subsidies for retirement savings are a prominent feature of all modern tax systems. Although the details differ from country to country, the core principle is the same: capital returns to assets held in accounts specially designated for retirement savings pay reduced (or no) tax. Many countries grant the underlying income originally deposited in the account favorable tax treatment as well.

In the United States, tax subsidies for retirement savings have existed since the very beginning of the permanent income tax system in 1913 (Georgetown University Law Center 2010). As retirement savings have grown, these subsidies have become increasingly costly; figure 10.1 shows this rapid growth over the past two decades and the projected growth going forward. Tax expenditures for retirement savings totaled \$146 billion in FY2014, which is nearly double the inflation-adjusted level in 1993; the Office of Management and Budget projects that this expense will grow by an incredible 7.6% annually over the next decade to a total of \$303 billion in 2024 (US Government 2015). Retirement subsidies from states increase this by another 20% (Ghilarducci 2015). All of this is despite the fact that the per-dollar subsidy for retirement savings has been flat or even shrinking over the past twenty years (Burtless and Toder 2010).

Supporters argue for these retirement tax subsidies based on a perceived deficit of savings, at both the national and the household level. Saving rates in the United States have fallen from 12.9% to 4.8% over the past forty years, as shown in figure 10.2, while at the same time the US population has rapidly aged. The result is that an increasing number of households reach retirement without sufficient funds to support adequate consumption (Poterba 2014). By one calculation, 52% of working households have sufficiently few assets that, on current trend, they will be forced into a sharp consumption drop at retirement (Munnell, Hou, and Webb 2014). Traditional sources of support in retirement are also shrinking. Looking forward, the Social Security Administration projects that Social Security replacement rates for middle-income workers will be just 40%, down from roughly 50% in the 1980s. Defined benefit plans are also in sharp retreat; just 13% of workers participated in such plans in 2013, down from 32% in 1989. All of these changes place ever more emphasis on individual retirement savings, which are the focus of these large tax subsidies.

This chapter reviews the economics literature on savings to assess the impact and efficiency of tax subsidies for retirement. Relative to previous reviews on this subject

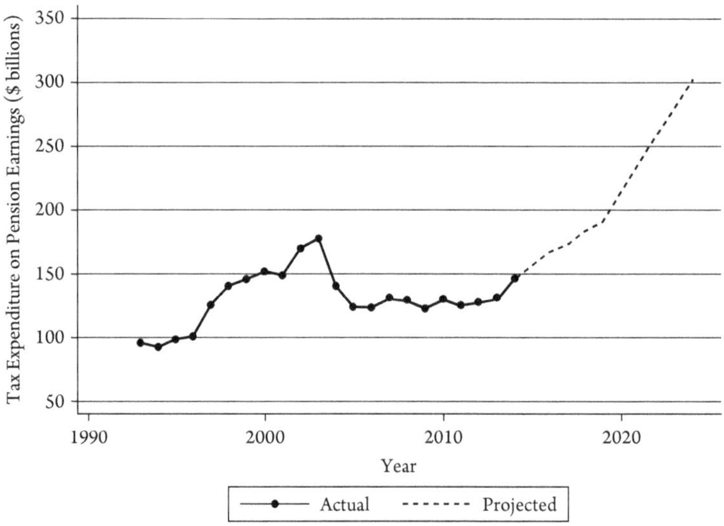

Figure 10.1 Tax expenditures on pension contributions and earnings in the United States, 1993–2024

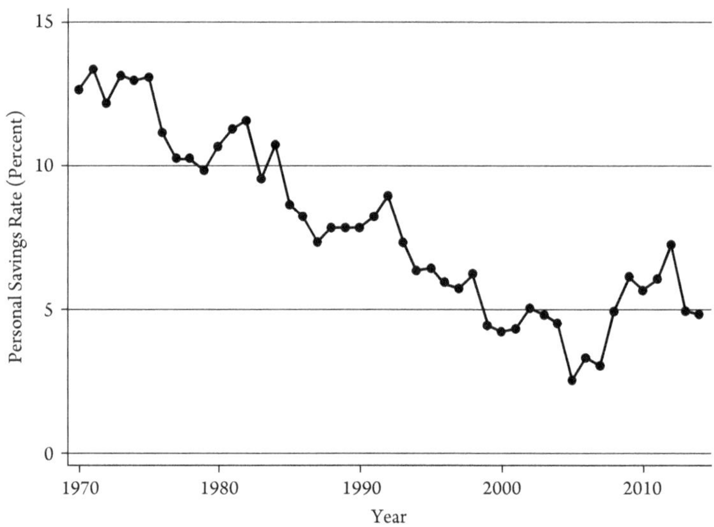

Figure 10.2 Savings rate in the United States, 1970–2014

(e.g., Attanasio and Wakefield 2010; Bernheim 2002), I highlight two recent advances in the literature that have important implications for our understanding of retirement tax policy. First, there has been much recent progress in this literature due to the rapidly expanding availability of high-quality administrative data, especially from tax records, retirement plan administrators, and large fund managers. In these data sets, measurement error of many important variables is essentially zero, and coverage is often near 100%. This high data administrative quality stands in contrast to the increasing problem of non-response and measurement error in more traditional survey data sets; for instance, 34% of dollars reported for major transfer programs are imputed, and 20% of individuals in the most recent Current Population Survey declined to answer questions about income (Meyer, Mok, and Sullivan 2015). Large sample sizes in administrative data also permit more plausible identification strategies.

Second, the literature on retirement savings has grown increasingly sophisticated in the ways that it models non-traditional or "behavioral" effects that are outside the canonical optimizing model. These innovations both help us understand observed responses to traditional tax subsidies for savings and also motivates new types of policies. For instance, by manipulating choice architecture in retirement plans, policies such as default settings, auto-escalation, and default asset allocations have potentially powerful effects on behavior. Following Thaler and Sunstein (2008), I will refer to these policies collectively as "nudges," that is policies that may affect savings but do not affect an individual's budget set. Although tax policies have not traditionally focused on such nudges, there is a rising chorus (including the President's FY2016 Budget) that advocates such reforms.

To organize this review, I begin with a simple model of an individual's retirement savings decision and the government policies that might affect it. Using this framework, I demonstrate how the efficacy of tax subsidies for increasing retirement savings depends on three key parameters. The first one is the extent to which tax subsidies drive increases or decreases in total savings for optimizing consumers (alternatively known as "pass-through" or "crowd-out" in much of the savings literature). Because of countervailing effects that both increase and decrease individual savings, tax subsidies have a theoretically ambiguous effect on savings, and so this parameter must be estimated empirically. The second is the extent to which individuals pay attention to tax subsidies or interest rates at all when choosing retirement savings. There is increasing evidence that individuals are not responsive to many different aspects of tax policy for behavioral reasons, either because of inattention (Chetty 2009) or a lack of information (Chetty, Friedman, and Saez 2013; Chetty and Saez 2013). The third is the extent to which tax subsidies increase savings most for those individuals who have the greatest savings deficit, which measures the quality of targeting. I also show how the effectiveness of savings nudges depends on three similar parameters, but in the opposite direction. Conditions under which tax subsidies are highly effective—for instance, when individuals are most attentive to government savings policy and increase savings in response to subsidies—are exactly the circumstances when mandates or nudges will be ineffective. The converse is also the case.

Next, I summarize and evaluate the empirical literature on these three key parameters. I present a wide range of studies and highlight differences in the quality of identification or in the exact parameter identified. Of particular importance in this empirical literature is the ability to distinguish between instances when individuals truly reduce consumption, and thus increase savings, and those when individuals simply reallocate funds from one account to another or reallocate savings from one year to the next. I also review the effect of tax subsidies on savings in a wide variety of contexts, including both very broad tax subsidies for retirement (such as IRAs) and also much more targeted savings policies (such as the Saver's Credit). Where possible, I draw from papers that study employer policies (such as contribution matches) that closely mimic government policies. Given the recent interest in more "behavioral" tax policies, I also review the literature on savings nudges (which relies almost exclusively on employer policies).

Although there is a diversity of estimates and opinions in the literature, the weight of the evidence suggests that tax subsidies are not effective policies for addressing retirement savings inadequacy. First, although tax subsidies generate moderate increases in savings within designated accounts, the best evidence suggests that these contributions primarily reflect savings that would have occurred (or borrowing that would not have occurred) absent the tax subsidies. Total savings do not increase. Second, the evidence suggests that the vast majority of savers are inattentive, for one reason or another, to tax subsidies for savings, and thus do not respond at all (even in the tax-favored account). Third, the literature suggests that individuals who undersave are less likely to be attentive to tax policy, which implies that tax subsidies do not target those individuals with the greatest savings deficits. Conversely, these parameter estimates from the literature suggest that mandates and savings nudges are effective at increasing savings, and especially for those households who need it the most. As a result, the literature suggests that the tax subsidy could roughly be cut in half without seriously affecting savings (although the literature has very little to say on the potential effects of more drastic changes that would entirely eliminate the tax expenditure).

Finally, in light of increasing talk of comprehensive tax reform in the United States, the last section of this chapter describes and analyzes key retirement tax policies and proposals in the United States in light of the lessons from the literature. Courtesy of the Tax Policy Center, I present distributional scores of key proposals to reform the tax treatment of retirement savings in the United States, including a rate limitation on the deductibility of retirement savings contributions and a conversion of the tax deduction into a tax credit for retirement savings contributions. The literature suggests that the United States focuses too much on tax subsidies, as opposed to other policies, in order to increase savings. In addition, the literature highlights several ways in which current savings incentives may be unnecessarily complex in ways that limit effectiveness. Although there is a lack of direct evidence on key alternative proposals, the literature suggests that expanding savings "nudges" could be more effective at increasing savings for those who need it. In addition to government policy, employers play an important role in encouraging savings through the provision of payroll-deduction retirement plans with features such as auto-enrollment and auto-escalation, but there is little good evidence on the determinants of employer plan design.

The chapter is organized as follows. Section 10.1 presents a stylized model to organize the analysis of the effects of tax policy on retirement savings, as well as to highlight the empirical parameters that are most important for gauging the success of tax policies. Section 10.2 reviews the rich empirical literature studying retirement savings and tax policy. Section 10.3 analyzes key retirement-related tax policies in light of the empirical evidence from the literature. Section 10.4 concludes.

10.1 CONCEPTUAL FRAMEWORK

In this section, I write down a simple two-type model of savings behavior. The goal of this model is not to capture all aspects of the savings decision but rather to highlight the importance of key parameters that bear on the tax treatment of savings. Importantly, I focus on the determinants of individual savings choice, holding constant savers' access to savings plans. In this simple framework there are three such key parameters: (1) the fraction α of savers who are potentially responsive to tax policy, who we will label as "active"; (2) the elasticity of total savings with respect to the tax subsidy ε, which controls the extent to which individuals increase savings in response to tax subsidies; and (3) the correlation ρ between an individual's propensity to undersave for retirement β_i and the consumption gains in retirement that result from the tax subsidies.

10.1.1 Setup

Individuals live for two periods. They earn a fixed amount W in period 1, which they can either consume or save in one of two risk-free accounts: a retirement account or a taxable savings account. Let r denote the net-of-tax interest rate that individuals earn in the taxable account. The government offers a subsidy ψ that increases the return to saving in the retirement account to $r + \psi$. To simplify notation, we abstract from income and capital gains taxes and let ψ represent the net subsidy to retirement accounts taking all taxes into account. We assume that the subsidy is financed by a tax on future generations, so that the financing has no direct effect on national or private savings. Therefore, the subsidy as a whole has no effect on national savings absent an increase in private savings (i.e., a decrease in consumption) in response to the tax incentive. I also assume that the return r is set exogenously to the model; in practice, any changes in retirement savings due to policy would have only small effects on the national capital stock, and so the returns to capital should not be affected. Finally, the individuals pay no tax in this model, and so here I abstract away from the traditional versus Roth treatment of tax-preferred savings. I return to this distinction in section 10.3.

Let S_i represent the amount that individual i saves in the non-retirement (taxable) savings account. Let P_i denote the amount that individual i contributes to the retirement account. Consumption in the two periods is given by

$$c_{i,1}(S_i, P_i) = W - S_i - P_i \tag{1}$$

$$c_{i,2}(S_i, P_i) = (1+r)S_i + (1+r+\psi).$$

In this simple setting, saving in the retirement account strictly dominates saving in taxable accounts, and hence all individuals would optimally set $S_i = 0$ (or even less than 0 if institutional constraints allow). In practice, retirement accounts are illiquid and cannot be accessed prior to retirement, leading many individuals to save outside retirement accounts despite their tax disadvantage. We model the value of liquidity as a concave benefit $g(S_i)$ of saving in the non-retirement account.[1]

Accounting for the value of liquidity, individuals have utility

$$u(c_{i,1}) + \beta_i \delta u(c_{i,2}) + g(S_i), \tag{2}$$

where $u(c)$ is a smooth, concave function, $\delta < 1$ denotes the individual's rational discount factor, and $\beta_i \leq 1$ denotes the extent to which an individual underweights the future (relative to the society's weight). An individual with $\beta_i = 1$ weights the future the same as society, while individuals with $\beta_i < 1$ place too little weight on the future and will, as a result, save too little. While I assume away any heterogeneity in δ, for the sake of parsimony, I allow β_i to vary across individuals to capture the fact that undersaving may be concentrated among certain subgroups of the population.

In this model, the "irrational" discount factor β_i is the sole driver of savings inadequacy. The most natural explanations for this discrepancy between individual and social discount factors are psychological factors such as myopia (Kaplow 2015) or hyperbolic discounting (e.g., Carroll et al. 2009; Laibson 1997), although there are also others (Kaplow 2011). In these cases, governments simply seek to help individuals maximize their own "experienced" utility, which differs from "decision" utility, and in the case of hyperbolic discounting this is precisely how individuals would want government to act from behind the veil of ignorance.

In practice, there are many other theories for why individuals may undersave that do not rely on individual optimization errors (Feldstein and Liebman 2002). For instance, some arguments focus on the government's inability to commit to social insurance schemes that could leave citizens destitute in retirement (Buchanan 1975; Kotlikoff 1987). Other arguments rely on externalities from savings on productivity through an increase in the capital stock (Feldstein 1974). While the weight of the evidence certainly suggests that psychological factors are the primary driver of savings inadequacy, the results that follow do not depend on which of these micro-foundations prevails.

An alternative justification of tax subsidies for savings is that r is too low due to the presence of capital taxation. A capital tax may be part of an optimal tax system (for instance, in the Mirrlees framework), if higher-ability individuals have a larger preference for savings (Golosov et al. 2013; Gruber and Saez 2002), in which case r would not be too low. But instead if a capital tax is an exogenous part of the tax system then policymakers may seek to increase certain types of savings by increasing returns.[2] It

[1] Gale and Scholz (1994) develop a three-period model in which individuals face uncertainty in the second period, motivating them to keep some assets in a liquid buffer stock. This model can be loosely interpreted as a reduced-form of the Gale and Scholz model.

[2] For instance, political economy may demand a capital income tax due to the concentration of capital income at the top of the income distribution and the desire for redistribution. In such circumstances, it would be consistent (both politically and economically) for policymakers to attempt to increase retirement savings, especially for middle-income families.

is well known in the literature that a constant linear tax on capital income generates a distortion on the intertemporal allocation of consumption that grows exponentially with time. Suppose that τ is the tax rate on capital income; then the post-tax return over one period is $(1-\tau)\, r$, and after N periods grows to $(1-\tau)^N r$. Note that the Euler equation governing the choice of pension savings is that $u'(c_{i,1}) = \beta_i (1 + r + \psi)\, u'(c_{i,2})$. Therefore functional form aside, β_i too low and r too low are isomorphic rationales for government policies that increase saving.[3]

Active versus Passive Savers. Another potentially important feature of savings policy is savers who are inattentive to or otherwise choose savings without regard to the particular savings policies in place. To model this in a simple way, suppose that there are two types of agents, active savers and passive savers, who differ in the way they choose S_i and P_i. In particular, let $P_i = \theta_i\, P_i^*(\psi) + (1-\theta_i)\, \overline{P}_i$, where $\theta_i \in \{0, 1\}$ denotes whether savers are active or passive. Active savers ($\theta_i = 1$) choose S_i and P_i to maximize utility (2) given ψ as in the neoclassical model, so that $P_i = \theta_i P_i^*(\psi)$.

Passive savers ($\theta_i = 0$) set retirement contributions at an exogenous level $P_i = \overline{P}_i$ that does not vary with ψ. Again, there are several models in the literature for why individuals' retirement savings plans are insensitive to incentives, such as fixed costs of adjustment that generate inertia, hyperbolic discounting that leads to procrastination in updating plans (Carroll et al. 2009), or a lack of information. Once again, the results that follow do not depend upon which of these micro-foundations drives passive behavior, and I therefore do not specify a particular model of passive choice. Let $a = E[\theta_i]$ denote the fraction of active savers.

Regardless of how passive savers make choices, they must satisfy the budget constraint in (1), which can be rewritten as

$$C_{i,1} + S_i = W - \overline{P}_i \tag{3}$$

that is, consumption plus taxable saving equals income net of pension contributions. I assume that passive savers choose S_i (or, equivalently, $c_{i,1}$) as a function of net income $W - \overline{P}_i$, so that changes in retirement savings policies affect behavior in period 1 only if they affect retirement contributions. As before, I do not posit a specific model of how passive savers choose S_i. Instead, we show how the impacts of government policy depend upon the way in which passive savers adjust $c_{i,1}$ and S_i when net income changes.

10.1.2 Results

10.1.2.1 Tax Subsidies for Savings

Consider now the effect of the tax subsidies for savings ψ on behavior. By assumption, tax subsidies impact neither pension contributions $\overline{P}_i$ nor total savings $(\overline{P}_i + S_i)$ of

[3] To see this, note that one could rewrite the tax subsidy for savings as a proportional increase in the gross return, so that the return on pension savings was $(1 + r)\,\psi$, in which case a proportional reduction in β is exactly isomorphic to a proportional decrease in $(1 + r)$.

passive savers. The interesting economics therefore lie in studying the behavior of the active savers.

The effects of an increase in the subsidy on pension savings for active savers occur in two ways, as is well known in the literature (Bernheim 2002; Gale and Scholz 1994). First, tax subsidies reduce the price of consumption in retirement, $c_{i,2}$, relative to consumption while working, $c_{i,1}$, which also leads to an increase in pension savings. Second, the tax subsidy increases lifetime wealth, which in turn may increase consumption earlier in life and in fact reduce pension savings. To see the intuition behind this latter effect, consider an extreme case where ψ is very large, for instance 1 million. In this case, an individual would only need to save a few dollars in order to guarantee a rich and comfortable retirement; very soon the saver would hit diminishing marginal utility of consumption in retirement and decide to stop saving and instead to spend the money today. Therefore the effect of tax subsidies on pension savings is theoretically ambiguous. I denote the parameter measuring the combination of these two effects as $\varepsilon = d(P + S)/d\psi$ for active savers. This parameter is closely related to the elasticity of intertemporal substitution (EIS) in the broader consumption literature.

Combining across the two types of savers, the total impact of tax subsidies on savings, which I denote by Δ_{TAX}, can be written as:

$$\Delta_{TAX} = \alpha\varepsilon. \tag{4}$$

Intuitively, this net force combines two separate effects; first, the fraction of savers a who are active and thus respond at all to tax subsidies in the first place, and the extent to which active savers increase or decrease savings as a result of the tax subsidy ε. These two parameters a and ε will therefore be critical to estimate empirically in order to assess the impact of tax subsidies on savings.

Note that we can also decompose the responsiveness parameter $\varepsilon = dP/d\psi * d(S + P)/dP$, where $d(S + P)/dP$ is a pass-through rate—that is, what fraction of an increase in pension savings driven by the tax subsidy is reflected in total savings.[4] While the direct effect of any particular policy $dP/d\psi$ may vary depending on the particular tax incentive, the pass-through rate is a relatively stable parameter that permits comparison across settings. Note further that for pass-through equal to or less than one (which is the sensible case) the direct effect of tax subsidies on pension savings provides an upper bound on the true effect on total savings. Intuitively, this is because tax subsidies may induce shifting from taxable savings into pension savings, which, of course, has no effect on total savings. Indeed, one can construct cases where $dP/d\psi > 0$ but $\varepsilon < 0$.

It is also important to consider the distributional effects of tax subsidies. Like many tax expenditures, the tax preference for retirement savings redistributes income from certain demographic groups to others. However, it is very difficult to assess the

[4] Pass-through $d(S + P)/dP$ is also mathematically equivalent to one minus "offset," which is dS/dP.

impact of this redistribution in isolation, since what really matters is the transfers from the whole tax system. Such an analysis is beyond the scope of this chapter. What has received less attention, though, is the extent to which tax subsidies help those individuals who are not saving enough for retirement. For individuals with $\beta_i = 1$, savings is sufficient without government intervention, and government intervention to increase savings is not just unnecessary but also wasteful, since it may distort savings choices. In contrast, individuals for whom $\beta_i < 1$ save too little, and government policies that increase savings can yield first order gains in welfare.

The effect of tax subsidies on consumption in retirement can, to first order, be written as

$$\frac{dc_{i,2}}{d\psi} = (r + \psi) * \theta_i \varepsilon + P_i \tag{5}$$

There are two distinct effects, captured in the two terms in the equation 5. First, tax subsidies can increase consumption in retirement by encouraging additional private savings, if $\theta_i \varepsilon > 0$. Note that this first force is only relevant for active savers who might potentially respond to the tax subsidies if $\varepsilon > 0$. Second, tax subsidies have the mechanical effect of paying out an additional return on existing pension savings. This second effect operates on both active and passive savers who have pension savings; however, it is less helpful for those individuals with $\beta_i < 1$, since the exact problem was that such workers saved too little (and perhaps nothing at all, if $\beta_i = 0$ in the first place). Therefore, the final key parameter in assessing tax subsidies for retirement savings is $1 - \rho = 1 - Corr\ (\theta_i, \beta_i)$, which is the extent to which those individuals who undersave the most are in fact those who are most responsive to tax subsidies.

10.1.2.2 Savings Nudges

Alongside tax subsidies, governments frequently attempt to influence savings behavior through mandates or nudges, which are elements of choice architecture—for instance, automatic enrollment or active decision policies—that change savings without changing the budget set. As I will show, a similar set of parameters as identified in section 10.1.2.1 for tax subsidies will determine the efficacy of nudges in increasing savings.

To incorporate nudges into the model, I simply decompose pension savings into nudged savings N_i and then revisions to the nudge $P_i' = P_i - N_i$, so that total savings is $P_i' + N_i + S_i$. The budget constraint (Equation 1) becomes:

$$c_{i,1}(S_i, P_i) = W - S_i - P_i' - N_i \tag{6}$$

$$c_{i,2}(S_i, P_i) = (1 + r)S_i + (1 + r + \psi)(P_i' + N_i).$$

I assume that active savers choose their saving and consumption in the standard way, while passive savers choose $P_i' = 0$ and so just go with the nudge. Note that individual revisions P_i' and savings nudges N_i are perfect substitutes in this model. One can also model mandates in a similar way, except that total savings equals $P_i' + M_i + S_i$, where M_i is mandated savings and P_i is pension savings in addition to the mandate. For mandates, I assume that passive individuals choose other pension savings $\overline{P}_i$ without reference to government policy, and therefore without regard to the mandate.

Consider now how savings nudges or mandates affect behavior. For active individuals, who rationally set P_i without regard to the nudge, the value of the nudge has no effect on either pension savings or total savings. (In the case of a mandated savings, this also applies for individuals who would choose to save more than the mandate.) Therefore (in contrast with tax subsidies), it is active savers who are essentially unaffected by nudges or mandates. Passive savers, on the other hand, do not change voluntary pension savings beyond the nudge (or ignore the mandate). Therefore, passive savers increase total pension savings dollar-for-dollar with the government mandates. Nudges are more complicated, since passive savers who would otherwise have saved $P_i > N_i$ would decrease savings, but in practice nudges seem to also increase savings almost unambiguously.

Importantly, though, it is ambiguous (as before) whether total savings will increase or not in response to nudges and mandates. Because total pension savings have increased, the budget constraint implies that either taxable savings or consumption (or both) must decrease to reflect the drop in disposable income. Therefore a key parameter in assessing the effect of mandates is $\varepsilon^N = d[P_i' + S_i + N_i]/dN_i$, the extent to which nudged increases in pension savings result in increased total savings for passive individuals.

Combining the responses for the two types of savers, the total impact of nudges on savings, which I denote by Δ_{NUDGE}, can be written as

$$\Delta_{NUDGE} = (1-\alpha)\varepsilon^N. \tag{7}$$

Intuitively, this net force combines two separate effects that are essentially the opposite to those in section 10.1.2.1 for tax subsidies; first, the fraction of savers $1 - \alpha$ who are passive and thus respond at all to nudges or mandates in the first place, and the extent to which passive savers increase or decrease savings as a result of the nudge ε^N.

Mandates, in particular, also provide an opportunity to estimate α directly by studying $d(P' + M)\ /dM$, which is the effect of mandates on total pension contributions. To see this, note that the perfect substitutability between M_i and P_i' implies that $d(P' + M)/dM = 0$ for active savers, while the assumptions of the model imply that $d(P' + M)/dM = 1$ for passive savers. Therefore, in aggregate, $d(P' + M)/dM = \alpha * 0 + (1 - \alpha) * 1 = 1 - \alpha$. We can estimate α as one minus the pass-through rate of mandates to total savings.

The correlation $\rho = Corr\ (\theta_i, \beta_i)$ will also reveal the extent to which nudges and mandates produce favorable distributional effects. When active savers are those in most need of additional savings, so when ρ is negative, nudges will be ineffective;

when passive savers face the largest savings deficits, so when ρ is large and positive, nudges effectively target individuals with inadequate savings. This demonstrates how the conditions under which saving mandates will be effective—that is when α is low, ε^N is large, and ρ is large—are essentially the opposite of those where tax subsidies will be effective.

10.2 EMPIRICAL EVIDENCE

The stylized framework in section 10.1 shows that there are three key parameters that determine the efficacy of tax subsidies and mandates at increasing savings: (1) the effect of tax subsidies on total savings for active savers, as well as the same parameter for mandates on passive savers; (2) the fraction of active savers; and (3) the correlation between passivity and undersaving across individuals. I now provide a critical review of the literature to generate estimates of these crucial parameters. Table 10.1 provides a summary of some of the key papers in this literature which I discuss in section 10.2.

10.2.1 Elasticity of Savings to Interest Rate Subsidies

10.2.1.1 Evidence from Tax Subsidies

There is a large literature studying the relationship between tax subsidies and savings. The primary challenge in all of these papers is to credibly identify increases in savings caused by tax subsidies, as separate from differences in savings driven instead by a taste for saving, differences in wealth or disposable income, or differences in the need for current expenditure. The ideal design would exploit large changes in tax policy, which would be credibly exogenous to individual circumstances. Alternatively, researchers could exploit cross-sectional differences in eligibility for tax subsidies, provided that one can identify credibly exogenous variation in eligibility, which has proven quite difficult in practice.

Another challenge faced by this literature is limited data quality. Analysis of savings requires a comprehensive measure of both the stock of wealth and annual savings or dissavings flows, including such variables as credit card debt, home equity or mortgage debt, bank balances, retirement account contributions, and other stock market holdings (e.g., Charles Schwab account). Unfortunately, these data are not present in many survey data sets, at least in a complete way, or measured in a very noisy way. In addition, these variables are traditionally not all present together in administrative data, since the IRS (for instance) maintains no comprehensive records of wealth or debt. As a result, even in more recent years, many researchers have instead relied on much smaller and noisier survey data sets. This limits the scope of feasible identification strategies, since empirical strategies that focus too tightly on a narrowly defined treatment and control group lose power.

Much of the early literature focuses on Individual Retirement Accounts (IRAs), which were first permitted in the United States to individuals without pensions in

Table 10.1 Summary of empirical papers on retirement tax incentives

Study	*Main Question/ Study's Goal*	*Data and Design*	*Result*
		Papers on the Effect of Tax Subsidies	
Engen, Gale, and Scholz 1994	Studies the effects of saving incentives on private and national saving using empirical and simulation analyses.	Data on 401(k) participation from the SIPP, and data on IRA participants come from the IRS-Michigan Tax Panel. Between 1986–1991, 401(k) participants had expanded saving incentives and IRA participants had reduced savings opportunities. The authors compare wealth measures between 401(k) participants and IRA participants who are not eligible for a 401(k), to estimate the effect of 401(k) plans on private savings.	401(k) plans have not stimulated private saving or wealth. IRAs, 401(k) plans, and other retirement saving plans are, to some extent, substitutes in households' portfolios. A small proportion of IRA contributions represents new private saving; however, coupled with the revenue losses created, which is offset by tax revenue losses for no net national savings.
Venti and Wise 1990	Examines if IRAs contributed to new US savings.	Data come from the Consumer Expenditure Survey (CES) 1980– 1985. Examine the correlation between IRA contributions and other savings, controlling for observables such as past saving and current income. The assumption required is that observables fully control for heterogeneity in taste for savings.	IRA and non-IRA savings are positively correlated, suggesting that IRA saving represents net new saving.

Feenberg and Skinner 1989	Studies differences in the behavior of individuals with varying take-up of IRA accounts over 1982–1986.	The authors use the IRS-University of Michigan taxpayer sample for income tax returns during 1980– 1984 to estimate the correlations between IRA contributions and other types of saving, controlling for observables. The assumption required is that observables fully control for heterogeneity in taste for savings.	IRA and non-IRA savings are positively correlated, suggesting that IRA saving represents mostly new saving, with some reshuffling through increased borrowing. In addition, IRA participants did not take full advantage of its provisions, suggesting that a lack of public information about IRA limits led to underutilization of IRAs.
Gale and Scholz 1994	Examines the effects of Individual Retirement Accounts (IRAs) on private and national saving.	The authors construct a model of dynamic utility maximization that generates closed-form equations for IRA and other saving, and estimate this model using data come from the 1983–1986 Survey of Consumer Finances (SCF) and the University of Michigan/Ernst and Young Tax Research Data Base.	Of the increased IRA contributions that would have resulted from increases in contribution limits, roughly 2% would represent net additions to national saving, if the accompanying tax cut were entirely saved. If one half of the tax cut were consumed in the first year, this estimate falls to −14%.

(*continued*)

Table 10.1 Continued

Study	*Main Question/ Study's Goal*	*Data and Design*	*Result*
Poterba, Venti, and Wise 1994	Studies the extent to which 401(k) contributions represent new saving.	Data are total assets of 401(k) participants over time from the SIPP (1984–1986). The authors: (1) examine whether differences in length of exposure to 401(k) plans affect savings, by comparing savings across demographically similar samples from different years (1984 vs. 1987), and (2) exploit exogeneity of 401(k) eligibility (determined by employers) by comparing saving among eligible and ineligible individuals, holding income constant.	401(k) plan contributions represent a net addition to saving, rather than transfers from other stores of wealth or displacement of other forms of saving. Individuals in the "treatment" group of both empirical strategies did not have lower IRA assets or other savings balances as a result of 401(k) exposure or eligibility.
Poterba, Venti, and Wise 1995	Describes patterns of participation in 401(k) plans, contrast these patterns with IRA participation, and evaluate the net impact of 401(k) contributions on personal saving.	Using data from SIPP (1984, 1987, 1991), the authors: (1) compare the financial assets of families who are eligible for 401(k) saving with the assets of those who are not eligible (for a given income), and (2) consider the change over time in the assets of similar groups of savers.	Authors find little evidence that 401(k) contributions substitute for other forms of personal saving, including IRA contributions. Results suggest that the promotion of savings plans may have an important effect on their use, and that an up-front tax deduction may be an important determinant of contribution behavior.

Benjamin 2003	Compares 401(k) eligible and ineligible households' wealth to estimate impact on private and national savings.	Data comes from 1991 SIPP. Improves on previous research (e.g., Engel 2000) by using propensity score subclasses instead of income-brackets to control for observed household characteristics; and by adjusting dependent variable (household wealth) to reduce measurement error caused by DB Contributions missing from the SIPP data.	On average, about 50% of 401(k) balances represent new private savings, and about 25% represent new national savings. Responses to eligibility vary considerably: households who normally save the most and who are most educated contribute funds they would have saved anyway.
Gelber 2011	Investigates the effect of 401(k) eligibility on saving.	Uses the 1996 SIPP. Exploits changes in eligibility due to the expiry of initial waiting periods that limit enrollment for new employees. Change in savings from Year 1 to 2 of households who are initially ineligible for 401(K) but later become eligible, is compared to the change in saving from Year 1 to Year 2 of those who are always eligible.	401(k) eligibility raises 401(k) contributions substantially. There is no evidence that eligibility impacts savings in other financial assets or significantly increases liabilities, but the confidence intervals are large enough that substantial changes in other assets or liabilities cannot be ruled out.

(*continued*)

Table 10.1 Continued

Study	*Main Question/ Study's Goal*	*Data and Design*	*Result*
Chetty, Friedman, Leth- Petersen, Nielsen, and Olsen 2014	Studies the effect of a reduction in tax subsidies on pension savings and total savings.	Uses administrative tax data on the full Danish population, including third-party reported data on total savings and wealth. Uses a difference-in-difference approach to analyze the effects of a rate limitation on the deductibility of retirement savings that effected taxpayers in the top bracket but not below.	The rate limitation causes a sharp drops in retirement savings, but total savings fall by only 1% as much. The confidence interval can rule out an effect larger than 28%. These responses are driven by 19% of savers; the other 81% are non- responsive to the tax change.
Duflo, Gale, Liebman, Orszag, and Saez 2006	Analyzes the effect of matching incentives to taxpayers on participation and contributions to IRAs.	A large, randomized field experiment carried out on H&R Block clients, predominantly low- and middle-income neighborhoods in the St. Louis metro area. Taxpayers were randomly offered {50%, 20%, 0%} match rate for contributions to an IRA account.	Take-up rates were 3% for the control group, 8% for those getting a 20% match, and 14% for the 50% match group. Average IRA contributions (including those who decided not to put money in the IRA, but excluding the "matches") for the 20% and 50% match groups were four and seven times higher than the control group, respectively.

Engelhardt and Kumar 2007	Studies the effect of firm match rates on 401(k) contributions.	The authors develop a model of 401(k) savings including matching, and estimate the effect of employer vs. employee contribution changes on savings, using data from the first wave of HRS and linked to SSA data (including W2s), over 1951–91.	An increase in the match rate by 25 cents per dollar of employee contribution raises 401(k) participation by 5 percentage points. The parametric and semi-parametric estimates for saving indicate that an increase in the match rate by 25 cents per dollar of employee contribution raises 401(k) saving by $365 (in 1991 dollars).
Papers on the Effect of Mandates and Nudges			
Madrian and Shea 2001	Analyzes the impact of automatic enrollment on 401(k) savings behavior.	Data are from a Fortune 500 company in the health care and insurance industry, which implemented a change in 401(k) enrollment and eligibility on April 1, 1998.	401(k) participation is 50 percentage points higher under automatic enrollment. In addition, a substantial fraction of 401(k) participants hired under automatic enrollment retain both the default contribution rate and fund allocation even though few employees hired before automatic enrollment picked this particular outcome.

(*continued*)

Table 10.1 Continued

Study	*Main Question/ Study's Goal*	*Data and Design*	*Result*
Card and Ransom 2011	Studies the effect of employer non-elective contributions on individual contributions to retirement accounts for university faculty.	Using a data set combining ten years of salary and pension information for older faculty at a sample of colleges and universities with TIAA-CREF pensions, the authors test for differential responses in employee savings to changes in mandated employee vs. employer contributions.	Supplementary savings are reduced by 60 to 80 cents per dollar of employee contributions to the regular pension, but only by one-half as much per dollar of employer contributions.
Attanasio and Brugiavini 2003	Studies the substitutability between private savings and public pensions in Italy	The authors exploit differential effects of a 1992 Italian pension reform on individuals belonging to different birth cohorts and occupational groups. They use a difference-in-difference approach to estimate increase in saving rates as a result of a reduction in pension wealth. Data comes from the Survey on Household Income and Wealth.	Pension wealth is a substitute for private saving, though estimates of pass-through vary greatly across the age distribution in ways that depend strongly on specification. Average pass-through coefficients are about 0.4.
Attanasio and Rohwedder 2003	Studies the substitutability between private savings and public pensions in the United Kingdom	The authors exploit a set of UK pension reforms as natural experiments to investigate the relationship between public pensions and discretionary private savings. They use a life-cycle model to scale the effects on each household depending on the effects on future wealth and timing of the reforms. Data comes from the Family Expenditure Survey.	Results indicate a considerable degree of substitutability (i.e., crowd- out) of 0.65–0.75 for private savings and earnings-related pensions, but essentially no crowd-out for the flat- rate pensions.

Chetty, Friedman, Leth- Petersen, Nielsen, and Olsen 2014	Studies the effect of savings mandates and employer non-elective contributions on pension savings and total savings.	Uses administrative tax data on the full Danish population, including third-party reported data on total savings and wealth. Uses changes in employer contributions as workers move between firms in an event study design. Also uses a regression discontinuity around a threshold for mandatory 1% contribution to a new government-sponsored account.	For each dollar in mandated savings from employers, individuals increase total pension savings by 95 cents and total savings by 77 cents. Government mandates generate full pass-through to total savings, but the effect is imprecisely estimated.
	Papers on Heterogeneity of Effects		
Engen and Gale 2000	Examines the impact of 401(k) plans on household wealth, allowing the impact to vary over time and earnings groups.	The authors provide a new econometric specification, and use data patterns to reject modeling constraints posed by previous authors. Data come from SIPP, 1987 and 1991.	The effects of 401(k)s on household wealth vary significantly by earnings level. 401(k)s held by groups with low earnings, who hold a small portion of 401(k) balances, are more likely to represent additions to net wealth than 401(k)s held by high-earning groups, who hold the bulk of 401(k) assets. Between 0 and 30% of 401(k) balances represent net additions to private saving in the sample period.

(continued)

Table 10.1 (*Continued*)

Study	*Main Question/ Study's Goal*	*Data and Design*	*Result*
Chernozhukov and Hansen 2004	Studies impact of 401(k) plans on wealth by analyzing the effect of 401(k) participation on the entire wealth distribution, instead of just the mean or median.	Authors use the 1991 SIPP. 401(k) eligibility is used as an instrument for 401(k) participation. Authors use a Quantile Treatment Estimator (QTE) to analyze heterogeneity in the effects of 401(k) savings on total savings.	Participation in 401(k)s increases total wealth and that there is little substitution between financial assets in 401(k)s and other financial assets. In addition, the results suggest that there is substitution between assets held in 401(k) s and other components of wealth in the upper tail of the wealth distribution, but that most financial assets held in 401(k)s in the lower tail of the distribution represent new savings.

1974. These accounts remained quite small until Congress extended eligibility to all workers in 1981, before restricting access again for higher income households in the Tax Reform Act of 1986 (TRA86). It was therefore in just the narrow window 1982–1986 that IRA contributions boomed, even accounting for roughly 20% of all personal savings in 1986. Many papers in the early literature focused on whether this five-year explosion of IRA contributions represented new savings. Some papers focused on the changes in eligibility in 1982 and 1986 (e.g., Engen, Gale, and Scholz 1994; Joines and Manegold 1995), while others looked at cross-sectional comparisons between the behavior of individuals with varying take-up of IRA accounts between 1982 and 1986 (e.g., Attanasio and DeLeire 2002; Feenberg and Skinner 1989; Gale and Scholz 1994; Venti and Wise 1990). Unfortunately, limitations on data and econometric methods available at the time led to a series of results that, by modern standards, are not reliable (Bernheim 2002).

Another branch of the early literature focused on 401(k) accounts, which gained in popularity very quickly following TRA86. The 401(k) accounts are in many ways a more attractive policy to study. For instance, 401(k)s feature much higher contribution limits—in 2015, $18,000 for individuals and $53,000 for the combination of individual and employer contributions—that are hit by only a small fraction of individuals. In addition, unlike IRAs, which feature essentially universal eligibility (conditional on income), 401(k) accounts operate under ERISA through a worker's employer. Even today there remain vast differences in access within populations of essentially similar individuals, which might provide proper identification for research. Finally, 401(k)s often differ across employers—for instance, in the employer matching provisions or in the choice architecture—and I return to consider these elements below.

The early literature on 401(k)s—most notably Poterba, Venti, and Wise (1994, 1995)—struggled with a number of critical data issues that made them rely on strong assumptions about the nature of selection into 401(k) eligibility. For instance, these papers attempt to use policy changes in TRA86 as an instrument for eligibility, but they do so using the Survey of Information and Program Participation (SIPP), which provides only repeated cross-sections of data, generating a number of econometric problems (Bernheim 2002). In another analysis, these authors made the very strong assumption that 401(k) eligibility was exogenous, conditional on observables, and found essentially all of 401(k) contributions were new savings. More recently, Benjamin (2003) used a propensity score approach to control more nonparametrically for observables and found that roughly 50% of 401(k) contributions represented new savings. Although more reliable than previous estimates, this analysis still relies critically on the assumption that observable controls are sufficient to eliminate bias, as opposed to the more preferred approach of identifying credibly exogenous variation in eligibility.

Gelber et al. (2011) instead seek to identify credibly exogenous variation in 401(k) eligibility that does not rely on observable controls. They exploit the fact that some companies prevent new employees from contributing to 401(k)s until they have worked at the company for a minimum period (e.g., one year). They find that eligibility significantly increases 401(k) contributions and find no offsetting reduction in other savings, but these latter estimates are quite imprecise and do not rule out significant shifting of assets. Setting aside the lack of precision with the estimates, Gelber's approach raised another concern of interpretation. The variation in 401(k) eligibility is temporary and expected, since workers know that they will gain eligibility soon. These estimates may therefore include significant shifting of 401(k) contributions from one period to another, leading to an overestimate of the effect of eligibility on savings and an underestimate of the extent to which 401(k) saving crowds out other asset accumulation. In contrast, the best identification for the policy-relevant effect of tax subsidies would be a permanent yet unexpected change.

Chetty et al. (2014b) analyze such a permanent unexpected change using administrative data from Denmark. Denmark has a similar retirement savings system to the United States, with a social security system providing a consumption floor for all elderly, plus both employer- and employee-funded tax-preferred pensions that supplement social security for middle- and high-income households. Denmark also has similar national savings rates to the United States, more broadly suggesting that responses to savings policy in Denmark can bear on such policies in the United States (Chetty et al. 2014a). Unlike in the United States, Denmark tax authorities receive third-party information reports on household wealth due to the one-time existence of a wealth tax (which had been phased out before their study period). They exploit a tax reform in 1999 that reduced the tax subsidy with lower deductibility of retirement savings contributions for individuals in the top tax bracket, but not lower down in the income distribution. Using a difference-in-difference approach, they demonstrate both a significant decrease in contributions to retirement accounts and also offsetting increases in other savings. On net, they estimate that only 1% of changes in retirement account contributions represent changes to total savings. Their estimates are also quite precise; they can rule out pass-through more than 28%.

The literature points to a relatively low pass-through of pension savings to total savings. This limits the effectiveness of tax subsidies that increase pension savings, but other work suggests that tax subsidies may have quite limited power to increase pension contributions in the first place. Freed from the need for data on total savings, papers in this literature have used large administrative data sets and correspondingly higher standards for identification. For instance, Duflo et al. (2006) implement a randomized experiment at H&R Block, offering taxpayers randomly chosen match rates to contribute to a type of IRA. They find that a 25% match rate increases participation by roughly 5 percentage points, but increasing the match rate to 50% has no marginal effect. Engelhardt and Kumar (2007) study similarly high-quality variation in company match rates within 401(k) plans, also estimating that a 25 percentage point increase in the match rate (e.g., 25% to 50%) increases participation in 401(k) by roughly 5 percentage points. Choi et al. (2002, 2004) and Choi, Laibson, and Madrian (2006) also study variation in match rates within and across a select number of companies and reach similar conclusions on the effectiveness of matching contributions for increasing participation and contribution rates.

In sum, then, the literature provides a wide variety of estimates that differ greatly in method. On balance, however, the most reliable estimates suggest that pass-through from pension savings to total savings is very low. Furthermore, the initial effect on pension savings may not be large either. Combining these two effects, I conclude that ε is likely to be quite small.

10.2.2 Effects of Nudges and Mandates on Savings

Despite the very large literature studying the effect of tax subsidies on total savings, very few papers examine this question for mandates or nudges. Most of the literature focuses solely on the effects of such policies on retirement savings contributions, finding very large effects of these policies on the retirement savings account that include the nudge. For instance, Madrian and Shea (2001) find that default enrollments can increase the participation rate within a 401(k) plan by 50 percentage points relative to employers with slightly more tenure who did not face a default. Choi et al. (2004) also showed large effects, but find that the effect shrinks over time. At one level, it was a striking finding that such policies had any effect at all, as they signal significant deviations from the rational model. As discussed in section 10.1, such findings are necessary but not sufficient for these policies to increase savings.

Card and Ransom (2011) took a first step toward total savings by studying substitution patterns across different retirement savings accounts. They show that academics moving from one university to another often experience very large changes in the employer-provided pensions, but that employee contributions do not come close to offsetting these differences. In particular, they find that differences in employer contributions have very little effect on individual retirement contributions. This suggests complete pass-through of mandated saving to total retirement savings and is suggestive that pass-through might be similarly large for total savings. Chetty et al. (2014b) use a similar design to study pass-through to total savings. Using individuals who move between all different firms in Denmark, they show that approximately 80% of mandated savings from the employer ends up as an increase in total savings. This estimate is also quite precise, and the authors can rule out pass-through less than 72%.

Other papers study changes in mandates for savings through reforms to government pensions. For instance, a number of papers study the effects of changes to mandatory government pension schemes on private household savings in European countries (Attanasio and Brugiavini 2003; Attanasio and Rohwedder 2003). These papers find that, as pension wealth decreases, households increase private savings, which would imply crowd-out of mandated savings. These results rely on assumptions about age-specific trends in savings, however, that by modern standards are rather strong. More recently, Chetty et al. (2014b) also study a Danish government mandate that workers above an income threshold deposit 1% of earnings in a special savings account. Using a regression discontinuity around this income threshold, they show that this 1% contribution was entirely new savings, although the estimates are quite imprecise (they cannot rule out pass-through of just 65%). In sum, in contrast to the much larger literature on the effect of tax subsidies, this smaller literature paints a more consistent picture: the effect of mandates on total savings ε^N is large, with the pass-through of increases in mandated savings to total savings closer to 100% than 50%.

10.2.3 Active versus Passive Savers

10.2.3.1 Fraction of Active Savers

The second crucial parameter is the fraction of savers who are active versus passive. As noted in section 10.1, one way to estimate this number is by looking at the pass-through of mandated savings to total pension savings. The pass-through cited from Card and Ransom (2011) suggests that $a = 1 - 67\% = 33\%$. Chetty et al. (2014b) estimate the pass-through of mandated employer savings to total pension savings at 95%, so that $a = 1 - 95\% = 5\%$.

One criticism of these estimates is that savers may be differentially passive with respect to tax subsidies and nudges. Chetty et al. (2014b) therefore develop an alternative estimator for a using behavior from changes in tax subsidies alone. The key to this approach is to note that all active savers with positive pension savings must strictly prefer to change their contributions following an increase in the tax subsidy. To see this, note that such savers will allocate their savings between taxable and pension accounts by balancing the higher returns from the tax subsidy against the value of liquidity from taxable savings. An increase in the tax subsidies further increases the returns to savings in the pension account, while (before reallocation) the value of taxable savings remains the same. Therefore pension contributions must increase, at least due to this reallocation effect (if not also because of an increase in total savings).[5] The fraction of savers who do not respond at all to a change in the tax subsidy is therefore an alternative estimate of the fraction of passive savers. Chetty et al. (2014b) implement this estimator when studying the reduction in deductibility of pension contributions in Denmark. Among current savers (that is, excluding those not making any contributions), they find only 19% adjust their savings rates at all, while the remaining 81% do nothing. This provides an estimate of $\alpha = 19\%$ that is specific to tax subsidies. The similarity to the mandate-based measure of α also suggests that this may be a relatively stable parameter across settings that is quite small.

10.2.3.2 Correlation between Responsiveness and Undersaving

A number of papers also study the correlation between responsiveness to government policies and undersaving. Undersaving is difficult to measure directly, and so most of this literature uses demographic characteristics such as education and income to proxy for undersaving (where poorer and less educated individuals have larger undersaving problems). In one recent paper, Beshears et al. (2015a) study heterogeneity in the effects of default settings. This effort is more difficult than it might seem because

[5] It is theoretically possible that individuals do not respond at all if income effects exactly cancel out price effects, but this is a knife-edge case that is rejected unambiguously by the data.

different types of households may prefer different contribution rates, even in the absence of default settings. But adjusting for this potential confound, the authors find that low-income households are significantly more likely to be swayed by the default. In this setting it is not clear that lower-income households have larger savings inadequacy, so these results are intriguing but difficult to interpret. Chetty et al. (2014b) also investigate heterogeneity in the fraction of active savers. They find that wealthier and more educated individuals (but not higher income individuals, conditional on wealth) were significantly more likely to be active savers. This evidence collectively suggests that $\rho > 0$, that is the individuals who suffer the largest savings deficit also are least likely to be active.

A different literature has explored heterogeneity in the responsiveness of total savings to tax subsidies. Using repeated cross-sections from the SIPP, Engen and Gale (2000) estimate than 401(k) contributions are more likely to represent new savings for lower income households but a reallocation of savings for higher income households. Chernozhukov and Hansen (2004) use a Quantile Treatment Estimator (QTE) to study heterogeneity in the 1991 SIPP. These authors find that the pension savings increases from 401(k) eligibility generated new wealth primarily for poor households, while mainly driving substitution from other sources of wealth for richer households. Although the underlying identification in these studies is somewhat weaker due to the lack of plausibly exogenous variation in tax subsidies (as discussed in section 10.2), the results suggest a correlation between ε, the effect of tax subsidies on total savings, and β. Although the model above does not explicitly discuss such a correlation, it would increase the efficiency of tax subsidies all else equal, since it would target the savings effects better (similar to a negative correlation $\rho < 0$ between passivity and savings inadequacy).

10.3 ANALYSIS OF TAX POLICIES ON RETIREMENT

10.3.1 General Tax Preferences for Retirement Savings

The most prominent tax policy to promote retirement savings is the series of tax preferences that apply to various retirement savings accounts, including IRAs, 401(k) s, and other retirement accounts. Contributions to such accounts are not only fully tax-deductible but are also "above the line" deductions, in the sense that they directly reduce adjusted gross income and so are not subject to various limitations on deductions present in the code. Although defined benefit accruals do not directly appear in the individual tax statement, these same tax preferences effectively apply to those retirement savings as well (setting aside some details of corporate accounting issues). In 2014, the Joint Committee on Taxation (JCT) estimated these tax preferences to cost \$146 billion per year (about 0.85% of GDP), and they are projected to grow over the coming decade to more than 1% of GDP. Figure 10.3 shows that the retirement tax expenditure is also highly concentrated in the top tail of the income distribution; CBO (2013) has estimated that two-thirds of the money spent goes to the top 20% of the income distribution, and more than one-third of the benefit to the top 5%. This

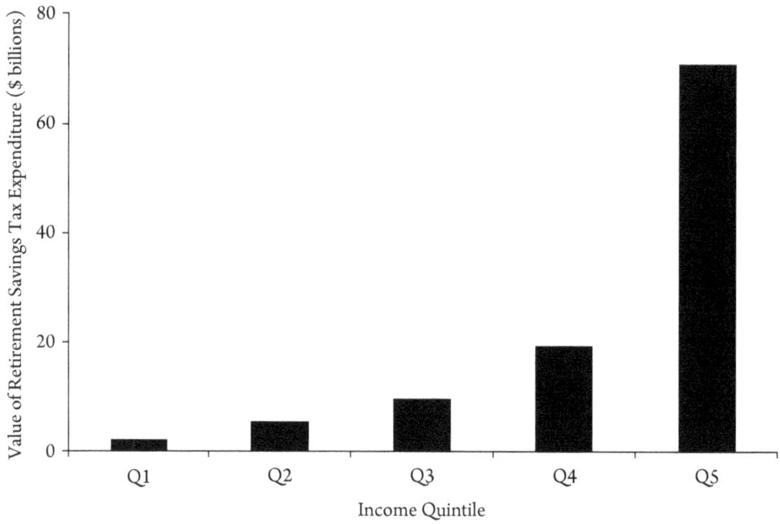

Figure 10.3 Distribution of tax expenditure for retirement savings across income quintiles

distribution is the result not only of higher levels of savings at higher incomes but also of the fact that a tax deduction provides a larger value per dollar saved to richer households, who pay higher marginal tax rates on both earned and capital income.

The parameters estimated in the empirical literature on retirement suggest that this large subsidy may not be effective, since each of the three parameters that measure this effect are quite small. First, the literature suggests that the effect of tax subsidies on total savings ε is not large. This is both because of a limited initial effect of tax subsidies on pension contributions, but more importantly because any increases in pension contributions do not translate into large effects on total savings. Second, the literature suggests that most savers, perhaps 80%–85%, are passive, so that $\alpha = 0.2$. Because tax subsidies rely on active savers to respond by increasing savings, a low value of α implies that relatively few individuals base savings decisions on tax subsidies to begin with. Third, the literature suggests that the correlation between savings deficits and inattention to tax subsidies ρ is positive. This implies that the particular households that are most attentive to tax subsidies are not those most in need of government support in increasing savings. There is also weaker evidence in the literature that the pass-through of pension contributions to total savings is higher for poor households, which is a point in favor of the targeting efficiency of tax subsidies. Importantly, these effects have primarily been estimated in a range around the current scope of the tax incentives; while this evidence suggests that cutting the tax incentive roughly in half would do little to reduce savings, we have essentially no evidence on the effects of completely eliminating the subsidy.

Outside of the framework discussed in section 10.1, there are also other arguments in favor of the tax subsidy. For instance, a number of authors have argued that the illiquidity of retirement accounts is critical, lest households withdraw much of the money before retirement (Munnell, Webb, et al. 2015). Theoretically, the tax subsidy might be necessary in order to compensate consumers ex ante for their use of artificially illiquid accounts. It is probably true that individuals do need some tax subsidy to make retirement accounts "a good deal," but for savers with higher marginal tax rates (who receive most of the tax expenditure) this subsidy is far larger than necessary solely for this purpose.

Another important caveat for this analysis is that it studies the individual response of savers, holding fixed the institutions through which savers access retirement accounts. But it is possible that changing the tax subsidy could alter those institutions as well; without further policy changes, this could negatively impact saving for a number of reasons. First, retirement accounts accessible as workplace pensions (such as 401(k)s, 403(b)s, and 401(a)s) have considerably higher contribution limits than IRAs that can be accessed directly by consumers. Workplace pensions allow workers to benefit from the convenience of payroll-deduction accounts, which evidence suggests increase pension savings; in contrast, most IRAs do not offer such convenience. Second, nondiscrimination rules for workplace pensions then give employers an incentive to encourage participation among employees, since the managers themselves would otherwise be barred from contributions. Certainly increasing participation in workplace pensions is a laudable goal, as only 51% of private-sector workers aged 21 to 64 had such access in 2013 (Copeland 2014).

While the importance of access to payroll-deduction accounts is clear, the evidence is less clear that such employer responses are a serious problem for potential reforms to the tax expenditure for retirement savings. First, most employers provide workplace pensions in order to compete for workers, suggesting it is mostly employee demand that drives provision; in any case, firms bear very little cost for providing such access to their employees, so that an economy-wide tax subsidy for retirement savings is grossly out of proportion to the type of targeted tax credits that would accomplish the same thing. Taking a step back, however, the inefficiency of workers relying on firms for access to retirement savings accounts has prompted several proposals to directly mandate such provisions or to decouple retirement savings from firms, both of which I discuss in section 10.3.1.1. More evidence on the determinants of the behavior of employers in this area, such as Bubb and Warren (2016), would be valuable to understand these concerns more thoroughly.

10.3.1.1 Alternative Policy Options

Motivated by the seeming inefficiency of tax expenditure on retirement savings—or perhaps by the need to cut spending in the budget for other purposes—a number of proposals have emerged to reform this large tax preference. Most prominently, President Obama proposed a 28% rate limitation for all deductions as part of the American Jobs Act of 2011, a proposal repeated in each Budget since. The literature suggests that this reform would have little effect on the savings of wealthy individuals. There is no publicly available score of the cost and distributional effects of such a change for just retirement savings, but the Tax Policy Center has recently produced such estimates for somewhat more stringent rate limitations of 15%, 20%, and 25%. A 25% (15%) limit would generate between $12.8 ($46.8) billion of additional revenue in the first full year in effect, with 99.5% (86.2%) of revenue coming from the top quintile of the income distribution.

A similar style of reform would reduce allowable contribution to retirement savings accounts, either by reducing annual contribution limits directly or by setting an asset cap beyond which individuals cannot make further contributions to tax-preferred accounts. Since FY2014, the President's Budget has included such lifetime limits on savings. Conceptually, a lifetime cap is both better targeted (by focusing on the stock rather than the flow) and also more flexible (by allowing individuals to re-allocate contributions across years in a more flexible way), but the implementation details of a lifetime cap are considerably more complicated.

A more far-reaching alternative would be to convert the tax deduction into a tax credit, so that the tax subsidy per dollar of retirement savings would be fully equalized across the income distribution. New estimates from the Urban-Brookings Tax Policy Center, generously provided at the request of the author, show that such policies would generate moderate gains especially for middle-income households.[6] For instance, replacing the deduction with a 25% non-refundable tax credit would generate $13.2 billion of annual tax cuts for households outside the top quintile, almost exactly offsetting the $12.7 billion of additional revenue from households in the top quintile (for whom the policy is exactly the same as the 25% rate-limitation). A refundable version of the same tax credit would generate an additional $7.2 billion of annual tax cuts for middle-income households. In contrast, similar policies that offer 15% tax credit (either refundable or non-refundable) generate essentially the same net revenue as the 15% rate limitation. This is because few households below the 15% tax bracket (who would potentially benefit from the credit) save in retirement accounts.

10.3.1.2 Post-Tax versus Pretax Contributions

Among the many different flavors of retirement savings accounts, perhaps the most important distinction is between those for which contributions are made with pretax versus post-tax dollars. For Roth IRAs, individuals receive no tax deduction for contributions but then pay no tax on earnings. For 401(k)s, traditional IRAs, and most other retirement accounts, individuals instead pay no tax on contributions up front, but pay full income tax on the gross value of withdrawals. Under certain circumstances—specifically, when income tax rates are constant and when individuals allocate a fixed

[6] See Urban-Brookings TPC Tables T15-0156 through T15-0168. Precisely, the policy would limit the rate for deductions to 25% while giving non-refundable or refundable tax credits at a rate equal to the difference between 25% and a household's marginal statutory tax rate, to those households below the 25% bracket. A policy which attempted to completely replace the deduction with a tax credit would generate substantially more complex effects due to the interaction with the Alternative Minimum Tax (AMT) and various phase-ins and phase-outs.

amount of pretax dollars for saving—it is economically irrelevant whether taxes are paid upfront or upon withdrawal.

In practice, however, there are a number of important differences between the two types of accounts, most obviously when individuals expect a different marginal tax rate in retirement. One source of such a difference is the progressive nature of the US tax system. Typically individuals plan to have about 30% less income in retirement than in their final working years; even adjusting for a rising real wage throughout the lifecycle, this should imply lower tax rates in retirement than during most working years (and especially the later working years in which retirement contributions are largest) and so a preference for pretax contributions. On the other hand, households may also expect an increase in tax rates in the future, either due to political forces or the projection of large future deficits, in which case they would prefer post-tax contributions.

Another set of differences relates to the potential for tax gaming. For instance, if an individual can redirect labor earnings into dividends paid on an asset held in a Roth IRA, then that income becomes tax-free. Similarly, any asset that is undervalued at the time of purchase will yield excess returns that are untaxed. Another way of expressing this difference is that, while neither account taxes the normal return to investment, pretax accounts tax the excess return but post-tax accounts do not. In practice, however, these forces likely affect only a small fraction of wealthy taxpayers; the vast majority of excess returns earned in retirement savings accounts likely reflects just the equity premium (in which the government could easily co-invest if it chose).

Post-tax versus pretax contributions also differ importantly in the frame of the contribution. Savers choose the number of dollars (or the fraction of income) to contribute to a retirement account, but a dollar contributed to a post-tax account is worth more in retirement consumption that a dollar contributed to a pretax account (since one has yet to pay tax). In a recent paper, Beshears et al. (2015b) demonstrate the intriguing possibility that confusion about this issue leads savers to contribute more, on an equivalent post-tax basis, to post-tax accounts than pretax accounts.[7]

Their estimates suggest that savers essentially ignore the pre-tax versus post-tax distinction, so that savings increase by roughly the marginal tax rate. If extrapolated nationally, post-tax accounts would increase savings by an average of 26% (the average marginal tax rate). Unfortunately, the progressive tax schedule would generate the largest increase in savings for the wealthiest taxpayers, so this policy would not be well targeted.

10.3.1.3 Revenue Timing and Tax Policy for Retirement

A final important difference between pre-tax and post-tax contributions is the timing of tax revenue. Holding all other economic forces constant, retirement savings

[7] This argument is opposite to that suggested by Feenberg and Skinner (1989), who argued that the immediacy of the tax deduction under a pre-tax contribution system would increase savings relative to a Roth system.

accounts that take pretax contributions delay the receipt of taxes on that income typically until the owner retires, if not long after. Conversely, a shift from pre-tax to post-tax accounts brings forward substantial tax revenue, often by many decades. These timing shifts, of course, do not actually change the net present value of revenue collected. But under current budgetary scoring conventions, which look at the effects of policies only for the first ten years, such revenue retiming appears the same as true revenue, making such timing shifts politically attractive.

One notable recent proposal that relied on such revenue retiming was the comprehensive tax reform bill proposed by now-retired Representative Dave Camp (R-MI). This proposal included a partial shift from pre-tax to post-tax contributions, a provision that would generate $143 billion in additional revenue over the first ten years of the reform.[8] Essentially all of this money reflected a shift forward of revenue rather than any actual increase in revenue.

At least the revenue timing included in Camp's reform package would not do active harm to the retirement system; the same cannot be said for more pernicious tactics, such as "pension smoothing," which may do real harm. This provision allows employers to use artificially high interest rates when calculating future pension liabilities, thereby reducing the current contributions to maintain adequate funding levels. Because firms contribute less to pension plans, they pay more in current profit taxes (as well as potentially higher dividend and capital gains taxes from the distribution of those profits), raising revenue that has, in recent years, been directed to fund transportation spending (in 2012 and 2014). Of course, this revenue too is simply the result of budget rules that do not capture the reduction in future revenue; what is worse, this maneuver contributes to the underfunding of pensions, potentially generating additional liabilities for the federal government not included in the official budget scores.

In all of these cases, there may be legitimate policy reasons to enact policies that shift the timing of revenue across years. However, it is unfortunate that current budgetary rules do not adjust. At best, Congress may misestimate the budgetary consequences of the underlying reforms; at worst, politicians may take advantage of these budgetary gimmicks in a way that generates real harm.

10.3.2 Targeted Tax Subsidies for Retirement Savings

In addition to the general tax subsidy for retirement savings, the tax code features several more powerful targeted tax incentives for savings. The most notable such policy is the Saver's Credit, which provides tax credits for up to $2,000 in contributions to retirement accounts for single/married households with adjusted gross income below $30,000/$60,000 in 2014. Contributions earn a 50% tax rate—which is economically equivalent to a 100% match—for the poorest households, and the tax credit rate shrinks to 20% and then 10% as households have more income. Take-up of the Saver's Credit is quite low; although it is difficult to measure broad eligibility, Duflo

[8] See Joint Committee on Taxation, JCX-14-20.

et al. (2006) report that just 15% of eligible households made a contribution even at the highest tax credit rate. The tax expenditure for the Saver's Credit was $1.2 billion in 2014.

Many of the general issues with retirement tax subsidies apply as well to the Saver's Credit, which might thus be expected to have a relatively small effect on net savings. In addition, a number of papers suggest that the particular form of the Saver's Credit reduces response, perhaps because it is too complicated. Duflo et al. (2006) compare the effect of the Saver's Credit to their randomized match rates and find that households were four times more responsive to subsidies framed as match rates, as compared with economically equivalent tax credits. This may be because taxpayers do not understand or do not know about the Saver's Credit, which has been shown to be an important determinant of tax credit take-up by low-income households in the context of the EITC (Chetty and Saez 2013). Saez (2009) also demonstrates that savers are more responsive to matches that are deposited in the retirement account, as opposed to the same incentive given as cash. The importance of the design of tax credits is not surprising, given recent results on the crucial role that choice architecture plays in 401(k) participation and contribution rates. In fact, many of these lessons might be applied to the general tax preference for retirement savings.

Another problem with the Saver's Credit, as currently constituted, is the nonrefundability of the credit. This provision effectively restricts eligibility to households with positive tax liability, which may make as many as 25% of otherwise eligible households effectively unable to benefit from the credit (Duflo et al. 2007).[9] This problem is especially acute for poorer households with children, since the Child Tax Credit (CTC) often eliminates residual tax liability. President Obama's 2011 Budget proposed to make the Saver's Credit fully refundable. This proposal, which also changed the credit structure to a 50% flat credit for the first $500 of contributions per individual for single/married households with AGI below $32,500/$65,000, would have cost $29.8 billion over ten years. While refundability of the Saver's Credit would certainly expand the potentially eligible population, it is not clear that such a policy would be substantially more successful than the current credit given the general problems with tax subsidies.

Research on other forms of targeted savings subsidies is less well developed. One notable example is the literature on Individual Development Accounts (IDAs), which are savings accounts, paired with financial education and counseling, that offer matching funds as an incentive if withdrawals are used for particular purposes (e.g., homeownership, business formation). While these accounts were not dedicated to retirement savings, their similarity might lead to some impact on total savings. Grinstein-Weiss et al. (2015) studies the long-term effects on savings of randomized

[9] In practice, the Saver's Credit is "stacked" before several refundable tax credits such as the Earned Income Tax Credit (EITC), so that households might still benefit from the Saver's Credit while owning no federal income tax. Technically, households must have a positive "total tax" balance in order to benefit from the Saver's Credit.

access to an IDA in Tulsa, Oklahoma. They find that, six years after the experiment ended, the IDA participants were no more likely to hold a retirement account or have sufficient balances to support stable consumption in retirement.

10.3.3 Tax Policies that Support "Nudges"

The literature is unambiguous in its support for nudges as powerful tools for increasing retirement savings. It is perhaps not surprising, then, that various recent proposals attempt to harness tax policy to support the use of nudges. For instance, Iwry and John (2009) proposed Auto-IRA accounts, into which firms that do not offer retirement savings plans would be required to default workers. This proposal was subsequently taken up by the President's FY2010 Budget (and included in all subsequent Budgets). This proposal would help address the fact that just 51% of private sector workers aged 21–64 have access to a workplace retirement account. Research has also shown that payroll deduction—which is only available through one's employer—increases savings, so it is critically important to get firms involved. The primary criticism of the auto-IRA proposal is that it includes a mandate that firms provide access for workers.

Although the auto-IRA proposal has faced opposition in Congress, a number of states are moving forward on similar initiatives. Illinois looks on track to be the first state to implement such a proposal. Specifically, Illinois will require employers with twenty-five or more employees and no other plan to set up auto-IRAs starting in 2017. The default rate will be 3% of salary, and the funds will be invested by default in lifecycle investment funds. A number of other states, including California, Massachusetts, Oregon, and Washington, have passed bills to implement similar systems and are working on implementation. In some cases the accounts would be standard IRAs; in others the accounts would be managed within existing pension infrastructures. For instance, California's system provides for the accounts to be managed within the California Public Employees Retirement System (CalPERS). Five more states have created commissions to study the feasibility of such schemes, with many other states actively considering the issue.

One of the largest holdups has been the potential that such plans might generate fiduciary duty or other responsibilities for either employers or the state government under the Employee Retirement Income Security Act (ERISA); in fact most state legislation explicitly authorizes the creation of a system only if the accounts receive some form of exemption from ERISA. Most recently, in November 2015, the Department of Labor published a notice of proposed rule-making (NPRM) in order to provide a safe harbor from for state-sponsored auto-IRAs, clearing the path for the states to proceed. The roll-out of these systems should provide fertile ground for the study of nudges in a public policy setting.

An alternative approach to mandated provision by employers would be to incentivize firms to provide access. New proposals in the President's FY2016 Budget would provide small tax credits for small firms that choose to start retirement savings plans, and additional credits for firms that auto-enroll workers in these plans. Friedman (2015) proposes a much larger permanent scheme of such incentives, funded by a rate limitation for the deductibility of retirement contributions.

10.4 CONCLUSION

The literature on tax policy and retirement has benefited greatly from recent research. Particularly by incorporating behavioral effects into models of tax response, and by utilizing rich new administrative data sets, we now understand in far greater detail how tax policy can, and cannot, influence savings. Applying consensus views within the literature suggests that tax subsidies for retirement savings, especially in their current form, are ineffective in addressing undersaving. In contrast, nudges such as default savings rates appear far more effective.

The challenge for tax policy is to find new more effective policies based on these results. Many authors have proposed alternative policies involving savings nudges, based on the successes in private firms, but there has yet to be a large-scale public policy trial of such an approach. Others have proposed financial education as a more direct attack on savings inadequacy. Yet other authors have suggested that a combination of savings subsidies, nudges, and education is the best approach. There will be great value in learning which of these proposed approaches works best as public policy.

This review also highlights several areas in which further research is crucial. First, the literature is clear on the importance of choice architecture for retirement savings, but relatively few papers have studied similar approaches to make tax subsidies more effective. It is possible that alternative frames might increase their efficiency. More generally, the literature would benefit greatly from more work on heterogeneity in the effects of tax incentives, though, of course, this is a very challenging task given the difficulty in properly identifying their basic effect. Second, more work is needed to understand the effects of nudges on total savings. While several papers have studied conceptually similar mandates, the literature lacks direct estimates for policies like defaults. Third, the literature needs more work on why some firms offer or do not offer retirement savings plans as in Bubb and Warren (2016) and how employers may respond in their plan choice to changes in government policy.

ACKNOWLEDGMENTS

This chapter was prepared for the Economics of Tax Policy Conference, held at The Brookings Institution on December 3–4, 2015. I especially thank Surachai Khitatrakun at the Tax Policy Center for help with policy scores, as well as Alan Auerbach, Bill Gale, Elizabeth Kelly, Brigitte Madrian, and Eric Toder for helpful feedback. Frina Lin and Jimmy Narang provided outstanding research assistance.

REFERENCES

Attanasio, Orazio P., and Agar Brugiavini. 2003. "Social Security and Households' Saving." *Quarterly Journal of Economics* 118 (3): 1075–119.

Attanasio, Orazio P., and Thomas DeLeire. 2002. "The Effect of Individual Retirement Accounts on Household Consumption and National Saving." *Economic Journal* 112 (481): 504–38.

Attanasio, Orazio P., and Susann Rohwedder. 2003. "Pension Wealth and Household Saving: Evidence from Pension Reforms in the United Kingdom." *American Economic Review* 93 (5): 1499–521.

Attanasio, Orazio P., and Matthew Wakefield. 2010. "The Effects on Consumption and Saving of Taxing Asset Returns." In *Dimensions of Tax Design: the Mirrlees Review*, edited by James A. Mirrlees, Stuart Adam, Tim Besley, Richard Blundell, Steve Bond, Robert Chote, Malcolm Gammie, Paul Johnson, Gareth Myles, and James Poterba, 675–736. Oxford: Oxford University Press.

Benjamin, Daniel J. 2003. "Does 401 (k) Eligibility Increase Saving?: Evidence from Propensity Score Subclassification." *Journal of Public Economics* 87 (5): 1259–90.

Bernheim, B. Douglas. 2002. "Taxation and Saving." In *Handbook of Public Economics* vol. 3, edited by Alan J. Auerbach and Martin Feldstein, 1173–249. New York, NY: Elsevier.

Beshears, John, James J. Choi, David Laibson, Brigitte C. Madrian, and Katherine L. Milkman. 2015a. "The Effect of Providing Peer Information on Retirement Savings Decisions." *Journal of Finance* 70 (3): 1161–201.

Beshears, John, James J. Choi, David Laibson, Brigitte C. Madrian, and Sean Wang. 2015b. "Who is Easier to Nudge?" NBER SSA-RRC Paper. http://www.nber.org/programs/ag/rrc/rrc2015/papers/7.3%20-%20Beshears,%20Choi,%20Laibson,%20Madrian,%20Wang.pdf

Bubb, Ryan, and Patrick Warren. 2016. "A Positive Theory of Retirement Plan Design." New York University School of Law.

Buchanan, James M. 1975. "The Samaritan's Dilemma." In *Altruism, Morality, and Economic Theory*, edited by Edmund S. Phelps, 71–85. New York, NY: Russell Sage Foundation.

Burtless, Gary, and Eric Toder. 2010. "The Shrinking Tax Preference for Pension Savings: An Analysis of Income Tax Changes, 1985–2007." Center for Retirement Research.

Card, David, and Michael Ransom. 2011. "Pension Plan Characteristics and Framing Effects in Employee Savings Behavior." *Review of Economics and Statistics* 93 (1): 228–43.

Carroll, Gabriel D., James J. Choi, David Laibson, Brigitte C. Madrian, and Andrew Metrick. 2009. "Optimal Defaults and Active Decisions." *Quarterly Journal of Economics* 124 (4): 1639–74.

Chernozhukov, Victor, and Christian Hansen. 2004. "The Effects of 401(k) Participation on the Wealth Distribution: An Instrumental Quantile Regression Analysis." *Review of Economics and Statistics* 86 (3): 735–51.

Chetty, Raj. 2009. "The Simple Economics of Salience and Taxation." National Bureau of Economic Research.

Chetty, Raj, John Friedman, Soren Leth-Petersen, Torben Nielsen, and Tore Olsen. 2014a. "Is the Danish Savings Experience Applicable to the US? Response to Banerjee and Adams (2013) Ebri Report." Retrieved from http://www.rajchetty.com/chettyfiles/crowdout_EBRI_response.pdf

Chetty, Raj, John N. Friedman, Søren Leth-Petersen, Torben Heien Nielsen, and Tore Olsen. 2014b. "Active vs. Passive Decisions and Crowd-Out in Retirement Savings Accounts: Evidence from Denmark." *Quarterly Journal of Economics* 129 (3): 1141–219.

Chetty, Raj, John N. Friedman, and Emmanuel Saez. 2013. "Using Differences in Knowledge across Neighborhoods to Uncover the Impacts of the EITC on Earnings." *American Economic Review* 103 (7): 2683–721.

Chetty, Raj, and Emmanuel Saez. 2013. "Teaching the Tax Code: Earnings Responses to an Experiment with EITC Recipients." *American Economic Journal: Applied Economics* 5 (1): 1–31.

Choi, James, David Laibson, and Brigitte Madrian. 2006. "Reducing the Complexity Costs of 401(k) Participation Through Quick Enrollment (TM)." National Bureau of Economic Research.

Choi, James J., David Laibson, Brigitte C. Madrian, and Andrew Metrick. 2002. "Defined Contribution Pensions: Plan Rules, Participant Choices, and the Path of Least Resistance." In *Tax Policy and the Economy*, vol. 16, edited by Jeffrey R. Brown, 67–114. Cambridge, MA: MIT Press.

Choi, James J., David Laibson, Brigitte C. Madrian, and Andrew Metrick. 2004. "Consumption-Wealth Comovement of the Wrong Sign." National Bureau of Economic Research.

Copeland, Craig. 2014. "Employment-Based Retirement Plan Participation: Geographic Differences and Trends, 2013." *EBRI Issue Brief No. 405.*

Duflo, Esther, William Gale, Jeffrey Liebman, Peter Orszag, and Emmanuel Saez. 2006. "Saving Incentives for Low- and Middle-Income Families: Evidence from a Field Experiment with H&R Block." *Quarterly Journal of Economics* 121 (4): 1311–46.

Duflo, Esther, William Gale, Jeffrey Liebman, Peter Orszag, and Emmanuel Saez. 2007. "Savings Incentives for Low- and Moderate-Income Families in the United States: Why Is the Saver's Credit Not More Effective?" *Journal of the European Economic Association* 5 (2–3): 647–61.

Engelhardt, Gary V., and Anil Kumar. 2007. "Employer Matching and 401(k) Saving: Evidence from the Health and Retirement Study." *Journal of Public Economics* 91 (10): 1920–43.

Engen, Eric M., and William G. Gale. 2000. "The Effects of 401(k) Plans on Household Wealth: Differences across Earnings Groups." National Bureau of Economic Research.

Engen, Eric M., William G. Gale, and John Karl Scholz. 1994. "Do Saving Incentives Work?" *Brookings Papers on Economic Activity* 1994 (1): 85–180.

Feenberg, Daniel, and Jonathan Skinner. 1989. "Sources of IRA Saving." In *Tax Policy and the Economy*, vol. 3, edited by Lawrence Summers, 25–46. Cambridge, MA: National Bureau of Economic Research.

Feldstein, Martin. 1974. "Social Security, Induced Retirement, and Aggregate Capital Accumulation." *Journal of Political Economy* 82 (5): 905–26.

Feldstein, Martin, and Jeffrey B. Liebman. 2002. "Social Security." In *Handbook of Public Economics*, vol. 4, edited by Alan J. Auerbach and Martin Feldstein, 2245–324. New York, NY: Elsevier.

Friedman, John N. 2015. "Building on What Works: A Proposal to Modernize Retirement Savings." The Hamilton Project.

Gale, William G., and John Karl Scholz. 1994. "IRAs and Household Saving." *American Economic Review* 84 (5): 1233–60.

Gelber, Alexander M., et al. 2011. "How Do 401(k)s Affect Saving? Evidence from Changes in 401(k) Eligibility." *American Economic Journal: Economic Policy* 3 (4): 103–22.

Georgetown University Law Center. 2010. "A Timeline of the Evolution of Retirement in the United States." Workplace Flexibility.

Ghilarducci, Teresa, Bridget Fisher, and Ismael Cid-Martinez. 2015. "Retirement Savings Tax Expenditures: The Need for Refundable Tax Credits." Schwartz Center for Economic Policy Analysis and Department of Economics, The New School.

Golosov, Mikhail, Maxim Troshkin, Aleh Tsyvinski, and Matthew Weinzierl. 2013. "Preference Heterogeneity and Optimal Capital Income Taxation." *Journal of Public Economics* 97 (1): 60–75.

Grinstein-Weiss, Michal, Michael Sherraden, William G. Gale, William M. Rohe, Mark Schreiner, Clinton Key, and Jane E. Oliphant. 2015. "Effects of an Individual Development Account Program on Retirement Saving: Follow-Up Evidence from a Randomized Experiment." *Journal of Gerontological Social Work* 58 (6): 572–89.

Gruber, Jon, and Emmanuel Saez. 2002. "The Elasticity of Taxable Income: Evidence and Implications." *Journal of Public Economics* 84 (1): 1–32.

Iwry, Mark J., and David C. John. 2009. "Pursuing Universal Retirement Security Through Automatic IRAs." Brookings Institute Retirement Security Project Paper.

Joines, Douglas H., and James G. Manegold. 1995. "IRAs and Saving: Evidence from a Panel of Taxpayers." Unpublished manuscript, University of Southern California, Los Angeles.

Kaplow, Louis. 2011. "Targeted Savings and Labor Supply." *International Tax and Public Finance* 18 (5): 507–18.

Kaplow, Louis. 2015. "Myopia and the Effects of Social Security and Capital Taxation on Labor Supply." *National Tax Journal* 68 (1): 7–32.

Kotlikoff, Laurence J. 1987. "Justifying Public Provision of Social Security." *Journal of Policy Analysis and Management* 6 (4): 674–96.

Laibson, David. 1997. "Golden Eggs and Hyperbolic Discounting." *Quarterly Journal of Economics* 112 (2): 443–77.

Madrian, Brigitte C., and Dennis F. Shea. 2001. "The Power of Suggestion: Inertia in 401(k) Participation and Savings Behavior." *Quarterly Journal of Economics* 116 (4): 1149–187.

Meyer, Bruce D., Wallace K. C. Mok, and James X. Sullivan. 2015. "Household Surveys in Crisis." *Journal of Economic Perspectives* 29 (4): 199–226.

Munnell, Alicia H., Wenliang Hou, and Anthony Webb. 2014. "NRRI Update Shows Half Still Falling Short." Chesnutt Hill, MA: Center for Retirement Research.

Munnell, Alicia H., Anthony Webb, et al. 2015. "The Impact of Leakages from 401(k)s and IRAs." Center for Retirement Research.

Poterba, James M. 2014. "Retirement Security in an Aging Population." *American Economic Review* 104 (5): 1–30.

Poterba, James M., Steven F. Venti, and David A. Wise. 1994. "401(k) Plans and Tax-Deferred Saving." In *Studies in the Economics of Aging*, edited by David A. Wise, 105–142. Chicago, IL: University of Chicago Press.

Poterba, James M., Steven F. Venti, and David A. Wise. 1995. "Do 401(k) Contributions Crowd Out Other Personal Saving?," *Journal of Public Economics* 58 (1): 1–32.

Saez, Emmanuel. 2009. "Details Matter: The Impact of Presentation and Information on the Take-up of Financial Incentives in Retirement Savings." *American Economic Journal: Economic Policy* 1 (1): 204–28.

Thaler, Richard H., and Cass R. Sunstein. 2008. *Nudge: Improving Decisions about Health, Wealth, and Happiness.* New Haven, CT: Yale University Press.

US Government. 2015. "Analytical Perspectives, Budget of the United States Government, Fiscal Year 2016."

Venti, Steven F., and David A. Wise. 1990. "Have IRAs Increased US Saving?: Evidence from Consumer Expenditure Surveys." *Quarterly Journal of Economics* 105 (3): 661–98.

COMMENTARY ON CHAPTER 10

Brigitte C. Madrian

In his chapter "Tax Policy and Retirement Savings," John Friedman examines the effectiveness of two different policy tools to encourage retirement savings: tax preferences for savings, and savings nudges such as a higher default retirement savings contribution rate. Friedman first makes the point that for either of these savings policies to make sense, there is an implied presumption that some (perhaps many) individuals will under save for retirement in their absence. He then outlines a conceptual framework that articulates the conditions necessary for either of these two policies to improve retirement savings outcomes. These conditions can be stated in terms of parameters that, with appropriate data and sources of identification, can be estimated. Table 10C.1 summarizes these parameters and their relationship to the effectiveness of tax preferences and default savings contributions as policies to improve retirement savings outcomes.

The effectiveness of these two policies depends on three parameters. The first is the fraction of individuals who actively respond to the policy. In the case of a tax preference, this is the fraction of individuals who change the amount that they save in response to the tax rules. In the case of a higher default retirement savings contribution, this is the fraction of individuals who adjust their savings in response to the new default, either by opting out of the default (if that is an option), or by reducing savings elsewhere in order to offset the increased savings that mechanically follows from a higher default contribution rate. The second parameter of interest is how responsive the active savers are to the policy in question: Is their behavioral response large or small? The final parameter of interest is how well targeted the policy is: Does it primarily impact those who are most likely to under save (the intended targets of the policy), or does it primarily impact those who would save sufficiently in the absence of any policy to promote greater retirement savings. Tax preferences are more effective at improving retirement savings outcomes if the fraction of active savers is high, if their responsiveness to the tax preference is high, and if the individuals who would otherwise under save are the ones who are most likely to respond to the policy. Higher default contribution rates, in contrast, are more effective at improving retirement savings outcomes if the fraction of active savers is low, if their responsiveness to changes in the default is low, and if the individuals who would otherwise under save are the ones who are least likely to respond to the policy.

Table 10C.1 Behavioral parameters that impact the effectiveness of policies to promote retirement savings

Behavioral Parameter	*Conditions under Which Policy Below Will Be Most Effective at Increasing Retirement Savings for Those Who Under Save*		*Empirical Evidence on Parameter Value*
	Tax Preferences for Retirement Savings	*Higher Default Retirement Savings Contributions*	
Fraction of individuals who actively respond to the policy ("active" vs. "passive" savers)	More effective if high	More effective if low	Low
Responsiveness of savings to the policy (for active savers)	More effective if high	More effective if low	Low
Correlation between responsiveness to the policy and under saving in the absence of the policy (targeting)	More effective if high	More effective if low	Low

Friedman then surveys the empirical literature to draw conclusions about the actual magnitude of these parameters (the last column of table 10C.1). By and large, the evidence suggests that few individuals are active savers, and that the correlation between actively saving and under saving in the absence of policies to promote retirement savings is low. The implication that follows is that tax preferences are a weak instrument for improving retirement savings outcomes. Most individuals don't respond to tax preferences, and those that do would largely save enough to begin with. In short, tax preferences are a poorly targeted policy: they help the people who don't need help, and they don't help the people who do need help.

The parameter values that make tax preferences such a weak instrument, however, are *exactly* the parameter values that make higher default retirement savings contributions a particularly effective tool. That most people are passive savers implies that a higher default retirement contribution will largely "stick," and those who are most likely to persist at the default are those who are most likely to under save. The policy is well targeted, and results in the largest changes for those who most are in greatest need of a policy to encourage greater retirement savings.

One institutional feature missing from the conceptual framework in Friedman's chapter is the role of employers as institutional facilitators of retirement savings through their sponsorship of workplace retirement savings plans. Indeed, it is the power of payroll deduction that makes default retirement savings contributions so effective—the money that people never see is the money they never miss. With employers playing such a central role in the retirement savings system in the United States (and in some other countries as well), the success of any retirement savings policy depends not only on how *individuals* respond to the policy but also on how *firms* respond to the policy. Friedman's chapter bypasses the role of firms and focuses entirely on how individuals respond to the two policies of interest: tax preferences and higher default retirement contributions.

If firms also respond to these policies, any comparative assessment of their merits needs to account for firm behavior as well. So, in addition to the individual behavioral parameters that are the central issue of interest in Friedman's chapter, we need to also consider a set of firm behavioral parameters as well:

(1) ***How does firm sponsorship of workplace savings plans change in response to the policy?*** In a Senate Finance Committee hearing held in September 2014, Senator Orrin Hatch (R-UT) asked Scott Betts, the Senior Vice President of National Benefit Services, LLC, a retirement plan provider and administrator, the following question: "Mr. Betts, you have real-life experience trying to convince small employers to adopt a retirement plan for their workers. Can you explain further: (1) what are their motivations when they make a decision to offer a plan, and (2) what sort of things convince them to say 'no' to setting up a new plan?" Mr. Betts responded with: "Working with employers for many years, it has been the incentives that the government has included in these plans that have incentivized employers to set them up. These incentives have motivated the employers to

provide this retirement plan for their employees, so the effect of the incentive is very powerful." In short: firms provide retirement plans to their workers because of governmental tax preferences. The evidence that we have on what motivates firms to sponsor retirement savings plans is limited, but, if firms sponsor savings plans because of the tax benefits to their employees from doing so, limiting those tax preferences would paradoxically reduce the effectiveness of policies to encourage higher default contribution rates in employer-sponsored savings plans by reducing the number of firms that sponsor such plans. If true, it may be that tax preferences and higher default contributions rates are complementary policies: the tax preferences provide the incentive for firms to offer plans even though the primary beneficiaries of these plans may not be those who are most likely to under save, but once the plans are in place, policies to encourage a higher default contribution rate extend the benefits of these plans to those employees who would otherwise under save.

(2) ***How does the firm's choice of the default contribution rate change in response to the policy?*** When firms set up an employer-sponsored retirement savings plan, one plan design decision they face is the choice of a default contribution rate. The Pension Protection Act of 2006 included provisions to encourage firms to adopt automatic enrollment in their retirement savings plans at a non-zero contribution rate, and to encourage firms to automatically escalate employee contribution rates over time. Figure 10C.1 shows a rapid increase in the fraction of firms adopting automatic enrollment following this reform, as well as sizable increases in the savings plan participation rate of newly hired employees (those with 0–1 years of tenure) and in the fraction of plans with an overall participation rate higher than

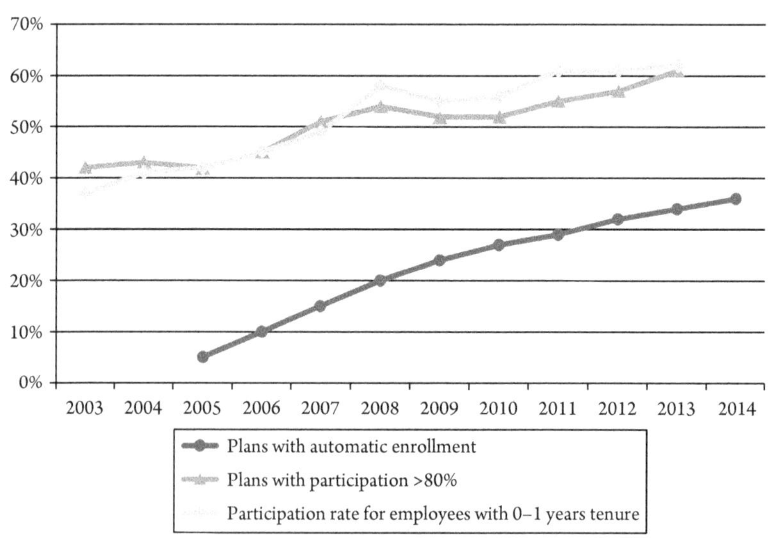

Figure 10C.1 Automatic enrollment and savings plan outcomes in the United States over time. *Source:* Vanguard (2013, 2015).

80%. These data suggest a certain amount of responsiveness by firms to a specific government policy to encourage higher default contribution rates; this responsiveness on the part of firms is a necessary condition for such policies to have an ultimate impact on their employee beneficiaries.

(3) ***How does the employer contribution change in response to the policy?*** Most employers who sponsor a retirement savings plan in the United States provide an employer contribution to the plan in addition to the elective contributions made by participants out of their compensation. Typically this employer contribution takes the form of a match that is tied to the level of the employees' own contributions; less often, employers make a contribution, either a flat dollar amount or a percentage of pay, that is not contingent on any employee contribution to the plan. These employer contributions are an important source of retirement savings for employees, and disproportionately so for lower-income savers. If firms respond to policy changes by altering the amount or structure of their employer contribution, the extent to which they do so is an important parameter in evaluating the impact of any retirement savings policy change. For example, some researchers have suggested that employers respond to a higher default retirement contribution rate by decreasing the generosity of their employer contribution to the plan (Butrica and Karamcheva 2015; Soto and Butrica 2009). If so, the benefits of higher default contribution rates for passive savers could be partially undone by the active response of firms that reduce their employer contribution.

(4) ***How correlated is firm responsiveness to the policy with the level of employee under saving in the absence of the policy?*** When firms change the structure of their savings plan, or whether or not they even offer a savings plan, do these changes largely impact the employees who would save a sufficient amount in the absence of any policy, or do these changes largely impact the employees who would otherwise under save? Changes in firm behavior that disproportionately impact the employees who under save are particularly problematic from a policy standpoint.

The potential for firms to change their savings plan design, or whether they offer a plan, complicates the analysis of the relative merits of tax preferences versus higher default contribution rates as policy tools to foster improved retirement savings outcomes. The individual behavioral parameters analyzed in Friedman's chapter all point in the same direction: higher default retirement contributions dominate tax preferences as a policy tool for changing the amount that individuals save. When we account for the potential behavioral responses by firms, the policy conclusions are more nuanced. Employer-sponsored savings plans provide their greatest net benefit to individuals who are likely to under save, but anything that undermines firms' willingness to offer retirement savings plans, or the generosity of their employer contributions to these plans, also has the greatest impact on the individuals who are likely to under save. It may well be that in the absence of mandates, tax preferences are necessary to induce firms to offer the types of plans that facilitate using default contributions to improve savings outcomes for the individuals most in need of help.

REFERENCES

Butrica, Barbara, and Nadia S. Karamcheva. 2015. "Automatic Enrollment, Employer Match Rates, and Employee Compensation in 401(k) Plans." *Monthly Labor Review*, May 2015. http://www.bls.gov/opub/mlr/2015/article/automatic-enrollment-employer-match-rates-and-employee-compensation-in-401k-plans.htm

"Retirement Savings 2.0: Updating Savings Policy for the Modern Economy." 2014. Hearing before the Committee on Finance, United States Senate, September 16, 2014. http://www.finance.senate.gov/hearings/retirement-savings-20-updating-savings-policy-for-the-modern-economy

Soto, Mauricia, and Barbara A. Butrica. 2009. "Will Automatic Enrollment Reduce Employer Contributions to 401(k) Plans?." Urban Institute Discussion Paper (09-04). http://www.urban.org/sites/default/files/alfresco/publication-pdfs/411995-Will-Automatic-Enrollment-Reduce-Employer-Contributions-to--k-Plans-.PDF

Vanguard. 2013. "How America Saves 2015." The Vanguard Group (Valley Forge, PA). https://institutional.vanguard.com/iam/pdf/HAS13.pdf

Vanguard. 2015. "How America Saves 2015." The Vanguard Group (Valley Forge, PA). https://institutional.vanguard.com/iam/pdf/HAS15.pdf

11

FUNDAMENTAL TAX REFORM
A COMPARISON OF THREE OPTIONS

Alan D. Viard

11.1 INTRODUCTION

Increased federal revenue will likely be required to finance the projected growth of entitlement spending in upcoming decades. The anticipated rise in revenue needs heightens the importance of having a more efficient tax system. One commonly discussed reform strategy is a move toward consumption taxation, which would avoid income taxation's penalties on saving and investment and the complications of measuring capital income. However, such a strategy must address distributional concerns, particularly in light of recent increases in economic inequality. The complete replacement of the income tax system with a retail sales tax or a value added tax (VAT) would constitute a troubling move away from tax progressivity.

This chapter compares three options that would adopt a federal consumption tax while ensuring that the overall federal tax system remains progressive, with higher average tax rates on those with higher incomes. The first option would replace part of the income tax system with a VAT. The second option would completely replace the income tax system with a Bradford X tax, a progressive modification of the VAT. The third option would completely replace the income tax system with a personal expenditure tax (PET).

The three options would differ in many of their economic effects. Some of the more important differences, particularly those pertaining to the open economy, are rather subtle. Further investigation of fundamental tax reform options is needed to help inform the policy choices posed by the need to finance rising entitlement spending.

11.2 THREE REFORM OPTIONS

For present purposes, a tax is a consumption tax if its broad conceptual outline features an aggregate tax base that is either consumption or consumption plus net exports. Of course, details of the plan might cause the actual tax base to deviate from that ideal in some respects.

With constant tax rates over time, consumption taxes impose a zero effective tax rate on the marginal returns to new saving. Consumption taxation also eliminates the need to measure capital income, sweeping away an array of income tax complications, including depreciation, amortization, and inventory accounting. Consumption taxation can also avoid the disparate tax treatment of different types of capital and financing methods generally observed under income tax systems. These gains would be greater under the two full-replacement options than under the partial-replacement-VAT option.

Setting aside government purchases and international trade, consumption equals net income minus net investment. Net income equals wages plus net capital income (business profits plus business interest payments). Consumption can therefore be expressed as wages plus business cash flow, where business cash flow is defined as net capital income minus net investment. A consumption tax can therefore be viewed as a wage tax plus a business cash flow tax.

If the tax rate is constant over time, a business cash flow tax does not penalize new investment on the margin. The cash flows from a marginal new investment have zero ex ante market-value because the reduction in cash flows from the initial investment offset, in present value, the future cash flows expected to be generated by the investment. Nevertheless, a business cash flow tax raises revenue from two sources. Inframarginal investments with above-normal returns generate positive ex ante business cash flows.[1] Also, capital in existence when the tax is introduced generates positive future cash flows. The cash flow tax is, at least in principle, a lump-sum tax because it is imposed on inframarginal investments and investments that have already been made.

11.2.1 Partial-Replacement Value Added Tax

The first option would replace part of the income tax system with a VAT. Recent proposals of this type include Graetz (2008), Bipartisan Policy Center (2010, 38–41), and Gale and Harris (2013).

Under a VAT, each business firm remits tax on its value added. Under the subtraction method, each firm is taxed on its sales to consumers and other firms minus its purchases from other firms. Under the credit-invoice method, each firm is taxed on its sales, but claims credit for taxes paid on its purchases, provided that it receives invoices documenting the payment of tax. Neither method allows a deduction or credit for wages. A VAT can be viewed as a retail sales tax that is collected in installments at each stage of production. Approximately 180 countries have VATs, generally imposed through the credit-invoice method. Because the credit-invoice and subtraction methods are equivalent if firms comply with the tax and if the tax features a uniform tax rate with no exemptions, they are treated as equivalent in this chapter.

[1] As Carroll and Viard (2012: 48–49) explain, above-normal returns are risk-adjusted returns earned by private parties that are greater than the marginal risk-adjusted return available in the economy. They emphasize (51–52) that lucky returns on risky investments are *not* above-normal returns if the same risky returns are available on a marginal investment. The revenue from taxing such risky returns has the same ex ante market value as the revenue from taxing risk-free returns even if the risky investment's expected rate of return is higher than the risk-free rate of return.

Because a VAT is collected at the business level and does not distinguish between wages and business cash flow, it can be viewed as an employer payroll tax plus a business cash flow tax, both imposed at the VAT rate. Each firm's value added equals its business cash flow plus the wages paid to its employees.

11.2.2 Full-Replacement X Tax

The second option would completely replace the income tax system with a Bradford X tax. Recent proposals include the Growth and Investment Tax proposal of the President's Advisory Panel on Federal Tax Reform (2005), Carroll and Viard (2012), and Antos et al. (2015).

The X tax is a modification of the Hall-Rabushka flat tax, which, in turn, is a modification of the VAT. Hall and Rabushka (1983, 1995) proposed to bifurcate a VAT into taxes on wages and business cash flow. Households are taxed on their wages and business firms are taxed on their business cash flows. Each firm computes value added as it would under a subtraction-method VAT, but deducts its wage payments. The cash flow on which each firm is taxed plus the wages on which its workers are taxed sum to the firm's value added.

Under the Hall-Rabushka flat tax, firms are taxed at a single flat rate on business cash flow. Workers are taxed at the same rate on wages, but only above an exemption amount. The flat tax is distributionally more attractive than the VAT for two reasons. First, the exemption offered under the wage tax provides some progressivity between high-paid and low-paid workers. Second, the exemption lowers the tax burden on wages relative to the tax burden on business cash flow; as discussed in section 11.7.2, the business cash flow tax falls on equity holders, who are generally well off. Despite these features, replacing the current income tax system with a flat tax would significantly redistribute the tax burden downward.

To promote progressivity, Bradford (1986: 81–82) proposed modifying the flat tax to feature a full set of graduated rates on wages and possibly refundable tax credits. The top wage tax rate equals the flat tax rate imposed on business cash flow. Bradford referred to this tax as the X tax.[2] Compared to the flat tax, the X tax offers further progressivity between high-paid and low-paid workers and further increases the tax burden on business cash flow relative to the tax burden on wages.

From an administrative perspective, the flat tax and X tax look similar to an income tax. Nevertheless, they differ from an income tax in two important respects. Their individual tax applies only to wages, not to investment income, and their business tax applies to cash flow rather than net income, expensing rather than depreciating investments and offering no interest expense deduction.

[2] It may seem unnecessary to assign distinct names to the flat tax and the X tax when they differ only in their rate structures. After Hall and Rabushka named the flat tax after its rate structure, however, Bradford's modification of the rate structure necessitated a new name.

The X tax has an optical problem because it features no *visible* tax on households living off of capital income. Although no consumption tax system imposes a marginal tax on capital income from new saving, consumption taxes do tax above-normal returns and the capital in existence when the tax is introduced. Although the X tax imposes such a tax, it does so at the firm level through the cash-flow tax rather than at the household level. A related concern is that the X tax does not look like a consumption tax because the tax's visible household component is imposed on wages rather than consumption.

11.2.3 Full-Replacement Personal Expenditure Tax

The third option would completely replace the income tax system with a PET. Recent PET proposals include the Unlimited Savings Allowance (USA) plan described by Alliance USA (1995), McCaffery and Hines (2010), and Heritage Foundation (2011).[3]

Under a PET, each household files an annual tax return on which it reports income, deducts saving (deposits into savings accounts, asset purchases, amounts lent to others, and payments, both interest and principal, made on outstanding debts), and adds dissaving (withdrawals from savings accounts, gross proceeds of asset sales, amounts borrowed from others, and payments, both interest and principal, received on outstanding loans). The resulting measure equals the household's before-tax consumption, which is then taxed at graduated rates. To further increase progressivity, refundable tax credits can be provided to households with low consumption.

Seidman (1997: 11–16) and Kaldor (1955: 11–13) discuss the PET's long history. Fisher (1937: 42–47) sketched the broad outlines of an "income tax" computed under PET principles and Kaldor (1955) extensively discussed a PET. Proposals were outlined by Treasury Blueprints, US Department of the Treasury (1977) and the Meade Report, Institute for Fiscal Studies (1978). As discussed by Toye (1989) and Pressman (1995), two countries briefly adopted the PET. India's PET was in place from 1957 to 1962 and 1964 to 1966 and Ceylon's was in place from 1959 to 1963. Each country concluded that the tax, which applied only to a small number of high-spending households and supplemented the income tax, was too costly to administer relative to its small revenue yield.

The PET's lack of a tax on business firms may be an optical problem. The PET also faces an optical challenge with respect to the tax treatment of borrowing. In accord with income tax principles, the current tax system does not tax the proceeds of borrowing. In contrast, a pure form of the PET taxes households on the proceeds of borrowing, but allows the borrower to deduct all subsequent loan payments, both principal and interest. Although those deductions offset the initial tax in present discounted value (if the household remains in the same tax bracket), the initial tax on borrowing may still be unpopular. Modifying the PET to remove the tax on borrowing can lead to complexity and unintended results, as Seidman (1997: 102–104) discussed.

[3] The USA plan would have imposed a VAT alongside the PET and the Heritage Foundation's plan would have imposed a business cash flow tax alongside the PET.

11.3 GENERAL ECONOMIC EFFECTS

11.3.1 Progressivity and Efficiency

The X tax and the PET take different approaches to achieving progressivity. It is useful to compare each tax to the VAT, which is not progressive. The VAT is a real-based tax that tracks only the production activity of firms, the PET is a real-plus-financial tax system that also tracks financial transactions, and the X tax is a real-based tax that tracks the activities of both firms and workers.

The VAT's real-based approach makes household tax returns unnecessary. However, the lack of household information precludes rate graduation, which makes it difficult to achieve progressivity. (VATs sometimes achieve a limited progressivity through the cumbersome and economically inefficient practice of imposing high tax rates on luxuries and zero tax rates on necessities.) The VAT must impose a flat tax rate on all consumption because it does not track consumption to its final recipients. At the other extreme, the PET requires that all financial transactions be reported on household tax returns. Obtaining that information allows the PET to tax consumer spending at graduated rates, which makes it easy to achieve progressivity.

The X tax seeks to capture both taxes' advantages by tracking wages, but not business cash flow, to final recipients. Unlike the VAT, the X tax requires household tax returns. But, they are far simpler than PET household returns because households report only wages, not their financial transactions. The X tax therefore achieves much, but not all, of the VAT's simplicity. The X tax's more limited information set means that it, unlike the PET, cannot calibrate marginal tax rates to a household's consumer spending. Instead, the X tax calibrates marginal tax rates on wages to a household's wage level and sets a high flat rate for the firm-level business cash flow tax, which largely falls on those who are well off. It thereby achieves progressivity in a less refined manner than the PET.

By modifying the VAT to tax wages at the household level, the X tax achieves much greater progressivity than the VAT with a modest loss of simplicity. Because the treatment of wages is the X tax's sole underlying difference from the VAT, any advantage or disadvantage of a full-replacement X tax, relative to a full-replacement VAT, must arise, directly or indirectly, from that feature. Nevertheless, the treatment of wages turns out to be quite important, with implications for monetary policy, Social Security, the taxation of business firms and cross-border transactions, and transition policy. Of course, a full-replacement X tax further differs from a partial-replacement VAT because the income tax is eliminated.

Because the X tax has graduated rates linked to annual wages, it penalizes workers with volatile wages. The extra taxes that workers pay in their high-wage years generally outweigh the tax savings in their low-wage years because they are likely to be in higher tax brackets in the high-wage years. Because the PET has graduated rates linked to annual consumption, it imposes a similar penalty on households with volatile consumption. Either the X tax or the PET could adopt averaging provisions, but doing so would offer only partial relief and would add complexity.

Because consumption is significantly smaller than income for well-to-do households, revenue and distributional neutrality might require that the top statutory tax rates under the X tax or the PET be markedly higher than the corresponding statutory income tax rates. Of course, the relative levels of statutory tax rates would also depend upon the degree of base broadening adopted under each system. High statutory tax rates would pose less economic harm under a consumption tax than under an income tax, as the effective marginal tax rate on saving would remain zero and work disincentives would be smaller. Carroll and Viard (2012: 18–19) note that, although the statutory rate increase would amplify the tax wedge between leisure and current consumption, the elimination of capital income taxation would reduce the tax wedge between leisure and future consumption. Nevertheless, high statutory tax rates would create some distortions, including increased incentives to evade tax, difficulties with the treatment of negative cash flows under the X tax, and transfer pricing problems and penalties on locating investments with above-normal returns in the United States under an origin-based X tax. High statutory tax rates might also pose political problems.[4]

11.3.2 Monetary Policy

Nominal wages appear to be downwardly rigid in the United States and other countries. As Viard (2014) discussed, the rigidity applies to the quoted wage that the firm pays to the worker, which is net of employer-level taxes on labor (including employer payroll taxes, excise taxes, retail sales taxes, and VATs) and gross of employee-level taxes on labor (including employee payroll taxes and individual income taxes). The abrupt introduction of an employer-level tax, which would reduce the market-clearing real value of the quoted wage, might prompt the Federal Reserve to implement a one-time increase in the consumer price level, to allow real wages to decline without having to force down nominal wages. Such a one-time price increase is referred to as monetary accommodation of the tax.

Because the VAT would reduce the market-clearing real value of the quoted wage by taxing the output produced by workers, the Fed would be likely to accommodate the VAT. Carroll and Viard (2012: 168) note that other countries' central banks have often, but not always, accommodated VATs. In contrast, the wage-tax component of the X tax would be imposed at the household level, similar to the individual income tax and the employee payroll tax. Similarly, the PET would tax households on their wages as they spent them. Accordingly, the Fed would not need to accommodate an X tax or PET.

[4] The political problem would be mitigated because the X tax and the PET would quote their tax rates in tax-inclusive form, rather than the higher tax-exclusive form. Consider an X tax under which a business with $100 of before-tax cash flow must pay $35 tax, leaving it with $65 of after-tax cash flow. The tax rate would be quoted as 35%, which would be the tax-inclusive rate, as the $35 tax would be 35% of the $100 gross-of-tax cash flow. The tax rate would not be quoted as 53.8%, which would be the tax-exclusive rate, as the $35 tax would be 53.8% of the $65 net-of-tax cash flow.

I now consider a wide range of economic effects for the three reform options. Due to space considerations, not all issues receive full attention. Also, some relevant issues, including the treatment of financial intermediation, are not examined.

11.4 SELECTED TAX POLICY ISSUES

11.4.1 Public and Private Transfer Payments

The logic of consumption taxation suggests that consumption financed from gifts and bequests should be taxed in the same manner as other consumption, implying that they should be included in either the donor's or the recipient's tax base, but not both. (Any concerns about wealth concentration could be better addressed through an estate and gift tax targeted at large estates and gifts rather than by double-taxing all gifts and bequests.) Under a PET or X tax, the choice between donor taxation and recipient taxation would determine the applicable tax bracket, but would not determine the economic incidence of the tax, which would depend on whether donors adjusted the size of the net-of-tax gift in response to the tax. Under a PET, the most natural treatment would allow donors to deduct gifts and bequests and require recipients to include them in their tax base. Because the household component of the X tax is a wage tax, the most natural treatment would deny donors a deduction and exempt recipients from tax. Similar considerations apply to the treatment of compulsory private transfer payments, such as child support and alimony.

Exemption would be the natural treatment of public transfer payments under an X tax. Carroll and Viard (2012: 60) recommended that approach, but the President's Advisory Panel (2005: 87–89) proposed partial taxation of Social Security benefits and Antos et al. (2015: 4) proposed full taxation of Social Security and unemployment insurance benefits. Inclusion would be the natural treatment of public transfer payments under a PET, but exemption of means-tested transfer payments would be a sensible simplification measure.

The impact of a VAT on recipients of public and private transfers would depend on whether and how the real value of the transfers responded to the VAT. Regardless of whether the VAT was accommodated, it would not change the real value of inflation-indexed transfers that do not depend upon wage levels, such as Social Security benefits for cohorts attaining age 60 before the VAT was introduced. The VAT would reduce the real value of fixed nominal benefits, such as TANF, child support, and alimony, if (and only if) it was accommodated. Regardless of whether it was accommodated, the VAT would reduce the real value of wage-indexed benefits, such as Social Security benefits for cohorts attaining age 60 after the VAT was introduced.[5] In each case, however, legislative adjustments could be made to the relevant programs to offset any undesired changes in the real value of the transfers.

[5] See Toder, Nunns, and Rosenberg (2011: 9–11) and Viard (2015) for further discussion of a VAT's effects on Social Security. The reduction in the real wage caused by a VAT would also cause

Many public transfer programs determine eligibility and benefits though means tests that rely on a mixture of labor income, capital income, and assets, with the income information often verified from income tax returns. As Carroll and Viard (2012: 63–64) note, such means tests would be harder to enforce under an X because household tax returns would report only wages. They suggest that some means-tested programs for the elderly base benefits on lifetime wages, as computed from Social Security records, but they note the limitations of that approach.[6]

11.4.2 Owner-Occupied Housing and Consumer Durables

A tax system that follows income-tax principles must measure and tax imputed rent on the same terms as other investment returns. A consumption tax can also measure and tax imputed rent while allowing a deduction for home and durable purchases. Unlike an income tax, however, a consumption tax system can choose a simpler alternative, the prepayment method. This method ignores imputed rents and treats purchases, improvement, and maintenance of homes and durables as consumption. If tax rates remain constant over time, the prepayment method results in a zero expected effective tax rate on new homes and durables because the purchase price equals the present value of the expected future imputed rents.

The prepayment method is broadly similar to the current income tax system's treatment of homes and durables, in which these assets are purchased with after-tax dollars and there is no tax on the imputed rent or on most sales. (Interestingly, the current tax system effectively applies consumption-tax treatment to homes and durables, avoiding the complexity that would arise from applying income-tax treatment.) The prepayment method would be easy to apply under a VAT or X tax, as it would simply require taxing the construction of houses and durables in the same manner as the production of consumer goods. Purchases and sales of existing houses and durables would be disregarded in the same manner as financial transactions.

If the prepayment method was employed in its pure form under the PET, purchases of homes and durables would be treated as positive consumption and sales of

a reduction in real payroll tax revenue; because the revenue reduction would begin immediately, but the benefit reduction would apply only to cohorts that reached age 60 after the VAT was implemented, the net effect would be an impairment of the Social Security trust fund's financial status.

[6] A PET could accommodate consumption-based means tests, but Carroll and Viard (2012: 62–64) argue that such tests would be undesirable. As previously discussed, consumption taxation is neutral with respect to the timing of consumption if (and only if) the tax rate is constant over time. Although a consumption-based means test would be a form of consumption taxation, it would not feature the necessary constant tax rate. Instead, the means test would impose positive marginal tax rates on households in years in which they are on the program and zero marginal tax rates in other years, thereby giving households an incentive to reduce consumption in selected years to qualify for the program. Carroll and Viard also argue that there is a moral imperative to prevent households that fail to save from falling into severe destitution and note that such an imperative necessitates some saving disincentives in transfer programs.

existing homes and durables would be treated as negative consumption. A household buying a home would not deduct the purchase cost, but would have to add to its tax base any asset draw-downs and borrowing used to finance the purchase. Conversely, a household selling a home would not be taxed on the sale, but would deduct any assets purchased or debt retired with the sale proceeds. Households would also deduct mortgage payments, both principal and interest, in the same manner as payments on other loans. As a result, the tax base could be very large in the year of purchase and could be negative in the year of sale, possibly moving the household between tax brackets. Also, the need to make a large up-front tax payment when the home is purchased might be seen as a liquidity problem, although a household that borrows to buy the house should be able to borrow to pay the tax. Fortunately, the volatility can be addressed relatively easily. Seidman (1997: 79–80 and 83) proposed that the PET ignore mortgage debt, so that there would be no inclusion of the borrowing and no deduction for interest and principal payments.

Carroll and Viard (2012: 154–55) argued that capital gains on homes should not be taxed under the prepayment method. If homeowners earn only a normal rate of return and there is no uncertainty, the prepayment method already taxes all future imputed rents because their value is reflected in the purchase price. In the actual economy, to be sure, some homeowners may earn unexpectedly high returns on homes. Nevertheless, taxing realized capital gains would not be a good way to tax these lucky returns, as it would be difficult to separate out expected capital gains that formed part of the normal return or to offer offsetting relief for homeowners with unexpectedly low returns. Moreover, realization-based capital gains taxation would create a lock-in effect, disrupting efficient allocation of the housing stock and impeding mobility, and would require that home improvement costs be tracked and capitalized. Nevertheless, the USA plan would have taxed capital gains on home sales and Seidman (1997: 81–82) endorsed that approach.

11.4.3 Other Household Tax Issues

The options for the treatment of the family are similar across the X tax, the PET, and the current income tax. With graduated tax rates, the familiar conflict between marriage neutrality and equal taxation of couples with equal incomes arises in each case. However, the X tax is somewhat simpler than the PET because non-wage income and financial flows need not be allocated between spouses and property settlements in divorce can be ignored. Also, the PET, like the current income tax, but unlike the X tax, is likely to require a "kiddie tax" to ensure that capital income is not shifted to children who are in lower tax brackets. The VAT need not address the treatment of the family.

The VAT, the X tax, the PET, and the income tax can each tax all, some, or no non-savings fringe benefits at the household level. The X tax and the income tax have an additional option to tax fringe benefits at the firm level by denying or limiting the firm's deduction for the costs of the benefits. In contrast, the PET, which has no tax on firms, can tax fringe benefits only at the household level. Both the X tax and the PET can provide tax relief for work-related expenses on household tax returns. The VAT can provide relief only through zero tax rates on types of goods and services thought to be work-related; it cannot distinguish among households purchasing a particular type of good or service based on whether their circumstances suggest a stronger or weaker connection between their purchases and work.

The VAT can ignore pensions. Under the PET, households deduct employee contributions and pay tax on withdrawals and benefit payments and employer contributions are disregarded. The treatment of pensions under the X tax is more difficult. The approach most consistent with the X tax's logical structure would allow firms to deduct, and would tax workers on, the market value of pension benefit accruals, but that approach would pose formidable valuation difficulties. Antos et al. (2015: 4) proposed that employees not be taxed on pension benefits or employer contributions, but that employers be allowed to deduct only half of contributions, effectively subjecting contributions to a flat firm-level tax at half the business cash flow tax rate. Carroll and Viard (2012: 56) recommended that firms deduct contributions to pension funds and that workers pay tax on benefits and withdrawals, in line with current law.

11.4.4 Political Concerns

All of the taxes are likely to be subject to political pressure to narrow the tax base. Many countries' VATs have experienced significant base narrowing, with zero tax rates for food and other necessities. Exclusions, deductions, and credits that appear on household tax returns under the income tax could generally be provided under the household tax returns used by the X tax and PET. As Carroll and Viard (2012: 60–61) note, base narrowing under the X tax would need to diverge in one respect from base narrowing under the income tax and the PET. Because households would be taxed only on wages under the X tax, tax preferences provided on household returns would be unavailable to households living off of investments unless the preferences were structured as refundable tax credits. The adoption of the X tax would dramatically transform the debate over refundable tax credits, with investors, as well as low-income households, pressing for refundability. While the need to adopt refundable tax credits might deter the addition of undesirable tax preferences to household tax returns, it might also impede the proper functioning of desirable tax preferences.

A common concern about the VAT, vividly expressed by Christian and Robbins (2011), is that it might function as a money machine that fuels the growth of federal spending. It is difficult to assess the validity of this concern. Although countries with VATs tend to have larger public sectors than those without, this correlation does not demonstrate that the VAT *caused* an expansion of government.

Of course, there would be little concern if a benevolent government raised more revenue because the VAT's greater efficiency reduced the social costs of raising revenue. The fear, however, appears to be that the VAT's lack of visibility to voters might enable the government to expand in ways that fully informed voters would not have accepted. If the VAT were not listed on customer receipts, it would be a highly invisible tax. Nevertheless, the VAT could be separately listed on customer receipts, a practice followed by some countries' VATs and by state and local retail sales taxes in the United States. Sullivan (2010) argued that the visibility of Canada's VAT, which is listed on receipts, has prevented it from serving as a money machine.

11.5 NONPROFIT ORGANIZATIONS AND GOVERNMENTS

11.5.1 Tax Treatment of Nonprofit Organizations

The appropriate treatment of nonprofit organizations is clearest under the X tax. The analysis for the X tax can be used to clarify the appropriate treatment under the other taxes.

Under the X tax, nonprofit organizations should be exempt from the business cash flow tax on the production of goods and services that they do not sell at market value because there would be no way to accurately value those goods and services. As discussed in section 11.7.3, that treatment would also spare those entities from the X tax's capital levy. Carroll and Viard (2012: 148) recommended that the organizations' commercial enterprises also be exempt from the cash flow tax to avoid the need to separate the enterprises from the entities' other operations. Nonprofit organizations' employees should be subject to the household wage tax on the same terms as other workers. That policy would resemble current law, as those employees pay the same individual income taxes as other workers. As Carroll and Viard (2012: 146–47) explain, exempting nonprofit organizations' employees from the wage tax would artificially lower hiring costs for the organizations and artificially encourage them to produce in-house when it might be more efficient to contract production out to businesses.

A VAT simply combines the two components of the X tax while moving the wage tax to the employer level and equalizing the tax rates on wages and business cash flow. Those changes do not alter the above logic. Accordingly, nonprofit organizations should be subject only to the wage-tax component of the VAT. As Carroll and Viard (2012: 145–48) explain, rather than paying VAT, the organizations should pay an employer payroll tax at the VAT rate.[7] Similarly, under a PET, the organizations' employees would include their wages in the computation of their taxable consumption.

[7] An interesting question arises as to the treatment of goods that a nonprofit organization sells to a business. The sale price might well exceed the taxed wages spent in the production of the goods, as part of the price could reflect untaxed business cash flow. The simplest approach would be to allow the business purchaser to deduct the full price under an X tax or to claim a credit based on the full price under a credit-invoice VAT.

Under current law, gifts to charitable 501(c)(3) organizations are deducted by the donor and excluded by the recipient. That treatment can be continued under the PET, if desired. In line with the discussion of tax preferences under the X tax, any preference for charitable contributions would need to be delivered through a refundable tax credit, to make the preference available to investors.[8]

11.5.2 Tax Treatment of State, Local, and Tribal Governments

Wages and business cash flow of state, local, and tribal governments should be treated the same as those of nonprofit organizations. Accordingly, under a VAT, these governments should be subject to an employer payroll tax.[9] Unfortunately, the imposition of such a tax has drawn strong objections by those who mistakenly view it as a new burden on state and local governments. The absence of such a payroll tax would be a significant shortcoming of a VAT.

The current income tax system exempts municipal bond interest from the tax imposed on other interest income. The income tax reduction under the VAT option would diminish the value of this preference and the income tax repeal under the X tax and PET options would eliminate it. If desired, a municipal bond preference could be provided under the PET by excluding such interest from the computation of taxable consumption. The VAT and X tax would have no ready mechanism to provide a tax preference for municipal bonds, although state and local government borrowing could be subsidized through a spending program. The elimination of the preference or its restructuring as a spending program would likely be beneficial, even in the absence of fundamental tax reform.

The current income tax system allows an itemized deduction for a household's property taxes and the larger of its sales taxes or income taxes. If desired, the PET could allow a similar deduction. It might be somewhat more difficult to provide a similarly broad deduction under the X tax, as households would be taxed only on wages.

[8] Carroll and Viard (2012: 181–82 n. 8) allude to a potential constitutional difficulty. If cash payments under a refundable tax credit are viewed as similar to direct government spending, a credit for contributions to religious organizations may be held to violate the establishment clause of the First Amendment.

[9] It would make no economic difference whether or not a similar payroll tax was imposed on the federal government, as the government would pay any such tax to itself. As Carroll and Viard (2012: 172) observe, the federal government's recorded outlays currently include gross-of-individual income-tax wage payments to its employees and its recorded receipts currently include the income taxes collected on those wages. Imposing the payroll tax, with offsetting inclusions in both outlays and receipts, would therefore maintain continuity in budgetary accounting.

11.5.3 Impact on State and Local Tax Systems

States could face challenges in maintaining their current tax systems under each of the three options. Because states often piggyback on the federal tax system, any change in federal taxes could alter the range of taxes that states could easily impose.

Some partial-replacement VAT proposals, such as Graetz (2008), would eliminate the federal individual income tax for a large group of middle-income households and maintain it only for a relatively small group of high-income households, which might make it administratively difficult for states to maintain income tax systems with broader coverage. States might also find it easier to conform to the federal VAT than to maintain their retail sales taxes. States that conformed to the federal VAT would probably apply some type of apportionment rule, which would not yield the same geographic division of the tax base as the current regime in which the purchaser's state generally imposes retail sales tax.

State and local tax systems would likely face greater challenges under the full-replacement options. Under the X tax, states would face considerable pressure to conform to the new system, as it might be administratively difficult for them to maintain conventional individual income taxes (that apply to capital income) and conventional corporate income taxes (that use depreciation rather than expensing and allow an interest deduction). The business cash flow tax would probably be apportioned in the same manner as current state corporate income taxes. States would face similar pressure to conform to the PET, as it might be administratively difficult for them to maintain conventional individual income taxes (that distinguish between interest and principal) and corporate income taxes. Without any federal business tax with which to conform, states might adopt simpler, but economically flawed, types of business taxes, such as gross receipts taxes.

11.6 BUSINESS TAXATION UNDER THE X TAX

The X tax faces two potential difficulties in its treatment of business firms. The PET avoids these problems because it has no separate tax on firms and the VAT also generally avoids them.

11.6.1 Negative Business Cash Flows

The X tax must address the treatment of firms with negative business cash flows. The cash-flow tax imposes a zero effective tax rate on a marginal new investment only if the firm's expensing deduction provides tax savings equal in present value to the taxes imposed on the investment's future cash flows. Problems arise if firms with negative cash flows are not accorded refundability or equally generous treatment. Without such treatment, a firm that is in negative-cash-flow status when making an investment and positive-cash-flow status when it receives the investment's payoffs would face a positive effective marginal tax rate on the investment.

Unfortunately, a significant number of firms may have negative cash flows in any given year. Moreover, because cash flow is taxed at the firm level, the X tax would not allow an individual who owns equity in two firms to deduct negative cash flows from one firm against positive cash flows from the other. In contrast, the current income tax system allows owners of flow-through firms to net losses from one firm against gains from other firms.

Allowing refunds for negative cash flows might facilitate fraud and attempts to deduct hobby losses. Also, direct cash payments to firms with losses might be perceived as corporate welfare, an objection that proved fatal to the safe-harbor leasing arrangement sanctioned by the 1981 tax law, which effectively allowed firms with losses to sell certain tax deductions. Carroll and Viard (2012: 80) recommended five to ten years of carryback and unlimited carryforward with interest and Hall and Rabushka (1995: 144–45) and the President's Advisory Panel (2005: 166) recommended unlimited carryforward with interest. Although extended carryback and unlimited carryforward with interest should result in effective tax rates close to zero for many firms, the effective tax rate would remain positive for liquidity-constrained firms and firms that faced a risk of going out of business before the carryforwards can be used.

The VAT would largely avoid this problem because negative value added is much less common than negative business cash flow. Moreover, some countries' VATs provide at least limited refundability for negative value added.

11.6.2 Distinguishing Wages from Business Cash Flow

The X tax must distinguish wages from business cash flow because wages are taxed more favorably than cash flow, except for workers in the top bracket. Owners who work for closely held firms would have an incentive to overstate their wages if they are not in the top bracket and such overstatements might be difficult to detect and correct. The VAT avoids these problems because it applies the same flat tax rate to wages and business cash flow.

A similar difficulty arises under the current income tax system. Capital income generated by firms subject to the corporate income tax faces double income taxation at the firm and household levels (although at preferential rates at the household level) while wages face income tax only at the household level (although they are also subject to payroll tax). To prevent corporate income tax avoidance, the IRS attempts to limit corporations' wage deductions to a reasonable level.

In one respect, the problem would be less severe under the X tax than under the current income tax. For owners in the top bracket, it would make no difference whether payments were classified as wages or business cash flow. In another respect, though, the problem would be more severe under the X tax than under the income tax because it would arise for all closely held firms, including firms that are not currently subject to the corporate income tax.

Carroll and Viard (2012: 73–74) recommended that firms be required to limit wage payments to owners to "reasonable compensation." The self-employment tax would be abolished, with payroll tax applying to the reasonable compensation paid by firms. Their acknowledgement that "there may be some difficulties in applying the above rules" might understate the challenges posed by setting reasonable compensation levels for closely held firms throughout the economy.

Carroll and Viard recommended a special rule for sole proprietorships, allowing them to treat all of their cash flow as wages. Antos et al. (2015: 5) would extend this treatment to other owners who work more than 500 hours during the year for the firm. They proposed that owners, other than sole proprietors, who work less than 500 hours would be subject to a reasonable-compensation rule. That approach might still be problematic because it relies on reasonable-compensation rules for some owners and (like the current passive-loss rules) relies on measuring hours worked and has a cliff effect at the 500-hour point.

In general, it would not be crucial for all wages and cash flow to be "correctly" distinguished, although doing so would minimize the distortion between arrangements in which the owners and the worker were the same person and arrangements in which they were different people. The primary reason to distinguish the two types of payments is to allow wages, which are often received by taxpayers who are less well off, to receive the benefits of graduated rates, which are denied to business cash flow, which tends to go to those who are well off. It seems reasonable to give the benefit of graduated rates to any owner who performed substantial work. Of course, any owner who received very large payments would move into the top bracket anyway.

11.7 TRANSITION IN CLOSED ECONOMY

This section considers the three options' transitional wealth effects in a closed economy. Income tax repeal or reduction would likely increase the value of existing wealth, with the gains accruing to equity holders. The introduction of a consumption tax would impose a capital levy on existing wealth that would outweigh the increase in value from income tax reduction or repeal. The incidence of the capital levy would vary across the three options.

11.7.1 Wealth Gain from Income Tax Reduction or Repeal

The Johansson (1969)–Samuelson (1964) theorem establishes that income tax repeal or reduction leaves the values of existing capital unchanged when both of two conditions hold. First, an unlimited amount of new capital that substitutes perfectly for existing capital can be produced as quickly as desired at constant replacement cost and with no adjustment costs. Changes in the demand for capital then translate fully and immediately into changes in the quantity of capital and the price remains fixed at the constant replacement cost. Second, the income tax on capital is collected concurrently, with a constant ratio of tax payments to net income throughout each capital asset's lifetime. Under these assumptions, income tax reduction or repeal would not increase the value of existing capital. Instead, the increased volume of saving and investment would reduce before-tax cash flows and drive up discount rates to keep the present discounted value of after-tax cash flows unchanged.

However, the constant-cost assumption generally does not hold in the actual economy. When income tax reduction or repeal caused more capital to be produced, the production cost of new capital would likely rise, increasing the value of existing capital. The increase in firms' demand for capital would not instantly increase the quantity of capital with no price change; instead, quantity would rise sluggishly and price would also rise. The concurrent-tax assumption also does not hold for the US tax system. Business income taxes are generally back-loaded due to accelerated depreciation and up-front credits. Because taxes are a higher fraction of net income late in each asset's life, existing capital carries deferred tax liabilities and is valued below replacement cost. If the King (1974)–Auerbach (1979)–Bradford (1981) new view is partly or fully correct, individual income taxes on dividends also create deferred tax liabilities. Income tax reduction or repeal would forgive part or all of the deferred tax liabilities, raising the value of existing capital relative to its replacement cost.

The wealth gains from income tax reduction or repeal would generally accrue to equity holders. Because equity holders are the firm's residual claimants, they capture the gains from the forgiveness of the firm's deferred tax liabilities and the increase in the value of its capital due to increased production with rising replacement costs. And, corporate shareholders reap the benefits of the forgiveness of any deferred dividend taxes. Holders of the firm's debt would be largely unchanged, at least if the debt had a very short time remaining before maturity (so that its value would not be affected by interest rates or the tax treatment of interest payments).[10]

11.7.2 Capital Levy

In the absence of transition relief, consumption taxes generally impose capital levies on existing wealth because consumption out of that wealth is subject to tax.

Simulation studies estimate larger long-run output gains from tax reform that impose larger capital levies. The gains arise from two sources. First, the capital levy is borne by older generations alive when it is imposed and permits a lighter tax burden on subsequent generations; that redistribution stimulates saving and increases long-run output. This effect improves social welfare if, and only if, current policy is viewed as assigning too few resources to future generations, relative to current generations. This redistribution to future generations could be achieved through other budgetary policies and could be offset by such policies. Second, the capital levy is lump-sum, and therefore yields efficiency gains, if it is unexpected and does not alter expectations of future policy.

[10] The value of a firm's debt would be affected if the tax changes altered the probability that the firm would default.

Despite these gains, it is not clear that capital levies are desirable. Kaplow (2008) and Carroll and Viard (2012: 126–27) argue that deliberate attempts to impose unexpected taxes are antithetical to the rule of law. It is not immediately apparent that a household should be taxed twice merely because it earns income while an income tax is in effect and consumes while a consumption tax is in effect. Of course, even if a capital levy is undesirable, it may be appropriate to recapture the gains that owners of existing capital receive from income tax reduction or repeal.

The capital levy imposed by a PET has a quite different form and incidence from the capital levy imposed by an X tax. The following stylized example, borrowed from Carroll and Viard (2012: 123), permits a comparison of the capital levy in a closed economy. (As discussed below, additional considerations arise in an open economy.) There are two individuals, Smith and Jones, and a single firm. The firm holds $100 of capital and has issued $30 of bonds, so its equity is worth $70. Jones holds the $30 of bonds issued by the firm and has also loaned $20 to Smith, so her net worth is $50. Smith holds the $70 equity issued by the firm and owes $20 to Smith, so her net worth is $50. The debt has a very short time remaining before maturity. There is no nonbusiness capital (owner-occupied homes and durables or capital held by governments or nonprofit organizations). The two individuals' combined wealth is $100, which equals the value of the capital stock, as it must in a closed economy.

The PET's capital levy would be relatively simple. Because each household would be taxed on its consumption, it would face a capital levy on its net worth on the effective date. Household borrowers would receive a capital subsidy because they would deduct interest and principal payments on their debt. In the example, Smith and Jones would each face a capital levy on their $50 net worth. The primary transition relief under the PET would likely be a deduction by households of their pre-enactment income-tax basis in their asset holdings. As Seidman (1997: 101) and Kaplow (1995) note, households should deduct pre-enactment basis on a fixed schedule independent of whether or when they sell the assets.

The X tax's capital levy would be quite different because it would be imposed at the firm level through the business cash flow tax. The levy would reduce the value of the firm's capital stock by a fraction equal to the flat tax rate on business cash flow. Although the aggregate size of the capital levy would be the same as that arising from a PET with the same tax rate, the incidence would be quite different. Equity holders would bear the burden as the firms' residual claimants, with little impact on holders of the firm's debt or household borrowers and lenders. In the example, Smith owns all $70 of the firm's equity and would therefore bear the full capital levy on the firm's entire $100 capital stock.

The primary transition relief under the X tax would likely be deductions by firms of part or all of their pre-enactment depreciable basis in their capital stock, both inventories and fixed business capital. Hall and Rabushka (1995: 78–79), the President's Advisory Panel (2005: 173–74), Carroll and Viard (2012: 131), and Antos et al. (2015: 6) all propose relief of this type. The equity holders would receive the benefit of this firm-level transition relief, which seems appropriate because they would bear the firm-level capital levy. As under the PET, the deduction should be claimed on a fixed schedule that does not depend on whether or when the firm sells its capital. As discussed in section 11.8.3, however, the transition issues posed by the X tax become significantly more complicated in an open economy.

If the Federal Reserve did not accommodate the VAT, its capital levy would have the same incidence as the X tax's capital levy. The value of business capital would be reduced by a fraction equal to the VAT rate and borrowers and lenders would be unaffected. As previously discussed, however, the VAT would likely be accommodated. The price increase would reduce the real value of the nominal debt, which would harm lenders and help borrowers and equity holders. With full accommodation, the incidence of the capital levy would be the same as under the PET. The levy would be smaller, however, because the partial-replacement VAT would have a lower tax rate than the full-replacement PET.

It is difficult to assess the proper division of the burden of any capital levy between debt holders and equity holders. There may be a case for placing higher proportional burdens on equity holders because they would reap the gains from the higher asset values induced by income tax repeal, because they contractually agreed to be the firm's residual claimants and to bear the risk of unexpected changes in its financial status (arguably including tax changes), and because they tend to be more affluent, on average, than debt holders.

11.7.3 Other Transition Issues

Non-business capital would not be subject to the capital levy under any of the three options. The prepayment method would spare existing owner-occupied homes and consumer durables from the capital levy. Because the method treats the consumption from those assets as having already taken place, the future imputed rents from existing homes and durables would not be subject to VAT, the X tax's business cash flow tax, or PET. On balance, sparing homeowners from the capital levy seems appropriate. Homeowners are less affluent, on average, than the business equity holders who would bear the capital levy under the X tax or the general holders of net worth (exclusive of non-business capital) who would bear it under the PET or an accommodated VAT. Furthermore, tax reform would likely reduce the demand for owner-occupied homes and durables at the same time that it would increase the demand for business capital because the former assets would lose their tax-favored status. If the constant-cost assumption does not hold, the replacement cost, and hence the value, of existing homes and durables would fall even as the replacement cost of existing business capital rose. For homes and durables, imposing a capital levy would amplify a decline in before-tax values, not offset a rise in before-tax values. Exempting nonprofit organizations and state, local, and tribal governments from the business cash flow tax would similarly spare their initial capital holdings from the capital levy, a result that also seems appropriate.

As Carroll and Viard (2012: 148–51) discuss, rules would be required to prevent tax-motivated migration by capital to the non-business sector (such as conversions of homes from rental to owner-occupied status) after the reform is announced and before it takes effect. The tax system would also need to ensure that similar movements of capital after the reform took effect were done at arm's length prices.

Another significant transition issue under the X tax concerns the treatment of interest on existing debt contracts. Many proposals would maintain, at least in part, the inclusion of interest income and the deduction of business and mortgage interest payments for existing contracts. Also, because all bonds would receive the same interest exclusion that municipal bonds currently enjoy, municipal bonds would lose their tax-preferred status, triggering a decline in the value of existing municipal bonds. Most proposals would not offer any transition relief for holders of existing municipal bonds, perhaps because the value decline would result from changes in their own tax treatment of competing assets rather than a change in their own tax treatment.

Numerous other transition issues would arise. Cash hoarding prior to enactment would pose a transition problem for the PET, as discussed by Seidman (1997: 106–7). The X tax would need to specify a treatment for firms' unused credits and net-operating-loss carryforwards. Still another issue concerns existing tax-preferred retirement accounts. Antos et al. (2015: 6 n. 6) proposed that existing front-loaded tax-preferred savings accounts, for which contributions are deductible and withdrawals are taxable, be closed to new contributions and that withdrawals from such accounts be subject to the household X tax. They proposed that existing Roth-type accounts, for which contributions are nondeductible and withdrawals are tax-free, be converted to ordinary accounts, which would allow contributions to remain nondeductible and withdrawals to remain tax-free in accord with the standard X tax rules.

11.8 THE OPEN ECONOMY

The VAT, X tax, and PET would have further differences in an open economy. A key issue is whether each tax would be a destination-based tax on domestic consumption or an origin-based tax on domestic production. That choice has important implications for tax administration, for the location of investments with above-normal returns, and for transitional wealth effects.

11.8.1 The Competitiveness Fallacy

The PET would be destination-based because it would tax consumption by domestic residents. The VAT would also surely be destination-based. Other countries' VATs are universally imposed as destination-based taxes, a result achieved through border adjustments that impose tax on imports and rebate tax on exports.

In contrast, the X tax would lend itself most naturally to an origin basis, although it could be placed on a destination basis through a border adjustment. If a border adjustment was adopted, the percentage value of the import tax and the export rebate would presumably be set equal to the tax rate on business cash flow. The President's Advisory Panel (2005: 167–72) recommended border adjustment for the X tax and the Heritage Foundation (2011) proposed the same for its cash-flow tax, but Carroll and Viard (2012: 115) recommend that the X tax not be border adjusted. Hufbauer (1996: 47–61 and 69–70) notes that an X tax border adjustment would likely violate international trade agreements. Nevertheless, the United States might be able to renegotiate international trade agreements to allow border adjustment of an X tax.

A common motivation for border adjustment is the belief that destination-based taxes improve competitiveness by boosting exports and reducing imports. As Viard (2009) notes, however, economists have long recognized that this belief is mistaken. Because the United States' future exports must be equal in present value to its future imports plus its current net debt to foreigners, a border adjustment could not increase exports without increasing imports. The real exchange rate would adjust in response to the border adjustment, with the dollar appreciating to choke off the putative increase in exports and reduction in imports. If the tax was not accommodated and the US price level remained fixed, the nominal exchange rate (the value of the dollar relative to foreign currencies) would rise. If the US price level rose due to full monetary accommodation, the nominal exchange rate would remain unchanged. In either case, American consumers would pay higher prices than foreign consumers on world markets, reflecting a real appreciation of the dollar.

It is just as well that the border adjustment would not permanently boost exports and reduce imports. Achieving that mercantilist goal would mean forever producing more goods to send abroad while receiving fewer goods in return. The competitiveness argument provides only a political, not an economic, advantage for destination-based taxes.[11] The border adjustment's actual virtue is that it would eliminate transfer pricing problems, which are the bane of origin-based taxes, and would attract mobile investments with above-normal returns to the United States.

11.8.2 Transfer Pricing and Above-Normal Returns

Following Carroll and Viard (2012: 112–13), suppose that an American has an idea that will produce future cash flows with a present value of $1 million. A destination-based tax would be neutral with respect to the location at which the idea is developed because the American's consumption would be taxed, no matter where she develops the idea. In contrast, an origin-based tax might deter the development of the idea inside the United States because the tax would apply only to returns earned in the United States.

As Bradford (2004: 19–20) explained, this problem can theoretically be avoided. A well-designed origin-based tax would create no incentive for the American to sell or lease her idea to an *unrelated* foreign firm for $1 million rather than developing it

[11] The PET's destination basis might not give it a political advantage because proponents of the competitiveness fallacy attribute the imagined competitiveness advantages to the explicit collection of taxes on imports and the rebate of taxes on exports, which does not occur under the PET. Indeed, Hartman (2004: 1081) criticizes the PET on the grounds that international trade agreements prohibit it from being border adjusted.

in the United States because the American's $1 million receipt would be taxed as the proceeds from the export of an intangible asset. If the American instead developed the idea through a foreign firm she wholly owns, the firm should, in principle, make a similar $1 million payment to the American, on which she should be taxed. If such a payment was made, the origin-based tax would create no incentive to develop the idea abroad.

Because the American owns the firm, though, the price she "charges" it would merely be a transfer price that she could easily understate. An understated payment would allow the wholly-owned firm to earn additional profits, which would ultimately be paid to the American as dividends that the X tax would not tax. The origin-based tax might therefore prompt the American to develop the idea abroad and to understate the value of the idea.

Due to its use of expensing, the X tax would not penalize locating normal-returns investments in the United States. But, an origin-based X tax would penalize locating investments with above-normal returns in the United States. Mobile investments with above-normal returns could escape US tax by locating outside the United States.

For two reasons, transfer pricing problems and the tax disincentive to locate investments with above-normal returns in the United States might be larger under an origin-based X tax than under the current income tax system. First, the X tax might feature a business cash flow tax rate higher than the current corporate income tax rate. Second, the X tax would not impose a repatriation tax on foreign subsidiaries' dividend payments. Weisbach (2000) argued that an origin-based flat tax or X tax would face severe transfer pricing and related complications. The use of a destination basis therefore would have the major advantages of eliminating transfer pricing problems and attracting mobile investments with above-normal returns to the United States. Although destination-based taxes would have their own compliance challenges, including tax evasion on imports and fraudulent export rebate claims, those challenges would likely be relatively modest.

The greatest drawback of destination-based taxes is that they would shift part of the tax burden from foreigners to Americans. Destination-based taxes would be imposed on Americans' consumption while origin-based taxes would be imposed on consumption financed by US production, including the consumption of foreign holders of US capital and excluding the consumption of American holders of foreign capital. The failure of destination-based taxes to tax foreigners' above-normal returns from US investments may be viewed as an unduly generous policy, particularly for immobile investments. Destination-based taxes would also reduce the tax burden on foreigners' existing holdings of US capital, giving rise to potentially undesirable cross-border wealth effects.

11.8.3 Cross-Border Wealth Effects

As previously discussed, income tax reduction or repeal would benefit business equity owners. In an open economy, part of those gains would accrue to foreign holders of equity in American firms. Unless foreigners bear a sufficient portion of the capital levy from the new consumption tax, tax reform would result in a net wealth transfer from Americans to foreigners.

The following stylized framework may shed some light on the cross-border wealth effects of a VAT, a PET, an origin-based X tax, and a border-adjusted X tax. Full monetary accommodation of the VAT is assumed. The taxes are assumed to provide no transition relief.[12]

The US capital stock is assumed to be $70 trillion and the foreign capital stock (whose value does not affect the analysis) is assumed to be $200 trillion. Based on very rough inference from recent Bureau of Economic Analysis data,[13] foreigners are assumed to hold $15 trillion of US capital and $15 trillion of US debt and Americans are assumed to hold $18 trillion of foreign capital and $5 trillion of foreign debt. Americans' wealth is $63 trillion and the US net external liability is $7 trillion. The top panel of table 11.1 shows the assumed holdings. The remainder of the table shows the size of the base on which each tax would impose a capital levy; the table does not show the gains to American and foreign holders of US capital from repeal or reduction of the corporate income tax.

The accommodated VAT would leave the nominal exchange rate unchanged; the increase in the US price level would provide the necessary real appreciation of the dollar. The nominal value of existing US capital would be unchanged, with the price increase reducing its real value. As shown in the second panel of the table, a capital levy would be imposed on Americans' holdings of all four assets, a total base of $63 trillion. There would be no change in the real value of foreigners' holdings of any assets.

In this framework, the PET would have the same real effects as the VAT. Like the VAT, the PET would increase the effective price paid by American consumers (although the increase would take the form of tax obligations reported on annual tax returns rather than an increase in quoted prices) and would leave the nominal exchange rate unchanged.

Under the origin-based X tax, there would be no change in the US price level or in nominal and real exchange rates. The nominal value of US capital would decline, reducing its real value for both American and foreign holders. As shown in the third

[12] The analysis makes several other assumptions. All US debt is nominal and dollar-denominated and all foreign debt is nominal and denominated in foreign currency. All debt has a very short remaining time to maturity, so that its value is unaffected by interest rates or the tax treatment of interest payments. The exchange rate is flexible and the foreign price level is unaffected by the US tax reform.

[13] Westmoreland (2016) reports that, at the end of the third quarter of 2015, foreigners held $30.6 trillion of US assets, including $10.7 trillion of equity, and Americans held $23.3 trillion of foreign assets, including $12.1 trillion of equity. The analysis treats all non-equity assets as debt and treats each $100 of equity as a claim on $150 of capital net of $50 debt. Foreigners are therefore treated as holding $20 trillion of US debt and claims on $15 trillion of US capital, net of $5 trillion of US debt, yielding net holdings of $15 trillion of US capital and $15 trillion of US debt. Similarly, Americans are treated as holding $11 trillion of foreign debt and claims on $18 trillion of foreign capital, net of $6 trillion of foreign debt, yielding net holdings of $18 trillion of foreign capital and $5 trillion of foreign debt.

Table 11.1 Stylized example of cross-border wealth effects ($ trillions)

	US Capital	*Foreign Capital*	*Cross-Border US Debt*	*Cross-Border Foreign Debt*	*Total*
			Holdings		
Americans	55	18	−15	5	**63**
Foreigners	15	182	15	−5	**207**
			Capital Levy Base Under VAT and PET		
Americans	55	18	−15	5	**63**
Foreigners					**0**
			Capital Levy Base Under Origin-Based X Tax		
Americans	55				**55**
Foreigners	15				**15**
			Capital Levy Base Under Border-Adjusted X Tax		
Americans	55	18		5	**78**
Foreigners			−15		**−15**

Source: Author's calculations.

panel of the table, the capital levy would fall on the $70 trillion US capital stock, both the $55 trillion held by Americans and the $15 trillion held by foreigners.

Under the border-adjusted X tax, there would be no change in the US price level. The dollar would appreciate relative to foreign currencies, which would increase the real value of foreigners' claims on Americans and reduce the real value of Americans' claims on foreigners. As under the origin-based X tax, the nominal value of US capital would decline, reducing its real value for American holders. However, there would be no decline in the real value of US capital for foreign holders because the strengthening of the dollar would offset the decline in the nominal dollar value. The nominal value of US debt, and its real value for American holders, would be unchanged, but its real value for foreign holders would *rise* due to the strengthening of the dollar. The real value of foreign capital and foreign debt for foreign holders would be unchanged, but their real values for American holders would decline due to the strengthening of the dollar. As shown in the bottom panel of the table, the capital levy would fall on a net base of $63 trillion, with a levy on $78 trillion held by Americans and a subsidy to $15 trillion held by foreigners.

The effects of monetary accommodation can be seen by comparing the VAT (which is accommodated) to the border-adjusted X tax (which is not accommodated). Accommodation would not change the size of the capital levy base, but would reallocate $15 trillion of the base from Americans to foreigners by benefiting issuers of US debt and harming its foreign holders.

The effects of border adjustment can be seen by comparing the two X tax options. The border adjustment would add to the tax base the $23 trillion of Americans' holdings of foreign assets and would remove from the tax base the $30 trillion of foreigners' holdings of US assets. The tax base would shrink by $7 trillion, reflecting the net US external liability. However, Americans would pay tax on $23 billion more and foreigners would pay tax on $30 trillion less, reflecting each group's gross cross-border holdings. The reduction in Americans' tax payments to the US government would merely reallocate wealth among Americans, but the reduction in foreigners' tax burdens would constitute a wealth transfer from Americans to foreigners. Auerbach (2007: 45–46, 2008: 19–20), Viard (2009), and Carroll and Viard (2012: 110–11) discuss the dependence of the cross-border wealth transfer on foreigners' *gross* holdings of American assets and provide illustrative calculations of the large magnitudes involved.

Although gross rather than net holdings matter, the effects might not be as large as those computed above because the BEA data do not necessarily reflect the ultimate household ownership. If a foreign parent owns a US company, but American shareholders own some shares in the foreign parent, the BEA data count all of the parent's ownership interest as a foreign claim on Americans. Nevertheless, there would be no wealth transfer to foreigners with respect to the portion of the holdings that are ultimately owned by American shareholders.

11.8.4 Policy Options in the Open Economy

Tax reform in the open economy poses difficult trade-offs. Policymakers must weigh the disadvantageous cross-border wealth effects of destination-based taxes against the challenges posed by origin-based taxes.

The origin-based X tax would maximize the capital levy imposed on foreigners. The levy would be smaller than shown in table 11.1, however, if firm-level transition relief was provided, as foreign equity holders would receive part of the transition relief. A focus on reducing the tax burden on Americans would point toward the adoption of an origin-based X tax, although the tax would face transfer pricing complications and would discourage locating investments with above-normal returns in the United States.

Bradford (2003, 2004: 34–35) proposed to address these challenges of an origin-based X tax by taxing related-party cross-border transactions on a real-plus-financial basis. Under this method, which Carroll and Viard (2012: 113–14) endorsed, a US firm would deduct all payments made to its foreign affiliates, including financial payments, and would be taxed on all receipts from them, including financial receipts. Any mispricing of real transactions would be automatically reversed through the inclusion of the accompanying financial flows. In the example previously considered, the excess dividends would eventually be taxed, correcting the understatement of the value of the idea. The method would effectively tax related-party transactions, which are the transactions for which origin-based taxation is problematic, on a destination basis while taxing transactions between unrelated parties on an origin basis.

The method might not offer an ideal solution. The method would likely be accompanied by transition rules that would effectively remove the capital levy from foreign parent companies' investments in their US affiliates, thereby diminishing the origin-based X tax's principal advantage. The method's practicality has also been questioned. Sullivan (2012: 810) aptly commented that the approach would seem "revolutionary" to transfer pricing practitioners and would have "serious transition problems that are not easily solved." He reasonably concluded that "if a consumption tax without border tax adjustments became law, we would probably still be stuck with the same transfer pricing problems that we have now."

The PET, the VAT, and the border-adjusted X tax would avoid the problems posed by origin-based taxation, but would have the potential to transfer wealth to foreigners. One way to limit the wealth transfers under the PET or the VAT would be to impose a windfall recapture tax at the firm level to offset the forgiveness of deferred tax liabilities caused by repeal or reduction of the corporate income tax; such a tax was proposed by the Treasury Department in 1985, in conjunction with corporate tax rate reduction, as discussed by Zodrow (1988). Foreign equity holders would bear part of the burden of the recapture tax. Household-level transition relief would then be offered to Americans, who would bear the capital levy from the new tax.

A similar approach could be pursued under a border-adjusted X tax, but it would be more difficult because transition relief would probably need to be administered at the firm level. One possibility would be to impose the recapture tax while providing imputation credits that would flow through to American, but not foreign, equity holders.

11.9 CONCLUSION

Although the VAT, the X tax, and the PET have each received extensive consideration in the tax reform literature, less attention has been devoted to comparisons of their effects. This analysis has touched on only some of the relevant issues. It would be useful, for example, to consider the treatment of financial intermediation and to further examine compliance and administration issues. It would also be valuable to consider hybrid options, particularly those in which a business cash flow tax is adopted alongside a PET, as proposed by Institute for Fiscal Studies (1978: 227–58) and Heritage Foundation (2011).

Nevertheless, this analysis makes clear that each option has significant advantages and disadvantages. A choice between the options requires careful consideration of numerous effects, some of which (particularly the cross-border wealth effects) have received little attention. In light of the fiscal imbalance confronting the United States, tax economists should place a high priority on the careful analysis of fundamental tax reform options.

ACKNOWLEDGMENTS

American Enterprise Institute, Washington, DC, 202-419-5202, aviard@aei.org.
I am grateful to Veronika Polakova for research assistance and to James Alm, Alan J. Auerbach, William G. Gale, James Hines, Adele Hunter, Matt Jensen, Regan

Kuchan, Adam Looney, Daniel N. Shaviro, Michael Strain, Victor Thuronyi, Eric Toder, Michael Udell, and participants at a Congressional Budget Office seminar, the Tulane University Fiscal Trilemma conference, an AEI seminar, the NYU Law School Tax Policy Colloquium, the Duke Law School Tax Policy Seminar, the Georgetown University Law Center's Tax Law and Public Finance Workshop, and the Burch Center/Penn Wharton Public Policy Initiative/Urban-Brookings Tax Policy Center conference on the economics of tax policy for helpful comments. I am solely responsible for any errors or omissions.

REFERENCES

Alliance USA. 1995. "Unlimited Savings Allowance (USA) Tax System." *Tax Notes* 66 (11) (supplement): 1485–575.

Antos, Joseph, Andrew Biggs, Alex Brill, and Alan D. Viard. 2015. "Tax and Spending Reform for Fiscal Stability and Economic Growth." *AEI Economic Perspectives*, May.

Auerbach, Alan J. 1979. "Wealth Maximization and the Cost of Capital." *Quarterly Journal of Economics* 93 (3): 433–36.

Auerbach, Alan J. 2007. "Tax Reform in the 21st Century." In *Fundamental Tax Reform: Issues, Choices, and Implications*, edited by John W. Diamond and George R. Zodrow, 27–59. Cambridge, MA: MIT Press.

Auerbach, Alan J. 2008. "The Choice between Income and Consumption Taxes: A Primer." In *Institutional Foundations of Public Finance: Economic and Legal Perspectives*, edited by Alan J. Auerbach and Daniel Shaviro, 13–46. Cambridge, MA: Harvard University Press.

Bipartisan Policy Center. 2010. "Restoring America's Future: Reviving the Economy, Cutting Spending and Debt, and Creating a Simple, Pro-Growth Tax System." http://www.bipartisanpolicy.org/sites/default/files/BPC%20FINAL%20REPORT%20FOR%20PRINTER%2002%2028%2011.pdf

Bradford, David F. 1981. "The Incidence and Allocation Effects of a Tax on Corporate Distributions." *Journal of Public Economics* 15 (1): 1–22.

Bradford, David F. 1986. *Untangling the Income Tax*. Cambridge, MA: Harvard University Press.

Bradford, David F. 2003. "Addressing the Transfer Pricing Problem in an Origin-Basis X Tax." *International Tax and Public Finance* 10 (5): 591–610.

Bradford, David F. 2004. *The X Tax in the World Economy: Going Global with a Simple, Progressive Tax*. Washington, DC: AEI Press.

Carroll, Robert, and Alan D. Viard. 2012. *Progressive Consumption Taxation: The X Tax Revisited*. Washington, DC: AEI Press.

Christian, Ernest S., and Gary A. Robbins. 2011. "A Value-Added Tax Fuels Big Government." *Wall Street Journal*, August 24.

Fisher, Irving. 1937. "Income in Theory and Income Taxation in Practice." *Econometrica* 5 (1): 1–55.

Gale, William G., and Benjamin H. Harris. 2013. "Creating an American Value-Added Tax." In *15 Ways to Rethink the Federal Budget*, edited by Michael Greenstone, Max Harris, Karen Li, Adam Looney, and Jeremy Patashnik, 57–62. Washington, DC: Brookings Institution Hamilton Project.

Graetz, Michael J. 2008. *100 Million Unnecessary Returns: A Simple, Fair, and Competitive Tax Plan for the United States*. New Haven, CT: Yale University Press.

Hall, Robert E., and Alvin Rabushka. 1983. *Low Tax, Simple Tax, Flat Tax*. New York: McGraw Hill.

Hall, Robert E., and Alvin Rabushka. 1995. *The Flat Tax*. 2d ed. Stanford, CA: Hoover Institution Press.

Hartman, David A. 2004. "The Urgency of Border-Adjusted Federal Taxation." *Tax Notes* 104 (10): 1075–88.

Heritage Foundation. 2011. "Saving the American Dream: The Heritage Plan to Fix the Debt, Cut Spending, and Restore Prosperity." http://www.heritage.org/research/reports/2011/05/saving-the-american-dream-the-heritage-plan-to-fix-the-debt-cut-spending-and-restore-prosperity

Hufbauer, Gary Clyde, assisted by Carol Gabyzon. 1996. *Fundamental Tax Reform and Border Adjustments*. Washington, DC: Institute for International Economics.

Institute for Fiscal Studies. 1978. *The Structure and Reform of Direct Taxation*. London: Allen and Unwin.

Johansson, Sven-Erik. 1969. "Income Taxes and Investment Decisions." *Swedish Journal of Economics* 71 (2): 104–10.

Kaldor, Nicholas. 1955. *An Expenditure Tax*. London: Allen and Unwin.

Kaplow, Louis. 1995. "Recovery of Pre-Enactment Basis under a Consumption Tax: The USA Tax System." *Tax Notes* 68 (9): 1109–18.

Kaplow, Louis. 2008. "Capital Levies and Transition to a Consumption Tax." In *Institutional Foundations of Public Finance: Economic and Legal Perspectives*, edited by Alan J. Auerbach and Daniel Shaviro, 112–46. Cambridge, MA: Harvard University Press.

King, Mervyn A. 1974. "Taxation and the Cost of Capital." *Review of Economic Studies* 41 (1): 21–35.

McCaffery, Edward J., and James R. HinesJr. 2010. "The Last Best Hope for Progressivity in Tax." *Southern California Law Review* 83 (5): 1031–98.

President's Advisory Panel on Federal Tax Reform. 2005. *Simple, Fair, and Pro-Growth: Proposals to Fix America's Tax System*. Washington, DC: Government Printing Office.

Pressman, Steven. 1995. "The Feasibility of an Expenditure Tax." *International Journal of Social Economics* 22 (8): 3–15.

Samuelson, Paul. 1964. "Tax Deductibility of Economic Depreciation to Ensure Invariant Valuations." *Journal of Political Economy* 72 (6): 604–6.

Seidman, Laurence S. 1997. *The USA Tax: A Progressive Consumption Tax*. Cambridge, MA: MIT Press.

Sullivan, Martin A. 2010. "VAT Lessons from Canada." *Tax Notes* 103 (5): 493–96.

Sullivan, Martin A. 2012. "The Holy Grail of Tax Reform." *Tax Notes* 135 (7): 807–11.

Toder, Eric, Jim Nunns, and Joseph Rosenberg. 2011. *Methodology for Distributing a VAT*. Washington, DC: Urban Institute.

Toye, John. 1989. "Tax Reform in South Asia: Yesterday and Today." *Modern Asian Studies* 23 (4): 797–813.

US Department of the Treasury. 1977. *Blueprints for Basic Tax Reform*. Washington, DC: Government Printing Office.

Viard, Alan D. 2009. "Border Tax Adjustments Won't Stimulate Exports." *Tax Notes* 122 (9): 1139–43.

Viard, Alan D. 2014. "Tax Increases and the Price Level." *Tax Notes* 142 (1): 115–26.

Viard, Alan D. 2015. "How Would Cardin's VAT Affect Social Security Recipients?" *Tax Notes* 149 (5): 717–22.

Weisbach, David A. 2000. "Ironing out the Flat Tax." *Stanford Law Review* 52 (3): 599–664.

Westmoreland, Kyle L. 2016. "The International Investment Position of the United States at the End of the Third Quarter of 2015." *Survey of Current Business* 96 (1). https://www.bea.gov/scb/toc/0116cont.htm

Zodrow, George R. 1988. "The Windfall Recapture Tax: Issues of Theory and Design." *Public Finance Quarterly* 16 (4): 387–424.

COMMENTARY ON CHAPTER 11

James R. Hines Jr.

Alan Viard's chapter, "Fundamental Tax Reform: A Comparison of Three Options" is a thoughtful, even-handed, and most worthwhile contribution to the analysis of major reforms that, if adopted, would move the tax system strongly in the direction of taxing consumption. The chapter nicely illustrates the complexity of the tax reform problem by exposing a range of available reform options, with an accompanying range of welfare implications. Even among tax reforms with common objectives, there can be strongly differing economic and distributional consequences. Furthermore, otherwise-similar reforms can and do appeal to very different political constituencies.

The economic arguments in favor of consumption taxation are by now well known, and rest largely on the potential to avoid the distortions that income tax systems create by compounding taxes on normal returns to longer-term investments. The inefficiency of existing taxation carries two implications for the desirability of tax reform. The first, and most direct, potential benefit of moving in the direction of a consumption-oriented tax system is that such a reform can improve resource allocation and thereby generate economic benefits that, in concept, can be widely shared among the population. The second potential benefit is more subtle and less commonly noted. It is that by decoupling the taxation of the normal return to investment from the taxation of other types of income, the tax system acquires design flexibility that permits the imposition of greater tax progressivity without producing the economic distortions that would accompany taxing capital income at damagingly high rates.

Both of these benefits make tax reform attractive, though it is noteworthy that realizing either requires the adoption of sensible plans that balance competing interests and benefits to different groups in the population. Identifying the effects of tax reform on the welfares of different groups in the population is indeed part of the chapter's point. It is worth stressing, however, that in order to obtain the available benefits of tax reform, and to generate the political support that a major tax reform requires, it is necessary for reform advocates and others to design reforms with these considerations in mind. One of the challenges of tax reform lies in crafting plans that appropriately address the concerns and interests of different groups, including those in the future as well as the present.

11C.1 REFORM TRANSITIONS AND REFORM ROBUSTNESS

The chapter rightly devotes attention to transitions from the current system of taxing income to alternatives that would tax consumption. Transitions are conceptually complicated and therefore analytically challenging, more so even than comparisons of the steady states of idealized potential reforms. Naturally, there are potential winners and losers from any reform, and it is often possible to craft reforms with features that mitigate distributional consequences—not perfectly, but enough to offer what may be rough justice.

Usually transition relief is predicated on the idea that a tax reform will be in place forever, which is entirely unrealistic, even in the case of a "fundamental" reform such as one that would move the system in the direction of taxing consumption. Experience confirms that tax reforms have finite life: tax reforms are followed by subsequent reforms, and these by yet further reforms. Furthermore, the direction of post-reform change cannot be predicted with certainty, since while it may be the case that in subsequent years governments decide to undo some previous reforms, the opposite also happens. For example, some of the reforms introduced by the US Tax Reform Act of 1986 were dampened or even reversed by subsequent US tax legislation, making these 1986 reforms temporary, and offering evidence of a form of regression to the mean in tax policy. But the world's experience with value added taxes (VATs) is the opposite, since most countries adopted VATs at low rates that were later increased, thereby effectively doubling down on the initial reforms that introduced the VATs.

Given that any tax reform is temporary, and that specific reforms may be partially or entirely unanticipated, many believe that the calculation of transition relief that makes taxpayers whole may require an estimate of how long a reform will be in place, and an estimate of what had been expected, and what policies and prices would have prevailed in the absence of reform. It is difficult to say with certainty because in order to know what information is needed it is critical to understand what function transition relief is intended to serve. Alas the literature is uniformly vague on this subject, in part reflecting the unrealistic premise that any contemplated reform will be the last time the government ever changes the tax laws.

Viewed from the standpoint of frequent, or at least episodic, tax reforms, it is possible to take a more principled stand on the subject of appropriate transition relief. The standard, and static, optimal tax problem as formulated by Ramsey, Mirrlees, and others has the government choosing tax laws and tax parameters to maximize social welfare. Once the policy is chosen, agents are informed of the government's choices and make their own decisions accordingly. One could imagine insisting on transition relief in this setting, in which the transition is understood to be the movement from a diffuse and unspecified tax policy to the one that the government chooses; but that is not how transition relief is typically understood, and there appears to be little support for the notion that taxpaying individuals in a Mirrlees- or Ramsey-style optimal tax setting are entitled to relief. The primary reason why taxpayers in these settings do not receive relief is that they are not blindsided by the policy the government adopts: taxpayers are fully aware of the tax environment, whether or not it is favorable to them, and behave accordingly.

This reasoning suggests that transition relief is a function of the element of surprise rather than the design of the tax system or the nature of the burdens that different taxpayers bear. Individuals who accurately predict the course of tax changes are not surprised when they happen, and have little if any claim for relief. Those who are surprised do have a claim based on the difference between the welfare they would have enjoyed if the government had told them what was coming, and the welfare they get with the policy surprise; though one might ask why this case differs from other economic surprises, such as changes in market prices or other economic conditions. It is widely accepted that it is incumbent on market actors to anticipate future developments in the economy; might the same be true of future developments in tax policy?

It is illustrative to consider a setting in which the government credibly announces that in twenty years it will introduce a VAT along with monetary policy that together implies a 20% rise in nominal prices. Young workers just entering the labor force would then be aware that any income they earn over the next twenty years and save for retirement will have 20% less purchasing power than otherwise, and presumably their labor supply and saving decisions will adjust accordingly. This may be unwelcome news, and may be perceived as unfair compared to the tax burdens of other generations, but it will not be a surprise when the VAT in fact is introduced twenty years hence. Would these workers be entitled to transition relief? They would seem to have a weak case for relief, no more than others whose economic situations or dates of birth or other circumstances led to heavier than average tax burdens. In the Mirrlees optimal nonlinear income tax model workers at different income levels face higher or lower tax rates based in part on how responsive to taxation is the labor supply of other workers at different points in the income distribution. From the standpoint of any one taxpayer, the tax burdens implied by these population characteristics may seem arbitrarily high or low, and the reality that the government chooses the tax schedule to further noble goals may offer cold comfort to those who feel aggrieved; but taxpayers facing high rates of Mirrlees taxation have little case for relief. The same reasoning applies to those who are warned in advance that a VAT is coming.

Of course, in reality major tax reforms are not perfectly anticipated, and as a result there are those who face unexpected burdens. More specifically, as the Viard chapter notes, the introduction of consumption-style taxes tends to impose unanticipated burdens on older generations and others who have accumulated significant saving in advance of the reform. Viewed from the perspective of one-time tax reform, these burdens are lump sum taxes; viewed from the perspective of frequent tax reforms, these burdens have incentive effects that are characteristic of any other taxes, with income and substitution effects that very likely discourage saving and certainly produce economic inefficiencies. Governments are well advised to treat transition effects this way in evaluating and crafting reforms.

For example, if once every twenty years a government will introduce a reform that imposes a 30% tax on the value of accumulated capital, then this policy is roughly equivalent to imposing a regular property tax of 1.5% per annum. This is likely an undesirable tax policy, since it is almost surely dominated by income and consumption tax alternatives, but it may be an intrinsic aspect of introducing what would otherwise be a desirable reform. The costs of implementing such a capital tax can be weighed against any benefits of the contemplated reform, understanding that the reform will not be in place forever. In this framework, the function of any transition relief is to change the ex ante incentive effects created by adopting a reform strategy, as well as to change the ex post consequences of reform. As long as the government is not deceptive—as long as it is understood that the tax system may be reformed, and that reform will create winners and losers—then adherence to customary principles in setting tax policy should create outcomes that have the same claim to fairness as any other optimal tax policy. True, market actors will need to anticipate the frequency and nature of tax reforms, but this is just one of many future economic conditions that economic actors must anticipate in order to make rational decisions.

Back to the example of an infrequent reform that imposes a 30% tax on the value of accumulated capital, one could imagine offering transition relief to capital owners that would have the effects of reducing the disincentive to accumulate capital during the years between reforms, and addressing some of the undesired welfare consequences of reforms. One difficulty is that there may not be tax instruments available that would tailor this relief so that it is delivered to all of the affected taxpayers and not to others, so the government may need to resort to blunt tools, such as providing tax benefits to low-income elderly taxpayers who might be most adversely affected by consumption-oriented tax reforms. These corrective gestures can be evaluated on their own terms for their effects on incentives and welfare, but they should not be evaluated on a one-time basis, given the prospects for frequent subsequent tax reforms.

11C.2 TAX REFORM ROBUSTNESS

The chapter offers valuable suggestions about the extent to which fundamental tax reforms are robust to errors, modification or subsequent changes. Realistically, tax reforms are seldom implemented the way that they are conceived by academics, so it is useful to consider the potential values of partial reform, reforms that fail to incorporate full information, or reforms that are gradually introduced, or introduced and subsequently repealed. As the chapter notes, the United States might benefit from the introduction of a VAT (and an accompanying reduction in other taxes) that at the time of introduction seemed permanent but that, for political or other reasons, wound up lasting only three years—though the possibility of such limited persistence may influence the desirability and design of any accompanying transition relief.

It is worth further considering to what extent there are experimental versions of any of these fundamental reforms, and the nature of information that might be gleaned from pilot tax reform programs. It is safe to say that we do not have full information about the practical realities of some of these consumption-oriented tax reforms in the US context, but how best to gather such information is still rather uncertain. One question raised by some of the chapter's analysis is whether such information gathering is better directed at tax policy analysts, who are uncertain of some of the behavioral effects of the reforms, or the general public, who may seek reassurance that the reforms are workable and fair.

The political process has its own dynamics, ones that typically entail adopting tax reform plans that differ in significant ways from the stark versions implied by theory. This reflects many considerations, including political realities, but also including that academics overlook important practical considerations and may discount significant distributional consequences of reforms. Furthermore, academics and politicians make mistakes. Reform alternatives are commonly evaluated on the basis of their projected effects, but it is surely also valuable to evaluate reform options based on the extent to which they are robust to plan changes, mistakes, politically driven carve-outs, and initially misjudged revenue needs that make it necessary to change provisions subsequently.

11C.3 THE POLITICS OF TAX REFORM

Chapter 11 offers interesting nuggets about the political attractiveness of tax reform alternatives, though fundamental consumption-oriented tax reform may fare better with American voters than some advocates fear is the case. There are controversial tax alternatives over which voters are understandably divided; and there are complicated analytical features of these tax alternatives that are seldom publicly discussed in much depth, and about which many voters may not have very well developed opinions. Despite this unpromising background, the politicians who voters elect very often implement reasonable tax policies, and it may be that sound tax alternatives play better in elections than the low level of public discourse would otherwise suggest. Just as economic actors very often adopt close to optimal plans without explicitly embracing economic methodology, voters may surprise analysts in their ability to evaluate the desirability of tax alternatives. If so, it bodes well for the prospects of fundamental tax reform, and suggests that substance rather than optics should guide the design of such reform.

Of course, politics is still politics. A question that must be asked of fundamental tax reform, or any other large legislative reform, is whether there are sufficiently large coalitions of winners from fundamental tax reform, with sufficiently large (perceived) gains, that they can overcome the natural inertia of the system. And more generally, the benefits of fundamental tax reform should be compared not to existing taxes, but to existing taxes that are improved with modest reforms that may be more feasible than fundamental reform. If the choice lies between wholesale reform and devoting a portion of the available political energy to modest fixes to the current system, it is worthwhile knowing just how much more one gets from the larger reforms, and how long the benefits are apt to persist once reform is implemented.

There are other uncertainties. If the fundamental tax reform project is a twenty-, or thirty-, or fifty-year plan, then it is difficult to know how much additional revenue will be needed compared to what is available from current taxes. Surely future revenue needs are different—and quite possibly greater—than what the government now collects. If this is true, then one of the compelling justifications for fundamental tax reform could be that the need to finance entitlements and at least some non-entitlement spending in the future entails such significant tax increases compared to today that more radical, and more efficient, alternatives need to be considered. This suggests that it may be most fruitful to think more broadly about a fundamental tax reform strategy rather than a package of specific alternatives, a strategy that includes ongoing information gathering and education, and the evolution of reform plans. Given the way the world works, there is an exciting future for tax reform efforts.

INDEX

Page references for figures are indicated by *f* and for tables by *t*.

www.ingramcontent.com/pod-product-compliance
Ingram Content Group UK Ltd.
Pitfield, Milton Keynes, MK11 3LW, UK
UKHW021348290925
8127UKWH00003B/105

9 780190 619725

Michael Geitner | Alexandra Schmid

Be Strict

+ 30 Karten mit Trainingstipps

Einbandgestaltung: Kornelia Erlewein
Titelbild: CAVALLO
Bildnachweis – Booklet: CAVALLO S.5; Kerstin Diacont S. 6, 8, 16, 25; alle übrigen Fotos stammen aus dem Archiv Geitner/Schmid
Karten: Kerstin Diacont: 1 vorne, 4 vorne, 6 hinten, 8 vorne+hinten, 9 vorne, 10 vorne, 14 vorne+hinten, 16 vorne, 27 hinten, 30 hinten; alle übrigen Fotos stammen aus dem Archiv Geitner/Schmid

ISBN 978-3-275-01966-3

Postfach 103743, 70032 Stuttgart
Ein Unternehmen der Paul Pietsch Verlage GmbH & Co. KG
Lizenznehmer der Bucheli Verlags AG, Baarerstr. 43, CH-6304 Zug

1. Auflage 2014

Sie finden uns im Internet unter www.mueller-rueschlikon-verlag.de

Lektorat: Claudia König
Innengestaltung: Kerstin Diacont
Druck und Bindung: Druck- und Medienzentrum Gerlingen GmbH
Printed in Germany